SIXTH EDITION

The Norton

Field Guide
to Writing

SIXTH EDITION

The Norton
Field Guide
to Writing

Richard Bullock
WRIGHT STATE UNIVERSITY

Deborah Bertsch
COLUMBUS STATE COMMUNITY COLLEGE

W. W. NORTON & COMPANY
Independent Publishers Since 1923

W. W. NORTON & COMPANY has been independent since its founding in 1923, when William Warder Norton and Mary D. Herter Norton first published lectures delivered at the People's Institute, the adult education division of New York City's Cooper Union. The firm soon expanded its program beyond the Institute, publishing books by celebrated academics from America and abroad. By mid-century, the two major pillars of Norton's publishing program—trade books and college texts—were firmly established. In the 1950s, the Norton family transferred control of the company to its employees, and today—with a staff of four hundred and a comparable number of trade, college, and professional titles published each year—W. W. Norton & Company stands as the largest and oldest publishing house owned wholly by its employees.

Editor: Sarah Touborg
Project Editor: Christine D'Antonio
Senior Associate Editor: Claire Wallace
Assistant Editor: Emma Peters
Manuscript Editor: Alice Vigliani
Managing Editor, College: Marian Johnson
Managing Editor, College Digital Media: Kim Yi
Production Managers: Liz Marotta, Stephen Sajdak
Media Editor: Joy Cranshaw
Media Project Editor: Cooper Wilhelm
Media Editorial Assistants: Katie Bolger, Maria Qureshi

Ebook Production Manager: Sophia Purut
Marketing Manager, Composition: Michele Dobbins
Design Director: Rubina Yeh
Book Designers: Anna Palchik, Jen Montgomery
Photo Editor: Ted Szczepanski
Photo Research: Dena Digilio Betz
Director of College Permissions: Megan Schindel
College Permissions Manager: Bethany Salminen
Permissions Clearing: Josh Garvin
Composition: Graphic World
Manufacturing: Transcontinental—Beauceville

Permission to use copyrighted material is included in the Credits section of this book, which begins on page C-1.

Library of Congress Cataloging-in-Publication Data

Names: Bullock, Richard H. (Richard Harvey), author. | Bertsch, Deborah,
    author.
Title: The Norton field guide to writing / Richard Bullock,
    Wright State University ; Deborah Bertsch.
Description: Sixth edition. | New York : W. W. Norton & Company, [2022] |
    Includes bibliographical references and index.
Identifiers: LCCN 2021033654 | **ISBN 9780393533057** (paperback) | ISBN 9780393883794 (epub)
Subjects: LCSH: English language--Rhetoric--Handbooks, manuals, etc. |
    English language--Grammar--Handbooks, manuals, etc. | Report
    writing--Handbooks, manuals, etc.
Classification: LCC PE1408 .B883824 2022 | DDC 808/.042--dc23
LC record available at https://lccn.loc.gov/2021033654

W. W. Norton & Company, Inc., 500 Fifth Avenue, New York, NY 10110
wwnorton.com
W. W. Norton & Company Ltd., 15 Carlisle St., London W1D 3BS

1 2 3 4 5 6 7 8 9 0

Preface

The Norton Field Guide to Writing began as an attempt to offer the kind of writing guides found in the best rhetorics in a format as user-friendly as the best handbooks, and on top of that, to be as flexible as possible. We wanted to create a handy guide to help college students with all their written work. Just as there are field guides for bird watchers, for gardeners, and for accountants, this would be one for writers.

In its first five editions the *Field Guide* has obviously touched a chord with many writing instructors, and it remains the best-selling college rhetoric—a success that leaves us humbled and grateful, but also determined to improve the book with each new edition. To that end, we've added new chapters on writing explorations, creating remixes, organizing your writing and guiding your readers, and reflecting on your writing; new student examples throughout; improved advice on evaluating sources; and (we hope) improved writing in every chapter. New and expanded resources, envisioned and cowritten by Deborah Bertsch, provide practical and inspiring support for instructors and students. But it's not just us: this new edition has also been shaped by our community of adopters and their students. Through formal and informal reviews, emails and letters, and conversations with teachers and students using the *Field Guide*, we've learned from you what you need to teach effectively and what your students need to learn.

The Norton Field Guide still aims to offer both the guidance new teachers and first-year writers need and the flexibility many experienced teachers want. In our own teaching we've seen how well explicit guides to writing work for students and novice teachers. But too often, writing textbooks provide far more information than students need or instructors can assign and as a result are bigger and more expensive than they should be. So we've tried to provide enough structure without too much detail—to give the information college writers need to know while resisting the temptation to tell them everything there is to know.

Most of all, we've tried to make the book easy to use, with menus, directories, a glossary/index, and color-coded links to help students find what they're looking for. The links are also the way we keep the book brief: chapters are short, but the links send students to pages elsewhere in the book if they need more detail.

This new edition also marks an important change in the *Field Guide*'s authorship—we want to welcome Deborah Bertsch as a coauthor. Deb, who teaches at Columbus State Community College, has a background rich in excellent teaching, has directed Columbus State's writing center, and has been an important innovator in dual-credit course design and delivery and in various technologies of teaching writing, including instructional video and online instruction. Deb has contributed new chapters, Remixes (Chapter 22) and Reflecting on Your Writing (Chapter 35), substantially revised the Taking Stock of Your Work questions throughout the book, and led the creation of new videos and interactive activities in InQuizitive for Writers that offer multiple ways for students to understand and apply the book's advice. Along with making numerous other improvements throughout the book and its resources, Deb also re-envisioned the instructor's guide to respond to today's teaching challenges. Thank you, Deb. It's good to have you on the team.

WHAT'S NEW IN THE SIXTH EDITION

Two new Genres chapters help first-year writers adapt to new rhetorical situations:

- A new chapter on Explorations offers advice on using writing to explore approaches to problems (Chapter 21).

- A new chapter on Remixes provides guidance on how to transform writing in one genre to another medium or for another audience (Chapter 22).

New and revised Taking Stock of Your Work questions appear in each genre chapter:

- Every Taking Stock question now connects back to key rhetorical concepts, explicitly encouraging students to reflect on their writing knowledge and experience so that they can draw on these concepts for future composing tasks.

Three new Processes chapters guide students in using writing as a tool for thinking:

- Writing as a Process offers a succinct and reassuring overview of the different ways writers approach composing tasks (Chapter 26).

- Organizing Your Writing, Guiding Your Readers offers practical advice on creating effective paragraphs, thesis statements, and topic sentences; crafting beginnings and titles and appropriate endings; and tying ideas together with transitions (Chapter 29).

- Reflecting on Your Writing shows students how to reflect on their writing in drafting, in peer review, and in editing what they write; it then walks students through how to write formal reflections (Chapter 35).

New readings throughout.   As in previous editions, the *Field Guide* features authentic student writing from a range of two-year and four-year schools across the country, along with high-interest professional writing that demonstrates how the genres and processes learned in first-year writing transfer outside the classroom. These readings reflect the kinds of writing most commonly assigned in first-year composition, and all student writing is documented in the latest MLA or APA style. There are eleven new readings in the rhetoric, including seven by students: new essays in nearly every genre, including two new literacy narratives, a visual-text analysis of how inequality is conveyed through the architecture in the movie *Parasite*, a report on sleep deprivation in college students, an argument advocating for actors with disabilities, and many more (see asterisked readings in the table of contents).

Updated coverage of digital tools
- The Processes chapters have been updated with information on digital tools that support writers' processes, like web-based concept mapping tools that help students generate ideas and text, as well as voice-recording tools, notes apps, and transcription apps for capturing ideas generated on the fly. (See Chapters 26–35.)

- The Processes chapters also include information about ways to use storyboards and mockups as generative tools for multimedia and other types of writing. (See Chapter 28.)

- The Doing Research part now includes more information about online tools for collecting, analyzing, and organizing source material.

- The Media/Design part offers an expanded and thoroughly updated chapter, Writing and Learning Online, with advice on participating in synchronous and asynchronous classes, tips on productivity, and more.

Norton Field Guide **ebook.**   All new print copies of *The Norton Field Guide* now include access to the interactive ebook, with embedded videos from the new collection (see below). Standalone ebook access is available at digital.wwnorton.com/fieldguide6 or can be offered through Inclusive Access programs on many campuses.

A collection of new videos.   The Sixth Edition offers a new collection of videos on key concepts—from thesis statements to the rhetorical situation—that help students visualize and apply the book's advice. Each video is two to three minutes long, making them ideal for streaming in class or for independent viewing as a quick refresher. Videos are also embedded directly in the ebook, and many are assignable through InQuizitive for Writers activities.

New InQuizitive activities.   New activities on Thesis Statements, Elements of Argument, Rhetorical Situations, Paragraph Development, and Critical Reading Strategies complement the widely used activities on working with sources and editing sentences. Many of the new questions feature embedded videos from the new collection, and direct links to relevant pages in the *Little Seagull Handbook* ebook provide additional support. Access to InQuizitive for Writers and the *Little Seagull Handbook* ebook is now included with all new copies of *The Norton Field Guide to Writing*, and both can be integrated directly into most campus learning management systems.

Norton Teaching Tools.   All of the popular resources from A *Guide to Teaching* The Norton Field Guides to Writing can now be downloaded from the searchable and sortable Norton Teaching Tools site in formats that are editable and easier than ever to use. The site also provides guidance for effective use of the new video collection, InQuizitive for Writers assignments, and the *Little Seagull Handbook* ebook, whether in person or online. Highlights include:

- A new collection of common writing assignments comes with transparent prompts that highlight purpose, task, and criteria; templates for peer review; sample rubrics; and sample student responses to assignments.

- New *PowerPoint* slides incorporate suggested class activities; chapter teaching tips have been fully updated as well as reformatted for easier application and assignability, and they now include guidance for dual-enrollment courses.

- New chapters in Norton Teaching Tools and the printed *Guide* support instructors interested in culturally responsive teaching, antiracist pedagogy, transparent assignment design, trauma-informed teaching, and more. Chapters on teaching writing online and contract (labor-based) grading have been extensively updated.

WAYS OF TEACHING WITH
THE NORTON FIELD GUIDE TO WRITING

The Norton Field Guide is designed to give you both support and flexibility. It has clear assignment sequences if you want them, or you can create your own. If, for example, you assign a position paper, there's a full chapter. If you want students to use sources, you can add the appropriate research chapters. If you want them to submit a topic proposal, you can add that chapter.

If you're a new teacher, the Genres chapters offer explicit assignment sequences—and the color-coded links will remind you of detail you may want to bring in. The Norton Teaching Tools site offers advice on creating a syllabus, responding to writing, and more.

If you focus on genres, there are complete chapters on all the genres college students are often assigned. Color-coded links will help you bring in details about research or other writing strategies as you wish.

If you teach a corequisite, IRW, or stretch course, the Academic Literacies chapters offer explicit guidelines to help students write and read in academic contexts, summarize and respond to what they read, and develop academic habits of mind that will help them succeed in college.

If you teach a dual-credit course, the Norton Teaching Tools site offers advice on supporting students in various dual-enrollment contexts, including online, in high schools, and on college campuses.

If you organize your course thematically, Chapter 28 on generating ideas and text can help get students thinking about a theme. You can also assign them to do research on the theme, starting with Chapter 47 on finding sources, or perhaps with Chapter 27 on writing as inquiry. If they then write in a particular genre, there will be a chapter to guide them.

If you want students to do research, there are nine chapters on the research process, including guidelines and sample papers for MLA and APA styles.

If you teach for transfer, three chapters about fields of study help students connect what they're reading, writing, and learning in your class to other college courses. The Considering the Rhetorical Situation questions that appear throughout the book prompt students to reflect on the key concepts of audience, purpose, genre, stance, and media/design, thus helping students develop a framework for analyzing future writing tasks.

If you teach writing about writing, you might use the chapter on literacy narratives as an introduction to your course—and use the Fields section to help students research and analyze the key features of writing in particular disciplines or careers.

If you focus on modes, you'll find chapters on using narration, description, and so on as strategies for many writing purposes, and links that lead students through the process of writing an essay organized around a particular mode.

WHAT'S IN THE BOOK

The Norton Field Guide covers twelve genres often assigned in college. Much of the book is in the form of guidelines, designed to help students consider the choices they have as writers. The book is organized into eight parts:

- **ACADEMIC LITERACIES.** Chapters 1–4 focus on writing and reading in academic contexts, summarizing and responding, and developing academic habits of mind.

- **RHETORICAL SITUATIONS.** Chapters 5–9 focus on purpose, audience, genre, stance, and media and design. In addition, almost every chapter includes tips to help students focus on their rhetorical situations.

- **GENRES.** Chapters 10–21 cover twelve genres, four of them—literacy narrative, textual analysis, report, and argument—treated in greater detail.

- **FIELDS.** Chapters 23–25 cover the key features of major fields of study and give guidance on reading and writing in each of those fields.

- **PROCESSES.** Chapters 26–35 offer advice for generating ideas and text, drafting, revising and rewriting, editing, proofreading, reflecting, compiling a portfolio, collaborating with others, and writing as inquiry.

- **STRATEGIES.** Chapters 36–45 cover ways of developing and organizing text—comparing, describing, taking essay exams, and so on.

- **RESEARCH / DOCUMENTATION**. Chapters 46–54 offer advice on how to do academic research; work with sources; quote, paraphrase, and summarize source materials; and document sources using MLA and APA styles. Chapter 53 presents the "official MLA style" introduced in 2021.

- **MEDIA / DESIGN**. Chapters 55–59 give guidance on choosing the appropriate print, digital, or spoken medium; designing text; using images and sound; giving spoken presentations; and writing online.

HIGHLIGHTS

It's easy to use. Menus, directories, and a glossary/index make it easy for students to find what they're looking for. Color-coded templates and documentation maps even make MLA and APA documentation easy.

It has just enough detail, with short chapters that include color-coded links sending students to more detail if they need more.

It's uniquely flexible for teachers. Short chapters can be assigned in any order—and color-coded links help draw from other chapters as need be.

RESOURCES

Like the book itself, the resources that accompany *The Norton Field Guide to Writing* are designed to provide flexibility, with a wealth of options for student learning and for new and experienced instructors alike.

Ebooks. Included with all new Sixth Edition copies of the print book, *Norton Field Guide* ebook access can also be purchased standalone from the Norton website and can be offered through Inclusive Access programs on many campuses. The ebook's built-in highlighting and note-taking capabilities help students engage with and respond to what they read, and instructors can share notes, videos, or external links with students using the instructor annotation tool. Norton ebooks can be viewed on—and synced among—all computers and mobile devices, and they can be made available for offline reading.

Videos. New to the Sixth Edition, short videos are now available in the ebook and for streaming online. Informed by feedback from hundreds of composition instructors, topics include the writing process, rhetorical situations, specific kinds of writing, critical reading strategies, and more. Videos are easily assigned from InQuizitive activities or short multiple-choice quizzes—available in Norton Testmaker and for import into an LMS.

InQuizitive for Writers. Included with all new copies of the *Field Guide*, InQuizitive gives students practice with writing, editing, and research in a low-stakes, feedback-driven environment. The activities are adaptive: students receive additional practice and feedback in the areas where they need more help, with links to relevant pages in the *Little Seagull Handbook* ebook. After practicing with InQuizitive, students will be better prepared to start drafting, find and evaluate sources, and edit their own writing. InQuizitive for the Sixth Edition includes new activities on Rhetorical Situations, Elements of Argument, Thesis Statements, Paragraph Development, Critical Reading Strategies, and Fact-Checking Sources.

Norton Teaching Tools. Available for the first time with the Sixth Edition, the Norton Teaching Tools site for *The Norton Field Guide* is your first stop when looking for creative, engaging resources to refresh your syllabus or design a new one. All of the revised contents from the popular *A Guide to Teaching with* The Norton Field Guides to Writing can now be found here, including the comprehensive guide to teaching first-year writing, advice for teaching every chapter and reading in the text, and new multimedia like videos and *PowerPoint* slides. Norton Teaching Tools are searchable and can be filtered by chapter or by resource type, making it easy to find exactly what you need, download and customize it, and import it into your LMS course. Contents for the Sixth Edition include:

- A comprehensive guide to teaching first-year writing, with chapters on developing a syllabus, responding to student writing, and more.

- Significantly revised chapters on teaching writing online, contract (labor-based) grading, and more.

- New chapters that address culturally responsive teaching, antiracist pedagogy, trauma-informed teaching, and more.

- An expanded collection of sample writing assignments with new peer-review templates, rubrics, and sample student essays.

- Thoroughly revised tips for teaching every chapter and reading in the book, with new suggestions for teaching dual-enrollment courses.

- *PowerPoint* slides for each chapter with classroom and online activities, as well as genre flowcharts and documentation maps from the book.

- A new collection of videos on topics including thesis statements, rhetorical situations, critical reading strategies, and commonly assigned genres.

- Expanded support for assigning InQuizitive for Writers.

- A collection of sample student essays organized by genre, rhetorical mode, and field, including some that are documented and annotated.

- Worksheets and templates in Word and PDF formats with guidance on editing paragraphs, responding to a draft, and more.

A Guide to Teaching with *The Norton Field Guides*. Written by Richard Bullock, Deborah Bertsch, Maureen Daly Goggin, and numerous other teachers and scholars, this is a comprehensive guide to teaching first-year writing, from developing a syllabus to facilitating group work, teaching multimodal writing to assessing student writing. It also includes teaching tips for every chapter and reading in the book. The *Guide* is available in both print and PDF formats; the contents are also available in downloadable, editable form on the Norton Teaching Tools site.

Quizzes. Over 150 quizzes on sentences, language, punctuation/mechanics, paragraph editing, plagiarism, and MLA and APA documentation, including several pre- and post-diagnostics, can be easily imported into your LMS. Additional quizzes for each chapter and reading in the *Field Guide* are also available.

Plagiarism Tutorial. Now available for integration directly into most campus learning management systems, the Plagiarism Tutorial guides students through why plagiarism matters, what counts as plagiarism, and how to avoid plagiarizing, with activities and short quizzes to assess what they've learned. Students earn 90 percent for completing the tutorial and an additional 10 percent based on their quiz performance. You can see your students' scores, how much time they spent working, and when they finished in your Class Activity Report.

Resources for Your LMS. Easily add high-quality Norton digital resources to your online, hybrid, or lecture courses. Get started building your course with our easy-to-use integrated resources. All activities can be accessed right within your existing learning management system. Graded activities can be configured to report to the LMS course gradebook. Integration links are available for the *Norton Field Guide* ebook, InQuizitive for Writers, the *Little Seagull Handbook* ebook, the Plagiarism Tutorial, and all videos. Instructors can also add customizable quizzes to their LMS or upload additional resources from the Norton Teaching Tools site, including *PowerPoint* slides, worksheets, sample writing assignments and rubrics, peer-review templates, and model student essays. All resources can be found at digital.wwnorton.com/fieldguide6.

ACKNOWLEDGMENTS

As we've traveled around the country and met many of the students, teachers, and WPAs who are using *The Norton Field Guide*, we've been gratified to hear that so many find it helpful, to the point that some students tell us that they aren't going to sell it back to the bookstore when the term ends—the highest form of praise. As much as we like the positive response, though, we are especially grateful when we receive suggestions for ways the book might be improved. In this sixth edition, as we did in the fifth edition, we have tried to respond to the many good suggestions we've gotten from students, colleagues, reviewers, and editors. Thank you all, both for your kind words and for your good suggestions.

Some people need to be singled out for thanks, especially Marilyn Moller, the guiding editorial spirit of the *Field Guide* through all six editions. When we presented Marilyn with the idea for this book, she encouraged us and helped us conceptualize it—and then taught us how to write a textbook. The quality of the *Field Guide* is due in large part to her knowledge of the field of composition, her formidable editing and writing skills, her sometimes uncanny ability to see the future of the teaching of writing—and her equally formidable, if not uncanny, stamina.

Editor Sarah Touborg guided us through this new edition with good humor and better advice. Just as developmental editor John Elliott did with the third and fourth editions, Sarah shepherded the fifth, and now sixth, editions through revisions and additions with a careful hand and a clear eye for appropriate content and language. Her painstaking editing shows throughout this book, and we're grateful for her ability to make us appear to be better writers than we are.

Many others have contributed, too. Thanks to project editor Christine D'Antonio for her energy, patience, and great skill in guiding the book from manuscript to final pages. Claire Wallace brought her astute eye and keen judgment to all of the readings, while Emma Peters managed the extensive reviewing process and took great care of the manuscript at every stage. *The Norton Field Guide* is more than just a print book, and we thank Joy Cranshaw, Katie Bolger, Maria Qureshi, Sophia Purut, Kim Yi, and Cooper Wilhelm for creating and producing the superb ebook and instructors' site. Anna Palchik designed the award-winning, user-friendly, and attractive interior, Pete Garceau created the beautiful new cover design, and Debra Morton Hoyt and Rubina Yeh further enhanced the design for accessibility in print and online. Liz Marotta and Stephen Sajdak transformed a scribbled-over manuscript into a finished product with extraordinary speed and precision, while Alice Vigliani copyedited. Megan Schindel and Josh Garvin cleared text permissions, coping efficiently with ongoing changes, and Ted Szczepanski cleared permission for the images found by Dena Digilio Betz. Michele Dobbins, Lib Triplett, Elizabeth Pieslor, Annie Stewart, Erin Brown, Kim Bowers, and Emily Rowin helped us all keep our eyes on the market. Thanks to all, and to Mike Wright, Ann Shin, and Julia Reidhead for supporting this project in the first place. Last but not least, our profound gratitude goes to the tireless Norton travelers, led so energetically by Erik Fahlgren.

Rich has many, many people at Wright State University to thank for their support and assistance. Jane Blakelock taught Rich most of what he knows about electronic text and writing on and for the web and assembled an impressive list of useful links for the book's website. Adrienne Cassel (now at Sinclair Community College) and Catherine Crowley read and commented on many drafts. Peggy Lindsey shared her students' work and the idea of using charts to show how various genres might be organized. Brady Allen, Deborah Bertsch (now at Columbus State Community College), Vicki Burke, Melissa Carrion, Jimmy Chesire, Carol Cornett, Mary Doyle, Byron Crews, Deborah Crusan, Sally DeThomas, Stephanie Dickey, Scott Geisel, Karen Hayes, Chuck Holmes, Beth Klaisner (now at Colorado State University), Nancy Mack, Marty Maner, Cynthia Marshall, Sarah McGinley, Kristie McKiernan, Michelle Metzner, Kristie Rowe, Bobby Rubin, Cathy Sayer, David Seitz, Caroline Simmons, Tracy Smith, Rick Strader, Mary Van Loveren, and A. J. Williams responded to drafts, submitted good models of student writing, contributed to the instructor's manual, tested the *Field Guide* in their classes, provided support, and shared with Rich some of their best teaching ideas. Henry Limouze and then Carol Loranger, chairs of the English Department, gave him room to work on this project with patience and good humor. Sandy Trimboli, Becky Traxler, and Lynn Morgan, the secretaries to the writing programs, kept him anchored. And he thanks especially the more than 300 graduate teaching assistants and 10,000 first-year students who class-tested various editions of the *Field Guide* and whose experiences helped—and continue to help—to shape it.

Deb is grateful to Columbus State's dean of Arts and Sciences, Allysen Todd, and to current and former English Department chairs Amanda Gradisek and Robyn Lyons-Robinson, who encouraged and supported her work on the *Field Guide*; to her fellow faculty members in the English Department, who show her every day what it means to be a good teacher, writer, collaborator, and colleague; to her high school teaching partners, who help her navigate the world of dual credit, enriching her own teaching in the process; and to her students, whose wit, work ethic, and writing regularly dazzle her. Deb is also incredibly grateful to Rich

Bullock, Joy Cranshaw, Michele Dobbins, Maureen Daly Goggin, Emma Peters, Sarah Touborg, and Lib Triplett for welcoming her to the *Field Guide* team and for teaching her—with patience and kindness—how to do the work.

The Norton Field Guide has also benefited from the good advice and conversations we've had with writing teachers across the country, including (among many others) Anne Champion, Sarah Fish, and Diana Gingo at Collin College; Polina Chemishanova, Cyndi Miecznikowski, and Melissa Schaub at the University of North Carolina at Pembroke; Maureen Mathison, Susan Miller, Tom Huckin, Gae Lyn Henderson, and Sundy Watanabe at the University of Utah; Christa Albrecht-Crane, Doug Downs, and Brian Whaley at Utah Valley State College; Anne Dvorak and Anya Morrissey at Longview Community University; Jeff Andelora at Mesa Community College; Robin Calitri at Merced College; Lori Gallinger, Rose Hawkins, Jennifer Nelson, Georgia Standish, and John Ziebell at the Community College of Southern Nevada; Stuart Blythe at Indiana University–Purdue University Fort Wayne; Janice Kelly at Arizona State University; Jeanne McDonald at Waubonsee Community College; Web Newbold, Mary Clark-Upchurch, Megan Auffart, Matt Balk, Edward James Chambers, Sarah Chavez, Desiree Dighton, Ashley Ellison, Theresa Evans, Keith Heller, Ellie Isenhart, Angela Jackson-Brown, Naoko Kato, Yuanyuan Liao, Claire Lutkewitte, Yeno Matuki, Casey McArdle, Tibor Munkacsi, Dani Nier-Weber, Karen Neubauer, Craig O'Hara, Martha Payne, Sarah Sandman, and Kellie Weiss at Ball State University; Patrick Tompkins at Tyler Community College; George Kanieski and Pamela Hardman at Cuyahoga Community College; Daniela Regusa, Jeff Partridge, and Lydia Vine at Capital Community College; Elizabeth Woodworth, Auburn University–Montgomery; Stephanie Eason at Enterprise Community College; Kate Geiselman at Sinclair Community College; Ronda Leathers Dively at Southern Illinois University; Debra Knutson at Shawnee State University; Guy Shebat and Amy Flick at Youngstown State University; Martha Tolleson, Toni McMillen, and Patricia Gerecci at Collin College; Sylva Miller at Pikes Peak Community College; Dharma Hernandez at Los Angeles Unified School District; Ann Spurlock at Mississippi State University; Luke Niiler at the University of Alabama; and Jeff Tix at Wharton County Junior College.

REVIEWERS

The authors and editors at W. W. Norton are grateful to the many instructors across the country whose astute feedback helped shape this new edition of the *Field Guide* and its digital resources: Carmela Abbruzzese, Regis College; Susan Achziger, Community College of Aurora; Liz Aguilar, Alamo Community College; Shazia Ali, Eastfield College; Kelly Allen, Northampton Community College; Emily Anderson, Columbus State Community College; Susan Austin, Johnston Community College; Stuart Barbier, Delta College; Elizabeth Barnes, Johnston Community College; William Beckham, Horry-Georgetown Technical College; Alyse Bensel, Brevard College; Betty Bettacchi, Collin College; Deb Bloom, Kirkwood Community College; Dean Blumberg, Horry-Georgetown Technical College; Brett Bodily, Dallas College North Lake Campus; Ethel Bowden, Central Maine Community College; Rachel Bragg, West Virginia University Institute of Technology; Laura Brandenburg, Wayland Baptist University; April Brannon, California State University, Fullerton; Crystal Brantley, Louisburg College; Jane Brockman, Rogue Community College; Mark Brumley, Randolph Community College; Keely Byars-Nichols, University of Mount Olive; Robert Canipe, Catawba Valley Community College; Anna Matsen Cantrell, Pellissippi State Community College; Neeta Chandra, Cuyahoga Community College; Catherine Childress, Lees-McRae College; Minda Chuska, Horry-Georgetown Technical College; Heather Clark, Ivy Tech Community College; Billy Clem, Waubonsee Community College; Alison Cope, Lone Star College; Virginia Crisco, California State University, Fresno; Amy Cruickshank, Cuyahoga Community College; Sarah Crump, Southern State Community College; John Daniel, Henry Ford College; Shemika Davis, Johnston Community College; LeeAnn Derdeyn, Dallas College Cedar Valley Campus; Heather Detzner, Spartanburg Community College; Amber Dinquel, Rappahannock Community College; Ivan Dole, Dallas College North Lake Campus; Katie Doughty, Mississippi State University; Holly Dykstra, Laredo College; Sara Edgell, Tarrant County College–Southeast Campus; Ashley Edlin, Wayland Baptist University; Kayleigh Few, Mississippi State University; Maureen Fitzpatrick, Johnson County Community College; Sue Fox, Central New Mexico Community College; Katie Franklin, University of New Orleans; Janet

Frye-Burleigh, San Jacinto College–Generation Park; Jo Gibson, Cuyahoga Community College–Western Campus; Brian Gogan, Western Michigan University; Anival Gonzalez, Northwest Vista College; Marti Grahl, Hagerstown Community College; Barbara Griest-Devora, Northwest Vista College; Kaleena Gross, Columbus State Community College; John Guthrie, Southeastern Community College; Bernabe Gutierrez, Laredo College; Stephanie Hamilton, University of Idaho; Amara Hand, Norfolk State University; Michael Hedges, Horry-Georgetown Technical College; Chelsea Hicken, Dixie State University; Ean High, University of Tennessee at Martin; Lee Ann Hodges, Tri-County Community College; Elizabeth Hogan, University of New Orleans; Monica Hogan, Johnson County Community College; Rachael Holloway, Johnston Community College; Michael Horton, Marshall High School; Deana Hueners, Dakota State University; Kenneth Huffer, Tarrant County College District; Paige Huskey, Clark State College; Patricia Ireland, Pellissippi State Community College; Neshon Jackson, Houston Community College; Kim Jacobs-Beck, University of Cincinnati Clermont; Jo Johnson, Ivy Tech Community College; Lori Johnson, Rappahannock Community College; Margaret Johnson, Langston University; Christine Junker, Wright State University–Lake Campus; Katie Kalisz, Grand Rapids Community College; William Keeth, Mansfield University of Pennsylvania; Jessica Kidd, University of Alabama; Danielle Klafter, Southeast Community College; Stacey Koller, Dixie State University; Christine Kozikowski, Central New Mexico Community College; Jennifer Kraemer, Collin College–Frisco Preston Ridge Campus; Julie Kratt, Cowley College; Alexander Kurian, Dallas College North Lake Campus; Katherine Kysar, University of Alaska Fairbanks; Nina Lambert, Dallas College Eastfield Campus; Kayla Landers, Lehigh University; Linda Lawson, Concord High School; Lindsey Light, University of Dayton; Bronwen Llewellyn, Daytona State College; Kelly Lovelace, Isothermal Community College; Juliette Ludeker, Howard Community College; Crystal Manboard, Northwest Vista College; Terri Mann, El Paso Community College; Diane Marcincin, Northampton Community College; Kelly Ann Martin, Collin College–Plano Campus; Adrienne McClain, Dallas College; Laura McClister, Volunteer State Community College; Jeanne McDonald, Waubonsee Community College; Kerry McGinnis, Columbus State Community College; Megan McIntyre, Sonoma State University; Gena McKinley, Rappahannock

Community College; James McWard, Johnson County Community College; Eileen Medeiros, Johnson & Wales University; Lora Meredith, Colorado Mountain College; Ashley Merrill, Wayne Community College; Dalia El Metwally, Wharton County Junior College; Harriet Millan, Drexel University; Kellie Miller, Santa Fe College; Rosemary Mink, Mohawk Valley Community College; Millie Moncada, Los Angeles Valley College; Michael Morris, Dallas College Eastfield Campus; Rhonda Morris, Santa Fe College; Damon Murrah, Pellissippi State Community College; Mary Newbegin, Lehigh University; Luke Niiler, University of Alabama; Annette Nusbaum, Aiken Technical College; Fabiana Oliveira, Normandale Community College; Tamra Painter, Kanab High School / CE Dixie State University; Diana Paquette, Waukesha County Technical College; Catherine Parisian, University of North Carolina at Pembroke; Teresa Paul, North Arkansas College; Andrea Peck, Cuyahoga Community College; Laurie Phillips, Dallas College El Centro Campus; Dan Portincaso, Waubonsee Community College; Britt Posey, Northwest Vista College; Chris Prentice, Central New Mexico Community College; Sharon Prince, Wharton County Junior College; Jessica Rabin, Anne Arundel Community College; Erin Radcliffe, Central New Mexico Community College; Yasmin Ramirez, El Paso Community College; Kassandra Ramirez-Buck, Eastfield College; Brian Reeves, Lone Star College–University Park; Eric Reyes, Wharton County Junior College; Cynthia Cox Richardson, Central State University; Jim Richey, Tyler Junior College; Jared Riddle, Ivy Tech Community College; Jennifer Riske, Northeast Lakeview College; Kelly Rivers, Pellissippi State Community College; Danielle Roach, Clark State College; Andrew Roback, Illinois Institute of Technology; Michelle Roberti, Rappahannock Community College; Natasha Robinson, Collin College; Brian Roffino, Eastfield College; Andrea Rogers, University of Arkansas; Mark Rooze, Florence-Darlington Technical College; Kathie Russell, Santa Fe College; Mary Rutledge-Davis, Dallas College North Lake Campus; Kelly Savage, Dallas College Eastfield Campus; Molly Scanlon, Nova Southeastern University; Matthew Schmeer, Johnson County Community College; Jessica Schreyer, University of Dubuque; Marcea Seible, Hawkeye Community College; Marilyn Senter, Johnson County Community College; Margaret Shaw, Johnson & Wales University; Chase Sisk, Pellissippi State Community College; Zahir Small, Santa Fe College; Tiffany Smith, Arkansas State University Beebe;

Jason Snart, College of DuPage; Jessi Snider, Wharton County Junior College; Cynthia Soueidan, Gloucester High School / Rappahannock Community College; Pam Stone, North Arkansas College; James (Ty) Stumpf, Central Carolina Community College; Allison Suber, Spartanburg Community College; Eric Sullivan, Metropolitan Community College; Karen Summey, Catawba Valley Community College; Ashley Supinski, Northampton Community College; Gerard Teichman, Bunker Hill Community College; Harun Karim Thomas, Daytona State College; Jessica Thompson, Mississippi State University; Tara Thompson, Johnston Community College; Jeff Tix, Wharton County Junior College; Susan Todd, Jefferson College; Andrew Tolle, Dallas College Eastfield Campus; Tyler Trimm, Mississippi State University; Jennifer Turner, Patrick County High School; Michael Walker, Santa Fe College; Mary Wallen, Big Sandy Community & Technical College; Maureen Walters, Vance-Granville Community College; Angie Weaver, South Beloit High School; Sharon West, Spartanburg Community College; Stephen Whitley, Collin College; Sabine Winter, Dallas College Eastfield Campus; Paul Wise, University of Toledo; Karen Wright, Pellissippi State Community College; Sue Yamin, Pellissippi State Community College; Jason Ziebart, Central Carolina Community College.

We owe a special thanks to the instructors and their students who reviewed this edition of the *Field Guide*, some of whom class-tested it: Jenna Bazzell, Monroe County Community College; Mary Anne Bernal, San Antonio College; Carrie Buttler, Del Mar College; Susan Muaddi Darraj, Harford Community College; Janice Filer, Shelton State Community College; Andrea Green, Motlow State Community College; Yolanda Gonzalez, McLennan Community College; Peaches Henry, McLennan Community College; Lennie Irvin, San Antonio College; Kent Lenz, Del Mar College; Carrie Nartker-Kantz, Monroe Community College; Jim Richey, Tyler Junior College; Ryan Shepherd, Ohio University; Wes Spratlin, Motlow State Community College.

It's customary to conclude by expressing gratitude to one's spouse and family, and for good reason. Writing and revising *The Norton Field Guide* over the past several years, we have enjoyed the loving and unconditional support of our spouses, Barb and Todd, who provide the foundation for all we do. Thank you. We couldn't have done it without you.

How to Use This Book

There's no one way to do anything, and writing is no exception. Some people need to do a lot of planning on paper; others write entire drafts in their heads. Some writers compose quickly and loosely, going back later to revise; others work on one sentence until they're satisfied with it, then move on to the next. And writers' needs vary from task to task, too: sometimes you know what you're going to write about and why, but need to figure out how to do it; other times your first job is to come up with a topic. *The Norton Field Guide* is designed to allow you to chart your own course as a writer, offering guidelines that suit your writing needs. It is organized in eight parts:

1. **ACADEMIC LITERACIES**: The chapters in this part will help you know what's expected in the reading and writing you do for academic purposes, and in summarizing and responding to what you read. One chapter even provides tips for developing habits of mind that will help you succeed in college, whatever your goals.

2. **RHETORICAL SITUATIONS**: No matter what you're writing, it will always have some purpose, audience, genre, stance, and medium and design. This part will help you consider each of these elements, as well as the particular kinds of rhetorical situations created by academic assignments.

3. **GENRES**: Use these chapters for help with specific kinds of writing, from abstracts to explorations to evaluations and more. You'll find more detailed guidance for four especially common assignments: literacy narratives, textual analyses, reports, and arguments.

4. **FIELDS**: The chapters in this part will help you apply what you're learning in this book to your other general education courses or courses in your major.

5. **PROCESSES**: These chapters offer general advice for all writing situations—from generating ideas and text to drafting, organizing, revising and rewriting, compiling a portfolio—and more.

6. **STRATEGIES**: Use the advice in this part to develop and organize your writing—to use comparison, description, dialogue, and other strategies as appropriate.

7. **RESEARCH / DOCUMENTATION**: Use this section for advice on how to do research, work with sources, and compose and document research-based texts using MLA and APA styles.

8. **MEDIA / DESIGN**: This section offers guidance in designing your work and using visuals and sound, and in deciding whether and how to deliver what you write on paper, on screen, or in person.

WAYS INTO THE BOOK

The Norton Field Guide gives you the writing advice you need, along with the flexibility to write in the way that works best for you. Here are some of the ways you can find what you need in the book.

Brief menus.   Inside the front cover you'll find a list of all the chapters; start here if you are looking for a chapter on a certain kind of writing or a general writing issue.

Complete contents.   Pages xxvii–xliv contain a detailed table of contents. Look here if you need to find a reading or a specific section in a chapter.

Guides to writing.   If you know the kind of writing you need to do, you'll find guides to writing twelve common genres in Part 3. These guides are designed to help you through all the decisions you have to make—from coming up with a topic to editing and proofreading your final draft.

Color-coding.   The parts of this book are color-coded for easy reference: light blue for **ACADEMIC LITERACIES**, orange for **RHETORICAL SITUATIONS**, green for **GENRES**, gray for **FIELDS**, lavender for **PROCESSES**, red for **STRATEGIES**, blue for **RESEARCH/DOCUMENTATION**, and pink for **MEDIA/DESIGN**. You'll find a key to the colors on the front cover flap and also on each left-hand page. When you see a word highlighted in a color, that tells you where you can find additional detail on the topic.

Glossary/index. At the back of the book is a combined glossary and index, where you'll find full definitions of key terms and topics, along with a list of the pages where everything is covered in detail.

Directories to MLA and APA documentation. A brief directory inside the back cover will lead you to guidelines on citing sources and composing a list of references or works cited. The documentation models are color-coded so you can easily see the key details.

WAYS OF GETTING STARTED

If you know your genre, simply turn to the appropriate genre chapter. There you'll find model readings, a description of the genre's Key Features, and a Guide to Writing that will help you come up with a topic, generate text, organize and write a draft, get response, revise, edit, and proofread. The genre chapters also point out places where you might need to do research, use certain writing strategies, design your text a certain way—and direct you to the exact pages in the book where you can find help doing so.

If you know your topic, you might start with some of the activities in Chapter 28, Generating Ideas and Text. From there, you might turn to Chapter 47, for help finding sources on the topic. When it comes time to narrow your topic and come up with a thesis statement, Chapter 29 can help. If you get stuck at any point, you might turn to Chapter 27, Writing as Inquiry; it provides tips that can get you beyond what you already know about your topic. If your assignment or your thesis defines your genre, turn to that chapter; if not, consult Chapter 27 for help determining the appropriate genre, and then turn to that genre chapter.

Contents

Preface *v*

How to Use This Book *xxiii*

✴ **Part 1   Academic Literacies   1**

1 Writing in Academic Contexts   3

What's expected of academic writing   3
What's expected of college writers: The WPA outcomes   8

2 Reading in Academic Contexts   11

Taking stock of your reading   11
Reading strategically   12
Thinking about what you want to learn   12
Previewing the text   13
Adjusting your reading speed to different texts   13
Looking for organizational cues   14
Thinking about your initial response   14
Dealing with difficult texts   15
Annotating   16
Coding   17
Summarizing   20
Reading critically   20
Believing and doubting   20
Thinking about how the text works: what it says, what it does   21
Identifying patterns   23
Reading rhetorically   25
Considering the rhetorical situation   25

Analyzing the argument   26
Considering the larger context   27
Reading visual texts   28
Reading onscreen   31

**3 Summarizing and Responding:
Where Reading Meets Writing**   33

Summarizing   33
Responding   36
Deciding how to respond   36
Writing a summary and response essay   40
JACOB MACLEOD, *Guns and Cars Are Different*   40

KEY FEATURES   42

*A clearly identified author and title / A concise summary of the text /
An explicit response / Support for your response*

Ways of organizing a summary and response essay   44

4 Developing Academic Habits of Mind   46

Engage   46
Be curious   48
Be open to new ideas   48
Be flexible   49
Be creative   50
Persist   51
Reflect   52
*Collaborate   52
Take responsibility   55

Part 2   Rhetorical Situations   57

5 Purpose   59

Identifying your purpose   60
Thinking about purpose   60

New to this edition

6 **Audience** 61

Identifying your audience 62
Thinking about audience 63

7 **Genre** 65

Choosing the appropriate genre 66
Dealing with ambiguous assignments 68
*Combining genres 69
Thinking about genre 70

8 **Stance** 72

Identifying your stance 73
Thinking about stance 74

9 **Media/Design** 75

Identifying your media and design needs 76
Thinking about media 76
Thinking about design 77

▲ **Part 3   Genres** 79

10 **Writing a Literacy Narrative** 81

*REA KARIM, *Becoming an American Girl* 81
*KARLA MARIANA HERRERA GUTIERREZ,
    Reading, Writing, and Riding 85
ANA-JAMILEH KASSFY, *Automotive Literacy* 91

KEY FEATURES 93

*A well-told story / Vivid detail / Some indication of
the narrative's significance*

A GUIDE TO WRITING 94

Choosing a topic 94
Considering the rhetorical situation 95

* New to this edition

Generating ideas and text   96
Ways of organizing a literacy narrative   98
Writing out a draft   99
Considering matters of design   100
Getting response and revising   100
Editing and proofreading   101
Taking stock of your work   102

11 Analyzing Texts   104

*PAT FINN, *The Architecture of Inequality:
On Bong Joon-ho's* Parasite   105
DANIELLE ALLEN, *Our Declaration*   111
ROY PETER CLARK, *Why It Worked: A Rhetorical
Analysis of Obama's Speech on Race*   116

KEY FEATURES   123

A summary or description of the text / Attention to the context / A clear
interpretation or judgment / Reasonable support for your conclusions

A GUIDE TO WRITING   124

Choosing a text to analyze   124
Considering the rhetorical situation   124
Generating ideas and text   124
Coming up with a thesis   134
Ways of organizing a textual analysis   134
Writing out a draft   136
Considering matters of design   137
Getting response and revising   138
Editing and proofreading   138
Taking stock of your work   139

12 Reporting Information   140

*RENAE TINGLING, *Sleepless Nights of a University Student*   140
FRANKIE SCHEMBRI, *Edible Magic*   146
JON MARCUS, *The Reason College Costs More Than You Think*   149

* *New to this edition*

KEY FEATURES   152

A tightly focused topic / Well-researched information / Synthesis of ideas / Various writing strategies / Clear definitions / Appropriate design

A GUIDE TO WRITING   154

Choosing a topic   154
Considering the rhetorical situation   155
Generating ideas and text   156
Ways of organizing a report   157
Writing out a draft   158
Considering matters of design   160
Getting response and revising   160
Editing and proofreading   161
Taking stock of your work   162

13 Arguing a Position   164

*KELLY CORYELL, All Words Matter: The Manipulation behind
    "All Lives Matter"   164
*BRIANNA SCHUNK, Come Look at the Freaks: Examining
    and Advocating for Disability Theatre   171
NICHOLAS KRISTOF, Our Blind Spot about Guns   177

KEY FEATURE   180

*A clear and arguable position / Background information /
Good reasons / Convincing evidence / Appeals to readers /
A trustworthy tone / Consideration of other positions*

A GUIDE TO WRITING   182

Choosing a topic   182
Considering the rhetorical situation   184
Generating ideas and text   185
Ways of organizing an argument   189
Writing out a draft   190
Considering matters of design   192

Getting response and revising 193
Editing and proofreading 194
Taking stock of your work 194

14 Abstracts 196

INFORMATIVE ABSTRACTS 196

PROPOSAL ABSTRACTS 197

KEY FEATURES / ABSTRACTS 198
A summary of basic information / Objective description / Brevity

A BRIEF GUIDE TO WRITING ABSTRACTS 198
Considering the rhetorical situation 198
Generating ideas and text 199
Ways of organizing an abstract 199
Taking stock of your work 200

15 Annotated Bibliographies and Reviews of Scholarly Literature 201

ANNOTATED BIBLIOGRAPHIES 201
MICHAEL BENTON, MARK DOLAN, AND REBECCA ZISCH, *Teen Film$* 202
KELLY GREEN, *Researching Hunger and Poverty* 203

KEY FEATURES OF ANNOTATED BIBLIOGRAPHIES 204
A clear scope / Complete bibliographic information / A concise description of the work / Relevant commentary / Consistent presentation

A BRIEF GUIDE TO WRITING ANNOTATED BIBLIOGRAPHIES 205
Considering the rhetorical situation 205
Generating ideas and text 206
Ways of organizing an annotated bibliography 208
Taking stock of your work 209

REVIEWS OF SCHOLARLY LITERATURE 209

CAMERON CARROLL, *Zombie Film Scholarship:
A Review of the Literature* 210

KEY FEATURES OF REVIEWS OF SCHOLARLY LITERATURE 212

*Thorough research / Objective summaries of the literature /
Critical evaluation / Synthesis / A clear focus*

Taking stock of your work 213

16 **Evaluations** 214

*OLIVIA MAZZUCATO, *Difficult-to-Follow Narrative Redeemed
by Well-Executed Comedy in The Lovebirds* 215

KEY FEATURES 217

*A concise description of the subject / Clearly defined criteria /
A knowledgeable discussion of the subject /
A balanced and fair assessment / Well-supported reasons*

A BRIEF GUIDE TO WRITING 219

Choosing something to evaluate 219
Considering the rhetorical situation 219
Generating ideas and text 219
Ways of organizing an evaluation 221
Taking stock of your work 222

17 **Literary Analyses** 223

ROBERT FROST, *The Road Not Taken* 223
MATTHEW MILLER, *Frost's Broken Roads* 224

KEY FEATURES 228

*An arguable thesis / Careful attention to the language of the text / Attention
to patterns or themes / A clear interpretation / MLA style*

A BRIEF GUIDE TO WRITING 229

Considering the rhetorical situation 229

New to this edition

Generating ideas and text 229
Organizing a literary analysis 234
Taking stock of your work 234

18 Memoirs 236

RICK BRAGG, *All Over but the Shoutin'* 236

KEY FEATURES 240

A good story / Vivid details / Clear significance

A BRIEF GUIDE TO WRITING 241

Choosing an event to write about 241
Considering the rhetorical situation 241
Generating ideas and text 242
Ways of organizing memoirs 243
Taking stock of your work 243

19 Profiles 245

*RYAN JONES, *A Fighter's Chance* 245

KEY FEATURES 252

*An interesting subject / Any necessary background / An interesting angle /
A firsthand account / Engaging details*

A BRIEF GUIDE TO WRITING 253

Choosing a suitable subject 253
Considering the rhetorical situation 254
Generating ideas and text 254
Ways of organizing a profile 256
Taking stock of your work 257

20 Proposals 258

*CHRISTIAN B. MILLER, *Just How Dishonest Are Most Students?* 258

KEY FEATURES 262

*A well-defined problem / A recommended solution / A convincing argument
for your solution / Possible questions / A call to action / An appropriate tone*

* New to this edition

A BRIEF GUIDE TO WRITING   263

Deciding on a topic   263
Considering the rhetorical situation   263
Generating ideas and text   264
Ways of organizing a proposal   264
Taking stock of your work   265

TOPIC PROPOSALS   266

CATHERINE THOMS, Social Media and Data Privacy   266

KEY FEATURES   267

A concise discussion of the subject / A statement of your intended focus /
A rationale for choosing the topic / Mention of resources

*21 Explorations   269

*BRIAN DIEHL, Talking with Granddad   269

KEY FEATURES   274

A topic that intrigues you / Some kind of structure / Specific details /
A questioning, speculative tone

A BRIEF GUIDE TO WRITING   276

Deciding on a topic   276
Considering the rhetorical situation   276
Generating ideas and text   277
Ways of organizing an exploratory essay   278
Taking stock of your work   279

*22. Remixes   280

*Original text: A print profile   280
*TODD JONES, Rare Earth   281
*Remix 1: A Video Profile   285
*Remix 2: An Explainer Video   286

KEY FEATURES   287

A connection to the original subject / A modification of the earlier
work / Attention to genre and media/design expectations

* New to this edition

SOME TYPICAL WAYS OF REMIXING   287

A BRIEF GUIDE TO CREATING REMIXES   289
Determining what will change in your remix   289
Considering the rhetorical situation   289
Generating ideas and text   290
Ways of organizing a remix   291
Taking stock of your work   292

● Part 4   Fields   293

23 Fields of Study   295
Academic fields and general education   295
Studying, reading, and writing in academic fields   296
Thinking about reading and writing in the fields   297

24 Reading across Fields of Study   298
Considering the rhetorical situation   298
Advice for reading across fields of study   299
Tips for reading in various fields of study   304
*The humanities / The social sciences / The sciences / A note
on career-focused fields*

25 Writing in Academic Fields of Study   309
Considering the rhetorical situation   309
Writing in academic fields of study   311
*Arts and humanities / Science and mathematics / Social sciences / Business /
Education / Engineering and technology / Health sciences and nursing*

⁝ Part 5   Processes   325

*26. Processes of Writing   327

27 Writing as Inquiry   329
Starting with questions   329

* New to this edition

Keeping a journal 332
Keeping a blog 332

28 Generating Ideas and Text 333

Freewriting 333
Looping 334
Listing 334
Clustering or mapping ideas 335
*Talking 336
Cubing 336
Questioning 337
*Using visuals 337
Using genre features 340
Outlining 340
Letter writing 342
Keeping a journal 343
Discovery drafting 344

*29. Organizing Your Writing, Guiding Your Readers 345

Outlining 345
Beginning 346
Thesis statements 347
More ways of beginning 350
Ending 354
Ways of ending 355
Paragraphs 358
Topic sentences 358
Paragraph length and number 360
Transitions 361
Titles 363

30 Drafting 364

Establishing a schedule with deadlines 364
Getting comfortable 364
Starting to write 365
Dealing with writer's block 366

New to this edition

31 Assessing Your Own Writing 367

Considering the rhetorical situation 367
Examining the text itself 368
For focus / Argument / Organization / Clarity
Assessing a body of your work 371

32 Getting Response and Revising 372

Giving and getting peer response 372
Getting effective response 373
Revising 375
Rewriting 378

33 Editing and Proofreading 380

Editing 380
Proofreading 383

34 Compiling a Portfolio 385

Considering the rhetorical situation 385

A WRITING PORTFOLIO 386

What to include in a writing portfolio 386
Organizing 387
Paper portfolios / Electronic portfolios
Assessing your writing portfolio 388

A LITERACY PORTFOLIO 389

What to include in a literacy portfolio 389
Organizing 390
Reflecting on your literacy portfolio 390

*35. Reflecting on Your Writing 391

Reflecting while writing 391
Reflecting after writing 392
Considering the rhetorical situation 393
Generating insights for your reflection 394
Providing support for your reflection 396
Ways of organizing a reflection 398

* *New to this edition*

◆ **Part 6   Strategies** *403*

36 Analyzing Causes and Effects   *405*

Determining plausible causes and effects   405
Arguing for causes or effects   406
Ways of organizing an analysis of causes and effects   407
Considering the rhetorical situation   408

37 Arguing   *410*

Reasons for arguing   410
Arguing logically   411
Claims / Reasons / Evidence
Arguing with a hostile audience   422
Convincing readers you're trustworthy   423
Appealing to readers' emotions   426
Checking for fallacies   427
Considering the rhetorical situation   429

38 Classifying and Dividing   *431*

Classifying   431
Dividing   432
Creating clear and distinct categories   433
Considering the rhetorical situation   435

39 Comparing and Contrasting   *437*

Two ways of comparing and contrasting   438
The block method / The point-by-point method
Using graphs and images   440
Using figurative language   441
Considering the rhetorical situation   443

40 Defining   *445*

Formal definitions   445
Extended definitions   447

Stipulative definitions   453
Considering the rhetorical situation   454

41 Describing   456

Detail   456
Objectivity and subjectivity   459
Vantage point   460
Dominant impression   461
Organizing descriptions   462
Considering the rhetorical situation   463

42 Using Dialogue   464

Why add dialogue?   464
Integrating dialogue into your writing   465
Interviews   466
Considering the rhetorical situation   468

43 Explaining Processes   469

Explaining clearly   469
Explaining how something is done   469
Explaining how to do something   470
Explaining visually   471
Considering the rhetorical situation   473

44 Narrating   474

Sequencing   474
Including pertinent detail   478
Opening and closing with narratives   480
Considering the rhetorical situation   482

45 Taking Essay Exams   483

Considering the rhetorical situation   483
Analyzing essay questions   484
Some guidelines for taking essay exams   486

Part 7 Doing Research 489

46 Getting a Start on Research 491

Establishing a schedule and getting started 491
Considering the rhetorical situation 492
Coming up with a topic 493
Consulting with librarians and doing preliminary research 494
Coming up with a research question 495
Drafting a tentative thesis 496
Creating a rough outline 497
Keeping a working bibliography 497
Keeping track of your sources 499

47 Finding Sources 501

Kinds of sources 501
Searching effectively using keywords 506
*Searching using popular sites and search engines 509
*Searching in academic libraries 511
Reference works 512
Books / searching the library catalog 514
Ebooks / finding books online 515
Periodicals / searching indexes and databases 516
Images, sound, and more 518
Doing field research 518
Interviews / Observation / Questionnaires and surveys

48 Evaluating Sources 524

Considering whether a source might be useful 524
*Fact-checking popular sources online 526
Reading sources with a critical eye 532
Comparing sources 533

New to this edition

49 Synthesizing Ideas   535

Reading for patterns and connections   535
Synthesizing ideas using notes   539
Synthesizing information to support your own ideas   541
Entering the conversation   541

50 Quoting, Paraphrasing, and Summarizing   542

Taking notes   542
Deciding whether to quote, paraphrase, or summarize   544
Quoting   544
Paraphrasing   547
Summarizing   550
Introducing source materials using signal phrases   551

51 Acknowledging Sources, Avoiding Plagiarism   555

Acknowledging sources   555
Avoiding plagiarism   558

52 Documentation   560

Understanding documentation styles   560
MLA style   562
APA style   562

53 MLA Style   564

A DIRECTORY TO MLA STYLE   564

MLA in-text documentation   567
Notes   574
MLA list of works cited   574

Documentation Maps
Article in a print journal   583 / *Article in an online magazine*   584 /
Article accessed through a database   587 / *Print book*   591 / *Work on
a website*   596

Formatting a research paper   605
Sample research paper, MLA style   607

54 APA Style   615

A DIRECTORY TO APA STYLE   615

APA in-text documentation   618
Notes   622
APA reference list   623

Documentation Maps
Article in a journal with DOI   631 / *Webpage*   633 / *Book*   635

Formatting a paper   645
Sample research paper, APA style   647

● Part 8   Media/Design   657

55 Choosing Media   659

Print   660
Digital   660
Spoken   660
Multimedia   661
Considering the rhetorical situation   662

56 Designing Text   664

Considering the rhetorical situation   664
Some basic principles of design   665
Consistency / Simplicity / Balance / Color and contrast / Templates
Some elements of design   668
Fonts / Layout / Headings / White space
Evaluating a design   672

57 Using Visuals, Incorporating Sound   673

Considering the rhetorical situation   674
Using visuals   674
Incorporating sound   680
Adding links   681
Editing carefully—and ethically   682

58 Writing and Learning Online 684

Writing Online 684
Email and texts 685
Social media 685
Websites 685
Blogs 687
Learning online 688
Keeping track of files 688
Finding basic course information 689
Using learning management systems 689
*Managing challenges of online learning 691
*Using web conferencing tools 693

59 Giving Presentations 694

ABRAHAM LINCOLN, *Gettysburg Address* 694
JUDY DAVIS, *Ours Was a Dad . . .* 695

KEY FEATURES 697

A clear structure / Signpost language / A tone to suit the occasion / Repetition and parallel structure / Slides and other media

Considering the rhetorical situation 698

A BRIEF GUIDE TO WRITING 699

Delivering a presentation 704

Credits C-1

Glossary/Index G/I-1

The Norton Writer's Prize

Directory to MLA Style

Directory to APA Style

New to this edition

SIXTH EDITION

The Norton

Field Guide
to Writing

Part 1
Academic Literacies

Whenever we enter a new community—start a new job, move to a new town, join a new club—there are certain things we need to learn. The same is true upon entering the academic world. We need to be able to **READ** and **WRITE** in certain ways. We're routinely called on to **SUMMARIZE** something we've heard or read and to **RESPOND** in some way. And to succeed, we need to develop certain **HABITS OF MIND**—everyday things such as asking questions and being persistent. The following chapters provide guidelines to help you develop these fundamental academic literacies—and know what's expected of you in academic communities.

Academic Literacies

1 Writing in Academic Contexts 3

2 Reading in Academic Contexts   11

3 Summarizing and Responding 33

4 Developing Academic Habits of Mind 46

1 Writing in Academic Contexts

Write an essay arguing whether genes or environment do more to determine people's intelligence. Research and write a report on the environmental effects of electricity-generating windmills. Work with a team to write a proposal and create a multimedia presentation for a sales campaign. Whatever you're studying, you're surely going to be doing a lot of writing, in classes from various disciplines—the above assignments, for example, are from psychology, environmental science, and marketing. Academic writing can serve a number of different purposes—to **ARGUE** for what you think about a topic and why, to **REPORT** on what's known about an issue, to **PROPOSE A SOLUTION** for some problem, and so on. Whatever your topics or purposes, all academic writing follows certain conventions, and learning about them will help you join the conversations going on across campus. This chapter describes what's typically expected of academic writing—and of academic writers.

▲ 164–95
140–63
258–68

What's Expected of Academic Writing

Evidence that you've considered the subject thoughtfully. Whether you're composing a report, an argument, or some other kind of writing, you need to demonstrate that you've thought seriously about the topic and done any necessary research. You can use various ways to show that you've considered the subject carefully, from citing authoritative sources to incorporating information you learned in class to pointing out connections among ideas.

An indication of why your topic matters.   You need to help your readers understand why your topic is worth exploring and why your writing is worth reading. Even if you are writing in response to an assigned topic, you can better make your point and achieve your purpose by showing your readers why your topic is important and why they should care about it. For example, in the prologue to *Our Declaration*, political philosopher Danielle Allen explains why her topic, the Declaration of Independence, is worth writing about:

> The Declaration of Independence matters because it helps us see that we cannot have freedom *without* equality. It is out of an egalitarian commitment that a people grows—a people that is capable of protecting us all collectively, and each of us individually, from domination. If the Declaration can stake a claim to freedom, it is only because it is so clear-eyed about the fact that the people's strength resides in its equality.
>
> The Declaration also conveys another lesson of paramount importance. It is this: language is one of the most potent resources each of us has for achieving our own political empowerment. The men who wrote the Declaration of Independence grasped the power of words. This reveals itself in the laborious processes by which they brought the Declaration, and their revolution, into being. It shows itself forcefully, of course, in the text's own eloquence.

By explaining that the topic matters because freedom and equality matter—and language gives us the means for empowering ourselves—Allen gives readers reason to read her careful analysis.

A response to what others have said.   Whatever your topic, it's unlikely that you'll be the first one to write about it. And if, as this chapter assumes, all academic writing is part of a larger conversation, you are in a way adding your own voice to that conversation. One good way of doing that is to present your ideas as a response to what others have said about your topic—to begin by quoting, paraphrasing, or summarizing what others have said and then to agree, disagree, or both.

✳ academic literacies	⬣ fields	⬤ research
◼ rhetorical situations	⦂ processes	⬤ media/design
▲ genres	◆ strategies	

For example, in an essay arguing that the phrase "all lives matter" is manipulative, Diablo Valley College student Kelly Coryell says, "It should be acknowledged that some of those who used the phrase did so naively attempting to unify people in a time of division." But then she responds—and disagrees, arguing that "The phrase 'all lives matter' belies the current racial inequality in America by implying that all lives are at equal risk."

A clear, appropriately qualified thesis. When you write in an academic context, you're usually expected to state your main point explicitly, often in a THESIS STATEMENT. Kelly Coryell states her thesis clearly in her essay "All Words Matter: The Manipulation behind 'All Lives Matter'": "Saying 'all lives matter' as a response to "Black lives matter" is, in reality, sending a dangerous message: it steals attention from the systematic oppression of Black Americans and actively distorts the message behind the BLM movement, manipulating the American people into maintaining the oppressive status quo." Often you'll need to QUALIFY your thesis statement to acknowledge that the subject is complicated and there may be more than one way of seeing it or exceptions to the generalization you're making about it. Here, for example, is a qualified thesis, from an essay evaluating the movie *The Lovebirds* by Olivia Mazzucato, a student at UCLA: "Though the film's story gets convoluted, Rae and Nanjiani are able to salvage the muddy plot with their razor-sharp comedic wit and hilarious chemistry." Mazzucato makes a claim that *The Lovebirds* achieves success, while acknowledging at the beginning of the sentence that the film's plot is flawed.

347–49

348–49

Good reasons supported by evidence. You need to provide good reasons for your thesis and evidence to support those reasons. For example, Kelly Coryell offers several reasons why saying "all lives matter" as a response to "Black lives matter" sends a dangerous message: systemic racism disproportionately affects the Black community and "Black lives matter" does not mean "only" Black lives matter, but that Black lives need to matter as much as White lives. Evidence to support your reasons sometimes comes

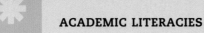

from your own experience but more often from published research and scholarship, research you do yourself, or firsthand accounts by others.

Compared with other kinds of writing, academic writing is generally expected to be more objective and less emotional. You may find *Romeo and Juliet* deeply moving or cry when you watch *A Dog's Journey*—but when you write about the play or the film for a class, you must do so using evidence from the text to support your thesis. You may find someone's ideas deeply offensive, but you should respond to them with reason rather than with emotional appeals or personal attacks.

Acknowledgment of multiple perspectives. Debates and arguments in popular media are often framed in "pro/con" terms, as if there were only two sides to any given issue. Once you begin seriously studying a topic, though, you're likely to find that there are several sides and that each of them deserves serious consideration. In your academic writing, you need to represent fairly the range of perspectives on your topic—to explore three, four, or more positions on it as you research and write. For example, in her report, "Sleepless Nights of a University Student," Drexel University student Renae Tingling examines sleep deprivation in several ways: through academic research, a survey of students, and a personal sleep-deprivation experiment.

A confident, authoritative stance. If one goal of academic writing is to contribute to a larger conversation, your tone should convey confidence and establish your authority to write about your subject. Ways to achieve such a tone include using active verbs ("X claims" rather than "it seems"), avoiding such phrases as "in my opinion" and "I think," and writing in a straightforward, direct style. Your writing should send the message that you've done the research, analysis, and thinking and know what you're talking about. For example, here is the first paragraph of Wilkes University student Brianna Schunk's essay advocating for the casting of actors with disabilities in the roles of characters with disabilities:

※ academic literacies   ● fields   ● research

■ rhetorical situations   ∴ processes   ● media/design

▲ genres   ◆ strategies

> When I first saw Gaten Matarazzo in the TV show *Stranger Things* and some of the first words out of his toothless little mouth were, "I have cleidocranial dysplasia," I actually cried with joy. Until then, I had never seen another human not related to my family who had cleidocranial dysplasia on television in a popular TV show. I was so shocked, I made my friend rewind the episode so I could hear him say it again. Having cleidocranial dysplasia myself, it is so much easier to be able to compare myself to Matarazzo when explaining my condition to other people, and I only wish he could have come into my life earlier. Representation—how we portray ourselves and are portrayed by others—is incredibly important to all groups of people, but especially to people with disabilities.

Schunk's use of vivid language ("toothless little mouth," "I was so shocked") and her strong final sentence ("Representation . . . is incredibly important to all groups of people, but especially to people with disabilities") lend her writing a confident tone. Her stance sends the message that she knows what she's talking about.

Carefully documented sources. Clearly acknowledging sources and documenting them carefully and correctly is a basic requirement of academic writing. When you use the words or ideas of others—including visuals, video, or audio—those sources must be documented in the text and in a works-cited or references list at the end. (If you're writing something that will appear online, you may also refer readers to your sources by using hyperlinks in the text; ask your instructor if you need to include a list of references or works cited as well.)

Careful attention to style expectations. In academic contexts, you should almost always write in complete sentences, use capitalization and punctuation as recommended in a handbook or other guide, check your spelling by consulting a dictionary, proofread carefully, and avoid any abbreviations used in texting or other informal writing. Grammar conventions are important, and it's a good idea to follow them in most kinds of academic writing. If you choose not to, however, you should make clear that you are doing so intentionally, for a particular purpose.

What's Expected of College Writers: The WPA Outcomes

Writing is not a multiple-choice test; it doesn't have right and wrong answers that are easily graded. Instead, your readers, whether they're teachers or anyone else, are likely to read your writing with various questions in mind: does it make sense, does it meet the demands of the assignment, are sources documented appropriately, to name just a few of the things readers may look for. Different readers may notice different things, so sometimes it may seem to you that their response—and your grade—is unpredictable. It should be good to know, then, that writing teachers across the nation have come to some agreement on certain "outcomes," what college students should know and be able to do by the time they finish a first-year writing course. These outcomes have been defined by the National Council of Writing Program Administrators (WPA). Here's a brief summary of these outcomes and how *The Norton Field Guide* can help you meet them:

Knowledge of Rhetoric

- *Understand the rhetorical situation of texts that you read and write.* See Chapters 5–9 and the many prompts for Considering the Rhetorical Situation throughout the book.

- *Read and write texts in a number of different genres, and understand how your purpose may influence your writing.* See Chapters 10–22 for guidelines on writing in twelve genres and remixing what you write in one genre to another.

- *Adjust your voice, tone, level of formality, design, and medium as is necessary and appropriate.* See Chapter 8 on stance and tone and Chapter 9 for help thinking about medium and design.

- *Choose the media that will best suit your audience, purpose, and the rest of your rhetorical situation.* See Chapters 9 and 55.

Critical Thinking, Reading, and Composing

- *Read and write to inquire, learn, think critically, and communicate.* See Chapters 1 and 2 on academic writing and reading, and Chapter 27 on writing as inquiry. Chapters 10–22 provide genre-specific prompts to help you think critically about a draft.

- *Read for content, argumentative strategies, and rhetorical effectiveness.* Chapter 2 provides guidance on reading texts with a critical eye, Chapter 11 teaches how to analyze a text, and Chapter 48 shows how to evaluate sources.

- *Find and evaluate popular and scholarly sources.* Chapter 47 teaches how to use databases and other methods to find sources, and Chapter 48 shows how to evaluate the sources you find.

- *Use sources in various ways to support your ideas.* Chapter 37 suggests strategies for supporting your ideas, and Chapter 50 shows how to incorporate ideas from sources into your writing to support your ideas.

Processes

- *Use writing processes to compose texts and explore ideas in various media.* Part 5 covers all stages of the processes writers use, from generating ideas and text to drafting, getting response and revising, and editing and proofreading. Each of the thirteen genre chapters (10–22) in Part 3 includes a guide that leads you through the process of writing in that genre or remixing your writing into another genre.

- *Collaborate with others on your own writing and on group tasks.* Chapter 4 offers guidelines for working with others, Chapter 32 provides general prompts for getting and giving response, and Chapters 10–22 provide genre-specific prompts for reading a draft with a critical eye.

- *Reflect on your own writing processes.* Chapters 10–22 provide genre-specific questions to help you take stock of your work, and Chapter 35 offers guidance in reflecting on your writing processes and products.

Knowledge of Conventions

- *Use appropriate grammar, punctuation, and spelling.* Chapter 33 provides tips to help you edit and proofread your writing. Chapters 10–22 offer genre-specific advice for editing and proofreading.

- *Understand and use genre conventions and formats in your writing.* Chapter 7 provides an overview of genres and how to think about them. Part 3 covers twelve genres, describing the key features and conventions of each one, and includes one chapter on remixes.

- *Understand intellectual property and document sources appropriately.* Chapter 51 offers guidance on the ethical use of sources, Chapter 52 provides an overview of documentation styles, and Chapters 53 and 54 provide templates for documenting in MLA and APA styles.

✳ academic literacies   ● fields   ● research
■ rhetorical situations   ⁞ processes   ● media/design
▲ genres   ◆ strategies

2 Reading in Academic Contexts

We read news sites to know about the events of the day. We read textbooks to learn about history, chemistry, and other academic topics—and other academic sources to do research and develop arguments. We read tweets and blogs to follow (and participate in) conversations about issues that interest us. And as writers, we read our own writing to make sure it says what we mean it to say and proofread our final drafts to make sure they say it the way we intended. In other words, we read many kinds of texts for many different purposes. This chapter offers a number of strategies for various kinds of reading you do in academic contexts.

TAKING STOCK OF YOUR READING

One way to become a better reader is to understand your reading process; if you know what you do when you read, you're in a position to decide what you need to change or improve. Consider the answers to the following questions:

- What do you read for pleasure? for work? for school? Consider all the sorts of reading you do: books, magazines, and newspapers, websites, *Facebook*, texts, blogs, product instructions.

- When you're facing a reading assignment, what do you do? Do you do certain things to get comfortable? Do you play music or seek quiet? Do you plan your reading time or set reading goals for yourself? Do you flip through or skim the text before settling down to read it, or do you start at the beginning and work through it?

- When you begin to read something for an assignment, do you make sure you understand the purpose of the assignment—why you must read this text? Do you ever ask your instructor (or whoever else assigned the reading) what its purpose is?

- How do you motivate yourself to read material you don't have any interest in? How do you deal with boredom while reading?

- Does your mind wander? If you realize that you haven't been paying attention and don't know what you just read, what do you do?

- Do you ever highlight, underline, or annotate text as you read? Do you take notes? If so, what do you mark or write down? Why?

- When you read text you don't understand, what do you do?

- As you anticipate and read an assigned text, what attitudes or feelings do you typically have? If they differ from reading to reading, why do they?

- What do you do when you've finished reading an assigned text? Write out notes? Think about what you've just read? Move on to the next task? Something else?

- How well do your reading processes work for you, both in school and otherwise? What would you like to change? What can you do to change?

The rest of this chapter offers advice and strategies that you may find helpful as you work to improve your reading skills.

READING STRATEGICALLY

Academic reading is challenging because it makes several demands on you at once. Textbooks present new vocabulary and new concepts, and picking out the main ideas can be difficult. Scholarly articles present content and arguments you need to understand, but they often assume that readers already know key concepts and vocabulary and so don't generally provide background information. As you read more texts in an academic field and begin to participate in its conversations, the reading will become easier, but in the meantime you can develop strategies that will help you read effectively.

Thinking about What You Want to Learn

To learn anything, we need to place new information into the context of what we already know. For example, to understand photosynthesis, we

---

❉ academic literacies   ● fields   ● research
■ rhetorical situations   ⦂ processes   ● media/design
▲ genres   ◆ strategies

need to already know something about plants, energy, and oxygen, among other things. To learn a new language, we draw on similarities and differences between it and any other languages we know. A method of bringing to conscious attention our current knowledge on a topic and of helping us articulate our purposes for reading is a list-making process called KWL+. To use it, create a table with three columns:

K: What I <u>K</u>now	W: What I <u>W</u>ant to Know	L: What I <u>L</u>earned

Before you begin reading a text, list in the "K" column what you already know about the topic. Brainstorm ideas, and list terms or phrases that come to mind. Then group them into categories. Also before reading, or after reading the first few paragraphs, list in the "W" column questions you have that you expect, want, or hope to be answered as you read. Number or reorder the questions by their importance to you.

Then, as you read the text or afterward, list in the "L" column what you learned from the text. Compare your "L" list with your "W" list to see what you still want or need to know (the "+")—and what you learned that you didn't expect.

Previewing the Text

It's usually a good idea to start by skimming a text—read the title and subtitle, any headings, the first and last paragraphs, the first sentences of all the other paragraphs. Study any illustrations and other visuals. Your goal is to get a sense of where the text is heading. At this point, don't stop to look up unfamiliar words; just mark them in some way to look up later.

Adjusting Your Reading Speed to Different Texts

Different texts require different kinds of effort. Some that are simple and straightforward can be skimmed fairly quickly. With academic texts, though, you usually need to read more slowly and carefully, matching the pace of your reading to the difficulty of the text. You'll likely need to skim the text for an overview of the basic ideas and then go back to read it closely. And then you may need to read it yet again. (But do try always to read quickly enough to focus on the meanings of sentences and paragraphs, not just individual words.) With visual texts, too, you'll often need to look at them several times, moving from gaining an overall impression to closely examining the structure, layout, and other visual features—and exploring how those features relate to any accompanying verbal text.

Looking for Organizational Cues

As you read, look for cues that signal the way the text's ideas are organized and how each part relates to the ones around it.

The introductory paragraph and thesis often offer a preview of the topics to be discussed and the order in which they will be addressed. Here, for example, is a typical thesis statement for a report: *Types of prisons in the United States include minimum and medium security, close security, maximum security, and supermax.* The report that follows should explain each type of prison in the order stated in the thesis.

361-62 **Transitions** help GUIDE READERS in following the direction of the writer's thinking from idea to idea. For example, "however" indicates an idea that contradicts or limits what has just been said, while "furthermore" indicates one that adds to or supports it.

Headings identify a text's major and minor sections, by means of both the headings' content and their design.

Thinking about Your Initial Response

Some readers find it helps to make brief notes about their first response to a text, noting their reaction and thinking a little about why they reacted as they did.

What are your initial reactions? Describe both your intellectual reaction and any emotional reaction, and identify places in the text that caused you to react as you did. An intellectual reaction might consist of an evaluation ("I disagree with this position because . . ."), a connection ("This idea

academic literacies   fields   research
rhetorical situations   processes   media/design
genres   strategies

reminds me of . . ."), or an elaboration ("Another example of this point is . . ."). An emotional reaction could include approval or disapproval ("YES! This is exactly right!" "NO! This is so wrong!"), an expression of feeling ("This passage makes me so sad"), or one of appreciation ("This is said so beautifully"). If you had no particular reaction, note that, too.

What accounts for your reactions?   Are they rooted in personal experiences? aspects of your personality? positions you hold on an issue? As much as possible, you want to keep your opinions from interfering with your understanding of what you're reading, so it's important to try to identify those opinions up front.

Dealing with Difficult Texts

Let's face it: some texts are difficult. You may have no interest in the subject matter, or lack background knowledge or vocabulary necessary for understanding the text, or simply not have a clear sense of why you have to read the text at all. Whatever the reason, reading such texts can be a challenge. Here are some tips for dealing with them:

Look for something familiar.   Texts often seem difficult or boring because we don't know enough about the topic or about the larger conversation surrounding it to read them effectively. By skimming the headings, the abstract or introduction, and the conclusion, you may find something that relates to something you already know or are at least interested in—and being aware of that prior knowledge can help you see how this new material relates to it.

Look for "landmarks."   Reading a challenging academic text the first time through can be like driving to an unfamiliar destination on roads you've never traveled: you don't know where you're headed, you don't recognize anything along the way, and you're not sure how long getting there will take. As you drive the route again, though, you see landmarks along the way that help you know where you're going. The same goes for reading a difficult text: sometimes you need to get through it once just to get some idea of what it's about. On the second reading, now that you have "driven the route," look for the ways that the parts of the text relate to one another, to other texts or course information, or to other knowledge you have.

Monitor your understanding.   You may have had the experience of reading a text and suddenly realizing that you have no idea what you just read. Being able to monitor your reading—to sense when you aren't understanding the text and need to reread, focus your attention, look up unfamiliar terms, take some notes, or take a break—can make you a more efficient and better reader. Keep these questions in mind as you read: What is my purpose for reading this text? Am I understanding it? Does it make sense? Should I slow down, reread, annotate? skim ahead and then come back? pause to reflect?

Be persistent.   Research shows that many students respond to difficult texts by assuming they're "too dumb to get it"—and quitting reading. Successful students, on the other hand, report that if they keep at a text, they will come to understand it. Some of them even see difficult texts as challenges: "I'm going to keep working on this until I make sense of it." Remember that reading is an active process, and the more you work at it the more successful you will be.

Annotating

Many readers find it helps to annotate as they read: highlighting keywords, phrases, sentences; connecting ideas with lines or symbols; writing comments or questions in the margin or on sticky notes; circling new words so you can look up the definitions later; noting anything that seems noteworthy or questionable. Annotating forces you to read for more than just the surface meaning. Especially when you are going to be writing about or responding to a text, annotating creates a record of things you may want to refer to.

Annotate as if you're having a conversation with the author, someone you take seriously but whose words you do not accept without question. Put your part of the conversation in the margin, asking questions, talking back: "What's this mean?" "So what?" "Says who?" "Where's evidence?" "Yes!" "Whoa!" or even 😐 or 😑 or texting shorthand like LOL or INTRSTN. If you're reading a text online, you can use a digital annotation

✳ academic literacies   ● fields   ● research
■ rhetorical situations   ∴ processes   ● media/design
▲ genres   ◆ strategies

tool like *Hypothes.is* or *Diigo* to highlight portions of the text and make notes electronically—and even share your annotations with others.

What you annotate depends on your **PURPOSE**, or what you're most interested in. If you're analyzing a text that makes an explicit argument, you would probably underline the **THESIS STATEMENT** and then the **REASONS** and **EVIDENCE** that support that statement. It might help to restate those ideas in your own words in the margins—in order to understand them, you need to put them in your own words! If you're trying to **IDENTIFY PATTERNS**, you might highlight each pattern in a different color or mark it with a sticky note and write any questions or notes about it in that color. You might annotate a visual text by circling and identifying important parts of the image.

■ 59–60

⁙ 347–49

◆ 413–14

   414–22

✳ 23–25

There are some texts that you cannot annotate, like library books. Then you will need to use sticky notes or make notes elsewhere, and you might find it useful to keep a reading log for this purpose.

Coding

You may also find it useful to record your thoughts as you read by using a coding system—for example, using "X" to indicate passages that contradict your assumptions, or "?" for ones that puzzle you. You can make up your own coding system, of course, but you could start with this one*:

✔   Confirms what you thought

X   Contradicts what you thought

?   Puzzles you

??   Confuses you

!   Surprises you

☆   Strikes you as important

➔   Is new or interesting to you

You might also circle new words that you'll want to look up later and highlight or underline key phrases.

---

*Adapted from Harvey Daniels and Steven Zemelman, *Subjects Matter: Every Teacher's Guide to Content-Area Reading* (Heinemann, 2004).

A Sample Annotated Text

Here is an excerpt from Justice: What's the Right Thing to Do?, *a book by Harvard professor Michael J. Sandel, annotated by a writer who was doing research for a report on the awarding of military medals:*

What Wounds Deserve the Purple Heart?

✔

On some issues, questions of virtue and honor are too obvious to deny. Consider the recent debate over who should qualify for the Purple Heart. Since 1932, the U.S. military has awarded the medal to soldiers wounded or killed in battle by enemy action. In addition to the honor, the medal entitles recipients to special privileges in veterans' hospitals.

PTSD increasingly common among veterans.

Since the beginning of the current wars in Iraq and Afghanistan, growing numbers of veterans have been diagnosed with post-traumatic stress disorder and treated for the condition. Symptoms include recurring nightmares, severe depression, and suicide. At least three hundred thousand veterans reportedly suffer from traumatic stress or major depression. Advocates for these veterans have proposed that they, too, should qualify for the Purple Heart. Since psychological injuries can be at least as debilitating as physical ones, they argue, soldiers who suffer these wounds should receive the medal.

Argument: Vets with PTSD should be eligible for PH because psych. injuries are as serious as physical.

No PH for PTSD vets? Seems unfair!

After a Pentagon advisory group studied the question, the Pentagon announced, in 2009, that the Purple Heart would be reserved for soldiers with physical injuries. Veterans suffering from mental disorders and psychological trauma would not be eligible, even though they qualify for government-supported medical treatment and disability payments. The Pentagon offered two reasons for its decision: traumatic stress disorders are not intentionally caused by enemy action, and they are difficult to diagnose objectively.

Argument: PTSD is like punctured eardrums, which do get the PH.

Did the Pentagon make the right decision? Taken by themselves, its reasons are unconvincing. In the Iraq War, one of the most common injuries recognized with the Purple Heart has been a punctured eardrum, caused by explosions at close range. But unlike bullets and bombs, such explosions are not a deliberate enemy tactic intended to injure or kill; they are (like traumatic stress) a damaging side effect of

❋ academic literacies   ⬤ fields   ⬤ research
◼ rhetorical situations   ⦂ processes   ⬤ media/design
▲ genres   ◆ strategies

battlefield action. And while traumatic disorders may be more difficult to diagnose than a broken limb, the injury they inflict can be more severe and long-lasting.

As the wider debate about the Purple Heart revealed, the real issue is about the meaning of the medal and the virtues it honors. What, then, are the relevant virtues? Unlike other military medals, <u>the Purple Heart honors sacrifice, not bravery</u>. It requires no heroic act, only an injury inflicted by the enemy. The question is what kind of injury should count.

PH "honors sacrifice, not bravery." Injury enough. So what kind of injury?

A veteran's group called the Military Order of the Purple Heart opposed awarding the medal for psychological injuries, claiming that doing so would "debase" the honor. A spokesman for the group stated that "shedding blood" should be an essential qualification. He didn't explain why bloodless injuries shouldn't count. But Tyler E. Boudreau, a former Marine captain who favors including psychological injuries, offers a compelling analysis of the dispute. He attributes the opposition to a deep-seated attitude in the military that views post-traumatic stress as a kind of weakness. "The same culture that demands tough-mindedness also encourages skepticism toward the suggestion that the violence of war can hurt the healthiest of minds. . . . Sadly, <u>as long as our military culture bears at least a quiet contempt for the psychological wounds of war, it is unlikely those veterans will ever see a Purple Heart</u>."

Wow: one vet's group insists that for PH, soldier must bleed!

☆

So the debate over the Purple Heart is more than a medical or clinical dispute about how to determine the veracity of injury. At the heart of the disagreement are rival conceptions of <u>moral character and military valor</u>. Those who insist that only bleeding wounds should count believe that post-traumatic stress reflects a weakness of character unworthy of honor. Those who believe that psychological wounds should qualify argue that veterans suffering long-term trauma and severe depression have sacrificed for their country as surely, and as honorably, as those who've lost a limb. The dispute over the Purple Heart illustrates the moral logic of Aristotle's theory of justice. We can't determine who deserves a military medal without asking what virtues the medal properly honors. And to answer that question, we have to assess competing conceptions of character and sacrifice.

Argument based on different ideas about what counts as a military virtue.

—Michael J. Sandel, *Justice: What's the Right Thing to Do?*

Summarizing

Writing a summary, boiling down a text to its main ideas, can help you understand it. To do so, you need to identify which ideas in the text are crucial to its meaning. Then you put those crucial ideas into your own words, creating a brief version that accurately sums up the text. Here, for example, is a summary of Sandel's analysis of the Purple Heart debate:

> In "What Wounds Deserve the Purple Heart?," Harvard professor Michael J. Sandel explores the debate over eligibility for the Purple Heart, the medal given to soldiers who die or are wounded in battle. Some argue that soldiers suffering from post-traumatic stress disorder should qualify for the medal because psychological injuries are as serious as physical ones. However, the military disagrees, since PTSD injuries are not "intentionally caused by enemy action" and are hard to diagnose. Sandel observes that the dispute centers on how "character" and "sacrifice" are defined. Those who insist that soldiers must have had physical wounds to be eligible for the Purple Heart see psychological wounds as reflecting "weakness of character," while others argue that veterans with PTSD and other psychological traumas have sacrificed honorably for their country.

READING CRITICALLY

When we read critically, we apply our analytical skills in order to engage with a text to determine not only what a text says but also what it means and how it works. The following strategies can help you read texts critically.

Believing and Doubting

One way to develop a response to a text is to play the believing and doubting game, sometimes called reading with and against the grain. Your goal is to **LIST** or **FREEWRITE** notes as you read, writing out as many reasons as you can think of for believing what the writer says (reading with the grain) and then as many as you can for doubting it (reading against the grain).

334–35
333–34

First, try to look at the world through the writer's perspective. Try to understand their reasons for arguing as they do, even if you strongly disagree. Then reread the text, trying to doubt everything in it: try to find every flaw in the argument, every possible way it can be refuted—even if you

---

* academic literacies ● fields ● research

■ rhetorical situations ⁂ processes ● media/design

▲ genres ◆ strategies

totally agree with it. Developed by writing theorist Peter Elbow, the believing and doubting game helps you consider new ideas and question ideas you already have—and at the same time see where you stand in relation to the ideas in the text you're reading.

Thinking about How the Text Works: What It Says, What It Does

Sometimes you'll need to think about how a text works, how its parts fit together. You may be assigned to analyze a text, or you may just need to make sense of a difficult text, to think about how the ideas all relate to one another. Whatever your purpose, a good way to think about a text structure is by **OUTLINING** it, paragraph by paragraph. If you're interested in analyzing its ideas, look at what each paragraph *says*; if, however, you're concerned with how the ideas are presented, pay attention to what each paragraph *does*.

340–42

What it says.   Write a sentence that identifies what each paragraph says. Once you've done that for the whole text, look for patterns in the top-ics the writer addresses. Pay attention to the order in which the topics are presented. Also look for gaps—ideas the writer has left unsaid. Such paragraph-by-paragraph outlining of the content can help you see how the writer has arranged ideas and how that arrangement builds an argument or develops a topic. Here, for example, is an outline of Christian B. Miller's proposal, "Just How Dishonest Are Most Students?" (see p. 258). The numbers in the left column refer to the essay's paragraphs.

1   To give exams in online classes is to invite cheating.

2   Papers are good ways to assess learning in philosophy courses but not in the sciences and other fields, so what can be done to deter cheating on exams in online courses?

3   Remote proctoring using tools that monitor the students and their web browsing is one solution, but it assumes that students are dishonest, may infringe on students' privacy, and may be racially biased.

4   A better solution is to extend to online learning honor pledges, which reduce cheating and promote honesty by allowing students to choose not to cheat.

5   Honor pledges and codes can have problems: they may only be instituted for public relations reasons, they may be imposed on faculty and students by administrators, or they may be given lip service but mostly ignored.

6   However, empirical research studies show that cheating is much less common at schools at all levels that take honor codes seriously.

7   Two researchers found that cheating of various types, including plagiarism, crib notes, help with test answers, and other forms of unauthorized help, were all done much less at schools with honor codes than at schools without them.

8   The researchers emphasized that students must be seriously committed to the honor code for it to work.

9   A few schools hold a ceremony at which the students pledge to uphold the code and may also require that the code be affirmed on every assignment.

10   Research as well as our experience in life shows that most people will cheat if they think it will go undetected; but at the same time most people consider themselves honest and know that it's wrong to cheat, even if they sometimes are tempted to do so. A way to create a moral reminder of those basic values is to ask students to sign an honor code.

11   Another research study paid students taking a difficult test money for each correct answer. One group was graded by the researchers, a second group graded themselves, and a third group also graded themselves—but signed an honor pledge before taking the test. Some in the second group cheated by inflating their scores, but no one in the third group did.

12   The research done in face-to-face class environments shows that honor codes work, but their results should be extended to online instruction as well.

13   Honor codes are not a perfect solution, as some "deeply dishonest" students will cheat no matter what; but research and teachers' experience agree that most students, with moral reminders through honor pledges, will behave with honesty.

What it does. Identify the function of each paragraph. Starting with the first paragraph, ask, What does this paragraph do? Does it introduce a topic? provide background for a topic to come? describe something? define something? entice me to read further? something else? What does the second paragraph do? the third? As you go through the text, you may identify groups of paragraphs that have a single purpose. Here is a functional outline of Miller's essay (again, the numbers on the left refer to the paragraphs):

1	Introduces the topic by defining a problem; author establishes credibility
2	Describes a flawed solution
3	Describes a second flawed solution
4	States the thesis; introduces a recommended solution
5	Describes potential problems with this solution
6	Offers a reason for adopting the solution
7	Presents evidence: describes a research study's results
8	Outlines what the proposed solution requires to be successful
9	Describes how the proposed solution is implemented
10	Offers another reason: summarizes how the proposed solution achieves its purpose
11	Presents evidence: describes a research study that shows the solution's effectiveness
12	Concludes with a call to action
13	Acknowledges and refutes a counterargument to the proposal

Identifying Patterns

Look for notable patterns in the text—recurring words and their synonyms, as well as repeated phrases, metaphors and other images, and types of sentences. Some readers find it helps to highlight patterns in various colors. Does the author repeatedly rely on any particular writing strategies: **NARRATION**? **COMPARISON**? Something else?

474–82

437–44

Another kind of pattern that might be important to consider is the kind of evidence the text provides. Is it more opinion than facts? nothing but statistics? If many sources are cited, is the information presented in

542–54 ●

any patterns—as **QUOTATIONS**? **PARAPHRASES**? **SUMMARIES**? Are there repeated references to certain experts or sources?

In visual texts, look for patterns of color, shape, and line. What's in the foreground, and what's in the background? What's completely visible, partly visible, or hidden? In both verbal and visual texts, look for omissions and anomalies: What isn't there that you would expect to find? Is there anything that doesn't really fit in?

If you discover patterns, then you need to consider what, if anything, they mean in terms of what the writer is saying. What do they reveal about the writer's underlying premises and beliefs? What do they tell you about the writer's strategies for persuading readers to accept the truth of what they are saying?

See how color-coding an essay by *New York Times* columnist William Safire on the meaning of the Gettysburg Address reveals several patterns in the language Safire uses. In this excerpt from the essay, which was published just before the first anniversary of the September 11, 2001, terrorist attacks, Safire develops his analysis through several patterns. Religious references are colored yellow; references to a "national spirit," green; references to life, death, and rebirth, blue; and places where Safire directly addresses the reader, gray.

> But the selection of this poetic political sermon as the oratorical centerpiece of our observance need not be only an exercise. . . . Now, as then, a national spirit rose from the ashes of destruction.
>
> Here is how to listen to Lincoln's all-too-familiar speech with new ears.
>
> In those 266 words, you will hear the word *dedicate* five times. . . .
>
> Those five pillars of dedication rested on a fundament of religious metaphor. From a president not known for his piety—indeed, often criticized for his supposed lack of faith—came a speech rooted in the theme of national resurrection. The speech is grounded in conception, birth, death, and rebirth.
>
> Consider the barrage of images of birth in the opening sentence. . . .
>
> Finally, the nation's spirit rises from this scene of death: "that this nation, under God, shall have a new birth of freedom." Conception, birth, death, rebirth. The nation, purified in this fiery trial of war, is resurrected. Through the sacrifice of its sons, the sundered nation would be reborn as one. . . .

✳ academic literacies   ● fields   ● research
■ rhetorical situations   ⁘ processes   ● media/design
▲ genres   ◆ strategies

Do not listen on Sept. 11 only to Lincoln's famous words and comforting cadences. Think about how Lincoln's message encompasses but
goes beyond paying "fitting and proper" respect to the dead and the
bereaved. His sermon at Gettysburg reminds "us the living" of our
"unfinished work" and "the great task remaining before us"—to
resolve that this generation's response to the deaths of thousands of
our people leads to "a new birth of freedom."

The color coding helps us to see patterns in Safire's language, just as Safire
reveals patterns in Lincoln's words. He offers an interpretation of Lincoln's
address as a "poetic political sermon," and the words he uses throughout
support that interpretation. At the end, he repeats the assertion that Lincoln's
address is a sermon, inviting us to consider it differently. Safire's repeated
commands ("Consider," "Do not listen," "Think about") offer additional
insight into how he wishes to position himself in relation to his readers.

READING RHETORICALLY

To read academic texts effectively, you need to look beyond the words on
the page or screen to the **RHETORICAL CONTEXT** of the text and the argument it makes. Academic texts—both the ones you read and the ones
you write—are parts of ongoing scholarly conversations, in which writers respond to the ideas and assertions of others in order to advance
knowledge. To enter those conversations, you must first read carefully and
critically to understand the rhetorical situation, the larger context within
which a writer wrote, and the argument the text makes.

▲ 125–26

Considering the Rhetorical Situation

As a reader, you need to think about the message that the writer wants
to articulate, including the intended audience and the writer's attitude
toward that audience and the topic, as well as about the genre, medium,
and design of the text.

PURPOSE   What is the writer's purpose? To entertain? inform? persuade readers to think something or take some action?
What is *your* purpose for reading this text?

■ 59–60

61–64 ■
AUDIENCE   Who is the intended audience? Are you a member of that group? If not, should you expect that you'll need to look up unfamiliar terms or concepts or that you'll run into assumptions you don't necessarily share? How is the writer addressing the audience—as an expert addressing those less knowledgeable? as an outsider addressing insiders?

65–71 ■
GENRE   What is the genre? Is it a report? an argument? an analysis? something else? Knowing the genre can help you to anticipate certain key features.

72–74 ■
STANCE   Who is the writer, and what is their stance? Critical? Curious? Opinionated? Objective? Passionate? Indifferent? Something else? Knowing the stance affects the way you understand a text, whether you're inclined to agree or disagree with it, to take it seriously, and so on.

75–77 ■
MEDIA/DESIGN   What is the medium, and how does it affect the way you read? If it's a print text, what do you know about the publisher? If it's on the web, who sponsors the site, and when was it last updated? Are there any headings, summaries, or other elements that highlight key parts of the text?

Analyzing the Argument

All texts make some kind of argument, claiming something and then offering reasons and evidence as support for any claim. As a critical reader, you need to look closely at the argument a text makes—to recognize all the claims it makes, consider the support it offers for those claims, and decide how you want to respond. What do you think, and why? Here are some questions to consider when analyzing an argument:

347–49 ⁙
5 ✳
- *What claim is the text making?* What is the writer's main point? Is it stated as a **THESIS** or only implied? Is it limited or **QUALIFIED** somehow? If not, should it have been?

413–14 ◆
414–22
- *How is the claim supported?* What **REASONS** does the writer provide for the claim, and what **EVIDENCE** is given for the reasons? What kind of

---

⁙ academic literacies   ● fields   ● research
■ rhetorical situations   ⁙ processes   ● media/design
▲ genres   ◆ strategies

evidence is it? Facts? Statistics? Examples? Expert opinions? Images? How convincing do you find the reasons and evidence? Is there enough evidence?

- *What appeals besides logical ones are used?* Does the writer appeal to readers' **EMOTIONS**? try to establish **COMMON GROUND**? demonstrate their **CREDIBILITY** as trustworthy and knowledgeable? How success-ful are these appeals?
426–27
424
423–26

- *Are any* **COUNTERARGUMENTS** *acknowledged?* If so, are they presented accurately and respectfully? Does the writer concede any value to them or try to refute them? How successfully does the writer deal with them?
424–25

- *What outside sources of information does the writer cite?* What kinds of sources are they, and how credible do they seem? Are they current and authoritative? How well do they support the argument?

- *Do you detect any* **FALLACIES**? Fallacies are arguments that involve faulty reasoning. Because they often seem plausible, they can be per-suasive. It is important, therefore, that you question the legitimacy of such reasoning when you run across it.
427–29

Considering the Larger Context

All texts are part of ongoing conversations with other texts that have dealt with the same topic. An essay arguing for an assault-weapons ban is part of an ongoing conversation on gun legislation, which is itself part of a con-versation on individual rights and responsibilities. Academic texts document their sources in part to show their relationship to the ongoing scholarly conversation on a particular topic. In fact, anytime you're reading to learn, you're probably reading for some larger context. Whatever your reading goals, being aware of that larger context can help you better understand what you're reading. Here are some specific aspects of the text to pay attention to:

Who else cares about this topic?   Especially when you're reading in order to learn about a topic, the texts you read will often reveal which people or groups are part of the conversation—and might be sources of further read-ing. For example, an essay describing the formation of Mammoth Cave in Kentucky could be of interest to geologists, cave explorers, travel writers, or tourists. If you're reading such an essay while doing research on the cave, you should consider how the audience to whom the writer is writing determines the nature of the information provided—and its suitability as a source for your research.

What conversations is this text part of? Does the text refer to any concepts or ideas that give you some sense that it's part of a larger conversation? An argument on airport security measures, for example, is part of larger conversations about government response to terrorism, the limits of freedom in a democracy, and the possibilities of using technology to detect weapons and explosives, among others.

What terms does the writer use? Do any terms or specialized language reflect the writer's allegiance to a particular group or academic discipline? If you run across words like *false consciousness*, *ideology*, and *hegemony*, for example, you might guess that the text was written by a Marxist scholar.

What other writers or sources does the writer cite? Do the other writers have a particular academic specialty, belong to an identifiable intellectual school, share similar political leanings? If an article on politics cites Paul Krugman and Gail Collins in support of its argument, you might assume that the writer holds liberal opinions; if it cites Ross Douthat and Jennifer Rubin, the writer is likely a conservative.

READING VISUAL TEXTS

Photos, drawings, graphs, diagrams, and charts are frequently used to help convey important information and often make powerful arguments themselves. So learning to read and interpret visual texts is just as necessary as it is for written texts.

Taking visuals seriously. Remember that visuals are texts themselves, not just decoration. When they appear as part of a written text, they may introduce information not discussed elsewhere in the text. Or they might illustrate concepts hard to grasp from words alone. In either case, it's important to pay close attention to any visuals in a written text.

✳ academic literacies	● fields	● research
■ rhetorical situations	⁖ processes	● media/design
▲ genres	◆ strategies	

Looking at any title, caption, or other written text that's part of a visual will help you understand its main idea. It might also help to think about its purpose: Why did the writer include it? What information does it add or emphasize? What argument is it making? See, for example, how a psychology textbook uses visuals to help explain two ways that information can be represented:

Analogical and Symbolic Representations

When we think about information, we use two basic types of internal representations: analogical and symbolic.

   Analogical representations usually correspond to images. They have some characteristics of actual objects. Therefore, they are analogous to actual objects. For example, maps correspond to geographical layouts. Family trees depict branching relationships between relatives. A clock corresponds directly to the passage of time. **Figure 2.1a** is a drawing of a violin from a particular perspective. This drawing is an analogical representation.

Figure 2.1 Analogical versus Symbolic Representations
(a)   (b)

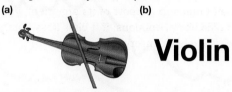

(a) Analogical representations, such as this picture of a violin, have some characteristics of the objects they represent.
(b) Symbolic representations, such as the word "violin," are abstract and do not have relationships to the physical qualities of objects.

   By contrast, **symbolic representations** are abstract. These representations usually consist of words or ideas. They do not have relationships to physical qualities of objects in the world. The word "hamburger" is a symbolic representation that usually represents a cooked patty of beef served on a bun. The word "violin" stands for a musical instrument (**Figure 2.1b**).   —Sarah Grison, Todd Heatherton, and Michael Gazzaniga, *Psychology in Your Life*

The headings tell you the topic: analogical and symbolic representations. The paragraphs define the two types of representation, and the illustrations present a visual example of each type. The visuals make the information in the written text easier to understand by illustrating the differences between the two.

Reading charts and graphs.   To read the information in charts and graphs, you need to look for different things depending on what type of chart or graph you're considering. A line graph, for example, usually contains certain elements: title, legend or clearly labeled parts, *x* axis (horizontal), *y* axis (vertical), and source information. Figure 2.2 shows one such graph taken from a sociology textbook.

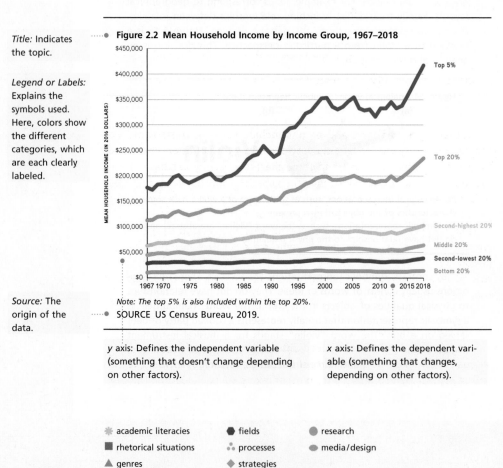

Title: Indicates the topic.

Legend or Labels: Explains the symbols used. Here, colors show the different categories, which are each clearly labeled.

Source: The origin of the data.

Figure 2.2 Mean Household Income by Income Group, 1967–2018

Note: The top 5% is also included within the top 20%.
SOURCE US Census Bureau, 2019.

y axis: Defines the independent variable (something that doesn't change depending on other factors).

x axis: Defines the dependent variable (something that changes, depending on other factors).

✳ academic literacies   ● fields   ● research

■ rhetorical situations   ⁖ processes   ● media/design

▲ genres   ◆ strategies

Figure 2.3 Women's Participation in the Labor Force in the United States

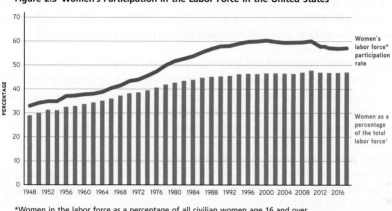

*Women in the labor force as a percentage of all civilian women age 16 and over.
†Women in the labor force as a percentage of the total workforce (both men and women) age 16 and over.
SOURCE US Bureau of Labor Statistics, 2018.

Other types of charts and graphs include some of these same elements. But the specific elements vary according to the different kinds of information being presented, and some charts and graphs can be challenging to read. For example, the chart in Figure 2.3, from the same textbook, includes elements of both bar and line graphs to depict two trends at once: the red line shows the percentage of women in the United States who were in the labor force over a sixty-eight-year period, and the blue bars show the percentage of US workers who were women during that same period. Both trends are shown in two-year increments. To make sense of this chart, you need to read the title, the y-axis legend, and the labels and their definitions carefully.

Reading Onscreen

Research shows that we tend to read differently onscreen than we do when we read print texts: we skim and sample, often reading a sentence or two and then jumping to another site, another text. If we need to scroll the page to continue, we often don't bother. In general, we don't read as carefully as we do when reading print texts, and we're less likely to reread or take other steps if we find that we don't understand something. Following are some strategies that might help you read effectively onscreen.

Adjust your reading speed and effort to your purpose.   Many students use the web to get an overview of a topic and find potential sources. In that case, skimming and browsing are sensible and appropriate tactics. If you're reading to evaluate a source or find specific information on a topic, though, you probably need to read more slowly and carefully.

Keep your purpose in mind as you read.   Clicking on hyperlinks and jumping from site to site can be tempting. Resist the temptation! Making a list of specific questions you're seeking to answer can help you stay focused and on task.

Print out longer texts.   Some people find reading online to be harder on their eyes than reading pages of print, and many find that they comprehend and remember information in longer texts better if they read them in print. Reading a long text is similar to walking through an unfamiliar neighborhood: we form a mental map of the text as we read and then associate the information with its location in the text, making remembering easier. Since forming such a map is more difficult when reading an electronic text, printing out texts you need to read carefully may be a good strategy.

If you need more help

524–34
333–44
367–71
372–79
380–84

See Chapter 48, **EVALUATING SOURCES**, for questions to help you analyze a text's rhetorical situation. See also Chapter 28 on **GENERATING IDEAS AND TEXT**; you can adapt those methods as ways of looking at texts, especially clustering and cubing. And see also Chapter 31 on **ASSESSING YOUR OWN WRITING**, Chapter 32 on **GETTING RESPONSE AND REVISING**, and Chapter 33 on **EDITING AND PROOFREADING** if you need advice for reading your own writing.

* academic literacies   ● fields   ● research
■ rhetorical situations   ∴ processes   ● media/design
▲ genres   ◆ strategies

3 Summarizing and Responding
Where Reading Meets Writing

Summarizing a text helps us to see and understand its main points and to think about what it says. Responding to that text then prompts us to think about—*and say*—what we think. Together, summarizing and responding to texts is one way that we engage with the ideas of others. In a history course, you might summarize and respond to an essay arguing that Civil War photographers did not accurately capture the realities of the battle-field. In a philosophy course, you might summarize Plato's "Allegory of the Cave" and respond to its portrayal of knowledge as shadows on a wall.

And in much of the writing that you do, you'll need to cite the ideas of others, both as context for your own thinking and as evidence to support your arguments. In fact, there's probably no topic you'll write about that someone else hasn't already written about—and one way of intro-ducing what you have to say is as a response to something others have said about your topic. A good way of doing that is by summarizing what they've said, using the summary as a launching pad for what you say. This chapter offers advice for summarizing and responding, writing tasks you'll have occasion to do in many of your college classes—and provides a short guide to writing a summary and response essay, a common assignment in composition classes.

SUMMARIZING

In many of your college courses, you'll likely be asked to summarize what someone else has said. Boiling down a text to its basic ideas helps you focus on the text, figure out what the writer has said, and understand (and remember) what you're reading. In fact, summarizing is an essential academic skill, a way to incorporate the ideas of others into your own writing. Following are some guidelines for summarizing effectively:

Read the text carefully. To write a good summary, you need to read the original text carefully to capture the writer's intended meaning as clearly and evenhandedly as you can. Start by **SKIMMING** the text to get a general sense of what it's saying. If some parts don't make sense, don't worry; at this point, you're reading just to get the gist. Then reread the text more slowly, **ANNOTATING** it paragraph by paragraph. If there's an explicit **THESIS** stating the main point, highlight it in some way. Then try to capture the main idea of each paragraph in a single sentence.

13

16–17

347–49

State the main points concisely and accurately. Summaries of a complete text are generally between 100 and 250 words in length, so you need to choose your words carefully and to focus only on the text's main ideas. Leave out supporting evidence, anecdotes, and counterarguments unless they're crucial to understanding the text. For instance, in summarizing "A Fighter's Chance" (see p. 245), Ryan Jones's profile of Rebecca Maine, a student, runner, and boxer, you would omit the lengthy description of her tattoo and her mother's description of her personality.

Describe the text accurately and fairly—and using neutral language. Present the author's ideas evenhandedly and fairly; a summary isn't the place to share your opinion of what the text says. Use neutral verbs such as "states," "asserts," or "concludes," not verbs that imply praise or criticism like "proves" or "complains."

551–54

Use SIGNAL PHRASES to distinguish what the author says from what you say. Introducing a statement with phrases such as "He says" or "The essay concludes" indicates explicitly that you're summarizing what the author said. When first introducing an author, you may need to say something about their credentials. For example:

* academic literacies   ● fields   ● research
■ rhetorical situations   ⋮ processes   ● media/design
▲ genres   ◆ strategies

In "Our Declaration," political philosopher Danielle Allen analyzes the language of the Declaration of Independence.

Jason Stanley, a Rutgers University philosophy professor, explains the many ways language can be used as a tool for suppression in his *New York Times* opinion piece, "The Ways of Silencing."

Later in the text, you may need to refer to the author again as you summarize specific parts of the text. These signal phrases are typically briefer: "In Stanley's view . . . ," "Allen then argues . . ."

Use quotations sparingly, if at all. You may need to **QUOTE** keywords or memorable phrases, but most or all of a summary should be written in your own words, using your own sentence structures.

544–47

DOCUMENT any text you summarize in a works-cited or references list. A summary of a lengthy work should include **IN-TEXT DOCUMENTATION** noting the pages summarized; they aren't needed with a brief text like the one summarized below (see p. 149).

560–63
MLA 567–74
APA 618–22

An Example Summary

In "The Reason College Costs More Than You Think," Jon Marcus, a higher-education editor at the *Hechinger Report*, reports that a major reason why college educations are so expensive is the amount of time students stay in college. Although almost all first-year students and their families assume that earning a bachelor's degree will take four years, the reality is that more than half of all students take longer, with many taking six years or more. This delay happens for many reasons, including students changing majors, having to take developmental courses, taking fewer courses per term than they could have, and being unable to register for required courses. As a result, their expenses are much greater—financial aid seldom covers a fifth or sixth year, so students must borrow money to finish—and the additional time they spend in college is time they aren't working, leading to significant losses in wages.

This summary begins with a signal phrase stating the author's name and credentials and the title of the text being summarized. The summary includes only the main ideas, in the summary writer's own words.

RESPONDING

When you summarize a text, you show that you understand its main ideas; responding to a text pushes you to engage with those ideas—and gives you the opportunity to contribute your own ideas to a larger conversation. You can respond in various ways, for instance, by taking a **POSITION** on the text's argument, by **ANALYZING THE TEXT** in some way, or by **REFLECTING** on what it says.

164–95 ▲
104–39
391–401 ⋮

Deciding How to Respond

You may be assigned to write a specific kind of response—an argument or analysis, for instance—but more often than not, the nature of your response is left largely up to you. If so, you'll need to read closely and critically to understand what the text says, to get a sense of how—and how well—it does so, and to think about your own reaction to it. Only then can you decide how to respond. You can respond to what the text says (its ideas), to how it says it (the way it's written), or to where it leads your own thinking (your own personal reaction). Or you might write a response that mixes those ways of responding. You might, for example, combine a personal reaction with an examination of how the writing caused that reaction.

If you're responding to what a text says, you might agree or disagree with the author's argument, supporting your position with good reasons and evidence for your response. You might agree with parts of the argument and disagree with others. You might find that the author has ignored or downplayed some important aspect of the topic that needs to be discussed or at least acknowledged. Here are some questions to consider that can help you think about what a text says:

- What does the writer claim?

413–14 ◆
414–22

- What **REASONS** and **EVIDENCE** does the writer provide to support that claim?

- What parts of the text do you agree with? Is there anything you disagree with—and if so, why?

✳ academic literacies   ● fields   ● research
■ rhetorical situations   ⋮ processes   ● media/design
▲ genres   ◆ strategies

- Does the writer represent any views other than their own? If not, what other perspectives should be considered?

- Are there any aspects of the topic that the writer overlooks or ignores?

- If you're responding to a visual text, how do the design and any images contribute to your understanding of what the text "says"?

Here is a brief response to Jon Marcus's "The Reason College Costs More Than You Think," one that responds to his argument:

> It's true that one reason college costs so much more is that students take longer than four years to finish their degrees, but Jon Marcus's argument in "The Reason College Costs More Than You Think" is flawed in several ways. He ignores the fact that over the past years state governments have reduced their subsidies to state-supported colleges and universities, forcing higher tuition, and that federal scholarship aid has declined as well, forcing students to pay a greater share of the costs. He doesn't mention the increased number of administrators or the costs of fancy athletic facilities and dormitories. Ultimately, his argument places most of the blame for higher college costs on students, who, he asserts, make poor choices by changing majors and "taking fewer courses per term than they could." College is supposed to present opportunities to explore many possible career paths, so changing majors should be considered a form of growth and education. Furthermore, many of us are working full-time to pay the high costs of college, leaving us with little extra time to study for four or five courses at once and sometimes forcing us to take fewer classes per term because that's all we can afford. Marcus is partly right—but he gets much of the problem wrong.

If you're focusing on the way a text is written, you'll consider what elements the writer uses to convey their message—facts, stories, images, and so on. You'll likely pay attention to the writer's word choices and look for any patterns that lead you to understand the text in a particular way. To think about the way a text is written, you might find some of these questions helpful:

- What is the writer's message? Is there an explicit statement of that message?

- How well has the writer communicated the message?

- How does the writer support what they say: by citing facts or statistics? by quoting experts? by noting personal experiences? Are you persuaded?

- Are there any words, phrases, or sentences that you find notable and that contribute to the text's overall effect?

128–34 ▲
- How does the text's design affect your response to it? If it's a **VISUAL TEXT** —a photo or ad, for example—how do the various parts of the text contribute to its message?

Here is a brief response to Marcus's essay that analyzes the various ways it makes its argument:

> In "The Reason College Costs More Than You Think," *Time* magazine writer Jon Marcus argues that although several factors contribute to high college costs, the main one is how long it takes students to graduate. Marcus introduces this topic by briefly profiling a student who is in his fifth year of school and has run out of financial aid because he "changed majors and took courses he ended up not needing." This profile gives a human face to the topic, which Marcus then develops with statistics about college costs and the numbers of students who take more than four years to finish. Marcus's purpose is twofold: to inform readers that the assumption that most students finish college in four years is wrong and to persuade them that poor choices like those this student made are the primary reason college takes so long and costs so much. He acknowledges that the extra costs are "hidden" and "not entirely the student's fault" and suggests that poor high school preparation and unavailable required courses play a role, as do limits on financial aid. However, his final paragraph quotes the student as saying of the extra years, "That's time you're wasting that you could be out making money." As the essay's final statement, this assertion that spending more time in school is time wasted and that the implicit goal of college is career preparation reinforces Marcus's argument that college *should* take only four years and that students who take longer are financially irresponsible.

If you're reflecting on your own reaction to a text, you might focus on how your personal experiences or beliefs influenced the way you understood the text or on how it reinforced or prompted you to reassess some of those beliefs. You could also focus on how it led you to see the topic in new ways—or note questions that it's led you to wonder about. Some questions that may help you reflect on your own reaction to a text include:

- How did the text affect you personally?
- Is there anything in the text that really got your attention? If so, what?
- Do any parts of the text provoke an emotional reaction—make you laugh or cry, make you uneasy? What prompted that response?
- Does the text bring to mind any memories or past experiences? Can you see anything related to yourself and your life in the text?
- Does the text remind you of any other texts?
- Does the text support (or challenge) any of your beliefs? How?
- Has reading this text given you any new ideas or insight?

Here is a brief response to Jon Marcus's essay that reflects on an important personal issue:

> Jon Marcus's "Why College Costs More Than You Think" made me think hard about my own educational plans. Because I'm working to pay for as much of my education as I can, I'm taking a full load of courses so I can graduate in four years, but truth be told I'm starting to question the major I've chosen. That's one aspect of going to college that Marcus fails to discuss: how your major affects your future career choices and earnings—and whether or not some majors that don't lead immediately to a career are another way of "wasting" your time. After taking several courses in English and philosophy, I find myself fascinated by the study of literature and ideas. If I decide to major in one or both of those subjects, am I being impractical? Or am I "following my heart," as Steve Jobs said in his Stanford commencement speech? Jobs did as he told those graduates to do, and it worked out well for him, so maybe majoring in something "practical" is less practical than it seems. If I graduate in four years and am "out making money" but doing something I don't enjoy, I might be worse off than if I take longer in college but find a path that is satisfying and enriching.

WRITING A SUMMARY AND RESPONSE ESSAY

You may be assigned to write a full essay that summarizes and responds to something you've read. Following is one such essay. It was written by Jacob MacLeod, a student at Wright State University, and responds to a *New York Times* column by Nicholas Kristof, "Our Blind Spot about Guns" (see p. 177).

JACOB MacLEOD

Guns and Cars Are Different

In "Our Blind Spot about Guns," *The New York Times* columnist Nicholas Kristof compares guns to cars in order to argue for sensible gun regulation. Kristof suggests that gun regulations would dramatically decrease the number of deaths caused by gun use. To demonstrate this point, he shows that the regulations governments have instituted for cars have greatly decreased the number of deaths per million miles driven. Kristof then argues that guns should be regulated in the same way that cars are, that car regulation provides a model for gun regulation. I agree with Kristof that there should be more sensible gun regulation, but I have difficulty accepting that all of the regulations imposed on cars have made them safer, and I also believe that not all of the safety regulations he proposes for guns would necessarily have positive effects.

Kristof is right that background checks for those who want to buy guns should be expanded. According to Daniel Webster, director of the Johns Hopkins Center for Gun Policy and Research, state laws prohibiting firearm ownership by members of high-risk groups, such as perpetrators of domestic violence and the mentally ill, have been shown to reduce violence. Therefore, Webster argues, universal background checks would significantly reduce the availability of guns to high-risk groups, as well as reducing the number of guns diverted to the illegal market by making it easier to prosecute gun traffickers.

Kristof also argues that lowering the speed limit made cars safer. However, in 1987, forty states raised their top speed limit from 55 to

❋ academic literacies   ● fields   ● research
■ rhetorical situations   ⁝ processes   ● media/design
▲ genres   ◆ strategies

65 miles per hour. An analysis of this change by the University of California Transportation Center shows that after the increase, traffic fatality rates on interstate highways in those forty states decreased between 3.4 percent and 5.1 percent. After the higher limits went into effect, the study suggested, some drivers may have switched to safer interstates from other, more dangerous roads, and highway patrols may have focused less on enforcing interstate speed limits and more on activities yielding greater benefits in terms of safety (Lave and Elias 58–61). Although common sense might suggest that lowered speed limits would mean safer driving, research showed otherwise, and the same may be true for gun regulation.

Gun control advocates argue that more guns mean more deaths. However, an article by gun rights advocates Don Kates and Gary Mauser argues that murder rates in many developed nations have no relation to the rate of gun ownership (6). The authors cite data on firearms ownership in the United States and England that suggest that crime rates are lowest where the density of gun ownership is highest and highest where gun density is lowest (8) and that increased gun ownership has often coincided with significant reductions in violence. For example, in the United States in the 1990s, criminal violence decreased, even though gun ownership increased (11–12). However, the authors acknowledge that "the notion that more guns reduce crime is highly controversial" (12).

In fact, a RAND Corporation study of recent research on the relationship between the number of guns and violent crime in the United States concluded that while "most of the new studies provide evidence consistent with the hypothesis that gun prevalence increases violent crime," the difficulty of measuring gun prevalence and other problems with the studies make showing a relationship difficult (Karimov).

All in all, then, Kristof is correct to suggest that sensible gun regulation is a good idea in general, but the available data suggest that some of the particular measures he proposes should not be instituted. I agree that expanding background checks would be a good way to regulate guns and that failure to require them would lead to more guns in the hands of criminals. While background checks are a good form of regulation, however, lower speed limits and trigger locks are not. The problem with this solution is that although it is based on commonsense thinking, the empirical data show that it may not work.

Works Cited

Karimov, Rouslan I. "The Relationship between Firearm Prevalence and Violent Crime." *RAND Corporation: Gun Policy in America*, 2 Mar. 2018, www.rand.org/research/gun-policy/analysis/essays /firearm-prevalence-violent-crime.html.

Kates, Don B., and Gary Mauser. "Would Banning Firearms Reduce Murder and Suicide? A Review of International Evidence." *bepress Legal Repository*, 2006, law.bepress.com/expresso /eps/1564. PDF download, working paper.

Kristof, Nicholas. "Our Blind Spot about Guns." *The New York Times*, 31 July 2014, www.nytimes.com/2014/07/31/opinion/nicholas -kristof-our-blind-spot-about-guns.html.

Lave, Charles, and Patrick Elias. "Did the 65 mph Speed Limit Save Lives?" *Accident Analysis and Prevention*, vol. 26, no. 1, Feb. 1994, pp. 49–62, www.sciencedirect.com/science/article /pii/000145759490068X.

Webster, Daniel. "Why Expanding Background Checks Would, in Fact, Reduce Gun Crime." Interview by Greg Sargent. *The Washington Post*, 3 Apr. 2013, www.washingtonpost.com/blogs/ plum-line/wp/2013/04/03/why-expanding-background-checks -would-in-fact-reduce-gun-crime.

In his response, MacLeod both agrees and disagrees with Kristof's argument, using several sources to support his argument that some of Kristof's proposals may not work. MacLeod states his thesis at the end of the first paragraph, after his summary, and ends with a balanced assessment of Kristof's proposals. He cites several sources, both in the text with signal phrases and in-text documentation and at the end in a works-cited section.

Key Features of Summary and Response Essays

A clearly identified author and title. Usually the author and title of the text being summarized are identified in a signal phrase in the first sentence. The author (or sometimes the title) may then be referred to in an abbreviated form if necessary in the rest of the essay: for example, "Kristof argues . . ." or "According to 'Our Blind Spot about Guns' . . ."

❋ academic literacies   ● fields   ● research

■ rhetorical situations   ⁝ processes   ● media/design

▲ genres   ◆ strategies

A concise summary of the text.   The summary presents the main and supporting ideas in the text, usually in the order in which they appear. MacLeod, for example, reduces Kristof's argument to four sentences that capture Kristof's main points while leaving out his many examples.

An explicit response.   Your essay should usually provide a concise statement (one sentence if possible) of your overall response to the text.

- *If you're responding to the argument,* you'll likely agree or disagree (or both), and so your response itself will constitute an argument, with an explicit thesis statement. For example, MacLeod first agrees with Kristof that "there should be more sensible gun regulation," but then introduces a two-part thesis: that not all automobile regulations have made cars safer and that not all gun regulations would make guns safer.

- *If you're analyzing the text,* you'll likely need to explain what you think the author is saying and how the text goes about conveying that message. An analysis of Kristof's text, for example, might focus on his comparison of automobile regulations with gun regulations.

- *If you're responding with a reflection,* you might explore the ideas, emotions, or memories that the text evokes, the effects of its ideas on your own beliefs, or how your own personal experiences support or contradict the author's position. One response to Kristof's essay might begin by expressing surprise at the comparison of guns to cars and then explore the reasons you find that comparison surprising, leading to a new understanding of the ways regulations can work to save lives.

Support for your response.   Whatever your response, you need to offer reasons and evidence to support what you say.

- *If you're responding to what the text says,* you may offer facts, statistics, anecdotal evidence, and textual evidence, as MacLeod does. You'll also need to consider—and acknowledge—any possible counterarguments, positions other than yours.

- *If you're responding to the way the text is written,* you may identify certain patterns in the text that you think mean something, and you'll need to cite evidence from the text itself. For example, Kristof twice invokes a popular slogan among gun rights advocates, "Guns don't kill people. People kill people," changing "guns" to "cars" to advance his argument that regulating guns may make them safer, just as has happened with cars.

- *If you're reflecting on your own reaction to the text,* you may connect its ideas with your own experiences or beliefs or explore how the text reinforced, challenged, or altered your beliefs. A staunch gun-rights advocate, for example, might find in Kristof's essay a reasonable middle ground too often lacking in polarized debates like the one on gun control.

Ways of Organizing a Summary and Response Essay

You can organize a summary and response essay in various ways. You may want to use a simple, straightforward structure that starts out by summarizing the text and then gives the **THESIS** of your response followed by details that develop the thesis.

347–49 ⁂

[Summary, followed by response]

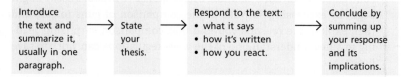

| Introduce the text and summarize it, usually in one paragraph. | → | State your thesis. | → | Respond to the text:
 • what it says
 • how it's written
 • how you react. | → | Conclude by summing up your response and its implications. |

Or you may want to start out with the thesis and then, depending on whether your response focuses on the text's argument or its rhetorical choices, provide a paired summary of each main point or each aspect of the writing and a response to it.

✳ academic literacies   ● fields   ● research
■ rhetorical situations   ⁂ processes   ● media/design
▲ genres   ◆ strategies

[Introduction and thesis, followed by point-by-point summary and response]

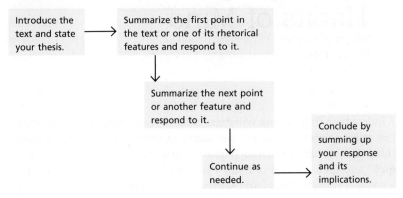

Introduce the text and state your thesis. → Summarize the first point in the text or one of its rhetorical features and respond to it. ↓ Summarize the next point or another feature and respond to it. ↓ Continue as needed. → Conclude by summing up your response and its implications.

If you need more help

See Chapter 30 for guidelines on **DRAFTING** and Chapter 29 for help writing a thesis and coming up with a title. See Chapter 31 on **ASSESSING YOUR OWN WRITING**, Chapter 32 on **GETTING RESPONSE AND REVISING**, and Chapter 33 on **EDITING AND PROOF-READING**. See Chapter 51 on **ACKNOWLEDGING SOURCES, AVOIDING PLAGIARISM**.

364–66
367–71
372–79
380–84
555–59

4 Developing Academic Habits of Mind

A little advice from Serena Williams: "Stick to it and work hard." She wasn't just talking about tennis, and her words resonate for all of us, for everything we set out to do. And here's Michael Jordan, who tells us "Never quit!" and then goes on to issue a warning: "If you quit once, it becomes a habit." Serena Williams and Michael Jordan may be two of the greatest athletes ever, but neither of them was born a champion. They became great by working hard, hanging in there, never giving up.

They succeeded, in other words, by developing certain habits of mind that can serve us all well—and that are especially valuable when it comes to succeeding in school. This chapter is about developing *academic habits of mind*. Just as Serena Williams wasn't born with her powerful serve, none of us was born knowing how to write academic papers or ace exams. But we, too, can learn and can develop the habits we need to succeed. This chapter offers advice for developing habits of mind that writing teachers nationwide have identified as essential for college success.

Engage

We all know people who see school as a series of hoops to jump through, who seem uninvolved—and even bored. We also know people who are passionate about something—a video game, a hobby, a profession—and who invest themselves, their time, and their emotions wholeheartedly in those activities. Successful students make that investment in school. In other words, they engage with what they're studying, what they're doing, and what they're learning.

✳ academic literacies   ● fields   ● research

■ rhetorical situations   ⁝ processes   ● media/design

▲ genres   ◆ strategies

Think about your purpose for being in college.   What are your goals? To get a degree? To qualify for a particular job or profession? To find intellectual stimulation? To explore life? Try to define why you are in school, both in larger terms ("to get a degree in accounting") and in terms of the specific courses you're taking ("Learning to write better will help me be a better student in general and communicate effectively at work").

Fight off boredom.   Every job, including the job of being a student, involves some tasks that are dull but need to be done. When you encounter such a task, ask yourself how it helps you reach a larger goal. Shooting a hundred free throws for practice may not seem interesting, but it can help you win games. When you're listening to a lecture or reading a textbook, take notes, highlight, and annotate; doing that forces you to pay attention and increases what you remember and learn. Trying to identify the main ideas as you listen to a lecture will help you stay focused. When you're studying, try alternating between different tasks: reading, writing, doing problem sets, drawing, and so on.

If you get distracted, figure out ways to deal with it.   It's hard to engage with what you're reading or studying when you're thinking about something else—paying a tuition bill, the last episode of *The Walking Dead,* whatever. Try taking a few moments to write out what's on your mind, in a journal or somewhere else. Sometimes that simple act frees your mind to think about your work, even if it doesn't solve anything.

Raise your hand.   When you think you know the answer to a teacher's question (or when you yourself have a question), raise your hand. Most teachers appreciate students who take chances and who participate in class. At the same time, be polite: don't monopolize discussion or interrupt others when they're speaking.

Get involved.   Get to know other students; study with them; join a campus organization. People who see themselves as part of something larger, even just a study group with three or four others, engage more in what they're doing than those who try to go it alone.

Be Curious

When we're young, we're curious about everything, and we learn by asking questions (why? why *not?*) and by exploring our surroundings (digging holes, cutting up magazines, investigating attics and basements). As we get older, though, we focus on things that interest us—and may as a result start to ignore other things or even to forget how to explore. In college, you'll be asked to research, study, and write about many topics you know nothing about. Seize the opportunity. Be curious! And take a tip from Dr. Seuss: "The more that you read, the more things you will know. / The more that you learn, the more places you'll go."

Ask questions. It's tempting to stay within our comfort zones, thinking about things we know and like, listening to those whose views we tend to agree with—to say what we already believe rather than to stop and think. Resist that temptation! Take every opportunity to ask questions, to learn more about things you're already interested in, and especially to learn about things you don't (yet) know anything about. As marine biologist Sylvia Earle says, "The best scientists and explorers have the attributes of kids! They ask questions and have a sense of wonder. They have curiosity. Who, what, where, why, when, and how! They never stop asking questions, and I never stop asking questions, just like a five year old."

Listen! Pay attention to what others say, including those who you don't necessarily agree with. The words and ideas of others can challenge the way we think, prompt us to rethink what we think—and spark our curiosity: Why does X think that? What do *I* think—*and why?* Why do my neighbors oppose the Common Core academic standards? What do educators think about it? Paying attention to all sides of an argument, doing research to find out what others have said about a topic, or searching social media to see the latest postings on a trending topic are all ways you can listen in on (and engage in) conversations on important issues of all kinds.

Be Open to New Ideas

No matter where you're in school, you're going to encounter ideas and concepts and even facts that challenge your own beliefs; you're also likely to meet people whose backgrounds and ways of looking at life are very

academic literacies   fields   research
rhetorical situations   processes   media/design
genres   strategies

different from your own. Be open-minded, open to new ideas and to what others think and say. Consider the perspectives and arguments of others. Learning involves accepting new ideas, acknowledging the value of different perspectives, and coming to understand our own beliefs in new ways. Listen to what others say, and think before you respond.

- *Treat the ideas of others with respect,* whether you agree with them or not, and encourage others to do the same. We don't open up if we don't feel safe.

- *Try to withhold judgment.* Be willing to listen to the thoughts of others and to consider ideas that may at first seem alien or weird (or wrong). Remember that your weird is likely someone else's normal—and the reverse.

- *Look for common ground between your perspectives and those of others*— places where you can agree, even in the midst of serious disagreement.

Be Flexible

Being flexible means being adaptable. In college, you'll likely face novel situations and need to find new ways to address problems, such as juggling school, work, and family; adjusting to roommates and making new friends; and figuring out how to do unfamiliar new assignments and how to take tests. You'll even have to do new kinds of writing: lab reports, reflections, literacy narratives, and many, many more; if your school writing up until this point has usually (or always) called for a five-paragraph theme, that's not going to be the case anymore.

Look for new ways to do things.   As the saying goes, "If all you have is a hammer, everything looks like a nail." Look for other tools to add to your toolbox: try solving math problems with words or by drawing, or starting a writing project by sketching out the parts.

Try not to see things as right or wrong, good or bad.   Be willing to consider alternative points of view and to withhold judgment. Often ideas or actions can only be judged in context; they may be true in some cases or in part, and you often need to understand the larger situation or take into account various perspectives. For example, you may believe that lying is wrong, but is it excusable if telling the truth will cause someone pain? You find a required reading assignment boring and useless, but why, then, did your instructor assign it?

Approach academic assignments rhetorically.   Analyze each assignment's purpose, intended audience, and the rest of its **RHETORICAL SITUATION**. Think about what's required in terms of content and format—and also about what's appropriate in terms of language and style. And what's expected in the discipline: informal language, sentence fragments, and photographs without captions might be appropriate for a sociology blog, for example, whereas a research project for a history course might have different requirements for how it's organized, formatted, and documented.

Be Creative

If you think that creativity is something artists have (and are born with), think again. From the young man selling homemade granola at a local farm market to the woman who puts together an eye-catching outfit from thrift-store bins, many of us are at work expressing ourselves in distinctive ways. Psychologists tell us that acting creatively opens us up to becoming more creative—and it's safe to say that doing so will make your work more productive and very likely more fun.

- *Play with ideas.* Freewrite. Make lists. Try looping, clustering, and the other ways of **GENERATING IDEAS** covered in this book. Take some time to think about the ideas you come up with.

- *Don't wait until the last minute.* Some students say they do better under the pressure of a deadline. Don't believe it! It's *always* better to give yourself time to think, to explore ideas, to "sleep on" assignments that first stump you.

- *Take risks!* Explore questions and topics that you haven't thought about before. Try out methods you haven't used previously. Challenge yourself to come up with ten ideas. Or twenty.

- *Ask questions.* And remember that there's no such thing as a dumb question.

57 ■

333–44 ⁖

✳ academic literacies   ● fields   ● research
■ rhetorical situations   ⁖ processes   ● media/design
▲ genres   ◆ strategies

Persist

Sometimes the key to success is simply sticking to the task at hand: ignoring distractions, hanging in there, forgetting frustration, getting the work done even in the face of setbacks and failures. Here's some advice from actress and singer Julie Andrews: "Perseverance is failing 19 times and succeeding the 20th."

- *Don't quit.* Assume that you can complete the task, and make up your mind to do it. If you're reading a book that seems hopelessly confusing or over your head, for example, keep at it until it starts to make sense. Reread, **OUTLINE CHAPTERS**, **SUMMARIZE**, **ANNOTATE**, and do whatever else you need to do to understand it.

340–42
20
16–17

- *Remember that sometimes you'll encounter setbacks*—and that the goal (a passing grade, a degree, a job) is still reachable if you keep trying. Those who play video games know that failing is an inherent part of playing them; the same is true of many other things as well.

- *Make a plan and establish a schedule,* and stick to them.

- *Break large projects into smaller goals.* Especially with assignments that call for a huge amount of work, approach it in stages: focus on getting through the next chapter, the next draft, the next whatever. It may be good to "keep your eyes on the prize," but it's usually best to take it one step at a time.

- *When you're working on several assignments, tackle the hardest ones first.* Work on them when you're fresh and your mind is clear.

- *If you don't understand something, ask for clarification.* Better to admit to confusion than to act as if you know something when you don't.

- *Ask for help when you need it.* Teachers are usually happy to help students during office hours or by appointment, before or after class, or over email. Get to know your teachers: they're there to help you.

- *Take advantage of whatever help is available* at your school's writing center or learning center and in class. An important part of being persistent is getting help when you need it.

Reflect

Pay attention to the ways you work and make decisions. Reflect on the ways you think and on how you think about the world. This kind of "meta-cognitive" thinking is one of the most important habits of mind, and it's one that will continue to serve you well throughout your life.

- *Figure out when you are most efficient* and do your best work—and try to schedule your work accordingly.

11–32 ✳

- *Pay attention to what you're reading and how you're doing it.* Think about why you're reading x, and use **READING STRATEGIES** appropriate to your purpose. If you lose the thread of an explanation or argument, figure out where you got lost and why.

- *After completing an assignment, reflect in writing* on what you did well, what problems you had, and how you solved them (or not). What would you do differently next time—or if you had more time? You'll find prompts for "Taking Stock of Your Work" at the end of Chapters 10–22 that can help.

- *Troubleshoot.* Pay attention to bumps in the road as you encounter them. Try to understand what caused the problem, what you did to solve it, how successful you were and why.

- *Try to focus on your achievements, what you can do*, rather than on what you may not be able to do or to do as well as you'd like.

Collaborate

Whether you're working in a face-to-face group, posting on an online discussion board, or exchanging drafts with a classmate for peer review, you likely spend a lot of time working with others on writing tasks. Even if you do much of your writing sitting alone at a computer, you probably get help from others at various stages in the writing process—and provide help as well. Two (or more) heads can be better than one—and learning to work well with a team is as important as anything else you'll learn in college.

✳ academic literacies   ● fields   ● research
■ rhetorical situations   ⁖ processes   ● media/design
▲ genres   ◆ strategies

Working with others face-to-face.   While informal groups can sometimes accomplish a lot, it's often better to be organized.

- Make sure everyone is facing everyone else and is physically part of the group. Doing that makes a real difference in the quality of the interactions—think how much better conversation works when you're sitting around a table than it does when you're sitting in a row.

- Thoughtfulness, respect, and tact are key, since most writers (as you know) are sensitive and need to be able to trust those commenting on their work. Respond to the contributions of others as you would like others to respond to yours.

- Each meeting needs an agenda—and careful attention paid to time. Appoint one person as timekeeper to make sure all necessary work gets done in the available time.

- Appoint another person to be group leader or facilitator. That person needs to make sure everyone gets a chance to speak, no one dominates the discussion, and the group stays on task.

- Appoint a member of the group to keep a record of the group's discussion, jotting down the major points as they come up and afterward writing a **SUMMARY** of the discussion that the group members then approve. 33–35

Working with others online.   You're likely to work with one or more people online. When sharing writing or collaborating with others online in other ways, consider the following suggestions:

- As with all online communication, remember that you need to choose your words carefully to avoid inadvertently hurting someone's feelings. Without facial expressions, gestures, and other forms of body language and without tone of voice, your words carry all the weight.

- Remember that the **AUDIENCE** for what you write may well extend beyond your group—your work might be forwarded to others, so there's no telling who else might read it. 61–64

- Decide as a group how best to deal with the logistics of exchanging drafts and comments. You can cut and paste text directly into email, send it as an attachment to a message, or post it to your class course management system site or a file-sharing site like *Dropbox* or *Google Docs*. You may need to use a combination of methods, depending on each group member's access to equipment and software. In any case, name your files carefully so that everyone knows which version to use.

- If you're using conferencing software like *Zoom* or *Microsoft Teams*, be aware that only one person at a time can speak and those who chime in quickly can dominate the conversation, sometimes silencing quieter members of the group. Be sure that everyone has a chance to contribute.

Creating group projects.   Creating a document with a team is common in business and professional work and in some academic fields as well. Here are some tips for making collaboration of this kind work well:

- *Define the task as clearly as possible.* Make sure everyone understands and agrees with the stated goals.

- *Divide the task into parts.* Decide which parts can be done by individuals, which can be done by a subgroup, and which need to be done by everyone together.

- *Assign each group member certain tasks.* Try to match tasks to each person's skills and interests and to divide the work equally.

- *Establish a deadline for each task.* Allow time for unforeseen problems before the project deadline.

- *Try to accommodate everyone's style of working.* Some people value discussion; others want to get right down to the writing. There's no best way to get work done; everyone needs to be conscious that their way is not the only way.

- *Work for consensus—not necessarily total agreement.* Everyone needs to agree that the plan to get the writing accomplished is doable and appropriate—if not exactly the way you would do the project if you were working alone.

❋ academic literacies	● fields	● research
■ rhetorical situations	⁘ processes	◖ media/design
▲ genres	◆ strategies	

- *Make sure everyone performs.* In some situations, your instructor may help, but in others the group itself may have to develop a way to make sure that the work gets done well and fairly. During the course of the project, it's sometimes helpful for each group member to write an assessment both of the group's work and of individual members' contributions.

Making the most of writing conferences.   Conferences with instructors or writing tutors, whether face-to-face or online, can be an especially helpful kind of collaboration. These one-on-one sessions often offer the most strongly focused assistance you can get—and truly valuable instruction. Here are some tips for making the most of conference time:

- *Be prepared.* Have at hand all necessary materials, including the draft you'll be discussing, your notes, any outlines—and, of course, any questions.

- *Be prompt.* Your instructor or tutor has set aside a block of time for you, and once that time is up, there's likely to be another student writer waiting.

- *Listen carefully, discuss your work seriously, and try not to be defensive.* Your instructor or tutor is only trying to help you produce the best piece possible. If you sense that your work is being misunderstood, explain what you're trying to say. Don't get angry! If a sympathetic reader who's trying to help can't understand what you mean, maybe you haven't conveyed your meaning well enough.

- *Take notes.* During the conference, jot down keywords and suggestions. Immediately afterward, flesh out your notes so you'll have a complete record of what was said.

- *Reflect on the conference.* Afterward, think about what you learned. What do you have to do now? Create a plan for revising or doing further work, and write out questions you will ask at your next conference or in a follow-up email or text.

Take Responsibility

In one way or another, all the habits of mind discussed above involve taking responsibility for your own actions. It may be tempting to blame others or society or bad luck for problems in your academic life, but the more you take ownership of your own learning, the more control you have over the results. Some ways you can enhance your sense of responsibility and demonstrate it include these:

- *Acknowledge that how much you learn and what grades you get depend mostly on you.* Teachers often say that they don't *give* grades, students *earn* grades—an important difference.

- *Treat school as you do a job,* one for which you must show up on time, perform tasks at a certain level of competence, and meet deadlines. In college, where your time is mostly unstructured, you have to become your own boss. So attend class regularly, follow instructions, and turn in assignments on time.

- *Get organized.* Maintain a calendar so you know what's due when. Create a schedule for your day that includes time for class, studying, working, and personal activities. Develop a system for organizing your written work and notes for each course you're taking. Learn where to find the materials you need to do your classwork.

542–54
560–63
- *Use research sources responsibly.* QUOTE, PARAPHRASE, and SUMMA-RIZE the work of others accurately, and DOCUMENT it correctly. Give appropriate credit to those whose ideas and words you are using.

✳ academic literacies ● fields ● research
■ rhetorical situations ⦙ processes ● media/design
▲ genres ◆ strategies

Part 2
Rhetorical Situations

Whenever we write, whether it's a text to a friend or a toast for a wedding, an English essay or a résumé, we face some kind of rhetorical situation. We have a **PURPOSE**, a certain **AUDIENCE**, a particular **STANCE**, a **GENRE**, and a **MEDIUM** to consider—and, as often as not, a **DESIGN**. All are important elements that we need to think about carefully. The following chapters offer brief discussions of those elements of the rhetorical situation, along with questions that can help you make the choices you need to as you write. See also the **GENRE** chapters for guidelines for considering your rhetorical situation in each of these specific kinds of writing.

Rhetorical Situations

5 Purpose   59

6 Audience   61

7 Genre   65

8 Stance   72

9 Media/Design   75

5 Purpose

All writing has a purpose. We write to explore our thoughts and emotions, to express ourselves, to entertain; we write to record words and events, to communicate with others, to try to persuade others to believe as we do or to behave in certain ways. In fact, we often have several purposes at the same time. We may write an essay in which we try to *explain* something to an audience, but at the same time we may be trying to *persuade* that audience of something. Look, for example, at this passage from a *New York Times* opinion essay by Christian B. Miller, a professor of philosophy at Wake Forest University. Miller explores the question of how cheating on exams can be discouraged, especially in online courses and homeschooling, and states, "I suggest that a practice that has been used widely in other educational contexts be extended to the world of online testing: pledging one's honor." He then explores honor codes "from elementary to graduate level":

> Donald McCabe at Rutgers Business School and Linda Treviño at the Smeal College of Business at Penn State found a 23 percent rate of helping someone with answers on a test at colleges without an honor code, versus only 11 percent at schools with an honor code. They reported impressive differences as well for plagiarism (20 percent versus 10 percent), unauthorized crib notes (17 percent versus 11 percent), and unpermitted collaboration (49 percent versus 27 percent), among other forms of cheating.
>
> A serious commitment to the honor code is crucial to its efficacy. As Professors McCabe and Treviño insist, an honor code should be "well implemented and strongly embedded in the student culture."
>
> What does that look like in practice? A few schools start the academic year with an actual commitment ceremony, where each student has to publicly pledge to uphold the school's code. To this can be added a requirement to affirm the honor code on each graded assignment.
>
> —Christian B. Miller, "Just How Dishonest Are Most Students?"

Miller is reporting information here, outlining how honor codes affect students' honesty in schooling. He is also making an argument that honor codes are preferable to other, surveillance- or punishment-focused methods of curbing cheating because "Most students are not deeply dishonest." His main purpose, then, is to persuade readers that schools should adopt honor codes.

Even though our purposes may be many, knowing our primary reason for writing can help us shape that writing and understand how to proceed with it. Our purpose can determine the genre we choose, our audience, even the way we design what we write.

Identify your purpose. While a piece of writing often has many purposes, a writer usually focuses on one. When you get an assignment or see a need to write, ask yourself what the primary purpose of the writing task is: to entertain? to inform? to persuade? to demonstrate your knowledge or your writing ability? What are your own goals? What are your audience's expectations, and do they affect the way you define your purpose?

Thinking about Purpose

- *What do you want your audience to do, think, or feel?* How will your readers use what you tell them?

- *What does this writing task call on you to do?* Do you need to show that you have mastered certain content or skills? Do you have an assignment that specifies a particular **STRATEGY** or **GENRE** — to compare two things, perhaps, or to argue a position?

- *What are the best ways to achieve your purpose?* What **STANCE** should you take? Should you write in a particular genre? Do you have a choice of **MEDIUM**, and does your text require any special format or **DESIGN** elements?

403 ◆
79 ▲
72–74 ■
657 ●

✳ academic literacies   ● fields   ● research
■ rhetorical situations   ⁖ processes   ● media/design
▲ genres   ◆ strategies

6 Audience

Who will read (or hear) what you are writing? A seemingly obvious but crucially important question. Your audience affects your writing in various ways. Consider a piece of writing as simple as a text from a mother to her son:

Pls. take chicken out to thaw and feed Annye. Remember Dr. Wong at 4.

On the surface, this brief note is a straightforward reminder to do three things. But in fact it is a complex message filled with compressed information for a specific audience. The writer (the mother) counts on the reader (her son) to know a lot that can be left unsaid. She expects that he knows that the chicken is in the freezer and needs to thaw in time to be cooked for dinner; she knows that he knows who Annye is (a pet?), what they are fed, and how much; she assumes that he knows who (and where) Dr. Wong is. She doesn't need to spell out any of that because she knows what her son knows and what he needs to know—and in her text she can be brief. She understands her audience. Think how different such a reminder would be were it written to another audience—a babysitter, perhaps, or a friend helping out while Mom is out of town.

What you write, how much you write, how you phrase it, even your choice of **GENRE** (essay, email, text, social media post, speech)—all are influenced by the audience you envision. And your audience will interpret your writing according to their own expectations and experiences, not yours.

65–71

When you are a student, your audience is most often your teachers, so you need to be aware of their expectations and learn about the conventions (rules, often unstated) for writing in specific academic fields. You may make statements that seem obvious to you, not realizing that your instructors may consider them assertions that must be proved with evidence of one sort or another. Or you may write more or less formally than teachers expect. Understanding your audience's expectations—by asking outright, by reading materials in your field of study, by trial and error—is important to your success as a college writer.

This point is worth dwelling on. You're probably reading this textbook for a writing course. As a student, you'll be expected to edit and proofread your essays carefully. But if you correspond with family, friends, or coworkers using email and texts, you might not proofread your messages much (or at all)—and your readers are probably fine with that. Whatever the rhetorical situation, your writing must meet the expectations of your audience.

Identify your audience.   Audiences may be defined as *known*, *multiple*, or *unknown*. *Known audiences* can include people with whom you're familiar as well as people you don't know personally but whose needs and expectations you do know. You yourself are a known, familiar audience, and you write to and for yourself often. Class notes, to-do lists, reminders, and journals are all written primarily for an audience of one: you. For that reason, they are often in shorthand, full of references and code that you alone understand.

Other known, familiar audiences include anyone you actually know—friends, relatives, teachers, classmates—and whose needs and expectations you understand. You can also know what certain readers want and need, even if you've never met them personally, if you write for them within a specific shared context. Such a known audience might include PC gamers who read cheat codes that you've posted on the internet for beating a game; you don't know those people, but you know roughly what they know about the game and what they need to know, and you know how to write about it in ways they will understand.

You often have to write for *multiple audiences*. Business memos or reports may be written initially for a supervisor, who may pass them along to others. Grant proposals may be reviewed by four to six levels of readers—each, of course, with its own expectations and perspectives. Even writing for a class might involve multiple audiences: your instructor and your classmates.

※ academic literacies   ● fields   ● research

■ rhetorical situations   ⁘ processes   ● media/design

▲ genres   ◆ strategies

Unknown audiences can be the most difficult to address since you can't be sure what they know, what they need to know, how they'll react. Such an audience could be your downstairs neighbor, with whom you've chatted occasionally in the laundry room. How will she respond to your letter asking her to sponsor you in an upcoming charity walk? Another unknown audience — perhaps surprisingly — might be many of your instructors, who want — and expect! — you to write in ways that are new to you. While you can benefit from analyzing any audience, you need to think most carefully about those you don't know.

Thinking about Audience

- *Whom do you want to reach?* To whom are you writing (or speaking)?

- *What is your audience's background — their education and life experiences?* It may be important for you to know, for example, whether your readers attended college, fought in a war, or have young children.

- *What are their interests?* What do they like? What motivates them? What do they care about?

- *Is there any demographic information that you should keep in mind?* Consider whether race, gender, sexual orientation, disabilities, occupation, religious beliefs, economic status, and so on should affect what or how you write. For example, writers for *Men's Health*, *InStyle*, and *Out* must consider the particular interests of each magazine's readers.

- *What political circumstances may affect their reading?* What attitudes — opinions, special interests, biases — may affect the way your audience reads your piece? Are your readers conservative, liberal, or middle of the road? Politics may take many other forms as well — retirees on a fixed income may object to increased school taxes, so a letter arguing for such an increase would need to appeal to them differently than would a similar letter sent to parents of young children.

- *What does your audience already know — or believe — about your topic? What do you need to tell them? What is the best way to do so?* Those retirees who oppose school taxes already know that taxes are a burden for them; they may need to know why schools are justified in asking for more money every few years. A good way to explain this may be with a bar graph showing how property values benefit from good schools with adequate funding. Consider which **STRATEGIES** will be effective—narrative, comparison, something else?

403 ◆

- *What's your relationship with your audience, and how should it affect your language and tone?* Do you know them, or not? Are they friends? colleagues? mentors? adversaries? strangers? Will they likely share your **STANCE**? In general, you need to write more formally when you're addressing readers you don't know, and you may address friends and colleagues more informally than you would a boss.

72–74 ■

- *What does your audience need and expect from you?* Your history professor, for example, may need to know how well you can discuss the economy of the late Middle Ages in order to assess your learning; he may expect you to write a carefully reasoned argument, drawing conclusions from various sources, with a readily identifiable thesis in the first paragraph. Your boss, on the other hand, may need an informal email that briefly lists your sales contacts for the day; she may expect that you list the contacts in the order in which you saw them, that you clearly identify each one, and that you briefly say how well each contact went. What **GENRE** is most appropriate?

79 ▲

- *What kind of response do you want?* Do you want readers to believe or do something? to accept as valid your information on a topic? to understand why an experience you once had still matters to you now?

657 ●

- *How can you best appeal to your audience?* Is there a particular **MEDIUM** that will best reach them? Are there any **DESIGN** requirements? (Elderly readers may need larger type, for instance.)

✳ academic literacies   ⬣ fields   ● research

■ rhetorical situations   ⁘ processes   ⬭ media/design

▲ genres   ◆ strategies

7 Genre

Genres are kinds of writing. Letters, profiles, reports, position papers, poems, blog posts, instructions, parodies—even jokes—are genres. For example, here is the beginning of a **PROFILE** of a mechanic who repairs a specific kind of automobile:

▲ 245–57

> Her business card reads Shirley Barnes, M.D., and she's a doctor, all right—a Metropolitan Doctor. Her passion is the Nash Metropolitan, the little car produced by Austin of England for American Motors between 1954 and 1962. Barnes is a legend among southern California Met lovers—an icon, a beacon, and a font of useful knowledge and freely offered opinions.

A profile offers a written portrait of someone or something that informs and sometimes entertains, often examining its subject from a particular angle—in this case, as a female mechanic who fixes old cars. While the language in this example is informal and lively ("she's a doctor, all right"), the focus is on the subject, Shirley Barnes, "M.D." If this same excerpt were presented as a poem, however, the new genre would change our reading:

> Her business card reads
> Shirley Barnes, M.D.,
> and she's a doctor, all right
> —a Metropolitan Doctor.
> Her passion is the Nash Metropolitan,
> the little car produced by Austin of England
> for American Motors between 1954 and 1962.
> Barnes is a legend
> among southern California Met lovers
> —an icon,

a beacon,
and a font of useful knowledge and
freely offered opinions.

The content hasn't changed, but the different presentation invites us to read not only to learn about Shirley Barnes but also to explore the significance of the words and phrases on each line, to read for deeper meaning and greater appreciation of language. The genre thus determines how we read and how we interpret what we read.

Genres help us write by establishing features for conveying certain kinds of content. They give readers clues about what sort of information they're likely to find and so help them figure out how to read ("This article begins with an abstract, so it's probably a scholarly source" or "Thank goodness! I found the instructions for editing videos on my phone"). At the same time, genres are flexible; writers often tweak the features or combine elements of different genres to achieve a particular purpose or connect with an audience in a particular way. Genres also change as writers' needs and available technologies change. For example, computers have enabled us to add audio and video content to texts that once could appear only on paper.

Choosing the Appropriate Genre

How do you know which genre you should choose? Often the words and phrases used in writing assignments can give you clues to the best choice. Here are typical terms used in assignments and the genres they usually call for.

81–103 ▲
LITERACY NARRATIVE If you're assigned to explore your development as a writer or reader or to describe how you came to be interested in a particular subject or career, you'll likely need to write a literacy narrative or a variation on one. Some terms that might signal a literacy narrative: "describe a learning experience," "tell how you learned," "trace your development," "write a story."

104–39 ▲
223–35
TEXTUAL ANALYSIS or **LITERARY ANALYSIS** If your assignment calls on you to look at a nonfiction text to see not only what it says but also how it works, you likely need to write a textual analysis. If the text is a short story,

✳ academic literacies   ● fields   ● research
■ rhetorical situations   ⦂ processes   ● media/design
▲ genres   ◆ strategies

novel, poem, or play, you probably need to write a literary analysis. If you are analyzing a text or texts in multiple media, you might choose either genre or mix the two. Some terms that might signal that a textual or literary analysis is required: "analyze," "examine," "explicate," "read closely," "interpret."

REPORT If your task is to research a topic and then tell your audience in a balanced, neutral way what you know about it, your goal is probably to write a report. Some terms that might signal that a report is required: "define," "describe," "explain," "inform," "observe," "record," "report," "show." ▲ 140–63

POSITION PAPER or **ARGUMENT** Some terms that might signal that your instructor wants you to take a position or argue for or against something: "agree or disagree," "argue," "claim," "criticize," "defend," "justify," "position paper," "prove." ▲ 164–95

SUMMARY If your assignment is to reduce a text into a single paragraph or so, a summary is called for. Some terms that might signal that a summary is expected: "abridge," "boil down," "compress," "condense," "recap," "summarize." ✳ 33–35

EVALUATION If your instructor asks you to say whether or not you like something or whether it's a good or bad example of a category or better or worse than something else, an evaluation is likely required. Some terms that might signal that an evaluation is expected: "assess," "critique," "evaluate," "judge," "recommend," "review." ▲ 214–22

MEMOIR If you're asked to explore an important moment or event in your life, you're probably being asked to write a memoir. Some terms that likely signal that a memoir is desired: "autobiography," "chronicle," "narrate," "a significant personal memory," "a story drawn from your experience." ▲ 234–44

PROFILE If your instructor assigns you the task of portraying a subject in a way that is both informative and entertaining, you're likely being asked to write a profile. Some terms that might indicate that a profile is being asked for: "angle," "describe," "dominant impression," "interview," "observe," "report on." ▲ 245–57

258–68 ▲ **PROPOSAL** If you're asked to offer a solution to a problem, to suggest some action—or to make a case for pursuing a certain project, a proposal is probably in order. Some terms that might indicate a proposal: "argue for [a solution or action]," "propose," "put forward," "recommend."

269–79 ▲ **EXPLORATION** If your assignment calls on you to think in writing about something or to play with ideas, you are likely being asked to write an exploratory essay. Some terms that may mean that an exploration is called for: "consider," "explore," "ponder," "probe," "reflect," "speculate."

280–92 ▲ **REMIX** If you're asked to adapt something you've written to create something new—perhaps for a new purpose, audience, or medium—a remix is probably in order. Some terms that might indicate a remix is asked for: "convert," "modify," "recast," "reimagine," "transform."

Dealing with Ambiguous Assignments

Sometimes even the key term in an assignment doesn't indicate clearly which genre is wanted, so you need to read such an assignment especially carefully. A first step might be to consider whether it's asking for a report or an argument. For example, here are two sample assignments:

> Discuss ways in which the invention of gas and incandescent lighting significantly changed people's daily lives in the nineteenth century.

> Discuss why Willy Loman in *Death of a Salesman* is, or is not, a tragic hero.

Both assignments use the word "discuss," but in very different ways. The first may simply be requesting an informative, researched report: the thesis—new forms of lighting significantly changed people's daily lives in various ways—is already given, and you may just be expected to research and explain what some of these changes were. It's also possible, though, that this assignment is asking you to make an argument about which of these changes were the most significant ones.

In contrast, "discuss" in the second assignment is much more open-ended. It does not lead to a particular thesis but is more clearly asking you to present an argument: to choose a position (Willy Loman is a tragic hero; Willy Loman is *not* a tragic hero; even, possibly, Willy Loman both

---

✳ academic literacies   ⬤ fields   ⬤ research
■ rhetorical situations ⦂⦂ processes   ⬤ media/design
▲ genres   ◆ strategies

is and is not a tragic hero) and to marshal reasons and evidence from the play to support your position. A clue that an argument is being asked for lies in the way the assignment offers a choice of paths.

Other potentially ambiguous words in assignments are "show" and "explore," both of which could lead in many directions. If after a careful reading of the entire assignment you still aren't sure what it's asking for, ask your instructor to clarify the appropriate genre or genres.

Combining Genres

Often your writing will include more than one genre. An **EVALUATION** of mining practices might include a **PROFILE** of a coal company CEO. A **PROPOSAL** to start a neighborhood watch might begin with a **REPORT** on crime in the area. In fact, genres are seldom "pure." When you write, you'll need to consider how you'll choose aspects of various genres to achieve your purpose.

▲ 214–22
245–57
258–68
140–63

Your writing situation will often call for a certain genre that is appropriate for your purpose—an argument, a proposal, a report, a textual analysis, and so forth. Additional genres then play supporting roles. Each genre must contribute to your main point: one genre may serve as the introduction, and others may be woven throughout the text in other ways, but all must address some aspect of the topic and support your central claim. When a text includes several genres, those genres need to fit together clearly and be connected in some way. **TRANSITIONS** do that, and in so doing, they help readers make their way through the text.

361–62

It's possible to mix almost any genres together. Following are some of the most commonly mixed genres and how they combine with other genres.

Memoirs. Sometimes a personal anecdote can help support an **ARGUMENT** or enhance a **REPORT**. Stories from your personal experience can help readers understand your motivations for arguing a certain position and can enhance your credibility as a writer.

▲ 164–95
140–63

Profiles. One way to bring a **REPORT** on an abstract topic to life is to include a profile of a person, place, or event. For example, if you were

▲ 140–63

writing a report for your boss on the need to hire more sales representatives, including a profile of one salesperson's typical day might drive home the point that your sales force is stretched too thin.

Textual analyses. You might need to analyze a speech or other document as part of an **ARGUMENT**, especially on a historical or political topic. For instance, you might analyze speeches by Abraham Lincoln and Jefferson Davis if you're writing about the causes of the Civil War, or an advertisement for e-cigarettes if you're making an argument about teen smoking.

164–95 ▲

Evaluations. You might include an evaluation of something when you write a **PROPOSAL** about it. For example, if you were writing a proposal for additional student parking on your campus, you would need to evaluate the current parking facilities to discuss their inadequacy.

258–68 ▲

Thinking about Genre

- *How does your genre affect what content you can or should include?* Objective information? Researched source material? Your own opinions? Personal experience? A mix?

403 ◆
214–22 ▲
437–44 ◆

- *Does your genre call for any specific* **STRATEGIES**? Profiles, for example, usually include some narration; **EVALUATIONS** often require **COMPARING AND CONTRASTING**.

258–68 ▲
236–44 ▲
81–103

- *Does your genre require a certain organization?* **PROPOSALS**, for instance, usually need to show a problem exists before offering a solution. Some genres leave room for choice. **MEMOIRS** and **LITERACY NARRATIVES** might begin at the beginning, middle, or end of the story.

73–74 ■

- *Does your genre affect your tone?* An abstract of a scholarly paper calls for a different **TONE** than a memoir. Should your words sound serious and scholarly? brisk and to the point? objective? opinionated? Some-

72–74 ■

  times your genre affects the way you communicate your **STANCE**.

- *Does the genre require formal (or informal) language?* A letter to the mother of a friend asking for a summer job in her bookstore calls for

---

❋ academic literacies   ● fields   ● research

■ rhetorical situations   ⁙ processes   ● media/design

▲ genres   ◆ strategies

more formal language than does an email or text to the friend thanking them for the lead.

- *Do you have a choice of medium?* Some genres call for print; others for an electronic medium. Sometimes you have a choice: a résumé, for instance, can be printed to bring to an interview, or it may be downloaded or emailed. Some teachers want reports turned in on paper; others prefer that they be emailed or posted in the class course management system. If you're not sure what **MEDIUM** you can use, ask.

  657

- *Does your genre have any design requirements?* Some genres call for paragraphs; others require lists. Some require certain kinds of fonts—you wouldn't use **impact** for a personal narrative, nor would you likely use chiller for an invitation to Grandma's sixty-fifth birthday party. Different genres call for different **DESIGN** elements.

  657

8 Stance

Whenever you write, you have a certain stance, an attitude toward your topic. The way you express that stance affects the way you come across to your audience as a writer and a person. This email from a college student to his father, for example, shows a thoughtful, reasonable stance for a carefully researched argument:

> Hi Dad,
> I'll get right to the point: I'd like to buy a car. I saved over $4,500 from working this summer, and I've found three different cars that I can get for under $3,000. That'll leave me $1,400 to cover the insurance. I can park in Lot J, over behind Monte Hall, for $75 for both semesters. And I can earn gas and repair money by upping my hours at the cafeteria. It won't cost you any more, and if I have a car, you won't have to come and pick me up when I want to come home. May I buy it?
> Love,
> Michael

While such a stance can't guarantee that Dad will give permission, it's more likely to produce results than this version:

> Hi Dad,
> I'm buying a car. A guy in my Western Civ course has a cool Nissan he wants to get rid of. I've got $4,500 saved from working this summer, it's mine, and I'm going to use it to get some wheels. Mom said you'd freak out at me if I did, but I want this car and I'm getting it.
> Michael

The writer of the first email respects his reader and offers reasoned arguments and evidence of research to convince him that buying a car is an action that will benefit them both. The writer of the second, by contrast, seems impulsive, ready to buy the first car that comes along, and defiant—he's picking a fight. Each email reflects a certain stance that shows the writer as a certain kind of person dealing with a topic in a certain way and establishing a certain relationship with his audience.

Identify your stance. What is your attitude toward your topic? Objective? Critical? Curious? Opinionated? Passionate? Indifferent? Your stance may be affected by your relationship to your **AUDIENCE**. How do you want them to see you? As a colleague sharing information? a good student showing what you can do? an advocate for a position? Often your stance is affected by your **GENRE**: for example, lab reports require an objective, unemotional stance that emphasizes the content and minimizes the writer's own attitudes. Memoir, by comparison, allows you to reveal your feelings about your topic. Your stance is also affected by your **PURPOSE**, as the two emails about cars show. Your stance in a piece written to entertain will likely differ from the stance you'd adopt to persuade.

61–64

79

59–60

You communicate (or downplay) your stance through your tone—through the words you use and other ways your text expresses an attitude toward your subject and audience. For example, in an academic essay you would state your position directly—"*The Bachelor* reflects the values of American society today"—using a confident, authoritative tone. In contrast, using qualifiers like "might" or "I think" can give your writing a wishy-washy, uncertain tone: "I think *The Bachelor* might reflect some of America's values." A sarcastic tone might be appropriate for a comment on a blog post but isn't right for an academic essay: "*The Bachelor*'s star has all the personality of a bowling ball."

Like every other element of writing, your tone must be appropriate for your rhetorical situation.

Just as you likely alter what you say depending on whether you're speaking to a boss, an instructor, a parent, or a good friend, so you need to make similar adjustments as a writer. It's a question of appropriateness: we behave in certain ways in various social situations, and writing is a social situation. You might sign an email to a friend with an XO, but in an email to your supervisor you'll likely sign off with a "Many thanks" or "Sincerely." To write well, you need to write with integrity, to say as much as possible what you wish to say; yet you also must understand that in writing, as in speaking, your stance and tone need to suit your purpose, your relationship to your audience, the way in which you wish your audience to perceive you, and your medium.

In writing as in other aspects of life, the Golden Rule applies: "Do unto audiences as you would have them do unto you." Address readers respectfully if you want them to respond to your words with respect.

Thinking about Stance

- *What is your stance, and how does it relate to your purpose for writing?* If you feel strongly about your topic and are writing an argument that tries to persuade your audience to feel the same way, your stance and your **PURPOSE** fit naturally together. But suppose you're writing about the same topic with a different purpose—to demonstrate the depth of your knowledge about the topic, for example, or your ability to consider it in a detached, objective way. You will need to adjust your stance to meet the demands of this different purpose.

59–60 ■

- *How should your stance be reflected in your tone?* Can your tone grow directly out of your stance, or do you need to "tone down" your attitude toward the topic or take a different tone altogether? Do you want to be seen as reasonable? angry? thoughtful? gentle? funny? ironic? If you're writing about something you want to be seen as taking very seriously, be sure that your language and even your font reflect that seriousness. Check your writing for words that reflect the tone you want to convey—and for ones that do not (and revise as necessary).

61–64 ■

- *How is your stance likely to be received by your audience?* Your tone and especially the attitude it projects toward your **AUDIENCE** will affect how they react to the content of what you say.

- *Should you openly discuss your stance?* Do you want or need to announce your own perspective on your topic? Will doing so help you reach your audience, or would it be better not to say directly where you're coming from?

※ academic literacies   ● fields   ● research
■ rhetorical situations   ⁚ processes   ● media/design
▲ genres   ◆ strategies

9 Media/Design

In its broadest sense, a medium is a go-between: a way for information to be conveyed from one person to another. We communicate through many media, verbal and nonverbal: our bodies (we catch someone's eye, wave, nod); our voices (we whisper, talk, shout, groan); and various technologies, including handwriting, print, phone, radio, video, and digital media.

Each medium has unique characteristics that influence both what and how we communicate. As an example, consider this message: "I haven't told you this before, but I love you." Most of the time, we communicate such a message in person, using the medium of voice (with, presumably, help from eye contact and touch). A phone call will do, though most of us would think it a poor second choice, and a handwritten letter or note would be acceptable, if necessary. Few of us would break such news on a website, with a tweet, or during a radio call-in program.

By contrast, imagine whispering the following sentence in a darkened room: "By the last decades of the nineteenth century, the territorial expansion of the United States had left almost all Native Americans confined to reservations." That sentence starts a chapter in a history textbook, and it would be strange indeed to whisper it into someone's ear. It is appropriate, however, in the textbook, in print or in an e-book, or as a quotation in an oral presentation.

As you can see, we can often choose among various media depending on our purpose and audience. In addition, we can often combine media to create **MULTIMEDIA** texts. And different media enable us to use different ways or modes of expressing meaning, from words to images to sound to hyperlinks, that can be combined in various ways.

661–62

No matter the medium or media, a text's design affects the way it is received and understood. A typed letter on official letterhead sends a different message than the same words handwritten on pastel stationery.

674–80
Classic type sends a different message than *flowery italics*. Some genres and media (and audiences) demand **PHOTOS**, **DIAGRAMS**, or color. Some information is easier to explain—and read—in the form of a **PIE CHART** or a **BAR GRAPH** than in the form of a paragraph. Some reports and documents are so long and complex that they need to be divided into sections, 670–72 which are then best labeled with **HEADINGS**. These are some of the elements to consider when thinking about how to design what you write.

Identify your media and design needs.   Does your writing situation call for a certain medium and design? A printed essay? An oral report with visual aids? A blog? A podcast? Academic assignments often assume a particular medium and design, but if you're unsure about your options or the degree of flexibility you have, check with your instructor.

Thinking about Media

403

- *What medium are you using*—print? spoken? electronic? a combination?—and how does it affect the way you will create your text? A printed résumé is usually no more than one page long; an electronic résumé posted on an employer's website has no length limits. An oral presentation should contain detailed information; accompanying slides should provide only an outline.

- *How does your medium affect your organization and* **STRATEGIES***?* Long paragraphs are fine on paper but don't work well on the web. On presentation slides, phrases or keywords work better than sentences. In print, you need to define unfamiliar terms; on the web, you can sometimes just add a link to a definition found elsewhere.

- *How does your medium affect your language?* Some print documents require a more formal voice than spoken media; email and texting often invite greater informality.

- *How does your medium affect what modes of expression you use?* Should your text include photos, graphics, audio or video files, or links? Do you need slides, handouts, or other visuals to accompany an oral presentation?

* academic literacies   ● fields   ● research
■ rhetorical situations ⁙ processes   ● media/design
▲ genres   ◆ strategies

Thinking about Design

- *What's the appropriate look for your* RHETORICAL SITUATION? Should your text look serious? whimsical? personal? something else? What design elements will suit your audience, purpose, stance, genre, and medium?

- *What elements need to be designed?* Is there any information you would like to highlight by putting it in a box? Are there any key terms that should be boldfaced? Do you need navigation buttons? How should you indicate links?

- *What font(s) are appropriate* to your audience, purpose, stance, genre, and medium?

- *Are you including any* VISUALS? Should you? Will your AUDIENCE expect or need any? Is there any information in your text that would be easier to understand as a chart or graph? If you need to include video or audio clips, how should the links be presented?

- *Should you include headings?* Would they help you organize your materials and help readers follow the text? Does your GENRE or MEDIUM require them?

- *Should you use a specific format?* MLA? APA?

57

674–80
61–64

65–71
75–77

MLA 564–614
APA 615–55

Part 3
Genres

When we make a shopping list, we automatically write each item we need in a single column. When we email a friend, we begin with a salutation: "Hi, Jordan." Whether we are writing a letter, a résumé, or a proposal, we know generally what it should contain and what it should look like because we are familiar with each of those genres. Genres are kinds of writing, and texts in any given genre share goals and features—a proposal, for instance, generally starts out by identifying a problem and then suggests a certain solution. The chapters in this part provide guidelines for writing in twelve common academic genres. First come detailed chapters on four genres often assigned in writing classes—**LITERACY NARRATIVES**, **TEXTUAL ANALYSES**, **REPORTS**, and **ARGUMENTS**—followed by brief chapters on **EIGHT OTHER GENRES** and one on **REMIXES**.

Genres

10 Writing a Literacy Narrative   81

11 Analyzing Texts   104

12 Reporting Information   140

13 Arguing a Position   164

14 Abstracts   196

15 Annotated Bibliographies and
Reviews of Scholarly Literature   201

16 Evaluations   214

17 Literary Analyses   223

18 Memoirs   236

19 Profiles   245

20 Proposals   258

21 Explorations   269

22 Remixes   280

10 Writing a Literacy Narrative

Narratives are stories, and we read and tell them for many different purposes. Parents read their children bedtime stories as an evening ritual. College applicants write about significant moments in their lives. In *psychology* courses, you may write a personal narrative to illustrate how individuals' stories inform the study of behavior. In *education* courses, you may share stories of your teaching experiences. And in *computer science* courses, you may write programming narratives to develop programming skills.

This chapter provides detailed guidelines for writing a specific kind of narrative: a literacy narrative. Writers of literacy narratives traditionally explore their experiences with reading or writing, but we'll broaden the definition to include experiences with various literacies, which might include learning an academic skill, a sport, an artistic technique, or something else. For example, the third narrative in this chapter explores one writer's realization that she needs "automotive literacy" to work in her parents' car repair shop. Along with this essay, this chapter includes two additional good examples, the first annotated to point out the key features found in most literacy narratives.

REA KARIM
Becoming an American Girl

Rea Karim earned an associate's degree in arts and sciences at Bellevue College, where she wrote this literacy narrative. It was nominated for the Norton Writer's Prize. Karim plans to major in political science at a university and then go to law school.

Attention-getting opening.

I stood on the monument's marble steps, surveying my country's capital. Elizabeth eagerly tugged on my denim jacket, "You gotta see this!"

I turned around to see her smiling at the scene before us. We stood, mesmerized by the beauty of the golden hour, as the sun set over Washington, DC, in the summer of 2017. Like all the other girls surrounding me, I belonged here. I was the walking embodiment of my ancestors' hopes and dreams.

In 2005, though, I felt far from belonging. I was four years old, and I could not speak. My life was filled with words in English, Urdu, Hindi, and Bengali. These four languages painted my dining room table and added zest into my young life, but while I could understand, none of the words came out of my mouth. My mom was extremely concerned about my inability to talk but found reassurance from a linguistics professional who told us that my speaking abilities would develop late because of the diversity of voices within our household. But once I could talk, I still felt difference from the kids around me.

Here Karim describes the setting—what hindered her literacy.

I was the only child on my block whose parents came from two different South Asian countries. My dinner plate was a battle between Indian curried vegetables and the juice of Bengali kebabs. Even though I was born in Seattle, I often felt like I was from another planet, struggling to integrate into my Cascadian hometown. At the same time, I didn't feel like I fit in with the other south Asian kids I knew either. I had roots from both India and Bangladesh, and while those countries are close in proximity, their competition could stretch for miles. On top of that, my classmates introduced me to the "Indian" stereotype that all brown kids are naturally smart, good at math, and excellent students. As hard as I tried, I could not fit in to that image. I was late to start speaking, and I couldn't read.

Mama would sit with me for hours trying to get me to give up TV and learn to read with her from one of the Dot books, but I didn't like Dot the dog. He was boring, and I was stubborn. Studying always seemed like a chore, and reading didn't spark the same interest in me that it did for my classmates. Kids my age were cruising through Dot and picking up Lemony Snicket, while I was still learning the difference between p and q. 5

Clearly described details.

Because of my reading level, I didn't feel smart enough to be around the students in my class. Even though I made friends, a huge part of me felt like I couldn't fit in. I didn't feel American enough to live in my predominantly white community, and I didn't feel "brown" enough

---

☀ academic literacies   ● fields   ● research

■ rhetorical situations   ⁂ processes   ● media/design

▲ genres   ◆ strategies

to hang out with the kids of my parents' friends. Instead of socializing with my peers, I sought refuge in my elementary school library.

The library's tall walls covered with princess and dragon murals, the dozens of birch bookshelves, and the solitude gave me comfort. Every morning, as soon as the bus parked in the roundabout, I dashed to the library's glass doors. The librarian, Ms. McEldowney, always let me in with a comforting smile. She knew I wasn't the best reader, but she still narrated the blurbs from the newly arrived books and introduced me to some of her old favorites. Usually, I snatched whatever was on display, found a quiet spot next to a shelf, and ran my fingers over the words, trying to sound them out. In that way, I started building a friendship with books. I touched the pictures on the front and back cover, imagining that I was a part of the adventures I held in my hand.

A key person in Karim's narrative.

The library became my safe haven. Days quickly turned into months, and soon I could read a book without pictures. Every day I practiced running my fingers through sentences, absorbing whatever was in front of me and reading the sentences aloud. In a matter of a few months and a dozen McEldowney recommendations, I could read.

The library is a key to her literacy development.

Yet, a huge part of me could not relate to the characters in front of me. I still felt like an outsider. I lacked the courage of the main characters from my books, often feeling like a token side character. I wanted to be fearless like the boys and girls in my stories, but sometimes I felt as if a distant force was holding me back from being fearless outside of the library. I wanted to embody red, white, and blue like the heroes American history books told me about. More than anything, I wanted to belong. Even though I had found a place among these imaginary books, I desired a place in the real world around me.

The conflict in the story.

The perceptions I had about being American were all about to change one crisp fall morning during library hour when Ms. McEldowney pulled out a thick set of chapter books. Once a glistening white, their faded covers were now coated in a thick gray dust.

"These" she said with a enthusiastic tone, "are the American Girls."

Ms. McEldowney explained to our class that each book was about a different girl in a different period of American History. As she held each one up for us to see, I noticed that not all the girls on the covers were white. Each girl had a unique outfit, her own personality, and her own story.

Her story.

My friends and I rushed to the books. Among the piles, I found *Meet Molly*. On the cover a quirky-looking girl with thick glasses, braided pigtails, and a checkered dress looked back at me. I spent that evening sitting at the dining table reading about Molly's family, her friends, and the new girl from England living with her who was seeking shelter during World War II. I read about how the two girls first felt a cultural clash between them but grew to be fascinated by each other's experiences. Their struggles reminded me of the cultural differences I had with some of my friends. Instead of viewing our lives as polar opposites, I considered sharing with them some of my household's celebrations like Chaand Raat and learning more about holidays like Easter.

What started with just a book became my lifestyle. I went to the library every morning, checked out whatever American Girl book was available, and finished it by the afternoon. From the story of Addy I learned of a family's escape from slavery. From Josephine I learned about living without a mother and having the sole responsibility of raising her Mexican American family in 1824. From Kaya I learned about the impact of the settlers on the Native Americans and the struggle of holding on to what is yours. Each book shaped my perspective of what it means to be an American. I learned that life in this country isn't on one set path. Rather, our country is a mixture of different paths, and each story matters. I started to believe that my story mattered.

After elementary school, I kept reading. My avid obsession with books grew from the American Girl books to Louisa May Alcott and Ta-Nehisi Coates. Once I entered high school, I pursued the passion for history that the American Girl books instilled in me and tried my hand at AP United States History, World Government, and Comparative Politics.

This brief paragraph emphasizes the moment's significance.

More specific details.

The significance of Karim's reading becomes clear to her.

* academic literacies   ● fields   ● research
■ rhetorical situations   ⋮ processes   ● media/design
▲ genres   ◆ strategies

In the summer of 2017, I was accepted to a program that invited sixty girls from all over the country to visit Washington, DC, and learn what it takes for a woman to run for a seat in Congress. As I packed for the trip, I glanced at the old American Girl novels I had purchased, once new and now dusty like the ones I read as a child. I thought about how I spent so much of my childhood wrapped up in the stories of other girls. I realized, then, that I was ready to live my life as the main character. I kept that realization in mind when I met and grew close to the other girls in DC. They came from diverse backgrounds like me, and we shared our passions and stories with each other, each one of us the heroine. By putting myself at the center of my own story, I finally belonged.

As I stood at the steps of the Lincoln Memorial underneath the setting sun, I reflected on my journey to get to that moment. I had fallen in love with the roots my parents planted in Seattle, and I was a smart South Asian American in my own way, well versed not in math, but in history. I was no longer confined to a stereotype. Instead, I embodied the brown color of my skin and belonged to the United States—on my own terms.

The end refers back to the opening anecdote but deepens its significance.

In this literacy narrative, Karim tells the story of how learning to read and reading American Girl novels helped her understand her identity as an American of South Asian heritage. The significance of her story lies in the role that reading played in developing her sense of who she is and where she belongs.

KARLA MARIANA HERRERA GUTIERREZ

Reading, Writing, and Riding
A Literacy Narrative

Karla Mariana Herrera Gutierrez recently graduated from Austin College with a triple major in English, Spanish, and public health. Her literacy narrative was nominated for the Norton Writer's Prize and is documented in MLA style.

Eight faces sleep peacefully as my grandmother surveys the bedroom and closes the door before going outside. Out on the street, the sky is shattered by the soft yellows and pinks that break through the clouds, indicating the start of a new day. My grandmother walks down the sidewalk with her hands grasping her black bag as her mind processes recent events and tries to focus on the task at hand today. *"Toma el autobus a la oficina y pide la pension,"* my grandmother whispers to herself as she approaches the bus stop to go to the police office for her pension.

It's early in the day, but slowly more and more people begin to crowd the streets of Mexico City. The sounds of people talking and the angry honking of horns envelop my grandmother as she looks frantically down the road for the bus. It's only been a few minutes, but she has no time to lose. They told her to be at the office at a certain time, and as a recent widow she does not want to make a bad impression on the people who could make it harder for her to secure the money she needs. Finally, the white and green speck she had fixated on grows closer until she sees it's the bus she has been waiting for. Adjusting her bag, she prepares to step forward but scrunches her brow in concern when the bus doesn't seem to be slowing down. I can picture my grandmother's confused look as the bus passes by without picking her up. My mother said this was my grandmother's breaking point, and she began to cry on the side of the road. "By God's grace," my mother continued, "a lady happened to pass by, and upon seeing my mother's agitated state, she offered her assistance." A simple arm signal stopped the next bus so my grandmother could get on and go to the police department.

During the following two weeks my grandmother learned to no longer fear taking the bus; she got used to traveling downtown to the police station, to the chief's office, sometimes twice in the same day. But her obstacles were only beginning. The process involved in receiving my deceased grandfather's pension was a struggle. The police were reluctant to give it to my grandmother, hoping to wear her out because they didn't care that she had to leave her children to make these trips downtown; they only worried about the money they'd lose.

I can't imagine my grandmother's will to hide her worry as she withstood the harsh glares of the police officers with her back straight and a stone face, determined to fight for what was her family's due. I can't imagine having to trust that the legal documents a stranger presented to her were a written representation of what he was telling

✳ academic literacies   ● fields   ● research
■ rhetorical situations   ⁚● processes   ● media/design
▲ genres   ◆ strategies

her and not a trap that would make her lose her pension. But I can imagine my grandmother realizing then the importance of knowing how to read and write.

Similar to the collective history of the May family described in literacy scholar Deborah Brandt's article "Accumulating Literacy," my maternal grandmother's experiences provided opportunities for learning that piled up from the moment she hailed that bus. The many obstacles my grandmother faced began with the unfamiliarity of having to navigate new experiences and then intensified when she found herself at the mercy of government officials because she was illiterate.

The importance of literacy became apparent in my mother's household, but obtaining an education was still not a priority. My mother and her siblings learned to read and write, but none finished high school, though one of my uncles later received his GED when he moved to the United States. Literacy and education were two separate things in my mother's youth—but that changed once she moved to the United States with my father and needed to help me when I started school. My own experiences navigating two languages and two cultures expanded my literacy as reading became a key tool not only in learning school subjects but also in learning to navigate a new environment.

I started kindergarten being thrown to the sharks—that is, the English native sharks. Like the *Jaws* theme song, any English word that reached my ears quickened my heartbeat as I turned my head from side to side, hoping to identify the source of such frightening, unfamiliar sounds. I flailed around in the uncharted waters, sobbing and crying for my mother. Every morning my stomach groaned in protest at going to this institution that filled me with dread. However, I wasn't in this alone. In the afternoons I pored over my textbooks and worksheets with my mother and her English-to-Spanish dictionary by my side. Together we conquered my homework, and the sounds that had first put me in fight-or-flight mode gradually became parts of my second language.

It takes more than learning a new language to fully assimilate into a new culture, however. Literacy constitutes more than reading and writing; it also involves the ability to understand and become a part of one's environment. Linguist James Paul Gee calls our "ways of being in the world" Discourses, beginning with the "primary Discourse" we learn at home; he defines literacy as "the mastery or fluent control over a secondary Discourse," the discourse or discourses that include the social practices and behaviors that allow us to communicate effectively with others and that we learn through becoming members of social institutions, like churches, stores, community groups—and schools (6–9). For the most part, reading books about "typical" non-Hispanic households uncovered the norms of a culture I knew little about, and it also opened a place for conflict to arise when there were conflicting cultural ideas.

Such was the case after I read a book from my favorite series, Junie B. Jones. When Junie B. gets invited to a sleepover, the idea of spending the night at another person's house riveted seven-year-old me. In the book, the sleepover takes place in the giant house of Junie B.'s rich friend, Lucille; however, Junie B.'s crazy antics alter the experience of the sleepover in the way only she knows how to do (Park). I thought my dream would come true when a school friend invited me to come over to her house. I asked my mother for permission even though I was sure she was going to say yes—but I got a lecture instead. My mother refused my request and in fast-spoken Spanish listed all the horrible things that could happen to me if I went to a sleepover. Red-faced and slightly out of breath, she ended her sermon by asking me what was wrong with my bed that I felt the need to sleep in someone else's. My mother, and father, rejected some of the freedoms other kids my age had, such as staying at each other's houses or hanging out after school, because they focused on the potential dangers that could come of such activities. I didn't want to upset my parents, so I only saw my friends at school and read my books to experience what I couldn't in real life.

If reading sometimes caused conflict at home, it was my method 10 for success at school. I was an avid reader and when the school set up a reading program, I took full advantage of it. My school hoped to present reading as a fun activity, so it promoted what was called the Star Program, which offered prizes to students for progressing in the program, with the ultimate prize a ride in a limousine. When the program ended, the twenty kids who had completed the course pressed our young, eager faces against our classroom window as the giant white limo pulled up to the front of the school building. We waited, bouncing in anxious joy, for the teachers to open the school doors and show the wonders of this marvelous car. The driver, in a black suit and sunglasses, walked to the back of the limo and opened the car's door. It could have been the glare of the blazing sun or my young, imaginative mind, but

* academic literacies   ● fields   ● research
■ rhetorical situations   ∴ processes   ● media/design
▲ genres   ◆ strategies

the limo seemed to come alive as we caught a glimpse of its sleek black interior. Upon being released to climb in and enjoy our prize, we felt a blast of cold air that cut against the warmth of that spring afternoon. The flash of a camera redirected our attention to our teachers, who positioned us for a picture for the school newspaper.

The Star Program focused on a ride in a limousine, but it failed to mention the bonus prize: feeling like a superstar. My eyes bulged as I took in all the features of this elegant white car as we drove away. The many buttons and compartments for food and drinks (which this ride unfortunately failed to provide) were a novelty to me. Feeling the cold leather of the seats, I traced the shape of the interior until I reached the buttons on the door. With one push the window went down, revealing to the world my awestruck face. The breeze whipped my curly hair around, but I didn't care. I can still see the wondering faces of the people in the cars next to us doing double takes when they saw the stretched car pulling up beside them. As we drove through a roundabout, I felt regal and waved a royal wave to all my subjects because I ruled the world . . . at least for the ride's thirty minutes.

In my elementary years, I thought the Star Program was the epitome of what reading could do, and that limousine ride was only a small taste of what I could achieve by reading and focusing on my academics. Many people would assume that literacy begins like this, by an educational institution, but our literacy actually begins before our time. Brandt observes that literacy "piles up," so that "many generations of literacy . . . now occupy the same social space" (652). This piling up of earlier and more recent literacies produces a "propelling effect"; as Brandt explains, "Schooling typically brings into a family's possession books, manuals, typewriters, and the like that then become the first forms of literacy that the next generation encounters" (659). My literacy began with my grandmother, but it evolved over two generations to include more than simply learning how to read and write—it also meant assimilating into a new culture. Unlike my grandmother's experience with the bus, my ride in the limousine was a marker of my assimilation. It was the first moment that I can remember when I stood out not because of my different background, but because of the reading I had accomplished in a program open to all.

Not only did reading help me assimilate into a new culture, it also helped me with learning a new language. There wasn't someone at home who could teach me how to properly speak and write English, so it was difficult for me to become fluent. While my mother did her best to help me with her English-to-Spanish dictionary, she couldn't teach me anything that wasn't a part of my homework. It was only through reading that I managed to expand my vocabulary and use the grammar rules I learned in school. By contrast, it was easier for my sister to learn English than it was for me because she had me to converse with at home. My sister's earlier comprehension of English led to her "graduating" from ESL classes in just one year, instead of the four years it took me. My sister had me as her source of English at home, and integrating this new language into our household created a culturally diverse environment that differed from the one my parents had grown up with.

In accumulating new literacies, we improve ourselves for the next generation, and what we improve is our ability to immerse ourselves in new situations because in doing so we elevate the standards of our education to reflect our experiences. But the piling up of literacies isn't an individual effort. My grandmother learned to ride the bus after receiving help from a stranger, and the legal obstacles she faced because she was illiterate pushed her to make sure that my mom and her siblings learned to read. Because my mother knew how to read, she could help me with my homework, and because I learned English, I could converse with my sister in our new language. Each generation is shaped by the collective history of people's literacies because of the opportunities we have to learn from those who came before us and to contribute to those who follow us.

Works Cited

Brandt, Deborah. "Accumulating Literacy: Writing and Learning to Write in the Twentieth Century." *College English*, vol. 57, no. 6, 1995, pp. 649–66.

Gee, James Paul. "Literacy, Discourse, and Linguistics: Introduction." *Journal of Education*, vol. 171, no. 1, 1989, pp. 5–25.

Park, Barbara. *Junie B. Jones Is a Party Animal*. Illustrated by Denise Brunkus, Scholastic, 1997.

Gutierrez traces her literacy development not just to her own life and experiences but to the literacies, or lack of them, of her mother and grandmother as well. Her references to scholarly work on literacy deepen her story and show its significance for many, not just her personally.

* academic literacies   ● fields   ● research
■ rhetorical situations   ⁂ processes   ● media/design
▲ genres   ◆ strategies

ANA-JAMILEH KASSFY

Automotive Literacy

In the following literacy narrative, Ana-Jamileh Kassfy describes an experience that taught her that literacy takes many forms, as well as the importance of knowing what goes on in the family business, auto repair. She wrote this essay in a college writing class at the University of Texas at El Paso and posted it on her class blog.

My father runs a well-known family-owned auto shop here in El Paso, Texas. I come from a family of five, which consists of me, two older brothers, and my parents. My father manages the place, while one of my brothers works as a mechanic in charge of most of the heavy labor and the other spends all day standing by a state inspection machine making sure the cars can run safely on the streets of El Paso. My mother works as the shop's secretary, answering the phone and handling all paperwork. I, on the other hand, was not given the option of being a part of the family business; my job is to graduate from college. And I'll gladly accept going to school and learning in place of spending my days working on cars, even though I spent a lot of time at the shop throughout my childhood.

Since I come from a family whose life revolves around cars, and since I practically lived at the auto shop until I was able to drive, you'd think that I'd understand most of the jargon a mechanic would use, right? Wrong. During my first sixteen years of life, I did manage to learn the difference between a flathead and a Torx screwdriver. I also learned what brake pads do and that a car uses many different colorful fuses. However, rather than paying attention to what was happening and what was being said around me, most of the time I chose to focus on the social aspect of the business. While everyone was running around ordering different pads, filters, and starters or explaining in precise detail why a customer needed a new engine, I preferred to sit and speak with customers and learn their life stories. Being social worked for me—until it didn't.

One day my mother couldn't come to work and decided to have me fill in for her. That was fine with me. I thought to myself, "How hard could it be to answer a phone and say, 'Good afternoon, M & J

Service, how may I help you?' or to greet customers and then turn them over to my dad?"

My morning went by pretty smoothly. I thought I had my duties down to a science. I figured aside from the permanent ringing in my ear from the annoyingly loud air compressors, a few minor paper cuts, and the almost perpetual stench of gasoline and burnt oil, my day was going to fly by.

Then, around lunchtime, my dad left to pick up a part at a car 5 dealership and my brothers went out for lunch. A woman pulled up in a '01 Hyundai Elantra that was desperately in need of a new paint job and walked into the shop. The woman seemed to be in her late forties and was wearing professional clothing with green eye shadow and bright orange lipstick. Her copper-brown hair was feathered out and she wore extremely large gold earrings. And she was angry. She demanded I tell her why she was having a difficult time starting her car. As I began to dust off the file stored in my memory as "Automotive Terms I Will Never Use," I attempted to calm her down, and then I made the mistake of asking her what the problem was.

She said in a harsh tone, "My car doesn't start, your dad just replaced the spark plugs and the motor head, and now my 'blah blah blah' is making noise! I took it to my friend who's a mechanic and he told me your dad fixed the wrong part."

I took a few seconds and just stood there looking at her, trying to add up what I had learned in my life as a "mechanic" and recall what spark plugs were. But it was useless. After a few moments, I gave up. I told her that I couldn't help her, but that she was more than welcome to wait for a mechanic to return.

After giving me an unpleasant look, she proceeded to say, while waving her hands in front of me, "I want my money back! Here is my receipt. I'm taking my car elsewhere. Your dad screwed me over. I told him it was the 'blah blah blah.' Why did he take out the 'blah blah blah'? WHY CAN'T YOU HELP ME? WHY ARE YOU HERE? BLAH BLAH BLAH!"

I stood there, overwhelmed. I began to fidget and push my hair back nervously as I wished some knowledge would kick in. It seemed unbelievable, but despite growing up in a family that lived and breathed automobiles, there was nothing I could do to help her. And my sixteen years of socializing with customers hadn't even paid off because I couldn't calm her down. When I saw my dad walk in, I sighed with

* academic literacies   ● fields   ● research
■ rhetorical situations   ∴ processes   ● media/design
▲ genres   ◆ strategies

relief, explained the problem to him, and it was resolved. But standing in front of that woman like a deer caught in headlights was so embarrassing. Having somebody shout, "Why can't you help me?" and "Why are you here?" made me feel so ignorant.

Unfortunately, that was only the first of many occasions when 10 people have automatically expected that I know how to take apart and rebuild an engine, or perform some other auto-related task. In reality, I know as much about cars as the next person. After that incident, it became clear to me that I could be literate on very different levels. I'm an expert at running social networks like my *Twitter* feed, and I can zip through and analyze an entire novel written in Spanish, but in other subjects, like automobiles, I am completely illiterate. And when I'm expected to know them, I feel anything but competent.

A confrontation with an irate costumer forces Kassfy to realize that she could be very literate in some situations but almost illiterate in others, and that her lack of knowledge in a workplace context put her at a real disadvantage.

Key Features / Literacy Narratives

A well-told story.   As with most narratives, those about literacy often set up some sort of situation that needs to be resolved. That need for resolution makes readers want to keep on reading. We want to know how Kassfy will deal with an irate customer. Some literacy narratives simply explore the role that developing literacy of some kind played at some time in someone's life, as when Karim discovered the school library and American Girl novels. And some, like Gutierrez's, explore the writer's literacy development in a larger context.

Vivid detail.   Details can bring a narrative to life for readers by giving them vivid mental sensations of the sights, sounds, smells, tastes, and textures of the world in which your story takes place. The details you use when describing something can help readers picture places, people, and events; dialogue can help them hear what is being said. We grasp the importance of books for Karim as she "touched the pictures on the front and back cover." Similarly, we can picture and hear Gutierrez as a little girl who speaks only Spanish in an English-language kindergarten, "sobbing and crying for my mother."

Some indication of the narrative's significance. By definition, a literacy narrative tells something the writer remembers about learning to read, write, or gain competence in a specific area. In addition, the writer needs to make clear why the incident matters to them. You may reveal its significance in various ways. Kassfy comes to understand that to work in an auto repair shop, she needs to understand automotive repair terms. Gutierrez places her literacy in a tradition going back generations—and continuing with her sister's relationship with her. Karim's narrative shows that her literacy was a key to understanding her place in society.

A GUIDE TO WRITING LITERACY NARRATIVES

Choosing a Topic

In general, it's a good idea to focus on a single event that took place during a relatively brief period of time—though sometimes learning to do or understand something may take place over an extended period. In that case, several snapshots or important moments may be needed. Here are some suggestions for topics:

- any early memory about writing, reading, speaking, or another form of literacy that you recall vividly
- someone who taught you to read or write
- someone who helped you understand how to do something
- a book, video game, recording, or other text that has been significant for you in some way
- an event at school that was related to your literacy and that you found interesting, humorous, or embarrassing
- a literacy task that you found (or still find) especially difficult or challenging
- a memento that represents an important moment in your literacy development (perhaps the start of a **LITERACY PORTFOLIO**)
- the origins of your current attitudes about writing, reading, speaking, or doing something

385–90 ⁖

※ academic literacies   ● fields   ● research ·

■ rhetorical situations   ⁖ processes   ● media/design

▲ genres   ◆ strategies

- learning to text, learning to write an email appropriately, creating and maintaining a *Facebook* page or blog

Make a list of possible topics, and then choose one that you think will be interesting to you and to others—and that you're willing to share with others. If several seem promising, try them out on a friend or classmate. Or just choose one and see where it leads; you can switch to another if need be. If you have trouble coming up with a topic, try **FREEWRITING**, **LISTING**, **CLUSTERING**, or **LOOPING**.

333–36

Considering the Rhetorical Situation

PURPOSE   Why do you want to tell this story? To share a memory with others? To fulfill an assignment? To teach a lesson? To explore your past learning? Think about the reasons for your choice and how they will shape what you write.

59–60

AUDIENCE   Are your readers likely to have had similar experiences? Would they tell similar stories? How much explaining will you have to do to help them understand your narrative? Can you assume that they will share your attitudes toward your story, or will you have to work at making them see your perspective? How much about your life are you willing to share with this audience?

61–64

STANCE   What attitude do you want to project? Affectionate? Neutral? Critical? Do you wish to be sincere? serious? humorously detached? self-critical? self-effacing? something else? How do you want your readers to see you?

72–74

MEDIA / DESIGN   Will your narrative be in print? presented orally? online? Should you use photos, tables, graphs, or video or audio clips? Is there a font that conveys the right tone? Do you need headings?

75–77

Generating Ideas and Text

Good literacy narratives share certain elements that make them interesting and compelling for readers. Remember that your goals are to tell the story as clearly and vividly as you can and to convey the meaning the incident has for you today. Start by thinking about what you already know about writing a literacy narrative. Then write out what you remember about the setting of your narrative and those involved, perhaps trying out some of the methods in the chapter on **GENERATING IDEAS AND TEXT**. You may also want to **INTERVIEW** a teacher or parent or other person who figures in your narrative.

333–44
518–20

Explore what you already know about writing a literacy narrative. Think about recent occasions when you've had to narrate a story, either orally or in writing, in school or out. Take a few moments to think about a couple of those occasions, especially ones involving your reading, writing, speaking, or learning to do something. Why and to whom were you telling these stories? How successful do you think your narratives were? What aspects of telling the story did you feel most confident about or do especially well? What could you have done better? What do you still need to learn about writing a literacy narrative?

Describe the setting. Where does your narrative take place? List the places where your story unfolds. For each place, write informally for a few minutes, **DESCRIBING** what you remember:

456–63

- *What do you see?* If you're inside, what color are the walls? What's hanging on them? What can you see out any windows? What else do you see? Books? Lined paper? Red ink? Are there people? places to sit? a desk or a table?

- *What do you hear?* A radiator hissing? Leaves rustling? The wind howling? Rain? Someone reading aloud? Shouts? Cheers? Children playing? Music? The chime of a text arriving on your phone?

- *What do you smell?* Sweat? Perfume? Incense? Food cooking?

- *How and what do you feel?* Nervous? Happy? Cold? Hot? A scratchy wool sweater? Tight shoes? Rough wood on a bench?

- *What do you taste?* Gum? Mints? Graham crackers? Juice? Coffee?

✸ academic literacies   ● fields   ● research
■ rhetorical situations   ⁘ processes   ● media/design
▲ genres   ◆ strategies

Think about the key people. Narratives include people whose actions play an important role in the story. In your literacy narrative, you are probably one of those people. A good way to develop your understanding of the people in your narrative is to write about them:

- *Describe each person in a paragraph or so.* What do the people look like? How do they dress? How do they speak? Quickly? Slowly? With an accent? Do they speak clearly, or do they mumble? Do they use any distinctive words or phrases? You might begin by describing their movements, their posture, their bearing, their facial expressions. Do they have a distinctive scent?

- *Recall (or imagine) some characteristic dialogue.* A good way to bring people to life and move a story along is with **DIALOGUE**, to let readers hear them rather than just hearing about them. Try writing six to ten lines of dialogue between two people in your narrative. If you can't remember an actual conversation, make up one that could have happened. (After all, you are telling the story, and you get to decide how it is to be told.) Try to remember (and write down) some of the characteristic words or phrases that the people in your narrative used.

◆ 464–68

Write about "what happened." At the heart of every good **NARRATIVE** is the answer to the question "What happened?" The action in a literacy narrative may be as dramatic as winning a spelling bee or as subtle as a conversation between two friends; both contain action, movement, or change that the narrative tries to capture for readers. A good story dramatizes the action. Try **SUMMARIZING** the action in your narrative in a paragraph—try to capture what happened. Use active and specific verbs ("pondered," "shouted," "laughed") to describe the action as vividly as possible.

◆ 474–82

● 550–51

Consider the significance of the narrative. You need to make clear the ways in which any event you are writing about is significant for you now. Write a page or so about the meaning it has for you. How did it change or otherwise affect you? What aspects of your life now can you trace to that event? How might your life have been different if this event had not happened or had turned out differently? Why does this story matter to you?

Ways of Organizing a Literacy Narrative

340–42

Start by **OUTLINING** the main events in your narrative. Then think about how you want to tell the story. Don't assume that the only way to tell your story is just as it happened. That's one way—starting at the beginning of the action and continuing to the end. But you could also start in the middle—or even at the end. Karla Gutierrez, for example, could have begun her narrative by discussing her current literacy and then gone back to trace the influences of her family. Several ways of organizing a narrative follow.

[Chronologically, from beginning to end]

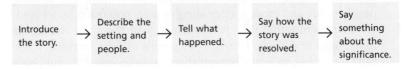

Introduce the story. → Describe the setting and people. → Tell what happened. → Say how the story was resolved. → Say something about the significance.

[Beginning in the middle]

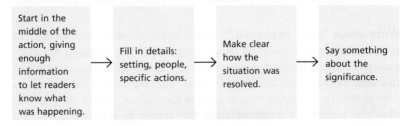

Start in the middle of the action, giving enough information to let readers know what was happening. → Fill in details: setting, people, specific actions. → Make clear how the situation was resolved. → Say something about the significance.

[Beginning at the end]

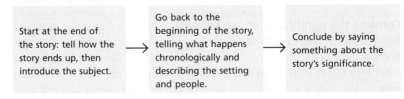

Start at the end of the story: tell how the story ends up, then introduce the subject. → Go back to the beginning of the story, telling what happens chronologically and describing the setting and people. → Conclude by saying something about the story's significance.

* academic literacies
■ rhetorical situations
▲ genres
● fields
∴ processes
◆ strategies
● research
● media/design

Writing Out a Draft

Once you have generated ideas and thought about how you want to organize your narrative, it's time to begin DRAFTING. Do this quickly—try to
write a complete draft in one sitting, concentrating on getting the story on
paper or screen and on putting in as much detail as you can. Some writers
find it helpful to work on the beginning or ending first. Others write out
the main event first and then draft the beginning and ending.

364–66

Draft a BEGINNING. A good narrative grabs readers' attention right from
the start. Here are some ways of beginning:

346–54

- *Create a question to be answered.* Karim begins her narrative at the
  Lincoln Memorial in Washington, D.C., leading readers to wonder how
  this scene connects to her literacy.

- *Describe the context.* You may want to provide background information
  at the start of your narrative, as Gutierrez does with an anecdote about
  her illiterate grandmother's struggle to collect a pension.

- *Describe the setting, especially if it's important to the narrative.* Kassfy
  begins by describing her family's roles working in her father's auto
  shop.

Draft an ENDING. Think about what you want readers to read last. An
effective ending helps them understand the meaning of your narrative.
Here are some possibilities:

354–58

- *End where your story ends.* It's up to you to decide where a narrative
  ends. Karim ends on a field trip in high school.

- *Say something about the significance of your narrative.* Gutierrez explores
  the meaning of her experience over several paragraphs, and Kassfy
  discusses her ignorance and resulting embarrassment. The trick is to
  touch on the narrative's significance without stating it too directly.

- *Refer back to the beginning.* Karim refers back to her trip to Washington,
  D.C., and Gutierrez to her grandmother and the "piling up" of literacies
  over several generations.

383–84　**Consider REWRITING.** If you have time and want to explore alternatives, you might try rewriting your draft to see if a different plan or approach might work better.

363　**Come up with a title.** A good **TITLE** indicates something about the subject of your narrative—and makes readers want to take a look. Kassfy's title joins two terms—"automotive" and "literacy"—that aren't usually seen together. Gutierrez uses wordplay—"Reading, Writing, and Riding," to suggest the multiple roles literacy plays in our lives.

Considering Matters of Design

You'll probably write your narrative in paragraph form, but think about the information you're presenting and how you can design it to enhance your story and appeal to your audience.

668–69　• What would be an appropriate **FONT**? Something serious, like Times Roman? Something whimsical, like *Comic Sans*? Something else?

670–72　• Would it help your readers if you added **HEADINGS** in order to divide your narrative into shorter sections?

674–80　• Would photographs or other **VISUALS** show details better than you can describe them with words alone? If you're writing about learning to read, for example, you might scan in an image of one of the first books you read. Or if your topic is learning to write, you could include something you wrote. You could even include a video or audio recording. Would your narrative best be conveyed as a multimedia composition that combines written text, images, and video or audio?

Getting Response and Revising

The following questions can help you study your draft with a critical eye. **GETTING RESPONSE** from others is always good, and these questions can guide their reading, too. Make sure they know your purpose and audience.

372–74

✳ academic literacies　　● fields　　● research

■ rhetorical situations　　⁘ processes　　● media/design

▲ genres　　◆ strategies

- Do the title and first few sentences make readers want to read on? If not, how else might you begin?

- Is the sequence of events in the narrative clear? Does it flow, and are there effective transitions? Does the narrative get sidetracked at any point?

- Is anything confusing?

- Is there enough detail, and is it interesting? Will readers be able to imagine the setting? Can they picture the characters and sense what they're like? Would it help to add some dialogue so that readers can "hear" them?

- Are visuals used effectively and integrated smoothly with the written text? If there are no visuals, would using some strengthen the narrative?

- Have you made the narrative meaningful enough for readers so that they wonder and care about what will happen?

- Do you narrate any actions clearly? vividly? Does the action keep readers engaged?

- Is the significance of the narrative clear?

- Is the ending satisfying? What are readers left thinking?

The preceding questions should identify aspects of your narrative you need to work on. When it's time to **REVISE**, make sure your text appeals to your audience and achieves your purpose as successfully as possible.

375–77

Editing and Proofreading

Once you've revised your draft, follow these guidelines for **EDITING** a narrative:

380–83

- Make sure events are **NARRATED** in a clear order and include appropriate time markers, **TRANSITIONS**, and summary phrases to link the parts and show the passing of time.

474–82
361–62

- Be careful that verb tenses are consistent throughout. If you start your narrative in the past tense ("he *taught* me how to use a computer"), be careful not to switch to the present ("So I *look* at him and *say* . . .") along the way.

- Check to see that verb tenses correctly indicate when an action took place. If one action took place before another action in the past, for example, you should use the past perfect tense: "I forgot to dot my i's, a mistake I *had made* many times before."

464–68
- Punctuate **DIALOGUE** correctly. Whenever someone speaks, surround the speech with quotation marks ("No way," I said). Periods and commas go inside quotation marks; exclamation points and question marks go inside if they're part of the quotation, outside if they're part of the whole sentence:

  INSIDE Opening the door, Ms. Cordell announced, "Pop quiz!"
  OUTSIDE It wasn't my intention to announce "I hate to read"!

383–84
- **PROOFREAD** your finished narrative carefully before turning it in.

Taking Stock of Your Work

Take stock of what you've written by considering to these questions:

- How did you go about coming up with ideas and generating text? Did you try freewriting, looping, mapping, something else? Which activities were most productive for you?

- How effectively did you use dialogue, description, or other narrative strategies in your writing?

- Did you use photographs or other visual or audio elements? If so, what did they add? If not, why not?

- Did you take any risks with your writing, or did you experiment in some way? Was the experiment a success? A failure? What can you learn from it?

- How did others' responses influence your writing?

- What did you learn about reading, writing, or other literacies as you worked on your piece? How might you use this learning in the future?

- Overall, what did you do well in this piece? What could still be improved? What would you do differently next time?

If you need more help

See also **MEMOIRS** (Chapter 18), a kind of narrative that focuses more generally on a significant event from your past, and **EXPLORATIONS** (Chapter 21), a kind of essay for thinking about a topic in writing. See Chapter 34 if you are required to submit your literacy narrative as part of a writing **PORTFOLIO**.

236–44
269–79

385–90

11 Analyzing Texts

Both *HuffPost* and *National Review* cover the same events, but each one interprets them differently. All toothpaste ads claim to make teeth "the whitest." The Environmental Protection Agency is a guardian of America's air, water, and soil—or an unconstitutional impediment to economic growth, depending on which politician is speaking. Those are but three examples that demonstrate why we need to be careful, analytical readers of magazines, newspapers, blogs, websites, ads, political documents, even textbooks.

Text is commonly thought of as words, as a piece of writing. In the academic world, however, text can include not only writing but images—photographs, illustrations, videos, films—and even sculptures, buildings, and music and other sounds. And many texts combine words, images, and sounds. We are constantly bombarded with texts: on the web, in print, on signs and billboards, even on our clothing. Not only does text convey information, but it also influences how and what we think. We need to read, then, to understand not only what texts say but also how they say it and how they try to persuade or influence what we think.

Because understanding how texts say what they say and achieve their effects is so crucial, assignments in many disciplines ask you to analyze texts. You may be asked to analyze candidates' speeches in a *political science* course or to analyze the imagery in a poem for a *literature* class. In a *statistics* course, you might analyze a set of data—a numerical text—to find the standard deviation from the mean.

This chapter offers detailed guidelines for writing an essay that closely examines a text both for what it says and for how it does so, with the goal of demonstrating for readers how—and how well—the text achieves its effects. We'll begin with three good examples, the first annotated to point out the key features found in most textual analyses.

☀ academic literacies   ◆ fields   ● research

■ rhetorical situations   ⁖ processes   ● media/design

▲ genres   ◆ strategies

PAT FINN

The Architecture of Inequality
On Bong Joon-ho's Parasite

Pat Finn writes for Architizer, *an online resource for architects.*

In Bong Joon-ho's Academy Award–winning film *Parasite*, architecture isn't silent, it speaks. Again and again, the built environment indicates where people fit into the social hierarchy—or if there is a place for them at all.

> A clear thesis.

The film opens in the apartment of the Kim family, the movie's protagonists. This is a semi-basement apartment, or *banjiha*, a common type of working-class residence in South Korea. "It really reflects the psyche of the Kim family," Bong told Rachel Wallace for *Architectural Digest*. "You're still half overground, so there's this hope and this sense that you still have access to sunlight and you haven't completely fallen to the basement yet. It's this weird mixture of hope and this fear that you can fall even lower."

> The meaning behind the design is explained in a quote by the filmmaker.

An early rendering of the Kim family's semi-basement apartment.

Clear description
of the apartment
and how the family
lives in it.

From the first shot of the film, the viewer can see that this is an improvised living situation, a space where nothing ever feels settled. As the opening credits flash across the screen, the camera lingers over socks hanging from a light fixture that is being used as a makeshift drying rack.

In the next shot, we see the two youngest members of the Kim family, siblings Ki-jung and Ki-woo, frantically scanning the apartment with their phones, searching for an unsecured wi-fi signal they can connect to. They eventually find service in the strange bathroom, in which the toilet is elevated on a tiled platform. Now, it seems, the bathroom will become a new communal space where the family will hang out and browse the internet.

The way the Kim family lives in their space, improvising as necessary, reflects the way they exist economically. Without stable jobs, the Kim family is forced to constantly hustle, make adjustments, and find new ways to make money. If they slow down, even for a second, it might prevent them from making ends meet.

Park So-dam, left, and Choi Woo-shik play the two children of the Kim family.

* academic literacies   ● fields   ● research
■ rhetorical situations   ⁝ processes   ● media/design
▲ genres   ◆ strategies

The Kims' stressful lifestyle is emblematic of the so-called "gig economy" that has emerged in recent years. In his now-classic 2009 book *Capitalist Realism*, the late theorist and blogger Mark Fisher argued that the proliferation of "gig" work in the twenty-first century has taken a serious psychological toll on workers worldwide. "To function effectively as a component of just–in-time production you must develop a capacity to respond to unforeseen events, you must learn to live in conditions of total instability, or 'precarity,' as the ugly neologism has it," Fisher explained. "Periods of work alternate with periods of unemployment. Typically, you find yourself employed in a series of short-term jobs, unable to plan for the future" (38).

This passage, like many others in the book, could have been written about the Kims.

In *Parasite*, the crucial difference between the experience of the working class and the upper class is not opulence but stability. The only other living space that features prominently in the film is a gleaming modern estate enclosed by concrete walls. It belongs to the Park

> *The family's life is analyzed with support from a scholarly source.*

The Kim family's most recent "gig" is folding pizza boxes.

family, for whom the Kims' college-age son, Ki-woo, goes to work as an English tutor. (With fabricated credentials, of course; like his other family members, Ki-woo is adept at hustling, or doing what he needs to survive.)

Much has been written about the Parks' gorgeous house, which is said in the film to have been designed by a famous architect named Namgoong Hyeonja. The space is so convincing that many viewers of the film assumed it was a real house, an architectural marvel. However, it is actually a series of sets designed by Lee Ha Jun, the film's production designer.

"Bong left it all to me in terms of its architectural style," Lee explained in an interview with *Dezeen*. "He showed me a simple floor plan which he sketched whilst writing the script." Instead of sticking to one architectural style, Lee took inspiration from multiple homes that had a minimalist design. The key element he wanted to capture was "great space arrangement."

The fact that the Parks' house was supposedly designed by a famous architect is a significant detail. As soon as Ki-woo steps into the house,

The residence of the wealthy Park family is said to have been built by a famous architect. This is an early rendering developed by production designer Lee Ha Jun.

※ academic literacies ● fields ● research
■ rhetorical situations ⦂ processes ● media/design
▲ genres ◆ strategies

The illustrations and photos replace written descriptions of the set.

The sets were designed to convey "great space arrangement," according to production designer Lee Ha Jun.

he is leaving the chaotic and improvisatory space of working-class Seoul and entering planned, architectural space. Here, light fixtures do not double as drying racks and bathrooms aren't used for surfing the web. In contrast, every detail of the Parks' house speaks to the logic of its overall design.

Analysis of the significance of the home, contrasted with the apartment.

In *Parasite*, secrets lurk even in spaces that appear meticulously logical in their design.

This is a living space that has carved out its niche in the social order. It asserts its right to exist.

Clear interpretation of the significance of the two dwellings.

However, the seeming stability of the Park household ultimately proves to be an illusion. The shocking ending of the film illustrates that dark secrets lurk in every house, even ones with open floor plans. It also shows that class tensions can only be tamped down for so long. If inequality persists, and workers continue to be unable to take control of their lives, something is eventually going to crack.

Works Cited

Fisher, Mark. *Capitalist Realism: Is There No Alternative?* Zero Books, 2009.

Lee Ha Jun. "*Parasite* House Designed from 'Simple Floor Plan' Sketched by Bong Joon-ho." Interview by Bridget Cogley. *Dezeen*, 16 Apr. 2020, www.dezeen.com/2020/04/16/parasite -film-set-design-interview-lee-ha-jun-bong-joon-ho.

Parasite. Directed by Bong Joon-ho, Barunson E and A, 2019.

Wallace, Rachel. "Inside the House from Bong Joon-ho's *Parasite*." *Architectural Digest,* 31 Oct. 2019, www.architecturaldigest.com /story/bong-joon-ho-parasite-movie-set-design-interview.

※ academic literacies   ⬟ fields   ● research
■ rhetorical situations   ⁘ processes   ◖ media/design
▲ genres   ◆ strategies

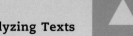

Finn's analysis of the film centers on the two main sets—one family's squalid apartment and another family's lovely home. He compares and contrasts the two dwellings but, interestingly, does not reveal the feature of the house that leads to the "shocking ending of the film."

DANIELLE ALLEN

Our Declaration

Danielle Allen is a political theorist, teaches at Harvard University, and directs Harvard's Edmond J. Safra Center for Ethics. This analysis is a chapter from her book Our Declaration: A Reading of the Declaration of Independence in Defense of Equality.

There's something quite startling about the phrase "We hold these truths to be self-evident." Perhaps it can be made visible most easily with a comparison.

The Catholic Church, too, is committed to a set of truths. At every mass priest and parishioners together recite a list of their beliefs called the *Credo*. One version, called the Apostles' Creed, starts like this: "I believe in God, the Father almighty, creator of heaven and earth. I believe in Jesus Christ, his only son and Lord." Each section begins with the words "I believe," and that's why this recitation is called the *Credo*. Latin, "credo" simply means "I believe."

The Declaration launches its list of truths altogether differently. Jefferson and his colleagues do not say, "I believe," or even "we believe," that all men are created equal. Instead, they say, "We hold these truths to be self-evident," and then they give us a set of either three or five truths, depending on how you count.

What's the difference between "We believe" and "We hold these truths to be self-evident"? In the Catholic *Credo*, when one says, "I believe," the basis for that belief is God's revealed word. In contrast, when Jefferson and his colleagues say, "We hold these truths to be self-evident," they are claiming to know the truths thanks to their own powers of perception and reasoning. These truths are self-evident, and so humans can grasp and hold them without any external or divine assistance.

In order to understand what "We hold these truths to be self-evident" [5]
really means, then, it is important to know what "self-evident" means.

Sometimes people take it to mean that we can instantly understand an idea, but that's not really right. It's true that sometimes the
idea of self-evidence is used for things that we simply perceive. For
instance, when I look out my window I immediately perceive that the
world includes things like trees and flowers. If outside my window
there are many different kinds of tree—hickory and maple and oak,
for instance—when I look at them, I nonetheless rapidly perceive that
they are all the same kind of thing. That many different kinds of a
particular sort of growing thing are all trees is self-evident. We can call
this self-evidence from sense perception.

The immediacy of perception, though, is not the same as instantly
understanding an idea. And, in fact, to call a proposition self-evident
is not at all to say that you will instantly get it. It means instead that
if you look into the proposition, if you entertain it, if you reflect upon
it, you will inevitably come to affirm it. All the evidence that you need
in order to believe the proposition exists within the proposition itself.

This second kind of self-evidence comes not from perception but
from logic and how language works.

For instance, we define a chair as an object with a seat and some
structure of legs to hold that seat up; and the artifact serves the purpose
of having someone sit on it. Then, if I say that a chair is for sitting on,
I am expressing a self-evident truth based only on the definition of a
chair. Of course a chair is for sitting on! That is how I've defined the
word, after all. That's a pretty trivial example of self-evidence. If that
were all there were to the idea of self-evidence, it wouldn't be very
interesting.

So here is where matters get more interesting: one can string [10]
together more than one kind of self-evident proposition—let's call
them "premises"—in order to lead to a new piece of knowledge, a conclusion, which will also count as self-evident, since it has been deduced
from a few basic self-evident premises.

Aristotle called this method of stringing together valid premises to
yield a self-evident conclusion, a syllogism. . . . Here is a basic example:

> FIRST PREMISE: *Bill Gates is a human being.*
> SECOND PREMISE: *All human beings are mortal.*
> CONCLUSION: *Bill Gates is mortal.*

* academic literacies   ● fields   ● research
■ rhetorical situations   ∴ processes   ● media/design
▲ genres   ◆ strategies

This is a bit like math. We can use a Venn diagram to show how the syllogism works. Venn diagrams represent sets of things and how they overlap, and the argument of a syllogism can be thought of as expressing facts about sets and their members. Bill Gates is in the set of human beings. And the set of human beings is entirely contained within the set of mortals. It follows that Bill Gates is in the set of mortals. The validity of this syllogism becomes self-evident when those facts are represented as in this Venn diagram:

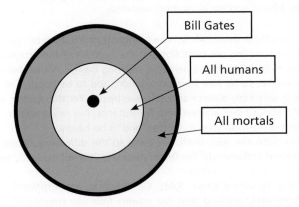

Now, in this syllogism, our two premises are both self-evident truths based on sense perception. We know Bill Gates is a human being by looking at and listening to him. As to the idea that human beings are mortal, we know that human beings die by seeing it happen all around us and never seeing a counterexample. Then we take these two premises, each self-evident through sense perception, and generate a third self-evident proposition, in this case a conclusion, through deduction. From the two premises, we can deduce the certain conclusion that Bill Gates will die.

The Declaration introduces a similar kind of argument when it says, "We hold these truths to be self-evident." At first glance, it looks as if we just have three separate self-evident truths. But if we look closer, we notice that our truths also represent an argument with two premises, which are true from sense perception, and a conclusion that is deduced from them.

Here's how it works. 15

After the Declaration says, "We hold these truths to be self-evident," the text proceeds to identify three truths: one about human beings, one about government, and one about revolution. The truth about human beings, though, is a three-part truth.

It is self-evidently true:

> *that all men are created equal, that they are endowed by their Creator with certain unalienable Rights, that among these are Life, Liberty and the pursuit of Happiness.*

How do these three claims make a single truth? Human beings are equal in all acquiring the same rights at the moment of their creation. From the moment of their emergence as living beings, human beings seek to survive, to be free from domination, and to be happy. This is something we simply observe about human beings. For that matter, we observe it about other animals, too. For instance, I've never seen a cat that didn't want to survive, to be free, and to be happy.

Then, with the next truth, we come to the difference between human beings and animals. The Declaration says, it is self-evidently true

> —*That to secure these rights, Governments are instituted among Men, deriving their just powers from the consent of the governed.*

This is a truly salient point. The signers are saying that, in contrast to the animal kingdom, the world of human beings is indeed full of kingdoms and other kinds of governments. The so-called animal kingdom is a kingdom only metaphorically. There are no governments among animals. Animals have social hierarchies, and they have their own methods for seeking their survival, freedom, and happiness, but human beings use politics. Human beings display self-conscious thought about social organization, and politics is the activity that flows from that self-consciousness about power. Again, this is simply a matter of observation. From the beginning of time to the present day, human beings have formed governments. Human beings have done this just as regularly as birds build nests.

Then the Declaration puts these first two truths together. Since human beings seek their own survival, freedom, and happiness, and since they have a special tool for doing so—namely, the ability to form

20

governments—it makes sense for them to stick with any particular version of that tool, any particular government, only if it's doing the work it's been built to do.

Compare it to a bird with a nest. What's the point of a bird's staying in a nest if it turns out that the nest has been built out of material inimical or poisonous to the bird? What's the use, in other words, of having a government, if it doesn't serve the purposes of protecting life, liberty, and the pursuit of happiness for which governments are set up in the first place?

The Declaration puts it this way: It is self-evidently true

> —That whenever any Form of Government becomes destructive of these ends, it is the Right of the People to alter or to abolish it, and to institute new Government, laying its foundation on such principles and organizing its powers in such form, as to them shall seem most likely to effect their Safety and Happiness.

From the facts, first, that people are simply wired, as are all animals, to seek their survival, freedom, and happiness, and, second, that human beings use governments as their central instrument for protecting their life, liberty, and pursuit of happiness, we can deduce that people have a right to change governments that aren't working for them.

This makes an argument that goes like this:

PREMISE 1: All people have rights to life, liberty, and the pursuit of happiness.

PREMISE 2: Properly constituted government is necessary to their securing these rights.

CONCLUSION: All people have a right to a properly constituted government.

In fact, a philosopher would say that a premise is missing from that argument and that the full formally valid syllogism would look like this: 25

PREMISE 1: All people have rights to life, liberty, and the pursuit of happiness.

PREMISE 2: Properly constituted government is necessary to their securing these rights.

PREMISE 3: [All people have a right to whatever is necessary to secure what they have a right to.]

CONCLUSION: All people have a right to a properly constituted government.

Politicians often craft maxims simply by dropping out pieces of their argument. With the missing premise inserted, the Declaration's truths fit together almost like the pieces of a mathematical equation; we intuitively feel the puzzle pieces snap together. That is how self-evidence should feel.

Allen's analysis focuses on the Declaration's second sentence, unpacking its logic through a careful examination of its key term, "self-evident," and explaining how the rest of the sentence forms a syllogism that "snaps together." She looks carefully at every word, restricting her analysis here to a very brief part of the text—but provides insights that illuminate the whole document.

ROY PETER CLARK

Why It Worked
A Rhetorical Analysis of Obama's Speech on Race

Roy Peter Clark teaches writing at the Poynter Institute. This essay, which Clark describes as "an X-ray reading of the text," appeared online on the Poynter Institute's website, first in 2008 and again in 2017, with a new introduction.

The National Conference of Teachers of English (NCTE) has declared today [October 20, 2017] a National Day on Writing. I celebrate such a day. The introduction of my book *Writing Tools* imagines what America might look like and sound like if we declared ourselves a "nation of writers." After all, what good is freedom of expression if we lack the means to express ourselves?

To mark this day—and to honor language arts teachers everywhere—Poynter is republishing an essay I wrote almost a decade ago.

✳ academic literacies   ⬟ fields   ⬤ research

◼ rhetorical situations   ⁝⁝ processes   ⬤ media/design

▲ genres   ◆ strategies

Remember? It was the spring of 2008 and Barack Obama was running for president. Many of us wondered if America was ready to elect an African-American president (a man with the middle name Hussein).

To dispel the fears of some white Americans and to advance his chances for election, Obama delivered a major address on race in America, a speech that was praised even by some of his adversaries. Obama had / has a gift for language. He is a skilled orator. To neutralize that advantage, his opponents—including Hillary Clinton at one point—would characterize Obama's words as empty "rhetoric"—an elaborate trick of language.

The spring of 2008 seems like such a long time ago. A time just before the Great Recession [that affected the United States from 2008 to 2009]. A time just before the ascendancy of social networks and the trolls who try to poison them. A time before black lives were said to matter in a more assertive way. A time before fake news was anything more dangerous than a piece of satire in the *Onion*. A time before Colin Kaepernick took a knee—except when he was tired. A time before torch-bearing white supremacists marched through the night in Charlottesville, Virginia.

It feels like the perfect time for a restart on a conversation about 5 race. To prepare us, let's take another look at the words of Barack Obama before he was president. Let's review what he said, and, more important, how and why he said it. My X-ray analysis of that speech is meant not as a final word on that historical moment, but as an invitation, a doorway to a room where we can all reflect on American history and the American language.

Have a great National Day on Writing.

More than a century ago, scholar and journalist W. E. B. Du Bois wrote a single paragraph about how race is experienced in America. I have learned more from those 112 words than from most book-length studies of the subject:

After the Egyptian and Indian, the Greek and Roman, the Teuton and Mongolian, the Negro is a sort of seventh son, born with a veil, and gifted with second-sight in this American world, a world which yields him no true self-consciousness, but only lets him see himself through the revelation of the other world. It is a peculiar sensation, this double-consciousness, this sense of always looking at one's self through the eyes of others, of measuring one's soul by the tape of a world that looks on in amused contempt and pity. One ever feels his two-ness, —an American, a Negro; two souls, two thoughts, two unreconciled strivings; two warring ideals in one dark body, whose dogged strength alone keeps it from being torn asunder.

Much has been said about the power and brilliance of Barack Obama's March 18, 2008, speech on race, even by some of his detractors. The focus has been on the orator's willingness to say things in public about race that are rarely spoken at all, even in private, and his expressed desire to move the country to a new and better place. There has also been attention to the immediate purpose of the speech, which was to reassure white voters that they had nothing to fear from the congregant of a fiery African-American pastor, the Rev. Jeremiah Wright.

Amid all the commentary, I have yet to see an X-ray reading of the text that would make visible the rhetorical strategies that the orator and authors used so effectively. When received in the ear, these effects breeze through us like a harmonious song. When inspected with the eye, these moves become more apparent, like reading a piece of sheet music for a difficult song and finally recognizing the chord changes.

Such analysis, while interesting in itself, might be little more than a scholarly curiosity if we were not so concerned with the language issues of political discourse. The popular opinion is that our current president [George W. Bush], though plain spoken, is clumsy with language. Fair or not, this perception has produced a hope that our next president will be a more powerful communicator, a Kennedy or Reagan, perhaps, who can use language less as a way to signal ideology and more as a means to bring the disparate parts of the nation together. Journalists need to pay closer attention to political language than ever before.

Like most memorable pieces of oratory, Obama's speech sounds better than it reads. We have no way of knowing if that was true of Lincoln's Gettysburg Address, but it is certainly true of Dr. King's "I Have a Dream" speech. If you doubt this assertion, test it out. Read the speech[1] and then experience it in its original setting[2] recited by his soulful voice.

10

---

1. http://www.americanrhetoric.com/speeches/mlkihaveadream.htm
2. https://archive.org/details/MLKDream

academic literacies   ● fields   ● research
■ rhetorical situations   ⁙ processes   ● media/design
▲ genres   ◆ strategies

The effectiveness of Obama's speech rests upon four related rhetorical strategies:

1. The power of allusion and its patriotic associations.
2. The oratorical resonance of parallel constructions.
3. The "two-ness" of the texture, to use Du Bois's useful term.
4. His ability to include himself as a character in a narrative about race.

Allusion

Part of what made Dr. King's speech resonate, not just for black people, but for some whites, was its framing of racial equality in familiar patriotic terms: "This will be the day when all of God's children will be able to sing with new meaning, 'My country 'tis of thee, sweet land of liberty, of thee I sing. Land where my fathers died, land of the pilgrim's pride, from every mountainside, let freedom ring.'" What follows, of course, is King's great litany of iconic topography that carries listeners across the American landscape: "Let freedom ring from the snowcapped Rockies of Colorado! . . ."

In this tradition, Obama begins with "We the people, in order to form a more perfect union," a quote from the Constitution that becomes a recurring refrain linking the parts of the speech. What comes next is "Two hundred and twenty one years ago," an opening that places him in the tradition of Lincoln at Gettysburg and Dr. King at the Lincoln Memorial: "Five score years ago."

On the first page, Obama mentions the words democracy, Declaration of Independence, Philadelphia convention, 1787, the colonies, the founders, the Constitution, liberty, justice, citizenship under the law, parchment, equal, free, prosperous, and the presidency. It is not as well known as it should be that many black leaders, including Dr. King, use two different modes of discourse when addressing white vs. black audiences, an ignorance that has led to some of the hysteria over some of Rev. Wright's comments.

Obama's patriotic lexicon is meant to comfort white ears and soothe white fears. What keeps the speech from falling into a pandering sea of slogans is language that reveals, not the ideals, but the failures of the American experiment: "It was stained by this nation's original sin of slavery, a question that divided the colonies and brought the convention to a stalemate until the founders chose to allow the slave trade to continue for at least twenty more years, and to leave any final resolution to future generations." And "what would be needed were Americans in successive generations who were willing to do their part . . . to narrow that gap between the promise of our ideals and the reality of their time."

Lest a dark vision of America disillusion potential voters, Obama returns to familiar evocations of national history, ideals, and language:

— "Out of many, we are truly one."
— "survived a Depression."
— "a man who served his country"
— "on a path of a more perfect union"
— "a full measure of justice"
— "the immigrant trying to feed his family"
— "where our union grows stronger"
— "a band of patriots signed that document."

Parallelism

At the risk of calling to mind the worst memories of grammar class, I invoke the wisdom that parallel constructions help authors and orators make meaning memorable. To remember how parallelism works, think of equal terms to express equal ideas. So Dr. King dreamed that one day his four children "will not be judged by the color of their skin but by the content of their character." (*By the content of their character* is parallel to *by the color of their skin*.)

Back to Obama: "This was one of the tasks we set forth at the beginning of this campaign—to continue the long march of those who came before us, a march for a more just, more equal, more free, more caring and more prosperous America." If you are counting, that's five parallel phrases among 43 words.

And there are many more:

"... we may not have come from the same place, but we all want to move in the same direction."

"So when they are told to bus their children to a school across town; when they hear that an African American is getting an advantage in landing a good job or a spot in a good college

20

because of an injustice that they themselves never committed; when they're told that their fears about crime in urban neighborhoods are somehow prejudiced, resentment builds over time."

"... embracing the burdens of our past without becoming victims of our past."

Two-ness

I could argue that Obama's speech is a meditation upon Du Bois's theory of a dual experience of race in America. There is no mention of Du Bois or two-ness, but it is all there in the texture. In fact, once you begin the search, it is remarkable how many examples of two-ness shine through:

— "through protests and struggles"
— "on the streets and in the courts"
— "through civil war and civil disobedience"
— "I am the son of a black man from Kenya and a white woman from Kansas."
— "white and black"
— "black and brown"
— "best schools ... poorest nations"
— "too black or not black enough"
— "the doctor and the welfare mom"
— "the model student and the former gang-banger"
— "raucous laughter and sometimes bawdy humor"
— "political correctness or reverse racism"
— "your dreams do not have to come at the expense of my dreams"

Such language manages to create both tension and balance and, without being excessively messianic, permits Obama to present himself as the bridge builder, the reconciler of America's racial divide.

Autobiography

There is an obnoxious tendency among political candidates to frame their life story as a struggle against poverty or hard circumstances. As satirist Stephen Colbert once noted of presidential candidates, it is not enough to be an average millionaire. To appeal to populist instincts it becomes de rigueur to be descended from "goat turd farmers" in France.

Without dwelling on it, Obama reminds us that his father was black and his mother white, that he came from Kenya, but she came from Kansas: "I am married to a black American who carries within her the blood of slaves and slave owners—an inheritance we pass on to our two precious daughters. I have brothers, sisters, nieces, nephews, uncles, and cousins, of every race and every hue, scattered across three continents, and for as long as I live, I will never forget that in no other country on Earth is my story even possible."

The word "story" is a revealing one, for it is always the candidate's job (as both responsibility and ploy) to describe himself or herself as a character in a story of his or her own making. In speeches, as in homilies, stories almost always carry the weight of parable, with moral lessons to be drawn.

Most memorable, of course, is the story at the end of the speech—25 which is why it appears at the end. It is the story of Ashley Baia, a young, white Obama volunteer from South Carolina, whose family was so poor she convinced her mother that her favorite meal was a mustard and relish sandwich.

"Anyway, Ashley finishes her story and then goes around the room and asks everyone else why they're supporting the campaign. They all have different stories and reasons. Many bring up a specific issue. And finally they come to this elderly black man who's been sitting there quietly the entire time. . . . He simply says to everyone in the room, 'I am here because of Ashley.' "

During most of the 20th century, demagogues, especially in the South, gained political traction by pitting working class whites and blacks against each other. How fitting, then, that Obama's story points in the opposite direction through an old black man who feels a young white woman's pain.

Clark traces four patterns of rhetorical strategies used by President Obama in his speech: allusion, parallelism, W. E. B. Du Bois's "two-ness," and auto-biography. His analysis shows how these strategies combine to provide Obama with the opportunity to address and bring together a broad audience through memorable prose.

* academic literacies   ● fields   ● research
■ rhetorical situations ⁘ processes   ● media/design
▲ genres   ◆ strategies

Key Features / Textual Analysis

A summary or description of the text.   Your readers may not know the text you are analyzing, so you need to include it or tell them about it before you analyze it. Allen's text, the Declaration of Independence, is well known, so she assumes that her readers already know its first sentences. Texts that are not so well known require a more detailed summary or description. For example, Finn provides just enough information on *Parasite's* plot that readers can see how the sets fit into it.

Attention to the context.   Texts don't exist in isolation: they are influenced by and contribute to ongoing conversations, controversies, debates, and cultural trends. To fully engage a particular text, you need to understand its larger context. Clark begins by quoting a 1903 book on race in America, and Finn relates the film's characters and sets to contrasts between social classes.

A clear interpretation or judgment.   Your goal in analyzing a text is to lead readers through careful examination of the text to some kind of interpretation or reasoned judgment, sometimes announced clearly in a thesis statement. When you interpret something, you explain what you think it means, as Allen does when she carefully constructs the logical argument underlying the Declaration of Independence. Clark argues that through Obama's use of four rhetorical strategies, he "present[s] himself as the bridge builder, the reconciler of America's racial divide."

Reasonable support for your conclusions.   Written analysis of a text is generally supported by evidence from the text itself and sometimes from other sources as well. The writer might support their interpretation by quoting words or passages from a verbal text or referring to images in a visual text. Allen, for example, interprets the term "self-evident" by referring to formal logic, Venn diagrams, and the Catholic *Credo*. Finn offers photos of the sets and quotations from the director and set designer to support his argument. Clark provides lists of phrases from Obama's speech to support his thesis. Note that the support you offer for your interpretation need only be "reasonable"—there is never only one way to interpret something.

A GUIDE TO WRITING TEXTUAL ANALYSES

Choosing a Text to Analyze

Most of the time, you will be assigned a text or a type of text to analyze: a poem in a literature class, the work of a political philosopher in a political science class, a speech in a history or communications course, a painting or sculpture in an art class, a piece of music in a music theory course. If you must choose a text to analyze, look for one that suits the demands of the assignment—one that is neither too large or complex to analyze thoroughly (a Dickens novel or a Beethoven symphony is probably too big) nor too brief or limited to generate sufficient material (a ten-second TV news brief or a paragraph from *Hillbilly Elegy* would probably be too small). You might also choose to analyze three or four texts by examining elements common to all. Be sure you understand what the assignment asks you to do, and ask your instructor for clarification if you're not sure.

Considering the Rhetorical Situation

59–60 ■	**PURPOSE**	Why are you analyzing this text? To demonstrate that you understand it? To show how its argument works—or doesn't? Or are you using the text as a way to make some other point?
61–64 ■	**AUDIENCE**	Are your readers likely to know your text? How much detail will you need to supply?
72–74 ■	**STANCE**	What interests you (or not) about your text? Why? What do you know or believe about it, and how will your own beliefs affect your analysis?
75–77 ■	**MEDIA/DESIGN**	Will your analysis appear in print? on the web? How will your medium affect your analysis? If you are analyzing a visual text, you will probably need to include an image of it.

Generating Ideas and Text

In analyzing a written text, your goal is to understand what it says, how it works, and what it means. To do so, you may find it helpful to follow a

certain sequence: read, respond, summarize, analyze, and draw conclusions from your analysis.

Read to see what the text says.   Start by reading carefully, to get a sense of what it says. This means first skimming to **PREVIEW THE TEXT**, rereading for the main ideas, then questioning and **ANNOTATING**.

Consider your **INITIAL RESPONSE**. Once you have a sense of what the text says, what do you think? What's your reaction to the argument, the tone, the language, the images? Do you find the text difficult? puzzling? Do you agree with what the writer says? disagree? agree *and* disagree? Your reaction to a text can color your analysis, so start by thinking about how you react—and why. Consider both your intellectual and any emotional reactions. Identify places in the text that trigger or account for those reactions. If you think that you have no particular reaction or response, try to articulate why. Whatever your response, think about what accounts for it.

Next, consolidate your understanding of the text by **SUMMARIZING** what it says in your own words. You may find it helpful to **OUTLINE** its main ideas. For instance, Allen carefully maps out the parts of the syllogism at the heart of her analysis.

Decide what you want to analyze.   Having read the text carefully, think about what you find most interesting or intriguing and why. Does the argument interest you? its logic? its attempt to create an emotional response? its reliance on the writer's credibility or reputation? its use of design to achieve its aims? its context? Does the text's language, imagery, or structure intrigue you? something else? You might begin your analysis by exploring what attracted your notice.

Think about the larger context.   All texts are part of larger conversations with other texts that have dealt with the same topic. An essay arguing for handgun trigger locks is part of an ongoing conversation about gun regulation, which is itself part of a conversation on individual rights and responsibilities. Academic texts include documentation in part to weave in voices from the conversation. And, in fact, anytime you're reading to learn, you're probably reading for some larger context. Whatever your reading goals, being aware of that larger context can help you better understand

13
16–17
14–15

550–51
340–42

what you're reading. Here are some specific aspects of the text to pay attention to:

- *Who else cares about this topic?* Especially when you're reading in order to learn about a topic, the texts you read will often reveal which people or groups are part of the conversation—and might be sources of further reading. For example, an essay describing the formation of the Grand Canyon could be of interest to geologists, environmentalists, Native Americans, travel writers, or tourists. If you're reading such an essay while doing research on the canyon, you should consider how the audience addressed determines the nature of the information provided—and its suitability as a source for your research.

- *Ideas.* Does the text refer to any concepts or ideas that give you some sense that it's part of a larger conversation? An argument on airport security measures, for example, is part of larger conversations about government response to terrorism, the limits of freedom in a democracy, and the possibilities of using technology to detect weapons and explosives, among others.

- *Terms.* Is there any terminology or specialized language that reflects the writer's allegiance to a particular group or academic discipline? If you run across words like "false consciousness," "ideology," and "hegemony," for example, you might guess the text was written by a Marxist scholar.

- *Citations.* Whom does the writer cite? Do the other writers have a particular academic specialty, belong to an identifiable intellectual school, share similar political leanings? If an article on politics cites Michael Moore and Maureen Dowd in support of its argument, you might assume the writer holds liberal opinions; if it cites Ben Shapiro and Sean Hannity, the writer is likely a conservative.

Write a brief paragraph describing the larger context surrounding the text and how that context affects your understanding of the text.

Consider what you know about the writer. What you know about the person who created a text can influence your understanding of it. Their

525 ●

CREDENTIALS, other work, reputation, stance, and beliefs are all useful windows into understanding a text. You may need to conduct an online search

---

- ✳ academic literacies   ● fields   ● research
- ■ rhetorical situations   ⦂ processes   ● media/design
- ▲ genres   ◆ strategies

to find information on the writer. Then write a sentence or two summarizing what you know about the writer and how that information affects your understanding of the text.

Study how the text works. Written texts are made up of various components, including words, sentences, paragraphs, headings, lists, punctuation—and sometimes images as well. Look for patterns in the way these components are used and try to decide what those patterns reveal about the text. How do they affect its message? See the sections on THINKING ABOUT HOW THE TEXT WORKS and IDENTIFYING PATTERNS for specific guidelines on examining patterns this way. Then write a sentence or two describing the patterns you've discovered and how they contribute to what the text says.

21–23
23–25

Analyze the argument. Every text makes an argument and provides some kind of support for it. An important part of understanding any text is to recognize its argument—what the writer wants the audience to believe, feel, or do. Here are some questions you'll want to consider when you analyze an argument:

- *What is the claim?* What is the main point the writer is trying to make? Is there a clearly stated THESIS, or is the thesis merely implied? Is it appropriately qualified?

347–49

- *What support does the writer offer for the claim?* What REASONS are given to support the claim? What EVIDENCE backs up those reasons? Facts? Statistics? Examples? Testimonials by authorities? Anecdotes or stories? Are the reasons and evidence appropriate, plausible, and sufficient? Are you convinced by them? If not, why not?

413–14
414–22

- *How does the writer appeal to readers?* Do they appeal to your EMOTIONS? rely on LOGIC? try to establish COMMON GROUND? demonstrate CREDIBILITY?

426–27
411–22
424
423–426

- *How evenhandedly does the writer present the argument?* Is there any mention of COUNTERARGUMENTS? If so, how does the writer deal with them? By refuting them? By acknowledging them and responding to them reasonably? Does the writer treat other arguments respectfully? dismissively?

424–25

427–29 ◆

- *Does the writer use any logical* FALLACIES? Are the arguments or beliefs of others distorted or exaggerated? Is the logic faulty?

- *What authorities or other sources of outside information does the writer use?* How are they used? How credible are they? Are they in any way biased or otherwise unreliable? Are they current?

- *How does the writer address you as the reader?* Does the writer assume that readers know something about what is being discussed? Does their language include you or exclude you? (Hint: If you see the word "we," do you feel included?) Do you sense that you and the writer share any beliefs or attitudes? If the writer is not writing to you, what audience is the target? How do you know?

Then write a brief paragraph summarizing the argument the text makes and the main way the writer argues it, along with your reactions to or questions about that argument.

In analyzing a visual text, your goal is to understand its intended effect on viewers as well as its actual effect, the ways it creates that effect, and its relationship to other texts. If the visual text accompanies a written one, you need to understand how the texts work together to convey a message or make an argument.

Describe the text. Your first job is to examine the image carefully. Focus on specific details; given the increasing use of *Photoshop* and other digital image manipulation tools, you can usually assume that every detail in the image is intentional. Ask yourself these questions:

- What kind of image is it? Does it stand alone, or is it part of a group? Are there typical features of this kind of image that it includes—or lacks?

- What does the image show? What stands out? What is in the back-ground? Are some parts of the image grouped together or connected? Are any set apart from one another?

✳ academic literacies   ● fields   ● research
■ rhetorical situations   ⁂ processes   ⬤ media/design
▲ genres   ◆ strategies

- As you look at the image, does the content seem far away, close up, or in between? Are you level with it, looking down from above, or looking up from below? What is the effect of your viewing position?

- Does the image tell or suggest a story about what has happened or is about to happen?

- Does the image allude to or refer to anything else? For example, the Starbucks logo features the image of a Siren, a mythical being who lured sailors to their doom.

Explore your response.   Images, particularly those in advertisements, are often trying to persuade us to buy something or to feel, think, or behave a certain way. News photographs and online videos also try to evoke EMOTIONAL responses, from horror over murdered innocents to amusement at cute kittens. Think about your response:

◆ 426–27

- How does the image make you feel? What emotional response, if any, does the image make you feel? Sympathy? Concern? Anger? Happiness? Contentment? Something else?

- What does the image lead you to think about? What connections does it have to things in your life, in the news, in your knowledge of the world?

- Do the image and any accompanying words seem to be trying to persuade you to think or do something? Do they do so directly, such as by pointing out the virtues of a product (Buick Encore: "Sized to fit the way your life moves")? Or indirectly, by setting a tone or establishing a mood (many perfume ads, like this one for Christina Aguilera's Unforgettable: "The feminine essence of timeless fascination, sensual notes like night blooming jasmine make you unforgettable")?

- Does the GENRE affect your response? For example, do you expect to laugh at a comic? feel empathy with victims of a tragedy in a photo accompanying a news story? find a satirical editorial cartoon offensive?

▲ 79

Consider the context. Like written texts, visual texts are part of larger conversations with other texts that have dealt with the same topic or used similar imagery. This editorial cartoon on climate change, for example, is part of an ongoing conversation about how quickly we must act on climate change:

Consider what you know about the artist or sponsor. Editorial cartoons, like the one above, are usually signed, and information about the artist and their other work is usually readily available on the web. Many commercials and advertisements, however, are created by ad agencies, so the organization or company that sponsored or posted the image should be identified and researched. How does that information affect your understanding of the text?

✳ academic literacies   ⬤ fields   ⬤ research
■ rhetorical situations   ⦙⦙ processes   ⬤ media/design
▲ genres   ◆ strategies

Decide on a focus for your analysis. What do you find most interesting about the text, and why? Its details and the way they work together (or not)? The argument it makes? The way it uses images to appeal to its audience? The emotional response it evokes? The way any words and images work together to deliver a message? These are just some ways of thinking about a visual text, ones that can help you find a focus.

However you choose to focus your analysis, it should be limited in scope so that you can zero in on the details of the visual you're analyzing. Here, for example, is an excerpt from an essay from 2014 by an art historian responding to a statement made by former president Barack Obama that manufacturing skills may be worth more than a degree in art history:

> *"I promise you, folks can make a lot more potentially with skilled manufacturing or the trades than they might with an art history degree."* President Barack Obama

Charged with interrogating this quote from the president, I Google "Obama art history." I click on the first result, a video from CNN, in which the quote is introduced by a gray-haired man in a dark and serious suit, standing in front of a bank of monitors in a digitally created nonspace. The camera cuts from this man to President Obama, who stands in shirtsleeves, his tie slightly loosened. His undershirt is visible through his buttondown under the intense light from what I assume is the work-day sun.

Behind him is a crowd of men and women in more casual clothing, some wearing sweatshirts that have the name of a union printed across them. Their presence creates a spectrum of skin tones. Each person was clearly vetted for visual effect, as were the president's and the newscaster's costumes, the size of their flag lapel pins, the shape of the microphones they speak into, and the angle of the light on their faces. The president makes the comment in question, immediately declares his love for art history, and says that he doesn't want to get a bunch of angry emails from art historians. The crowd behind him laughs and the clip cuts off abruptly.

A click away, I find a digitized copy of a handwritten note from President Obama, apologizing to an angry art history professor who emailed him to complain about his comments. The card on which the note is written is plain, undecorated save for two lines of text printed in a conservative, serif font in a shade of blue that is just on the vibrant side of navy—THE WHITE HOUSE—and under it in smaller letters, WASHINGTON. Its tasteful, minimal aesthetic pulls double duty, meant to convey both populist efficiency (note the absence of gold gilding) and stern superiority (you know where Washington is, right?). It sets up a productive contrast with the friendliness of the president's own handwriting, particularly his looping signature, soft on the outside with a strong slash through the middle.

Like the video of the president's speech, it is a screen-scale tour de force of political imagecraft, certainly produced with the full knowledge that it would be digitized and go viral, at least among a particular demographic.

—Joel Parsons, "Richness in the Eye of the Beholder"

Parsons begins by describing the images—Obama's clothing, the people standing behind him, the letterhead on his note card, his "looping

Barack Obama speaking at a General Electric plant in Waukesha, Wisconsin, 2014.

THE WHITE HOUSE
WASHINGTON

Ann —

Let me apologize for my off-the-cuff remarks. I was making a point about the jobs market, not the value of art history. As it so happens, art history was one of my favorite subjects in high school, and it has helped me take in a great deal of joy in my life that

I might otherwise have missed.

So please pass on my apology for the glib remark to the entire department, and understand that I was trying to encourage young people who may not be predisposed to a four four year college experience to be open to technical training that can lead them to an honorable career.

Sincerely,

Obama's apology note to Ann Johns, art history professor at the University of Texas at Austin.

signature"—followed by an analysis of how every aspect of the video and the note card was "certainly produced with the full knowledge that it would be digitized and go viral." Notice as well that Parsons's analysis focuses more on the visual aspects of the video and note card than on what was said or written. And in a part of his essay not shown here, he notes that his analysis is grounded in "tools . . . he learned in a first-year art history course"—a not-so-subtle response to what President Obama said.

Coming Up with a Thesis

410–30 ◆

When you analyze a text, you are basically **ARGUING** that the text should be read or seen in a certain way. Once you've studied the text thoroughly, you need to identify your analytical goal: Do you want to show that the text has a certain meaning? uses certain techniques to achieve its purposes? tries to influence its audience in particular ways? relates to some larger context in some significant manner? should be taken seriously—or not?

347–49 ⁚⁚

something else? Come up with a tentative **THESIS** to guide your thinking and analyzing—but be aware that your thesis may change as you continue to work.

Ways of Organizing a Textual Analysis

Examine the information you have to see how it supports or complicates your thesis. Look for clusters of related information that you can use to

340–42 ⁚⁚

structure an **OUTLINE**. Your analysis might be structured in at least two ways. You might, as Clark does, discuss patterns, elements, or themes that run through the text. Alternatively, you might analyze each text or section of text separately, as Allen does. Following are graphic representations of some ways of organizing a textual analysis:

☀ academic literacies	● fields	● research
■ rhetorical situations	⁚⁚ processes	● media/design
▲ genres	◆ strategies	

[Thematically]

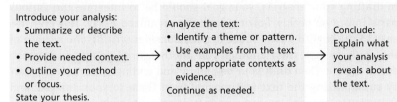

Introduce your analysis:
• Summarize or describe the text.
• Provide needed context.
• Outline your method or focus.
State your thesis. →

Analyze the text:
• Identify a theme or pattern.
• Use examples from the text and appropriate contexts as evidence.
Continue as needed. →

Conclude: Explain what your analysis reveals about the text.

[Part by part, or text by text]

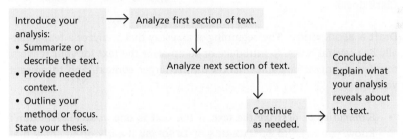

Introduce your analysis:
• Summarize or describe the text.
• Provide needed context.
• Outline your method or focus.
State your thesis. →

Analyze first section of text.
↓
Analyze next section of text.
↓
Continue as needed. →

Conclude: Explain what your analysis reveals about the text.

[Spatially, as the text is likely to be experienced by viewers]

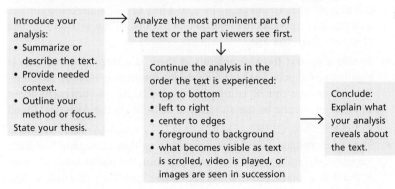

Introduce your analysis:
• Summarize or describe the text.
• Provide needed context.
• Outline your method or focus.
State your thesis. →

Analyze the most prominent part of the text or the part viewers see first.
↓
Continue the analysis in the order the text is experienced:
• top to bottom
• left to right
• center to edges
• foreground to background
• what becomes visible as text is scrolled, video is played, or images are seen in succession →

Conclude: Explain what your analysis reveals about the text.

Writing Out a Draft

In drafting your analysis, your goal should be to integrate the various parts into a smoothly flowing, logically organized essay. However, it's easy to get bogged down in the details. Consider writing one section of the analysis first, then another and another, until you've drafted the entire middle; then draft your beginning and ending. Alternatively, start by summarizing the text and moving from there to your analysis and then to your ending. However you do it, you need to support your analysis with evidence: from the text itself (as Finn's analysis of the "text" of a film does), or from **RESEARCH** on the larger context of the text (as Allen does), or by comparing the text you are analyzing to another text (as Clark does).

489

346–54

Draft a BEGINNING.   The beginning of an essay that analyzes a text generally has several tasks: to introduce or summarize the text for your readers, to offer any necessary information on the larger context, and to present your thesis.

550–51
456–63

- *Summarize or describe the text.* If the text is one your readers don't know, you need to **SUMMARIZE** or **DESCRIBE** it early on to show that you understand it fully. For example, as Finn describes the Kim family apartment and the Parks' house.

- *Show the text.* If you're analyzing a visual text online, consider starting off with an image, a video, or a link to it or something similar, as Finn does by including several illustrations of the sets and photos of scenes from the film.

- *Provide a context for your analysis.* If there is a larger context that is significant for your analysis, you might mention it in your introduction. Allen does this by comparing the Declaration's statement about self-evident truths to the statements of belief in the Apostles' Creed of the Catholic Church.

347–49

- *State your* **THESIS**. Finn begins by asserting that in *Parasite* "the built environment indicates where people fit into the social hierarchy—or if there is a place for them at all." Clark promises to analyze "the rhetorical strategies that the orator and authors used so effectively."

🌟 academic literacies   ⬤ fields   ⬤ research
⬛ rhetorical situations   ⦂ processes   ⬤ media/design
▲ genres   ◆ strategies

Draft an ENDING. Think about what you want your readers to take away from your analysis, and end by getting them to focus on those thoughts.

354–58

- *Restate your thesis—and say why it matters.* Finn, for example, begins by asserting that *Parasite's* sets show "where people fit into the social hierarchy" and ends by discussing the dangers of "class tensions" and inequality.

- *Explain what your analysis reveals.* Your analysis should tell your readers something about the way the text works or about what it means or says. Allen, for example, concludes by noting that "the Declaration's truths fit together almost like the pieces of a mathematical equation; we intuitively feel the puzzle pieces snap together. That is how self-evidence should feel."

Come up with a TITLE. A good title indicates something about the subject of your analysis—and makes readers want to see what you have to say about it. Finn's title provides a preview of his thesis that the architecture seen in *Parasite* reflects the social inequality at the core of the film, while Clark's title straightforwardly announces his topic.

363

Consider REWRITING. If you have time and want to explore alternatives, you might try rewriting your draft to see if a different plan or approach might work better.

378–79

Considering Matters of Design

- If you cite written text as evidence, be sure to set long quotations and **DOCUMENTATION** according to the style you're using.

560–63
670–72

- If your essay is lengthy, consider whether **HEADINGS** would make your analysis easier for readers to follow.

- If you're analyzing a visual text, include a copy of the image and a caption identifying it.

- If you're submitting your essay electronically, provide links to whatever text you are analyzing.

- If you're analyzing an image or a screen shot, consider annotating elements of it right on the image.

Getting Response and Revising

372–74

The following questions can help you and others study your draft with a critical eye. Make sure that anyone you ask to read and **RESPOND** to your text knows your purpose and audience.

- Is the beginning effective? Does it make a reader want to continue?
- Does the introduction provide an overview of your analysis? Is your thesis clear?
- Is the text described or summarized clearly and sufficiently?
- Is the analysis well organized and easy to follow? Do the parts fit together coherently? Does it read like an essay rather than a collection of separate bits of analysis?
- Does each part of the analysis relate to and support the thesis?
- Is anything confusing or in need of more explanation?
- Are all quotations accurate and correctly documented?
- Is it clear how the analysis leads to the interpretation? Is there adequate evidence to support the interpretation?
- Does the ending make clear what your analysis shows?

375–77

Then it's time to **REVISE**. Make sure your text appeals to your audience and think hard about whether it will achieve your purpose.

Editing and Proofreading

Once you've revised your draft, edit carefully:

347–49

- Is your **THESIS** clearly stated?

542–54
560–63

- Check all **QUOTATIONS**, **PARAPHRASES**, and **SUMMARIES** for accuracy and form. Be sure that each has the required **DOCUMENTATION**.

361–62

- Make sure that your analysis flows clearly from one point to the next and that you use **TRANSITIONS** to help readers move through your text.

383–84

- **PROOFREAD** your finished analysis carefully before turning it in.

※ academic literacies   ● fields   ● research
■ rhetorical situations   ⁂ processes   ● media/design
▲ genres   ◆ strategies

Taking Stock of Your Work

Take stock of what you've written and learned by considering these questions:

- What reading strategies did you use as you analyzed your text—annotating? coding? something else? Which strategies were most helpful?

- What writing strategies did you use to analyze your text—defining? comparing? others? Which ones helped you the most?

- Did you provide enough evidence to support your analysis? Can you point to a place in your text where you did an especially good job of providing evidence?

- Did you include any visuals, and if so, what did they add? Could you have shown the same thing with words?

- What did you learn from providing feedback on your peers' work? How did that learning affect your own writing?

- What kinds of analytical writing, if any, have you done in the past? How does your current work compare?

- Was anything new to you about this kind of writing? If so, how did you adapt to the task?

- Are you pleased with your analysis? What did it teach you about the text you analyzed? If you were to write another text analysis, what would you do differently?

If you need more help

See Chapter 30 for guidelines on **DRAFTING**, Chapter 31 on **ASSESSING YOUR OWN WRITING**, Chapter 32 on **GETTING RESPONSE AND REVISING**, and Chapter 33 on **EDITING AND PROOFREADING**. See Chapter 34 if you are required to submit your analysis in a writing **PORTFOLIO**. See Chapter 57 for help using **VISUALS**.

364–66
367–71
372–79
380–84
385–90
673–83

12 Reporting Information

Many kinds of writing report information. Newspapers report on local and world events; textbooks give information about biology, history, writing; websites provide information about products (jcrew.com), people (billieeilish .com), institutions (smithsonian.org). We write out a lot of information ourselves, from a note we post on our door saying we've gone to choir practice to a text we send to tell a friend where to meet us for dinner and how to get there.

College assignments often call for reporting information as well. In a *history* class, you may be assigned to report what you've learned about the state of US relations with Japan just before the bombing of Pearl Harbor. A *biology* course may require you to report the effects of an experiment in which plants are deprived of sunlight for different periods of time. In a *nursing* class, you may have to report the changes in a patient's symptoms after the administration of a particular drug.

This chapter focuses on reports that are written to inform readers about a particular topic. Very often this kind of writing calls for some kind of research: you need to know your subject in order to report on it! When you write to report information, you are the expert. We'll begin with three good examples, the first annotated to show the key features found in most reports.

RENAE TINGLING
Sleepless Nights of a University Student

In the following report, Drexel University student Renae Tingling explains how inadequate sleep can affect college students' performance. Her essay, which is documented in MLA style, originally appeared in The 33rd, *an anthology of student writing published by Drexel Publishing Group.*

* academic literacies   ● fields   ● research
■ rhetorical situations   ⁘ processes   ● media/design
▲ genres   ◆ strategies

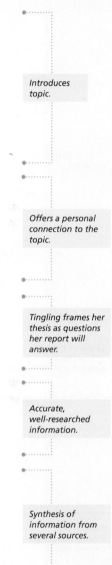

When can we say we've had "enough" sleep? Does the amount of sleep someone gets in a night make a difference? Is getting enough sleep even worth it? According to Newton's first law of motion, a body in motion will stay in motion unless acted upon by an opposing external force. The human body experiences this opposing force in the form of tiredness, slowly approaching as our day comes to an end. For most college students, every day is jam-packed with an infinite number of responsibilities, ranging from exam preparation and homework assignments to managing student organizations and completing chores. Many students find themselves trapped in a cycle of work and activities with rest on the back burner.

Introduces topic.

As a first-year student, I took on a list of new and exciting ventures during my first week. As the weeks progressed, the announcement of midterms marked the end of the adjustment period. I found myself adding more tasks to my to-do list than I was marking off, while time ran shorter by the day. Surrendering a portion of my sleeping hours to my work was unavoidable. Even though I felt satisfied to have completed my assignments, the lack of sleep did not go unnoticed by my body. My body's demand for compensation resulted in my waking up at some ungodly hour the following Saturday afternoon. This hadn't been common practice for me before college, making me wonder if the same could be said for other students. Is this something that most college students perpetually struggle with? If so, why? How does this kind of schedule affect their lives as students, if at all? It's best if we start by figuring out what the big deal is about sleep.

Offers a personal connection to the topic.

Tingling frames her thesis as questions her report will answer.

Sleep is indeed a big deal. It plays a crucial role in an individual's overall health and wellness. A good and consistent quantity and quality of sleep can help with the regulation of physiological processes (Kabrita and Hajjar-Muça 190), such as cardiovascular activity and glucose regulation (Cheng et al. 270). For students, sleep is in some ways like our very own pot of gold. It is essential for effective processing of information (Kabrita and Hajjar-Muça 190), memorization, and proper immune function (Carter et al. 315). As David Dinges, a professor of psychology and chief of the sleep and chronobiology division in the department of psychiatry at the University of Pennsylvania School of Medicine, notes:

Accurate, well-researched information.

Synthesis of information from several sources.

> We know, for example, that sleep is critical for waking cognition—
> that is, for the ability to think clearly, to be vigilant and alert, and

sustain attention. We also know that memories are consolidated during sleep, and that sleep serves a key role in emotional regulation. (qtd. in Worley 758)

So, what exactly is a good quality of sleep? Some would argue that it's almost entirely subjective. Some students find taking short and frequent naps is an effective way of getting all their hours in, while others couldn't disagree more. According to Dinges, for the average person, the target should be "ideally somewhere between seven to seven and a half hours" of uninterrupted sleep (qtd. in Worley 759). The National Sleep Foundation recommends that young adults get a total of seven to nine hours of sleep with no fewer than six and no more than ten. Anything below six hours and you've reached the danger zone (Suni). Sleep deficiency can have a severe and lasting impact on a student's academic performance. Poor sleep quality can also greatly impact our decision-making process (Pilcher et al.).

Ask any university student and they would probably agree that sleep is a privilege. Countless factors at play during a student's academic journey can heavily disrupt their sleep schedule. Habitual procrastination is a major cause of increased stress among university students (Sirois), which may result in health issues such as insomnia (difficulty falling and/or staying asleep). Drinking too much coffee can be a problem. A study conducted by two Turkish dieticians finds that though consumption of most caffeinated beverages had no correlation to poor quality of sleep, coffee was the exception: students with poor sleep quality consumed a notably larger amount of coffee than those with good sleep quality (Suna and Ayaz S132). Prolonged internet usage and cigarette smoking are other behavioral factors that can eat away at students' precious hours of sleep. This brings into question those factors that exist beyond the control of the student—and to determine those factors, who better to ask than the students themselves?

A total of thirty-three students participated in a survey I conducted, ranging from freshman to pre-junior year. The questionnaire collected information pertaining to participants' class level, sleep patterns, and factors that may disrupt their sleep schedule and how those factors affect them academically. Most students (eighty percent) reported sleeping for the recommended number of hours (seven to nine) either a few times or not at all. Behavioral influences, like prolonged internet usage and late-night studying for upcoming exams, were common reasons for

Sleep processes explained.

Causes of sleep difficulties outlined.

Tingling includes her own research study to give another perspective on the topic.

5

* academic literacies   ● fields   ● research
■ rhetorical situations   ⁞ processes   ● media/design
▲ genres   ◆ strategies

losing sleep. As for external influences, many students reported that disruptive roommates and outside noise hindered them from sleeping. Some students also pointed out that trying to complete assignments before their fast-approaching deadlines caused heavy stress and prevented them from getting more hours of sleep. Very few placed the blame on social activities. With habitual and external factors such as these, it is understandable that low quality of sleep can lead to poor academic performance (Carter et al. 315). Consequently, many students found it difficult to be attentive and involved during lectures (eighty-seven percent), successfully complete an exam (fifty-six percent), and maintain their involvement in student organizations (sixty-five percent) after a night of little or no sleep. Approximately half of the participants reported that they rely or have relied on medication and/or caffeinated beverages to feel alert during the day.

At this point I decided to try an experiment: for three days I would only allow myself half my normal hours of sleep to see how my mind and body would react. About halfway through my experiment, I didn't mind the thought of having a cup of coffee myself.

The author reports on a third kind of research, a self-study.

I'll admit, getting out of bed at 5:00 a.m. was a bit of a challenge, especially after sleeping for a total of four and a half hours. It wasn't by chance that by the start of the first day, I had already reached my quota of embarrassing absentminded mistakes after having pressed the wrong button on the elevator and wandered into the wrong classroom. This unusual behavior was due to the effect that lack of sleep had on my level of self-control and alertness (Pilcher et al.). This can greatly throw off a person's decision-making process—as it did mine.

By the second day, getting half a night's worth of sleep took a greater toll on me. Most of the day's lectures managed to slip right past me. Too often to count, I found myself opening eyes I hadn't even realized were closed. What little attention span I had left went to counting down the minutes until the end of each class session. Now, we can all agree that conducting an experiment like this during the exam period would not be the wisest thing to do. Knowing this, I was prepared to add this to my list of mistakes. Funnily enough, my lack of sleep did not have its way with the quiz I took that day. In that moment, the effects of my sleep deprivation seemingly vanished. It was as though my brain ensured that I was able to place all my efforts into not failing math. Sadly, those effects came back sometime afterward and with a vengeance. I became so demotivated to do just about anything

She clearly describes the process of sleep deprivation as she experienced it.

afterward that even having dinner with friends seemed like too much. I was completely against the idea of preparing for upcoming lectures and exams and used how tired I felt as an excuse. This response drives home the notion that sleep deprivation can have serious psychological impacts and weaken our ability to concentrate on academic material (Kabrita and Hajjar-Muça 190).

Oddly enough, I felt a lot less tired on the third day. Though I still felt somewhat tired, it was as if my body was getting used to the lack of sleep. At the end of the day my experiment came to a close, allowing me a well-deserved night's rest. What took me by surprise was how exhausted I felt the following morning after a full eight hours of rest. I initially expected to feel rested, having given myself the chance to get the recommended amount of sleep. But I felt as I had on the first morning of the experiment, even though I had double the amount of sleep. Thankfully, a few days of seven to eight hours of sleep was enough to get me back on track. I was able to focus on discussions during lectures and was more motivated to attend club meetings and study with friends for whatever the next exam would be. It was surprising to discover just how greatly each day was affected by the amount of sleep I got several nights before. It wasn't too hard for me to imagine the damaging effects that poor sleep habits would have over time.

Sleep is a beautiful thing; my experiment is a testament to this. Many of us see it as the easiest and most convenient thing to sacrifice on our journey to academic success. How ironic is it that, as we continue to undermine its significance, sleep can potentially determine whether we achieve that success. It should be mentioned that students often find themselves in situations where valuable hours of sleep are stolen from them by circumstances beyond their control. Whether deliberate or unintentional, lost sleep can take a lot more from us than we bargained for. If I had to summarize what I took from my research, it would be that we as students have fallen for the misconception that less sleep is the only way to stay on top of everything. As a result, we tend to make everything a priority except ourselves. We place getting those extra hours of studying above resting the brain that has to take the exam the following day. At the end of the day, the benefits of a good night's rest are limitless, so ask yourself this: Do I get enough sleep?

Conclusion: A summary of the research and its implication for Tingling's audience, college students.

10

* academic literacies
■ rhetorical situations
▲ genres

⬢ fields
⦂ processes
◆ strategies

● research
● media/design

Works Cited

Carter, Briana, et al. "An Analysis of the Sleep Quality of Undergraduate Students." *College Student Journal*, vol. 50, no. 3,
   2017, pp. 315-22. *Gale Academic Onefile*, go.galegroup.com.

Cheng, Shu Hui, et al. "A Study on the Sleep Quality of Incoming University Students." *Psychiatry Research*, vol. 197, Feb. 2012, pp. 270–74.

Kabrita, Colette S., and Theresa A. Hajjar-Muça. "Sex-Specific Sleep
   Patterns among University Students in Lebanon: Impact on
   Depression and Academic Performance." *Nature and Science of
   Sleep*, vol. 8, 2016, pp. 189–96. *DovePress*, https://doi.org/10.2147
   /NSS.S104383.

Pilcher, June J., et al. "Interactions between Sleep Habits and Self-Control."
   Frontiers in Human Neuroscience, vol. 9, 11 May 2015, www
   .frontiersin.org/articles/10.3389/fnhum.2015.00284/full.

Sirois, F. M., et al. "Is Procrastination Related to Sleep Quality?
   Testing an Application of the Procrastination–Health Model."
   Cogent Psychology, vol. 2, 2015. *Taylor and Francis Online*,
   https://doi.org/10.1080/23311908.2015.1074776.

Suna, G., and A. Ayaz. "Relationship between Caffeinated Beverages
   and Sleep Quality in University Students." *Clinical Nutrition*,
   vol. 37, Sept. 2018, pp. S131–S132. *ScienceDirect*, https://doi
   .org/10.1016/j.clnu.2018.06.1492. Supplement 1.

Suni, Eric. "How Much Sleep Do We Really Need?" *SleepFoundation
   .org*, 10 Mar. 2021, www.sleepfoundation.org/how-sleep-works
   /how-much-sleep-do-we-really-need.

Worley, Susan L. "The Extraordinary Importance of Sleep: The Detri-
   mental Effects of Inadequate Sleep on Health and Public Safety
   Drive an Explosion of Sleep Research." *Pharmacy and Therapeu-
   tics: A Peer-Reviewed Journal for Managed Care and Hospital
   Formulary Management*, vol. 43, no. 12, 2018, pp. 758–63.
   PubMedCentral, https://pubmed.ncbi.nlm.nih.gov/30559589.

Tingling's report draws on published research, her own survey research, and informal research using personal experience to provide a multifaceted view of the effects of inadequate sleep on college students' performance.

FRANKIE SCHEMBRI

Edible Magic

In the following report, written for a first-year writing class at Massachusetts Institute of Technology, Frankie Schembri explains the science behind how popcorn pops. Originally published in Angles 2016: Selected Essays from Introductory Writing Subjects at MIT, *this report is documented in APA style.*

Life is studded with little pockets of magic. These are the moments with mysterious emergent qualities, when the whole is greater than the sum of the parts, when one plus one somehow equals three. Such magic is even better when it comes in edible form.

When an unassuming little kernel of corn meets hot oil, it is transformed. It is elevated with an unmistakable "pop!" into a fluffy cloud of goodness ready to be dressed with butter, caramel, or whatever your heart desires.

This magic is called popcorn.

Popcorn exploded in popularity in the early 20th century but surprisingly only made it into movie theaters with the advent of sound films, or "talkies," in 1927. Silent films catered to a smaller, more exclusive clientele and owners worried that the sound of the snack being munched would detract from the experience (Geiling, 2013).

By the 1940s, popcorn had become an inextricable part of going to the movies, and from then on, over half of the popcorn consumed yearly in America was eaten at movie theaters (Geiling, 2013). Fast-forward some 70 years and the relationship remains unbreakable. Step into any movie theater lobby across America and your senses are bombarded with the unmistakable scent of salt and butter. 5

Popcorn snuck into the American household in the

1960s with Jiffy Pop, a self-contained stovetop popper including kernels, oil, and even the pan, and it flourished with the popularity of microwave ovens in the 1970s (Smith, 1999, p. 124). Popcorn cultivated an important relationship with microwaves in the latter half of the 20th century, important enough that popcorn was eventually given the rare honor of its own designated microwave button (Smith, 1999, p. 127).

"But how?" you might ask. How do these ordinary kernels magically spring to life with a little heat and oil, enchanting kids and grown-ups alike?

Like most acts of magic, popcorn's "pop" can be understood with a little science.

Botanically speaking, popcorn is a type of maize, the only domesticated subgroup in the genus *Zea*, a group of plants in the grass family. The different types of maize are classified based on their kernel's size, shape, and composition (Smith, 1999, p. 6).

Corn kernels have three main structural components. First, there is the germ (from the Latin *germen*, meaning seed or sprout), a small pocket of genetic material that is essentially a baby corn plant waiting to grow. The germ is surrounded by the endosperm (the Greek *endon*, within, and *sperma*, seed), a larger parcel of water mixed with soft and hard starch granules that make up most of the kernel's weight and would provide food for the corn plant if it were to sprout. Finally, the germ-endosperm complex is surrounded by the pericarp (from the Greek *peri*, around, and *karpos*, fruit), the hard shell that winds up stuck between your molars after you enjoy a bag of popcorn (Ghose, 2015).

Popcorn kernels are unique in that they are relatively small, they have endosperms containing a larger number of hard starch granules, and their pericarps are hard and impermeable, essentially sealing off the contents of the kernel from the outside environment. These characteristics have endowed popcorn kernels with the ability to pop (Ghose, 2015).

In an attempt to better understand the physics of popcorn, aeronautical engineer Emmanuel Virot and physicist Alexandre Ponomarenko, who seem to have also fallen under popcorn's spell (judging by the language of their published report), experimented with the temperature at which a kernel pops. As Virot and Ponomarenko (2015) explained, when heat is applied to the kernels via hot oil on a stovetop or in a microwave, the temperature of the kernels begins to rise accordingly. Most affected by this increase in heat is the water stored between the starch granules in the endosperm. Much like a bubbling pot of water brought to a boil, the water in the kernel begins to change from liquid into gas.

While liquid water is content to stay put, gaseous water in the form of steam craves space to move, but the hard shell of the pericarp effectively keeps the water trapped inside the kernel. As a result, the kernel acts like a tiny steamer and the starch granules inside are cooked into a gooey mass. As the mass gets hotter and hotter, the steam presses harder and harder on the inside surface of the kernel's shell like the hands of a million tiny creatures trapped inside a bubble (Virot & Ponomarenko, 2015).

The tension is palpable. The kernel begins to shake with anticipation. It rocks back and forth, back and forth, faster and faster, and faster still. Then finally . . . pop! The bubble bursts, the lid flies off the pot, and fireworks explode as the hard shell of the pericarp cracks and the steam breaks free from its kernel prison. The starchy goop also bubbles out into the world, where it meets cold, fresh air and rapidly hardens into spongy cloudlike shapes. Just like that, in just one-fifteenth of a second, a new piece of popcorn is born (Virot & Ponomarenko, 2015).

Virot and Ponomarenko (2015) determined that the temperature at which kernels typically pop is 180 degrees Celsius. The pair also determined that the resulting popped kernel can be up to 40 times its un-popped volume, although usually the kernel's radius merely doubles.

But what propels the kernel, with what Virot and Ponomarenko (2015) called "all the grace of a seasoned gymnast," into the air as it pops? When the pericarp fractures, it does so in only one place first, giving some of the steam and starchy goop a head start on escaping. The starch released first extends to create a leg of sorts, off of which the rest of the kernel springboards, launching it somersaulting into the air like an Olympic gymnast. Popcorn jumps typically only reach a height of a few centimeters, but still manage to create endless entertainment for the hungry viewer.

Where does the "pop" sound come from? Arguably the most important part of the whole experience, popcorn's characteristic noise is not, contrary to popular belief, the sound of the kernel's shell breaking open. The popping sound is created by the release of trapped water vapor resonating in the kernel, similar to how, when removed, a champagne cork makes a popping sound that resonates in the glass bottle (Virot & Ponomarenko, 2015).

15

* academic literacies
■ rhetorical situations
▲ genres

● fields
∴ processes
◆ strategies

● research
● media/design

Making popcorn hardly seems like an opportunity to learn about physics, but the kernels' unique transformation illustrates some principles of thermodynamics, biomechanics, and acoustics, as the properties of different materials dictate how they respond to pressure and heat.

Life is studded with little pockets of magic. From the enticing smell during a night at the movies to the rising staccato sound of a bag coming to life in your microwave, popcorn is magic-meets-science in its most delicious form. And it always leaves you hungry for more.

References

Geiling, N. (2013, October 3). Why do we eat popcorn at the movies? *Smithsonianmag.com*. https://www.smithsonianmag.com/arts-culture/why-do-we-eat-popcorn-at-the-movies-475063/

Ghose, T. (2015, February 10). *The secret acrobatics of popcorn revealed*. Live Science. https://www.livescience.com/49768-mechanics-of-popcorn.html

Smith, A. (1999). *Popped culture: A social history of popcorn in America*. University of South Carolina Press.

Virot, E., & Ponomarenko, A. (2015). Popcorn: Critical temperature, jump and sound. *Journal of the Royal Society Interface, 12*(104). https://doi.org/10.1098/rsif.2014.1247

Schembri introduces her subject by placing it in a cultural context of the movies, Jiffy Pop, and microwave popcorn. She then distinguishes popcorn from other varieties of corn or maize and goes on to describe what happens when popcorn kernels are heated, pop, and fly into the air. To explore her subject from these various perspectives, she draws on scientific, historical, and popular sources.

JON MARCUS

The Reason College Costs More Than You Think

Writing online for Time *in 2014, Hechinger Report editor Jon Marcus examines the length of time students take to graduate and how that affects the cost of getting a degree.*

When Alex Nichols started as a freshman at the University of Mississippi, he felt sure he'd earn his bachelor's degree in four years. Five years later, and Nichols is back on the Oxford, Mississippi, campus for what he hopes is truly his final semester.

"There are a lot more students staying another semester or another year than I thought there would be when I got here," Nichols says. "I meet people once a week who say, 'Yes, I'm a second-year senior,' or, 'I've been here for five years.'"

They're likely as surprised as Nichols still to be toiling away in school.

Nearly nine out of 10 freshmen think they'll earn their bachelor's degrees within the traditional four years, according to a nationwide survey conducted by the Higher Education Research Institute at UCLA. But the U.S. Department of Education reports that fewer than half that many actually will. And about 45 percent won't have finished even after six years.

That means the annual cost of college, a source of so much anxi-   5
ety for families and students, often overlooks the enormous additional expense of the extra time it will actually take to graduate.

"It's a huge inconvenience," says Nichols, whose college career has been prolonged for the common reason that he changed majors and

The Lyceum, the oldest building at the University of Mississippi.

* academic literacies   ● fields   ● research
■ rhetorical situations   ⁑ processes   ● media/design
▲ genres   ◆ strategies

took courses he ended up not needing. His athletic scholarship—Nichols was a middle-distance runner on the cross-country team—ran out after four years. "I had to get some financial help from my parents."

The average added cost of just one extra year at a four-year public university is $63,718 in tuition, fees, books, and living expenses, plus lost wages each of those many students could have been earning had they finished on time, according to the advocacy group Complete College America.

A separate report by the Los Angeles–based Campaign for College Opportunity finds that the average student at a California State University campus who takes six years instead of four to earn a bachelor's degree will spend an additional $58,000 and earn $52,900 less over their lifetime than a student who graduates on time, for a total loss of $110,900.

"The cost of college isn't just what students and their families pay in tuition or fees," says Michele Siqueiros, the organization's executive director. "It's also about time. That's the hidden cost of a college education."

So hidden that most families still unknowingly plan on four years for a bachelor's degree, says Sylvia Hurtado, director of the Higher Education Research Institute at UCLA. 10

Although the institute does not poll parents in its annual survey, "that high percentage of freshmen [who are confident they'll finish in four years] is probably reflecting their parents' expectation—'This is costing me a lot, so you're going to be out in four years.' So the students think, 'Sure, why not?' I don't think the parents even initially entertain or plan for six years or some possible outcome like that."

Yet many students almost immediately doom themselves to taking longer, since they register for fewer courses than they need to stay on track. Surveys of incoming freshmen in California and Indiana who said they expected to graduate in four years found that half signed up for fewer courses than they'd needed to meet that goal, according to a new report by the higher-education consulting firm HCM Strategists.

It's not entirely the students' fault.

More than half of community-college students are slowed down by having to retake subjects such as math and reading that they should have learned in high school, says Complete College America. And at some schools, budget cuts have made it difficult to register for the courses students do need to take. Two-thirds of students at one California State University campus weren't able to get into their required courses, according to a 2010 study by the University of California's Civil Rights Project.

Most state financial-aid programs, meanwhile, cover only four years. "They do not fund a fifth or sixth year," says Stan Jones, president of Complete College America and a former Indiana commissioner of higher education. "And by that time the parents' resources and the students' resources have run out. So that fifth year is where you borrow."

Students at the most elite colleges and universities tend not to have this problem, which means that schools with some of the highest annual tuition can turn out to be relative bargains. These schools "would have a revolt if their students had to go a fifth year," Jones says. "But that recognition has really not hit the public sector yet, about the hidden cost of that extra year."

Policymakers urge speeding students through remedial classes more quickly, adding more sections of required courses so students can get in when they need them, and encouraging students to take 15 credits per semester instead of the typical 12.

Change won't come soon enough for Nichols, who is determined that it won't take more than one extra semester to finish his degree in integrated marketing communications.

"That's time you're wasting," he says, "that you could be out making money."

Marcus combines information from various research institutes, advocacy groups, surveys, and academic sources to support his argument. His statistics are given a human face by quotations from a student who is taking longer to graduate than he expected.

Key Features / Reports

A tightly focused topic.   The goal of this kind of writing is to inform readers about something without digressing—and without, in general, bringing in the writer's own opinions. All three examples focus on a particular topic—sleep deprivation, popping popcorn, and the cost of college—and present information about the topics evenhandedly.

* academic literacies   ● fields   ● research
■ rhetorical situations   ⠶ processes   ● media/design
▲ genres   ◆ strategies

Accurate, well-researched information. Reports usually require research. The kind of research depends on the topic. Sometimes internet research will suffice, though reports done for college courses may require library research to locate scholarly sources—Tingling, for example, uses various sources available through her university library's databases, and Schembri uses a mix of scholarly and popular sources. Other topics may require or benefit from field research—interviews, observations, surveys, and so on. In addition to doing library and online research, for example, Marcus interviewed a student, and Tingling conducted a survey of students.

A synthesis of ideas. Reports seldom rely on a single source of information. Rather, they draw on several sources, making connections among the facts and ideas found in them. For example, Schembri combines information from a magazine article and a book to provide a brief history of the growth of popcorn's popularity in the United States. Marcus compares undergraduate students' expectations of finishing college in four years with statistics showing that more than half will take longer, using information from a university study and a government report as well as an interview with a student.

Various writing strategies. Presenting information usually requires various organizing patterns—defining, comparing, classifying, explaining processes, analyzing causes and effects, and so on. Schembri explains the process governing popcorn popping and classifies different kinds of maize. Marcus analyzes the financial effects of delaying graduation, and Tingling traces the effects of inadequate sleep on college students' performance.

Clear definitions. Reports need to provide clear definitions of any key terms that their audience may not know. Schembri defines several components of corn kernels, including the germ, endosperm, and pericarp. Tingling includes a definition of "waking cognition."

Appropriate design. Reports often combine paragraphs with information presented in lists, tables, diagrams, and other illustrations. When you're presenting information, you need to think carefully about how to design it —numerical data, for instance, can be easier to understand and remember in a table than in a paragraph. Often a photograph can bring a subject to life, as does the photo on page 146, which accompanies "Edible Magic." Online reports offer the possibility of video and audio clips as well as links to source materials and more detailed information.

A GUIDE TO WRITING REPORTS

Choosing a Topic

Whether you get to choose your topic or are working with an assigned one, see if you can approach the topic from an angle that interests you.

If you get to choose.   What interests you? What do you wish you knew more about? The possible topics for informational reports are limitless, but the topics that you're most likely to write well on are those that engage you. They may be academic in nature or reflect your personal interests or both. If you're not sure where to begin, here are some places to start:

- an intriguing technology: driverless cars, touchscreens, tooth whiteners
- sports: soccer, snowboarding, ultimate Frisbee, basketball
- an important world event: the Arab Spring, the fall of Rome, the COVID-19 pandemic
- a historical period: the African diaspora, the Middle Ages, the Ming dynasty, the Great Depression
- a common object: hoodies, gel pens, mascara, Post-it notes
- a significant environmental issue: melting Arctic ice, deer overpopulation, mercury and the fish supply
- the arts: rap, outsider art, the Crystal Bridges Museum of American Art, Savion Glover, Mary Cassatt

334–35 ∴ **LIST** a few possibilities, and then choose one that you'd like to know more about—and that your audience might find interesting, too. You might start

---

⁂ academic literacies   ● fields   ● research
■ rhetorical situations   ∴ processes   ● media/design
▲ genres   ◆ strategies

out by phrasing your topic as a question that your research will attempt to answer. For example:

How is *Google* different from *Yahoo!*?

How was the Great Pyramid constructed?

What kind of training do football referees receive?

If your topic is assigned. If your assignment is broad—"Explain some aspect of the US government"—try focusing on a more limited topic within the larger topic: federalism, majority rule, political parties, states' rights. Even if an assignment seems to offer little flexibility—"Explain the physics of roller coasters"—your task is to decide how to research the topic, and sometimes even narrow topics can be shaped to fit your own interests and those of your audience.

Considering the Rhetorical Situation

PURPOSE	Why are you presenting this information? To teach readers about the subject? To demonstrate your research and writing skills? For some other reason?	59–60
AUDIENCE	Who will read this report? What do they already know about the topic? What background information do they need in order to understand it? Will you need to define any terms? What do they want or need to know about the topic? Why should they care about it? How can you attract their interest?	61–64
STANCE	What is your own attitude toward your subject? What interests you most about it? What about it seems important?	72–74
MEDIA/DESIGN	What medium are you using? What is the best way to present the information? Will it all be in paragraph form, or is there information that is best presented as a chart, table, or infographic? Do you need headings? Would diagrams, photographs, or other illustrations help you explain the information?	75–77

Generating Ideas and Text

Good reports share certain features that make them useful and interesting to readers. Remember that your goal is to present information clearly and accurately. Start by exploring your topic.

333–36

Explore what you already know about your topic. Write out whatever you know or want to know about your topic, perhaps by **FREEWRITING**, **LISTING**, or **CLUSTERING**. Why are you interested in this topic? What questions do you have about it? Such questions can help you decide what you'd like to focus on and how you need to direct your research efforts.

501–23

Narrow your topic. To write a good report, you need to narrow your focus—and to narrow your focus, you need to know a fair amount about your subject. If you are assigned to write on a subject like biodiversity, for example, you need to know what it is, what the key issues are, and so on. If you do, you can simply list or brainstorm possibilities, choose one, and start your research. If you don't know much about the subject, though, you need to do some research to discover focused, workable topics. This research may shape your thinking and change your focus. Start with **SOURCES** that can give you a general sense of the subject, such as a *Wikipedia* entry, a magazine article, a website, perhaps an interview with an expert. Your goal at this point is simply to find out what issues your topic might include and then to focus your efforts on an aspect of the topic you will be able to cover.

347–49

Come up with a tentative thesis. Once you narrow your topic, write out a statement that explains what you plan to report or explain. A good **THESIS** is potentially interesting (to you and your readers) and limits your topic enough to make it manageable. Schembri phrases her thesis as a question: "How do these ordinary kernels magically spring to life with a little heat and oil?" Marcus presents detailed information on the effects of taking six years to earn a bachelor's degree and then offers a simple thesis: "It's not entirely the students' fault." At this point, however, you need only a tentative thesis that will help focus any research you do.

---

* academic literacies   ● fields   ● research
■ rhetorical situations   ∴ processes ● media/design
▲ genres   ◆ strategies

Do any necessary research, and revise your thesis. To focus your research efforts, **OUTLINE** the aspects of your topic that you expect to discuss. Identify any aspects that require additional research, and develop a research plan. Expect to revise your outline as you do your research, since more information will be available for some aspects of your topic than others; some may prove irrelevant to your topic, and some may turn out to be more than you need. You'll need to revisit your tentative thesis once you've done any research, to finalize your statement.

340–42

Ways of Organizing a Report

Reports can be organized in various ways. Here are three common organizational structures:

[Reports on topics that are unfamiliar to readers]

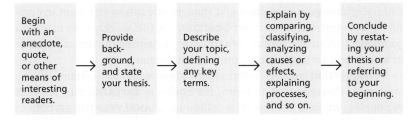

[Reports on events or procedures]

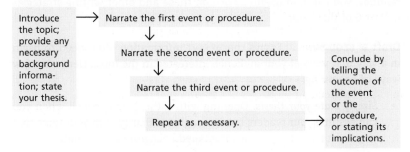

[Reports that compare and contrast]

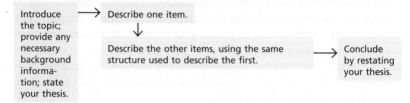

Many reports use a combination of organizational structures; don't be afraid to use whatever method of organization best suits your material and your purpose.

Writing Out a Draft

364–66

Once you have generated ideas and thought about how you want to organize your report, it's time to start **DRAFTING**. Do this quickly—try to write a complete draft in one sitting, concentrating on getting the report on paper or screen and on putting in as much detail as you can.

469–73
405–9
437–44

Writing that reports information often calls for certain writing strategies. The report on popcorn, for example, **EXPLAINS THE PROCESS** of popping, whereas the report on college costs **ANALYZES THE EFFECTS** of delaying college graduation. When you're reporting on a topic your readers aren't familiar with, you may wish to **COMPARE** it with something more familiar; you can find useful advice on these and other writing strategies in Part 6 of this book.

346–54

Draft a BEGINNING. Essays that report information often need to begin in a way that will get your audience interested in the topic. Here are a few ways of beginning:

- *Simply state your thesis.* Opening with a thesis works well when you can assume your readers have enough familiarity with your topic that you don't need to give much detailed background information.

✷ academic literacies   ● fields   ● research

■ rhetorical situations ⦂ processes   ● media/design

▲ genres   ◆ strategies

- *Begin by providing a context for your report.* Tingling starts her report on sleep deprivation by describing college students' busy lives, which often cause them to get inadequate sleep.

- *Start with something that will provoke readers' interest.* Marcus's report begins with an anecdote about a college student.

- *Begin with an illustrative example.* Schembri evokes the childhood wonder of popping corn before exploring its history and physics.

Draft an ENDING. Think about what you want your readers to read last. An effective ending leaves them thinking about your topic.

354–58

- *Summarize your main points.* This is a good way to end when you've presented several key points you want readers to remember. Tingling ends this way, summarizing the results of her research.

- *Point out the implications of your report.* Tingling ends by noting that lost sleep can have greater effects than simply sleepiness: it "can take a lot more than bargained for."

- *Frame your report by referring to its introduction.* Marcus begins and ends his report by quoting the same student, and Schembri returns to her introductory evocation of popcorn as "little pockets of magic."

- *Tell what happened.* If you are reporting on an event, you could conclude by telling how it turns out.

Come up with a title. You'll want a title that tells readers something about your subject—and makes them want to know more. Tingling's title, "Sleepless Nights of a University Student," clearly indicates what's to come in her report. Marcus suggests that his essay will disclose the reason college costs more than you think—but doesn't tell us in the title. See the chapter on **ORGANIZING YOUR WRITING AND GUIDING YOUR READERS** for tips on coming up with titles that are informative and enticing enough to make readers wish to read on.

345–63

Considering Matters of Design

You'll probably write the main text of your report in paragraph form, but think about what kind of information you're presenting and how you can design and format it to make it as easy as possible for your readers to understand. You might ask yourself these questions:

668–69
- What is an appropriate **FONT**? A font like Times New Roman that is easy to read in print? A font like Arial or Verdana that looks good onscreen? Something else?

670–72
- Would it help your readers if you divided your report into shorter sections and added **HEADINGS**?

669–70
- Is there any information that would be easier to follow in a **LIST**?

676
- Could any of your information be summarized in a **TABLE** or **FIGURE**?

676
- Do you have any data that readers would more easily understand in the form of a bar **GRAPH**, line graph, or pie chart?

674–80
- Would **ILLUSTRATIONS** (diagrams, photos, drawings, and so on), video or audio clips, or links help you explain anything in your report?

Getting Response and Revising

The following questions can help you study your draft with a critical eye. **GETTING RESPONSE** from others is always good, and these questions can guide their reading, too. Make sure they know your purpose and audience.

372–74

- Do the title and opening sentences get readers' interest? If not, how might they do so?
- What information does this text provide, and for what purpose?
- Does the introduction explain why this information is being presented? Does it place the topic in a larger context?
- Are all key terms defined that need to be?
- Do you have any questions? Where might more explanation or an example help you understand something better?

❋ academic literacies   ● fields   ● research
■ rhetorical situations   ⁝ processes   ● media/design
▲ genres   ◆ strategies

- Is any information presented visually, with a chart, graph, table, drawing, or photograph? If so, is it clear how the illustration relates to the written text? Is there any text that would be more easily understood if it were presented visually?

- Is any information presented through digital media, such as hyperlinks, video clips, or audio files? If so, is the relation of these elements to the written text made clear? Would any aspect of the report be clearer if presented using such elements?

- Does the organization help make sense of the information? Does the text include description, comparison, or any other writing strategies? Does the topic or rhetorical situation call for any particular strategies that should be added?

- If the report cites any sources, are they quoted, paraphrased, or summarized effectively (and with appropriate documentation)? Is information from sources introduced with **SIGNAL PHRASES**? 551–54

- Does the report end in a satisfying way? What are readers left thinking?

These questions should identify aspects of your report you need to work on. When it's time to **REVISE**, make sure your report appeals to your audience and achieves your purpose as successfully as possible. If you have time and want to explore alternatives, you might try **REWRITING** your draft to see if a different plan or approach might work better. 375–77 378–79

Editing and Proofreading

Once you've revised your draft, follow these guidelines for **EDITING** a report: 380–83

- Check your use of key terms. Repeating key words is acceptable in reports; using synonyms for unfamiliar words may confuse readers, while the repetition of key words or the use of clearly identified **PRONOUNS** for them can be genuinely helpful. Glossary

- Check to be sure you have **TRANSITIONS** where you need them. 361–62

- 670–72 If you have included **HEADINGS**, make sure they're parallel in structure and consistent in design.
- 674–80 Make sure that any photos or other **ILLUSTRATIONS** have captions, that charts and graphs have headings—and that all are referred to in the main text. Use white space as necessary to separate sections of your report and to highlight graphic elements.
- 560–63 Check any **DOCUMENTATION** to see that it follows the appropriate style.
- 383–84 **PROOFREAD** and spell-check your report carefully.

Taking Stock of Your Work

Take stock of what you've written by considering these questions:

- How well did you convey the information? Is it complete enough for your audience's needs?
- What writing strategies (for example, defining, comparing, classifying) did you rely on, and how did they help you achieve your purpose?
- What element of your rhetorical situation (purpose, audience, genre, stance, media/design) was the easiest to figure out for this writing project? What element was the hardest to figure out? Why?
- How did you go about researching the information for this piece?
- How did you go about drafting this piece? For example, did you write out an outline or plan? Do something else? How could you make the drafting process more productive in the future?
- How well did you synthesize information from your sources? Can you point to a specific place in your text where you did an especially good job of making connections among the facts and ideas in your sources?
- Did you use tables, graphs, diagrams, photographs, illustrations, or other graphics? If so, what did they add to the piece? If not, can you think of such elements you might have used?

✳ academic literacies   ● fields   ● research
■ rhetorical situations   ⁖ processes   ● media/design
▲ genres   ◆ strategies

- What did you do to keep yourself engaged with your writing task? If you weren't engaged, how could you improve in the future?

- What did you learn about yourself as a writer through your work on this project? How can you apply that learning to future writing tasks?

If you need more help

See Chapter 34 if you are required to submit your report in a writing **PORTFOLIO**. See also Chapter 14 on **ABSTRACTS** if your report requires one; and Chapter 19 on **PROFILES**, a report based on firsthand research.

385–90
196–200
245–57

13 Arguing a Position

Everything we say or do presents some kind of argument, takes some kind of position. Often we take overt positions: "Everyone in the United States is entitled to affordable health care." "The university needs to offer more language courses." "Photoshopped images should carry disclosure notices." But arguments can be less direct and specific as well, from empty chairs that honor fallen veterans and COVID-19 victims to a yellow smiley face, which might be said to argue for a good day.

In college course work, you are constantly called on to argue positions: in an *English* class, you may argue for a certain interpretation of a poem; in a *business* course, you may argue for the merits of a flat tax; in a *linguistics* class, you may argue that English is now a global language. All of those positions are arguable—people of goodwill can agree or disagree with them and present reasons and evidence to support their positions.

This chapter provides guidelines for writing an essay that argues a position. We'll begin with three good examples, the first one annotated to point out key features of this kind of writing.

KELLY CORYELL

All Words Matter
The Manipulation behind "All Lives Matter"

Kelly Coryell wrote this essay in her first-year writing course at Diablo Valley College in Pleasant Hill, California. An English major, Coryell works as a tutor in the college's learning center and serves as a supplemental instruction leader for multilingual students. This essay was nominated for the Norton Writer's Prize and is documented in MLA style.

* academic literacies   ● fields   ● research

■ rhetorical situations   ⁚ processes   ● media/design

▲ genres   ◆ strategies

I've never understood the popular saying "Sticks and stones may break my bones, but words will never hurt me." I grew up as a tomboy; I've had more than my fair share of scrapes, bruises, and stitches. But I've found that words inflict the most painful injuries. On sleepless nights when I toss and turn, I'm not replaying the time I broke my foot over and over in my head—I'm thinking about some embarrassing thing I said that still makes me physically cringe or a time someone said something hurtful to me. Broken bones heal—words stay with us.

This is because words have power. A skilled wordsmith can influence us by using evocative words that elicit an emotional response. The meanings of these "loaded" words aren't located in a dictionary. There is a context surrounding them that implies a meaning beyond the basic information they convey. Loaded words and phrases appeal to our emotions, not our logic—they enter our hearts, not our minds. They can manipulate, so sometimes people use loaded language to distract us from a flawed argument.

Coryell defines an underlying premise: words have power.

Such is the case when people use the phrase "all lives matter" to oppose the phrase "Black lives matter." In 2012, neighborhood watch coordinator George Zimmerman shot and killed Trayvon Martin, an unarmed African American teenager returning home from a late-night snack run. In 2013, Zimmerman was acquitted of all charges. This sparked the birth of the Black Lives Matter (BLM) movement, when activists Alicia Garza, Opal Tometi, and Patrisse Cullors, frustrated with the systemic inequality and oppression exemplified by Zimmerman's trial, started using the hashtag #BlackLivesMatter on *Twitter*. As more and more Black people died during police confrontations or in police custody—Eric Garner, Michael Brown, Tamir Rice, Walter Scott, Freddie Gray—the movement, and the phrase "Black lives matter," gained momentum, eventually becoming a major talking point in the 2016 presidential election. And in the spring of 2020, the deaths of Ahmaud Arbery, Breonna Taylor, George Floyd, Rayshard Brooks, Dominique "Rem'mie" Fells, and Riah Milton reignited the BLM movement, leading to an overdue reckoning with racism in the United States.

Background: Events leading to Black Lives Matter movement.

As a direct response, Americans who either disagreed with the BLM movement as a whole or supported the movement but were uncomfortable with its slogan began to chant their own phrase: "all lives matter." It should be acknowledged that some of those who have used the phrase "all lives matter" did so naïvely aiming to unify people in a time

Background: "All lives matter" as response to BLM.

A banner in Yellow Springs, Ohio.

Thesis: "All lives matter" sends a dangerous message.

of division, thinking of the words as a positive affirmation to which no one could object. However, saying "all lives matter" as a response to "Black lives matter" is, in reality, sending a dangerous message: it steals attention from the systematic oppression of Black Americans and actively distorts the message behind the BLM movement, manipulating the American people into maintaining the oppressive status quo.

First reason supporting thesis.

The phrase "all lives matter" belies racial inequality in America by implying that all lives are at equal risk. The racism and prejudice endured by African Americans didn't end when slavery was abolished in 1865, it didn't end when Congress passed the Civil Rights Act of 1964, and it didn't end when a Black man was elected president of the United States in 2008. Racial inequality in America persists to this day, ingrained and interwoven so deeply in American society that our prison systems and manufacturing industries depend on it. It's so expertly hidden under layers of celebrity gossip in our media and blatant and bold lies from our politicians, and so "normalized" in our culture, that many people may not even be aware of the plight of Black Americans.

Evidence to support first reason.

But the statistics speak for themselves. According to the NAACP, African Americans are incarcerated at six times the rate of White Americans for drug crimes ("Criminal Justice Fact Sheet"). The Center for American Progress reported that in 2016, the median wealth of Black families was only ten percent of the median wealth of White families (Hanks et al.). Police shoot and kill Black Americans at two and a half times the rate of White Americans, according to a 2016 report (Lowery). All these statistics point to the fact that Black lives

5

☀ academic literacies   ● fields   ● research
■ rhetorical situations ⁝ processes   ● media/design
▲ genres   ◆ strategies

in America are valued less than White lives. The BLM movement aims to change this depressing reality by insisting that "Black lives matter."

Responding to "Black lives matter" with "all lives matter" ignores the unique prejudices and discrimination Black people experience in America. In an essay explaining why she calls herself a feminist, Chimamanda Ngozi Adichie observes that "[f]eminism is, of course, part of human rights in general—but to choose to use the vague expression *human rights* is to deny the specific and particular problem of gender." Adichie's point, that not every human being suffers the oppression that women suffer, parallels the way that emphasizing *all* lives takes focus away from the oppression specifically felt only by Black Americans.

Second reason.

"All lives matter" implies that all lives endure an equal amount of hardship; therefore, the struggles of Black Americans deserve no more attention than the struggles of White Americans—which is statistically false. Daniel Victor illustrates the harmful way the phrase "all lives matter" removes focus from the hardships of Black Americans in his article "Why 'All Lives Matter' Is Such a Perilous Phrase." He writes:

> Those in the Black Lives Matter movement say black people are in immediate danger and need immediate attention. . . .
>
> Saying "All Lives Matter" in response would suggest to them that all people are in equal danger, invalidating the specific concerns of Black people.
>
> "You're watering the house that's not burning but you're choosing to leave the house that's burning unattended," said Allen Kwabena Frimpong, an organizer for the New York chapter of Black Lives Matter. "It's irresponsible."

Here she makes the analogy clear and extends her argument with another analogy.

To put it simply, focusing too much on the whole can divert much-needed attention from crises affecting a specific group.

Summary of this argument.

Using "all lives matter" as a response to "Black lives matter" perpetuates the misconception that BLM activists do not believe both sentiments. The core of the BLM movement is the belief that *all* lives matter—*including* Black lives, which are treated differently than White lives, not just by law enforcement but by America as a whole. As J. Clara Chan explains in her article "What Is 'All Lives Matter'? A Short Explainer":

Third reason: "All lives matter" misinterprets the meaning of "Black lives matter."

Here and below, evidence supporting the third reason. Also, an appeal to readers' shared values—in this case, fairness.

BLM supporters stress that the movement isn't about believing no other races matter. Instead, the movement seeks to highlight and change how racism disproportionately affects the black community, in terms of police brutality, job security, socioeconomic status, educational opportunities, and more.

The BLM movement's focus on particular inequities doesn't mean other races don't matter, but the phrase "all lives matter" is loaded language that implies they don't. As Dave Bry explains, "Understanding 'black lives matter' to mean 'only' black lives matter has been a misinterpretation from the beginning." "All lives matter" is the point of the BLM movement—that all lives do matter; therefore, Black lives need to matter as much as White lives. It isn't "*only* Black lives matter"; it's "Black lives matter, *too*."

The essay refers back to its underlying premise, that words have power—but focuses on the power of "all lives matter" to shape perception.

"All lives matter" manipulates people into believing those who say "Black lives matter" are against other lives. Jason Stanley explains the many ways language can be used as a tool for suppression: "Words are misappropriated and meanings twisted. I believe that these tactics are not really about making substantive claims, but rather play the role of silencing. They are, if you will, linguistic strategies for stealing the voices of others." In other words, a group can be silenced if the language vital to their ability to express themselves and their beliefs is co-opted by another group. Supporters of "all lives matter" co-opted the language of the BLM movement, forcing a separation between the two phrases. As a result, BLM activists cannot say "all lives matter" without sounding like they oppose the views of the BLM movement, since "all lives matter" is no longer just a phrase but a rebuttal—a counterargument.

10

Saying "all lives matter" is premature, since it presupposes that equality has already been achieved. If Black lives really did matter as much as White lives in American society, then saying so would be as uncontroversial as stating any other fact. In fact, America is not a postracial society: poverty, education, health, incarceration rates—all are unequal between different races in America. We must acknowledge this ugly truth if we are ever going to change it. "All lives matter" invokes a naïve reality in which all races are holding hands in a great big circle, singing "This Land Is Your Land" as the sun smiles down on

☀ academic literacies   ● fields   ● research

■ rhetorical situations   ⁚ processes   ● media/design

▲ genres   ◆ strategies

the world. "All lives matter," like the statement "I don't see race, I just see people," may, at first, seem like a beautiful sentiment. Those who say such things may truly do so with the intent of creating a world where everyone is treated equally—regardless of race, gender, creed, orientation, and so on.

But upon close examination, these phrases—however well-meaning—are harmful because, aside from robbing people of their racial identities, they ignore race-based discrimination. How can one notice racism when one does not "see race"? How can one point out discrimination against African Americans if the only response one gets is "everyone matters"? If one insists that a goal has already been met when it hasn't, why would anyone put in more effort toward reaching that goal? This is why "all lives matter" is so manipulative and damaging. It's an attempt to convince us we don't have to keep reaching for equality and justice, even though every fact around us tells us this is far from the case. Only by consciously acknowledging racial inequality will we ever be able to put an end to it.

The root of "all lives matter" boils down to one thing: privilege, and the reluctance to give it up in the name of equality. As Chris Boeskool puts it, "Equality can *feel* like oppression. But it's not. What you're feeling is just the discomfort of losing a little bit of your privilege." Evening the playing field can feel like a bad thing to the person benefiting from the imbalance. In the 1960s, a White bus rider may have felt oppressed when she started having to compete with Black bus riders for the front seat—she lost the privilege of getting a guaranteed front seat because of her race. In the 1970s, a man might have complained that he could no longer "compliment" his female coworkers without being accused of sexual harassment—he lost the privilege of being able to say offensive things because of his gender. If American society starts to accept that Black lives matter as much as White lives, White Americans will lose some of the privileges afforded to them as a result of the oppression of Black Americans. Therefore, people who either do not realize they have this privilege, or simply don't want to give it up, chant "all lives matter" in an effort to hold on to that privilege. If the BLM movement is silenced, the status quo of racial inequality will be maintained. The privileged must resist this unethical temptation and not mistake oppression for equality.

A counterargument is presented and refuted.

Strong conclusion.

Works Cited

Adichie, Chimamanda Ngozi. "I Decided to Call Myself a Happy Feminist." *The Guardian*, 17 Oct. 2014, www.theguardian.com /books/2014/oct/17/chimamanda-ngozi-adichie-extract-we-should -all-be-feminists.

Boeskool, Chris. "When You're Accustomed to Privilege, Equality Feels Like Oppression." *HuffPost*, 14 Mar. 2016, www.huffpost .com/entry/when-youre-accustomed-to-privilege_b_9460662.

Bry, Dave. "'All Lives Matter' Is and Always Was Racist—and This Weekend's Trump Rally Proved It." *The Guardian*, 23 Nov. 2015, www.theguardian.com/commentisfree/2015/nov/23/all-lives -matter-racist-trump-weekend-campaign-rally-proved-it.

Chan, J. Clara. "What Is 'All Lives Matter'? A Short Explainer." *The Wrap*, 13 July 2016, www.thewrap.com/what-is-all-lives -matter-a-short-explainer.

"Criminal Justice Fact Sheet." *NAACP*, www.naacp.org/criminal -justice-fact-sheet. Accessed 25 Feb. 2019.

Hanks, Angela, et al. *Systematic Inequality: How America's Structural Racism Helped Create the Black–White Wealth Gap.* Center for American Progress, Feb. 2018, cdn.americanprogress.org /content/uploads/2018/02/20131806/RacialWealthGap-report.pdf.

Lowery, Wesley. "Aren't More White People Than Black People Killed by Police? Yes, but No." *The Washington Post*, 11 July 2016, www.washingtonpost.com/news/post-nation/ wp/2016/07/11/arent-more-white-people-than-black-people -killed-by-police-yes-but-no.

Stanley, Jason. "The Ways of Silencing." *The New York Times*, 25 June 2011, opinionater.blogsnytimes.com/2011/06/25 /the-ways-of-silencing. Opinionator.

Victor, Daniel. "Why 'All Lives Matter' Is Such a Perilous Phrase." *The New York Times*, 15 July 2016, www.nytimes.com/2016/07 /16/us/all-lives-matter-black-lives-matter.html.

Coryell bases her argument on a clear premise, that "words have power" and that the phrase "all lives matter" reflects a misunderstanding and negative manipulation of the Black Lives Matter movement.

* academic literacies   ● fields   ● research

■ rhetorical situations   ⁝ processes   ● media/design

▲ genres   ◆ strategies

BRIANNA SCHUNK

Come Look at the Freaks
Examining and Advocating for Disability Theatre

In this essay, Wilkes University student Brianna Schunk argues that our culture should support disability theatre in various ways. Schunk's essay was nominated for the Norton Writer's Prize, and it is documented in MLA style.

When I first saw Gaten Matarazzo in the TV show *Stranger Things* and some of the first words out of his toothless little mouth were, "I have cleidocranial dysplasia" ("Chapter One" 00:35:21), I actually cried with joy. Until then, I had never seen another human not related to my family who had cleidocranial dysplasia on television in a popular TV show. I was so shocked, I made my friend rewind the episode so I could hear him say it again. Having cleidocranial dysplasia myself, it is so much easier to be able to compare myself to Matarazzo when explaining my condition to other people, and I only wish he could have come into my life earlier. Representation—how we portray ourselves and are portrayed by others—is incredibly important to all groups of people, but especially to people with disabilities.

Disability, until recently, has rarely been studied through the lens of culture. Up until the last fifty years, disability was studied in the fields of medicine and science by doctors and surgeons. However, the world has recently begun to publish works not related to science and medicine, and this study of the true experience of disability is called *disability culture*. Disability culture has taken root in many fields, such as fiction, nonfiction, the analysis of stories, sociological studies of the disability experience, and visual, musical, and theatre arts. Champions like Rosemarie Garland-Thomson have brought disability culture to a wider audience. In her book *Extraordinary Bodies*, Garland-Thomson uses the lens of feminist critique as well as comparison to the study of race and gender to explain disability culture in America. Her publications are regarded as some of the earliest works on the emerging field of disability culture. *Disability* refers to an incredibly wide spectrum of things, ranging from physical conditions to unseeable mental illnesses and cognitive impairment, but all are part of disability culture. Using studies and reports like Garland-Thomson's, we can share our experiences of being disabled with both able-bodied and disabled people.

Disability theatre is about making theatre for and with people with disabilities, and it is an important topic to me because I am an actor with a disability. Cleidocranial dysplasia affects me physically but is not immediately noticeable and manifests in less visible ways, such as hearing loss in my left ear and years of corrective orthodontic surgery. Throughout most of my life I didn't even consider myself disabled because my disability does not affect my life as much as some other people's disabilities affect theirs. In addition, people around me discouraged me from considering myself disabled, likely because the idea of disability is so stigmatizing. This stems from the power difference found between people with disabilities and people without. Garland-Thomson asserts that people who have "ordinary" (non-disabled) bodies are considered superior to those who do not, and these "normates" have social power and authority (8). However, by considering myself an actress with a disability—an identity important to me—I assert my power. Disability is not bad, it's just different. In the same way able-bodied people are different from one another, so people with disabilities are different from one another and from people who are able-bodied. However, people advocate less for people with disabilities than for any other minority group, and especially so in the theatre and entertainment world. As Lennard Davis notes in a *HuffPost* article, many people turn a blind eye when an able-bodied actor portrays a disabled person, but if anyone does blackface today it is widely acknowledged to be racist.

Many people in the field of disability theatre think it is acceptable for able-bodied actors to portray people with disabilities. This is a strange gray area for two main reasons. One, there are often not enough actors with disabilities available to play the roles; and two, sometimes the character needs to go through a period of time when they are not disabled, such as the story of Stephen Hawking (a role played by able-bodied actor Eddie Redmayne), whose disability developed as he grew older—a situation that has no definite solution. Unfortunately, "the current reality is that non-disabled actors get to

※ academic literacies   ● fields   ● research
■ rhetorical situations   ⁝ processes   ● media/design
▲ genres   ◆ strategies

play whatever roles they want whereas disabled actors don't" (Davis). That there aren't enough disabled actors stems from a vicious cycle identified by disability scholar Carrie Sandahl, who observes that most theatre departments are inaccessible to people with disabilities. They are often denied admission to acting programs because educators are not willing to work with them or the programs do not have the means to accommodate them (255). Also, many training programs can be a challenge to people with disabilities. Sandahl notes that the origin of the "neutral" body in many acting techniques stems from the study of body normalcy (261). Bodies were considered "damaged physically and emotionally from the process of living, and those bodies capable of cure are suitable actors" —disabled bodies could not be "cured" and therefore could not be actors (262). These limitations then lead to fewer actors with disabilities in the professional world. And directors are not willing to work with or adapt stories for actors with disabilities, thinking "their impairments would detract from the playwright's or director's intent for a nondisabled character" (255).

We can get to the root of the problem by recognizing and eliminating disability stereotypes. Marilyn Dahl's essay "The Role of the Media in Promoting Images of Disability" explores common metaphors surrounding people with disabilities, such as villains who are marked as evil because of a missing body part or victims who are completely helpless and dependent on others. However, Dahl's essay also highlights how news reports do the same thing in creating fantastic stories out of the lives of people with disabilities, creating what Dahl calls "heroes by hype." Jack Nelson has also done research into stereotyped characters, even going so far as to categorize them: the "supercrip," the disabled villain, the burden, the misfit, and the victim. However, Nelson gives examples of a few positive representations as well, such as Nemo and his "lucky fin" in the children's animated movie *Finding Nemo*. Nelson stresses that "what most people with disabilities ask is that they [should] be portrayed as real people with real problems that often are not connected to their disability" (289).

Some actors and directors worry that in casting people with disabilities in disabled roles they face "typecasting" them, an idea that stems from years of stereotyping characters with disabilities. When people deny actors with disabilities opportunities to expand their repertoire and play parts traditionally played by able-bodied actors, they close their minds to creating a whole new level of theatre. Having someone with a disability play a typically able-bodied role can add much depth to the character and to the story and can bring to life the character's journey and problems through the medium of the human body. For example, when I was in a local production of the musical *Side Show*, a story about a pair of conjoined twins on the freak show circuit who later achieved vaudeville and film performance fame, I played one of the "World's Tiniest Cossacks," among other ensemble roles. I resonated deeply with my character, because even though I do not have dwarfism, my short stature relates to my disability, and I took to playing a "freak" easily because my condition leads me to entertain people. Playing a character who makes a living by entertaining people with their different body structure was easy, because I drew on my real-life experience. It wasn't the best thing that we didn't have actors with dwarfism to play that part, but at least there was a disabled actor playing the part—a part that honored disability. In the same way that our having actual twin sisters play the main characters added a whole new level of connection between the sisters in our production, so I felt that my playing the part of a disabled character created a whole new connection to the show for myself and for the audience.

People with disabilities originally had a connection to disability theatre through the world of freak shows. Freak shows "challenged the boundaries of the individual" (Garland-Thomson 59) to audiences by presenting bodies different from their own. Those shows were among the early origins of the celebration of disability culture. They also provided a place for people to "identify with nonconformity" (Garland-Thomson 68)—specifically, people wounded and missing limbs from war. When the shows gradually shut down in the mid-twentieth century, people with disabilities couldn't find jobs to sustain themselves because the people who took away their celebration of bodily difference refused to hire them to work anywhere else. They found some work in the developing film industry, in films such as Tod Browning's 1932 movie *Freaks*. It features a cast of actors with disabilities, including people with dwarfism, a pair of conjoined twins, and "pinheads," or actors with microcephaly.

✳ academic literacies   ◆ fields   ● research
■ rhetorical situations   ⁖ processes   ● media/design
▲ genres   ◆ strategies

This movie, in addition to providing jobs and representation to actors with disabilities, also challenged traditional stereotypes about people with disabilities. As the movie progresses and one sees the freaks going about their daily lives, one comes to root for them and value their lives and ambitions as humans, not as freaks or disabled characters. The script even recognizes this, with the characters calling out the ableism of one able-bodied woman in the movie by saying, "Cleopatra ain't one of us. Why, we're just filthy things to her" (*Freaks* 00:25:21–23). Nowadays, we have countless organizations and forms of media that celebrate disability. Derrick Vanmeter, a theatre professor at Clayton State University, lists several organizations, such as Full Radius Dance, which puts on dance shows with people in wheelchairs, and That Uppity Theatre Company, which introduces artists with disabilities in their work *The DisAbility Project*. The Star Wars movies portray people losing limbs—becoming disabled—without any accompanying storylines or stereotypes, instead tying their disabilities to the overarching theme of keeping the universe in balance, which video blogger Hank Green of the vlogbrothers channel summarizes as "when someone cuts someone's hand off in *Star Wars* . . . they're gonna get their hand chopped off too" ("13 Severed Hands" 00:01:21–26). Even musicals such as *Sideshow, Next to Normal* (a story about a woman with bipolar disorder), and Deaf West's production of *Spring Awakening* create stories using characters with disabilities and support them as humans with desires and goals. In 2019, actor Ali Stroker, who played Ado Annie in the Broadway revival of the classic musical *Oklahoma!*, became the first person who uses a wheelchair to win a Tony award, proving actors with disabilities can excel in starring roles created for able-bodied characters.

I encourage other people with disabilities to do theatre and see theatre and seek out opportunities to participate in theatre, and I encourage everyone to support us in our endeavors and to support disability theatre on a whole. Directors: cast more disabled actors; open up your shows to a completely different take by using an actor with a disability. Choose to perform more shows about people with disabilities, and honor those roles with actors who truly know the disabled experience, not just able-bodied actors who can fake a limp. Theatre is the place for everyone to express themselves and tell their stories, and we as a

Ali Stroker as Ado Annie in the 2019 Broadway revival of *Oklahoma!*

theatre community need to honor all people. As a performer with a skeletal condition, my whole life is technically disability theatre. I am evidence that these two worlds can work together, and I want to show that to the world. No one can stop me from doing what I love to do, and I hope I can extend this confidence and belief to every other human that I meet. We can all be brilliant.

Works Cited

"Chapter One." *Stranger Things*, season 1, episode 1, 21 Laps Entertainment / Monkey Massacre, 2016. *Netflix*, www .netflix.com.

Dahl, Marilyn. "The Role of the Media in Promoting Images of Disability: Disability as Metaphor: The Evil Crip." *Canadian Journal of Communication*, vol. 18, no. 1, 1993. *ProQuest Central*, https://doi.org/10.22230/cjc.1993v18n1a718.

※ academic literacies   ● fields   ● research
■ rhetorical situations   ⁘ processes   ● media/design
▲ genres   ◆ strategies

Davis, Lennard J. "Let Actors with Disabilities Play Characters with
    Disabilities." *HuffPost*, 6 Dec. 2017, www.huffpost.com/entry
    /let-actors-with-disabilit_b_380266.
Freaks. Directed by Tod Browning, Metro-Goldwyn Mayer, 1932.
Garland-Thomson, Rosemarie. *Extraordinary Bodies: Figuring Physi-
    cal Disability in American Culture and Literature*. Columbia UP,
    1997.
Nelson, Jack A. "Invisible No Longer: Images of Disability in the
    Media." *Images That Injure: Pictorial Stereotypes in the Media*,
    edited by Susan Dente Ross and Paul Martin Lester, 3rd ed.,
    Praeger, 2011, pp. 274–91.
Sandahl, Carrie. "The Tyranny of Neutral: Disability and Actor Train-
    ing." *Bodies in Commotion: Disability and Performance*, edited
    by Sandahl and Philip Auslander, U of Michigan P, 2005, pp.
    255–67.
"13 Severed Hands!" *YouTube*, uploaded by vlogbrothers, 30 Sept.
    2009, youtube.com/watch?v=lDlqwbMCBg4.
Vanmeter, Derrick. "Disability and Theatre: Access for All." Southeast-
    ern Theatre Conference, 3 Mar. 2017, Hilton Hotel, Lexington,
    Kentucky.

*Schunk argues that actors with disabilities should be cast in the roles of
characters with disabilities—and in roles of nondisabled characters as well.
To make her argument, she draws on recent scholarship on disability culture
and her own experiences.*

NICHOLAS KRISTOF

Our Blind Spot about Guns

*In this essay, which first appeared in the New York Times in 2014, colum-
nist Nicholas Kristof argues that if guns and their owners were regulated
in the same way that cars and their drivers are, thousands of lives could
be saved each year.*

If we had the same auto fatality rate today that we had in 1921, by my calculations we would have 715,000 Americans dying annually in vehicle accidents.

Instead, we've reduced the fatality rate by more than 95 percent—not by confiscating cars, but by regulating them and their drivers sensibly.

We could have said, "Cars don't kill people. People kill people," and there would have been an element of truth to that. Many accidents are a result of alcohol consumption, speeding, road rage or driver distraction. Or we could have said, "It's pointless because even if you regulate cars, then people will just run each other down with bicycles," and that, too, would have been partly true.

Yet, instead, we built a system that protects us from ourselves. This saves hundreds of thousands of lives a year and is a model of what we should do with guns in America.

Whenever I write about the need for sensible regulation of guns, some readers jeer: *Cars kill people, too, so why not ban cars? Why are you so hypocritical as to try to take away guns from law-abiding people when you don't seize cars?*

That question is a reflection of our national blind spot about guns. The truth is that we regulate cars quite intelligently, instituting evidence-based measures to reduce fatalities. Yet the gun lobby is too strong, or our politicians too craven, to do the same for guns. So guns and cars now each kill more than 30,000 in America every year.

One constraint, the argument goes, is the Second Amendment. Yet the paradox is that a bit more than a century ago, there was no universally recognized individual right to bear arms in the United States, but there was widely believed to be a "right to travel" that allowed people to drive cars without regulation.

A court struck down an early attempt to require driver's licenses, and initial attempts to set speed limits or register vehicles were met with resistance and ridicule. When authorities in New York City sought in 1899 to ban horseless carriages in the parks, the idea was lambasted in the *New York Times* as "devoid of merit" and "impossible to maintain."

Yet, over time, it became increasingly obvious that cars were killing and maiming people, as well as scaring horses and causing accidents. As a distinguished former congressman, Robert Cousins, put it in 1910: "Pedestrians are menaced every minute of the days and nights by a

5

wanton recklessness of speed, crippling and killing people at a rate that is appalling."

Courts and editorial writers alike saw the carnage and agreed that 10 something must be done. By the 1920s, courts routinely accepted driver's license requirements, car registration and other safety measures.

That continued in recent decades with requirements of seatbelts and air bags, padded dashboards and better bumpers. We cracked down on drunken drivers and instituted graduated licensing for young people, while also improving road engineering to reduce accidents. The upshot is that there is now just over 1 car fatality per 100 million miles driven.

Yet as we've learned to treat cars intelligently, we've gone in the opposite direction with guns. In his terrific new book, *The Second Amendment: A Biography,* Michael Waldman, the president of the Brennan Center for Justice at the New York University School of Law, notes that "gun control laws were ubiquitous" in the nineteenth century. Visitors to Wichita, Kansas, for example, were required to check their revolvers at police headquarters.

And Dodge City, symbol of the Wild West? A photo shows a sign on the main street in 1879 warning: "The Carrying of Fire Arms Strictly Prohibited."

The National Rifle Association supported reasonable gun control for most of its history and didn't even oppose the landmark Gun Control Act of 1968. But, since then, most attempts at safety regulation have stalled or gone backward, and that makes the example of cars instructive.

"We didn't ban cars, or send black helicopters to confiscate them," 15 notes Waldman. "We made cars safer: air bags, seatbelts, increasing the drinking age, lowering the speed limit. There are similar technological and behavioral fixes that can ease the toll of gun violence, from expanded background checks to trigger locks to smart guns that recognize a thumbprint, just like my iPhone does."

Some of these should be doable. A Quinnipiac poll this month found 92 percent support for background checks for all gun buyers.

These steps won't eliminate gun deaths any more than seatbelts eliminate auto deaths. But if a combination of measures could reduce the toll by one-third, that would be 10,000 lives saved every year.

Dodge City, Kansas, 1879. The sign reads, "The Carrying of Fire Arms strictly prohibited."

A century ago, we reacted to deaths and injuries from unregulated vehicles by imposing sensible safety measures that have saved hundreds of thousands of lives a year. Why can't we ask politicians to be just as rational about guns?

Kristof argues that because regulating cars has made them much safer, guns should be regulated similarly. He supports his argument with data on fatality rates and the history of automobile and gun regulation in the United States.

Key Features / Arguments

A clear and arguable position. At the heart of every argument is a claim with which people may reasonably disagree. Some claims are not arguable because they're completely subjective, matters of taste or opinion ("I hate sauerkraut"), because they are a matter of fact ("The first *Star Wars* movie came out in 1977"), or because they are based on belief or faith ("There is life after death"). To be arguable, a position must reflect one of at least two points of view, making reasoned argument necessary: guns should (or should not) be regulated; selling human organs should be legal (or illegal). In college writing, you will often argue not that a position is correct but that it is plausible—that it is reasonable, supportable, and worthy of being taken seriously.

Necessary background information. Sometimes we need to provide some background on a topic we are arguing so that readers can understand what is being argued. Coryell recounts the origin of the phrase "Black lives matter" before launching her argument that "all lives matter" misrepresents the BLM phrase and movement; Kristof describes the history of automobile regulation.

Good reasons. By itself, a position does not make an argument; the argument comes when a writer offers reasons to back up the position. There are many kinds of good reasons. Kristof makes his argument by comparing cars to guns. Schunk offers several reasons why actors with disabilities should get more parts: using non-disabled actors in roles of characters with disabilities is discriminatory; if there is a shortage of actors with disabilities, it derives from barriers to participation of those actors; and stereotypes limit the roles available to actors with disabilities.

Convincing evidence. Once you've given reasons for your position, you then need to offer evidence for your reasons: facts, statistics, expert testimony, anecdotal evidence, case studies, textual evidence. All three arguments use a mix of these types of evidence. Coryell cites statistics on the differences between Black Americans and White Americans in terms of their incarceration, wealth, and incidence of being shot and killed by police. Kristof shows how regulating cars led to dramatic decreases in driving deaths and injuries. Both Schunk and Coryell cite anecdotes from their own experience to support their arguments.

Appeals to readers' values.   Effective arguers try to appeal to readers' values and emotions. Kristof appeals to the idea that reducing traffic deaths—and, by extension, shooting deaths—is a worthy goal. Coryell appeals to her readers' sense of fairness, that "Black lives matter, *too*"—as much as the lives of White people. These values are deeply held and may be seen as common ground we share with one another.

A trustworthy tone.   Arguments can stand or fall on the way readers perceive the writer. Very simply, readers need to trust the person who's making the argument. One way of winning this trust is by demonstrating that you know what you're talking about. Kristof offers plenty of facts to show his knowledge of the history of automotive regulation—and he does so in a self-assured tone. There are many other ways of establishing yourself (and your argument) as trustworthy—by showing that you have some experience with your subject, that you're fair, and of course that you're honest.

Careful consideration of other positions.   No matter how reasonable and careful we are in arguing our positions, others may disagree or offer counterarguments. We need to consider those other views and to acknowledge and, if possible, refute them in our written arguments. Coryell, for example, acknowledges some people's discomfort with the phrase "Black lives matter," but she counters that to say instead that "all lives matter" is to make a mistake—"Black lives matter" asserts that racism against Black people needs to be pointed out and that Black lives are as worthy as everyone else's lives.

A GUIDE TO WRITING ARGUMENTS

Choosing a Topic

A fully developed argument requires significant work and time, so choosing a topic in which you're interested is very important. Students often find that widely debated topics such as "animal rights" or "abortion" can

---

※ academic literacies   ● fields   ● research

■ rhetorical situations   ∴ processes   ● media/design

▲ genres   ◆ strategies

be difficult to write on because they don't feel any personal connection to them. Better topics include those that

- interest you right now
- are focused, but not too narrowly
- have some personal connection to your life

One good way to **GENERATE IDEAS** for a topic that meets those three criteria is to explore your own roles in life.

333–44

Start with your roles in life. Make four columns with the headings "Personal," "Family," "Public," and "School." Then **LIST** the roles you play that relate to each heading. Here is a list one student wrote:

334–35

Personal	Family	Public	School
gamer	son	voter	college student
dog owner	younger	homeless-shelter	work-study employee
old-car owner	brother	volunteer	dorm resident
male	grandson	American	primary-education major
White		resident of Texas	
middle class			

Identify issues that interest you. Think, then, about issues or controversies that may concern you as a member of one or more of those groups. For instance, as a primary-education major, this student cares about the controversy over whether teachers' jobs should be focused on preparing kids for high-stakes standardized tests. As a college student, he cares about the costs of a college education. Issues that stem from these subjects could include the following: Should student progress be measured by standardized tests? Should college cost less than it does?

Pick four or five of the roles you list. In five or ten minutes, identify issues that concern or affect you as a person who takes on of each of those roles. It might help to word each issue as a question starting with "Should."

Frame your topic as a problem.   Most position papers address issues that are subjects of ongoing debate—their solutions aren't easy, and people disagree on which ones are best. Posing your topic as a problem can help you think about the topic, find an issue that's suitable to write about, and find a clear focus for your essay.

For example, if you wanted to write an argument on the lack of student parking at your school, you could frame your topic as one of several problems: What causes the parking shortage? Why are the university's parking garages and lots limited in their capacity? What might alleviate the shortage?

Choose one issue to write about.   Remember that the issue should be interesting to you and have some connection to your life. It is a tentative choice; if you find later that you have trouble writing about it, simply go back to your list of roles or issues and choose another.

Considering the Rhetorical Situation

59–60 ■	**PURPOSE**	Do you want to persuade your audience to do something? Change their minds? Consider alternative views? Accept your position as plausible—see that you have thought carefully about an issue and researched it appropriately?
61–64 ■	**AUDIENCE**	Who is your intended audience? What do they likely know and believe about this issue? How personal is it for them? To what extent are they likely to agree or disagree with you—and with one another? Why? What common ground can you find with them?
72–74 ■	**STANCE**	What's your attitude toward your topic, and why? How do you want your audience to perceive your attitude? How do you want your audience to perceive you? As an authority on your topic? As someone much like them? As calm? reasonable? impassioned or angry? something else?

※ academic literacies   ◆ fields   ● research

■ rhetorical situations   ⁜ processes   ● media/design

▲ genres   ◆ strategies

MEDIA/DESIGN   What media will you use, and how do your media affect your argument? Does your print or online argument call for photos or charts? If you're giving an oral presentation, should you put your reasons and support on slides? If you're writing electronically, should you include audio or video evidence or links to counter-arguments or your sources?

▪ 75–77

Generating Ideas and Text

Most essays that successfully argue a position share certain features that make them interesting and persuasive. Remember that your goal is to stake out a position and convince your readers that it is plausible.

Explore what you already know about the issue.   Write out whatever you know about the issue by **FREEWRITING** or as a **LIST** or **OUTLINE**. Why are you interested in this topic? What is your position on it at this point, and why? What aspect do you think you'd like to focus on? Where do you need to focus your research efforts? This activity can help you discover what more you need to learn. Chances are you'll need to learn a lot more about the issue before you even decide what position to take.

∴ 333–34
334–35
340–42

Do some research.   At this point, try to get an overview. Start with one **GENERAL SOURCE** of information that will give you a sense of the ins and outs of your issue, one that isn't overtly biased. *The Atlantic*, *Time*, *Slate*, and other online newspapers and magazines can be good starting points on current issues. For some issues, you may need to **INTERVIEW** an expert. For example, one student who wanted to write about chemical abuse of animals at 4-H competitions interviewed an experienced show competitor. Use your overview source to find out the main questions raised about your issue and to get some idea about the various ways in which you might argue it.

● 513

● 518–20

Explore the issue strategically.   Most issues may be argued from many different perspectives. You'll probably have some sense of the different views that exist on your issue, but you should explore multiple perspectives before deciding on your position. The following methods are good ways of exploring issues:

445–55 ◆

- As a matter of **DEFINITION**. What is it? How should it be defined? How can "organic" or "genetically modified food" be defined? How do proponents of organic food define it—and how do they define "genetically modified food"? How do advocates of "genetically modified food" define it—and how do they define "organic food"? Considering such definitions is one way to identify different perspectives on the topic.

431–36 ◆

- As a matter of **CLASSIFICATION**. Can the issue be divided into categories? Are there different kinds of, or different ways of, producing organic foods and genetically modified foods? Do different categories suggest particular positions or perhaps a way of supporting a certain position? Are there other ways of categorizing foods?

437–44 ◆

- As a matter of **COMPARISON**. Is one subject being considered better than another? Is organic food healthier or safer than genetically modified food? Is genetically modified food healthier or safer than organic? Is the answer somewhere in the middle?

469–73 ◆

- As a matter of **PROCESS**. Should somebody do something? What? Should people buy and eat more organic food? More genetically modified food? Should they buy and eat some of each?

Reconsider whether the issue can be argued. Is this issue worth discussing? Why is it important to you and to others? What difference will it

410–30 ◆

make if one position or another prevails? Is it **ARGUABLE**? At this point, you want to be sure that your topic is worth arguing about.

Draft a thesis. Having explored the possibilities, decide your position, and write it out as a complete sentence. For example:

Parents should be required to have their children vaccinated.

Pod-based coffeemakers should be banned.

Genetically modified foods should not be permitted in the United States.

☀ academic literacies   ● fields   ● research

■ rhetorical situations   ⋰ processes   ● media/design

▲ genres   ◆ strategies

Qualify your thesis. Rather than taking a strict pro or con position, in most cases you'll want to **QUALIFY YOUR POSITION** —in certain circumstances, with certain conditions, with these limitations, and so on. This is not to say that we should settle, give in, sell out; rather, it is to say that our position may not be the only "correct" one and that other positions may be valid as well. **QUALIFYING YOUR THESIS** also makes your topic manageable by limiting it. For example:

◆ 412

⁂ 348–49

> Parents should be required to have their children vaccinated, with only medical exemptions allowed.

> Pod-based coffeemakers should be banned unless the pods are recyclable.

> Genetically modified foods should not be permitted in the United States if a link between GMOs and resistance to antibiotics is proven.

Come up with good reasons. Once you have a thesis, you need to come up with good **REASONS** to convince your readers that it's plausible. Write out your position, and then list several reasons. For instance, if your thesis is that pod-based coffeemakers should be banned, two of your reasons might be:

◆ 413–14

> The pods cannot be recycled.

> Other methods of making coffee are more environmentally sound.

Think about which reasons are best for your purposes. Which seem the most persuasive? Which are most likely to be accepted by your audience? Which seem to matter the most now? If your list of reasons is short or you think you'll have trouble developing them enough to write an appropriate essay, this is a good time to rethink your topic—before you've invested too much time in it.

Develop support for your reasons. Next you have to come up with **EVIDENCE** to support your reasons: facts, statistics, examples, testimony by authorities and experts, anecdotal evidence, scenarios, case studies and observation, and textual evidence. For some topics, you may want or need to use evidence in visual form like photos, graphs, and charts; online,

◆ 414–22

you could also use video or audio evidence and links to evidence in other websites.

What counts as evidence varies across audiences. Statistical evidence may be required in certain disciplines but not in others; anecdotes may be accepted as evidence in some courses but not in engineering. Some audiences will be persuaded by emotional appeals while others will not. For example, if you argue that foods produced from genetically modified organisms (GMOs) should be allowed to be sold because they're safe, you could support that reason with *facts*: GMOs are tested thoroughly by three separate US government agencies. Or you could support it with *statistics*: a study of 29 years of data on livestock fed GMO feed found that GMO-fed cattle had no adverse health effects on people who ate them. *Expert testimony* might include R. E. Goodman of the Department of Food Science and Technology at the University of Nebraska–Lincoln, who writes that "there is an absence of proof of harm to consumers from commercially available GMOs."

Identify other positions.   Now think about positions other than yours and the reasons people are likely to give for those positions. Be careful to represent their points of view as accurately and fairly as you can. Then decide whether you need to acknowledge or to refute each position.

424–25 ◆

Acknowledging other positions.   Some positions can't be refuted but are too important to ignore, so you need to **ACKNOWLEDGE** concerns and objections they raise to show that you've considered other perspectives. For example, in an essay arguing that vacations are necessary to maintain good health, medical writer Alina Tugend acknowledges that "in some cases, these trips—particularly with entire families in tow—can be stressful in their own way. The joys of a holiday can also include lugging around a ridiculous amount of paraphernalia, jet-lagged children sobbing on airplanes, hotels that looked wonderful on the Web but are in reality next to a construction site." Tugend's acknowledgment moderates her position and makes her argument appear more reasonable.

✳ academic literacies ⬟ fields ⬤ research
■ rhetorical situations ⁚ processes ⬮ media/design
▲ genres ◆ strategies

Refuting other positions. State the position as clearly and as fairly as you can, and then **REFUTE** it by showing why you believe it is wrong. Perhaps the reasoning is faulty or the supporting evidence inadequate. Acknowledge the merits of the position, if any, but emphasize its shortcomings. Avoid logical **FALLACIES** such as attacking the person holding the position or bringing up a competing position that no one seriously entertains.

◆ 426

◆ 427–29

Ways of Organizing an Argument

Readers need to be able to follow the reasoning of your argument from beginning to end; your task is to lead them from point to point as you build your case. Sometimes you'll want to give all the reasons for your argument first, followed by discussion of any other positions. Alternatively, you might discuss each reason and any opposing arguments together.

[Reasons to support your argument, followed by opposing arguments]

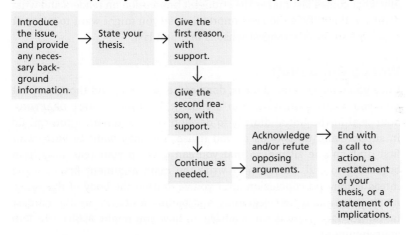

[Reason/opposing argument, reason/opposing argument]

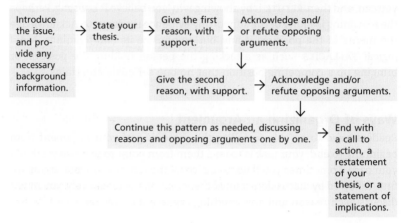

Introduce the issue, and provide any necessary background information. → State your thesis. → Give the first reason, with support. → Acknowledge and/or refute opposing arguments.

Give the second reason, with support. → Acknowledge and/or refute opposing arguments.

Continue this pattern as needed, discussing reasons and opposing arguments one by one. → End with a call to action, a restatement of your thesis, or a statement of implications.

Consider carefully the order in which you discuss your reasons. Usually what comes last makes the strongest impression on readers and what comes in the middle the least impression, so you might want to put your most important or strongest reasons first and last.

Writing Out a Draft

364–66

Once you have generated ideas, done some research, and thought about how you want to organize your argument, it's time to start **DRAFTING**. Your goal in the initial draft is to develop your argument—you can fill in support and transitions as you revise. You may want to write your first draft in one sitting, so that you can develop your reasoning from beginning to end. Or you may write the main argument first and the introduction and conclusion after you've drafted the body of the essay; many writers find that beginning and ending an essay are the hardest

346–58

tasks they face. Here is some advice on how you might **BEGIN AND END** your argument:

✳ academic literacies   ● fields   ● research
■ rhetorical situations   ⁛ processes   ● media/design
▲ genres   ◆ strategies

Draft a beginning. There are various ways to begin an argument essay, depending on your audience and purpose. Here are a few suggestions:

- *Offer background information.* You may need to give your readers information to help them understand your position. Coryell first establishes the truth of the assertion that "Words have power" and then provides a brief history of the events leading to the formation of the Black Lives Matter movement.

- *Begin with an anecdote.* Schunk starts by describing the first time she saw on television an actor who had the same disability that she has.

- *Define a key term.* You may need to show how you're using certain keywords. Coryell carefully defines "loaded" words as "evocative words that elicit an emotional response. . . . They can manipulate, so sometimes people use loaded language to distract us from a flawed argument."

- *Explain the context for your position.* All arguments are part of a larger, ongoing conversation, so you might begin by showing how your position fits into the arguments others have made. Kristof places his argument about guns in the **CONTEXT** of government regulation of other dangerous technologies.

▲ 125–26

- *Begin with something that will get readers' attention.* Kristof begins with an eye-popping statistic: "If we had the same auto fatality rate today that we had in 1921, by my calculations we would have 715,000 Americans dying annually in vehicle accidents."

Draft an ending. Your conclusion is the chance to wrap up your argument in such a way that readers will remember what you've said. Here are a few ways of concluding an argument essay:

- *Summarize your main points.* Especially when you've presented a complex argument, it can help readers to **SUMMARIZE** your main point. Schunk sums up her argument by stating, "Theatre is the place for

● 550–51

everyone to express themselves and tell their stories, and we as a theatre community need to honor all people."

- *Call for action.* Kristof does this by asking politicians to consider "sensible safety measures." Schunk calls for theater and film directors to cast more actors with disabilities.

- *Frame your argument by referring to the introduction.* Kristof ends by returning to the country's response "to death and injuries from unregulated vehicles," suggesting that "sensible safety measures" similar to those adopted 100 years ago for cars could be devised for guns.

Come up with a title.   Most often you'll want your title to tell readers something about your topic—and to make them want to read on. Kristof's title, "Our Blind Spot about Guns," entices us to find out what that blind spot is. Schunk's "Come Look at the Freaks: Examining and Advocating for Disability Theatre" offers a shocking suggestion—and then a subtitle phrased in scholarly language. Coryell also offers a two-part title, the first part a play on the two slogans she discusses in the essay and the second a clear description of the contents. See the chapter on 345–63 **ORGANIZING YOUR WRITING AND GUIDING YOUR READER** for more advice on composing a good title.

Considering Matters of Design

You'll probably write the main text of your argument in paragraph form, but think about what kind of information you're presenting and how you can design it to make your argument as easy as possible for your readers to understand. Think also about whether any visual or audio elements would be more persuasive than written words.

668–69
- What would be an appropriate **FONT**? Something serious like Times Roman? Something traditional like Courier? Something else?

670–72
- Would it help your readers if you divided your argument into shorter sections and added **HEADINGS**?

※ academic literacies   ● fields   ● research
■ rhetorical situations   ⁚ processes   ● media/design
▲ genres   ◆ strategies

- If you're making several points, would they be easier to follow if you set them off in a **LIST**?

  669–70

- Do you have any supporting evidence that would be easier to understand in the form of a bar **GRAPH**, line graph, or pie chart?

  676

- Would **ILLUSTRATIONS**—photos, diagrams, or drawings—add support for your argument? Online, would video, audio, or links help?

  674–80

Getting Response and Revising

At this point you need to look at your draft closely, and if possible **GET RESPONSE** from others as well. Following are some questions for looking at an argument with a critical eye.

372–74

- Is there sufficient background or context?
- Have you defined terms to avoid misunderstandings?
- Is the thesis clear and appropriately qualified?
- Are the reasons plausible?
- Is there enough evidence to support these reasons? Will readers accept the evidence as valid and sufficient?
- Can readers follow the steps in your reasoning?
- Have you considered potential objections or other positions? Are there any others that should be addressed?
- Have you cited enough sources, and are these sources credible?
- Are source materials documented carefully and completely, with in-text citations and a works-cited or references section?
- Are any visuals or links that are included used effectively and integrated smoothly with the rest of the text? If there are no visuals or links, would using some strengthen the argument?

Next it's time to **REVISE**, to make sure your argument offers convincing evidence, appeals to readers' values, and achieves your purpose. If you have

375–77

378–79 time and want to explore alternatives, you might try **REWRITING** your draft to see if a different plan or approach might work better.

Editing and Proofreading

380–83 Once you've revised your draft, follow these guidelines for **EDITING** an argument:

72–74
- Check to see that your tone is appropriate and consistent throughout, reflects your **STANCE** accurately, and enhances the argument you're making.

- Be sure readers will be able to follow the argument; check to see you've
361–62 provided **TRANSITIONS** and summary statements where necessary.
542–54
560–63
- Make sure you've smoothly integrated **QUOTATIONS**, **PARAPHRASES**, and **SUMMARIES** from source material into your writing and **DOCU-MENTED** them accurately.

- Look for phrases such as "I think" or "I feel" and delete them; your essay itself expresses your opinion.

673–83
- Make sure that **ILLUSTRATIONS** have captions and that charts and graphs have headings—and that all are referred to in the main text.

- If you're writing online, make sure all your links work.

383–84
- **PROOFREAD** and spell-check your essay carefully.

Taking Stock of Your Work

Take stock of what you've written by considering these questions:

- How did you go about researching your topic? What would you do differently next time?

- Did your stance change as you researched and wrote your argument? Why or why not?

- What types of evidence did you use in your argument—facts? statistics? expert testimony? something else? Why did you choose those types of evidence?

☀ academic literacies   ⬡ fields   ● research
■ rhetorical situations   ⁘ processes   ◗ media/design
▲ genres   ◆ strategies

- How did feedback from peers, teachers, tutors, or others influence your writing?

- In what ways were you open to other perspectives as you worked on your argument?

- If you were going to revise this argument for a different audience (say, a letter to an online forum or a newspaper), what changes would you need to make?

- What was most meaningful to you about this piece or about your experience of writing it?

If you need more help

See Chapter 34 if you are required to submit your argument as part of a writing **PORTFOLIO**. See also Chapter 11 on **ANALYZING TEXTS**, Chapter 16 on **EVALUATIONS**, and Chapter 20 on **PROPOSALS** for advice on writing those specific types of arguments.

385–90
104–39
214–22
258–68

14 Abstracts

140–63

Abstracts are summaries written to give readers the gist of a **REPORT** or presentation. Sometimes they are published in conference proceedings or databases. In courses in the *sciences*, *social sciences*, and *engineering*, you may be asked to create abstracts of your proposed projects and completed reports and essays. Abstracts are brief, typically 100–200 words, sometimes even shorter. Two common kinds are *informative abstracts* and *proposal abstracts*.

INFORMATIVE ABSTRACTS

Informative abstracts state in one paragraph the essence of a whole paper about a study or a research project. That one paragraph must mention all the main points or parts of the paper: a description of the study or project, its methods, the results, and the conclusions. Here is an example of the abstract accompanying a seven-page article that appeared in the *Journal of Clinical Psychology*:

> The relationship between boredom proneness and health-symptom reporting was examined. Undergraduate students ($N = 200$) completed the Boredom Proneness Scale and the Hopkins Symptom Checklist. A multiple analysis of covariance indicated that individuals with high boredom-proneness total scores reported significantly higher ratings on all five subscales of the Hopkins Symptom Checklist (Obsessive–Compulsive, Somatization, Anxiety, Interpersonal Sensitivity, and Depression). The results suggest that boredom proneness may be an important element to consider when assessing symptom reporting. Implications for

* academic literacies
■ rhetorical situations
▲ genres

● fields
∴ processes
◆ strategies

● research
● media/design

determining the effects of boredom proneness on psychological- and physical-health symptoms, as well as the application in clinical settings, are discussed.

—Jennifer Sommers and Stephen J. Vodanovich,
"Boredom Proneness"

The first sentence states the nature of the study being reported. The next summarizes the method used to investigate the problem, and the following one gives the results: students who, according to specific tests, are more likely to be bored are also more likely to have certain medical or psychological symptoms. The last two sentences indicate that the paper discusses those results and examines the conclusion and its implications.

PROPOSAL ABSTRACTS

Proposal abstracts contain the same basic information as informative abstracts, but their purpose is very different. You prepare proposal abstracts to persuade someone to let you write on a topic, pursue a project, conduct an experiment, or present a paper at a scholarly conference. This kind of abstract is not written to introduce a longer piece but rather to stand alone, and often the abstract is written before the paper itself. Titles and other aspects of the proposal deliberately reflect the theme of the proposed work, and you may use the future tense, rather than the past, to describe work not yet completed. Here is a possible proposal for doing research on boredom:

Undergraduate students will complete the Boredom Proneness Scale and the Hopkins Symptom Checklist. A multiple analysis of covariance will be performed to determine the relationship between boredom-proneness total scores and ratings on the five subscales of the Hopkins Symptom Checklist (Obsessive–Compulsive, Somatization, Anxiety, Interpersonal Sensitivity, and Depression).

Key Features / Abstracts

A summary of basic information. An informative abstract includes enough information to substitute for the report itself, and a proposal abstract gives an overview of the planned work.

Objective description. Abstracts present information on the contents of a report or a proposed study; they do not present arguments about or personal perspectives on those contents. The informative abstract on boredom proneness, for example, offers only a tentative conclusion: "The results *suggest* that boredom proneness *may* be an important element to consider."

Brevity. Although the length of abstracts may vary, journals and organizations often restrict them to 120–200 words—meaning you must carefully select and edit your words.

A BRIEF GUIDE TO WRITING ABSTRACTS

Considering the Rhetorical Situation

59–60 ■	**PURPOSE**	Are you giving a brief but thorough overview of a completed study? only enough information to create interest? a proposal for a planned study or presentation?
61–64 ■	**AUDIENCE**	For whom are you writing this abstract? What information about your project will your readers need?
72–74 ■	**STANCE**	Regardless of stance in the longer work, your abstract must be objective.
75–77 ■	**MEDIA / DESIGN**	How will you set off your abstract from the rest of the text? If you are publishing it online, should it be on a separate page? What format do your readers expect?

✳ academic literacies   ● fields   ● research

■ rhetorical situations   ⦂ processes   ● media/design

▲ genres   ◆ strategies

Generating Ideas and Text

Write the paper first, the abstract last. You can then use the finished work as the guide for the abstract, which should follow the same basic structure. *Exception:* you may need to write a proposal abstract months before the work it describes will be complete.

Copy and paste key statements. If you've already written the work, highlight your **THESIS**, objective, or purpose; basic information on your methods; your results; and your conclusion. Copy and paste those sentences into a new document to create a rough version of your abstract.

347–49

Pare down the rough abstract. **SUMMARIZE** the key ideas in the document, editing out any nonessential words and details. In your first sentence, introduce the overall scope of your study. Also include any other information that seems crucial to understanding your paper. Avoid phrases that add unnecessary words, such as "It is concluded that." In general, you probably won't want to use "I"; an abstract should cover ideas, not say what you think or will do.

550–51

Conform to any requirements. In general, an informative abstract should be at most 10 percent of the length of the entire work and no longer than the maximum length allowed. Proposal abstracts should conform to the requirements of the organization calling for the proposal.

Ways of Organizing an Abstract

Organizing abstracts is straightforward: in a single paragraph, briefly state the nature of the report or presentation, followed by an overview of the paper or the proposal.

[An informative abstract]

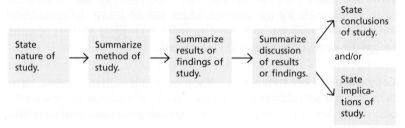

[A proposal abstract]

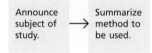

Taking Stock of Your Work

Take stock of what you've written by considering these questions:

- How did you decide on the type of abstract—informative or proposal—to write?

- Describe your process for writing your abstract. What was easy, and what was challenging?

- What writing skills did you develop or refine by working on this piece? How might you use those skills in other writing situations?

- What did you do well in this piece? What could still be improved? What would you do differently next time?

If you need more help

See Chapter 30 for guidelines on **DRAFTING**, Chapter 31 on **ASSESSING YOUR OWN WRITING**, Chapter 32 on **GETTING RESPONSE AND REVISING**, and Chapter 33 on **EDITING AND PROOFREADING**.

364–66
367–71
372–79
380–84

❋ academic literacies   ● fields   ● research
■ rhetorical situations   ⁖ processes   ● media/design
▲ genres   ◆ strategies

15 Annotated Bibliographies and Reviews of Scholarly Literature

When we do research, we may consult annotated bibliographies to evaluate potential sources and literature reviews when we need an overview of the important research ("literature") on a topic. In some courses, you may be asked to create annotated bibliographies or literature reviews to demonstrate that you have researched your topic thoroughly. This chapter offers advice on writing both.

ANNOTATED BIBLIOGRAPHIES

Annotated bibliographies describe, give publication information for, and sometimes evaluate each work on a list of sources. There are two kinds of annotations, *descriptive* and *evaluative*; both may be brief, consisting only of phrases, or more formal, consisting of sentences and paragraphs. Sometimes an annotated bibliography is introduced by a short statement explaining its scope.

Descriptive annotations simply summarize the contents of each work, without comment or evaluation. They may be very short, just long enough to capture the flavor of the work, like the examples in the following excerpt from a bibliography of books and articles on teen films, published in the *Journal of Popular Film and Television*.

MICHAEL BENTON, MARK DOLAN,
AND REBECCA ZISCH

Teen Film$

In the introduction to his book *The Road to Romance and Ruin*, Jon Lewis points out that over half of the world's population is currently under the age of twenty. This rather startling fact should be enough to make most Hollywood producers drool when they think of the potential profits from a target movie audience. Attracting the largest demographic group is, after all, the quickest way to box-office success. In fact, almost from its beginning, the film industry has recognized the importance of the teenaged audience, with characters such as Andy Hardy and locales such as Ridgemont High and the 'hood.

Beyond the assumption that teen films are geared exclusively toward teenagers, however, film researchers should keep in mind that people of all ages have attended and still attend teen films. Popular films about adolescents are also expressions of larger cultural currents. Studying the films is important for understanding an era's common beliefs about its teenaged population within a broader pattern of general cultural preoccupations.

This selected bibliography is intended both to serve and to stimulate interest in the teen film genre. It provides a research tool for those who are studying teen films and their cultural implications. Unfortunately, however, in the process of compiling this list we quickly realized that it was impossible to be genuinely comprehensive or to satisfy every interest.

Doherty, Thomas. *Teenagers and Teenpics: The Juvenilization of American Movies in the 1950s*. Unwin Hyman, 1988.
    Historical discussion of teenagers as a film market.

Foster, Harold M. "Film in the Classroom: Coping with 'Teenpics.'" *English Journal*, vol. 76, no. 3, Mar. 1987, pp. 86–88.
    Evaluation of the potential of using teen films such as *Sixteen Candles*, *The Karate Kid*, and *The Breakfast Club* to instruct adolescents on the difference between film as communication and film as exploitation.

✳ academic literacies　　● fields　　● research
■ rhetorical situations　　⁙ processes　　● media/design
▲ genres　　◆ strategies

Washington, Michael, and Marvin J. Berlowitz. "Blaxploitation Films and High School Youth: Swat Superfly." *Jump Cut*, vol. 9, Oct.–Dec. 1975, pp. 23–24.

> Marxist reaction to youth-oriented Black action films. Article seeks to illuminate the negative influences the films have on students by pointing out the false ideas about education, morality, and the Black family espoused by the heroes in the films.

These annotations are purely descriptive; the authors express none of their own opinions. They describe works as "historical" or "Marxist" but do not indicate whether they're "good." The bibliography entries are documented in MLA style.

Evaluative annotations offer opinions on a source as well as describe it. They are often helpful in assessing how useful a source will be for your own writing. The following evaluative annotations are from a bibliography by Kelly Green, a student at Arizona State University. Following her instructor's directions, she labeled each required part of her annotation—summary, degree of advocacy, credibility, and reliability.

KELLY GREEN
Researching Hunger and Poverty

Abramsky, Sasha. "The Other America, 2012: Confronting the Poverty Epidemic." *The Nation*, vol. 294, no. 20, 25 Apr. 2012, www.thenation.com/article/other-america-2012-confronting-poverty-epidemic/.

> The author presents the image of American poverty in 2012 with examples from various families living in poverty. The author explores the conditions that make up the new recession and suggests that people in America notice the scale of the issue and take action to solve it [Summary]. The author advocates poverty reform and shows bias toward the interests of low-income families. He acknowledges other perspectives on the issue respectfully [Degree of Advocacy]. Abramsky is a freelance journalist with experience in several magazines and newspapers. He has written several books on the topic of

poverty [Credibility]. *The Nation* is one of the oldest-running magazines in the United States and contains opinions on politics and culture [Reliability].

Ambler, Marjane. "Sustaining Our Home, Determining Our Destiny." *Tribal College Journal*, vol. 13, no. 3, spring 2002, www.tribalcollegejournal .org/sustaining-home-determining-destiny/.

> The author examines the causes of poverty on Native American reservations, the factors that lead to solutions to Native American poverty, and the ways in which tribal colleges have helped improve life on reservations [Summary]. The author is strongly biased toward Native American interests and advocates that effective solutions to poverty originate within the reservations, especially in tribal colleges and universities [Degree of Advocacy]. Marjane Ambler was an editor for the *Tribal College Journal* for nine years and worked in national park service for nearly a decade [Credibility]. This article was published in 2002 in the *Tribal College Journal*, a national magazine published by the American Indian Higher Education Consortium [Reliability].

These annotations not only summarize the sources in detail but also evaluate their bias, or "degree of advocacy"; credibility; and reliability.

Key Features / Annotated Bibliographies

A statement of scope. Sometimes you need or are asked to provide a brief introductory statement to explain what you're covering. The authors of the bibliography on teen films introduce their bibliography with three paragraphs establishing a context for the bibliography and announcing their purpose for compiling it.

Complete bibliographic information. Annotations should provide all the information about each source using one documentation system (MLA, APA, or another one) so that you, your readers, or other researchers will be able to find the source easily. It's a good idea to include sources' URLs or **PERMALINKS** to make accessing online sources easier.

499

A concise description of the work. A good annotation describes each item as carefully and objectively as possible, giving accurate information

☀ academic literacies   ● fields   ● research
■ rhetorical situations   ⁛ processes   ● media/design
▲ genres   ◆ strategies

and showing that you understand the source. These qualities will help to build authority—for you as a writer and for your annotations.

Relevant commentary.   If you write an evaluative bibliography, your comments should be relevant to your purpose and audience. The best way to achieve relevance is to consider what questions a potential reader might have about each source: What are the main points of the source? What is its argument? How even-handed or biased is it? How current and reliable is it? Will the source be helpful for your project?

Consistent presentation.   All annotations should follow a consistent pattern: if one is written in complete sentences, they should all be. Each annotation in the teen films bibliography, for example, begins with a phrase (not a complete sentence) characterizing the work.

A BRIEF GUIDE TO WRITING ANNOTATED BIBLIOGRAPHIES

Considering the Rhetorical Situation

PURPOSE	Will your bibliography need to demonstrate the depth or breadth of your research? Will your readers actually track down and use your sources? Do you need or want to convince readers that your sources are good?	▮ 59–60
AUDIENCE	For whom are you compiling this bibliography? What does your audience need to know about each source?	▮ 61–64
STANCE	Are you presenting yourself as an objective describer or evaluator? Or are you expressing a particular point of view toward the sources you evaluate?	▮ 72–74
MEDIA/DESIGN	If you are publishing the bibliography electronically, will you provide links from each annotation to the source itself? Online or offline, should you distinguish the bibliographic information from the annotation by using a different font?	▮ 75–77

Generating Ideas and Text

Decide what sources to include. You may be tempted to include in a bibliography every source you find or look at. A better strategy is to include only those sources that you or your readers may find potentially useful in researching your topic. For an academic bibliography, consider the qualities in the list below. Some of these qualities should not rule a source in or out; they simply raise issues you need to think about.

- *Appropriateness.* Is this source relevant to your topic? Is it a primary source or a secondary source? Is it aimed at an appropriate audience? General or specialized? Elementary, advanced, or somewhere in between?

- *Credibility.* Is the author reputable? Is the publication, publishing company, or sponsor of the site reputable? Do the ideas more or less agree with those in other sources you've read?

- *Balance.* Does the source present enough evidence for its assertions? Does it show any particular bias? Does it present opposing arguments fairly?

- *Timeliness.* Is the source recent enough? Does it reflect current thinking or research about the subject?

501–23

If you need help **FINDING SOURCES**, see Chapter 47.

MLA 564–614
APA 615–55

Compile a list of works to annotate. Give the sources themselves in whatever documentation style is required; see the guidelines for **MLA** and **APA** styles in Chapters 53 and 54.

Determine what kind of bibliography you need to write. Will your bibliography be descriptive or evaluative? Will your annotations be in the form of phrases? complete sentences? paragraphs? The form will shape your reading and note taking. If you're writing a descriptive bibliography, your reading goal will be just to understand and capture the writer's message as clearly as possible. If you're writing an evaluative bibliography, you will

✳ academic literacies   ● fields   ● research
■ rhetorical situations   ∴ processes   ● media/design
▲ genres   ◆ strategies

also need to assess the source as you read in order to include your own opinions of it.

Read carefully.   To write an annotation, you must understand the source's argument; but when writing an annotated bibliography as part of a **PROPOSAL**, you may have neither the time nor the need to read the whole text. Here's a way of quickly determining whether a source is likely to serve your needs:

- Check the publisher or sponsor (university press? scholarly journal? popular magazine? website sponsored by a reputable organization?).
- Read the preface (of a book), abstract (of a scholarly article), introduction (of an article in a nonscholarly magazine or a website).
- Skim the table of contents or the headings.
- Read the parts that relate specifically to your topic.

Research the writer, if necessary.   If you are required to indicate the writer's credentials, you may need to do additional research. You may find information by typing the writer's name into a search engine or looking up the writer in *Gale Literature: Contemporary Authors*. In any case, information about the writer should take up no more than one sentence in your annotation.

Summarize the work in a sentence or two.   **DESCRIBE** it as objectively as possible: even if you're writing an evaluative annotation, you can evaluate the central point of a work better by stating it clearly first. *If you're writing a descriptive annotation, you're done.*

Establish criteria for evaluating sources.   If you're **EVALUATING SOURCES** for a project, you'll need to evaluate them in terms of their usefulness for your project, their **STANCE**, and their overall credibility.

▲ 258–68

◆ 456–63

● 524–34

■ 72–74

Write a brief evaluation of the source. If you can generalize about the worth of the entire work, fine. You may find, however, that some parts are useful while others are not, and what you write should reflect that mix.

Be consistent—in content, sentence structure, and format.

- *Content.* Try to provide about the same amount of information for each entry. If you're evaluating, don't evaluate some sources and just describe others.

- *Sentence structure.* Use the same style throughout—complete sentences, brief phrases, or a mix.

668–69

- *Format.* Use one documentation style throughout; use a consistent **FONT** for each element in each entry—for example, italicize or underline all book titles.

Ways of Organizing an Annotated Bibliography

Depending on their purpose, annotated bibliographies may or may not include an introduction. Most annotated bibliographies cover a single topic and so are organized alphabetically by author's or editor's last name. When a work lacks a named author, alphabetize it by the first important word in its title. Consult the documentation system you're using for additional details about alphabetizing works appropriately.

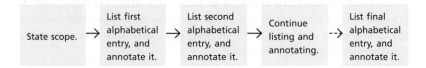

State scope. → List first alphabetical entry, and annotate it. → List second alphabetical entry, and annotate it. → Continue listing and annotating. ⇢ List final alphabetical entry, and annotate it.

Sometimes an annotated bibliography needs to be organized into several subject areas (or genres, periods, or some other category); if so, the entries are listed alphabetically within each category. For example, a bibliography about terrorism breaks down into subject categories such as "Global Terrorism" and "Weapons of Mass Destruction."

- ☀ academic literacies
- ■ rhetorical situations
- ▲ genres
- ● fields
- ⁘ processes
- ◆ strategies
- ● research
- ● media/design

[Multicategory bibliography]

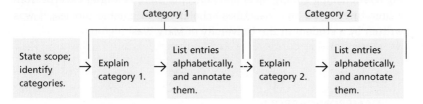

Taking Stock of Your Work

Take stock of what you've written by considering these questions:

- Did curiosity about your topic play a role in your research and writing? If so, how?

- What previous experience did you have with research? In what ways, if any, did you draw on that experience for your annotated bibliography?

- How did you go about researching the entries in this bibliography? What databases or other tools did you use? How did you decide on keywords for your search?

- How did you approach sources that were difficult to understand? What reading strategies did you use to make sense of them?

- How did you decide which sources to include in your bibliography and which ones to leave out?

- Did you cite sources accurately?

- Overall, what was challenging about writing an annotated bibliography? What was rewarding?

REVIEWS OF SCHOLARLY LITERATURE

Reviews of scholarly literature describe and evaluate important research ("literature") available on a topic. In writing a literature review, your goal is to give an overview of the literature on a topic. You do that by discussing the literature that is most relevant to your topic and your purposes, providing clear and accurate summaries of appropriate source material, and describing relationships among facts and concepts. Here is a brief excerpt from a literature review that describes scholarship in zombie movies; it was written by a student at the University of Mary Washington.

CAMERON CARROLL

Zombie Film Scholarship
A Review of the Literature

Zombies are the shambling undead creatures that attack in hordes and strike terror into the hearts of moviegoers with their mindless aggression. Monsters on the big screen fascinate American audiences and scholars alike as representations of cultural fears and reflections of public perceptions, and they have done so since they first shuffled into theaters. The walking dead first haunted cinemas in 1932 with the release of *White Zombie* and have gone through cycles of popularity both at the box office and in scholarly debate. Without a doubt, the height of zombie scholarship began in the mid-2000s with only shallow mentions made in horror analyses before then. Only the English discipline gave the zombie credit as a subject worthy of study. As author and English professor Kyle Bishop wrote in 2010, "The zombie phenomenon has yet to be plumbed to its depths by the academic and literary markets."[1] Although significant zombie research has only surfaced in the 2000s, a valiant effort is currently being made to explore zombie symbolism and its historical and cultural context across nontraditional scholarly fields, such as anthropology, psychology, sociology, and philosophy.

. . .

Zombies, as creatures that waver between living and dead, necessarily bring forth questions on the nature of being and thus also fall into the realm of philosophy as seen in *Zombies, Vampires, and*

✳ academic literacies   ⬤ fields   ⬤ research
◼ rhetorical situations   ⦙ processes   ⬤ media/design
▲ genres   ◆ strategies

Philosophy: New Life for the Undead published in 2010 and edited by Richard Greene and K. Silem Mohammed, professors of philosophy and English, respectively. Philosophers in the study of zombies seek to answer such questions as, is it better to be undead or dead? Richard Greene argues that since death is a state of nonexistence and Undeath is at least a primal existence, the question comes down to the classic "to be, or not to be?" For him, Undeath is the only option for a state of being, since death is nonexistence. Existence in any form is inherently better than utterly ceasing to be.[16] Greene's philosophy colleague, William Larkin, counters that zombies are driven to actions seen as evil and mindless, both states that humans do not usually choose. He cites how zombie films repeatedly depict survivors who ask their friends and family to kill them should it appear that they will turn into zombies, so desperate are they to avoid Undeath.[17] Simon Clark, a writer with a master's degree in Fine Arts, discusses morality in relation to zombies: if zombies are nonmoral and whether or not they are the freest creatures because of their lack of morality. Clark writes that they become ultimately free in their modern incarnations from turn-of-the-millennium cinema.[18] Zombies break through barriers that survivors put up to keep them confined and are so primal that they cannot be held accountable for their actions, making them truly liberated. A fictional creature encourages real discussions in philosophical debate, demonstrating yet another area that inspires scholars to reexamine their own field because of zombies.

. . .

The message to take away from zombie scholarship is that what it represents is evolutionary and infinitely debatable, but the victory for zombie studies is that zombies are being studied at all. After decades of being underrepresented in horror scholarship, zombies are finally getting their due as a cultural icon, complete with varying opinions and interpretations. Scholarly debate proves that the zombie is a valid resource for understanding American culture and worthy of the enthusiastic pursuit of interdepartmental scholarship. As shown within the scholarly works above, the debate over the meaning of the living dead is quite lively, indeed.

Notes

1. Kyle William Bishop, *American Zombie Gothic: The Rise and Fall (and Rise) of the Walking Dead in Popular Culture* (Jefferson, NC: McFarland, 2010), 7.

. . .

16. Richard Greene and K. Silem Mohammed, eds., *Zombies, Vampires, and Philosophy: New Life for the Undead* (Chicago: Open Court, 2010), 13.
17. Greene and Mohammed, 20.
18. Greene and Mohammed, 208.

Carroll begins by establishing a context for her discussion and then focuses on her topic, the scholarship of zombies in film. In her review, she discusses the history of zombie scholarship in general and then in psychology, social trends, fiction, and, in this excerpt, philosophy. A history major, she follows Chicago style; in addition to the notes, she included a bibliography listing all her sources, including the two noted here.

Key Features / Reviews of Scholarly Literature

Careful, thorough research.   A review of scholarly literature demands that you research all the major literature on the topic—or at least the major literature available to you, given the time you have.

Accurate, objective summaries of the relevant literature.   Readers expect a literature review to objectively summarize the main ideas or conclusions of the texts reviewed.

Critical evaluation for the literature.   A literature review offers considered selection of the most important, relevant, and useful sources of information on its topic, so you must evaluate each source to decide whether it should be included and then to determine how it advances understanding of the topic.

535–41

SYNTHESIS of the scholarship.   A literature review differs from an annotated bibliography in that the review identifies key concepts, similarities, and differences within the body of literature, showing how the sources relate to one another by method, study findings, themes, main ideas, or something else.

☀ academic literacies   ● fields   ● research

■ rhetorical situations   ⦂ processes   ● media/design

▲ genres   ◆ strategies

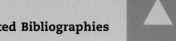

A clear focus.   Because a literature review provides an overview of your topic's main issues and explains the main concepts underlying your research, it must be carefully organized and clearly focused on your specific topic.

Taking Stock of Your Work

Take stock of what you've written by considering these questions:

- Did curiosity about your topic play a role in your research and writing? If so, how?

- What previous experience did you have with research? In what ways, if any, did you draw on that experience for your literature review?

- How did you approach sources that were difficult to understand? What reading strategies did you use to make sense of them?

- What helped you the most in finding, keeping track of, and evaluating the scholarship? What can you do next time to make the process more efficient and productive?

- How did you decide which sources to include in your literature review and which ones to leave out?

- What led you to group related sources together as you did?

- How did you go about synthesizing similar sources?

- Overall, what was challenging about writing a literature review? What was rewarding?

If you need more help

See Chapter 30 for guidelines on **DRAFTING**, Chapter 31 on **ASSESSING YOUR OWN WRITING**, Chapter 32 on **GETTING RESPONSE AND REVISING**, and Chapter 33 on **EDITING AND PROOFREADING**. See Chapter 34 if you are required to submit your bibliography in a writing **PORTFOLIO**.

364–66
367–71
372–79
380–84
385–90

16 Evaluations

Techspot reviews computer gaming equipment. The *Princeton Review* and *U.S. News & World Report* evaluate colleges and universities. You probably consult such sources to make decisions, and you probably evaluate things all the time—when you recommend a film (or not) or a teacher (ditto). An evaluation is basically a judgment; you judge something according to certain criteria, supporting your judgment with reasons and evidence. You need to give your reasons for evaluating it as you do because often your evaluation will affect your audience's actions: they must see this movie,

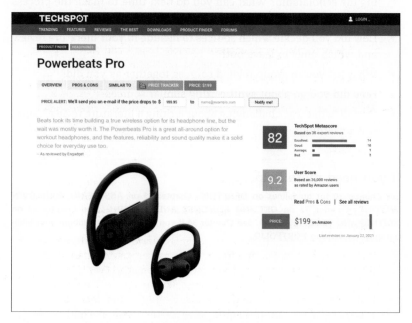

Techspot aggregates reviews of electronics from across the web and *Amazon*.

* academic literacies ● fields ● research
■ rhetorical situations ⦂ processes ● media/design
▲ genres ◆ strategies

needn't bother with this book, should be sure to have the Caesar salad at this restaurant, and so on.

In college courses, students in *literature, film, drama,* and *art* classes may be assigned to evaluate poems, fiction, movies, plays, and artwork, and those in *business* and *political science* classes may be asked to evaluate advertising or political campaigns or plans for business or public-policy initiatives. In a review that follows, written for *The Daily Bruin,* UCLA's student newspaper, Olivia Mazzucato offers her evaluation of the film *The Lovebirds.*

OLIVIA MAZZUCATO

Difficult-to-Follow Narrative Redeemed by Well-Executed Comedy in The Lovebirds

Issa Rae and Kumail Nanjiani are two of the brightest stars in modem comedy—pairing them together is an obvious winning combo.

The two play the beleaguered couple Leilani and Jibran in *The Lovebirds*, the first film to be released on Netflix after its theatrical premiere was canceled as a result of the coronavirus pandemic. The central pair unwittingly become accomplices to a murder just minutes after breaking up and quickly decide to work together to clear their names, leading them down a rabbit hole of blackmail and black-tie cult gatherings. Though the film's story gets convoluted, Rae and Nanjiani are able to salvage the muddy plot with their razor-sharp comedic wit and hilarious chemistry.

The plot of *The Lovebirds* starts out with an air of intrigue but is soon bogged down with unnecessary complications and loose threads, becoming less a mystery and more of a mess. Within minutes, Leilani and Jibran are wrapped up in a complex web of conspiracy, having to confront an absurd lineup of foes—a congressman and his wife, a blackmail ring operating out of a fraternity, and eventually a nefarious cult that's equal parts Illuminati, *The Handmaid's Tale,* and *Eyes Wide Shut.*

All the individual capers with one-off characters make for entertaining vignettes but fail to tie together cohesively. The final plot twist fails to make sense of the jumble, barely registering as an anticlimactic reveal. In a film full of inventive quips and conversations, the finale is

Rae and Nanjiani in a scene from *The Lovebirds*.

far from the most memorable scene in the film, which deflates a lot of
the momentum the story generates.

Luckily, Rae and Nanjiani's easy chemistry and awkward humor   5
transcend the narrative jumble. Whether they're arguing over the odds
of orgy schedulers using a calendar app or intimidating answers out of
a terrified fraternity brother, their back and forth feels effortless as they
operate on the same wavelength of frenetic, weird energy.

Their palpable onscreen connection makes it easy to both believe
the love between the two as well as understand why they've started to
grate on each other after four years together. They might argue with
comical conviction about whether or not they'd do well on *The Amazing
Race*, but the conversation hints at the deeper emotional insecurities
about incompatibility that plague their relationship.

The two comedians also bring versatility and depth to their characters. Within the first fifteen minutes of the movie, Leilani and Jibran are
falling in love, breaking up, and witnessing their first murder. The actors
take the fast pacing in stride, matching it with equally fast-paced jokes.

✴ academic literacies   ● fields   ● research
■ rhetorical situations   ⦂ processes   ◖ media/design
▲ genres   ◆ strategies

Though *The Lovebirds* isn't necessarily a traditional romantic comedy, the movie makes Leilani and Jibran's breakup more than just a plot point—it's a scene with heartbreaking gravity. The quiet tension that fills the car after another blowout argument adds a sense of realism to their relationship, making it impossible not to root for their reconciliation as they go on their adventure. The narrative arc of the film may fail, but the emotional arc is where the film finds its footing.

Not to mention, *The Lovebirds* is flat-out funny.

From the ridiculous scenarios Leilani and Jibran find themselves 10 in to the one-liners Rae and Nanjiani scatter throughout the film, *The Lovebirds* never fails to earn a laugh, even in its most serious scenes. The easily enjoyable film is able to span the range of comedy by blending physical slapstick comedy with witty dialogue to produce a compact eighty-six-minutes full of levity and heart. The film is in no way groundbreaking, but it puts Rae and Nanjiani firmly into the spotlight, demonstrating their potential for larger silver-screen roles.

The two transform an easily mediocre film into a fun, enjoyable comedy that offers a brief escape from reality.

Mazzucato provides a brief summary of the plot of The Lovebirds *and the context of its release and then evaluates the film using clear criteria: its plot, the chemistry between the leading actors, their comedic and acting skill, and its ability to generate laughs.*

Key Features / Evaluations

A concise description of the subject. You should include just enough information to let readers who may not be familiar with your subject understand what it is; the goal is to evaluate, not summarize. Depending on your topic and medium, some of this information may be in visual or audio form. In her introduction, Mazzucato briefly describes *The Lovebirds'* main plot to provide what readers need to understand the context of her evaluation, and then she goes into more detail when evaluating the plot and its shortcomings.

Clearly defined criteria.   You need to determine clear criteria as the basis for your judgment. In reviews or other evaluations written for a broad audience, you can integrate the criteria into the discussion as reasons for your assessment, as Mazzucato does in her evaluation of *The Lovebirds*. In more formal evaluations, you may need to announce your criteria explicitly. Mazzucato evaluates the film based on the stars' performances, the complexity and coherence (or lack thereof) of the plot, the acting ability of the main characters and their chemistry together, and the film's ability to generate laughs.

A knowledgeable discussion of the subject.   To evaluate something credibly, you need to show that you know it yourself and that you understand its context. Mazzucato cites many examples from *The Lovebirds*, demonstrating her knowledge of the film. Some evaluations require that you research what other authoritative sources have said about your subject. Mazzucato might have referred to other reviews of the film to show that she'd researched others' views.

A balanced and fair assessment.   An evaluation is centered on a judgment. Mazzucato concedes that "the film's story gets convoluted" and does not "tie together cohesively," and that "the finale . . . deflates a lot of the momentum the story generates." Nevertheless, the overall humorousness and the chemistry between the leads "transform an easily mediocre film into a fun, enjoyable comedy." It is important that any judgment be balanced and fair. Seldom is something all good or all bad. A fair evaluation need not be all positive or all negative; it may acknowledge both strengths and weaknesses. For example, a movie's soundtrack may be wonderful while the plot is not.

Well-supported reasons.   You need to argue for your judgment, providing reasons and evidence that might include visual and audio as well as verbal material. Mazzucato gives several reasons for her overall positive assessment of *The Lovebirds*—the problems with the plot, the strong performances of Issa Rae and Kumail Nanjiani, the film's emotional arc, that the film "is flat-out funny"—and she supports these reasons with several examples from the film.

---

* academic literacies   ● fields   ● research
■ rhetorical situations   •• processes   ● media/design
▲ genres   ◆ strategies

A BRIEF GUIDE TO WRITING EVALUATIONS

Choosing Something to Evaluate

You can more effectively evaluate a limited subject than a broad one: review certain dishes at a local restaurant rather than the entire menu; review one film or scene rather than all the films by Alfred Hitchcock or all seventy-three *Game of Thrones* episodes. The more specific and focused your subject, the better you can write about it.

Considering the Rhetorical Situation

PURPOSE   Are you writing to affect your audience's opinion of a   ■ 59–60
subject? to help others decide what to see, do, or buy?
to demonstrate your expertise in a field?

AUDIENCE   To whom are you writing? What will your audience   ■ 61–64
already know about the subject? What will they expect
to learn from your evaluation of it? Are they likely to
agree with you or not?

STANCE   What is your attitude toward the subject, and how will   ■ 72–74
you show that you have evaluated it fairly and appro-
priately? Think about the tone you want to use: Should
it be reasonable? passionate? critical?

MEDIA/DESIGN   How will you deliver your evaluation? In print? Elec-   ■ 75–77
tronically? As a speech? Can you show images or audio
or video clips? If you're submitting your text for publication, are there any format requirements?

Generating Ideas and Text

Explore what you already know.   FREEWRITE to answer the following   ⁘ 333–34
questions: What do you know about this subject or subjects like it? What
are your initial or gut feelings, and why do you feel as you do? How does
this subject reflect or affect your basic values or beliefs? How have others
evaluated subjects like this?

Identify criteria. Make a list of criteria you think should be used to evaluate your subject. Think about which criteria will likely be important to your **AUDIENCE**. You might find **CUBING** and **QUESTIONING** to be useful processes for thinking about your criteria.

61–64 ▪
336 ⁚⁚
337

Evaluate your subject. Study your subject closely to determine to what extent it meets each of your criteria. You may want to list your criteria and take notes related to each one, or you may develop a rating scale for each criterion to help stay focused on it. Come up with a tentative judgment.

Compare your subject with others. Often, evaluating something involves **COMPARING AND CONTRASTING** it with similar things. We judge movies in comparison with the other movies we've seen and french fries with the other fries we've tasted. Sometimes those comparisons can be made informally. For other evaluations, you may have to do research—to try on several pairs of jeans before buying any, for example—to see how your subject compares.

437–44 ◆

State your judgment as a tentative thesis statement. Your **THESIS STATEMENT** should be one that addresses both pros and cons. "*Hawaii Five-O* is fun to watch despite its stilted dialogue." "Of the five sport-utility vehicles tested, the Toyota 4Runner emerged as the best in comfort, power, and durability, though not in styling or cargo capacity." Both of these examples offer a judgment but qualify it according to the writer's criteria.

347–49 ⁚⁚

Anticipate other opinions. I think Anthony Anderson is a comic genius whose TV show *black·ish* is first-rate. You think Anderson is a terrible actor whose show is unwatchable. How can I write a review of his latest series that you will at least consider? One way is by **ACKNOWLEDGING** other opinions—and **REFUTING** those opinions as best I can. I may not persuade you to watch Anderson's show, but I can at least demonstrate that by certain criteria he should be appreciated. You may need to **RESEARCH** how others have evaluated your subject.

424–25 ◆
426
489 ●

※ academic literacies   ● fields   ● research
▪ rhetorical situations   ⁚⁚ processes   ● media/design
▲ genres   ◆ strategies

Identify and support your reasons. Write out all the **REASONS** you can
think of that will convince your audience to accept your judgment. Review
your list to identify the most convincing or important reasons. Then review
how well your subject meets your criteria, and decide how best to **SUPPORT**
your reasons: through examples, authoritative opinions, statistics, visual or
audio evidence, or something else.

◆ 413–14

◆ 414–22

Ways of Organizing an Evaluation

Evaluations are usually organized in one of two ways. One way is to introduce what's being evaluated, followed by your judgment, discussing your
criteria along the way. This is a useful strategy if your audience may not
be familiar with your subject.

[Start with your subject]

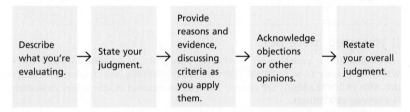

You might also start by identifying your criteria and then follow with a
discussion of how well your subject meets those criteria. This strategy
foregrounds the process by which you reached your conclusions.

[Start with your criteria]

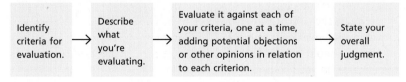

Taking Stock of Your Work

Take stock of what you've written by considering these questions:

- How did you decide on your stance for your evaluation? How well does your evaluation communicate that stance?

- How did you develop criteria for your evaluation?

- In working on this piece, did you use a process or strategy you've used before? If so, what was it? How well did it work? What new strategies or processes do you want to try in the future?

- What academic habits of mind—like creativity, flexibility, persistence, or another habit—did you need in order to write this evaluation? What specific examples can you give?

- How satisfied are you with your writing? What would you do differently next time?

If you need more help

364–66 See Chapter 30 for guidelines on **DRAFTING**, Chapter 31 on **ASSESSING YOUR OWN**
367–71 **WRITING**, Chapter 32 on **GETTING RESPONSE AND REVISING**, and Chapter 33 on **EDIT-**
372–79 **ING AND PROOFREADING**. See Chapter 34 if you are required to submit your evaluation
380–84 in a writing **PORTFOLIO**.
385–90

☀ academic literacies   ● fields   ● research
■ rhetorical situations   ⁖ processes   ● media/design
▲ genres   ◆ strategies

17 Literary Analyses

Literary analyses are essays that examine literary texts closely to understand their messages, interpret their meanings, appreciate their techniques, or understand their historical or social contexts. Such texts traditionally include novels, short stories, poems, and plays but may also include films, TV shows, videogames, music, and comics. You might read Gwendolyn Brooks's poem "We Real Cool" and notice how she uses slang to get across her message. You could explore the distinctive point of view in Ambrose Bierce's story "An Occurrence at Owl Creek Bridge." Or you could point out the differences between Stephen King's *The Shining* and Stanley Kubrick's screenplay based on that novel. In all these cases, you use specific analytical techniques to go below the surface of the work to deepen your understanding of how it works and what it means.

You may be assigned to analyze works of literature in courses in *English, film, drama,* and many other subjects. Here is a poem by the twentieth-century American poet Robert Frost, followed by a student's analysis of it written for a literature course at the University of South Dakota and chosen as a winner of the 2017 Norton Writer's Prize.

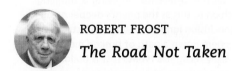

ROBERT FROST
The Road Not Taken

Two roads diverged in a yellow wood,
And sorry I could not travel both
And be one traveler, long I stood
And looked down one as far as I could
To where it bent in the undergrowth;   5

Then took the other, as just as fair,
And having perhaps the better claim,
Because it was grassy and wanted wear;
Though as for that the passing there
Had worn them really about the same,   10

And both that morning equally lay
In leaves no step had trodden black.
Oh, I kept the first for another day!
Yet knowing how way leads on to way,
I doubted if I should ever come back.   15

I shall be telling this with a sigh
Somewhere ages and ages hence:
Two roads diverged in a wood, and I—
I took the one less traveled by,
And that has made all the difference.   20

MATTHEW MILLER

Frost's Broken Roads

"The Road Not Taken" by Robert Frost is arguably one of the most popular poems ever written. Read at graduations, eulogies, even in movies
and car commercials, it is often interpreted as an ode to individualism.
Frost's image of the road "less traveled" has become synonymous with
daring life choices that make "all the difference" in living a fulfilling
life (lines 19–20). Some may latch on to this as the poem's deeper meaning. However, this convenient conclusion ignores several conflicting, yet
beautiful, details that lead the poem down a path of broken metaphor
and temporal inconsistency. To truly recognize what Frost is building in
this poem, a few nagging inconsistencies must be considered.

    In the first line of the poem, the traveler is depicted hiking in a
"yellow wood" wherein he finds a fork in his path (1). This setting is
the foundation of a common metaphor, but transposing familiar notions
of a figurative fork in the road onto Frost's poem requires acceptance
of the traveler's metaphoric natural world and its "temporal scheme,"

◉ academic literacies   ● fields   ● research
■ rhetorical situations   ⦂ processes   ● media/design
▲ genres   ◆ strategies

or some form of unified movement through time, as the critic Cleanth Brooks describes it in his classic book on poetic structure, *The Well Wrought Urn* (203). If the path that is covered "[i]n leaves no step had trodden black" (Frost, line 12) makes "all the difference" (20) in a life, common sense indicates the decision to choose that path has to occur early enough during a lifetime to properly affect its outcome. The speaker/traveler affirms this, telling the reader that he "shall be telling" them the story of his decision "with a sigh / Somewhere ages and ages hence" (16–17). In other words, the traveler must be fairly young, otherwise he wouldn't have "ages and ages" (17) left to tell his story. It may not be apparent at a surface level, but this complicates our understanding of the poem's implicit story.

It is common knowledge that morning, the beginning of the day, is often paralleled figuratively with the beginning of other things (e.g., "the dawn of civilization"). In this sense, the setting helps to solidify the poem's established temporal sense; the earliness of the day— "morning" (16)—parallels the early point in life when the traveler makes his life-altering decision. However, the description of the scene, the "yellow wood" (1) where the ground "lay / In leaves" (11–12), indicates that late autumn has set in around the forest. Parallels between seasonal progression and the human life cycle saturate literature and art with such metaphors as the "springtime of youth" and the "hoary winter of old age" (Kammen 23). With that in mind, the end of autumn represents the bitter end of productive years and the first step into the cold and death of winter. So, embedded in the poem is a temporal inconsistency; the traveler is young, with "ages and ages" yet to live, but the autumn setting implies his world is quickly coming to an end.

Another question that complicates a traditional understanding of the poem is that of identity. The narrator claims he is "sorry" he "could not travel both" paths "and be one traveler" (Frost, lines 2–3). For him to stray off his path would equal becoming a different person; he "could not travel both / *And be one traveler*" (2–3; emphasis added). However, one person can easily be two different travelers in a lifetime (i.e., one person can take both a cruise vacation and a backpacking trip: two very different traveling styles). The traveler/speaker even admits this is possible by saying he *could* keep "the first for another day" (13). His excuse for not traveling both paths was not that it was impossible but rather that "knowing how way leads on to way, / I doubted if I should ever come back" (14–15). Although he believes one of the paths has "the better claim, / Because it was grassy and wanted wear" (7–8), in practically the same breath he casts doubt on the claim that it is "less traveled" (19), admitting other travelers have worn down the two trails "really about the same" (10). The speaker in this poem is not Ralph Waldo Emerson's self-reliant transcendentalist, who can "speak what [he] think[s] to-day in words as hard as cannon balls, and to-morrow speak what to-morrow thinks in hard words again, though it contradict every thing [he] said to-day" (214).

Frost's syntax and punctuation add even more nuance. The poem consists of one sentence that takes up the first two stanzas and part of the third, in which our traveler deliberates and, eventually, makes his decision; and the three sentences of the third and fourth stanzas, in which our traveler lives with his choice. As the poem progresses to the point where our traveler makes his decision, we see punctuation that is irregular when compared with the rest of the poem: an exclamation point when the traveler finally makes a decision (possibly showing excess emotion); an em dash (—) followed by a repeated word when retelling his story that functions almost like a stutter, possibly showing regret/lack of confidence in his choice. With this in mind, it seems as though our traveler had a tough time making his decision, and afterward, there is no obvious approval or happiness with it, only that it "made all the difference" (Frost, line 20), which could be positive or negative. 5

Placing the poem in its historical context further complicates these questions. According to an article by the poet Katherine Robinson, "The Road Not Taken" was actually written "as a joke for a friend, the poet Edward Thomas." Robinson writes:

> Indeed, when Frost and Thomas went walking together, Thomas would often choose one fork in the road because he was convinced it would lead them to something. . . . In a letter, Frost goaded Thomas, saying, "No matter which road you take, *you'll always sigh*, and wish you'd taken another." (emphasis added)

Introducing the poet's biography might be considered by many a sin against the work, especially for those espousing Cleanth Brooks's celebration of poetic unity and universal meaning. However, knowing

---

✳ academic literacies   ● fields   ● research

■ rhetorical situations   ⁝ processes   ● media/design

▲ genres   ◆ strategies

this information fills in several gaps about the poem; instead of confusing inconsistencies and paradoxical meanings, the poem can now be
viewed—at least partly—as teasing from a friend. It is easy to imagine
an indecisive Thomas, standing and staring down the fork in the path,
afraid of what he'll miss if he picks the wrong trail, and then on the way
home "telling" Frost, "with a sigh" (Frost, line 16), about all he swore
he missed on *the road he didn't take*. This being said, Frost published
this work knowing full well of its depth and epistemological possibilities, saying in a letter, "My poems . . . are all set to trip the reader head
foremost into the boundless" (qtd. in Robinson).

Frost's timeless poem is an elegant narrative, filled with serene
imagery and laced with layers of mystery. Readers of this canonical
work can easily find themselves slipping into the easy, traditional
reading of an ode to individualism. Upon closer inspection, there is
only one thing clear about "The Road Not Taken," which is said best
in words Frost loved to tell his readers regarding his classic poem:
"[Y]ou have to be careful of that one; it's a tricky poem—very tricky"
(qtd. in Robinson).

Works Cited

Brooks, Cleanth. *The Well Wrought Urn: Studies in the Structure of
    Poetry*. Harcourt, 1975.
Emerson, Ralph Waldo. "Self-Reliance." *The Norton Anthology of
    American Literature*, Robert S. Levine et al., general editors,
    9th ed., vol. B, W. W. Norton, 2017, pp. 236–53.
Frost, Robert. "The Road Not Taken." *Poetry Foundation,* www
    .poetryfoundation.org/poems/44272/the-road-not-taken.
Kammen, Michael G. *A Time to Every Purpose: The Four Seasons in
    American Culture*. U of North Carolina P, 2004.
Robinson, Katherine. "Robert Frost: 'The Road Not Taken.'" *Poetry
    Foundation,* 27 May 2016, www.poetryfoundation.org/articles
    /89511/robert-frost-the-road-not-taken.

*Miller focuses his analysis on "tricky" aspects of Frost's poem. In addition, he
uses aspects of Frost's biography and letters to resolve some of the seeming
contradictions and tensions in the poem.*

Key Features / Literary Analyses

An arguable thesis.   A literary analysis is a form of argument; you are arguing that your analysis of a literary work is valid. Your thesis, then, should be arguable, as Miller's is: "To truly recognize what Frost is building in this poem, a few nagging inconsistencies must be considered." A mere summary—"Frost writes about someone trying to decide which road to take"—would not be arguable and therefore would not be a good thesis.

Careful attention to the language of the text.   The key to analyzing a text is looking carefully at the language, which is the foundation of its meaning. Specific words, images, metaphors—these are where analysis begins. You may also bring in contextual information, such as cultural, historical, or biographical facts, or you may refer to similar texts. But the words, phrases, and sentences that make up the text you are analyzing are your primary source when dealing with texts. That's what literature teachers mean by "close reading": reading with the assumption that every word of a text is meaningful.

Attention to patterns or themes.   Literary analyses are usually built on evidence of meaningful patterns or themes within a text or among several texts. These patterns and themes reveal meaning. In Frost's poem, images of diverging roads and yellow leaves create patterns of meaning, while the regular rhyme scheme ("wood"/"stood"/"could," "both"/"undergrowth") creates patterns of sound and structure that may contribute to the overall meaning.

A clear interpretation.   A literary analysis demonstrates the plausibility of its thesis by using evidence from the text and, sometimes, relevant contextual evidence to explain how the language and patterns found there support a particular interpretation. When you write a literary analysis, you show readers one way the text may be read and understood; that is your interpretation.

MLA style.   Literary analyses usually follow MLA style. Miller's essay includes a works-cited list and refers to line numbers using MLA style.

✳ academic literacies	⬢ fields	⬤ research
◼ rhetorical situations	⁖ processes	⬤ media/design
▲ genres	◆ strategies	

A BRIEF GUIDE TO WRITING LITERARY ANALYSES

Considering the Rhetorical Situation

PURPOSE   What do you need to do? Show that you have examined the text carefully? Offer your own interpretation?
Demonstrate a particular analytical technique? Or
some combination? If you're responding to an assignment, does it specify what you need to do?
59–60

AUDIENCE   What do you need to do to convince your readers that
your interpretation is plausible and based on sound
analysis? Can you assume that readers are already
familiar with the text you are analyzing, or do you
need to tell them about it?
61–64

STANCE   How can you see your subject through interested, curious eyes—and then step back in order to see what
your observations might mean?
72–74

MEDIA/DESIGN   Will your analysis focus on an essentially verbal text
or one that has significant visual content, such as a
graphic novel? Will you need to show visual elements
in your analysis? Will it be delivered in a print, spoken,
or electronic medium? Are you required to follow MLA
or some other style?
75–77

Generating Ideas and Text

Look at your assignment.   Does it specify a particular kind of analysis?
Does it ask you to consider a particular theme? To use any specific critical
approaches? Look for any terms that tell you what to do, words like "analyze," "compare," "interpret," and so on.

Study the text with a critical eye.   When we read a literary work, we
often come away with a reaction to it: we like it, we hate it, it made us cry
or laugh, it perplexed us. That may be a good starting point for a literary

21–23 ✳

analysis, but to write about literature you need to go beyond initial reactions, to think about **HOW THE TEXT WORKS**: What does it *say*, and what does it *do*? What elements make up this text? How do those elements work together or fail to work together? Does this text lead you to think or feel a certain way? How does it fit into a particular context (of history, culture, technology, genre, and so on)?

Choose a method for analyzing the text.   There are various ways to analyze your subject. Three common focuses are on the text itself, on your own experience reading it, and on other cultural, historical, or literary contexts.

445–55 ◆
456–63
474–82

- *The text itself*. Trace the development and expression of themes, characters, and language through the work. How do they help to create the overall meaning, tone, or effect for which you're arguing? To do this, you might look at the text as a whole, something you can understand from all angles at once. You could also pick out parts from the beginning, middle, and end as needed to make your case, **DEFINING** key terms, **DESCRIBING** characters and settings, and **NARRATING** key scenes. Miller's essay about "The Road Not Taken" offers a text-based analysis that looks at Frost's treatment of time in the poem. You might also examine the same theme in several different works.

- *Your own response as a reader*. Explore the way the text affects you or develops meanings as you read through it from beginning to end. By doing such a close reading, you're slowing down the process to notice how one element of the text leads you to expect something, confirming earlier suspicions or surprises. You build your analysis on your experience of reading the text—as if you were pretending to drive somewhere for the first time, though in reality you know the way intimately. By closely examining the language of the text as you experience it, you explore how it leads you to a set of responses, both intellectual and emotional. If you were responding in this way to the Frost poem, you might discuss how the narrator keeps trying to assert that one road is preferable to another but admits that both are the same, so that his willful assertion that one is "less traveled by" and that his choice "made all the difference" is no difference at all.

✳ academic literacies   ● fields   ● research
■ rhetorical situations   ⁝ processes   ● media/design
▲ genres   ◆ strategies

- *Context.* Analyze the text as part of some larger **CONTEXT** — as part of a certain time or place in history or as an expression of a certain culture (how does this text relate to the time and place of its creation?), as one of many other texts like it, a representative of a genre (how is this text like or unlike others of its kind? how does it use, play with, or flout the conventions of the genre?). A context-based approach to the Frost poem might look at Frost's friendship with another poet, Edward Thomas, for whom Frost wrote the poem, and its influence on Thomas's decision to enlist in the army at the start of World War I.

▲ 114

Read the work more than once. Reading literature, watching films, or listening to speeches is like driving to a new destination: the first time you go, you need to concentrate on getting there; on subsequent trips, you can see other aspects—the scenery, the curve of the road, other possible routes—that you couldn't pay attention to earlier. When you experience a piece of literature for the first time, you usually focus on the story, the plot, the overall meaning. By experiencing it repeatedly, you can see how its effects are achieved, what the pieces are and how they fit together, where different patterns emerge, how the author crafted the work.

To analyze a literary work, then, plan to read it more than once, with the assumption that every part of the text is there for a reason. Focus on details, even on a single detail that shows up more than once: Why is it there? What can it mean? How does it affect our experience of reading or studying the text? Also, look for anomalies, details that *don't* fit the patterns: Why are they part of the text? What can they mean? How do they affect the experience of the text? See the **READING IN ACADEMIC CONTEXTS** chapter for several different methods for reading a text.

✳ 11–32

Compose a strong thesis. The **THESIS** of a literary analysis should be specific, limited, and open to potential disagreement. In addition, it should be analytical, not evaluative: avoid thesis statements that make overall judgments, such as a reviewer might do: "Virginia Woolf's *The Waves* is a failed experiment in narrative" or "No one has equaled the achievement of *The Lego Movie.*" Rather, offer a way of seeing the text: "The choice presented

⁙ 347–49

in Robert Frost's 'The Road Not Taken' ultimately makes no difference"; "The plot of *The Lego Movie* reflects contemporary American media culture."

Read the text carefully.　When you analyze a text, you need to find specific, brief passages that support your interpretation. Then you should interpret those passages in terms of their language, their context, or your reaction to them as a reader. To find such passages, you must read the text closely, questioning it as you go, asking, for example:

- What language provides evidence to support your thesis?
- What does each word (phrase, passage) mean exactly?
- Why does the writer choose *this* language, *these* words? What are the implications or connotations of the language? If the language is dense or difficult, why might the writer have written it that way?
- What images, similes, or metaphors are used? What is their effect on the meaning?
- What patterns of language, imagery, or plot do you see? If something is repeated, what significance does the repetition have?
- How does each word, phrase, or passage relate to what precedes and follows it?
- How does the experience of reading the text affect its meaning?
- What words, phrases, or passages connect to a larger **CONTEXT**? What language demonstrates that this work reflects or is affected by that context?
- How do these various elements of language, image, and pattern support your interpretation?

Your analysis should focus on analyzing and interpreting your subject, not simply summarizing or paraphrasing it. Many literary analyses also use the strategy of **COMPARING** two or more works.

11–32 ✳

437–44 ◆

✳ academic literacies　　● fields　　● research

■ rhetorical situations　　⁚ processes　　● media/design

▲ genres　　◆ strategies

Find evidence to support your interpretation.   The parts of the text you examine in your close reading become the evidence you use to support your interpretation. Some think that we're all entitled to our own opinions about literature. And indeed we are. But when writing a literary analysis, we're entitled only to our own *well-supported* and *well-argued* opinions. When you analyze a text, you must treat it like any other **ARGUMENT**: you need to discuss how the text creates an effect or expresses a theme, and then you have to show **EVIDENCE** from the text—significant plot or structural elements; important characters; patterns of language, imagery, or action—to back up your argument.

◆ 410–30

◆ 414–22

Pay attention to matters of style.   Literary analyses have certain conventions for using pronouns and verbs.

- In informal papers, it's OK to use the first person: "I believe Frost's narrator has little basis for claiming that one road is 'less traveled.'" In more formal essays, make assertions directly; claim authority to make statements about the text: "Frost's narrator has no basis for claiming that one road is 'less traveled.'"

- Discuss textual features in the present tense even if quotations from the text are in another tense: "When Nick finds Gatsby's body floating in the pool, he says very little about it: 'the laden mattress moved irregularly down the pool.'" Describe the historical context of the setting in the past tense: "In the 1920s, such estates as Gatsby's were rare."

Cite and document sources appropriately.   Use **MLA** citation and documentation style unless told otherwise. Format **QUOTATIONS** properly, and use **SIGNAL PHRASES** to introduce quoted material.

● MLA 564–614
544–47
551–54

Think about format and design.   Brief essays do not require **HEADINGS**; text divisions are usually marked by **TRANSITIONS** between paragraphs. In longer papers, though, headings can be helpful.

● 670–72
⦂ 361–62

Organizing a Literary Analysis

[Of a single text]

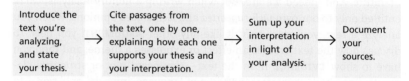

Introduce the text you're analyzing, and state your thesis. → Cite passages from the text, one by one, explaining how each one supports your thesis and your interpretation. → Sum up your interpretation in light of your analysis. → Document your sources.

[Comparing two texts]

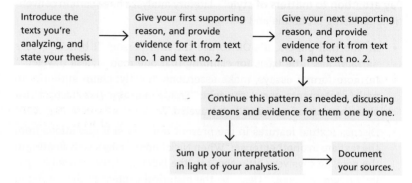

Introduce the texts you're analyzing, and state your thesis. → Give your first supporting reason, and provide evidence for it from text no. 1 and text no. 2. → Give your next supporting reason, and provide evidence for it from text no. 1 and text no. 2.

↓

Continue this pattern as needed, discussing reasons and evidence for them one by one.

↓

Sum up your interpretation in light of your analysis. → Document your sources.

Taking Stock of Your Work

Take stock of what you've written by considering these questions:

- How did you go about analyzing the text? Did you focus on the text itself? your own response? the larger context? something else? Why?

- How did you come up with your thesis? Did you need to revise, expand, or narrow it?

- Did you provide enough evidence from the text or its context to support your analysis?

✳ academic literacies   ● fields   ● research
■ rhetorical situations   ⁝ processes   ● media/design
▲ genres   ◆ strategies

- How did your audience affect the language and tone you used in your piece?

- Did you try anything new in your writing process for this piece? A new way of generating ideas and text? A new way of drafting or revising? Something else? If so, what was the result?

- How did you plan and manage your time for this project? How well did you stick to your plan? If changes were needed, how did you adapt?

- What did you learn about yourself as a reader through your work on this piece? How can you apply that learning to future reading tasks?

- Are you pleased with your analysis? What did it teach you about the text you analyzed? Did it make you want to read more works by the same author?

If you need more help

See Chapter 30 for guidelines on **DRAFTING**, Chapter 31 on **ASSESSING YOUR OWN WRITING**, Chapter 32 on **GETTING RESPONSE AND REVISING**, and Chapter 33 on **EDITING AND PROOFREADING**. See Chapter 34 if you are required to submit your analysis in a writing **PORTFOLIO**.

364–66
367–71
372–79
380–84
385–90

18 Memoirs

We write memoirs to explore our past—about shopping for a party dress with Grandma, or driving a car for the first time, or breaking up with our first love. Memoirs focus on events and people and places that are important to us. We usually have two goals when we write a memoir: to capture an important moment and to convey something about its significance for us. You may be asked to write memoirs or personal reflections that include memoirs in *psychology*, *education*, and *English* courses. The following example is from *All Over but the Shoutin'* by Pulitzer Prize–winning journalist Rick Bragg. Bragg grew up in Alabama, and in this memoir he recalls when, as a teenager, he paid a final visit to his dying father.

RICK BRAGG
All Over but the Shoutin'

He was living in a little house in Jacksonville, Alabama, a college and mill town that was the closest urban center—with its stoplights and a high school and two supermarkets—to the country roads we roamed in our raggedy cars. He lived in the mill village, in one of those houses the mills subsidized for their workers, back when companies still did things like that. It was not much of a place, but better than anything we had ever lived in as a family. I knocked and a voice like an old woman's, punctuated with a cough that sounded like it came from deep in the guts, told me to come on in, it ain't locked.

It was dark inside, but light enough to see what looked like a bundle of quilts on the corner of a sofa. Deep inside them was a ghost of a man, his hair and beard long and going dirty gray, his face pale and cut with deep grooves. I knew I was in the right house because

---

☀ academic literacies   ● fields   ● research

■ rhetorical situations   ∴ processes   ● media/design

▲ genres   ◆ strategies

my daddy's only real possessions, a velvet-covered board pinned with medals, sat inside a glass cabinet on a table. But this couldn't be him.

He coughed again, spit into a can and struggled to his feet, but stopped somewhere short of standing straight up, as if a stoop was all he could manage. "Hey, Cotton Top," he said, and then I knew. My daddy, who was supposed to be a still-young man, looked like the walking dead, not just old but damaged, poisoned, used up, crumpled up and thrown in a corner to die. I thought that the man I would see would be the trim, swaggering, high-toned little rooster of a man who stared back at me from the pages of my mother's photo album, the young soldier clowning around in Korea, the arrow-straight, good-looking boy who posed beside my mother back before the fields and mop handle and the rest of it took her looks. The man I remembered had always dressed nice even when there was no cornmeal left, whose black hair always shone with oil, whose chin, even when it wobbled from the beer, was always angled up, high.

I thought he would greet me with that strong voice that sounded so fine when he laughed and so evil when, slurred by a quart of corn likker, he whirled through the house and cried and shrieked, tormented by things we could not see or even imagine. I thought he would be the man and monster of my childhood. But that man was as dead as a man could be, and this was what remained, like when a snake sheds its skin and leaves a dry and brittle husk of itself hanging in the Johnson grass.

"It's all over but the shoutin' now, ain't it, boy," he said, and when 5 he let the quilt slide from his shoulders I saw how he had wasted away, how the bones seemed to poke out of his clothes, and I could see how it killed his pride to look this way, unclean, and he looked away from me for a moment, ashamed.

He made a halfhearted try to shake my hand but had a coughing fit again that lasted a minute, coughing up his life, his lungs, and after that I did not want to touch him. I stared at the tops of my sneakers, ashamed to look at his face. He had a dark streak in his beard below his lip, and I wondered why, because he had never liked snuff. Now I know it was blood.

I remember much of what he had to say that day. When you don't see someone for eight, nine years, when you see that person's life red on their lips and know that you will never see them beyond this day, you listen close, even if what you want most of all is to run away.

"Your momma, she alright?" he said.

I said I reckon so.

"The other boys? They alright?"   10

I said I reckon so.

Then he was quiet for a minute, as if trying to find the words to a question to which he did not really want an answer.

"They ain't never come to see me. How come?"

I remember thinking, fool, why do you think? But I just choked down my words, and in doing so I gave up the only real chance I would ever have to accuse him, to attack him with the facts of his own sorry nature and the price it had cost us all. The opportunity hung perfectly still in the air in front of my face and fists, and I held my temper and let it float on by. I could have no more challenged him, berated him, hurt him, than I could have kicked some three-legged dog. Life had kicked his ass pretty good.

"How come?"   15

I just shrugged.

For the next few hours—unless I was mistaken, having never had one before—he tried to be my father. Between coughing and long pauses when he fought for air to generate his words, he asked me if I liked school, if I had ever gotten any better at math, the one thing that just flat evaded me. He asked me if I ever got even with the boy who blacked my eye ten years ago, and nodded his head, approvingly, as I described how I followed him into the boys' bathroom and knocked his dick string up to his watch pocket, and would have dunked his head in the urinal if the aging principal, Mr. Hand, had not had to pee and caught me dragging him across the concrete floor.

He asked me about basketball and baseball, said he had heard I had a good game against Cedar Springs, and I said pretty good, but it was two years ago, anyway. He asked if I had a girlfriend and I said, "One," and he said, "Just one?" For the slimmest of seconds he almost grinned and the young, swaggering man peeked through, but disappeared again in the disease that cloaked him. He talked and talked and never said a word, at least not the words I wanted.

He never said he was sorry.

He never said he wished things had turned out different.   20

He never acted like he did anything wrong.

Part of it, I know, was culture. Men did not talk about their feelings in his hard world. I did not expect, even for a second, that he would bare his soul. All I wanted was a simple acknowledgment that he was wrong, or at least too drunk to notice that he left his pretty wife and sons alone again and again, with no food, no money, no way to get any, short of begging, because when she tried to find work he yelled, screamed, refused. No, I didn't expect much.

After a while he motioned for me to follow him into a back room where he had my present, and I planned to take it and run. He handed me a long, thin box, and inside was a brand-new, well-oiled Remington .22 rifle. He said he had bought it some time back, just kept forgetting to give it to me. It was a fine gun, and for a moment we were just like anybody else in the culture of that place, where a father's gift of a gun to his son is a rite. He said, with absolute seriousness, not to shoot my brothers.

I thanked him and made to leave, but he stopped me with a hand on my arm and said wait, that ain't all, that he had some other things for me. He motioned to three big cardboard egg cartons stacked against one wall.

Inside was the only treasure I truly have ever known.   25

I had grown up in a house in which there were only two books, the King James Bible and the spring seed catalog. But here, in these boxes, were dozens of hardback copies of everything from Mark Twain to Sir Arthur Conan Doyle. There was a water-damaged Faulkner, and the nearly complete set of Edgar Rice Burroughs's *Tarzan*. There was poetry and trash, Zane Grey's *Riders of the Purple Sage*, and a paperback with two naked women on the cover. There was a tiny, old copy of *Arabian Nights*, threadbare Hardy Boys, and one Hemingway. He had bought most of them at a yard sale, by the box or pound, and some at a flea market. He did not even know what he was giving me, did not recognize most of the writers. "Your momma said you still liked to read," he said.

There was Shakespeare. My father did not know who he was, exactly, but he had heard the name. He wanted them because they were pretty, because they were wrapped in fake leather, because they looked like rich folks' books. I do not love Shakespeare, but I still have those books. I would not trade them for a gold monkey.

"They's maybe some dirty books in there, by mistake, but I know you ain't interested in them, so just throw 'em away," he said. "Or at least, throw 'em away before your momma sees 'em." And then I swear to God he winked.

I guess my heart should have broken then, and maybe it did, a little. I guess I should have done something, anything, besides mumble "Thank you, Daddy." I guess that would have been fine, would not have betrayed in some way my mother, my brothers, myself. But I just stood there, trapped somewhere between my long-standing, comfortable hatred, and what might have been forgiveness. I am trapped there still.

Bragg's memoir illustrates all the features that make a memoir good: how the son and father react to each other creates the kind of suspense that keeps us reading; vivid details and rich dialogue bring the scene to life. His later reflections make the significance of that final meeting very clear.

Key Features / Memoirs

A good story.   Your memoir should be interesting, to yourself and others. It need not be about a world-shaking event, but your topic—and how you write about it—should interest your readers. At the center of most good stories stands a conflict or question to be resolved. The most compelling memoirs feature some sort of situation or problem that needs resolution. That need for resolution is another name for suspense. It's what makes us want to keep reading.

Vivid details.   Details bring a memoir to life by giving readers mental images of the sights, sounds, smells, tastes, and textures of the world in which your story takes place. The goal is to show as well as tell, to take readers there. When Bragg describes a "voice like an old woman's, punctuated with a cough that sounded like it came from deep in the guts," we can hear his dying father ourselves. A memoir is more than simply a report of what happened; it uses vivid details and dialogue to bring the events of the past to life, much as good fiction brings to life events that the writer makes up or embellishes. Depending on your topic and medium, you may want to provide some of the details in audio or visual form.

✳ academic literacies   ● fields   ● research
■ rhetorical situations   ⁚⁚ processes   ● media/design
▲ genres   ◆ strategies

Clear significance. Memories of the past are filtered through our view from the present: we pick out some moments in our lives as significant, some as more important or vivid than others. Over time, our interpretations change, and our memories themselves change.

A good memoir conveys something about the significance of its subject. As a writer, you need to reveal something about what the incident means to you. You don't, however, want to simply announce the significance as if you're tacking on the moral of the story. Bragg tells us that he's "trapped between [his] long-standing, comfortable hatred, and what might have been forgiveness," but he doesn't come right out and say that's why the incident is so important to him.

A BRIEF GUIDE TO WRITING MEMOIRS

Choosing an Event to Write About

LIST several events or incidents from your past that you consider significant in some way. They do not have to be earthshaking; indeed, they may involve a quiet moment that only you see as important—a brief encounter with a remarkable person, a visit to a special place, a memorable achievement (or failure), something that makes you laugh whenever you think about it. Writing about events that happened at least a few years ago is often easier than writing about recent events because you can more easily step back and see those events with a clear perspective. To choose the event that you will write about, consider how well you can recall what happened, how interesting it will be to readers, and whether you want to share it with an audience.

334–35

Considering the Rhetorical Situation

PURPOSE   What is the importance of the memory you are trying to convey? How will this story help you understand yourself and your readers understand you, as you were then and as you are now?

59–60

61–64 ■
AUDIENCE   Who are your readers? Why will they care about your memoir? What do you want them to think of you after reading it? How can you help them understand your experience?

72–74 ■
STANCE   What impression do you want to give, and how can your words contribute to that impression? What tone do you want to project? Sincere? Serious? Humorous? Detached? Self-critical?

75–77 ■
MEDIA/DESIGN   Will your memoir be a print document? a speech? Will it be posted on a website? Can you include photographs, audio or video clips, or other visual texts?

Generating Ideas and Text

Think about what happened.   Take a few minutes to write out an account of the incident: **WHAT** happened, **WHERE** it took place, **WHO** else was involved, what was said, how you feel about it, and so on. Can you identify any tension or conflict that will make for a compelling story? If not, you might want to rethink your topic.

337 ⁖

Consider its significance.   Why do you still remember this event? What effect has it had on your life? What makes you want to tell someone else about it? Does it say anything about you? What about it might interest someone else? If you have trouble answering these questions, you should probably find another topic. But in general, once you have defined the significance of the incident, you can be sure you have a story to tell—and a reason for telling it.

Think about the details.   The best memoirs connect with readers by giving them a sense of what it was like to be there, leading them to experience in words and images what the writer experienced in life. Spend some time **DESCRIBING** the incident, writing what you see, hear, smell, touch, and taste when you envision it. Do you have any photos or memorabilia or other **VISUAL** materials you might include in your memoir? Try writing out **DIALOGUE**, things that were said (or, if you can't recall exactly, things

456–63 ◆
674–80 ●
464–68 ◆

✳ academic literacies   ● fields   ● research
■ rhetorical situations   ⁖ processes   ● media/design
▲ genres   ◆ strategies

that might have been said). Look at what you come up with—is there detail enough to bring the scene to life? anything that might be called vivid? If you don't have enough detail, you might reconsider whether you recall enough about the incident to write about it. If you have trouble coming up with plenty of detail, try **FREEWRITING**, **LISTING**, or **LOOPING**.

333–35

Ways of Organizing Memoirs

[Tell about the event from beginning to end]

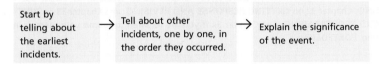

Start by telling about the earliest incidents. → Tell about other incidents, one by one, in the order they occurred. → Explain the significance of the event.

[Start at the end and tell how the event came about]

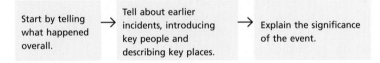

Start by telling what happened overall. → Tell about earlier incidents, introducing key people and describing key places. → Explain the significance of the event.

Taking Stock of Your Work

Take stock of what you've written by considering to these questions:

- How did you decide on your topic and determine the conflict or question to be resolved in your memoir?

- How effectively did you use dialogue, description, or other narrative strategies in your memoir?

- Did you use photographs or other visual or audio elements? What did they add? Can you think of such elements you might have used?

- How did you go about revising your work? How effective do you think your revisions were?

- What previous writing experiences, if any, did you draw on in writing your memoir? Did those experiences help you or hinder you?

- How much did you reflect on your story and what it means to you—and might mean to others?

- What was your most important achievement in this piece? What's the best part of this memoir? Why?

If you need more help

364–66
367–71
372–79
380–84
385–90

See Chapter 30 for guidelines on **DRAFTING**, Chapter 31 on **ASSESSING YOUR OWN WRITING**, Chapter 32 on **GETTING RESPONSE AND REVISING**, and Chapter 33 on **EDITING AND PROOFREADING**. See Chapter 34 if you are required to submit your memoir in a writing **PORTFOLIO**.

⚹ academic literacies   ● fields   ● research
■ rhetorical situations   ⁘ processes   ● media/design
▲ genres   ◆ strategies

19 Profiles

Profiles are written portraits—of people, places, events, or other things. We find profiles of celebrities, travel destinations, and offbeat festivals in magazines and newspapers, on radio and TV, on the web and through various social media. A profile presents a subject in an entertaining way that conveys its significance, showing us something or someone that we may not have known existed or that we see every day but don't know much about. In college *journalism* classes, students learn to create profiles using words and, in many cases, photos and video as well. Here is a profile of a young woman whose path to college included hopping freight trains, battling addiction, and becoming a boxer. This profile originally appeared in a longer version in *The PennStater,* the alumni magazine of Penn State University, where writer Ryan Jones is the senior editor.

RYAN JONES

A Fighter's Chance

The end of the world begins on Rebecca Maine's right shoulder, an apocalypse of skulls and trees and snarling beasts that wraps around her arm until it reaches the back of her hand, where a serpent clenches an eyeball in its jaws.

The scene is a tattoo depiction of Ragnarok, the violent denouement in ancient Norse mythology. Her mother has traced the family's genealogy back to the Vikings, and Maine appreciates the connection to her lineage. But mostly, she says, "I just think it's badass."

Maine began work on the tattoo nearly a decade ago, but only got it finished last year. She's got a number of other pieces—the comic-book

heroine Tank Girl on her left arm, others of varying complexity on her neck, legs, and back—but she's particularly fond of that full sleeve. "It's silly," she says, "but finishing it felt like an accomplishment." The greater achievement is that she lived long enough to see it through.

It's difficult to reconcile the 26-year-old dean's-list student-athlete Maine is today with the young woman—still a girl, really—she was eight or nine years ago, the one who left a difficult home life looking for adventure, acceptance, and escape. She carried little more than the clothes on her back and a burgeoning taste for substances that could numb her pain. She ended up hopping freight trains, traveling the country that way for the better part of three years. And she fell deep into the throes of heroin addiction that nearly killed her.

In March, near the end of her first year in the physical therapist assistant program at Penn State DuBois, she celebrated five years sober.   5

A few months earlier, Maine had completed an award-winning season on the campus cross-country team; in May, she fought in the national Golden Gloves tournament. Still, the darkest parts of her past are never far out of mind.

"I feel like I've had to keep accomplishing more and more, trying to kind of bury all that," she says. "But I can't get too removed from it. I need it, as a reminder."

So she has embraced the pain and loss and anger and guilt, because the future she's set her mind to requires nothing less. Talking about it took longer, because it meant exposing herself to judgment, but she has embraced that, too. She sees the value of sharing her experience, both for herself and, she hopes, for others, kids who are where she was: in a small town, without many options, in the midst of a national

* academic literacies   ● fields   ● research
■ rhetorical situations   •• processes   ● media/design
▲ genres   ◆ strategies

epidemic of opioid abuse, bearing emotional burdens that few around them are willing or able to understand. "I don't think she recognized how big of a deal her story is—it hits home for a lot of people, especially in our community," says DuBois cross-country coach Kyle Gordon. "It's a story of hope."

Rebecca started drinking in middle school in Punxsutawney, PA, both to fit in and to cope with the stress of family life: Though close with her mother, Rebecca describes her father as a functional alcoholic who was unfaithful, abusive, and often absent, and it was for the best when her parents' marriage ended when she was in high school. But it was an unrelated incident during her freshman year that helped send Rebecca spiraling: She describes herself as a reluctant member of the popular crowd, hanging with kids who "just drank all the time." Her mother, Louise—a teacher at the local high school—found photos of a booze-fueled underage party on Rebecca's phone, and decided her best move—the right move—would be calling the other kids' parents. "I thought I should talk to them about what was happening," Louise says. "But they didn't welcome that."

Instead, their kids targeted Rebecca for retribution. "They tor- 10 mented me for it," she says. Louise remembers her daughter coming to her classroom to eat lunch, moody and miserable but desperate to avoid the relentless bullying of the classmates she had once considered friends. Ostracized from her peer group, Rebecca began hanging out with older kids, many of whom had already moved beyond drinking to more dangerous substances. She followed suit: "By my sophomore year," Rebecca says, "I did anything I could get my hands on."

Around this time, Louise found drug paraphernalia in Rebecca's room, but she says she still didn't fully grasp the turmoil that was driving her daughter to self-medicate. Rebecca got a reprieve of sorts when her mother allowed her to finish high school via online courses. Louise was skeptical, thinking her daughter was just looking for a way to quit school altogether, but Rebecca stuck it out and finished ahead of schedule—a sign of the persistence she'd show years later.

But Rebecca was also entrenched in a social circle that enabled her worst tendencies, including substance abuse. Not long after she turned 18, she and her boyfriend moved 80 miles southwest to Pittsburgh. Once there, she toyed with the idea of culinary school or a veterinary tech program, but nothing took. And then, she says, "I pretty much snapped. I had suppressed so much, and I just felt like I had to do . . . something."

She sold everything she owned, minus a backpack full of clothes, and bought a plane ticket to New Orleans. She felt guilty leaving her mom and brother, and she hated herself for feeling like she deserved the turmoil that defined her life. She had no idea what came next. She only knew that running away felt like something she could control.

They were on the road to Scranton for a cross-country meet last fall, the coach and his three runners, one of them a 26-year-old freshman. Kyle Gordon was struck by the fact that the young woman beside him seemed so excited to visit a city famous for its train museum. "I thought it was a little bizarre," he says with a laugh. "That's when she told us about her train-hopping."

She had left Pittsburgh and landed in New Orleans and spent a   15
couple of months there with friends, thinking she'd hitchhike across the country. And then she linked up with the amorphous community of train-hoppers—"travelers," as she calls them, a group she describes as an underground society, hidden in plain sight. "I was a little punk rocker, and it was the most punk-rock thing I'd ever seen," she says. "I wanted in."

All these years later, there are aspects of her nearly three years on the rails that provide fond memories. She learned all the tricks, like which trains ran faster or offered better hiding places. How to wait until the conductors' shift change, when trains would generally be left unattended on the edge of a yard, and she and fellow hoppers would wait, hidden, until they were sure it was clear. And of course, she got to see so much of the country for free. But it was often dangerous, and always illegal, and it's impossible to fully separate the good parts from the bad. About a month into traveling, she says, she was "eating, sleeping, drinking heroin."

Money was always tight: Maine quickly burned through the money she'd made selling her things, and the spare change she made playing music on the mandolin she traveled with never lasted long. She remembers one bleak stretch near the high desert town of Twentynine Palms, a few hours east of Los Angeles, when it occurred to her that she'd barely eaten in two weeks. "Del Taco had 49-cent burritos, and

✳ academic literacies   ● fields   ● research
■ rhetorical situations   ⁝ processes   ● media/design
▲ genres   ◆ strategies

I'd get one of those, once or twice a week," she says. "All my money was going elsewhere."

There were other wake-up calls: Maine says she was "Narcanned" several times, referring to emergency doses of the medication carried by police and EMTs to block the effects of opioid overdose. There was the traveling companion, someone she thought she could trust, who she learned had offered to "sell" her for sex. There were friends whose addictions got the best of them, who weren't as tough, or as lucky, and who never made it home.

She never thought of herself as homeless, not as long as her mom was back in Punxsutawney, wishing for her safe return. They would talk by phone, and Louise held out hope that the travel might be good for Rebecca, that at least she'd be far from the roots of her problems. But Rebecca could only maintain the facade for so long.

More than once, Rebecca tried to get sober. She returned to Punxsutawney, moving back in with her mom until she started using again, then moving in with a friend. She tried Pittsburgh again, even tried Brooklyn, where she played in a folk-punk band that hoped to record an album. Each time, she backslid. "She would be OK for a while," Louise says, "but you always know when they relapse. It would be immediate." She tried therapy but hated it. She got a part-time job as a hospital housekeeper near her home. She made regular trips to and from Pittsburgh, scoring drugs for herself and occasionally re-selling the surplus to support her habit. She'd ruined the veins in her arms and started shooting into her neck.

Finally, Rebecca says, something—some combination of guilt, desperation, and exhaustion—clicked. She deleted her dealer's number from her phone. She took all the time off she could afford from her job at the hospital, and she went cold turkey. It was February in Punxsutawney, in a house with no heat, and she burrowed into her couch, chain-smoking cigarettes, flinging off the blankets when the sweats came, piling them back on when they passed. Her roommate had box sets of the first five seasons of *Sons of Anarchy*, and she watched every episode. It took two weeks before she was able to function, to keep any food down, and to tell her mom—and for the first time, mean it—that she needed help.

And here Rebecca knows her experience might not be fully transferable: She did this largely on her own. Her mom was a rock, family and close friends helped hold her accountable, but she never felt comfortable in 12-step programs, and so she focused instead on staying busy. She was about a month sober, still wracked with cold sweats, when she took seasonal work as a merchandiser for a garden wholesaler. Around the same time, she and her mom went to watch a local boxing showcase; Louise was dating the physician who sat ringside for the bouts, and she thought the discipline and physical activity would be good for her daughter. They were introduced to a trainer, who saw before him a young woman who was, in her own words, "un-athletic and a wreck."

She told him she wanted to learn how to fight.

Rebecca dove right in, going through an intensive workout her first day at the gym. The next day, she says with a laugh, "I couldn't walk." But she stuck with it, never missing practice, and along the way she found that the sport had a way of helping other issues. She had struggled for years with body image, and she'd battled both bulimia and anorexia; training for fights forced her to eat well and made her proud of the athlete she was becoming.

Through endless hours at the gym, Maine transformed her body   25
and her life, and before long she'd decided she wanted to try to make a career as a professional fighter. But that hope was nearly derailed with a pair of diagnoses, first hepatitis C—a relic from her days of sharing needles—and then endometriosis. She's since undergone treatment for both conditions and says the silver lining was that she developed a curiosity about her body—how it worked and how to take care of it. "Boxing was everything—boxing may have saved my life—but I didn't realize maybe it was a stepping stone to the next thing," Rebecca says. It turned out the next thing was Penn State.

The letter arrived not long before the start of the school year, informing Rebecca Maine that she could pick up two additional kinesiology credits if she participated in an intercollegiate sport at Penn State DuBois. *I want to go for a doctorate someday*, Maine thought to herself, *so I might as well get as many credits as I can.*

She had yet to complete a single credit in anything, of course, but Maine was thinking ahead. She was already running as part of her boxing training; joining the DuBois cross-country team didn't seem like too much of a stretch. The team featured just three runners, and Maine was

✳ academic literacies   ● fields   ● research
■ rhetorical situations   ⁝ processes   ● media/design
▲ genres   ◆ strategies

the only woman, a 26-year-old freshman who'd never raced competing against 18- and 19-year-olds fresh off their high school teams. She'd seen and endured so much more of life than most of her opponents ever would, and yet when she lined up for her first race, she was terrified.

"I'm on the starting line, and there's all these young people—all these young *athletes*," she says. "I was scared. I didn't know what to expect."

And yet she thrived, finishing sixth in her first race, and first among runners from Penn State campuses. She went on to finish fourth in the PSUAC championship meet, earning a spot on the all-conference team and a trip to nationals. And it was there that her coach finally convinced her to tell her story. Gordon asked Rebecca if she'd mind him nominating her for a conference award. As they'd gotten to know each other over the course of the semester, she had grudgingly offered Gordon bits of her past. For this, she agreed to open up a bit more.

It was in Virginia Beach in November, at the U.S. Collegiate Athletic 30 Association banquet, that strangers first heard pieces of Maine's story. In the write-up honoring her as the USCAA's Student-Athlete of the Year, the key details stood out: *addicted to heroin . . . hitchhiking and train-hopping . . . boxing as a means to turn her life around.*

And there were more achievements to come. Maine would go on to compete in the 2018 Golden Gloves boxing championship, winning two fights in her weight class before falling in the semifinals. Back at DuBois, she earned the highest GPA among first-semester freshmen, started a campus PT assistant's club, and led the campus LGBTQA support group.

When we first spoke last winter, Maine was reeling, her eyes welling a half dozen times as she laid out her story to a stranger for the first time. "It was things surfacing that I'd repressed, things I don't want to remember," she said then. "All the positive things people are saying now, it's new to me. It's very alien."

But by the spring, having had time to process her feelings and appreciate the value of her story, she had come around. She knew the stigma around issues like mental health and addiction, knew how it felt to believe there was something "wrong" with her, and not that she simply needed help. She understood that her story could help others and that telling it could help her, too.

Jones's profile traces Rebecca Maine's unusual life from her teen years to the present. Because it's a profile, the piece focuses on a part of her life, rather than trying to describe her entire life story. Jones provides details, from Maine's tattoos to her first boxing workout, that give us snapshots of Maine's life and character.

Key Features / Profiles

An interesting subject. The subject may be something unusual, or it may be something ordinary shown in an intriguing way. You might profile an interesting person (like a local celebrity), a place (like a company that makes paper straws), an event (like the rescue of a sea turtle), or an object (like a rare automobile).

Any necessary background. A profile usually includes just enough information to let readers know something about the subject's larger context. Jones provides some details about why Maine left home (an alcoholic and abusive father, ostracism by her peers), but he leaves out other details about her life that don't matter for this profile.

An interesting angle. A good profile captures its subject from a particular angle. Sometimes finding an angle will be fairly easy because your topic—like the history of a local coffee shop—is offbeat enough to be interesting in and of itself. Other topics, though, may require you to find a particular aspect that you can focus on. For example, a profile of a person might focus on the important work the person does or a challenging hobby they pursue; it would likely ignore aspects of the person's life that don't relate to that angle.

A firsthand account. Whether you're writing about a person, place, object, or event, you need to spend time observing and interacting with your subject. With a person, interacting means watching and conversing. Journalists tell us that "following the guy around," getting your subject to do something and talk about it at the same time, yields excellent material for a profile. When one writer met Theodor Geisel (Dr. Seuss) before profiling him, she asked him not only to talk about his characters but also to draw one—resulting in an illustration for her profile. With a place, object, or event, interacting may mean visiting and participating, although sometimes you may gather even more information by playing the role of the silent observer.

Engaging details.   You need to include details that bring your subject to life. These may include *specific information* ("She learned all the tricks, like which trains ran faster or offered better hiding places. How to wait until the conductors' shift change, when trains would generally be left unattended on the edge of a yard, and she and fellow hoppers would wait, hidden, until they were sure it was clear"); *sensory images* ("she burrowed into her couch, chain-smoking cigarettes, flinging off the blankets when the sweats came, piling them back on when they passed"); *figurative language* ("The end of the world begins on Rebecca Maine's right shoulder, an apocalypse of skulls and trees and snarling beasts"); *dialogue* ("'Boxing was everything—boxing may have saved my life—but I didn't realize maybe it was a stepping stone to the next thing,' Rebecca says"); and *anecdotes* (Rebecca started training for boxing, "going through an intensive workout her first day at the gym. The next day, she says with a laugh, 'I couldn't walk.'"). Choose details that show rather than tell—that let your audience see and hear your subject rather than merely read an abstract description of it. Sometimes you may let them see and hear it literally, by including *photographs* or *video and audio clips*. And be sure all the details create some *dominant impression* of your subject: the impression that we get out of this profile, for example, is of a strong-willed, ambitious young woman who has persevered despite many challenges and setbacks.

A BRIEF GUIDE TO WRITING PROFILES

Choosing a Suitable Subject
A person, a place, an object, an event—whatever you choose, make sure it's something that arouses your curiosity and that you're not too familiar with. Knowing your subject too well can blind you to interesting details. **LIST** five to ten interesting subjects that you can experience firsthand. Obviously,

334–35

you can't profile a person who won't be interviewed or a place or activity that can't be observed. So before you commit to a topic, make sure you'll be able to carry out firsthand research.

Considering the Rhetorical Situation

59–60 ■

PURPOSE Why are you writing the profile? What angle will best achieve your purpose? How can you inform and engage your audience?

61–64 ■

AUDIENCE Who is your audience? How familiar are they with your subject? What expectations of your profile might they have? What background information or definitions do you need to provide? How interested will they be—and how can you capture and hold their interest?

72–74 ■

STANCE What view of your subject do you expect to present? Sympathetic? Critical? Sarcastic? Will you strive for a carefully balanced perspective?

75–77 ■

MEDIA/DESIGN Will your profile be a print document? electronic? an oral presentation? Can (and should) you include images or any other visuals? Will it be recorded as an audio file or a multimodal text?

Generating Ideas and Text

Explore what you already know about your subject. Why do you find this subject interesting? What do you know about it now? What do you expect to find out about it from your research? What preconceived ideas about or emotional reactions to this subject do you have? Why do you have them? It may be helpful to try some of the activities in the chapter 333–44 ◦• on **GENERATING IDEAS AND TEXT**.

Visit your subject. If you're writing about an amusement park, go there; if you're profiling the man who runs the carousel, make an appointment to meet and interview him. Get to know your subject—if you profile the owner of a local BBQ place, sample the ribs! Take photos or videos if there's

---

✳ academic literacies	● fields	● research
■ rhetorical situations	◦• processes	● media/design
▲ genres	◆ strategies	

anything you might want to show visually in your profile. Find helpful hints for **OBSERVING** and **INTERVIEWING** in the chapter on finding sources.

● 520–21
518–20

If you're planning to interview someone, prepare questions. Jones likely asked Rebecca Maine such questions as, "What triggered your interest in train-hopping? You did it for three years; what are some of your good memories of that time? What are some of the bad ones?" See the **INTER-VIEWING** guidelines in Chapter 47 for help with planning good questions and conducting interviews.

● 518–20

Do additional research. You may be able to write a profile based entirely on your field research. You may, though, need to do some library or web **RESEARCH** as well, to deepen your understanding, get a different perspective, or fill in gaps. Often the people you interview can help you find sources of additional information; so can the sponsors of events and those in charge of places. To learn more about a city park, for instance, contact the government office that maintains it. Download any good photos of your subject that you find online, both to refer to as you write and to illustrate your profile.

● 489

Analyze your findings. Look for patterns, images, recurring ideas or phrases, and engaging details. Look for contrasts or discrepancies: between a subject's words and actions, between the appearance of a place and what goes on there, between your expectations and your research findings. Jones may have expected to meet an athlete with an unusual background—but he may not have expected Maine's life to be as difficult as it turned out to be. You may find the advice in the **READING IN ACADEMIC CONTEXTS** chapter helpful here.

✳ 11–32

Come up with an angle. What's most memorable about your subject? What most interests you? What will interest your audience? Jones focuses on the aspects of Maine's life that set her apart from most young women. Sometimes you'll know your angle from the start; other times you'll need to look further into your topic. You might try **CLUSTERING**, **CUBING**, **FREE-WRITING**, and **LOOPING**, to help you see your topic from many different angles.

⁙ 333–36

456–63
437–44
464–68

Note details that support your angle. Use your angle to focus your research and generate text. Try **DESCRIBING** your subject as clearly as you can, **COMPARING** your subject with other subjects of its sort, writing **DIALOGUE** that captures your subject. Jones, for instance, describes Maine's tattoos, compares her to the much younger runners on her team, and includes several quotes from Maine that capture her impressions—and her spirit. Engaging details will bring your subject to life for your audience. Together, these details should create a dominant impression of your subject.

Ways of Organizing a Profile

474–82

One common way to organize a profile is by **NARRATING**. For example, if you're profiling a chess championship, you may write about it chronologically, creating suspense as you move from start to finish.

[As a narrative]

| Introduce your subject and your angle on it; provide any necessary background. | → | Tell about various incidents or characteristics, one by one, that bring your subject to life. | → | Conclude by stating your overall impression — with an anecdote, a quote, a summary comment, or some other ending. |

456–63

Sometimes you may organize a profile by **DESCRIBING** —a person or a place, for instance.

[As a description]

| Introduce your subject and your angle on it, providing any necessary background. | → | Present details that create some dominant impression of your subject:
• sensory details
• examples
• dialogue
• anecdotes
• and so on | → | State your overall impression, offering a final anecdote or quote or finishing a description begun earlier. |

Taking Stock of Your Work

Take stock of what you've written by considering these questions:

- How did you go about choosing a subject—and an angle on that subject?

- What strategies did you use for the beginning and ending of your profile? How did you decide on those strategies?

- What design or media choices did you make? Why did you make them, and how effective were they?

- In what ways did you reflect on your writing as you worked on it? How did the act of reflecting help you in your writing?

- What setbacks did you face as you worked on your writing? How did you overcome them and persist as a writer?

- How did you use concepts or methods you learned elsewhere (in other classes, for example) as you worked on your profile?

- What were your writing goals for yourself in this piece? How well did you achieve them? How could you improve in the future?

If you need more help

See Chapter 30 for guidelines on **DRAFTING**, Chapter 31 on **ASSESSING YOUR OWN WRITING**, Chapter 32 on **GETTING RESPONSE AND REVISING**, and Chapter 33 on **EDITING AND PROOFREADING**. See Chapter 34 if you are required to submit your profile in a writing **PORTFOLIO**.

364–66
367–71
372–79
380–84
385–90

20 Proposals

Proposals are part of our personal lives: lovers propose marriage, friends propose sharing dinner and a movie, you offer to pay half the cost of a car and insurance if your parents will pay the other half. They are also part of our academic and professional lives: student leaders lobby for lights on bike paths. Musicians, artists, writers, and educators apply for grants. Researchers in all fields of the humanities, social sciences, sciences, and technology seek funding for their projects. In business, contractors bid on building projects, and companies and freelancers solicit work from potential clients. These are all examples of proposals, ideas put forward for consideration that say, "Here is a solution to a problem" or "This is what ought to be done." For example, here is a proposal for reducing cheating among college students, written by a philosophy professor at Wake Forest University who directs a team of scholars examining the role of honesty in our lives. The team's undertaking is called The Honesty Project.

CHRISTIAN B. MILLER

Just How Dishonest Are Most Students?

I teach philosophy to college students, and there was no way I was going to give them exams this semester, with our classes being held online. Why not? Simple—cheating. It is nothing personal with these particular students, but I have read enough psychological research to know that it would be very hard for them to resist looking for help in places where they are not supposed to, such as their notes, their friends, and the internet.

✳ academic literacies   ⬢ fields   ● research
■ rhetorical situations   ⦂ processes   ● media/design
▲ genres   ◆ strategies

I am fortunate that papers are a great alternative means of assessment in philosophy courses. But they do not work so well in certain other fields, like the sciences. In this time of widespread online learning and home-schooling, what can be done to curb cheating on exams?

One solution is remote proctoring, where the student is video-recorded during the exam, with any suspicious web browsing reported. That might be effective, but it strikes me as a crude approach, relying as it does on active surveillance, which creates an overt atmosphere of distrust. Naturally enough there are also privacy concerns (Hubler; Patil and Bromwich), as well as some anecdotal evidence (Patil and Bromwich; Swauger) that remote proctoring technology encodes racial biases.

Instead I suggest that a practice that has been used widely in other educational contexts be extended to the world of online testing: pledging one's honor. Honor pledges not only are surprisingly effective in curbing cheating; they also promote honesty. Students who abide by them refrain from cheating not because they can't, but because they choose not to.

It is easy to be cynical about honor pledges and honor codes. They 5
can seem to be—and sadly too often are—PR stunts for schools looking
to burnish their image. Or administrative mandates that do not have buy-
in from the faculty. Or just a formality, where students check a box on
a form during first-year orientation and then never give it any thought
for the rest of the year. Honor codes like these are indeed mere facades.

But many schools and programs, from elementary to graduate
level, take their honor codes seriously. And for good reason. Empirical research has repeatedly found that schools that are committed to
honor codes have significantly reduced cheating rates compared with
schools that are not.

Donald McCabe at Rutgers Business School and Linda Treviño at
the Smeal College of Business at Penn State found a 23 percent rate
of helping someone with answers on a test at colleges without an
honor code, versus only 11 percent at schools with an honor code. They
reported impressive differences as well for plagiarism (20 percent versus
10 percent), unauthorized crib notes (17 percent versus 11 percent), and
unpermitted collaboration (49 percent versus 27 percent), among other
forms of cheating (224).

A serious commitment to the honor code is crucial to its efficacy.
As Professors McCabe and Treviño insist, an honor code should be "well
implemented and strongly embedded in the student culture" (224).

What does that look like in practice? A few schools start the academic year with an actual commitment ceremony, where each student
has to publicly pledge to uphold the school's code. To this can be added
a requirement to affirm the honor code on each graded assignment.

When I was an undergraduate at Princeton, every paper we turned 10
in had to have the honor code written out and then signed. Now as a
professor at Wake Forest, I make my class recite aloud with me before
each exam our entire honor code and then sign it.

Signing an honor code can, among other things, serve as a moral
reminder. As we know from both ordinary life and recent experimental
findings, most of us are willing to cheat to some extent if we think it
would be rewarding and we can get away with it. At the same time,
we also want to think of ourselves as honest people and genuinely
believe that cheating is wrong. But our more honorable intentions can
be pushed to one side in our minds when tempting opportunities arise
to come out ahead, even if by cheating. What a moral reminder does,
then, is help to place our values front and center in our minds.

✳ academic literacies	⬤ fields	⬤ research
◼ rhetorical situations	⁘ processes	⬤ media/design
▲ genres	◆ strategies	

This is borne out by recent findings in the lab. In a widely cited study, Nina Mazar at the Questrom School of Business at Boston University and her colleagues had one group of students take a 20-problem test where they would be paid 50 cents per correct answer. It was a hard test—students averaged only 3.4 correct answers. A second group of students took the same test, but they graded their own work and reported their "scores" with no questions asked. The average in this group was 6.1 correct answers, suggesting some cheating. The third and most interesting group, though, began by signing an honor code and then took the test, followed by grading their own work. The result? An honorable 3.1 correct answers. Cheating was eliminated at the group level. Signing the honor code did the job (636–37).

Studies of honor codes and cheating have typically been conducted in face-to-face environments. But as we settle into the routine of online instruction, we should consider trying to extend the impact of an honor code virtually as well.

Honor codes won't eliminate cheating. Deeply dishonest students will not be deterred. But fortunately, the research confirms what experience suggests: most students are not deeply dishonest.

Works Cited

Hubler, Shawn. "Keeping Online Testing Honest? Or an Orwellian Overreach?" *The New York Times*, 10 May 2020, www.nytimes .com/2020/05/10/us/online-testing-cheating-universities -coronavirus.html.

Mazar, Nina, et al. "The Dishonesty of Honest People: A Theory of Self-Concept Maintenance." *Journal of Marketing Research*, vol. 45, 2008, pp. 633–44.

McCabe, Donald L., et al. "Cheating in Academic Institutions: A Decade of Research." *Ethics & Behavior*, vol. 11, no. 3, 2001, pp. 219–32.

Patil, Anushka, and Jonah Engel Bromwich. "How It Feels When Software Watches You Take Tests." *The New York Times*, 29 Sept. 2020, www.nytimes.com/2020/09/29/style/testing-schools -proctorio.html.

Swauger, Shea. "Software That Monitors Students during Tests Perpetuates Inequality and Violates Their Privacy." *MIT Technology Review*, 7 Aug. 2020, www.technologyreview .com/2020/08/07/1006132/software-algorithms-proctoring -onlinetests-ai-ethics.

This proposal clearly defines the problem—students cheat on exams—and offers a solution: honor pledges and honor codes. The author provides arguments and evidence from research to show why this is a good solution.

Key Features / Proposals

A well-defined problem.   Some problems are self-evident and relatively simple, and you would not need much persuasive power to make people act—as with the problem "This university discards too much paper." While some people might see nothing wrong with throwing paper away, most are likely to agree that recycling is a good thing. Other issues are controversial: some people see them as problems while others do not, such as this one: "Motorcycle riders who do not wear helmets risk serious injury and raise health-care costs for everyone." Some motorcyclists believe that wearing or not wearing a helmet should be a personal choice; you would have to present arguments to convince your readers that not wearing a helmet is indeed a problem needing a solution. Any written proposal must establish at the outset that there is a problem—and that it's serious enough to require a solution. For some topics, visual or audio evidence of the problem may be helpful.

A recommended solution.   Once you have defined the problem, you need to describe the solution you're suggesting and to explain it in enough detail for readers to understand what you are proposing. Again, photographs, diagrams, or other visuals may help. Sometimes you might suggest several solutions, weigh their merits, and choose the best one.

A convincing argument for your proposed solution.   You need to convince readers that your solution is feasible—and that it is the best way to solve the problem. Sometimes you'll want to explain in detail how your proposed solution would work: "The honor code proposal offers several reasons why honor codes work, drawing on both empirical research and understanding of human nature." Visuals may strengthen this part of your argument as well.

☀ academic literacies	● fields	● research
■ rhetorical situations	⸭ processes	● media/design
▲ genres	◆ strategies	

A response to anticipated questions. You may need to consider any questions readers may have about your proposal—and to show how its advantages outweigh any disadvantages. Had the honor code proposal been written for college judicial officers, it would have needed to anticipate and answer questions about how such a code would be implemented.

A call to action. The goal of a proposal is to persuade readers to accept your proposed solution. This solution may include asking readers to take action.

An appropriate tone. Since you're trying to persuade readers to act, your tone is important—readers will always react better to a reasonable, respectful presentation than to anger or self-righteousness.

A BRIEF GUIDE TO WRITING PROPOSALS

Deciding on a Topic

Choose a problem that can be solved. Complex, large problems, such as poverty, hunger, or terrorism, usually require complex, large solutions. Most of the time, focusing on a smaller problem or a limited aspect of a large problem will yield a more manageable proposal. Rather than tackling the problem of world poverty, for example, think about the problem faced by people in your community who have lost jobs and need help until they find employment.

Considering the Rhetorical Situation

PURPOSE	Do you have a stake in a particular solution, or do you simply want to eliminate the problem by whatever solution might be adopted?	■ 59–60
AUDIENCE	Do your readers share your view of the problem as a serious one needing a solution? Are they likely to be open to possible solutions or resistant? Do they have the authority to carry out a proposed solution?	■ 61–64

72–74
STANCE   How can you show your audience that your proposal is reasonable and should be taken seriously? How can you demonstrate your own authority and credibility?

75–77
MEDIA/DESIGN   How will you deliver your proposal? In print? Electronically? As a speech? Would visuals, or video or audio clips, help support your proposal?

Generating Ideas and Text

Explore potential solutions to the problem. Many problems can be solved in more than one way, and you need to show your readers that you've examined several potential solutions. You may develop solutions on your own; more often, though, you'll need to do **RESEARCH** to see how others have solved—or tried to solve—similar problems. Don't settle on a single solution too quickly—you'll need to **COMPARE** the advantages and disadvantages of several solutions in order to argue convincingly for one.

489

437–44

Decide on the most desirable solution(s). One solution may be head and shoulders above others—but it's important to be open to rejecting all the possible solutions on your list and starting over if you need to, or to combining two or more potential solutions in order to come up with an acceptable fix.

Think about why your solution is the best one. Why did you choose your solution? Why will it work better than others? What has to be done to enact it? What will it cost? What makes you think it can be done? Writing out answers to these questions will help you argue for your solution: to show that you have carefully and objectively outlined a problem, analyzed the potential solutions, weighed their merits, and determined the reasons the solution you propose is the best.

Ways of Organizing a Proposal

You can organize a proposal in various ways, but always you will begin by establishing that there is a problem. You may then identify several possible

※ academic literacies   ● fields   ● research
■ rhetorical situations   ∴ processes   ● media/design
▲ genres   ◆ strategies

solutions before recommending one of them or a combination of several. Sometimes, however, you might discuss only a single solution.

[Several possible solutions]

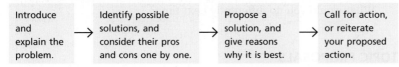

| Introduce and explain the problem. | → | Identify possible solutions, and consider their pros and cons one by one. | → | Propose a solution, and give reasons why it is best. | → | Call for action, or reiterate your proposed action. |

[A single solution]

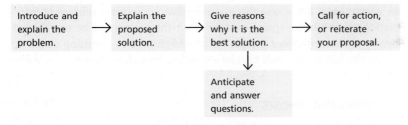

| Introduce and explain the problem. | → | Explain the proposed solution. | → | Give reasons why it is the best solution. | → | Call for action, or reiterate your proposal. |

Anticipate and answer questions.

Taking Stock of Your Work

Take stock of what you've written by considering these questions:

- How did you determine your audience for this piece?
- How did you decide on and limit your topic?
- How did you determine the best solution to the problem you defined?
- What writing strategies did you use to guide your reader through your text? How effectively did you use them?
- What editing and proofreading processes did you use, and how effective were they?
- Based on your experiences with this piece, what academic habit of mind—for example, being flexible, creative, and so on—do you want to work on as you tackle your next writing project?

- What did you learn about writing as you wrote your proposal? How might you use that learning as you write in other contexts now or in the future?

- What did you do well in this piece? What could still be improved? What would you do differently next time?

TOPIC PROPOSALS

Instructors often ask students to write topic proposals to ensure that their topics are appropriate or manageable. Some instructors may also ask for an **ANNOTATED BIBLIOGRAPHY** showing that appropriate sources of information are available—more evidence that the project can be carried out. Here a student proposes a topic for an assignment in a writing course in which she has been asked to take a position on a global issue.

201–9

CATHERINE THOMS

Social Media and Data Privacy

The relationship between social media and data privacy is an issue that has recently risen to the forefront of many social media users' concerns. While we have been posting and sharing online, major companies like Facebook, Twitter, and Google have been silently collecting information about our personal lives and leaving that data vulnerable to potentially harmful exposure. As someone who has had their private information compromised multiple times by large-scale data breaches, I feel compelled to share my research on the dangers of such security breaches and how they can happen.

In this paper, I will argue that it is crucial for consumers to be aware of the ways in which social media platforms can gain access to consumers' private data and what those platforms can do with that data. In March 2018, it was revealed that 87 million Facebook profiles were exposed to manipulation by the political consulting firm Cambridge

☀ academic literacies	● fields	● research
■ rhetorical situations	⁚ processes	● media/design
▲ genres	◆ strategies	

Analytica during the 2016 presidential election. I will use this scandal as an example of how the unlawful exposure of personal data can have far-reaching effects on external world events, and I plan to analyze how this scandal has functioned as a global catalyst for further scrutiny into the privacy mechanisms of social media.

I will concentrate on the specific ways personal data may be misused. Although sharing thoughts and pictures on social media may not seem like anything to think twice about, many people don't realize just how much is at stake should enough of that personal data fall into the wrong hands. Much of my research will be done on specific social media applications such as Facebook and Google Analytics, as that is where the heart of the issue resides and where consumers can learn the most about their personal data exposure and protection.

Thoms defines and narrows her topic (from data breaches to the specific ways consumers' data may be misused), discusses her interest, outlines her argument, and discusses her research strategy. Her goal is to convince her instructor that she has a realistic writing project and a clear plan.

Key Features / Topic Proposals

You'll need to explain what you want to write about, why you want to explore it, and what you'll do with your topic. Unless your instructor has additional requirements, here are the features to include:

A concise discussion of the subject.   Topic proposals generally open with a brief discussion of the subject, outlining any important areas of controversy or debate associated with it and clarifying the extent of the writer's current knowledge of it. In its first two paragraphs, Thoms's proposal includes a concise statement of the topic she wishes to address.

A clear statement of your intended focus.   State what aspect of the topic you intend to write on as clearly as you can, narrowing your focus appropriately. Thoms does so by stating her intended topic—data breaches—and then showing how she will focus on the specific ways consumers' data may be misused.

A rationale for choosing the topic. Tell your instructor why this topic interests you and why you want to write about it. Thoms both states what made her interested in her topic and hints at a practical reason for choosing it: plenty of information is available.

Mention of resources. To show your instructor that you can achieve your goal, you need to identify the available research materials.

If you need more help

364–66
367–71
371–79
380–84
385–90

See Chapter 30 for guidelines on **DRAFTING**, Chapter 31 on **ASSESSING YOUR OWN WRITING**, Chapter 32 on **GETTING RESPONSE AND REVISING**, and Chapter 33 on **EDITING AND PROOFREADING**. See Chapter 34 if you are required to submit your proposal in a writing **PORTFOLIO**.

※ academic literacies　　● fields　　● research

■ rhetorical situations　　⁚ processes　　● media/design

▲ genres　　◆ strategies

21 Explorations

Sometimes we write essays just to think about something—to play with an idea, develop a thought, explore possible solutions to a problem, or even to figure out what the problem is. Exploratory essays are our attempt to think something through by writing about it and to share our thinking—or the progression of our understanding—with others. In college, you might be asked in courses across the curriculum to write formal or informal exploratory essays, journals, design reports, or learning log entries. Have a look at one example of an exploratory essay written for a first-year composition class at Columbus State Community College. The author, Brian Diehl, was a high school student taking college courses when he wrote his exploration.

BRIAN DIEHL

Talking with Granddad

An overcast sky chokes the usual radiant light of summer on this Sunday afternoon—an ironic backdrop to the sign in front of me, which reads "Sunrise on the Scioto." Upon entering the nursing home's lobby, I'm met with a clash of two scents: the buttery aroma of a nearby popcorn machine and that distinct "old people" smell. The latter always seems to outlast its opponent and seeps into my nostrils around every corner of the building. I make sure to grab a few hard candies before taking an elevator up to the third floor.

Knock, knock, knock.

No answer. Peeking into the doorway, I see a man slouched in his bed absorbing the sounds of a televised college football game.

"Hey granddad, it's me!" A slow turn allows him to see the boy now in front of him. "You know who I am, right?"

He stares blankly.   5

"I'm Brian, your grandson!"

The scruff around his face rises, revealing a smile of recognition. ". . . Yes," he responds.

"How've you been holding up?" I ask. The drone of the TV fills the silence. "Hey, I have a girlfriend now! Would you like to see her?"

I bring the image on my phone closer to him. After some scrutiny, he exclaims, "Well, I'll be damned!"

"Has grandma stopped by recently?"   10

". . . Well, I'll be damned!"

He repeats this phrase after every question I ask. After a while, I lightly wrap my arms around his motionless body, and we part ways.

For the longest time, there has been no medical phenomenon more intriguing to me than dementia. One may be familiar with Alzheimer's disease, the most common type of dementia characterized by plaques and tangles that spread throughout the brain, destroying tissue and eventually affecting memory, language, and other neurological functions ("Dementia"). When my grandfather showed signs of Alzheimer's in its early stages, I found myself struggling in my attempts to talk with him; my words sometimes seemed to bounce off a brick wall. Knowing that my other grandparents could be at risk of dementia as well, I wondered: How could I communicate more effectively with family members who may exhibit memory loss in the future?

Of course, communication is a two-way street, so before I could explore verbal tactics on my end, I decided to first gain an understanding of how people with dementia might express their mental state—how *they* try to communicate their experiences and perceptions. This is when I came across the story of artist William Utermohlen, who was diagnosed with Alzheimer's in 1995. As a way of understanding the disease, the artist chose to paint himself. Below is a series of Utermohlen's self-portraits, revealing changes in his perception of himself over time.

Comparing the 1996 portrait to the one drawn pre-diagnosis, we   15
can notice an immediate disappearance of details such as hair texture and facial shadows. Utermohlen's unicolor portrayal of himself inside a green framework reflects neurologist Bruce Miller's comments on artistic

A collage showing details from William Utermohlen's self-portraits. The first (top left) was made in 1967, and the rest were made following his diagnosis of Alzheimer's disease: the top middle in 1996, the top right in 1997, and the bottom row, from left to right, in 1998, 1999, and 2000.

creativity among people with brain diseases: "Alzheimer's affects the right parietal lobe in particular, which is important for visualizing something internally and then putting it onto a canvas. The art becomes more abstract, the images are blurrier and vague, more surrealistic" (qtd. in Grady). This surrealism becomes more apparent in the next portrait, where the eyes are positioned far too low, the forehead and ear are enlarged, and the frown of the artist becomes more solemn. The true erasure of identity begins in the 1998 portrait, revealing a fragmented Utermohlen with his most melancholic facial expression yet. Perhaps the most devastating work is the fifth portrait; other than an oval serving as the bare structure of a human head, there is hardly a distinguishable facial feature contained in the canvas. The final portrait—with its pencil scratches, eraser smudges, and incompleteness—suggests a dramatic alteration of Utermohlen's sense of self. What can perhaps be represented by this artist's works are the combined voices of those just like him—those who cannot verbalize their reality. As heartbreaking as Utermohlen's portraits are, they offer caregivers and others a bridge toward understanding dementia from the perspective of those who experience it.

After gaining insight into the possible mental state of someone with dementia, I sought to find concrete methods of verbal communication that could best meet the needs of individuals with Alzheimer's. I came across a study published in the *Journal of Speech, Language, and Hearing Research* conducted by Jeff Small and colleagues, who set out to evaluate the effectiveness of ten common strategies for communicating with people with Alzheimer's. As part of the study, the researchers audio-recorded twenty-two couples—individuals with Alzheimer's and their spouses—as the couples engaged in everyday tasks like setting the table, getting an item upon request, and using the telephone. The success of each communication strategy was measured by the number of communication breakdowns that occurred after its usage. Small and colleagues report that "eliminating distractions, speaking in simple sentences, and employing yes/no questions" resulted in fewer breakdowns (364). On the other hand, using a slower rate of speech caused an increase in the number of breakdowns. This study suggests the viability of some verbal techniques over others, but I was still left with a burning question: Doesn't communication effectiveness ultimately depend on what personally works for the individual with Alzheimer's?

At this point, I decided to reach out to somebody who could shed light on my question: my grandmother, Andrea Diehl. Being the embodiment of positivity that she is, her continual presence by my grandfather's side at the nursing home was one of the greatest factors that helped keep him stable. Below is a portion of our interview that highlights their communication dynamic in the midst of his dementia.

> **Brian:** Did you make any changes to your communication with granddad during his state of dementia? If so, what methods worked for you?
>
> **Andrea:** Anything that worked for me was something that was familiar already to him, something that *he* wanted to say. I always made sure he was smiling. Anything that I knew was going to please him was the object of my time with him. I would give him a hot chocolate and give him a little hug, and then when I put a marshmallow in that hot chocolate, he would smile! There were many things that I tried to do to keep him above board and happy. There were many little tricks like that. I wanted him to have the memories that were still living in both of our minds.
>
> **Brian:** In what ways did grandpa communicate with you?

✳ academic literacies   ● fields   ● research
◼ rhetorical situations   ⦂ processes   ● media/design
▲ genres   ◆ strategies

Andrea: He would reminisce about old times. For example, we had taken seven cruises on one cruise line, and we would relive those because he remembered those! He would ask, "Do you remember that meal we had? Do you remember when I found just the right things to make the drink I wanted to make?" He could remember those things and then ask me if I remembered them! It was a joy, every minute.

Reflecting on my grandmother's experiences, it becomes clear that one does not need to be a master of psychological techniques in order to properly approach communication with a person affected by dementia. What's needed is a repeated effort to be present with the individual, expressing joy over what *they* say instead of sweating over anything *we* could ever say. Even if one were to find a golden strategy that makes conversation a breeze, its use alone will never mitigate the frustration of identity loss portrayed so vividly by Utermohlen. Instead, the most important action one can take is a demonstration of love. Ranging from hugs to marshmallow drops, small acts of kindness honor the humanity of the person with Alzheimer's. It is the enjoyment of their company that fosters communication. It is relationship, not repetition, that gives way to a signal of understanding, even if that signal is as simple as a smile.

Looking back on my initial visit with my grandfather, I knew that he processed every word I said. Those shining blue eyes and unwavering smile told me that he fully knew of my presence, but he was unable to express that awareness in my world. I like to think that my grandfather's mind found an entire universe overflowing with worlds unique to him, each planet representing a blissful memory of a life full of love.

Did dementia ever take his 20 universe away? No.

Well, I'll be damned!

Works Cited

"Dementia." *The Gale Encyclopedia of Psychology*, edited by Jacqueline L. Longe, 3rd ed., Gale, 2016. *Credo Reference*, search.credoreference.com/content/entry/galegp/dementia/0.

Diehl, Andrea. Interview with author. 11 Nov. 2020.

Grady, Denise. "Self-Portraits Chronicle a Descent into Alzheimer's." *The New York Times*, 24 Oct. 2006, www.nytimes.com/2006/10/24/health/24alzh.html.

Small, Jeff A., et al. "Effectiveness of Communication Strategies Used by Caregivers of Persons with Alzheimer's Disease during Activities of Daily Living." *Journal of Speech, Language, and Hearing Research*, vol. 46, no. 2, Apr. 2003, pp. 353–67. *EBSCOhost*, https://doi.org/10.1044/1092-4388(2003/028).

Diehl's challenges in conversing with a grandparent with Alzheimer's disease spur him to explore ways to communicate effectively with people with dementia. Through his exploration, Diehl ponders the merits of several communication strategies, including those recommended by experts and those used by his own grandmother.

Key Features / Explorations

A topic that intrigues you. An exploratory essay has a dual purpose: to ponder something you find interesting or puzzling, and to share your thoughts with an audience. Your topic may be anything that interests you. You might write about someone you've never met and are curious about, an object or occurrence that makes you think, a problem you need to solve—or one you need to define. Your goal is to explore the meaning that the person, object, event, or problem has for you in a way that will interest others. One way to do that is by making connections between your personal experience and more general ones that readers may share. Diehl writes about his interactions with his own grandfather, but in so doing he raises questions and offers insights about how others communicate with people affected by dementia.

※ academic literacies   ● fields   ● research
■ rhetorical situations   ∴ processes   ● media/design
▲ genres   ◆ strategies

Some kind of structure. An exploratory essay can be structured in many ways, but it needs to *be* structured. It may seem to wander, but all its paths and ideas should relate, one way or another. The challenge is to keep your readers' interest as you explore your topic and to leave readers satisfied that the journey was pleasurable, interesting, and profitable. Often doing this requires COMBINING GENRES. For example, Diehl begins with a narrative that includes snippets of dialogue, moves into a visual analysis of a series of self-portraits, summarizes a study of communication strategies, and then recounts an interview with his grandmother. He ends by proposing that demonstrating love for a person with dementia is more important than using any particular strategy for communication.

■ 69–70

Specific details. You'll need to provide specific details to help readers understand and connect with your subject, especially if it's an abstract or unfamiliar one. Diehl notes how his grandfather is "slouched in his bed, absorbing the sounds of a televised college football game" and how the "scruff around his face rises, revealing a smile of recognition." Later, Diehl captures an anecdote from his grandmother to help bring her relationship with her husband to life: "'I always made sure he was smiling. Anything that I knew was going to please him was the object of my time with him. I would give him a hot chocolate and give him a little hug, and then when I put a marshmallow in that hot chocolate, he would smile!'" In addition to details and anecdotes, exploratory essays may include researched information, as Diehl's does when it mentions a study of communication strategies among couples affected by Alzheimer's. In some cases, photographs or other visuals—like the self-portraits Diehl analyzes—help provide examples as well as set a certain tone for an exploration.

A questioning, speculative tone. In an exploratory essay, you are working toward answers, not providing them neatly organized and ready for consumption. So your tone is usually tentative and open, demonstrating a willingness to entertain, accept, and reject various ideas as your essay progresses from beginning to end. Often this tone is achieved by asking questions, like Diehl does: "Knowing that my other grandparents could be at risk of dementia as well, I wondered: How could I communicate more effectively with family members who may exhibit memory loss in the future?" "This study suggests the viability of some verbal techniques over others, but I was still left with a burning question: Doesn't communication effectiveness ultimately depend on what personally works for the individual with Alzheimer's?"

A BRIEF GUIDE TO WRITING EXPLORATIONS

Deciding on a Topic

Choose a subject you want or need to explore. Write a list of things that you think about, wonder about, find puzzling or annoying. They may be big things—life, relationships—or little things—quirks of certain people's behavior, curious objects, everyday events. Try clustering one or more of those things, or begin by freewriting to see what comes to mind as you write. If you need to define and solve a problem, try googling the topic to see what others have said about it and how you might think about it—and to see what potential solutions have already been proposed.

Considering the Rhetorical Situation

59–60 ■	**PURPOSE**	What's your goal in writing this essay? To explore a topic that interests you? To work through an issue or problem that concerns you? To provoke readers to think about something? What aspects of your subject do you want to ponder and reflect on?
61–64 ■	**AUDIENCE**	Who is the audience? How familiar are they with your subject? How will you introduce it in a way that will interest them? Even if your primary audience is yourself, how will you help readers understand your thinking?

☀ academic literacies	● fields	● research
■ rhetorical situations	⦂ processes	● media/design
▲ genres	◆ strategies	

72–74

STANCE   What is your attitude toward the topic you plan to
explore—questioning? playful? critical? curious? something else?

75–77

MEDIA/DESIGN Will your essay be a print document? an oral presentation? Will it be posted on a website or a blog? Would it
help to include any visuals or video or audio files?

Generating Ideas and Text

Explore your subject in detail.   Exploratory essays often include descriptive details. Diehl, for example, describes Utermohlen's self-portraits as he
speculates about their meaning and effect: "This surrealism becomes more
apparent in the next portrait, where the eyes are positioned far too low, the
forehead and ear are enlarged, and the frown of the artist becomes more
solemn." Diehl also compares and contrasts the portraits, pointing out the
changes between the pre-diagnosis portrait and those that follow. You may
also make your point by defining, narrating, even classifying. Virtually any
organizing pattern will help you explore your subject.

Back away.   Ask yourself why your subject matters: Why is it important
or intriguing or significant? You may try listing or outlining possibilities,
or you may want to start drafting to see where the first round of writing
takes your thinking. Your goal is to think onscreen (or on paper) about your
subject, to play with its possibilities.

Think about how to keep readers with you.   Explorations may seem
loose or unstructured, but they must be carefully crafted so that readers
can follow your train of thought. It's a good idea to sketch out a rough
thesis to help focus your thoughts. You might not include the thesis in the
essay itself, but every part of the essay should in some way relate to it. If
Diehl's essay has a thesis, it's this: "One does not need to be a master of
psychological techniques in order to properly approach communication
with a person affected by dementia. What's needed is a repeated effort to
be present with the individual, expressing joy over what *they* say instead
of sweating over anything *we* could ever say."

Ways of Organizing an Exploratory Essay

Exploratory essays may be organized in many ways because they mimic the way we think, associating one idea with another in ways that make sense but do not necessarily form a "logical" progression. In general, you might consider organizing an exploration using this overall strategy:

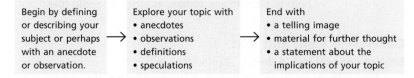

| Begin by defining or describing your subject or perhaps with an anecdote or observation. | Explore your topic with • anecdotes • observations • definitions • speculations | End with • a telling image • material for further thought • a statement about the implications of your topic |

Another way to organize this type of essay is as a series of brief anecdotes and ideas that together create an overall impression:

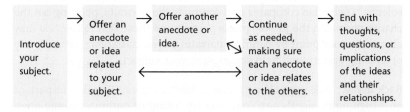

| Introduce your subject. | Offer an anecdote or idea related to your subject. | Offer another anecdote or idea. | Continue as needed, making sure each anecdote or idea relates to the others. | End with thoughts, questions, or implications of the ideas and their relationships. |

If you're pondering solutions to a problem, you might organize your essay like this:

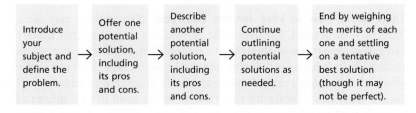

| Introduce your subject and define the problem. | Offer one potential solution, including its pros and cons. | Describe another potential solution, including its pros and cons. | Continue outlining potential solutions as needed. | End by weighing the merits of each one and settling on a tentative best solution (though it may not be perfect). |

Taking Stock of Your Work

Take stock of what you've written by considering these questions:

- How did you decide on your topic?

- Why did you organize your piece as you did?

- Describe your revision process for this piece. What worked, and what didn't work? Did you learn anything new—about your topic, about yourself, about something else—as you revised your piece?

- Did you use visual elements (photographs, diagrams, drawings), audio elements, or links? If so, what did they add? If not, what might you have used?

- How did curiosity play a role in the writing of your exploration? Can you point to a specific part of your text that illustrates your curiosity about your topic?

- What have you learned about your writing ability from writing this piece? What do you need to work on in the future?

- What was most rewarding about your work on this piece?

If you need more help

See Chapter 30 for guidelines on **DRAFTING**, Chapter 31 on **ASSESSING YOUR OWN WRITING**, Chapter 32 on **GETTING RESPONSE AND REVISING**, and Chapter 33 on **EDITING AND PROOFREADING**.

364–66
367–71
372–79
380–84

22 Remixes

Just as musicians alter existing tracks to create new ones, writers sometimes "remix" or refashion their writing for new contexts. A mechanical engineer uses elements of her technical report about a new engine part to write instructions for the machinists who assemble the part. A historian turns his scholarly article on slavery and disability into a podcast episode for the general public. A sociology student transforms her essay on food insecurity into an infographic to persuade her college administration to start a food pantry. In each case, the writer modifies all or part of their earlier work for a new purpose, audience, genre, stance, or medium.

In college courses across the curriculum, you might be asked to do the same—for example, by writing a researched report for a class assignment and then sharing your work through a multimedia presentation for your classmates or others. For a capstone project in your major, you might be asked to return to some earlier writing you've done, reimagining or extending it for a new purpose.

This chapter offers suggestions for creating remixes—texts that grow out of and "play on" earlier texts you've composed. Let's start by looking at an example: a profile originally published in a university alumni magazine that gets remixed into two different videos for the university's website.

Original Text: A Print Profile

"Rare Earth," a profile that inspired two remixes, traces Dr. Rattan Lal's path from refugee to premier soil scientist. Following is an excerpt from the piece, which appeared in the *Ohio State Alumni Magazine*. The author, Todd Jones, is a senior writer for the magazine.

* academic literacies   ● fields   ● research
■ rhetorical situations   ∴ processes   ● media/design
▲ genres   ◆ strategies

TODD JONES
Rare Earth

The thin man in the Ohio State ballcap hunches down near his home garden, in the backyard with the two buckeye trees. He's holding a clump of dirt. "No, no. Not dirt," he says. "This is soil. Soil is not the same as dirt. Soil is a living entity. That's the part we must understand."

His hands are cupped, as if holding a baby bird. He gazes in admiration, points to roots and a worm. He tells us a tablespoon of soil contains billions of microorganisms. "Soil is one. Indivisible. Interconnected," he says. "Soil is the basis of all terrestrial life. Every living thing on the planet depends on it, and yet this material is underappreciated and unrecognized."

His face is wrinkled and weathered, a testament to years spent researching in the fields, forging wisdom about our place in the world. "We belong to nature. We belong to soil," he says. "Therefore, we have a duty and obligation to soil." He has researched soil for five decades on five continents, traveling to 106 countries to spread a message: that we must "make an investment to restore [soil]. You always want to leave something behind," the concept underlying regenerative agriculture. But more work must be done to spread understanding about the critical role of soil in the health of the planet. "That challenge," he says, "is my motivator, my driving force."

Lal surveys an Ohio cornfield.

Thomson Reuters has long listed Dr. Rattan Lal, Ohio State Distinguished University Professor of Soil Science, among the top 1 percent of the most frequently cited agricultural researchers in the world. In 2007, Lal was recognized for his contributions to the Intergovernmental Panel on Climate Change, which shared the 2007 Nobel Peace Prize with former U.S. vice president Al Gore. In 2019, Lal was awarded the Japan Prize, one of the most prestigious honors in science and technology. That same year, he won the Alumni Medalist Award, the highest honor bestowed by The Ohio State University Alumni Association. Such status suggests that Lal deserves a gilded lair, but he sits behind an ordinary metal desk in a painted cinder-block room measuring 9 feet by 12 feet. "My office is fine," Lal says. "The office is in proportion to your contributions."

His modesty also masks a fierce inner drive. Three heart attacks   5
have not slowed him, and praise from international peers has not inflated him. He has more speeches to give, papers to write, conference calls to join, classes to teach, research to conduct, and students to mentor. "This is who he is," says Sukhvarsha Sharma, his wife of 48 years. "He has very high expectations of himself. He wants to make a difference in the environment, and through that, make a difference in peoples' lives."

There are times when Lal looks like a symphony conductor as he speaks, his voice accompanied by slowly moving hands, as if words about soil were notes in a musical sonnet. In those moments, your eyes might fall on an ancient symbol in faded blue ink on the back of Lal's right hand. He thinks he was about 8 years old when a stranger on a bicycle came to his school in India offering cheap tattoos. The boy couldn't resist. Nearly seven decades later, he regrets his choice. "I would not get it done now," Lal says. "But a small decision about a tattoo, that's very little in importance. Decisions about soil are very, very important. Those are decisions that influence other people's lives and have very long-lasting impact."

The impact is intensifying because the world's population is projected to increase nearly 50 percent in the next 80 years—an ominous forecast that Lal tells Ohio State students on a summer afternoon while lecturing in an Introduction to Soil Science class. Humanity, Lal warns, is facing a dire necessity to advance food security by protecting finite, fragile soil resources. "Agriculture and soil are, can be, and must be a solution," he says, clasping and shaking his hands for emphasis.

✳ academic literacies	⬢ fields	⬤ research
◼ rhetorical situations	⁘ processes	⬭ media/design
▲ genres	◆ strategies	

In that moment, you could see Lal's tattoo, an ink version of the symbol for om, considered the most sacred of mantras in his Hindu religion. Through the word's three distinct sounds—"a-u-m"—the speaker is meant to understand the essence of the universe: Everything is connected. Om is the sound of Lal's life.

"There's just kind of an equanimity, a sense of mental peace, about him," says Ellen Maas, one of Lal's current doctoral students. "His manner is not one that is focused on himself. He just cares so deeply about humanity and the planet. He finds an inner strength in caring about things bigger than himself."

Lal's family experience shaped his worldview. The youngest of three, 10 he was raised by his father after his mother died of an illness when Lal was 3 months old. When India was partitioned to form Pakistan in 1947, his family fled as refugees to the Indian village of Rajaund, about 120 miles northwest of New Delhi. They left a 9-acre farm and settled on one totaling only 1.5 acres, a change that marked Lal with a different tattoo, just as permanent but invisible.

Lal holds his undergraduate diploma from Punjab Agricultural University.

"It taught me that the land is very precious," Lal says. "You cannot let it waste. Your life depends on it. Our land was so small, but it was not a unique situation. There are right now in the world about 600 million farm families that have less than 2 acres. In a way, what I do and what I think relates back to those people and my experience."

Lal helped grow rice, wheat, cotton, and sugarcane on his family farm. But unlike his siblings, he also was sent to school by his father. The child felt chosen, obligated to make good on a privileged opportunity. In 1959, his diligence and excellent grades met

Ohio State in serendipity: he enrolled at the Government Agricultural College and Research Institute (which became Punjab Agricultural University his senior year). Ohio State had helped establish the institute only four years earlier. "One of the professors, Dr. [Dev Raj] Bhumbla, had just returned with a PhD from Ohio State, and he started teaching a soil class," Lal says. "I was in that class. My best subject was botany, but he told me to go into soil science. In fact, he recommended my name to faculty at Ohio State to be a student there."

In 1965, Lal boarded a plane for the first time and traveled alone 7,300 miles to pursue his doctorate. He brought along an insatiable hunger to succeed. At Punjab Agricultural University, he had run 4 miles— yes, run them—to school from home every day, studied by the light of a kerosene lamp, sometimes held up by his grandmother. He found an agricultural book in the library so essential that he spent two months hand-copying it to have his own edition. "Nothing can be achieved without the strongest possible desire to achieve it," Lal says.

His desire and degree mixed to fuel a career trek around the globe. Ohio State connections landed him research jobs, first in Sydney, Australia, for a year, and then in Nigeria, where the Rockefeller Foundation asked him to set up a soil science laboratory at the International Institute of Tropical Agriculture. Lal and his wife—only a year into their arranged marriage—went in spite of a bloody civil war. They stayed 18 years, even as three Nigerian governments were toppled by coups. "Once, I was at the house of a general," Lal says. "He had invited me to come talk about suggestions to control soil erosion. Two days later, he was hanged and his family shot. People have said if I was there when they came, I would not be here today."

One moment can make a difference. So can one person. This is 15 why he accepts invitations to speak about soil, whether the audience is filled with heads of power or young burgeoning minds. "The students are ambassadors of Ohio State," Lal says. "They represent us. They carry on the work that we do."

There are twenty-two students in this day's class. Lal speaks to them without notes, standing next to a podium, hand in pocket. His tone is

✹ academic literacies   ⬤ fields   ⬤ research
◼ rhetorical situations   ⦂ processes   ⬤ media/design
▲ genres   ◆ strategies

measured, but his message linking soil management to the nourishment of humankind is urgent. "The story has to be told in a language that farmers and policymakers understand and can relate to. That's critical," Lal says. "That's going to take education. We have to change opinions in a humble way. That falls on your generation."

Remix 1: A Video Profile

Eventually, the writer and photographer of "Rare Earth" collaborated with others to remix the article into a video profile. The remix uses recorded footage to showcase Dr. Lal in action as he and his students assess the results of no-till farming. Below are a few frames from the video; you can view the complete video at digital.wwnorton.com/fieldguide6.

(gentle music)

and what practices can be shown are not sustainable

And we're gonna quantify the total fresh weight

If we can do no-till and we can have better yields

Remix 2: An Explainer Video

The original profile piece was remixed into yet another video, this time a motion-graphics video that explains the science behind regenerative agriculture. Below are some frames from the full video, available at digital.wwnorton.com/fieldguide6.

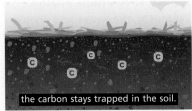

All three texts remix parts of the others, but each has a different purpose, audience, and medium/design. The print article is designed for magazine subscribers and aims to profile Dr. Lal's personal and professional achievements as an alumnus of the university. The video profile is produced for the web and provides a firsthand look at Dr. Lal's work in agriculture, while the explainer video helps viewers understand a crucial concept in Dr. Lal's research. Together the remixes offer a fuller picture of the scientist and his contributions to his field.

Key Features / Remixes

A connection to the original subject. A remix always hearkens back to the original subject in some way. Sometimes the connection is obvious—Dr. Lal takes center stage in both the video profile and the print profile, though each profile shares a different aspect of his story. Other times, just a fragment of the original subject inspires the remix. For example, the science behind Dr. Lal's work is mentioned only briefly in the print article but becomes the sole focus of the explainer video.

A modification of the earlier work. By definition, a remix involves change. Something in the writing situation changes—like the writer's purpose or audience—and that change requires other modifications as well. The writer might need to work within a new medium, or adopt a different stance, or write in a new genre to get their message across most effectively. When the creators of the "Rare Earth" article needed to explain the complex concept of regenerative agriculture, they determined that a visual medium would better suit their purpose than a print-based one.

Attention to genre and media / design expectations. Often remixes require a change in genre or a change in medium (or both), and effective remixes meet audience expectations for the new genre or medium. The profile video of Dr. Lal, for example, uses background music, on-screen titles, and clips of recorded footage—all of which are typical features of a profile (genre) delivered through a video (medium).

SOME TYPICAL WAYS OF REMIXING

Your writing situation—especially your purpose and audience—will determine the type of remix you might create. Following, though, are some common ways of remixing texts for new genres or media.

Memoirs. With their vivid details and scenes, print memoirs lend themselves to visual remixes as photo montages, graphic memoirs, comic strips, and digital stories. You might also repurpose parts of a memoir into a new genre—for example, by sharing an anecdote to support a point in an argument.

Profiles.   A print profile that showcases an interesting person, place, or event might get remixed into a mini documentary or a podcast to bring the subject to life even more fully for an audience. You could also incorporate a profile into another genre—like a report—to make an abstract concept more concrete.

Arguments.   With their focus on making and supporting claims, arguments are often remixed as newspaper op-eds, public service announcements (PSAs) for radio or television, or print or online petitions. With instructor permission, you might remix an argument you've written on gun control for your first-year writing class into a proposal for your public health class.

Proposals.   A written proposal might morph into a slide show for a presentation and then into a fund-raising letter to secure financial support for a proposed project. In your college classes, you might repurpose parts of a topic proposal for a report, an argument, or some other genre you're asked to write—as long as your instructors approve.

Reports.   Research findings from reports often get remixed into infographics, poster presentations, timelines, and listicles (articles presented in list form). In college courses, you might remix a report you've written into an oral presentation to your class.

In creating a remix as part of your college coursework, be sure to follow your school's academic integrity policies. Most policies forbid students from reusing or resubmitting their previous work without instructor permission. If you plan to remix something you've created for one class into a project for another class, get approval from *both* instructors beforehand.

A BRIEF GUIDE TO CREATING REMIXES

Determining What Will Change in Your Remix

When you compose a remix, you're not starting from scratch—you already have a general topic and a text to work from. Still, you need to determine how your remix will be different from your earlier work.

A good place to start is to think about what has changed in your writing situation. Has your instructor asked you to prepare a *Prezi* version of an academic essay you've written for your course? If so, the media/design elements of your rhetorical situation have changed. Or maybe you've written a report for a class assignment, and now you want to inspire a particular group of people to take action on your topic. In this case, your purpose and audience have changed. Usually, a change in one element of the rhetorical situation affects the others, so it's important to carefully consider all those elements as you plan your remix.

Considering the Rhetorical Situation

PURPOSE   Why are you creating the remix? To share the same message from your earlier work through a different genre or medium? To make a new point about your topic? To explain a concept from your earlier work? To reach a different audience? To reach the same audience in a new way? To persuade or inform or entertain?   ■ 59–60

AUDIENCE   Who will read, view, or listen to your remix? Are they the same audience as before? a different audience? Why should they care about your message? What will they already know? How can you engage their interest?   ■ 61–64

GENRE   Will you work within a new genre or the same one as earlier? Will you mix multiple genres? Which genres would work best for your purpose and audience? What expectations will your audience have for genre?   ■ 65–71

72–74 ■ **STANCE** Will your stance in the remix be the same as or different from your earlier stance? What is your relationship with your audience? Are you an equal, a student, an interested or concerned outsider, something else? What tone is appropriate—objective, impassioned, respectful, informal, something else?

75–77 ■ **MEDIA / DESIGN** Will you work within a new medium or the same one as earlier? What medium would be most appropriate for your audience and purpose? Will you use multiple media, combining sounds, visuals, words, movement? What expectations will your audience have for design and format? What steps can you take to make your
666–68 ● composition **ACCESSIBLE** to diverse audiences?

Generating Ideas and Text

Return to your earlier work. Remember, you're not starting from a blank slate. You can go back to your earlier work to decide what to keep, delete, change, or add as you create your remix. Are there key ideas you want to be sure to include in your remix? Will you need to condense some information from your earlier work? explore a new angle on your topic? reframe an argument? conduct more research? find or create images or
333–36 ⁘ sounds? Try **FREEWRITING**, **LISTING**, or **CLUSTERING** to figure out what you can use from your earlier work and what you'll need to reimagine or create anew.

If you're remixing for a new genre, examine sample texts in your chosen genre. Whether you're creating a brochure, a business plan, an infographic, or something else, find samples that you think are effective. Then study the genre features: What do you notice about the use of headings,
75–77 ■ bullets, photos, and other **DESIGN** elements? What do you notice about
73–74 the formality of the language, the lengths of sentences and paragraphs,
674–80 ● the **TONE**? How is source information documented? How are **VISUALS** or sounds acknowledged or cited? Consider how you'll make use of the genre features in your own remixed composition.

---

* academic literacies ⬡ fields ● research
■ rhetorical situations ⁘ processes ● media/design
▲ genres ◆ strategies

If you're remixing for a new medium, consider your capabilities and your options. Maybe you want to create a website, a video, a podcast, or some other digital text, but you don't have access to the tools you need or you're not skilled in using them. Your school might have a multimedia support center or other resources to help you get started. Another option: with your instructor's permission, you could perhaps create a "pre-production" document instead of a full-fledged multimedia piece. For example, you might make a mock-up of a website in a *Microsoft Word* document. Or you might write a script for a podcast or create a detailed **STORYBOARD** for a video.

338–39

Remember, too, that online tools and templates can make composing with sound and visuals easier. Some tools you might consider using (with a free trial) include:

For brochures, advertisements, posters
Adobe Spark, Canva

For infographics
Venngage, Piktochart, Canva

For interactive line charts
Knight Lab Storyline

For interactive timelines
Tiki Toki, Knight Lab Timeline

For photo montages
Fotor

For picture books
Storybird, Storyjumper

For podcasts
Podbean

For slide presentations
Prezi, Canva

For comics, storyboards, graphic novels
Pixton

For videos
Animoto, Powtoon

For virtual reality stories
Knight Lab Scene

For websites
Adobe Spark, Google Sites, Weebly, Wix

For free music and sound effects
Free Music Archive, Orange Free Sounds

For free images
Pexels, Pixabay

Ways of Organizing a Remix

Your organizational strategy will depend on your genre and medium, and you may be able to consult the relevant genre chapter as a guide. If appropriate, you might also consider creating a simple **STORYBOARD** to plan out a sequence of text and images for your remix.

338–39

Taking Stock of Your Work

Take stock of what you've created by considering these questions:

- What elements of your rhetorical situation changed as you moved from your original work to your remix—your purpose? audience? genre? stance? medium? In what specific ways does your remixed composition respond to those changes?

- What part of the composing process was most enjoyable as you worked on your remix? Why?

- What technological, logistical, design, or other challenges did you face in creating your remix, and how did you address them?

- What previous composing experiences (print-based and multimedia ones), if any, did you draw on in creating your remix? Did those experiences help you or hinder you?

- What resources did you use to complete your remix? How did those resources help you, and how might you use them in future composing situations?

- What new things did you learn about your topic in the process of remixing your earlier work?

- What new things did you learn about composing? about genres, media, and other elements of rhetorical situations?

- What are you most proud of in this piece?

If you need more help

659–63
664–72
673–83
684–93
391–401

See Chapter 55 for guidelines on **CHOOSING MEDIA**, Chapter 56 on **DESIGNING TEXT**, Chapter 57 on **USING VISUALS**, **INCORPORATING SOUND**, and Chapter 58 on **WRITING AND LEARNING ONLINE**. If you're required to write a formal **REFLECTION** to accompany your remix, see Chapter 35.

☀ academic literacies   ● fields   ● research

■ rhetorical situations   ⁖ processes   ● media/design

▲ genres   ◆ strategies

Part 4
Fields

When we study at a college or university, we take courses in many academic fields of study, or disciplines, in the humanities, social sciences, the sciences, and various career-oriented fields. Each field of study has its own methods of doing research and communicating, requiring us to learn how to **READ** and **WRITE** in the ways appropriate to that field. The chapters that follow offer advice on how to adapt your reading and writing to the demands of various fields of study.

Fields

23 Fields of Study   295

24 Reading across Fields of Study   298

25 Writing in Academic Fields of Study   309

23 Fields of Study

Most colleges and universities are organized around fields of study, often referred to as *disciplines*, that share ways of seeing the universe, doing research, and presenting information—each through a different lens. For example, historians and economists differ in the ways they examine human behavior; biologists and physicists differ in the ways they study the natural world. The various majors that colleges and universities offer invite you to learn to see the world in their distinctive ways and join professions that use distinctive skills. Marketing majors, for example, learn ways of influencing human behavior, while education majors learn ways of teaching students and music majors learn the intricacies of playing an instrument or singing. As you immerse yourself in a major, you come to see the world with a particular perspective.

Academic Fields and General Education

Your general education courses have a different goal: to prepare you for the demands of living in a complex and changing world—a world in which you'll need to use your ability to understand a wide range of facts, theories, and concepts to interact with a wide variety of people, work in various jobs, and make important decisions. In other words, these courses are designed to teach you how to learn and think. They are also helpful if you're not sure what you'd like to major in, because you can sample courses in various disciplines to help you decide. In your first couple of years, you will likely take general education courses in the following subject areas:

- the humanities, which include the arts, communications, history, literature, music, philosophy, and religion
- the social sciences, which may include anthropology, economics, political science, geography, psychology, and sociology

- the sciences, which usually include such disciplines as astronomy, biology, chemistry, geology, mathematics, and physics

It's important to note that these lists are far from comprehensive; schools differ in the courses and majors they offer, so some schools may offer courses in fields that aren't on any of these lists—and some of these courses might not be available at your school. You may also take courses in career-oriented fields such as education, business, engineering, and nursing.

Studying, Reading, and Writing in Academic Fields

Each field focuses on the study of particular subjects and issues. In *psychology*, you study the human mind—what it is and why we behave as we do. In *sociology*, you study the way society shapes our actions. In *biology*, you study life itself, from bacteria and fungi to organisms interacting with their environment. In *history*, you study the past to understand the present. In *nursing*, you study best ways of providing patient care within the health-care system. In *engineering*, you learn how to solve technical problems and design engineering systems.

Each field also examines the world through a distinctive lens, using its own methods to study and analyze those subjects. For example, scientists test hypotheses with experiments designed to prove or disprove their accuracy; sociologists study groups by using statistical evidence; and historians examine diaries, speeches, or photographs from the past. In addition, disciplines develop technical terms and ways of using language that allow scholars to understand one another—but that can be hard to understand. For example, consider the word "significant." When people say that something is *significant* in day-to-day conversation, they usually mean that it's important, a big deal; in statistics, though, a *significant* result is one that is probably true—but it may or may not be important.

Disciplines also present information using methods standard in that discipline. In *business* courses, you're likely to read case studies of specific companies and write business cases and other communications. In *education* courses, you'll read and write lesson plans; in *science* courses, you'll read and write laboratory reports; in *English* courses, you'll read fiction, poetry, and plays and write literary analyses. In each, you'll present information in ways used in conversations among scholars in the discipline. And that means that you may need to adapt your reading and writing to the genres, concepts, and methods of the various academic fields you encounter.

THINKING ABOUT READING AND WRITING IN THE FIELDS

- What reading assignments do you have in your other courses?
- What makes them easy or hard to read? What helps you read them?
- Do you enjoy reading some genres or subjects more than others? Why?
- What writing assignments do you have in your other courses?
- Do you alter or adjust your writing processes in different courses? Why or why not?
- What makes writing in some courses hard or easy?
- Do you enjoy writing in certain genres or on certain topics? Why?

24 Reading across Fields of Study

We read shopping lists differently from graphic novels and operating instructions differently from poems. For that matter, we read novels and poems differently—and go about reading textbooks differently still. Just as we write using various processes—generating ideas and text, drafting, getting responses and revising, editing, and proofreading—we vary our reading processes from task to task. We will likely read a mathematics textbook differently from a case study in nursing, and read a speech by Abraham Lincoln in a history course differently from the way we'd read it in a rhetoric course. This chapter offers advice on how to engage with texts in a variety of fields.

Considering the Rhetorical Situation

A good way to approach reading in academic fields is to treat reading as a process that you adapt to the demands of each new situation. Instead of diving in and focusing your reading on the details of the content, it's often useful to take some time to consider the text's purpose, your purpose, the audience, the author, the author's stance, the genre, and the medium and design. This information can help you decide how to get the most out of the text.

59–60

- *The text's* **PURPOSE**. When was the text written, and why? Is it a textbook? a classic work that lays out concepts that have become fundamental to the field? a work proposing a new way of looking at an issue?

- *Your purpose as a reader.* Why are you reading this text? To study for a test? To find sources for a research project? To learn about something on your own?

✹ academic literacies ● fields ● research
■ rhetorical situations ⁝ processes ● media/design
▲ genres ◆ strategies

- *The* **AUDIENCE**. For whom was the text written? Students like you? Scholars in the field? Interested nonspecialists? Readers who lived at some point in the past or in a particular location? What facts and concepts does the text assume its readers already know and understand?

- *The author.* Who wrote what you are reading? Does knowing the author's identity matter? Is the author reliable and credible? For example, is the author a respected scholar? Is the author known for a particular point of view?

- *The author's* **STANCE**. What is the author's stance toward the subject? toward the reader? Approving? Hostile? Critical? Passionate? What elements of the text reveal the author's stance?

- *The* **GENRE**. What is the text's genre? How was it meant to be read? Is that how you're reading it? What are the genre's key features? Knowing the key features of the genre can help you understand the text's content as you read and predict the text's organization.

- *The* **MEDIUM** *and* **DESIGN**. The medium and design of a text affect how you must read it. You may need to read a textbook differently from an article found on the internet, for example. An online textbook may require different commenting and note-taking strategies from a print text. Understanding the limitations and the advantages of a particular genre, medium, and design will help you get the most out of your reading.

61–64

72–74

65–71

75–77

Advice for Reading across Fields of Study

Becoming knowledgeable in a field of study requires learning its specialized ways of thinking, writing, and reading, including the terminology specific to the field and the kinds of texts the field is likely to produce and study. However, there is some general advice that can help you as you begin to read the kinds of texts you're likely to encounter in college.

Pay attention to vocabulary. All disciplines require that you learn their vocabulary, which includes not only concepts and facts but also the names of important figures in the field and what they represent. Scholars typically write for other scholars in the same field, so they may assume that readers understand these terms and references and refer to them without explanation—and even "popular" writing often makes the same assumption. You'll find that much of the work in all your courses consists of learning terms and concepts. So it's important to take good notes in lectures, writing down terms your instructor emphasizes as they are defined, or, if they aren't, writing them down to look up later. Your textbooks introduce and define key terms and often include a glossary in the back that provides definitions.

In addition, be aware that disciplinary vocabularies use different kinds of words. In the sciences, the language is likely very technical, with many terms based on Greek and Latin roots (for example, the Greek prefix *gastr-* forms "gastropod" [snail], "gastric" [stomach], and "gastroscopy" [examination of the abdomen and stomach]). In the humanities, the vocabulary often alludes to complex concepts. Consider, for example, these sentences from *The Swerve*, a book by literary historian Stephen Greenblatt:

> The household, the kinship network, the guild, the corporation—these were the building blocks of personhood. Independence and self-reliance had no cultural purchase.

Almost every term, from "household" to "guild" to "personhood" to "cultural purchase," carries a wealth of information that must be understood. While understanding the scientific terms requires a good dictionary, these particular terms require an encyclopedia—or the knowledge gained by much reading.

Consider the author—or not. In some disciplines, it's important to know who wrote a text, while in others the identity or **STANCE** of the author is considered irrelevant. Historians, for example, need to know who the author of a text is, and the perspective that author brings to the text is central to reading history. Literary scholars may try not to consider the author at all, focusing solely on a close reading of the text itself. Scientists may consider the author's identity or the school or lab where the author works to decide whether or not to read a text. Mathematicians resolutely ignore the author, focusing solely on the information in the text itself. So to make sense of a text in a discipline, you need to find out how that discipline sees the role of the author.

72–74 ■

✳ academic literacies	⬤ fields	⬤ research
■ rhetorical situations	⦂ processes	⬤ media/design
▲ genres	◆ strategies	

Identify key ideas and make comparisons.   Whatever the discipline, look for the main ideas its texts present. Rather than highlight or underline them, write out the key ideas in your own words. As you read texts on the same subject, you may want to develop a matrix to help you **COMPARE AND CONTRAST** as well as **SYNTHESIZE** the main ideas. The following chart, adapted from one developed by two librarians, presents the main ideas in two sources and then synthesizes the two versions. This example synthesizes one main idea found in each of two articles on how social media affect political participation among youths and then, in the third column, synthesizes those ideas:

◆ 437–44
● 535–41

Source #1: Skorik, M. M. "Youth Engagement in Singapore"	**Source #2:** Ahmad, K. "Social Media and Youth Participatory Politics"	**Synthesis: Main Ideas**
Summary of 1st main idea: Singapore's government has consistently applied controls on traditional media outlets but has left social media outlets untouched and unregulated.	**Summary of 1st main idea:** Online participation in political campaigns and issues was almost five times greater than traditional participation. Researchers concluded that this "could provide the participant with anonymity, in turn less vulnerability to political vengeance."	**Synthesis of 1st main ideas:** Government control and censorship of mainstream media has caused protesters to look for alternative communication tools.
Summary of 2nd main idea:	**Summary of 2nd main idea:**	**Synthesis of 2nd main ideas:**
Summary of 3rd main idea:	**Summary of 3rd main idea:**	**Synthesis of 3rd main ideas:**

Adapted from Michelle Chiles and Emily Brown, "Literature Review." Bristol Community College, Fall River, MA, 2015. Unpublished *PowerPoint*.

More main ideas can be summarized and synthesized in the rows below; add as many as needed.

You might also get into the habit of skimming the list of works cited or references at the end of articles and books. As you do so, you'll begin to see who the most important people are in the discipline and what counts as evidence.

Build a map of the discipline. To make sense of a new idea, you need to have some way of fitting it into what you already know. Reading in an unfamiliar discipline can be hard because you likely won't have a sense of where the information in the text fits into the conversations of the discipline, its history, or your goals—what you'd like to know or do in this field. It's useful to visualize the discipline so that you can place readings into the appropriate context. Possible ways of organizing a discipline follow.

Draw a word map. Using your textbook and perhaps some online sources as guides, draw an overview of the field. Here's one for psychology:

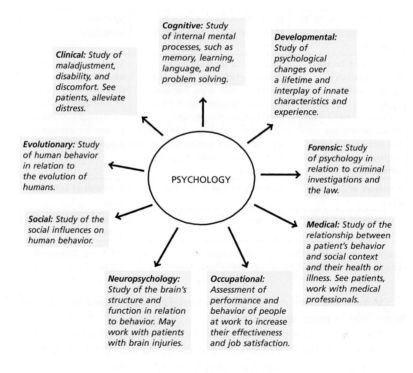

Cognitive: Study of internal mental processes, such as memory, learning, language, and problem solving.

Clinical: Study of maladjustment, disability, and discomfort. See patients, alleviate distress.

Developmental: Study of psychological changes over a lifetime and interplay of innate characteristics and experience.

Evolutionary: Study of human behavior in relation to the evolution of humans.

PSYCHOLOGY

Forensic: Study of psychology in relation to criminal investigations and the law.

Social: Study of the social influences on human behavior.

Medical: Study of the relationship between a patient's behavior and social context and their health or illness. See patients, work with medical professionals.

Neuropsychology: Study of the brain's structure and function in relation to behavior. May work with patients with brain injuries.

Occupational: Assessment of performance and behavior of people at work to increase their effectiveness and job satisfaction.

※ academic literacies ⬛ rhetorical situations ▲ genres ⬢ fields ⁚ processes ◆ strategies ● research ● media/design

Create a timeline. Sometimes it's helpful to understand how a discipline developed over time, how its research methods or emphases came to be, so you can place its texts and key developments within that history. Here, for example, is a timeline of the behaviorist approach in psychology:

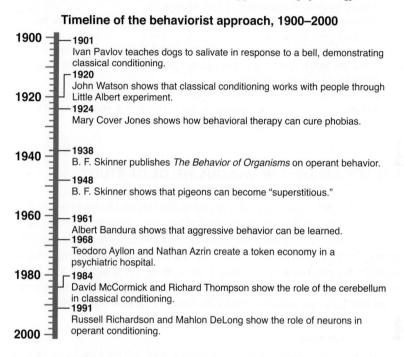

Timeline of the behaviorist approach, 1900–2000

1900
— **1901**
Ivan Pavlov teaches dogs to salivate in response to a bell, demonstrating classical conditioning.

— **1920**
John Watson shows that classical conditioning works with people through
1920 Little Albert experiment.

— **1924**
Mary Cover Jones shows how behavioral therapy can cure phobias.

— **1938**
1940 B. F. Skinner publishes *The Behavior of Organisms* on operant behavior.

— **1948**
B. F. Skinner shows that pigeons can become "superstitious."

1960
— **1961**
Albert Bandura shows that aggressive behavior can be learned.

— **1968**
Teodoro Ayllon and Nathan Azrin create a token economy in a psychiatric hospital.

1980
— **1984**
David McCormick and Richard Thompson show the role of the cerebellum in classical conditioning.

— **1991**
Russell Richardson and Mahlon DeLong show the role of neurons in
2000 operant conditioning.

Write a conversation among researchers. To better understand the similarities and differences among various schools of thought within a discipline, choose some of the most prominent proponents of each school and write a fictional conversation among them, outlining where they agree and disagree and where they published or disseminated their theories and findings. Here, for instance, is a snippet of a dialogue that might have taken place between developmental psychologist Jean Piaget and behavioral psychologist B. F. Skinner:

> **Piaget:** Children learn by adapting to conflicts between what they already know and challenges to that knowledge.
> **Skinner:** Bosh! We can't know what's in someone's mind; we have to focus on their behavior.
> **Piaget:** If a child sees something that doesn't match her preconceptions, she learns from it and through her behavior assimilates the new information into her thinking.
> **Skinner:** But if we reinforce a certain behavior by rewarding it, the child will do it more, and if we ignore it, the behavior will stop. It doesn't matter what, if anything, the child is thinking.

TIPS FOR READING IN VARIOUS FIELDS OF STUDY

Though groups of disciplines (the sciences, the arts and humanities, and so on) within each field share many similarities, each discipline has features unique to it. While you should expect to read difficult texts in any field several times, taking notes in your own words rather than highlighting or underlining, you need to be aware that reading, say, a biology text likely requires different reading techniques than a history text would. Here are some tips that can help you read effectively in various disciplines.

The Humanities

501–2

- Much of the scholarship in the humanities is based on texts of one sort or another—the Constitution, the Bible, Toni Morrison's novels, Mozart's piano concertos, Georgia O'Keeffe's paintings. When reading in the humanities, then, be aware of the differences between reading **PRIMARY SOURCES** like those and **SECONDARY SOURCES** (commentaries, analyses, evaluations, and interpretations of primary sources).

- When reading a primary source, you may need to ask questions like these: What kind of document is this? Who created it? When and

* academic literacies   ● fields   ● research
■ rhetorical situations   ⁝ processes   ● media/design
▲ genres   ◆ strategies

where was the source produced? Who was it intended for? What is its historical context? Why did the creator of the source create it? How was it received at the time of its creation? Has that reception changed?

- Read primary sources carefully and expect to reread them, perhaps several times. The way a text is organized, its sentence structure, its wording, and its imagery can all contribute to its overall message, and that's true of documents like the Declaration of Independence, the Torah, and Descartes's *Principles of Philosophy*.

- Similarly, plan to reread secondary sources. The argument of interpretations, analyses, or critical works requires close attention to their logic and use of evidence.

- Reading secondary sources requires that you examine them with a critical eye. The questions on pages 532–33 can help you understand the source and evaluate its accuracy, perspective or angle, and usefulness for your own work.

- Remember that in the humanities, "criticism" doesn't necessarily mean looking for flaws and errors. Rather, it's another term for analyzing or evaluating.

- Some key terms you need to know in order to read texts in the humanities include: "analogy," "allusion," "argument," "deductive reasoning," "inductive reasoning," "irony," "metaphor," "natural law," "natural rights," "political rights," "premise." If you don't understand the meaning of any of these terms, be sure to look up their definitions.

The Social Sciences

- As you read in the social sciences, you need to pay attention to the hypotheses, claims, reasons, and evidence presented in the texts. Are they persuasive? How do they compare or contrast with other arguments?

- Be sure you understand what a theory in the social sciences is: a way of organizing information to help enhance our understanding of behavior, events, phenomena, or issues. For example, in sociology, social exchange theory assumes that we behave according to our sense of whether we'll be rewarded or punished by those with whom we interact. Remember that a theory is not an unsupported opinion but rather a coherent, logical frame for understanding and describing.

209–13 ▲

- Many articles include a **LITERATURE REVIEW** that summarizes and critiques previous work on the topic. Since scholarly work always grows out of the work of others, authors need to connect their work to articles and books previously published on the topic. Many literature reviews discuss limitations and problems in previous studies, ultimately identifying missing elements or gaps in them (often identified with words like "but," "however," and "although"), leading to a rationale for why this new work is needed.

- The "Discussion" and "Conclusion" sections (which are sometimes combined into a single section) explain and interpret the results of a study in the context of the previous literature, note any limitations in the current study, and recommend future research to address those limitations. In other words, these sections discuss what the author thinks the study means. As you read, consider possible flaws or omissions in the author's thinking as well as in the research design; for example, the study is too broad, the research question is poorly defined, or the study doesn't address its significance—the "so what?" question. Your insights could lead you to a better understanding of the topic—or to a research project of your own.

- Some key terms you need to know in order to read texts in the social sciences include "adaptation," "aggregate," "alienation," "capital," "class system," "deviance," "interest," "markets," "motivation," "norm," "power," "schema," "supply and demand," and "value." If you don't understand the meaning of any of these terms, be sure to look up their definitions.

The Sciences

- Remember that scientific texts are not collections of established facts. They make claims and argue for them, using reasons and evidence to support those arguments. Scientific texts report the results of studies

✳ academic literacies   ● fields   ● research
■ rhetorical situations   ⁖ processes   ● media/design
▲ genres   ◆ strategies

and experiments and are written by scientists for an audience of other scientists in the same field. These texts are different from science writing, which is often a form of nonfiction sometimes written by scientists, journalists, or other writers and aimed at general audiences to inform about scientific topics.

- If you're examining potential sources for a research project, read selectively: use articles' **ABSTRACTS** to decide whether an article is likely to be useful for your project, and skim the text to find the information relating to your needs. Many scientific articles follow a structure nicknamed IMRaD (Introduction, Methods, Results, and Discussion), so you may need to read only the sections of the article that discuss what you're looking for.

▲ 196–200

- Pay attention to the sample size—the number of units of whatever is being studied that are included in the study (a larger sample size is generally better than a smaller one)—and error bars in graphs, which show the uncertainty in the findings of the study being described.

- Scientists often make their arguments through visuals as much as through words, so read images, graphs, and charts as carefully as you would the words in the text.

- For math problems or exercises, read the entire problem. Draw a picture or diagram to help visualize the problem. Read it again, identifying the most important information; be sure you understand what the problem is asking for. Then decide on a method for solving it, and come up with an answer. If you get stuck, think about how you'd deal with this information if it weren't a math problem. In that case, how would you go about solving it? Finally, reread the problem, and ask yourself if you've answered the question that was asked.

- Some key terms you need to know in order to read texts in the sciences include "skepticism," "data," "evidence/observation," "hypothesis," "variables," "biodiversity," "falsifiability," "theory," "evolution," "experimentation," "population," "qualitative," "quantitative," "repeatability," "empirical," "paradigm," "rational/agnostic," "cosmos." If you don't understand the meaning of any of these terms, be sure to look up their definitions.

A Note on Career-Focused Fields

In general, the advice here for reading texts in general-education courses holds for reading in every major, including career-oriented disciplines, such as business administration, nursing, teaching, and education. At the same time, it's worth paying attention to the ways of thinking and the priorities of every field as you read in them. Here are a few examples:

Both business administration and education focus on processes. In business, much reading discusses how businesspeople do things, manage workers, set up systems, follow best accounting practices, and the like; in education, your reading will likely focus on how to write lesson plans, how to present information appropriately, and so on. Drawing flowcharts and diagrams of processes can help you understand the steps involved and help you remember them.

Engineers solve problems. So when reading engineering texts, look for relationships among concepts and ideas, and think about ways those concepts can be used to solve complex problems. Pay close attention to charts, graphs, diagrams, and visuals, as they often pack considerable information into a single image. When reading a graph, for example, consider not only the data as presented but also relationships in the data, and look for inferences and predictions you can make from the data presented.

Engineering and nursing texts contain a lot of information, much of which you won't need right away, so don't try to master every fact or procedure. Instead, read the chapter introductions, summaries, and questions, and skim, looking for the answers to the questions. You might also review a study guide for the NCLEX nursing licensing exam or the NCEES PE exam in engineering and focus your reading on the subject areas the exam focuses on. In general, work to understand the concepts you need rather than trying to memorize an avalanche of information; look for patterns in the information and how concepts are interrelated.

✳ academic literacies ⬢ fields ⬤ research
◼ rhetorical situations ⁙ processes ⬤ media/design
▲ genres ◆ strategies

25 Writing in Academic Fields of Study

In a *literature* course, you're asked to write an analysis of a short story. In a *biology* course, you must complete several lab reports. In a *management* course, you may create a detailed business plan. In fact, just about every course you take in college will require writing, and to write successfully, you'll need to understand the rhetorical situation of your writing in the course—and in the larger field of study. That understanding will come in time, especially as you begin writing in your major. For now, this chapter offers help in determining the general expectations of writing done in various academic fields of study.

Considering the Rhetorical Situation

To write in academic fields, you need to use the same processes and strategies you're asked to use in your writing classes, including analyzing the **RHETORICAL SITUATION** in which you're writing. These questions can help:

■ 57

■ 59–60

PURPOSE   Why do people in this discipline write? To share scholarship and research findings? persuade? teach or provide guidance? show learning or mastery? track progress? propose solutions or plans of action? explore ideas or the self? earn grants or other rewards? something else?

61–64 **AUDIENCE**

To whom do people in this discipline write? To colleagues and other scholars? students? managers? employees? customers? clients? granting agencies? the public? others? What do they already know about the discipline and the topic? What specialized terms or concepts do they understand, and which ones need to be defined or explained? How much evidence or support is required, and what kinds (empirical data, research findings, logical analysis, personal testimony, something else) will they accept?

65–71 **GENRE**

What genres—reports, analyses, arguments, instructions, case studies, résumés, to name only a few—are typically used in this discipline? Are they organized in a certain way, and do they contain specific kinds of information? How much flexibility or room for innovation and creativity is allowed? What counts as evidence or support for assertions, and how is it cited (in citations in the text, in footnotes, in a works-cited page, informally in the text, or in some other way)?

72–74 **STANCE**

What attitude is considered appropriate in this discipline? Objective? Unemotional? Critical? Passionate? Should you write as a good student showing what you can do? an instructor of others? an advocate for a position? someone exploring an idea? something else? Does the discipline require a certain tone? formal or informal language? Can you include your personal perspective and write using "I"? Should you write only in the third person and use passive voice?

75–77 **MEDIA/DESIGN**

What media are typically used in this discipline? Print? Spoken? Electronic? A combination? Are certain design elements expected? to be avoided? Are visuals commonly used? What kinds—charts, graphs, photos, drawings, video or audio clips, or something else? In which genres? How much design freedom do you have?

✷ academic literacies   ● fields   ● research
■ rhetorical situations   ⁝ processes   ● media/design
▲ genres   ◆ strategies

WRITING IN ACADEMIC FIELDS OF STUDY

Generalizing about the requirements of writing in academic disciplines is tricky; what constitutes a discipline is sometimes unclear, and universities group academic fields together in various ways. For example, in some universities psychology is considered a science, while in others it's a social science. Economics is sometimes part of a college of business administration, sometimes in a college of arts and sciences. In addition, the writing required in, say, history differs from that required in English literature, though both are considered parts of the humanities.

Furthermore, certain genres of writing, like *case studies* and *research reports*, can share the same name but have very different organizational structures and content, depending on the discipline in which they're used. For example, research reports in psychology and the natural sciences include a review of relevant scholarly literature in the introduction; in reports in sociology and other social sciences, the literature review is a separate section. A case study in business identifies a problem or issue in an organization; provides background information; includes a section, "Alternatives," that discusses possible solutions to the problem and why they were rejected; outlines and argues for a proposed solution; and proposes specific strategies for achieving the proposed solution. A case study in nursing, on the other hand, includes three sections: patient status, which gives an overview of the patient's condition and treatment; the nurse's assessment of the patient's symptoms and their possible causes; and a plan for helping the patient improve. The guide below offers general advice on how to write in broad academic disciplines, but as the differences between two disciplines' expectations for case studies show, it's always a good idea to ask all your professors for guidance on writing for their particular fields.

WRITING IN THE ARTS AND HUMANITIES

The arts and humanities focus on human culture and the expressions of the human mind, and the purpose of writing in these fields is to explore and analyze aspects of the human experience across time and sometimes to create original works of literature, music, and art. The methods used in these disciplines include careful reading, critical analysis, historical research, interpretation, questioning, synthesis, and imitation. Courses in the arts and humanities typically include fine arts, architecture, music, dance, theater, film, photography, literature, history, classical and modern languages, linguistics, and philosophy.

Writing in the arts and humanities generally serves a broad audience that includes professors and scholars, other students, the general public, and oneself. Genres may include **ANNOTATED BIBLIOGRAPHIES**, **ANALYSES**, **ARGUMENTS**, essays, **EVALUATIONS**, **JOURNALS**, personal narratives, **REPORTS**, **PRESENTATIONS**, **PROPOSALS**, **REFLECTIONS**, and **LITERATURE REVIEWS**, as well as fiction and poetry. Support is often based on textual and observational evidence and personal insight, though in some fields empirical evidence and data are also valued. Writers in the arts and humanities tend to use modifiers (such as "arguably" or "perhaps") to acknowledge that their insights and conclusions are interpretive, not definitive. Documentation is usually done in **MLA** or Chicago style. Elements of style favored in writing in the arts and humanities may include the use of "I"; the active voice; an informal vocabulary, if appropriate; and vivid language.

201–9 ▲
104–39
164–95
214–22
343–44 ∴
140–63 ▲
694–705 ●
258–68 ▲
391–401 ∴
209–13 ▲

MLA 564–614 ●

A Sample of Writing in History: A Researched Essay

Identifies a problem in current understanding of a historical event.

The Pueblo Revolt of 1680 was one of the most significant yet misrepresented events in the history of American Indians. After three generations of being oppressed by Spanish rule, the Pueblo Indians throughout the southwest region of North America banded together,

Offers a narrative of a past event.

organizing a widespread rebellion in the blistering summer heat of 1680 and successfully liberating themselves from their oppressors by springtime. When examining the causes of the revolt, the lack of

Demonstrates familiarity with relevant sources.

authentic Pueblo voices within the written records challenges the validity of the available sources and makes one wonder if we will ever

---

✳ academic literacies   ● fields   ● research

■ rhetorical situations   ∴ processes   ● media/design

▲ genres   ◆ strategies

know what went on through the eyes of the Pueblo. Although in the traditional narrative, the Spaniards are regarded as missionaries sent by God to "save" the "barbaric" Pueblos, the event, if seen from the Pueblo perspective, can be understood as a violent retaliation by the Pueblo against the Spanish oppression. The Pueblo uprisings, from burning down churches to the violent deaths of Catholic friars, reveal spiritual abuse as the major cause of the revolt. Moreover, without texts written by the Pueblo, their architecture and spatial organization provide valuable insight into the causes of the revolt era and help to overcome the veneer of Spanish colonialism.

Offers a strong thesis.

Clear, engaging writing style.

Adapted from "Letting the Unspoken Speak: A Reexamination of the Pueblo Revolt of 1680," by E. McHugh, April 2015, Armstrong Undergraduate Journal of History 5, no. 1, digitalcommons.georgiasouthern.edu/aujh/vol5/iss1/5.

Typical Organization of Arts and Humanities Essays

Typical essays in the arts and humanities include these elements:

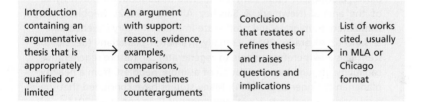

Introduction containing an argumentative thesis that is appropriately qualified or limited → An argument with support: reasons, evidence, examples, comparisons, and sometimes counterarguments → Conclusion that restates or refines thesis and raises questions and implications → List of works cited, usually in MLA or Chicago format

WRITING IN SCIENCE AND MATHEMATICS

The sciences include biology, chemistry, geology, earth sciences, and physics. Mathematics may include statistics and logic as well. All these fields aim to increase our knowledge of the physical and natural world and its phenomena through observation, experiment, logic, and computation.

196–200 ▲
209–13
140–63
164–95
694–705 ●
258–68 ▲
322 ⬢

APA 615–55 ●

Scientists and mathematicians typically write **ABSTRACTS**, **LITERATURE REVIEWS**, **REPORTS**, **ARGUMENTS**, poster **PRESENTATIONS**, **PROPOSALS**, and **LAB REPORTS** for audiences that may include other researchers, granting agencies, teachers, students, and the general public. Support in the sciences most often consists of repeatable empirical evidence; in mathematics, careful reasoning and the posing and solving of problems; in both, careful attention to the work of previous researchers. The writing in these fields focuses on the subject of the study, not the researcher, so most often the passive voice is used. Source material is paraphrased and summarized and cited in CSE or **APA** style.

A Sample of Scientific Writing: A Scientific Proposal in Biology

Careful reference to previous sentence.

Specialized disciplinary vocabulary.

Sources paraphrased and summarized.

Passive voice, third person.

Planarians, flatworms widely known for their incredible regenerative capabilities, are able to restore an entire organism from even a small fragment of tissue. This ability to regenerate is attributed solely to neoblasts, pluripotent adult stem cells located throughout the parenchyma of the animal (Newmark & Sanchez Alvarado, 2002). Neoblasts are stimulated to migrate and proliferate in times of injury (Guedelhoefer & Sanchez Alvarado, 2012). Lethally irradiated planarians (devoid of stem cells and therefore unable to regenerate) can restore regenerative capability through transplantation of a single neoblast from a healthy planarian (Wagner et al., 2011). Many studies have concluded that the population of neoblasts is not homogenous (Scimone et al., 2014), and there are different responses to different injury types. Wenemoser and Reddien (2012) observed a body-wide increase in mitotic activity, such as cell division and migration, with any injury.

Adapted from "Identifying Genes Involved in Suppression of Tumor Formation in the Planarian Schmidtea mediterranea," by E. Dorsten, 2015, Best Integrated Writing, 2, https://corescholar.libraries.wright.edu/biw/vol2/iss1/6/.

※ academic literacies   ● fields   ● research
■ rhetorical situations   ⁘ processes   ● media/design
▲ genres   ◆ strategies

Typical Organization of Research Reports in the Sciences

Typical reports in the sciences include elements that follow the IMRaD structure: Introduction, Methods, Results, and Discussion. They also include an abstract and a list of references.

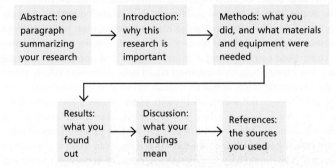

WRITING IN THE SOCIAL SCIENCES

Anthropology, archaeology, criminal justice, cultural studies, gender studies, geography, psychology, political science, and sociology are considered social sciences because they all explore human behavior and society using observation, experimentation, questionnaires, and interviews.

Social scientists typically write for fellow scholars, teachers, students, and the general public. They may write in several genres: **ABSTRACTS**, **ANNOTATED BIBLIOGRAPHIES**, **ANALYSES**, **ARGUMENTS**, case studies, ethnographies, **LITERATURE OR RESEARCH REVIEWS**, **REPORTS**, **SUMMARIES**, and **PRESENTATIONS**. Claims are typically supported by empirical evidence, fieldwork done in natural settings, observation, and interviews. Writers in these fields strive for an objective tone, often using the passive voice. Sources may be cited in **APA** or Chicago style.

▲ 196–200
201–9
104–39
164–95
209–13
140–63
✳ 33–35
● 694–705

● APA 615–55

A Sample of Writing in the Social Sciences: A Research Report

Traditional economic theory states that a minimum wage above the marginal product of labor will lead to increased unemployment. . . . This paper aims to look at a different but related question, namely, *Objective tone.* whether or not a minimum wage makes a population happier. Since people would arguably be happier if they could make enough money to cover their costs of living and less happy if the unemployment rate rose, the answer to such a question could help determine which effect *Research question.* is the dominant force and if an overall increase in the minimum wage is a good policy for society. Although scant research has been done *Specialized language.* on a minimum wage's effect on happiness, one could assume that research done on the size of the positive and negative effects of minimum wages could indicate whether or not it would leave a population *Literature review.* happier. Therefore, I begin by reviewing relevant economic theory and research on the effects of a minimum wage increase to provide background information and describe what related questions have been *Empirical method.* approached and answered. I then describe the data and method used to answer this question, followed by the interpretation of such results *Analysis and evaluation of results.* as well as the implications.

Adapted from "The Effect of Minimum Wages on Happiness," by J. Nizamoff, Beyond Politics 2014, pp. 85–95, beyondpolitics.nd.edu/wp-content/uploads /2015/03/2013-14-Full-Journal.pdf.

Typical Organization of a Research Report in the Social Sciences

Typical research reports in social science courses might include the following elements, though the order and names of the elements may differ from discipline to discipline. For example, in psychology, the literature review is part of the introduction, not a separate section as shown here.

※ academic literacies   ● fields   ● research
■ rhetorical situations   ⁝ processes   ● media/design
▲ genres   ◆ strategies

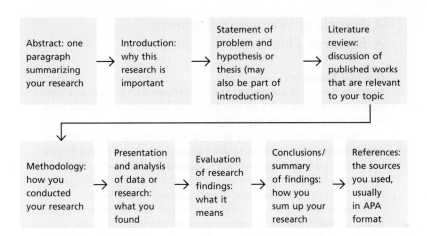

| Abstract: one paragraph summarizing your research | → | Introduction: why this research is important | → | Statement of problem and hypothesis or thesis (may also be part of introduction) | → | Literature review: discussion of published works that are relevant to your topic |

| Methodology: how you conducted your research | → | Presentation and analysis of data or research: what you found | → | Evaluation of research findings: what it means | → | Conclusions/ summary of findings: how you sum up your research | → | References: the sources you used, usually in APA format |

WRITING IN BUSINESS

The focus of the academic discipline of business is business-management principles and their application, and the purpose of writing in business is often to motivate readers to make a decision and then act on it. The primary methods used include problem solving, planning, and experiential learning, or learning by doing. Courses typically taught include finance, economics, human resources, marketing, operations management, and accounting.

The audiences for writing in business usually include colleagues, employees in other departments, supervisors, managers, clients, customers, and other stakeholders—often several at the same time as a text moves through an organization. Genres may include memos, emails, letters, case studies, executive summaries, **RÉSUMÉS**, business plans, **REPORTS**, and **ANALYSES**. Support usually takes the form of facts and figures, examples, narratives, and expert testimony, and documentation is usually done in **APA** or Chicago style. Elements of style favored in business writing include these features: the main point is presented early; the language is simple, direct, and positive; and the active voice is used in most cases.

Glossary
▲ 140–63
104–39
● APA 615–55

A Sample of Writing in Business: A Business Plan Executive Summary

Financial Projections

Precise numbers, confidently stated.

Based on the size of our market and our defined market area, our sales projections for the first year are $340,000. We project a growth rate of 10% per year for the first three years.

Clear, direct writing, free of jargon and hedging.

The salary for each of the co-owners will be $40,000. On start up we will have six trained staff to provide pet services and expect to hire four more this year once financing is secured. To begin with, co-owner Pat Simpson will be scheduling appointments and coordinating services, but we plan to hire a full-time receptionist this year as well.

Positive tone.

Already we have service commitments from over 40 clients and plan to aggressively build our client base through newspaper, website, social media, and direct mail advertising. The loving on-site professional care that Pet Grandma Inc. will provide is sure to appeal to cat and dog owners throughout the West Vancouver area.

Adapted from "Business Plan Executive Summary Sample," by S. Ward, March 29, 2017, The Balance, *www.thebalancesmb.com/business-plan -executive-summary-example-2948007*.

Typical Organization of Business Plans

A common assignment in business courses is a business plan. Business plans typically include these sections:

Executive summary: outlines your proposal and what makes it likely to succeed →

Company overview: includes a mission statement and describes the company's ownership, structure, and location →

Products and services: defines the problem your company will try to solve and how it will do so; the competition and how you can do better; what, specifically, you are selling

Target market: includes a list of who your customers are →

Marketing plan: specifies how you will reach your customers →

Implementation plan: provides a schedule, a management team, and a financial plan

✷ academic literacies   ● fields   ● research
■ rhetorical situations   ⁝ processes   ● media/design
▲ genres   ◆ strategies

WRITING IN EDUCATION

The focus of study in education is how people learn and how to teach effectively. Its primary methods include observation, problem solving, and practice teaching. Courses typically center on teaching methods, the philosophy of education, educational measurement and assessment, educational psychology, and instructional technology, among others.

Educators typically write for audiences that include their students, parents, other teachers, administrators, and the public. Genres may include lesson plans, **SUMMARIES**, **REPORTS**, **ANNOTATED BIBLIOGRAPHIES**, **PORTFOLIOS**, and **REFLECTIONS**. Support for claims may include facts, statistics, test scores, personal narratives, observations, and case studies. Sources are documented in **APA** style. Clarity and correctness are important in writing in education; "I" may be used in reflective writing and informal communication, while in formal writing the third person is preferred.

✳ 33–35
▲ 140–63
201–9
⁜ 385–90
391–401
● APA 615–55

A Sample of Writing in Education: A Teaching Philosophy Statement

My Image of the Child: ●···

Sections labeled with headings.

I believe that the student should be at the center of the instructional ●······· process. I have an image of children as strong and capable beings. The classroom is a place where the teacher serves as a facilitator and guide as the students construct their own understanding of the world around them. Although it is the teacher's role to plan lessons and evaluate students' progress, it is of the utmost importance to always take the children and their own unique needs into consideration. For my second field experience, I was placed at Margaret Manson Elementary. Their ●········ school motto is that "the children come first." When children are the priority in teaching, an amazing amount of learning can take place. I believe in creating opportunities for students to develop to their fullest potential while developing and expanding their horizons and worldviews. In order to accomplish this, there must be a welcoming, positive environment that is open and honest. When students feel comfortable

Argument is constructed to show teaching priorities.

Writing carefully crafted and proofread.

As a reflective piece, "I" is appropriate.

at school they will surely be more engaged and responsive to class activities. I also consider it essential to be passionate and enthusiastic about learning so that the students can have a most relevant and meaningful experience.

Discusses both teaching and personal qualities.

Adapted from "Statement of Teaching Philosophy," by K. Tams (n.d.), Kelly Tams' Teaching Portfolio, *tams.yolasite.com/my-philosophy-of-education .php.*

Typical Organization of Lesson Plans in Education

Frequent assignments in education courses are lesson plans, which typically include these elements:

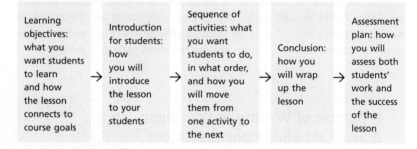

| Learning objectives: what you want students to learn and how the lesson connects to course goals | → | Introduction for students: how you will introduce the lesson to your students | → | Sequence of activities: what you want students to do, in what order, and how you will move them from one activity to the next | → | Conclusion: how you will wrap up the lesson | → | Assessment plan: how you will assess both students' work and the success of the lesson |

WRITING IN ENGINEERING AND TECHNOLOGY

In the fields of engineering and technology, the focus is how to create and maintain useful structures, systems, processes, and machines. Engineers and technicians define problems as well as solve them, weigh various alternatives, and test possible solutions before presenting them to clients. This is a broad set of disciplines that may include civil, computer, electrical, mechanical, and structural engineering; computer science; and various technology specialties such as HVAC and automotive technology.

* academic literacies   ● fields   ● research
■ rhetorical situations   ⁖ processes   ● media/design
▲ genres   ◆ strategies

Engineers and technicians typically write for their peers and team members, their clients, and the public. Writing tasks may include **ABSTRACTS**, **EVALUATIONS**, instructions, **LITERATURE REVIEWS**, memos, **PROPOSALS**, **REPORTS**, and **SUMMARIES**. Support usually includes data, examples, mathematical and logical reasoning, and experimental results, and sources are usually cited in **APA** format. Engineers and technicians value writing that includes logical ordering of ideas and precise language. Tables, charts, figures, illustrations, and headings and subheadings within the writing—all ways of quickly and efficiently conveying information—are also valued.

▲ 196–200
214–22
209–13
258–68
140–63
✳ 33–35
● APA 615–55

A Sample of Writing in Engineering: A Research Report

2. MATERIALS AND METHODS •⋯⋯⋯⋯⋯⋯⋯⋯⋯⋯⋯⋯ *Headings used.*
To begin testing, an ATV test bed was designed (see Figure 1). To secure •⋯⋯ *Charts, graphs, and photos included.*
the machine, a loose rope was attached to the front of the machine and then to the testing platform. An additional rope was then attached at •⋯ *Precise description of procedure.*
a 90° angle to the front of the machine to act as the lifting force. The test bed platform could be raised to a maximum of 60°, which simulated hills or steep terrain. Each test was started at 0° and then increased by increments of 10 (angles were determined by a digital level attached to platform). Once the machine was at the appropriate angle, a lift force •⋯ *Technical language used for precision.*
was applied to observe turnover weight. Once the machine's tires lifted off of the platform, the scale was read to determine the amount of weight. Each machine was tested from front to rear and side to side.

Adapted from "Analysis of All Terrain Vehicle Crash Mechanisms," by S. Tanner, M. Aitken, and J. N. Warnock, 2008–10, Journal of Undergraduate Research in Bioengineering, docplayer.net/32747021-Analysis-of-all-terrain-vehicle-crash-mechanisms.html.

Typical Organization of Lab Reports in Engineering

Lab reports, a typical assignment in engineering classes, usually include the IMRaD elements, along with an abstract and a list of references. This format may vary depending on the engineering field and the requirements of the experiment or task.

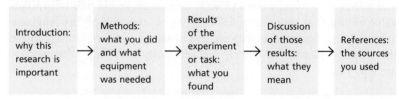

Introduction: why this research is important → Methods: what you did and what equipment was needed → Results of the experiment or task: what you found → Discussion of those results: what they mean → References: the sources you used

WRITING IN HEALTH SCIENCES AND NURSING

Health sciences and nursing is a broad set of fields that may include nursing, anatomy, physiology, nutrition, and pharmacology as well as athletic training, exercise science, physical or occupational therapy, and speech pathology. Consequently, the methods used are also broad and varied, and they may include study of theories and techniques, observation, role-playing, and experiential learning.

196–200 ▲
201–9
164–95
140–63
391–401 ⦂
209–13 ▲
33–35 ✳
456–63 ◆

APA 615–55 ●

Writing in these fields may include **ABSTRACTS**, **ANNOTATED BIBLIOGRAPHIES**, **ARGUMENTS**, case studies, instructions, personal narratives, **REPORTS**, **REFLECTIONS**, **LITERATURE OR RESEARCH REVIEWS**, **SUMMARIES**, and charts **DESCRIBING** patients' conditions and care. The audiences for this writing may include other patient care providers, clinic and hospital administrators and staff, insurance companies, and patients or clients. Support for assertions typically includes scholarly research, observation, and description, and high value is placed on accurate information and detail. Other aspects of this writing include a preference for writing in the third person, paraphrased source information, and the use of headings and subheadings. Sources are usually cited in **APA** format.

✳ academic literacies   ● fields   ● research

■ rhetorical situations   ⦂ processes   ● media/design

▲ genres   ◆ strategies

A Sample of Writing in Nursing: A Case Study

Patient status.

Ms. D is a morbidly obese 67 year old female, 240 lbs, 5'2" with type II diabetes mellitus. She was transferred from a nursing home to the hospital for pneumonia, but also suffers from congestive heart disease, sleep apnea, psoriasis, and osteoarthritis. She has a weak but productive cough with tonsil suction, and she was on breathing treatments with albuterol. Her skin is very dry and thin with several lesions and yeast infections, and the deep folds of her lower abdomen bled during the bed bath. She did not want to wear her breathing mask at night and refused to get out of bed. She cried when encouraged to use the bathroom or to move her legs. She expressed great fear of returning to the nursing home.

From the outset, we realized that Ms. D needed care beyond physical therapy and treatment for pneumonia; we realized that her obesity and refusal to participate in her health care expressed important patterns of her life. Morbid obesity does not happen overnight; it is a progressive pattern associated with activity levels, diet, and self-care practices, as well as other possible physiological and psychosocial dimensions. Johnson's (1980) Behavioral System Model, which outlines seven behavioral subsystems, was helpful in providing a perspective of the complexity of Ms. D's health needs. We also assessed that Ms. D lacked confidence in taking care of herself (reflecting the *achievement subsystem*) and lacked a sense of family support from her two sons (*affiliative subsystem*). Her fear of returning to the nursing home coupled with her need for ongoing care challenged her sense of interdependency as addressed in Johnson's *dependency subsystem*.

Careful description of patient's condition.

Detailed observation using precise terms.

Behavior as well as medical conditions taken into account.

Patient assessment.

Use of paraphrased scholarly source to aid assessment.

Adapted from "Esthetic Knowing with a Hospitalized Morbidly Obese Patient," by R. Brinkley, K. Ricker, and K. Tuomey, Fall 2007, Journal of Undergraduate Nursing Scholarship, 9, no. 1, http://www.juns.nursing .arizona.edu/articles/Fall%202007/Esthetic%20knowing.htm. Accessed July 21, 2010.

Typical Organization of Case Studies in Health Sciences and Nursing

Case studies, typical assignments in these fields, usually include the following elements:

Patient status: symptoms, lab findings, history, doctor's orders, how much help the patient needs	→	Assessment: why the patient is being cared for; origins of current situation; when symptoms started, how the patient has been treated, the expected outcome	→	Care plan: what has been done, how current care is working, how care might be improved

Part 5
Processes

To create anything, we generally break the work down into a series of steps. We follow a recipe (or the directions on a box) to bake a cake; we break a song down into different parts and the music into various chords to arrange a piece of music. So it is when we write. We rely on various processes to get from a blank screen or page to a finished product. The chapters that follow offer advice on some of these processes—from **WRITING AS INQUIRY** and **GENERATING IDEAS** to **DRAFTING** to **GETTING RESPONSE** to **EDITING** to **COMPILING A PORTFOLIO**, and more.

Processes

26 Processes of Writing   327

27 Writing as Inquiry   329

28 Generating Ideas and Text   333

29 Organizing Your Writing,
Guiding Your Readers   345

30 Drafting   364

31 Assessing Your Own Writing   367

32 Getting Response and Revising   372

33 Editing and Proofreading   380

34 Compiling a Portfolio   385

35 Reflecting on Your Writing   391

26 Processes of Writing

Many people think that good writers can just sit down in front of a screen or piece of paper and create a finished piece of writing. After all, in the movies, newspaper reporters pound out stories that then appear on the front page; novelists crank out hundreds of pages without breaking a sweat. That kind of talent for getting it right the first time happens on occasion, or for formulaic writing like business memos. Most of the time, though, most of us write the way we learn to draw, play piano, drive a car, or bake a cake: by working, practicing, making mistakes, and changing what we do as a result. In a way, because we usually need to generate ideas, draft, revise, and edit what we write, we learn to write every time we write.

You may have learned in school about a writing process that looks something like this: prewrite, outline, draft, revise, edit—five steps, to be done in order. That's the way the chapters in this book look, too; but that ordering is somewhat misleading. Sometimes we have to do considerable research before we can begin to figure out what we need to say. Sometimes we have to revise several times, getting responses from others between drafts. Sometimes we reach a certain point in our writing and realize that we need to stop, abandon the work in progress, and start over. And sometimes we can knock out a draft quickly, revising and editing as we go.

In other words, the processes writers use can vary from text to text, genre to genre, task to task. What is easy to describe as a set of lockstep activities:

research → generate ideas → write a draft → get response → revise → edit often looks more like this:

And it will differ from text to text, assignment to assignment. As writer and writing teacher Donald M. Murray once wrote, "Any process is legitimate if it produces an effective text."

Still, it's good to know the various processes you can use to create an effective text. The chapters that follow can help you understand writing as a way of learning; give you ways to generate ideas and text; offer advice on organizing, drafting, revising, and editing your writing; help you assess your own writing and get response from others; compile your writing into a portfolio; and reflect on your writing and learning.

27 Writing as Inquiry

Sometimes we write to say what we think. Other times, however, we write in order to figure out what we think. Much of the writing you do in college will be the latter. Even as you learn to write, you will be writing to learn. This chapter is about writing with a spirit of inquiry—approaching writing projects with curiosity, moving beyond the familiar, keeping your eyes open, tackling issues that don't have easy answers. It's about starting with questions and going from there—and taking risks. As Mark Twain once said, "Sail away from the safe harbor. . . . Explore. Dream. Discover." This chapter offers strategies for doing just that with your writing.

Starting with Questions

The most important thing is to start with questions—with what you *don't* know rather than with what you *do* know. Your goal is to learn about your subject and then to learn more. If you're writing about a topic you know well, you want to expand on what you already know. In academic writing, good topics arise from important questions, issues, and problems that are already being discussed. As a writer, you need to find out what's being said about your topic and then see your writing as a way of entering that larger conversation.

So start with questions, and don't expect to find easy answers. If there were easy answers, there would be no reason for discussion—or for you to write. For purposes of inquiry, the best questions can't be answered by looking in a reference book or searching online. Instead, they are ones that help you explore what you think—and why. As it happens, many of the strategies in this book can help you ask questions of this kind. Following are some questions to get you started:

445–55 **How can it be DEFINED?**   What is it, and what does it do? Look it up in a dictionary; check *Wikipedia*. Remember, though, that these are only starting points. How *else* can it be defined? What more is there to know about it? If your topic is being debated, chances are that its very definition is subject to debate. If, for instance, you're writing about gay marriage, how you define marriage will affect how you approach the topic.

456–63 **How can it be DESCRIBED?**   What details should you include? From what vantage point should you describe your topic? If, for example, your topic is the physiological effects of running a marathon, what are those effects—on the lungs, heart muscles, nerves, brain, and so on? How will you describe the physical experience of running over twenty-six miles from the runner's point of view?

469–73 **How can it be EXPLAINED?**   What does it do? How does it work? If you're investigating the use of performance-enhancing drugs by athletes, for example, what exactly are the effects of these drugs? What makes them dangerous—and are they always dangerous or only in certain conditions? Why are they illegal—and should they be illegal?

437–44 **What can it be COMPARED with?**   Again using performance-enhancing drugs by athletes as an example, how does taking such supplements compare with wearing high-tech footwear or uniforms? Does such a comparison make you see taking steroids or other performance-enhancing drugs in a new light?

405–9 **What may have CAUSED it? What might be its EFFECTS?**   Who or what does it affect? What causes cerebral palsy in children, for example? What are its symptoms? If children with cerebral palsy are not treated, what might be the consequences?

431–36 **How can it be CLASSIFIED?**   Is it a topic or issue that can be placed into categories of similar topics or issues? What categories can it be placed into? Are there legal and illegal performance-enhancing supplements (human growth hormone and steroids, for instance), and what's the difference? Are some safe and others less safe? Classifying your topic in this way can help you consider its complexities.

---

* academic literacies   ● fields   ● research

■ rhetorical situations   :● processes   ● media/design

▲ genres   ◆ strategies

How can it be ANALYZED ?   What parts can the topic be divided into? For example, if you're exploring the health effects of cell phone use, you might ask these questions: What evidence, if any, suggests that cell phone radiation causes cancer? What cancers are associated with cell phone use? What do medical experts and phone manufacturers say? How can cell phone users reduce their risk?

▲ 104–39

How can it be interpreted?   What does it really mean? How do you interpret it, and how does your interpretation differ from those of other writers? What evidence supports your interpretation, and what argues against it? Imagine you're exploring the topic of sports injuries among young women. Do these injuries reflect a larger cultural preoccupation with competition? anatomical differences between male and female bodies? something else?

What expectations does it raise?   What will happen next? What makes you think so? If this happens, how will it affect those involved? For instance, will the governing bodies of professional sports require more testing of athletes' blood, urine, and hair than they do now? Will such tests be unfair to athletes taking drugs for legitimate medical needs?

What are the different POSITIONS on it?   What controversies or disagreements exist, and what evidence is offered for the various positions? What else might be said? Are there any groups or individuals who seem especially authoritative? If so, you might want to explore what they have said.

▲ 164–95

What are your own feelings about it?   What interests you about the topic? How much do you already know about it? For example, if you're an athlete, how do you feel about competing against others who may have taken performance-enhancing supplements? If a friend has problems with drugs, do those problems affect your thinking about drugs in sports? How do you react to what others say about the topic? What else do you want to find out?

Are there other ways to think about it?   Is what seems true in this case also true in others? How can you apply this subject in another situation? Will what works in another situation also work here? What do you have to do to adapt it? Imagine you're writing about traffic fatalities. If replacing stop signs with roundabouts or traffic circles reduced traffic fatalities in England, could doing so also reduce accidents in the United States?

337

You can also start with the journalist's **QUESTIONS**: *Who? What? When? Where? Why? How?* Asking questions from these various perspectives can help you deepen your understanding of your topic by leading you to see it from many angles.

Keeping a Journal

343–44

One way to get into the habit of using writing as a tool for inquiry is to keep a **JOURNAL**. You can use a journal to record your observations, reactions, whatever you wish. Some writers find journals especially useful places to articulate questions or speculations. You may be assigned by teachers to do certain work in a journal, but in general you can use a journal to write for yourself. Note your ideas, speculate, digress—go wherever your thoughts lead you.

Keeping a Blog

687

You may also wish to explore issues or other ideas online in the form of a **BLOG**. Most blogs have a comments section that allows others to read and respond to what you write, leading to potentially fruitful discussions. You can also include links to other websites, helping you connect various strands of thought and research. The blogs of others, along with online discussion forums and groups, may also be useful sources of opinion on your topic, but keep in mind that they probably aren't authoritative research sources. There are a number of search engines that can help you find blog posts related to specific topics, including blogsearchengine.org and *Blogarama*. You can create your own blog on sites such as *Blogger*, *Tumblr*, *Svbtle*, or *WordPress*.

※ academic literacies   ● fields   ● research
■ rhetorical situations   ∴ processes   ● media/design
▲ genres   ◆ strategies

28 Generating Ideas and Text

All good writing revolves around ideas. Whether you're writing a job-application letter, a sonnet, or an essay, you'll always spend time and effort generating ideas. Some writers can come up with a topic, put their thoughts in order, and flesh out their arguments in their heads; but most of us need to write out our ideas, play with them, tease them out, and examine them from some distance and from multiple perspectives. This chapter offers activities that can help you do just that. *Freewriting*, *looping*, *listing*, *clustering*, and *talking* can help you explore what you already know about a subject; *cubing*, *questioning*, and *using visuals* nudge you to consider a subject in new ways; and *outlining*, *letter writing*, *journal keeping*, and *discovery drafting* offer ways to generate a text.

Freewriting

An informal method of exploring a subject by writing about it, freewriting ("writing freely") can help you generate ideas and come up with materials for your draft. Here's how to do it:

1. Write as quickly as you can without stopping for 5 to 10 minutes (or until you fill a screen or page).

2. If you have a subject to explore, write it at the top and then start writing about it; but if you stray, don't worry—just keep writing. If you don't have a subject yet, just start writing and don't stop until the time is up. If you can't think of anything to say, write that ("I can't think of anything to say") again and again until you do—and you will!

3. Once the time is up, read over what you've written, and underline or highlight passages that interest you.

4. Write some more, starting with one of those underlined or highlighted passages as your new topic. Repeat the process until you've come up with a usable topic.

Looping

Looping is a more focused version of freewriting; it can help you explore what you already know about a subject. You stop, reflect on what you've written, and then write again, developing your understanding in the process. It's good for clarifying your knowledge and understanding of a subject and finding a focus. Here's what to do:

1. Write for 5 to 10 minutes on whatever you know about your subject. This is your first loop.

2. Read over what you wrote, and then write a single sentence summarizing the most important or interesting idea. You might try completing one of these sentences: "I guess what I was trying to say was . . . " or "What surprises me most in reading what I wrote is . . ." This will be the start of another loop.

3. Write again for 5 to 10 minutes, using your summary sentence as your beginning and your focus. Again, read what you've written, and then write a sentence capturing the most important idea—in a third loop.

Keep going until you have enough understanding of your topic to be able to decide on a tentative focus—something you can write about.

Listing

Some writers find it useful to keep lists of ideas that occur to them while they're thinking about a topic. Follow these steps:

1. Write a list of potential ideas about a topic. Don't try to limit your list—include anything that interests you.

2. Look for relationships among the items on your list: What patterns do you see? If other ideas occur to you, add them to the list.

---

* academic literacies
■ rhetorical situations
▲ genres

● fields
⁘ processes
◆ strategies

● research
● media/design

3. Arrange the items in an order that makes sense for your purpose and can serve as the beginning of an outline for your writing.

Clustering or Mapping Ideas

Clustering (also called "idea mapping," "mind mapping," or "concept mapping") is a way of generating and connecting ideas visually. It's useful for seeing how various ideas relate to one another and for developing subtopics. You can create a cluster with pencil and paper or use an online mapping tool like *Coggle*, *Bubble.us*, or *MindMup*. Either way, the technique is simple:

1. Write your topic in the middle of a page or computer screen.

2. Write ideas relating to that topic around it, and connect them to the central idea with lines or shapes.

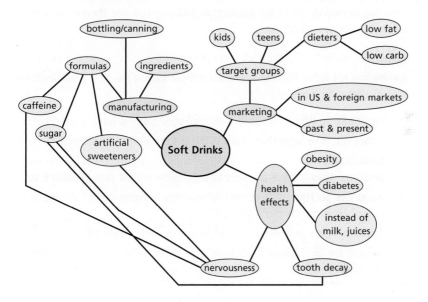

3. Write down examples, facts, or other details relating to each idea, and join them to connecting topics.

4. Keep going until you can't think of anything else relating to your topic.

You should end up with various ideas about your topic, and the clusters will enable you to see how they relate to one another. In the example cluster on the topic of "soft drinks" on the previous page, note how some ideas link not only to the main topic or related topics but also to other ideas.

Talking

Sometimes it's helpful to generate ideas by talking rather than writing. You might talk about your topic with a classmate, a teacher, a tutor, a friend—or even just talk out loud to yourself. If you do, be sure to take notes during or after talking, or use a voice-recording app to capture the conversation. You can also use free transcription apps, like *Otter* or *Google Voice*, to generate a print version of the conversation. Some apps, like *Otter*, even tag keywords from the transcript, helping you see themes and patterns in your conversation.

Cubing

A cube has six sides. You can examine a topic as you might a cube, looking at it in these six ways:

456–63 ◆
- **DESCRIBE** it. What's its color? shape? age? size? What's it made of?

437–44 ◆
- **COMPARE** it to something else. What is it similar to or different from?

431–36 ◆
104–39 ▲
- Associate it with other things. What does it remind you of? What connections does it have to other things? How would you **CLASSIFY** it?

- **ANALYZE** it. How is it made? Where did it come from? Where is it going? How are its parts related?

- Apply it. What is it used for? What can be done with it?

164–95 ▲
- **ARGUE** for or against it. Choose a position relating to your subject, and defend it.

✳ academic literacies   ● fields   ● research
■ rhetorical situations   ⠶ processes   ● media/design
▲ genres   ◆ strategies

Questioning

It's always useful to ask questions. One way is to start with *What? Who? When? Where? How?* and *Why?* A particular method of exploring a topic is to ask questions as if the topic were a play. This method is especially useful for exploring literature, history, the arts, and the social sciences. Start with these questions:

- *What?* What happens? How is it similar to or different from other actions?
- *Who?* Who are the actors? Who are the participants, and who are the spectators? How do the actors affect the action, and how are they affected by it?
- *When?* When does the action take place? How often does it happen? What happens before, after, or at the same time? Would it be different at another time? Does the time have historical significance?
- *Where?* What is the setting? What is the situation, and what makes it significant?
- *How?* How does the action occur? What are the steps in the process? What techniques are required? What equipment is needed?
- *Why?* Why did this happen? What are the actors' motives? What end does the action serve?

Using Visuals

Some writers use visuals—photographs, presentation slides, drawings—as tools for sparking or capturing ideas or for thinking about a topic in a new way. Here are some suggestions for doing so:

- Search for images related to your topic on a stock photo site like *Pixabay* or *Pexels*. Then freewrite about the images you find. What do the images make you think of? Do they help you see your topic in a different light? Do they suggest details you hadn't considered?

Here's an example of how a stock image helped one student generate ideas for a memoir about memories of her grandmother raising chickens and selling eggs.

Freewrite: This picture is beautiful, the way the eggs are almost glowing in the basket. It makes me think of bounty—of having more than enough. Maybe that's part of the significance of my story? I didn't realize it when I was young, but Grandma sold the eggs to make her own money—to afford "extras" and to have some financial freedom apart from Grandpa. And then there was all the bounty she left us in stories and memories and recipes. Maybe I can play on this theme somehow in my writing?

- Make a *PowerPoint* or *Keynote* slide about your topic. Choose keywords for headings and subheadings, find images or icons for each, and experiment with different arrangements of the material. Doing so might help you make new connections or associations among your ideas.

- Do what filmmakers and animators do when developing a new project: create a storyboard—a scene-by-scene plan of what the final product might look like. You could draw scenes by hand (stick figures are fine!) or use stock images to represent each scene or section of your draft. Search for storyboard templates online to get started.

Here's an example storyboard for the student memoir mentioned earlier. Created with a template and stock images from the graphic design app *Canva*, the storyboard helped the student generate memories and details and then organize them before drafting.

Storyboard: "Egg Money" Memoir

SCENE #1
I feed the chickens while Grandma gathers the eggs, placing them gently in the pockets of her tattered apron.

SCENE #2
Grandma shows me how to separate an egg, whisking out the last drop of egg white with her finger. "No use wasting," she says. Later, after we make our egg deliveries, we'll come home to Grandma's angel food cake.

SCENE #3
Grandma and I place the eggs in cartons and wrap each in newspaper and twine.

SCENE #4
We load up the old wheelbarrow with egg cartons and set out to deliver our goods to Grandma's customers.

SCENE #5
After the egg deliveries, Grandma records every transaction in her cash ledger. I sit next to her, eating my angel food cake.

SCENE #6
Going through Grandma's attic as an adult, I find her recipe books, her county-fair ribbons, her cash ledgers documenting forty years' worth of chicken raising and egg selling.

Using Genre Features

Genres typically include particular kinds of information and organize it in particular ways. One way to generate ideas and text, then, is to identify the key features of the genre in which you're writing and use them to guide you as you write. Of course, you may alter the genre's features or combine two or more genres in order to achieve your purpose, but the overall shape and content of the genre can give you a way to develop and organize your ideas and research.

Outlining

You may create an *informal outline* by simply listing your ideas and numbering them in the order in which you want to write about them. You might prefer to make a *working outline*, to show the hierarchy of relationships among your ideas. While still informal, a working outline distinguishes your main ideas and your support, often through simple indentation:

First main idea
  Supporting evidence or detail
  Supporting evidence or detail

Second main idea
  Supporting evidence or detail
  Supporting evidence or detail

A *formal outline* shows the hierarchy of your ideas through a system of indenting, numbering, and lettering. Remember that when you divide a point into more specific subpoints, you should have at least two of them—you can't divide something into only one part. Also, try to keep items at each level parallel in structure. Formal outlines work this way:

Thesis statement
  I. First reason
    A. Supporting evidence
      1. Detail of evidence
      2. Detail of evidence
    B. Supporting evidence
  II. Another reason

☀ academic literacies   ● fields   ● research
■ rhetorical situations   ⁛ processes   ● media/design
▲ genres   ◆ strategies

Here is a formal outline of the first part of the **MLA** research report by Dylan Borchers, "Against the Odds: Harry S. Truman and the Election of 1948," that shows how he organized it:

MLA 608–14

  I. Introduction: Outcome of 1948 election
  II. Bad predictions by pollsters
    A. Pollsters stopped polling.
    B. Dewey supporters became overconfident.
    C. Truman supporters were either energized or stayed home.
  III. Dewey's campaign overly cautious
    A. He was overconfident.
    B. His message was vague—he avoided taking stands.
  IV. Dewey's public appearances poor
    A. He was seen as aloof, uncomfortable with crowds.
    B. He made blunders.
    C. His speeches were dull.

Writing out a formal outline can be helpful when you're dealing with a complex subject; as you revise your drafts, though, be flexible and ready to change your outline as your understanding of your topic develops.

Another way to outline is to use an online organizing tool like *Trello*, *Jira*, or *Wrike*. These tools let you create a digital bulletin board to which you post "lists" and "cards." Below is an example *Trello* board that outlines Dylan Borchers's research report. Each color-coded "card" represents a supporting detail for the main point listed at the top of a column of cards. You can drag cards to different lists, depending on where the cards fit

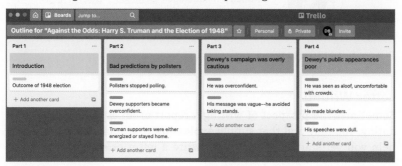

best. You can expand a card to jot down notes, save website links, and add attachments, as in the following example, which includes notes and links to sources that support one of Borchers's points.

 ## He was seen as aloof, uncomfortable with crowds.

in list Part 4

LABELS

+

≡ **Description** Edit

Comparison to plastic groom on top of a wedding cake -- Hamby.

Stiff and cold demeanor -- McCullough

⌗ **Attachments**

Hamby article ↗
Added a minute ago - <u>Comment</u> - <u>Delete</u> - <u>Edit</u>

▭ <u>Make cover</u>

McCullough book ↗
Added a minute ago - <u>Comment</u> - <u>Delete</u> - <u>Edit</u>

▭ <u>Make cover</u>

Add an attachment

Letter Writing

Sometimes the prospect of writing a report or an essay can be intimidating. You may find that simply explaining your topic to someone will help you get started. In that case, write a letter or an email or a text

* academic literacies   ● fields   ● research
■ rhetorical situations   ⁝ processes   ◖ media/design
▲ genres   ◆ strategies

to someone you know—your best friend, a parent or grandparent, a sibling—in which you discuss your subject. Explain it in terms that your reader can understand. Use the unsent letter to rehearse your topic; make it a kind of rough draft that you can then revise and develop to suit your actual audience.

Keeping a Journal

Some writers find that writing in a journal helps them generate ideas. Making note of your ideas, thoughts, feelings, or the events of your day can provide a wealth of topics, and a journal can also be a good place to explore what you think and why you think as you do.

Journals are private—you are the only audience—so you can feel free to write whatever comes to mind. And you can do more than write. If you choose a paper journal, doodle or draw in it, and keep clippings or scraps of paper between the pages; if you keep your journal on a computer, copy and paste interesting images or text you find online. Whatever form your journal takes, feel free to play with its contents, and don't worry about errors or grammar. The goal is to generate ideas; let yourself wander without censoring yourself or fretting that your writing is incorrect or incomplete or incoherent. That's OK.

One measure of the success of journaling and other personal writing is length: journal entries, FREEWRITING, LISTING, CUBING, and other types of informal writing are like warm-up exercises to limber you up and get you thinking. If you don't give them enough time and space, they may not do what you want them to. Often, students' best insights appear at the end of their journal entries. Had they stopped before that point, they would never have had those good ideas.

333–34
334–35
336

After you've written several journal entries, one way to study the ideas in them is to highlight useful patterns in different colors. For example, journal entries usually include some questioning and speculating, as well as summarizing and paraphrasing. Try color-coding each of these, sentence by sentence, phrase by phrase: yellow for summaries or paraphrases, green for questions, blue for speculations. Do any colors dominate? If, for example, your entries are mostly yellow, you may be restating the course content or quoting from the textbook too much and perhaps need to ask more questions. If you're generating ideas for an essay, you might assign colors to ideas or themes to see which ones are the most promising.

Discovery Drafting

364–66

Some writers do best by jumping in and writing. Here are the steps to take if you're ready to write a preliminary **DRAFT**:

1. Write your draft quickly, in one sitting if possible.

2. Assume that you are writing to discover what you want to say and how you need to say it—and that you will make substantial revisions in a later part of the process.

3. Don't worry about grammatical or factual correctness—if you can't think of a word, leave a blank space to fill in later. If you're unsure of a date or spelling, put a question mark in parentheses as a reminder to check it later. Just write.

If you need more help

79

See each of the **GENRE** chapters for specific strategies for generating text in each genre.

☀ academic literacies   ● fields   ● research
■ rhetorical situations   ⁂ processes   ● media/design
▲ genres   ◆ strategies

29 Organizing Your Writing, Guiding Your Readers

Traffic lights, street signs, and lines on the road help drivers find their way. Readers need similar guidance—to know, for example, whether they're reading a report or an argument, evaluation, or proposal. They also need to know what to expect: What will the report be about? What perspective will it offer? What will this paragraph cover? What about the next one? How do the two paragraphs relate to each other—and to the rest of the essay?

When you write, then, you need to organize your ideas and provide cues to help your readers navigate your text and understand the points you're trying to make. This chapter offers advice on organizing your writing and guiding your readers through it by organizing the text and its paragraphs; creating strong thesis statements, clear topic sentences, and helpful beginnings and titles; ending appropriately; and tying ideas together with transitions. See also the **GENRE** chapters for advice on organizing texts in specific genres.

▲ 79

Outlining

At some point as writers develop their ideas and collect their information, they often create an **OUTLINE** as a plan for drafting a text. You may create an *informal outline* by simply listing your ideas and numbering them in the order in which you want to write about them. You might prefer to make a *working outline* to show the hierarchy of relationships among your ideas. Or you might need to create a *formal outline*, which shows the hierarchy of your ideas through a system of indenting, numbering, and lettering. And you might use an online organizing tool.

340–42

Beginning

Whenever we pick up something to read, we generally start by looking at the first few words or sentences to see if they grab our attention, and based on them, we decide whether to keep reading. Beginnings, then, are important—both for attracting readers and for giving them some information about what's to come. How you begin depends on your **RHETORICAL SITUATION**, especially your purpose and audience. Academic audiences generally expect a text's introduction to establish context, explaining how the text fits into some larger conversation, addresses certain questions, or explores an aspect of the subject. Most introductions also offer a brief description of the text's content, often in the form of a thesis statement. The following opening paragraph of a report on cyberloafing—that is, using an employer's internet access to do non-work-related tasks—does all of this:

> Increased technological advances and widespread internet access have revolutionized the workplace. But all this innovation has come with at least one questionable stowaway: cyberloafing—the act of browsing the internet for personal use while at work. It's becoming essential for organizations to understand cyberloafing: what it is, which factors lead employees to do it, and how it affects productivity. At its worst, cyberloafing can jeopardize an organization's information security, so awareness about cyberloafing is essential to both employees and employers in order to prevent its most negative consequences.
>
> —Rocia Celeste Mejia Avila,
> "Cyberloafing: Distraction or Motivation?"

If you're writing for a nonacademic audience or genre—for a newspaper or a website, for example—your introduction may need to entice your readers to read on by connecting your text to their interests through shared experiences, anecdotes, or some other attention-getting device. Cynthia Bass, writing a newspaper article about the Gettysburg Address on its 135th anniversary, connects that date—the day her audience would read it—to Lincoln's address. She then develops the rationale for thinking about the

57 ■

* academic literacies   ● fields   ● research
■ rhetorical situations   ∴ processes   ● media/design
▲ genres   ◆ strategies

speech and introduces her specific topic: debates about the writing and delivery of the Gettysburg Address:

> November 19 is the 135th anniversary of the Gettysburg Address. On that day in 1863, with the Civil War only half over and the worst yet to come, Abraham Lincoln delivered a speech now universally regarded as both the most important oration in U.S. history and the best explanation—"government of the people, by the people, for the people"—of why this nation exists.
>
> We would expect the history of an event so monumental as the Gettysburg Address to be well established. The truth is just the opposite. The only thing scholars agree on is that the speech is short—only ten sentences—and that it took Lincoln under five minutes to stand up, deliver it, and sit back down.
>
> Everything else—when Lincoln wrote it, where he wrote it, how quickly he wrote it, how he was invited, how the audience reacted—has been open to debate since the moment the words left his mouth.
>
> —Cynthia Bass, "Gettysburg Address: Two Versions"

Thesis Statements

A thesis identifies the topic of a text along with the claim being made about it. A good thesis helps readers understand an essay. Working to create a sharp thesis can help you focus both your thinking and your writing. Here are four steps for moving from a topic to a thesis statement:

1. **State your topic as a question.** You may have an idea for a topic, such as "gasoline prices," "analysis of 'real women' ad campaigns," or "famine." Those may be good topics, but they're not thesis statements, primarily because none of them actually makes a statement. A good way to begin moving from topic to thesis statement is to turn your topic into a question:

    What causes fluctuations in gasoline prices?

    Are ads picturing "real women" who aren't models effective?

    What can be done to prevent famine in Somalia?

2. **Then turn your question into a position.** A thesis statement is an assertion—it takes a stand or makes a claim. Whether you're writing a report or an argument, you are saying, "This is the way I see . . ." or "My research shows . . ." or "This is what I believe about . . ." Your thesis statement announces your position on the question you're raising about the topic, so a relatively easy way of establishing a thesis is to answer your own question:

    Gasoline prices fluctuate for several reasons.

    Ads picturing "real women" instead of models are effective because most women can easily identify with them.

    The threat of famine in Somalia could be avoided if certain measures are taken.

3. **Narrow your thesis.** A good thesis is specific, guiding you as you write and showing readers exactly what your essay will cover. The preceding thesis statements need to be qualified and focused—they should be made more specific. For example:

    Gasoline prices fluctuate because of production procedures, consumer demand, international politics, and oil companies' policies.

    Dove's "Campaign for Self-Esteem" and Aerie's ads featuring Iskra Lawrence work because consumers can identify with the women's bodies and admire their confidence in displaying them.

    The current threat of famine in Somalia could be avoided if the government and humanitarian organizations increase the availability of water, provide shipments of food, and supply medical and nutrition assistance.

337

A good way to narrow a thesis is to ask **QUESTIONS** about it: *Why* do gasoline prices fluctuate? *How* could the Somalia famine have been avoided? The answers will help you craft a narrow, focused thesis.

4. **Qualify your thesis.** Sometimes you want to make a strong argument and state your thesis bluntly. Often, however, you need to acknowledge

---

* academic literacies   ● fields   ● research
■ rhetorical situations   ⁚ processes   ● media/design
▲ genres   ◆ strategies

that your assertions may be challenged or may not be unconditionally true. In those cases, consider limiting the scope of your thesis by adding to it such terms as "may," "probably," "apparently," "very likely," "sometimes," and "often."

Gasoline prices *very likely* fluctuate because of production procedures, consumer demand, international politics, and oil companies' policies.

Dove's and Aerie's ad campaigns featuring "real women" *may* work because consumers can identify with the women's bodies and admire their confidence in displaying them.

The current threat of famine in Somalia could *probably* be avoided if the government and humanitarian organizations increase the availability of water, provide shipments of food, and supply medical and nutrition assistance.

Thesis statements are typically positioned at or near the end of a text's introduction, to let readers know at the outset what is being claimed and what the text will be aiming to prove. A thesis doesn't necessarily forecast your organization, which may be more complex than the thesis itself. For example, Notre Dame University student Sarah Dzubay's essay, "An Outbreak of the Irrational," contains this thesis statement:

The movement to opt out of vaccinations is irrational and dangerous because individuals advocating for their right to exercise their personal freedom are looking in the wrong places for justification and ignoring the threat they present to society as a whole.

The essay that follows this thesis statement includes discussions of herd immunity; a socioeconomic profile of parents who choose not to have their children vaccinated; outlines of the rationales those parents use to justify their choice, which include fear of autism, fear of causing other health problems, and political and ethical values; and a conclusion that parents who refuse to have their children vaccinated are being unreasonable and selfish. The paper delivers what the thesis promises but includes important information not mentioned in the thesis itself.

More Ways of Beginning

Explain the larger context of your topic. Most essays are part of an ongoing conversation, so you might begin by outlining the context of the subject to which your writing responds. An essay exploring the "emotional climate" of the United States after Barack Obama became president begins by describing the national moods during some of his predecessors' administrations:

> Every president plays a symbolic, almost mythological role that's hard to talk about, much less quantify — it's like trying to grab a ball of mercury. I'm not referring to using the bully pulpit to shape the national agenda but to the way that the president, as America's most inescapably powerful figure, colors the emotional climate of the country. John Kennedy and Ronald Reagan did this affirmatively, expressing ideals that shaped the whole culture. Setting a buoyant tone, they didn't just change movies, music, and television; they changed attitudes. Other presidents did the same, only unpleasantly. Richard Nixon created a mood of angry paranoia, Jimmy Carter one of dreary defeatism, and George W. Bush, especially in that seemingly endless second term, managed to do both at once.
>
> —John Powers, "Dreams from My President"

Forecast your organization. You might begin by briefly summarizing the way in which you will organize your text. The following example from a scholarly paper on the role of immigrants in the US labor market offers background on the subject and describes the points that the writer's analysis will discuss:

> Debates about illegal immigration, border security, skill levels of workers, unemployment, job growth and competition, and entrepreneurship all rely, to some extent, on perceptions of immigrants' role in the U.S. labor market. These views are often shaped as much by politics and emotion as by facts.
>
> To better frame these debates, this short analysis provides data on immigrants in the labor force at the current time of slowed immigration,

---

* academic literacies   ● fields   ● research
■ rhetorical situations   ∴ processes   ● media/design
▲ genres   ◆ strategies

high unemployment, and low job growth and highlights eight industries where immigrants are especially vital. How large a share of the labor force are they and how does that vary by particular industry? How do immigrants compare to native-born workers in their educational attainment and occupational profiles?

The answers matter because our economy is dependent on immigrant labor now and for the future. The U.S. population is aging rapidly as the baby boom cohort enters old age and retirement. As a result, the labor force will increasingly depend upon immigrants and their children to replace current workers and fill new jobs. This analysis puts a spotlight on immigrant workers to examine their basic trends in the labor force and how these workers fit into specific industries and occupations of interest.

—Audrey Singer,
"Immigrant Workers in the U.S. Labor Force"

Offer background information. If your readers may not know as much as you do about your topic, giving them information to help them understand your position can be important, as journalist David Guterson does in an essay on the Mall of America:

Last April, on a visit to the new Mall of America near Minneapolis, I carried with me the public-relations press kit provided for the benefit of reporters. It included an assortment of "fun facts" about the mall: 140,000 hot dogs sold each week, 10,000 permanent jobs, 44 escalators and 17 elevators, 12,750 parking places, 13,300 short tons of steel, $1 million in cash disbursed weekly from 8 automatic-teller machines. Opened in the summer of 1992, the mall was built on the 78-acre site of the former Metropolitan Stadium, a five-minute drive from the Minneapolis–St. Paul International Airport. With 4.2 million square feet of floor space—including twenty-two times the retail footage of the average American shopping center—the Mall of America was "the largest fully enclosed combination retail and family entertainment-complex in the United States."

—David Guterson,
"Enclosed. Encyclopedic. Endured. One Week at the Mall of America"

A roller coaster in the Mall of America.

Visuals can also help provide context. For example, Guterson's essay on the Mall of America might have included a photo like the one above to convey the size of the structure.

Define key terms or concepts. The success of an argument often hinges on how key terms are DEFINED. You may wish to provide definitions up front—as an advocacy website, *Health Care without Harm*, does in a report on the hazards of fragrances in health-care facilities:

445–55 ◆

> To many people, the word "fragrance" means something that smells nice, such as perfume. We don't often stop to think that scents are chemicals. Fragrance chemicals are organic compounds that volatilize, or vaporize into the air—that's why we can smell them. They are added to products to give them a scent or to mask the odor of other ingredients. The volatile organic chemicals (VOCs) emitted by fragrance products can contribute to poor indoor air quality (IAQ) and are associated with a variety of adverse health effects.
>
> —"Fragrances," *Health Care without Harm*

Connect your subject to your readers' interests or values. You'll always want to establish COMMON GROUND with your readers, and sometimes you may wish to do so immediately, in your introduction, as in this example:

◆ 424

> We all want to feel safe. Most Americans lock their doors at night, lock their cars in parking lots, try to park near buildings or under lights, and wear seat belts. Many invest in expensive security systems, carry pepper spray or a stun gun, keep guns in their homes, or take self-defense classes. Obviously, safety and security are important issues in American life.
>
> —Andy McDonie, "Airport Security: What Price Safety?"

Start with something that will provoke readers' interest. Writer and columnist Anna Quindlen opens an essay on feminism with the following eye-opening assertion:

> Let's use the F word here. People say it's inappropriate, offensive, that it puts people off. But it seems to me it's the best way to begin, when it's simultaneously devalued and invaluable.
>   Feminist. Feminist, feminist, feminist.
>
> —Anna Quindlen, "Still Needing the F Word"

Start with an anecdote. Sometimes a brief NARRATIVE helps bring a topic to life for readers. See, for example, how an essay on student loans and their effects on individuals and society begins:

◆ 474–82

> Rodney Spangler first enrolled at the University of North Texas in 2001. There, he pursued a degree in what the school now calls "integrative studies," focusing on history, philosophy, and criminal justice. Rodney also worked full time, and so attended UNT off and on until 2007. For every semester of classes, Spangler took out student loans. When he left—without a degree—he estimates that he had about $30,000 in outstanding student debt.
>
> —Charles Fain Lehman,
> "The Student Loan Trap: When Debt Delays Life"

Ask a question. Instead of opening with a thesis statement, you might open with a question about the topic your text will explore, as this study of the status of women in science does:

> Are women's minds different from men's minds? In spite of the women's movement, the age-old debate centering around this question continues. We are surrounded by evidence of de facto differences between men's and women's intellects—in the problems that interest them, in the ways they try to solve those problems, and in the professions they choose. Even though it has become fashionable to view such differences as environmental in origin, the temptation to seek an explanation in terms of innate differences remains a powerful one.
>
> —Evelyn Fox Keller, "Women in Science: A Social Analysis"

Jump right in. Occasionally you may wish to start as close to the key action as possible. See how one writer jumps right in when opening his profile of a blues concert:

> Long Tongue, the Blues Merchant, strolls onstage. His guitar rides sidesaddle against his hip. The drummer slides onto the tripod seat behind the drums, adjusts the high-hat cymbal, and runs a quick, off-beat tattoo on the tom-tom, then relaxes. The bass player plugs into the amplifier, checks the settings on the control panel, and nods his okay. Three horn players stand off to one side, clustered, lurking like brilliant sorcerer-wizards waiting to do magic with their musical instruments.
>
> —Jerome Washington, "The Blues Merchant"

Ending

Endings are important because they're the last words readers read. How you end a text will depend in part on your **RHETORICAL SITUATION**. You may end by wrapping up loose ends, or you may wish to give readers something to think about. Some endings do both, as Nicholas Kristof's does in arguing that guns should be regulated in the same way cars are. In the first of two paragraphs, Kristof acknowledges that his proposals aren't a cure-all for gun violence but notes that thousands of lives would be saved. In the second, he sums up his entire argument:

57

☀ academic literacies   ● fields   ● research

■ rhetorical situations   ⁝ processes   ● media/design

▲ genres   ◆ strategies

These steps won't eliminate gun deaths any more than seatbelts eliminate auto deaths. But if a combination of measures could reduce the
toll by one-third, that would be 10,000 lives saved every year.

A century ago, we reacted to deaths and injuries from unregulated
vehicles by imposing sensible safety measures that have saved hundreds
of thousands of lives a year. Why can't we ask politicians to be just as
rational about guns?

—Nicholas Kristof, "Our Blind Spot about Guns"

Kristof's final question provides readers with food for thought and challenges legislators either to come up with "sensible safety measures" or to
provide reasons why they can't or won't.

Ways of Ending

Restate your main point. Sometimes you'll simply summarize your central idea, as in this example from an essay arguing that people have no
"inner" self and that they should be judged by their actions alone:

The inner man is a fantasy. If it helps you to identify with one, by all
means, do so; preserve it, cherish it, embrace it, but do not present it
to others for evaluation or consideration, for excuse or exculpation, or,
for that matter, for punishment or disapproval.

Like any fantasy, it serves your purposes alone. It has no standing in
the real world which we share with each other. Those character traits,
those attitudes, that behavior—that strange and alien stuff sticking out
all over you—*that's the real you!*

—Willard Gaylin, "What You See Is the Real You"

Discuss the implications of your argument. The following conclusion of
an essay on the development of Post-it notes leads readers to consider how
failure sometimes leads to innovation:

Post-it notes provide but one example of a technological artifact that
has evolved from a perceived failure of existing artifacts to function
without frustrating. Again, it is not that form follows function but,
rather, that the form of one thing follows from the failure of another
thing to function as we would like. Whether it be bookmarks that fail

to stay in place or taped-on notes that fail to leave a once-nice surface clean and intact, their failure and perceived failure is what leads to the true evolution of artifacts. That the perception of failure may take centuries to develop, as in the case of loose bookmarks, does not reduce the importance of the principle in shaping our world.

—Henry Petroski, "Little Things Can Mean a Lot"

474–82

End with an anecdote. If you take this approach, you might finish a NARRATIVE that was begun earlier in your text or add one that illustrates the point you're making. See how Sarah Vowell uses a story to end an essay on students' need to examine news reporting critically:

> I looked at Joanne McGlynn's syllabus for her media studies course, the one she handed out at the beginning of the year, stating the goals of the class. By the end of the year, she hoped her students would be better able to challenge everything from novels to newscasts, that they would come to identify just who is telling a story and how that person's point of view affects the story being told. I'm going to go out on a limb here and say that this lesson has been learned. In fact, just recently, a student came up to McGlynn and told her something all teachers dream of hearing. The girl told the teacher that she was listening to the radio, singing along with her favorite song, and halfway through the sing-along she stopped and asked herself, "What am I singing? What do these words mean? What are they trying to tell me?" And then, this young citizen of the republic jokingly complained, "I can't even turn on the radio without thinking anymore."
>
> —Sarah Vowell, "Democracy and Things Like That"

Refer to the beginning. One way to bring closure to a text is to bring up something discussed in the beginning; often the reference adds to or even changes the original meaning. For example, Amy Tan opens an essay on her Chinese mother's English by establishing herself as a writer and lover of language who uses many versions of English in her writing:

> I am not a scholar of English or literature. I cannot give you much more than personal opinions on the English language and its variations in this country or others.
> I am a writer. And by that definition, I am someone who has always loved language. I am fascinated by language in daily life. I spend a

* academic literacies
■ rhetorical situations
▲ genres

● fields
∴ processes
◆ strategies

● research
● media/design

great deal of my time thinking about the power of language—the way it can evoke an emotion, a visual image, a complex idea, or a simple truth. Language is the tool of my trade. And I use them all—all the Englishes I grew up with.

At the end of her essay, Tan repeats this phrase, but now she describes language not in terms of its power to evoke emotions, images, and ideas but in its power to evoke "the essence" of her mother. When she began to write fiction, she says,

> [I] decided I should envision a reader for the stories I would write. And the reader I decided upon was my mother, because these were stories about mothers. So with this reader in mind—and in fact she did read my early drafts—I began to write stories using all the Englishes I grew up with: the English I spoke to my mother, which for lack of a better term might be described as "simple"; the English she used with me, which for lack of a better term might be described as "broken"; my translation of her Chinese, which could certainly be described as "watered down"; and what I imagined to be her translation of her Chinese if she could speak in perfect English, her internal language, and for that I sought to preserve the essence, but neither an English nor a Chinese structure. I wanted to capture what language ability tests can never reveal: her intent, her passion, her imagery, the rhythms of her speech and the nature of her thoughts.
>
> —Amy Tan, "Mother Tongue"

Note how Tan not only repeats "all the Englishes I grew up with" but also provides parallel lists of what those Englishes can do for her: "evoke an emotion, a visual image, a complex idea, or a simple truth" on the one hand, and on the other, capture her mother's "intent, her passion, her imagery, the rhythms of her speech and the nature of her thoughts."

Propose some action. A good example of this strategy is the following conclusion of a report on the consequences of binge drinking among college students:

> The scope of the problem makes immediate results of any interventions highly unlikely. Colleges need to be committed to large-scale and

long-term behavior-change strategies, including referral of alcohol abusers to appropriate treatment. Frequent binge drinkers on college campuses are similar to other alcohol abusers elsewhere in their tendency to deny that they have a problem. Indeed, their youth, the visibility of others who drink the same way, and the shelter of the college community may make them less likely to recognize the problem. In addition to addressing the health problems of alcohol abusers, a major effort should address the large group of students who are not binge drinkers on campus who are adversely affected by the alcohol-related behavior of binge drinkers.

—Henry Wechsler et al.,
"Health and Behavioral Consequences of Binge Drinking in College: A National Survey of Students at 140 Campuses"

Paragraphs

Paragraphs are groups of sentences (and sometimes a single sentence) that relate to one main idea. Paragraphs in some of your textbooks may contain several hundred words, while paragraphs in news articles often contain just a single sentence or even, occasionally, a phrase. In English, we show paragraphs by indenting the first word; this is one way that the white space of a text conveys meaning. In fact, we sometimes use white space to create emphasis, especially with very brief paragraphs.

This one, for instance.

In academic writing, paragraphs usually contain a topic sentence that defines the main idea. Then the paragraph is developed by presenting examples or using defining, narrating, classifying, and other writing **STRATEGIES**. Following is advice on writing topic sentences and organizing paragraphs.

403 ◆

Topic Sentences

Just as a thesis statement announces the topic and position of an essay, a topic sentence states the subject and focus of a paragraph. Good paragraphs focus on a single point, which is summarized in a topic sentence. Usually, but not always, the topic sentence begins the paragraph:

※ academic literacies   ● fields   ● research
■ rhetorical situations   ⁑ processes   ● media/design
▲ genres   ◆ strategies

Graduating from high school or college is an exciting, occasionally even traumatic event. Your identity changes as you move from being a high school teenager to a university student or a worker; your connection to home loosens as you attend school elsewhere, move to a place of your own, or simply exercise your right to stay out later. You suddenly find yourself doing different things, thinking different thoughts, fretting about different matters. As recent high school graduate T. J. Devoe puts it, "I wasn't really scared, but having this vast range of opportunity made me uneasy. I didn't know *what* was gonna happen." Jenny Petrow, in describing her first year out of college, observes, "It's a tough year. It was for all my friends."

> —Sydney Lewis, *Help Wanted: Tales from the First Job Front*

Sometimes the topic sentence may come at the end of the paragraph or even at the end of the preceding paragraph, depending on the way the paragraphs relate to one another. At other times, a topic sentence will summarize or restate a point made in the previous paragraph, helping readers understand what they've just read as they move on to the next point. See how linguist Deborah Tannen does this in the first paragraphs of an article on differences in men's and women's conversational styles:

I was addressing a small gathering in a suburban Virginia living room—a women's group that had invited men to join them. Throughout the evening, one man had been particularly talkative, frequently offering ideas and anecdotes, while his wife sat silently beside him on the couch. Toward the end of the evening, I commented that women frequently complain that their husbands don't talk to them. This man quickly concurred. He gestured toward his wife and said, "She's the talker in our family." The room burst into laughter; the man looked puzzled and hurt. "It's true," he explained. "When I come home from work I have nothing to say. If she didn't keep the conversation going, we'd spend the whole evening in silence."

This episode crystallizes the irony that although American men tend to talk more than women in public situations, they often talk less at home. And this pattern is wreaking havoc with marriage.

> —Deborah Tannen, "Sex, Lies, and Conversation:
> Why Is It So Hard for Men and Women to Talk to Each Other?"

414–22 ◆

Glossary

Of course, simply stating the topic of a paragraph isn't enough; you need to support your main point with evidence to prove that your idea or claim is worth considering. Such **EVIDENCE** might include reasons, facts, statistics, quotations or citations from authorities, anecdotes, textual evidence, observations, and examples. For example, in the paragraph below, linguist Dennis Baron uses quotations and examples to make his point that **"THEY"** as a singular pronoun ("Everyone forgets *their* passwords," rather than "*his or her*" or merely "*his*") has been in use for a long time:

> Faced with the onslaught of coined pronouns in the 1880s, singular *they* began to seem less and less objectionable, and more observers recognized the old but much-maligned singular *they* as the people's choice. For example, a writer in 1884 recommended *they* as an interim solution to be used while experts pondered *thon* and *lin*. According to another writer, C. K. Maddox, there was no need for invented pronouns because *they* has been singular "for ages" in the writing of standard authors like Dickens. Maddox criticized experts who withheld their approval: "Our grammarians and dictionary makers are very conservative and often positively stupid" for rejecting a term "so natural to the genius of our language that hardly one in a hundred has noticed it as an intrusion."
>
> —Dennis Baron, *What's Your Pronoun? Beyond He and She*

The topic sentence begins the paragraph, and then information from two different sources—a paraphrase of one writer's solution and a quotation from another—provides support for the assertion made in the topic sentence.

Paragraph Length and Number

The simplest answer to the questions "How long should my paragraphs be?" and "How many paragraphs should my essays contain?" is this: "as long as you need" and "as many as you need." In other words, the length and number of paragraphs in a text depend on your content, on what you need to say. Generally, your paragraphs should signal that groups of sentences are related in meaning and should help readers make those connections. For those reasons, too many brief paragraphs may make a text hard to read because each sentence stands alone, unrelated to the surrounding sentences, while long paragraphs or an essay of a single, very long paragraph forces readers to try to group related ideas together themselves. In other words, the number of paragraphs and the number of sentences within a paragraph depend on the message you're trying to convey—not on some formula or arbitrary number. Here are some reasons to begin a new paragraph:

- to introduce a new subject or idea
- to emphasize an idea
- to give readers a needed pause
- to signal a new speaker when writing dialogue

Transitions

Transitions help readers move from thought to thought—from sentence to sentence, paragraph to paragraph. You're likely to use a number of transitions as you draft; when **EDITING**, you should make a point of checking transitions. Here are some common ones:

380–83

Causes and effects	Changes in direction or expectations	Comparisons
accordingly	although	also
as a result	but	in the same way
because	even though	like
consequently	however	likewise
hence	in contrast	similarly
so	instead	
then	nevertheless	**Examples**
therefore	nonetheless	for example
thus	on the contrary	for instance
	on the one hand . . . on the other hand	indeed
	still	in fact
	yet	such as

Sequences or similarities	Summary or conclusion	Time relations
again	as a result	after
also	as we have seen	as soon as
and	finally	at first
and then	in a word	at the same time
besides	in any event	before
finally	in brief	eventually
first, . . . second, . . . third, etc.	in conclusion	finally
furthermore	in other words	immediately
last	in short	later
moreover	in the end	meanwhile
next	in the final analysis	next
too	in the whole	simultaneously
	therefore	so far
	thus	soon
	to summarize	then
		thereafter

Transitions can also help readers move from paragraph to paragraph and, by summing up the previous paragraph's main point, show how the paragraphs are connected. A common way to summarize is to use phrases like "this _____" and "such _____." Here's an example from an anthropologist's study of American college students:

> When I asked students in interviews whether they felt they had a "community" at AnyU, most said yes. But what they meant by community were these personal networks of friends that some referred to as "my homeys." It was these small, ego-centered groups that were the backbone of most students' social experience in the university.
>
> On a daily basis these personal networks were easily recognizable within the dorm and on campus. "Where are you now?" says the cell phone caller walking back to the dorm from class. "I'm on my way home, so ask Jeffrey and Mark to come, and I'll meet you at my room at 8." Such conversations are everywhere.
>
> —Rebekah Nathan, *My Freshman Year*

"these personal networks" ties the second paragraph to the preceding one.

"Such conversations" sums up the example as a single concept.

* academic literacies
■ rhetorical situations
▲ genres

● fields
⁘ processes
◆ strategies

● research
● media/design

Titles

A title serves various purposes, naming a text and providing clues to the content. It also helps readers decide whether they want to read further, so it's worth your while to come up with a title that attracts interest. Some titles include subtitles. You generally have considerable freedom in choosing a title, but you'll always want to consider the **RHETORICAL SITUATION** to be sure your title serves your purpose and appeals to the audience you want to reach.

■ 57

Some titles simply announce the subject of the text:

"Black Men and Public Space"

The Pencil

"Why Colleges Shower Their Students with A's"

"Does Texting Affect Writing?"

Some titles provoke readers or otherwise entice them to read:

"Kill 'Em! Crush 'Em! Eat 'Em Raw!"

"Thank God for the Atom Bomb"

"Just How Dishonest Are Most Students?"

Sometimes writers add a subtitle to explain or illuminate the title:

Aria: Memoir of a Bilingual Childhood

"It's in Our Genes: The Biological Basis of Human Mating Behavior"

"From Realism to Virtual Reality: Images of America's Wars"

Sometimes when you're starting to write, you'll think of a title that helps you generate ideas and write. More often, though, a title is one of the last things you'll write, when you know what you've written and can craft a suitable name for your text.

30 Drafting

At some point, you need to write out a draft. By the time you begin drafting, you've probably written quite a bit—in the form of notes, lists, outlines, and other kinds of informal writing. This chapter offers some hints on how to write a draft—and reminds you that as you draft, you may well need to get more information, rethink some aspect of your work, or follow new ideas that occur to you as you write.

Establishing a Schedule with Deadlines

Don't wait until the last minute to write. Computers crash, printers jam. Life intervenes in unpredictable ways. You increase your chances of success immensely by setting and meeting deadlines: research done by ___; rough draft done by ___; revisions done by ___; final draft edited, proofread, and submitted by ___. How much time you need varies with each writing task; but trying to compress everything into twenty-four or forty-eight hours before the deadline is asking for trouble.

Getting Comfortable

When are you at your best? When do you have your best ideas? For major writing projects, consider establishing a schedule that lets you write when you stand the best chance of doing good work. Schedule breaks for exercise and snacks. Find a good place to write—a place where there's a good surface on which to spread out your materials, good lighting, a comfortable chair, and the right tools (computer, pen, paper) for the job. Often, however, we must make do: you may have to do your drafting in a busy computer lab or classroom. The trick is to make yourself as comfortable as you can manage. Sort out what you *need* from what you *prefer*.

* academic literacies
■ rhetorical situations
▲ genres
● fields
⁂ processes
◆ strategies
● research
● media/design

Starting to Write

All of the above advice notwithstanding, don't worry so much about the trappings of your writing situation that you don't get around to writing. Write. Start by **FREEWRITING**, start with a first sentence, start with awful writing that you know you'll discard later—but write. That's what gets you warmed up and going.

333–34

Write quickly in spurts. Write quickly with the goal of generating a complete draft, or a complete section of a longer draft, in one sitting. If you need to stop in the middle, make some notes about where you were headed when you stopped so that you can easily pick up your train of thought when you begin again.

Break down your writing task into small segments. Big projects can be intimidating. But you can always write one section or, if need be, one paragraph or even a single sentence—and then another and another. It's a little like dieting. If I think I need to lose twenty pounds, I get discouraged and head for the doughnuts; but if I decide that I'll lose one pound and I lose it, well, I'll lose another—*that* I can do.

Expect surprises. Writing is a form of thinking; the words you write lead you down certain roads and away from others. You may end up somewhere you didn't anticipate. Sometimes that can be a good thing—but sometimes you can write yourself into a dead end or out onto a tangent. Just know that this is natural, part of every writer's experience, and it's OK to double back or follow a new path that opens up before you.

Expect to write more than one draft. A first sentence, first page, or first draft represents your attempt to organize into words your thoughts, ideas, feelings, research findings, and more. It's likely that some of that first try will not achieve your goals. That's OK—having writing onscreen or on paper that you can change, add to, and cut means you're part of the way there. As you revise, you can fill in gaps and improve your writing and thinking.

Dealing with Writer's Block

You may sit down to write but find that you can't—nothing occurs to you; your mind is blank. Don't panic; here are some ways to get started writing again:

- Think of the assignment as a problem to be solved. Try to capture that problem in a single sentence: "How do I explain the context for my topic?" "What is the best way to organize my argument?" "What am I trying to do in the conclusion?"

- Start early and break the writing task into small segments drafted over several days. Waiting until the night before an assignment is due can create panic—and writer's block.

- Stop trying: take a walk, take a shower, do something else. Come back in a half hour, refreshed.

- Open a new document on your computer or get a fresh piece of paper and **FREEWRITE**, or try **LOOPING** or **LISTING**. What are you trying to say? Just let whatever comes come—you may write yourself out of your box.

- If you usually write on your computer, turn it off, get out paper and pencil, and write by hand.

- Try a graphic approach: try **CLUSTERING**, or draw a chart of what you want to say; draw a picture or a comic strip; doodle.

- Do some **RESEARCH** on your topic to see what others have said about it.

- **TALK** to someone about what you are trying to do. If there's a writing center at your school, talk to a tutor: **GET RESPONSE**. If there's no one to talk to, then talk to yourself. It's the act of talking—using your mouth instead of your hands—that can free you up.

333–35
335–36
489
336
372–74

If you need more help

333–44
367–71
372–79

See Chapter 28 on **GENERATING IDEAS AND TEXT** if you find you need more material. And once you have a draft, see Chapter 31 on **ASSESSING YOUR OWN WRITING** and Chapter 32 on **GETTING RESPONSE AND REVISING** for help evaluating your draft.

academic literacies · fields · research · rhetorical situations · processes · media/design · genres · strategies

31 Assessing Your Own Writing

In school and out, our work is continually assessed by others. Teachers judge whether our writing meets their expectations; supervisors decide whether we merit raises or promotions; even friends and relatives size up in various ways the things we do. As writers, we need to assess our own work—to step back and see it with a critical eye. By developing standards of our own and being conscious of the standards others use, we can assess—and shape—our writing, making sure it does what we want it to do. This chapter will help you assess your own written work.

What we write for others must stand on its own because we usually aren't present when it is read—we rarely get to explain to readers why we did what we did and what it means. So we need to make our writing as clear as we can before we submit, post, display, or publish it. It's a good idea to assess your writing in two stages, first considering how well it meets the needs of your particular rhetorical situation, then studying the text itself to check its focus, argument, organization, and clarity. Sometimes some simple questions can get you started:

What works?
What still needs work?
Where do I need to say more (or less)?

Considering the Rhetorical Situation

PURPOSE   What is your purpose for writing? If you have multiple   59–60
purposes, list them, and then note which ones are the most important. How well does your draft achieve your

purpose(s)? If you're writing for an assignment, what are its requirements, and does your draft meet those requirements?

61–64 **AUDIENCE** To whom are you writing? What do those readers need and expect, as far as you can tell? Does your draft answer their needs? Do you define any terms and explain any concepts they won't know?

65–71 **GENRE** What is the genre, and what are the key features of that genre? Does your draft include each of those features? If not, is there a good reason?

72–74 **STANCE** Is your attitude toward your topic and your audience clear? Does your language project the personality and tone that you want?

75–77 **MEDIA/DESIGN** What medium (print? spoken? electronic?) or combination of media is your text intended for, and how well does your writing suit it? How well does the design of the text suit your purpose and audience? Does it meet any requirements of the genre or of the assignment, if you're writing for one?

Examining the Text Itself

Look carefully at your text to see how well it says what you want it to say. Start with its focus, and then examine its support, organization, and clarity, in that order. If your writing lacks focus, the revising you'll do to sharpen the focus is likely to change everything else; if it needs more support, the organization may well change.

Consider your focus. Your writing should have a clear point, and every part of the writing should support that point. Here are some questions that can help you see if your draft is adequately focused:

※ academic literacies   ● fields   ● research
■ rhetorical situations   ∴ processes   ● media/design
▲ genres   ◆ strategies

- What is your main point? Even if it's not stated directly, you should be able to summarize it for yourself in a single sentence.

- If your genre calls for a thesis, is it narrow or broad enough to suit the needs and expectations of your audience?

- How does the **BEGINNING** focus attention on your thesis or main point?

346–54

- Does each paragraph support or develop that point? Do any paragraphs or sentences stray from your focus?

- Does the **ENDING** leave readers thinking about your main point? Is there another way of concluding the essay that would sharpen your focus?

354–58

Consider the support you provide. Your writing needs to give readers enough information to understand your points and see the logic of your thinking. How much information is enough will vary according to your audience. If they already know a lot about your subject or are likely to agree with your point of view, you may need to give less detail. If, however, they are unfamiliar with your topic or are skeptical about your views, you will probably need to provide much more.

- If your text makes an argument, what **REASONS** and **EVIDENCE** do you give to support your thesis? Where might more information be helpful? If you're writing online, could you provide links to it?

413–14
414–22

- What key terms and concepts do you **DEFINE**? Are there any other terms your readers might need to have explained? Could you do so by providing links?

445–55

- Where might you include more **DESCRIPTION** or other detail?

456–63

- Do you make any **COMPARISONS**? Especially if your readers won't be familiar with your topic, it can help to compare it with something more familiar.

437–44

- If you include **NARRATIVE**, how is it relevant to your point?

474–82

- See Part 6 for other useful **STRATEGIES**.

403

Consider the organization.   As a writer, you need to lead readers through your text, carefully structuring your material so that they will be able to follow your ideas.

340–43
- Analyze the structure by **OUTLINING** it. An informal outline will do since you mainly need to see the parts, not the details.

196–200
MLA 574–605
- Is your text complete? Does your genre require an **ABSTRACT**, a **WORKS-CITED LIST**, or any other elements?

361–62
- What **TRANSITIONS** help readers move from idea to idea and paragraph to paragraph? Do you need to add more?

670–72
- If there are no **HEADINGS**, would adding them help orient readers?

Check for clarity.   Nothing else matters if readers can't understand what you write. Following are some questions that can help you see whether your meaning is clear and your text is easy to read:

363
- Does your **TITLE** announce the subject of your text and give some sense of what you have to say? If not, would a more direct title give readers a better sense of your topic?

- If your writing requires a thesis, do you state it directly? If not, will readers easily understand your main point? Try stating your thesis outright, and see if it makes your ideas easier to follow.

346–54
354–58
- Does your **BEGINNING** tell readers what they need to understand your text, and does your **ENDING** help them make sense of what they've just read?

361–62
- How does each paragraph relate to the ones before and after? Are those relationships clear—or do you need to add **TRANSITIONS**?

- Do you vary your sentences? If all the sentences are roughly the same length or follow the same subject-verb-object pattern, your text probably lacks any clear emphasis and might even be difficult to read.

674–80
- Are **VISUALS** clearly labeled, positioned near the text they relate to, and referred to clearly in the text?

☀ academic literacies   ● fields   ● research
■ rhetorical situations   ⁘ processes   ● media/design
▲ genres   ◆ strategies

- If you introduce materials from other sources, have you clearly distinguished **QUOTED**, **PARAPHRASED**, or **SUMMARIZED** ideas from your own?

  542–54

- Do you **DEFINE** all the words that your readers may not know?

  445–55

- Does your punctuation make your writing more clear or less? Incorrect punctuation can make writing difficult to follow or, worse, change the meaning from what you intended. As a best-selling punctuation manual reminds us, there's a considerable difference between "eats, shoots, and leaves" and "eats shoots and leaves."

You may be asked to go into greater detail in an essay-length **REFLECTION** on your writing. If so, these questions may give you a good starting point.

391–401

Assessing a Body of Your Work

If you're required to submit a portfolio of your writing as part of a class, you'll likely need to write a reflective letter or essay that introduces the portfolio's contents, describes the processes you used to create them, and **ASSESSES THE WRITING IN YOUR PORTFOLIO**. See Chapter 35 for detailed advice.

385–90

32 Getting Response and Revising

If we want to learn to play a song on the guitar, we play it over and over again until we get it right. If we play basketball or baseball, we likely spend hours shooting foul shots or practicing a swing. Writing works the same way. Making meaning clear can be tricky, and you should plan on revising and, if need be, rewriting in order to get it right. When we speak with someone face-to-face or on the phone or text a friend, we can get immediate response and restate or adjust our message if we've been misunderstood. In most other situations when we write, that immediate response is missing, so we need to seek out responses from readers to help us revise. This chapter includes a list of guidelines for those readers to consider, along with various strategies for subsequent revising and rewriting.

Giving and Getting Peer Response

When you meet with other students in pairs or small groups to respond to one another's work, in class or online, you have the opportunity to get feedback on your work from several readers who can help you plan revisions. At the same time, you learn from reading others' work how they approached the writing task—you're not writing in a vacuum. Some students wonder why class time is being taken up by peer response, assuming that their instructor's opinion is the only one that counts, but seeing the work of others and learning how others see your work can help you improve the clarity and depth of your writing. The key to responding effectively is to be as specific in your response as possible and avoid being either too harsh or too complimentary. These guidelines can help:

* academic literacies
■ rhetorical situations
▲ genres
● fields
⦂ processes
◆ strategies
● research
● media/design

- Read your peer review partner's draft first from beginning to end as an interested reader, trying to understand the information and ideas. Don't look for problems. In fact, a good rule of thumb is this: read your partner's drafts in the same spirit that you want yours to be read.

- Before starting a second reading, ask your partner what questions they have about the draft or if you should focus on a particular aspect or part of the draft.

- As you read the draft again, take notes on a separate sheet of paper or save your comments to a different file. Your notes might include positive comments ("I like the way you . . . "), negative comments ("This sentence seems out of place"; "_____ doesn't seem like the best word to use"), and questions ("I'm not sure what you mean by _____"; "Would this paragraph work better on p. 2?").

- When you can, do more than identify issues. Offer suggestions or possible alternatives.

- When it's your draft's turn to be discussed, read or listen carefully to your partner's responses, take notes, and ask for clarification if necessary. Do not take issue with your partner's responses or argue over them; even if you're sure that what you wrote is perfectly clear, it's worth taking a second look if your partner has had trouble understanding it.

Getting Effective Response

Ask your readers to consider some of the specific elements in the list below, but don't restrict them to those elements. Caution: if a reader says nothing about any of these elements, don't be too quick to assume that you needn't think about them yourself.

- What did you think when you first saw the **TITLE**? Is it interesting? informative? appropriate? Will it attract other readers' attention?

363

- Does the **BEGINNING** grab your attention? If so, how does it do so? Does it give enough information about the topic? offer necessary background information? How else might the piece begin?

346–54

347–49
- Is there a clear **THESIS**, if the genre or assignment calls for one? What is it?

411–22

560–63
- Is there sufficient **SUPPORT** for the thesis? Is there anywhere you'd like to have more detail? Is the supporting material sufficiently **DOCUMENTED**?

345–63
- Does the text have a clear pattern of **ORGANIZATION**? Does each part relate to the thesis or main idea? Does each part follow from the one preceding it? Was the text easy to follow? How might the organization be improved?

354–58
- Is the **ENDING** satisfying? What did it leave you thinking? How else might the piece end?

72–74
- Can you tell the writer's **STANCE** or attitude toward the subject and audience? What words convey that attitude? Is it consistent throughout?

61–64

59–60
- How well does the text meet the needs and expectations of its **AUDIENCE**? Where might readers need more information, guidance, or clarification? How well does it achieve its **PURPOSE**? Does every part of the text help achieve the purpose? Could anything be cut? Should anything be added? Does the text meet the requirements of

65–71
  its **GENRE**? Should anything be added, deleted, or changed to meet those requirements?

445–55

464–68
- Do any terms need **DEFINING**? Would examples, additional detail, explanations, **DIALOGUE**, or some other strategies help you understand the draft?

676

673–83
- Are **CHARTS**, **GRAPHS**, or **TABLES** clear and readable? If there are no **VISUALS**, should there be?

361–62
- Are sentences complete and grammatical? Are **TRANSITIONS** helpful or needed? Is the punctuation correct?

- Can any words or phrases be sharpened? Are verbs mostly active? Is language that refers to others appropriate? Are all words spelled correctly?

---

* academic literacies　　● fields　　● research
■ rhetorical situations　　∴ processes　　● media/design
▲ genres　　◆ strategies

Revising

Once you have studied your draft with a critical eye and, if possible, gotten responses from other readers, it's time to revise. Major changes may be necessary, and you may need to generate new material or do some rewriting. But assume that your draft is good raw material that you can revise to achieve your purposes. Revision should take place on several levels, from global (whole-text issues) to particular (the details). Work on your draft in that order, starting with the elements that are global in nature and gradually moving to smaller, more particular aspects. This allows you to use your time most efficiently and take care of bigger issues first. In fact, as you deal with the larger aspects of your writing, many of the smaller ones will be taken care of along the way.

Give yourself time to revise. When you have a due date, set **DEADLINES** for yourself that will give you time—preferably several days, but as much as your schedule permits—to work on the text before it has to be delivered. Also, get some distance. Often when you're immersed in a project, you can't see the big picture because you're so busy creating it. If you can, get away from your writing for a while and think about something else. When you return to it, you're more likely to see it with fresh eyes. If there's not enough time to put a draft away for several days or more, even letting it sit overnight or for a few hours can help.

364

As you revise, assume that nothing is sacred. Bring a critical eye to all parts of a draft, not only to those parts your reviewers point out. Content, organization, sentence patterns, individual words—all are subject to improvement. Be aware that a change in one part of the text may require changes in other parts.

At the same time, don't waste energy struggling with writing that simply doesn't work; you can always discard it. Look for the parts of your draft that *do* work—the parts that match your purpose and say what you want to say. Focus your efforts on those bright spots, expanding and developing them.

368–69
59–60
340–42

Revise to sharpen your FOCUS. If your draft includes a thesis, make sure it matches your **PURPOSE** as you now understand it. Read each paragraph to ensure that it contributes to your main point; you may find it helpful to **OUTLINE** your draft to help you see all the parts. One way to do this is to highlight one sentence in each paragraph that expresses the paragraph's main idea. Then copy and paste the highlighted sentences into a new document. Does one state the thesis of the entire essay? Do the rest relate to the thesis? Are they in the best order? If not, you need to either modify the parts of the draft that don't advance your main idea or revise your thesis to reflect your draft's focus and to rearrange your points so they advance your discussion more effectively.

346–58

Read your **BEGINNING AND ENDING** carefully; make sure that the first paragraphs introduce your topic and provide any needed contextual information and that the final paragraphs provide a satisfying conclusion.

369

Revise to strengthen the argument. If readers find some of your claims unconvincing, you need to provide more information or more **SUPPORT**. You may have to define terms you've assumed they will understand, offer additional examples, or provide more detail by describing, explaining processes, adding dialogue, or using some other **STRATEGIES**. Make sure you show as well as tell—and don't forget that you might need to do so literally, with visuals like photos, graphs, or charts. You might try freewriting, clustering, or other ways of **GENERATING IDEAS AND TEXT**. If you have to provide additional evidence, you might need to do additional **RESEARCH**.

403
333–44
489

345–63

Revise to improve the ORGANIZATION. If you've outlined your draft, it helps to number each paragraph and make sure each one follows from the one before. If anything seems out of place, move it—or if necessary, cut it completely. Check to see if you've included appropriate **TRANSITIONS** or **HEADINGS** to help readers move through the text, and add them as needed. Check to make sure your text meets readers' expectations of the **GENRE** you're writing in.

361–62
670–72
65–71

370–71
363

Revise for CLARITY. Be sure readers will be able to understand what you're saying. Look closely at your **TITLE** to be sure it gives a sense of

* academic literacies
* rhetorical situations
▲ genres
● fields
⁘ processes
◆ strategies
● research
● media/design

what the text is about and at your **THESIS**, if you state one directly: Will readers recognize your main point? If you don't state a thesis directly, consider whether you should. Provide any necessary background information, and **DEFINE** any key terms. Make sure you've integrated any **QUOTATIONS**, **PARAPHRASES**, or **SUMMARIES** into your text smoothly. Are all **PARAGRAPHS** focused around one main point? Do the sentences in each paragraph contribute to that point? Finally, consider whether there are any data that would be more clearly presented in a **CHART**, **TABLE**, or **GRAPH**.

347–49

445–55
542–54
368–71

676

One way to test whether your text is clear is to switch audiences: write what you're trying to express as if you were talking to an eight-year-old. Your final draft probably won't be written that way, but the act of explaining your ideas to a young audience or readers who know nothing about your topic can help you discover any points that may be unclear.

Revise VISUALS. Make sure images are located as close as possible to the discussion to which they relate and that the information in each visual is explained in your text. Each image should be numbered and have a title or caption that identifies it and explains its significance. Each part of a **CHART**, **GRAPH**, or **TABLE** should be clearly labeled to show what it represents. If you didn't create the image yourself, make sure to cite its source, and if you're posting your work online, obtain permission from the copyright owner.

673–83

676

Read and reread—and reread. Take some advice from writing theorist Donald Murray:

> Nonwriters confront a writing problem and look away from the text to rules and principles and textbooks and handbooks and models. Writers look at the text, knowing that the text itself will reveal what needs to be done and what should not yet be done or may never be done. The writer reads and rereads and rereads, standing far back and reading quickly from a distance, moving in close and reading slowly line by line, reading again and again, knowing that the answers to all writing problems lie within the evolving text.
>
> —Donald Murray, *A Writer Teaches Writing*

Rewriting

Some writers find it useful to try rewriting a draft in various ways or from various perspectives just to explore possibilities. Try it! If you find that your original plan works best for your purpose, fine. But you may find that another way will work better. Especially if you're not completely satisfied with your draft, consider the following ways of rewriting. Experiment with your rhetorical situation:

- Rewrite your draft from different points of view—through the eyes of different people, perhaps, or through the eyes of an animal or even from the perspective of an object. See how the text changes (in the information it presents, its perspective, its voice).

61–64 ■

- Rewrite for a different **AUDIENCE**. How might an email detailing a recent car accident be written to a friend, an insurance agent, a parent?

73–74 ■

- Rewrite in a different **TONE**. If the first draft was written in formal academic prose, rewrite it more informally.

65–71 ■
75–77

- Rewrite the draft in a different **GENRE** or **MEDIUM**. Rewrite an essay as a letter, story, poem, speech, comic strip, *PowerPoint* presentation. Which genre and medium work best to reach your intended audience and achieve your purpose?

Ways of rewriting a narrative

464–68 ◆

- Rewrite one scene completely in **DIALOGUE**.

- Start at the end of the story and work back to the beginning, or start in the middle and fill in the beginning as you work toward the end.

Ways of rewriting a textual analysis

437–44 ◆

- **COMPARE** the text you're analyzing with another text (which may be in a completely different genre—film, TV, song lyrics, computer game, poetry, fiction, whatever).

- Write a parody of the text you're analyzing. Be as silly and as funny as you can while maintaining the structure of the original text. Alternatively, write a parody of your analysis, using evidence from the text to support an outrageous analysis.

✳ academic literacies   ● fields   ● research
■ rhetorical situations   ⁝ processes   ● media/design
▲ genres   ◆ strategies

Ways of rewriting a report

- Rewrite for a different **AUDIENCE**. For example, explain a concept to your grandparents; describe the subject of a profile to a visitor from another planet, a different time, or a different culture.

  61–64

- Be silly. Rewrite the draft as if for *The Onion* or a Dave Chappelle skit, or rewrite it as if it were written by Bart Simpson.

Ways of rewriting an argument

- Rewrite taking another **POSITION**. Argue as forcefully for that position as you did for your actual one, acknowledging and refuting your original position. Alternatively, write a rebuttal to your first draft from the perspective of someone with different beliefs.

  164–95

- Rewrite your draft as a **STORY** —make it real in the lives of specific individuals. (For example, if you were writing about abortion rights, you could write a story about a young pregnant woman trying to decide what she believes and what to do.) Or rewrite the argument as a fable or parable.

  474–82

- Rewrite the draft as a letter responding to a hostile reader, trying at least to make them understand what you have to say.

- Rewrite the draft as an angry letter to someone or as a table-thumping dinner-with-the-relatives discussion. Write from the most extreme position possible.

- Write an **ANALYSIS** of the topic of your argument in which you identify, as carefully and as neutrally as possible, the various positions people hold on the issue.

  104–33

Once you've rewritten a draft in any of these ways, see whether there's anything you can use. Read each draft, considering how it might help you achieve your purpose, reach your audience, and convey your stance. Revise your actual draft to incorporate anything you think will make the text more effective, whether it's other genres or a different perspective.

33 Editing and Proofreading

No matter what you write, you need to communicate in ways that are appropriate to your rhetorical situation. When you text your friends, for example, you might use minimal punctuation, incomplete sentences, and mainly lowercase letters—and your friends won't bat an eye. If you write a job application letter and résumé, on the other hand, your readers may expect clear, error-free writing in the belief that careful attention to editing—to grammar, punctuation, language, and formality—may indicate similar care in the work you do on the job. Most college instructors expect similar attention to editing and proofreading in formal assignments like research papers. This chapter offers strategies for editing and proofreading your writing carefully.

Editing

Editing is the stage where you work on the details of your paragraphs, sentences, words, and punctuation to make your writing as clear, precise, and appropriate as possible. Your goal is not to achieve "perfection" (whatever that may be) so much as to make your writing as effective as possible for your particular purpose and audience. Consult a good writing handbook for detailed advice, but use the following guidelines to help you check the paragraphs, sentences, and words in your draft.

Editing paragraphs

359–60

- Does each paragraph focus on one point? Does it have a **TOPIC SENTENCE** that announces that point, and if so, where is it located? If it's not the first sentence, should it be? If there's no clear topic sentence, should there be one?

- Does every sentence relate to the main point of the paragraph? If any sentences do not, should they be deleted, moved, or revised?

❋ academic literacies   ● fields   ● research
■ rhetorical situations   ⁘ processes   ● media/design
▲ genres   ◆ strategies

- Is there enough detail to develop the paragraph's main point? How is the point developed—with narrative? definition? some other **STRATEGY**?   ◆ 403

- Where have you placed the most important information—at the beginning? at the end? in the middle? The most emphatic spot is at the end, so in general that's where to put information you want readers to remember. The second most emphatic spot is at the beginning.

- Are any paragraphs especially long or short? Consider breaking long paragraphs if there's a logical place to do so—maybe an extended example should be in its own paragraph, for instance. If you have paragraphs of only a sentence or two, see if you can add to them or combine them with another paragraph, unless you're using a brief paragraph to provide emphasis.

- Check the way your paragraphs fit together. Does each one follow smoothly from the one before? Do you need to add any **TRANSITIONS**?   361–62

- Do the **BEGINNING** paragraphs catch readers' attention? In what other ways might you begin your text?   346–54

- Do the final paragraphs provide a satisfactory **ENDING**? How else might you conclude your text?   354–58

Editing sentences

- Is each sentence complete? Does it have someone or something (the subject) performing some sort of action or expressing a state of being (the verb)? Does each sentence begin with a capital letter and end with a period, question mark, or exclamation point?

- Check your use of the **PASSIVE VOICE**. Although there are some rhetorical situations in which the passive voice ("The prince was killed by a rival") is more appropriate than the active voice ("A rival killed the prince") because you want to emphasize an action rather than who performed it, you'll do well to edit it out unless you have a good reason for using it.   Glossary

- Check for **PARALLELISM**. Items in a list or series should be parallel in form—all nouns ("lions," "tigers," "bears"), all verbs ("hopped,"   Glossary "skipped," "jumped"), all clauses ("he came, he saw, he conquered"), and so on.

- Do many of your sentences begin with "it" or "there"? Too often these words make writing wordy and vague or even conceal needed information. Why write "There are reasons we voted for him" when you can say "We had reasons to vote for him"?

361–62

- Are your sentences varied? If they all start with the subject or are the same length, your writing might be dull and maybe even hard to read. Try varying your sentence openings by adding **TRANSITIONS**, introductory phrases, or clauses. Vary sentence lengths by adding detail to some or by combining some sentences.

- Make sure you've used **COMMAS** correctly. Is there a comma after each introductory element? ("After the lead singer quit, the group nearly disbanded. However, they then produced a string of hits.") Do commas set off nonrestrictive elements—parts that aren't needed to understand the sentence? ("The books I read in middle school, like the Harry Potter series, became longer and more challenging.") Are compound sentences connected with a comma? ("I'll eat broccoli steamed, but I prefer it roasted.")

Editing words

- Are you sure of the meaning of every word? Use a dictionary; be sure to look up words whose meanings you're not sure about. And remember your audience—do you use any terms they'll need to have defined?

- Is any of your language too general or vague? Why write that you competed in a race, for example, if you could say you ran the 4×200 relay?

73–74

- What about the **TONE**? If your stance is serious (or humorous or critical or something else), make sure that your words all convey that attitude.

Glossary

- Do any pronouns have vague or unclear **ANTECEDENTS**? If you use "he" or "they" or "it" or "these," will readers know whom or what the words refer to?

Glossary

- Have you used any **CLICHÉS**—expressions that are used so frequently that they're no longer fresh? "Live and let live," avoiding something

★ academic literacies   ● fields   ● research
■ rhetorical situations   ∴ processes   ● media/design
▲ genres   ◆ strategies

"like the plague," and similar expressions are so predictable that your writing will almost always be better off without them.

- Be careful with language that refers to others. Make sure that your words do not stereotype any individual or group. Mention age, gender, race, religion, sexual orientation, and so on only if they are relevant to your subject. When referring to an ethnic group, make every effort to use the terms members of the group prefer. Also, whenever possible, refer to people by the **PRONOUNS** they use for themselves. If you don't know their pronouns and you need to refer to them with pronouns, it's best to ask. If you can't ask or don't think you should, your best alternative is to use the **SINGULAR "THEY."**

Glossary

Glossary

- Edit out language that might be considered sexist. Have you used words like "manpower" or "policemen" to refer to people who may be female? If so, substitute less gendered words such as "personnel" or "police officers." Do your words reflect any gender stereotypes—for example, that all engineers are male, or all nurses female? If you mention someone's gender, is it even necessary? If not, eliminate the unneeded words.

- How many of your verbs are forms of "be" and "do"? If you rely too much on these words, try replacing them with more specific verbs. Why write "She did a proposal for" when you could say "She proposed"?

- Do you ever confuse "its" and "it's"? Use "it's" when you mean "it is" or "it has." Use "its" when you mean "belonging to it."

Proofreading

Proofreading is the final stage of the writing process, when you check for misspelled words, mixed-up fonts, missing pages, and so on. It's the time to pay extra attention to detail. Most readers will excuse an occasional error, but by and large, academic readers and many employers are an intolerant bunch: too many errors will lead them to declare your writing—and maybe your thinking—flawed. There goes your credibility. So careful proofreading helps ensure that your message is taken as seriously as you want it to be.

Up to this point, you've been told *not* to read individual words on the page and instead to read for meaning. Proofreading demands the opposite: you must slow down your reading so that you can see every word, every punctuation mark.

- Use your computer's grammar checker and spelling checker, but only as a first step, and know that they're not very reliable. Computer programs don't read writing; instead, they rely on formulas and banks of words, so what they flag (or don't flag) as mistakes may or may not be accurate. If you were to write, "My brother was diagnosed with a leaning disorder," "leaning" wouldn't be flagged as misspelled because it's a word (and might even be a disorder), even though it's the wrong word in that sentence.

- To keep your eyes from jumping ahead, place a ruler or piece of paper under each line as you read. Use your finger or a pencil as a pointer.

- Some writers find it helpful to read the text one sentence at a time, beginning with the last sentence and working backward.

- Temporarily change the font or size of your text as you proofread; doing so can help you notice problems you may have overlooked.

- Read the text out loud to yourself—or better, to others, who may *hear* problems you can't see. Alternatively, have someone else read your text aloud while you follow along on the screen or page.

- Ask someone else to read your text. The more important the writing is, the more important this step is.

- If you find a mistake after you've printed out your text and are unable to print out a corrected version, make the change as neatly as possible in pencil or pen.

✳ academic literacies   ● fields   ● research
■ rhetorical situations   ⁝ processes   ● media/design
▲ genres   ◆ strategies

34 Compiling a Portfolio

Artists maintain portfolios of their work to show gallery owners, collectors, and other potential buyers. Money managers work with investment portfolios of stocks, bonds, mutual funds, and other products. And often as part of a writing class, student writers compile portfolios of their work. As with a portfolio of paintings or drawings, a portfolio of writing includes a writer's best work and, sometimes, preliminary and revised drafts of that work, along with a statement by the writer articulating why they consider it good. The *why* is as important as the work, for it provides you with an occasion for assessing your overall strengths and weaknesses as a writer. This chapter offers guidelines to help you compile both a *writing portfolio* and a *literacy portfolio*, a project that writing students are sometimes asked to complete as part of a literacy narrative.

Considering the Rhetorical Situation

As with the writing you put in a portfolio, the portfolio itself is generally intended for a particular audience but could serve a number of different purposes. It's a good idea, then, to consider these and the other elements of your rhetorical situation when you begin to compile a portfolio.

PURPOSE   Why are you creating this portfolio? To show your learning? To create a record of your writing? As the basis for a grade in a course? To organize your research? To explore your literacy? For something else?

59–60

AUDIENCE   Who will read your portfolio? What will your readers expect it to contain? How can you help them understand the context or occasion for each piece of writing you include?

61–64

65–71 ■ **GENRE**

What genres of writing should the portfolio contain? Do you want to demonstrate your ability to write one particular type of writing or in a variety of genres? Will your introduction to or assessment of the portfolio be in the form of a letter or an essay?

72–74 ■ **STANCE**

How do you want to portray yourself in this portfolio? What items should you include to create this impression? What stance do you want to take in your written assessment of its contents? Thoughtful? Enthusiastic? Something else?

75–77 ■ **MEDIA/DESIGN**

Will your portfolio be in print? Or will it be electronic? Will it include multiple media? Whichever medium you use, how can you help readers navigate its contents? What design elements will be most appropriate to your purpose and medium?

A WRITING PORTFOLIO

What to Include

A portfolio developed for a writing course typically contains examples of your best work in that course, including any notes, outlines, preliminary drafts, and so on, along with your own assessment of your performance in the course. You might include any of the following items:

- freewriting, outlines, and other work you did to generate ideas
- drafts, rough and revised
- in-class writing assignments
- source material—copies of articles and online sources, observation notes, interview transcripts, and other evidence of your research
- tests and quizzes
- responses to your drafts

❋ academic literacies   ● fields   ● research
■ rhetorical situations   ∴ processes   ● media/design
▲ genres   ◆ strategies

- conference notes, error logs, lecture notes, and other course materials
- electronic material, including visuals, blogs, and multimedia texts
- reflections on your work

What you include will vary depending on what your instructor asks for. You may be asked to include three or four of your best papers or everything you've written. You may also be asked to show work in several different genres. In any case, you'll usually need to choose, and to do that you'll need to have criteria for making your choices. Don't base your decision solely on grades (unless grades are one criterion); your portfolio should reflect *your* assessment of your work, not your instructor's. What do you think is your best work? your most interesting work? your most ambitious work? Whatever criteria you use, *you* are the judge.

Organizing a Portfolio

If you set up a way to organize your writing at the start of the course, you'll be able to keep track of it throughout the course, making your job at term's end much easier. Remember that your portfolio presents you as a writer, presumably at your best. It should be neat, well organized, and easy to navigate. Your instructor may provide explicit guidelines for organizing your portfolio. If not, here are some guidelines:

Paper portfolios.   Choose something in which to gather your work. You might use a two-pocket folder, a three-ring binder, or a file folder, or you may need a box, basket, or some other container to accommodate bulky or odd-shaped items.

Label everything. Label each piece at the top of the first page, specifying the assignment, the draft, and the date: "Proposal, Draft 1, 9/12/21"; "Text Analysis, Final Draft, 10/10/21"; "Portfolio Self-Assessment, Final Draft, 11/11/21"; and so on. Write this information neatly on the page, or put it on a Post-it note. For each assignment, arrange your materials chronologically, with your earliest material (freewriting, for example) on the bottom, and each successive item (source materials, say, then your outline, then your first draft, and so on) on top of the last, ending with your final draft on top. That way, readers can see how your writing changed from draft to draft.

Electronic portfolios. You might also create an electronic portfolio, or

681–82
e-portfolio. E-portfolios typically consist of a network of **LINKED** documents that might include not only your writing and reflections on that writing, but also sources, writing, and art you did for other courses or for your own enjoyment; audio and video clips; and other resources. Tools that can help you create an e-portfolio include:

- *Courseware.* Your school may use a learning platform, such as *Blackboard*, *Canvas*, or *Moodle*, that allows you to create an e-portfolio of your work.

- *Online tools.* Several websites, including *Weebly* and *Wix*, offer free tools to help you create a preformatted e-portfolio. For example, *GoogleSites* provides templates you can use to build an e-portfolio, uploading documents, images, and videos from your computer.

- *Blogging tools.* You can create an e-portfolio using a blogging platform, like *Tumblr* or *WordPress*, which allows you to upload files and create a network of linked pages. Readers can then comment on your e-portfolio, just as they might on your blog entries.

It's also possible to create an electronic portfolio using word processing, spreadsheet, or presentation software. The programs available for your use and the requirements for publishing your portfolio vary from school to school and instructor to instructor; ask your instructor or your school's

684–93
help desk for assistance (and see Chapter 58 on **WRITING AND LEARNING ONLINE** for general guidance).

Assessing Your Writing Portfolio

An important part of your portfolio is your written self-assessment of your work. This is an opportunity to assess your work with a critical eye and to think about what you're most proud of, what you most enjoyed doing, what you want to improve. It's your chance to think about and say what you've learned during the class. Some instructors may ask you

367–71
to write out your **ASSESSMENT** in essay form, as an additional sample of your writing; others will want you to put it in letter form, which usually allows for a more relaxed and personal tone. See Chapter 31 for detailed

* academic literacies   ● fields   ● research
■ rhetorical situations ⋮ processes   ● media/design
▲ genres   ◆ strategies

advice on assessing your writing and Chapter 35 for advice on composing a formal reflection.

A LITERACY PORTFOLIO

As a writing student, you may be asked to think back to the time when you first learned to read and write or to remember significant books or other texts you've read, and perhaps to put together a portfolio that chronicles your development as a reader and writer. You may also be asked to put together a literacy portfolio to accompany a **LITERACY NARRATIVE**.

▲ 81–103

What you include in such a portfolio will vary depending on what you've kept over the years and what your family has kept. You may have all of your favorite books, stories you dictated to a preschool teacher, notebooks in which you practiced writing the alphabet. Or you may have almost nothing. What you have or don't have is unimportant in the end: what's important is that you gather what you can and arrange it in a way that shows how you think about your development and growth as a literate person. What have your experiences been with reading and writing? What's your earliest memory of learning to write? If you love to read, what led you to love it? Who was most responsible for shaping your writing ability? Those are some of the questions you'll ask if you write a literacy narrative. You might also compile a literacy portfolio as a good way to generate ideas and text for that assignment.

What to Include in a Literacy Portfolio
- school papers
- drawings and doodles from preschool
- favorite books
- photographs you've taken
- drawings
- poems
- letters

- journals and diaries
- lists
- reading records or logs
- electronic texts you've created
- marriage vows
- speeches you've given
- awards you've received
- workplace writing

Organizing a Literacy Portfolio

You may wish to organize your material chronologically, but there are other methods of organization to consider as well. For example, you might group items according to where they were written (at home, at school, at work), by genre (stories, poems, essays, letters, notes), or even by purpose (pleasure, school, work, church, and so on). Arrange your portfolio in the way that best conveys who you are as a literate person. Label each item you include, perhaps with a Post-it note, to identify what it is, when it was written or read, and why you've included it in your portfolio. Or you might create an e-portfolio, scanning print items to include in it along with electronic items.

Reflecting on Your Literacy Portfolio

- Why did you choose each item?
- Is anything missing? Are there any other important materials that should be here?
- Why is the portfolio organized as it is?
- What does the portfolio show about your development as a reader and writer?
- What patterns do you see? Are there any common themes you've read or written about? any techniques you rely on? any notable changes over time?
- What are the most significant items, and why?

☀ academic literacies	⬢ fields	⬤ research
■ rhetorical situations	⁙ processes	⬤ media/design
▲ genres	◆ strategies	

35 Reflecting on Your Writing

Reflecting on experiences—looking back on them to understand and learn from them—is an important part of our work, school, and personal lives. Employees reflect on their job performance as they develop goals for the future. Students reflect on their coursework and extracurricular activities as they prepare applications for scholarships or internships. Lots of people reflect on their daily lives in diaries or journals. And writers reflect on their writing—they look back on their work and consider what they've learned, what they've accomplished, and how they can use their new knowledge and experience in future writing situations. But reflection isn't just an activity that writers engage in *after* they've finished writing. It's also a powerful tool for thinking and learning throughout the writing process. This chapter gives advice for making the most of that tool.

REFLECTING WHILE WRITING

When teachers ask you to reflect during your writing process, they're asking you to pause, step back, and pay attention to what you're doing and thinking as you write. This activity—sometimes called "metacognition"—can help you solve problems in your writing, adjust or adapt your strategies, and make decisions about how to move forward.

Following are questions you can ask yourself in order to prompt reflection at several points in your writing process. You might record your reflections in a process log, or talk through them with someone else, or just mull them over in your mind.

- *Reflecting as you approach a new writing assignment or task.* Have you encountered a similar assignment or task in the past? If so, what processes or strategies worked for you then, and how might you adapt them for your new writing situation now? What goals can you set for yourself? What problems might you encounter, and what resources can help you solve them?

- *Reflecting as you generate ideas and compose a draft.* What's the most intriguing idea you've generated? the most puzzling or surprising? What connections do you see among ideas? What do you like about your draft so far?

- *Reflecting as you participate in peer review.* Which comments from your peers are most helpful? Which comments do you think you'll ignore, and why? What did you learn from reviewing your classmates' drafts, and how can you apply that learning to your own draft?

- *Reflecting as you revise and edit*: What feedback did your teacher provide on your previous work, and can you apply that feedback to your current writing situation? What revision strategies have worked for you in the past, and can you use or adapt them now? What resources can you draw on for help with editing and proofreading?

REFLECTING AFTER WRITING

At times, you may be asked to write a formal reflection on your work—perhaps after completing a writing project, after compiling a portfolio, or at the end of a course. Formal reflection assignments go by many names: portfolio cover letters, reflective self-assessments, companion pieces, statements of goals and choices, and others. Regardless of the name, reflection-after-writing assignments typically ask you to share insights about your work and the process you used to create it—and to support your insights with evidence. Considering your rhetorical situation will help you make decisions about how to approach your particular reflection task.

* academic literacies   ● fields   ● research
■ rhetorical situations   ⁘ processes   ● media/design
▲ genres   ◆ strategies

Considering the Rhetorical Situation

PURPOSE   Why are you writing your reflection? To examine your growth and development as a writer over time? To assess your achievement of course learning goals? To consider how you might use your new knowledge in future writing contexts? Are you reflecting on just one piece of writing or on a body of work?

■ 59–60

AUDIENCE   Who will read your reflection, and what's your relationship to your reader? Is your course instructor your primary reader? Does your audience include other instructors or external evaluators whom you may not know? Will you need to introduce or contextualize the writing you're reflecting on? What examples or evidence of your learning will your readers most want to see?

■ 61–64

GENRE   Has a genre been assigned to you? If so, what are the key features of the genre, and how can you use them in your reflection? Can you choose a genre? If so, what will you choose—a letter, a literacy narrative, a textual analysis, something else? What expectations will your audience have for your chosen genre?

■ 65–71

STANCE   How will you portray yourself in your reflection—as introspective? curious? self-critical? What stance will you take toward the work you're reflecting on—objective? evaluative? analytical? What tone will you use—relaxed and conversational? serious and formal?

■ 72–74

MEDIA/DESIGN   What medium will best suit your purpose and audience? A print document? An electronic text like a blog post, a video diary, or a podcast? Will visuals be helpful? Does your audience expect, or your instructor require, a certain format or type of documentation?

■ 75–77

Generating Insights for Your Reflection

If you've responded to the "Taking Stock of Your Work" prompts at the end of Chapters 10 through 22, you can return to those responses as a starting point to generate insights for an essay-length reflection. The following activities might also help you develop ideas and text:

Take an inventory of your writing. List everything you wrote for your course or for a particular project—freewrites, peer reviews, notes, drafts, revisions, and so on. Then gather as much of the material as you can, and read it carefully. Pretend you're looking at your writing as an outsider, and try **ANNOTATING** or **CODING** it: notice the strengths and weaknesses of individual pieces of writing; pay attention to the language, organization, and other choices you made; note whether your writing changed over time. In other words, *study* your own writing—be curious about it! Take notes so you can harness insights from your inventory.

16–19

Create a map or flowchart of your current writing process. Think about a writing project you recently completed, and make a visual representation of the process you engaged in to create the work. Begin by listing the writing tools you used, the spaces where you worked, the types of tasks you completed—anything you remember about your writing process. Then represent those items with stick figures, symbols, or something else. Use arrows to show how you moved from one point in your writing process to another, and perhaps mark the times when you struggled and the times when you felt productive. When you finish your map, ask yourself what it reveals: Which parts of your writing process were most and least enjoyable? What would you change about your process if you could? What insights can you gain about what you do when you write—and what you might do better in the future? The sample map on the next page represents one writer's process for a research assignment.*

---

* Adapted from Tim Lockridge and Derek Van Ittersum, *Writing Workflows: Beyond Word Processing*.

academic literacies   fields   research
rhetorical situations   processes   media/design
genres   strategies

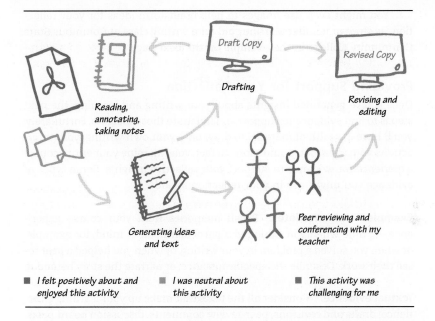

Reading, annotating, taking notes

Drafting

Draft Copy

Revised Copy

Revising and editing

Generating ideas and text

Peer reviewing and conferencing with my teacher

■ I felt positively about and enjoyed this activity

■ I was neutral about this activity

■ This activity was challenging for me

Think of words, phrases, or images that capture your experiences as a writer. Start by listing key activities or concepts that guided your work: maybe **REVISING** was especially important to your writing process, or **AUDIENCE AWARENESS** was something you worked hard to develop. Maybe a particular **ACADEMIC HABIT OF MIND**—like openness or curiosity—was a hallmark of your work. Think, too, about other words or phrases that represent your lived experiences as a writer—like the name of the café where you did your best writing, or the tool (blue notebook, *Google Docs*) that you relied on to get your work done, or the mantra that got you through your course. Freewrite about what those key words or phrases mean to you in the context of your writing and learning.

375–77

61–64

46–56

You might even use images to help brainstorm ideas for your reflection, as student Jennifer Martinez did for a writing class at Columbus State Community College in the example on the next page.

Providing Support for Your Reflection

Once you've generated insights about your writing and learning, the next step is to find evidence to support and illustrate those insights. Fortunately, you'll have a wealth of material to draw on—your own writing, your interactions with classmates, and more. In fact, you can mine your entire course experience for evidence to support your reflective insights. Some types of evidence you might use in your reflection include:

Examples and anecdotes. Recall memories from your course experience—a time when you exhibited a particular habit of mind, for example, or when you solved a problem in your writing, or when you helped a peer re-see their work. Describe the specific instance, or narrate the story behind it.

Textual evidence. Consider all the texts that make up your learning experience: drafts and revisions, peer-review comments, discussion board posts, written feedback from your teacher, and so on. All those texts provide fodder to support the insights you share in your reflection. For example, if you want to illustrate your revising skills, you might quote a passage from an early draft of a writing project and compare it to a revised passage from a later draft. If you want to support a claim about your rhetorical knowledge, you might quote from your writing to highlight particular language choices you made to meet readers' needs. To illustrate your openness to others' ideas, you could quote a comment a peer reviewer made, and then explain how you used that comment to rethink something in your own writing. To show your evolving self-awareness as a writer, you could quote from the "Taking Stock" responses you wrote throughout the course.

Jennifer's Reflection Brainstorming

This whole semester I struggled with **SELF-DOUBT** and overwhelming anxiety at times. Slowly I was able to overcome some of these issues by trusting the writing process and just knowing that I will get through it. I have learned to give myself more time by starting earlier so I am able to work through those moments and to also take breaks when I start to feel the anxiety creep in.

Before this class I would have dreaded the thought of writing a **JOURNAL** entry. Once writing became a normal routine, I started looking forward to our journal entries. I even decided I'm going to buy my mom a daily writing prompt book. You can't be wrong with a journal; it's just your thoughts and your feelings.

One of the most helpful lessons I received from this class was a more positive attitude toward the things I struggle with. After we watched the video on **GROWTH MIND-SET** at the beginning of this semester, something clicked and I started looking at all of my struggles a little differently; I understood that the struggles were helping to make me smarter. Once I accepted that my brain was like a muscle and that I should treat it that way, it was easier for me to work through rough times in my writing.

Statistics. Some students enjoy collecting and interpreting data about their writing processes and products. You might use the "Compare" feature in *Word* to tabulate the number of changes you made from one draft to the next. You might do a search through your process work to see how many times the word "genre" or "audience" or some other key term appeared. You might look for themes in your peer reviewers' comments and tabulate, for example, the percentage of comments related to focus or organization or editing. You might then use the numerical data as support for a particular insight you want to share or a claim you want to make in your reflection.

Visuals. Sometimes visual evidence can help support your reflective insights and claims. You might use photographs of notes, drafts, sketches, and storyboards to support an insight about your writing process. You might create a graph or chart to illustrate numerical data you've generated about your own writing, if you're using such data. You might develop

506–7 ●

a **WORD CLOUD** — a visual representation of words in a text — to highlight key themes in your writing. Remember that visuals almost never speak for themselves, so you'll need to explain them in your reflection. For example, if you include a graph, you might say something like, "The graph in figure 1 depicts how many times my peer reviewers and instructor mentioned key elements — like thesis, organization, or editing — in response to each of my essays."

Ways of Organizing a Reflection

The organization of your reflection will depend on your genre, and you may be able to consult the organizational diagrams in the genre chapters of this book for help. Some common genres used for reflections include letters,

81–103 ▲
104–39
269–79
140–63

LITERACY NARRATIVES , **TEXTUAL ANALYSES** , **EXPLORATIONS** , and **REPORTS** .

❋ academic literacies   ● fields   ● research
■ rhetorical situations   ⁑ processes   ● media/design
▲ genres   ◆ strategies

A Sample Reflection

In the letter below, Nathaniel Cooney reflects on the strengths and weaknesses of the writing he produced in his first-year composition class at Wright State University.

---

2 June 2021

Dear Reader,

It is my hope that in reading this letter you will gain an understanding of the projects contained in this portfolio. I enclose three works that I have submitted for an introductory writing class at Wright State University, English 102, Writing in Academic Discourse: an informative report, an argument paper, and a remix project based largely on the content of the argument paper. I selected the topics of these works for two reasons: First, they address issues that I believe to be relevant in terms of both the intended audience (peers and instructors of the course) and the times when they were published. Second, they speak to issues that are important to me personally. Below I present general descriptions of the works, along with my review of their strengths and weaknesses.

My purpose in writing the informative report "Higher Standards in Education Are Taking Their Toll on Students" was to present a subject in a factual manner and to support it with well-documented research. My intent was not to argue a point. However, because I chose a narrowly focused topic and chose information to support a thesis, the report tends to favor one side of the issue over the other. Because as a student I have a personal stake in the changing standards in the formal education system, I chose to research recent changes in higher education and their effects on students. Specifically, I examine students' struggles to reach a standard that seems to be moving further and further beyond their grasp.

I believe that this paper could be improved in two areas. The first is a bias that I think exists because I am a student presenting information from the point of view of a student. It is my hope, however, that my inclusion of unbiased sources lessens this problem somewhat and, furthermore, that it presents the reader with a fair and accurate collection of facts and examples that supports the thesis. My second area of concern is the overall balance in the paper between outside sources supporting my own thoughts and outside sources supporting opposing points of view. Rereading the paper, I notice many places where I may have worked too hard to include sources that support my ideas.

The second paper, "Protecting Animals That Serve," is an argument intended not only to take a clear position on an issue but also to argue for that position and convince the reader that it is a valid one. That issue is the need for legislation guaranteeing that certain rights of service animals be protected. I am blind and use a guide dog. Thus, this issue is especially important to me. During the few months that I have had him, my guide dog has already encoun-tered a number of situations where intentional or negligent treat-ment by others has put him in danger. At the time I was writing the paper, a bill was being written in the Ohio House of Represen-tatives that, if passed, would protect service animals and establish consequences for those who violated the law. The purpose of the paper, therefore, was to present the reader with information about service animals, establish the need for the legislation in Ohio and nationwide, and argue for passage of such legislation.

I think that the best parts of my argument are the introduction and the conclusion. In particular, I think that the conclusion does a good job of not only bringing together the various points but also convey-ing the significance of the issue for me and for others. In contrast, I think that the area most in need of further attention is the body of the paper. While I think the content is strong, I believe the overall organization could be improved. The connections between ideas are unclear in places, particularly in the section that acknowledges oppos-ing viewpoints. This may be due in part to the fact that I had difficulty understanding the reasoning behind the opposing argument.

✳ academic literacies   ● fields   ● research
■ rhetorical situations   ⁖ processes   ● media/design
▲ genres   ◆ strategies

The argument paper served as a starting point for the remix project, for which the assignment was to revise one paper written for this class in a different genre. My remix project consists of a poster and a brochure. As it was for the argument paper, my primary goal was to convince my audience of the importance of a particular issue and viewpoint—specifically, to convince my audience to support House Bill 369, the bill introduced in the Ohio legislature that would create laws to protect the rights of service animals in the state.

Perhaps both the greatest strength and the greatest weakness of the remix project is my use of graphics. Because of my blindness, I was limited in my use of some graphics. Nevertheless, the pictures were carefully selected to capture the attention of readers and, in part, to appeal to their emotions as they viewed and reflected on the material.

I put a great deal of time, effort, and personal reflection into each project. While I am hesitant to say that they are finished and while I am dissatisfied with some of the finer points, I am satisfied with the overall outcome of this collection of works. Viewing it as a collection, I am also reminded that writing is an evolving process and that even if these works never become exactly what I envisioned them to be, they stand as reflections of my thoughts at a particular time in my life. In that respect, they need not be anything but what they already are, because what they are is a product of who I was when I wrote them. I hope that you find the papers interesting and informative and that as you read them, you, too, may realize their significance.

Respectfully,

Nathaniel J. Cooney

Enclosures (3)

Cooney describes each of the works he includes in his portfolio and considers their strengths and weaknesses, citing examples from his texts to support his assessment and reflection.

Part 6

Strategies

Whenever we write, we draw on many different strategies to articulate what we have to say. We may **DEFINE** key terms, **DESCRIBE** people or places, and **EXPLAIN** how something is done. We may **COMPARE** one thing to another. Sometimes we may choose a pertinent story to **NARRATE**, and we may even want to include some **DIALOGUE**. The chapters that follow offer advice on how to use these and **OTHER BASIC STRATEGIES** for developing and organizing the texts you write.

Strategies

36 Analyzing Causes and Effects   405

37 Arguing   410

38 Classifying and Dividing   431

39 Comparing and Contrasting   437

40 Defining   445

41 Describing   456

42 Using Dialogue   464

43 Explaining Processes   469

44 Narrating   474

45 Taking Essay Exams   483

36 Analyzing Causes and Effects

Analyzing causes helps us think about why something happened, whereas thinking about effects helps us consider what might happen. When we hear a noise in the night, we want to know what caused it. Children poke sticks into holes to see what will happen. Researchers try to understand the causes of diseases. Writers often have occasion to consider causes or effects as part of a larger topic or sometimes as a main focus: in a PROPOSAL, we might consider the effects of reducing tuition or the causes of recent tuition increases; in a MEMOIR, we might explore why the person we had a date with failed to show up.

258–68
236–44

Usually we can only speculate about *probable* causes or *likely* effects. In writing about causes and effects, then, we are generally ARGUING for those we consider plausible, not proven. This chapter will help you analyze causes and effects in writing—and to do so in a way that suits your rhetorical situation.

410–30

Determining Plausible Causes and Effects

What causes ozone depletion? sleeplessness? obesity? And what are their effects? Those are of course large, complex topics, but whenever you have reason to ask why something happened or what could happen, there will likely be several possible causes and just as many predictable effects. There may be obvious causes, though often they will be less important than others that are harder to recognize. (Eating too much may be an obvious cause of being overweight, but *why* people eat too much has several less obvious causes: portion size, advertising, lifestyle, and psychological disorders are only a few possibilities.) Similarly, short-term effects are often less important than long-term ones. (A stomachache may be an effect of eating too much candy, but the chemical imbalance that can result from consuming too much sugar is a much more serious effect.)

334–35
335–36
340–43
489

LISTING, CLUSTERING, and OUTLINING are useful processes for analyzing causes. And at times you might need to do some RESEARCH to identify possible causes or effects and to find evidence to support your analysis. When you've identified potential causes and effects, you need to analyze them. Which causes and effects are primary? Which seem to be secondary?

59–60
61–64

Which are most relevant to your PURPOSE and are likely to convince your AUDIENCE? You will probably have to choose from several possible causes and effects for your analysis because you won't want or need to include all of them.

Arguing for Causes or Effects

410–30

Once you've identified several possible causes or predictable effects, you need to ARGUE that some are more plausible than others. You must provide convincing support for your argument because you usually cannot *prove* that x causes y or that y will be caused by z; you can only show, with good reasons and appropriate evidence, that x is *likely* to cause y or that y will *likely* follow from z. See, for example, how an essay on the psychological basis for risk taking speculates about two potential causes for the popularity of extreme sports:

> Studies now indicate that the inclination to take high risks may be hardwired into the brain, intimately linked to arousal and pleasure mechanisms, and may offer such a thrill that it functions like an addiction. The tendency probably affects one in five people, mostly young males, and declines with age. It may ensure our survival, even spur our evolution as individuals and as a species. Risk taking probably bestowed a crucial evolutionary advantage, inciting the fighting and foraging of the hunter-gatherer. . . .
>
> As psychologist Salvadore Maddi, PhD, of the University of California at Davis warns, "High-risk takers may have a hard time deriving meaning and purpose from everyday life." Indeed, this peculiar form of dissatisfaction could help explain the explosion of high-risk sports in America and other postindustrial Western nations. In unstable cultures, such as those at war or suffering poverty, people rarely seek

academic literacies   ● fields   ● research

■ rhetorical situations   .°. processes   ● media/design

▲ genres   ◆ strategies

out additional thrills. But in a rich and safety-obsessed country like America, land of guardrails, seat belts, and personal-injury lawsuits, everyday life may have become too safe, predictable, and boring for those programmed for risk taking.

—Paul Roberts, "Risk"

Roberts suggests that genetics is one likely cause of extreme sports and that an American obsession with safety is perhaps a cause of their growing popularity. Notice, however, that he presents these as likely or possible, not certain, by choosing his words carefully: "studies now *indicate*"; "the inclination to take high risks *may* be hardwired"; "[r]isk taking *probably* bestowed a crucial evolutionary advantage"; "this . . . dissatisfaction *could help* explain." Like Roberts, you'll almost always need to qualify what you say about causes and effects—to say that something *could explain* (rather than saying it "explains") or that it *suggests* (rather than "shows"). Causes and effects can seldom be proved definitively, so it's important to acknowledge that your argument is not the last word on the subject.

Ways of Organizing an Analysis of Causes and Effects

Your analysis of causes and effects may be part of a proposal or some other genre of writing, or you may write a text whose central purpose is to analyze causes or speculate about effects. While there are many ways to organize an analysis of causes and effects, three common ways are to state a cause and then discuss its effects, to state an effect and then discuss its causes, and to identify a chain of causes and effects.

Identify a cause and then discuss its effects.   If you were writing about climate change, you might first show that many scientists fear it will have several effects, including more violent storms, the extinction of various kinds of plants, and elevated sea levels.

Identify an effect and then trace its causes. If you were writing about school violence, for example, you might argue that it is a result of sloppy dress, informal teacher-student relationships, low academic standards, and disregard for rules.

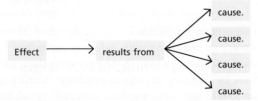

Identify a chain of causes and effects. You may sometimes discuss a chain of causes and effects. If you were writing about the right to privacy, for example, you might consider the case of Megan's law. A convicted child molester raped and murdered a girl named Megan; the crime caused New Jersey legislators to pass the so-called Megan's law (an effect), which requires that convicted sex offenders be publicly identified. As more states enacted versions of Megan's law, concern developed for the rights of those who are identified—the effect became a cause of further effects.

First cause → leads to → first effect, → which leads to → next effect. --→ Continue the chain as need be.

Considering the Rhetorical Situation

As a writer or speaker, it's important to think about the message you want to articulate, the audience you want to reach, and the larger context you are writing in.

59–60 ■

PURPOSE   Your main purpose may be to analyze the causes and effects of something. But sometimes you'll have another goal that calls for such analysis—a business report, for example, might need to explain what caused a decline in sales.

* academic literacies   ● fields   ● research
■ rhetorical situations   ⁚ processes   ● media/design
▲ genres   ◆ strategies

AUDIENCE Who is your intended audience, and how will analyzing causes help you reach them? Do you need to tell them why some event happened or what effects resulted?

61–64

GENRE Does your genre require you to analyze causes? Proposals, for example, often need to consider the effects of a proposed solution.

65–71

STANCE What is your stance, and could analyzing causes or effects show that stance? Could it help demonstrate your seriousness or show that your conclusions are reasonable?

72–74

MEDIA/DESIGN You can rely on words to analyze causes, but sometimes a drawing will help readers *see* how causes lead to effects.

75–77

If you need more help

See also the **PROCESSES** chapters for help with generating ideas, drafting, and so on if you need to write an entire text whose purpose is to analyze causes or speculate about effects.

325

37 Arguing

Basketball fans argue about who's better, LeBron James or Steph Curry. Political candidates argue that they have the most experience or best judgment. A toilet paper ad argues that "you deserve a little luxury in your life, and so does your bottom." As you likely realize, we are surrounded by arguments, and much of the work you do as a college student requires you to read and write arguments. When you write a **LITERARY ANALYSIS**, for instance, you argue for a particular interpretation. In a **PROPOSAL**, you argue for a particular solution to a problem. Even a **PROFILE** argues that a subject should be seen in a certain way. This chapter offers advice on some of the key elements of making an argument, from developing an arguable thesis and identifying good reasons and evidence that supports those reasons to building common ground and dealing with viewpoints other than your own.

223–35 ▲
258–68
245–57

Reasons for Arguing

We argue for many reasons, and they often overlap: to convince others that our position on a subject is reasonable, to influence the way they think about a subject, to persuade them to change their point of view or take some sort of action. In fact, many composition scholars and teachers believe that all writing makes an argument.

As a student, you'll be called on to make arguments continually: when you participate in class discussions, when you take an essay exam, when you post a comment to an online discussion or a blog. In all these instances, you're adding your opinions to some larger conversation, arguing for what you believe — and why.

* academic literacies   ● fields   ● research
■ rhetorical situations   ⁝ processes   ● media/design
▲ genres   ◆ strategies

Arguing Logically: Claims, Reasons, and Evidence

The basic building blocks of argument are claims, reasons, and evidence that supports those reasons. Using these building blocks, we can construct a strong logical argument, also known as *logos*.

Claims.   Good arguments are based on arguable claims—statements that reasonable people may disagree about. Certain kinds of statements cannot be argued:

- *Verifiable statements of fact.* Most of the time, there's no point in arguing about facts like "the earth is round" or "George H. W. Bush was America's forty-first president." Such statements contain no controversy, no potential opposition—and so no interest for an audience. However, you might argue about the basis of a fact. For example, until recently it was a fact that our solar system had nine planets; but when further discoveries led to a change in the definition of "planet," Pluto no longer qualified.

- *Issues of faith or belief.* By definition, matters of faith cannot be proven or refuted. If you believe in reincarnation or don't believe there is an afterlife, there's no way I can convince you otherwise. However, in a philosophy or religion course you may be asked to argue, for example, whether or not the universe must have a cause.

- *Matters of simple opinion or personal taste.* If you think cargo pants are ugly, no amount of arguing will convince you to think otherwise. If you've downloaded every Taylor Swift album and think she's the greatest singer ever, you won't convince your Nirvana-loving parents to like her, too. If matters of taste are based on identifiable criteria, though, they may be argued in an **EVALUATION**, where "Tom Cruise is a terrible actor" is more than just your opinion—it's an assertion you can support with evidence.

▲ 214–22

You may begin with an opinion: "I think wearing a helmet makes riding a bike more dangerous, not less." As it stands, that statement can't be considered a claim—it needs to be made more reasonable and informed. To do that, you might reframe it as a question—"Do bike riders who wear helmets get injured more often than those who don't?"—that may be answered as you do research and start to write. Your opinion or question should lead you to an arguable claim, however, one that could be challenged by another thoughtful person. In this case, for example, your research might lead you to a focused, qualified claim: "Contrary to common sense, wearing a helmet while riding a bicycle increases the chances of injury, at least to adult riders."

Qualifying a claim.   According to an old saying, there are two sides to every story. Much of the time, though, arguments don't sort themselves neatly into two sides, pro and con. No matter what your topic, your argument will rarely be a simple matter of being for or against; in most cases, you'll want to qualify your claim—that it is true in certain circumstances, with certain conditions, with these limitations, and so on. Qualifying your claim shows that you're reasonable and also makes your topic more manageable by limiting it. The following questions can help you qualify your claim:

- *Can it be true in some circumstances or at some times but not others?* For example: "Freedom of speech should generally be unrestricted, but individuals can sue for slander or libel."

- *Can it be true only with certain conditions?* For instance: "Cell phones and computer monitors should be recycled, but only by licensed, domestic recyclers."

- *Can it be true for some groups or individuals but not others?* For example: "The Keto and Atkins diets can lead to weight loss for many people, but people with kidney or liver conditions should avoid them."

SOME WORDS FOR QUALIFYING A CLAIM

sometimes	nearly	it seems/seemingly
rarely	usually	some
in some cases	more or less	perhaps
often	for the most part	possibly
routinely	in many cases	in most cases

※ academic literacies   ● fields   ● research

■ rhetorical situations   ⁝ processes   ● media/design

▲ genres   ◆ strategies

Drafting a thesis statement.   Once your claim is focused and appropriately qualified, it can form the core of your essay's **THESIS STATEMENT**, 347–49 which announces your position and forecasts the path your argument will follow. For example, here is the opening paragraph of an essay by the executive director of the National Congress of American Indians arguing that the remains of Native Americans should be treated with the same respect given to others. The author outlines the context of her argument and then presents her thesis (here, in italics):

> What if museums, universities and government agencies could put your dead relatives on display or keep them in boxes to be cut up and otherwise studied? What if you believed that the spirits of the dead could not rest until their human remains were placed in a sacred area? The ordinary American would say there ought to be a law—and there is, for ordinary Americans. *The problem for American Indians is that there are too many laws of the kind that make us the archeological property of the United States and too few of the kind that protect us from such insults.*
>
> —Suzan Shown Harjo, "Last Rites for Indian Dead:
> Treating Remains Like Artifacts Is Intolerable"

Reasons.   Your claim must be supported by reasons that your audience will accept. A reason can usually be linked to a claim with the word "because":

CLAIM	+	BECAUSE	+	REASON
College students should strive to graduate		because		they will earn far more over their lifetimes than those who do not.

Keep in mind that you likely have a further reason, a rule or principle that underlies the reason you link directly to your claim. In this argument, the underlying reason is that graduating from college leads to a boost in lifetime income because employers value college graduates. If your audience doesn't accept that principle, you may have to back it up with further reasons or evidence.

To come up with good reasons, start by stating your position and then answering the question "Why?"

CLAIM: College students should strive to graduate. *Why?*

REASON: (Because) They will earn far more over their lifetimes than those who do not. *Why?*

UNDERLYING REASON: The economy values college graduates and pays them more.

As you can see, this exercise can continue indefinitely as the underlying reasons grow more and more general and abstract. You can do the same with other positions:

CLAIM: Smoking should be banned. *Why?*

REASON: (Because) It is harmful to smokers and also to nonsmokers.

UNDERLYING REASON: People should be protected from harmful substances.

Evidence. Evidence to support your reasons can come from various sources. In fact, you may need to use several kinds of evidence to persuade your audience that your claim is true. Some of the most common types of evidence include facts, statistics, examples, authorities, anecdotes, scenarios, case studies, textual evidence, and visuals.

Facts are ideas that are proven to be true. Facts can include observations or scholarly research (your own or someone else's), but they need to be accepted as true. If your audience accepts the facts you present, they can be powerful means of persuasion. For example, an essay on the problems faced by people who lose their senses of smell and taste offers these facts to demonstrate the seriousness of this loss:

> Smell is intimately tied to both taste and appetite, and anosmia often robs people of the pleasure of eating. But the sudden absence also may have a profound impact on mood and quality of life.
> Studies have linked anosmia to social isolation and anhedonia, an inability to feel pleasure, as well as a strange sense of detachment and

isolation. Memories and emotions are intricately tied to smell, and the olfactory system plays an important though largely unrecognized role in emotional well-being, said Dr. Sandeep Robert Datta, an associate professor of neurobiology at Harvard Medical School.

—Roni Caryn Rabin,
"Some Covid Survivors Haunted by Loss of Smell and Taste"

Rabin quotes a specialist, which gives her facts credibility; citing the studies she refers to would provide even greater credibility.

Statistics are numerical data, usually produced through research, surveys, or polls. Statistics should be relevant to your argument, as current as possible, accurate, and obtained from a reliable source. An argument advocating that Americans should eat less meat presents these data to support the writer's contention that we eat far too much of it:

> Americans are downing close to 200 pounds of meat, poultry, and fish per capita per year (dairy and eggs are separate, and hardly insignificant), an increase of 50 pounds per person from 50 years ago. We each consume something like 110 grams of protein a day, about twice the federal government's recommended allowance; of that, about 75 grams come from animal protein. (The recommended level is itself considered by many dietary experts to be higher than it needs to be.) It's likely that most of us would do just fine on around 30 grams of protein a day, virtually all of it from plant sources.
>
> —Mark Bittman, "Rethinking the Meat-Guzzler"

Bittman's statistics demonstrate the extent to which Americans have increased their meat consumption over the last half century, the proportion of our diets that comes from meat, and, by comparison, how much protein our bodies require—and summarize the heart of his argument in stark numeric terms.

Examples are specific instances that illustrate general statements. In a book on life after dark in Europe, a historian offers several examples to demonstrate his point that three hundred years ago, night—without artificial lighting—was treacherous:

> Even sure-footed natives on a dark night could misjudge the lay of the land, stumbling into a ditch or off a precipice. In Aberdeenshire, a fifteen-year-old girl died in 1739 after straying from her customary path through a churchyard and tumbling into a newly dug grave. The Yorkshireman Arthur Jessop, returning from a neighbor's home on a cold December evening, fell into a stone pit after losing his bearings.
>
> —A. Roger Ekirch, *At Day's Close: Night in Times Past*

Ekirch illustrates his point and makes it come alive for readers by citing two specific individuals' fates.

Authorities are experts on your subject. To be useful, authorities must be reputable, trustworthy, and qualified to address the subject. You should carefully **EVALUATE** any authorities you consult to be sure they have the credentials necessary for readers to take them seriously. When citing experts, you should clearly identify them and the origins of their authority in a **SIGNAL PHRASE**, as does the author of an argument that deforested land can be reclaimed:

524–34

551–54

> Reed Funk, professor of plant biology at Rutgers University, believes that the vast areas of deforested land can be used to grow millions of genetically improved trees for food, mostly nuts, and for fuel. Funk sees nuts used to supplement meat as a source of high-quality protein in developing-country diets.
>
> —Lester R. Brown, *Plan B 2.0: Rescuing a Planet under Stress and a Civilization in Trouble*

Brown cites Funk, an expert on plant biology, to support his argument that humans need to rethink the global economy in order to create a sustainable world. Without the information on Funk's credentials, though, readers would have no reason to take his proposal seriously.

474–82

Anecdotes are brief **NARRATIVES** that your audience will find believable and that contribute directly to your argument. Anecdotes may come from your personal experience or the experiences of others. In an essay arguing that it's understandable when athletes give in to the temptation to use performance-enhancing drugs, sports blogger William Moller uses an anecdote to show that the need to perform can outweigh the potential negative consequences of using drugs:

I spent my high school years at a boarding school hidden among the apple orchards of Massachusetts. Known for a spartan philosophy regarding the adolescent need for sleep, the school worked us to the bone, regularly slamming us with six hours of homework. I pulled a lot more all-nighters (of the scholastic sort) in my years there than I ever did in college. When we weren't in class, the library, study hall, or formal sit-down meals, we were likely found on a sports field. We also had school on Saturday, beginning at 8 a.m. just like every other non-Sunday morning.

Adding kindling to the fire, the students were not your laid-back types; everyone wanted that spot at the top of the class, and social life was rife with competition. The type A's that fill the investment banking, legal, and political worlds—those are the kids I spent my high school years with.

And so it was that midway through my sophomore year, I found myself on my third all-nighter in a row, attempting to memorize historically significant pieces of art out of E. H. Gombrich's *The Story of Art*. I had finished a calculus exam the day before, and the day before that had been devoted to world history. And on that one cold night in February, I had had enough. I had hit that point where you've had so little sleep over such a long time that you start seeing spots, as if you'd been staring at a bright light for too long. The grade I would compete for the next day suddenly slipped in importance, and I began daydreaming about how easy the real world would be compared to the hell I was going through.

But there was hope. A friend who I was taking occasional study breaks with read the story in the bags beneath my eyes, in the slump of my shoulders, the nervous drumming of my fingers on the chair as we sipped flat, warm Coke in the common room. My personal *deus ex machina*,* he handed me a small white pill.

I was very innocent. I matured way after most of my peers, and was probably best known for being the kid who took all the soprano solos

---

* *Deus ex machina:* In ancient Greek and Roman drama, a god introduced into the plot to resolve complications.

away from the girls in the choir as a first-year student. I don't think I had ever been buzzed, much less drunk. I'd certainly never smoked a cigarette. And knowing full well that what I was doing could be nothing better than against the rules (and less importantly, illegal) I did what I felt I needed to do, to accomplish what was demanded of me. And it worked. I woke up and regained focus like nothing I'd ever experienced. Unfortunately, it also came with serious side effects: I was a hypersensitized, stuffed-up, sweaty, wide-eyed mess, but I studied until the birds started chirping. And I aced my test.

Later I found out the pill was Ritalin, and it was classified as a class 3 drug.* I did it again, too—only a handful of times, as the side effects were so awful. But every time it was still illegal, still against the rules. And as emphasized above, I was much more worried about the scholastic consequences if I were discovered abusing a prescription drug than the fact that I was breaking the law. Though I was using it in a far different manner than the baseball players who would later get caught with it in their systems, it was still very clearly a "performance-enhancing drug."

Just like every other person on this planet, I was giving in to the incentive scheme that was presented to me. The negative of doing poorly on the test was far greater than the negative of getting caught, discounted by the anesthetic of low probability.

—William Moller, "We, the Public,
Place the Best Athletes on Pedestals"

Moller uses this anecdote to demonstrate the truth of his argument—that given the choice between "breaking the rules and breaking my grades" or "getting an edge" in professional sports, just about everyone will choose to break the rules.

Scenarios are hypothetical situations. Like anecdotes, "what if?" scenarios can help you describe the possible effects of particular actions or offer new ways of looking at a particular state of affairs. For example, a mathematician presents this lighthearted scenario about Santa Claus in a tongue-in-cheek argument that Christmas is (almost) pure magic:

---

* Class 3 drug: Drug that is illegal to possess without a prescription.

academic literacies ● fields ● research

■ rhetorical situations ∴ processes ● media/design

▲ genres ◆ strategies

Let's assume that Santa only visits those who are children in the eyes of the law, that is, those under the age of 18. There are roughly 2 billion such individuals in the world. However, Santa started his annual activities long before diversity and equal opportunity became issues, and as a result he doesn't handle Muslim, Hindu, Jewish and Buddhist children. That reduces his workload significantly to a mere 15% of the total, namely 378 million. However, the crucial figure is not the number of children but the number of homes Santa has to visit. According to the most recent census data, the average size of a family in the world is 3.5 children per household. Thus, Santa has to visit 108,000,000 individual homes. (Of course, as everyone knows, Santa only visits good children, but we can surely assume that, on an average, at least one child of the 3.5 in each home meets that criterion.)

—Keith Devlin, "The Mathematics of Christmas"

Devlin uses this scenario, as part of his mathematical analysis of Santa's yearly task, to help demonstrate that Christmas is indeed magical—because if you do the math, it's clear that Santa's task is physically impossible.

Case studies and observations feature detailed reporting about a subject. Case studies are in-depth, systematic examinations of an occasion, a person, or a group. For example, in arguing that class differences exist in the United States, sociologist Gregory Mantsios presents studies of three "typical" Americans to show "enormous class differences" in their lifestyles.

Observations offer detailed descriptions of a subject. Here's an observation of the emergence of a desert stream that flows only at night:

At about 5:30 water came out of the ground. It did not spew up, but slowly escaped into the surrounding sand and small rocks. The wet circle grew until water became visible. Then it bubbled out like a small fountain and the creek began.

—Craig Childs, *The Secret Knowledge of Water*

Childs presents this and other observations in a book that argues (among other things) that even in harsh, arid deserts, water exists, and knowing where to find it can mean the difference between life and death.

542–54

Textual evidence includes QUOTATIONS, PARAPHRASES, and SUMMARIES. Usually, the relevance of textual evidence must be stated directly, as excerpts from a text may carry several potential meanings. For example, here is an excerpt from a student essay analyzing the function of the raft in *Huckleberry Finn* as "a platform on which the resolution of conflicts is made possible":

> [T]he scenes where Jim and Huck are in consensus on the raft contain the moments in which they are most relaxed. For instance, in chapter 12 of the novel, Huck, after escaping capture from Jackson's Island, calls the rafting life "solemn" and articulates their experience as living "pretty high" (Twain 75–76). Likewise, subsequent to escaping the unresolved feud between the Grangerfords and Shepherdsons in chapter 18, Huck is unquestionably at ease on the raft: "I was powerful glad to get away from the feuds. . . . We said there warn't no home like a raft, after all. Other places do seem so cramped up and smothery, but a raft don't. You feel mighty free and easy and comfortable on a raft" (134).
>
> —Dave Nichols, "'Less All Be Friends': Rafts as
> Negotiating Platforms in Twain's *Huckleberry Finn*"

Huck's own words support Nichols's claim that he can relax on a raft. Nichols strengthens his claim by quoting evidence from two separate pages, suggesting that Huck's opinion of rafts pervades the novel.

674–80

Visuals can be a useful way of presenting evidence. Remember, though, that charts, graphs, photos, drawings, and other VISUAL TEXTS seldom speak for themselves and thus must be explained in your text. For example, at the top of the facing page, is a photograph of a poster carried by demonstrators at the 2008 Beijing Summer Olympics, protesting China's treatment of Tibetans. If you were to use this photo in an essay, you would need to explain that the poster combines the image of a protester standing before a tank during the 1989 Tiananmen Square uprising with the Olympic logo, making clear to your readers that the protesters are likening China's

---

✳ academic literacies   ● fields   ● research
■ rhetorical situations   ⁚ processes   ● media/design
▲ genres   ◆ strategies

treatment of Tibetans to its brutal actions in the past. Similarly, you could use the image below of an American flag made from license plates in an argument about America's dependence on the auto industry.

Choosing appropriate evidence. The kinds of evidence you provide to support your argument depend on your **RHETORICAL SITUATION** . If your purpose is, for example, to convince readers to accept the need for a proposed solution, you'd be likely to include facts, statistics, and anecdotes. If you're writing for an academic audience, you'd be less likely to rely on anecdotes, preferring authorities, textual evidence, statistics, and case studies instead. And even within academic communities, different disciplines and genres may focus primarily on different kinds of evidence. If you're not sure what counts as appropriate evidence, ask your instructor for guidance.

Arguing with a Hostile Audience

Academic arguments are often presented to an audience that is presumed to be open-minded and fair, and the goal of such arguments is to demonstrate that your position is plausible and reasonable. Sometimes, though, your goal is to change people's minds, to try to get them to see some issue differently. That can be more of a challenge, because your audience likely has good reasons for thinking as they do, or their views reflect their basic values, and they may well feel defensive, angry, or threatened when you challenge them. These situations call for different argumentative strategies, such as Rogerian argument.

Rogerian argument. This method of presenting an argument is based on the work of psychologist Carl Rogers. The method assumes that common ground—areas of shared values or beliefs—exists between people who disagree. If they can find that common ground, they're more likely to come to some agreement or compromise position.

Since the goal of a Rogerian argument is to find compromise, it is organized differently than a traditional argument. First you must show that you understand your opponents' position, and then you offer your own position. Here's how a typical Rogerian argument is organized; be aware that each section may require several paragraphs:

* academic literacies   ● fields   ● research
■ rhetorical situations   ⁖ processes   media/design
▲ genres   ◆ strategies

Introduction. Here you introduce the issue, acknowledging the various sides of the controversy and being as fair as you can.

Describe the opposing view. In this section, you try to capture the opposing view as accurately and as neutrally as you can. There may be circumstances when that view might be valid, and you should include them, too. Your goal here is to show that you understand the opposing view, and why your readers hold that view, convincingly enough that they will agree that it's accurate. By doing so, you establish your credibility and honest desire to understand those whose views differ from yours.

State your THESIS and support it. Now it's time to outline your position and defend it with reasons and evidence. As with a traditional argument, your goal here is to show that you have thought carefully about your position and researched it thoroughly. As with all arguing, your TONE should show your openness to ideas and avoid sounding as if you and you alone know the truth about the issue or that you are intellectually or morally superior to your opponent.

347–49

73–74

Conclude. In your concluding section, you bring together the two perspectives you've just outlined to show how, while your opponent's views have merit, your position deals with the issue or solves the problem in a better way—or how a compromise position, somewhere in the middle, allows both sides to benefit.

You may find value in using Rogerian techniques in traditional arguments, including seeking common ground, describing issues and positions in neutral terms, and addressing those with opposing views respectfully and with goodwill.

Convincing Readers You're Trustworthy

For your argument to be convincing, you have to establish your own credibility with readers (also known as *ethos*)—to demonstrate your knowledge about the topic, to show that you and your readers share some common ground, and to show yourself to be evenhanded in the way you present your argument.

Building common ground. One important element of gaining readers' trust involves identifying some common ground, some values you and your audience share. For example, to introduce a book arguing for the compatibility of science and religion, author Chet Raymo offers some common memories:

> Like most children, I was raised on miracles. Cows that jump over the moon; a jolly fat man that visits every house in the world in a single night; mice and ducks that talk; little engines that huff and puff and say, "I think I can"; geese that lay golden eggs. This lively exercise of credulity on the part of children is good practice for what follows—for believing in the miracle stories of traditional religion, yes, but also for the practice of poetry or science.
>
> —Chet Raymo, *Skeptics and True Believers: The Exhilarating Connection between Science and Religion*

Raymo presents childhood stories and myths that are part of many people's shared experiences to help his readers find a connection between two realms that are often seen as opposed.

To show that you have carefully considered the viewpoints of others, including those who may agree or disagree with you, it's important to incorporate those viewpoints into your argument by acknowledging, accommodating, or refuting them.

Acknowledging other viewpoints. One essential part of establishing your credibility is to acknowledge that there are viewpoints different from yours and to represent them fairly and accurately. Rather than weakening your argument, acknowledging possible objections to your position shows that you've thought about and researched your topic thoroughly.

For example, in an essay about his experience growing up homosexual, writer Andrew Sullivan admits that not every young gay man or woman has the same experience:

> I should add that many young lesbians and homosexuals seem to have had a much easier time of it. For many, the question of sexual identity was not a critical factor in their life choices or vocation, or even a factor at all.
>
> —Andrew Sullivan, "What Is a Homosexual?"

In response to a reasonable objection, Sullivan qualifies his assertions, making his own stance appear to be reasonable.

Accommodating other viewpoints.   You may be tempted to ignore views you don't agree with, but in fact it's important to demonstrate that you're aware of them and have considered them carefully. You may find yourself conceding that opposing views have some merit and qualifying your claim or even making them part of your own argument. See, for example, how a philosopher arguing that torture is sometimes "not merely permissible but morally mandatory" addresses a major objection to his position:

> The most powerful argument against using torture as a punishment or to secure confessions is that such practices disregard the rights of the individual. Well, if the individual is all that important—and he is— it is correspondingly important to protect the rights of individuals threatened by terrorists. If life is so valuable that it must never be taken, the lives of the innocents must be saved even at the price of hurting the one who endangers them.
>
> —Michael Levin, "The Case for Torture"

Levin acknowledges his critics' argument that the individual is indeed important; but he then asserts that if the life of one person is important, the lives of many people must be even more important. In effect, he uses an opposing argument to advance his own.

Refuting other viewpoints. Often you may need to refute other arguments and make a case for why you believe they are wrong. Are the values underlying the argument questionable? Is the reasoning flawed? Is the evidence inadequate or faulty? For example, an essay arguing for the elimination of college athletics scholarships includes this refutation:

> Some argue that eliminating athletics scholarships would deny opportunity and limit access for many students, most notably black athletes. The question is, access to what? The fields of competition or an opportunity to earn a meaningful degree? With the six-year graduation rates of black basketball players hovering in the high 30% range, and black football players in the high 40% range, despite years of "academic reform," earning an athletics scholarship under the current system is little more than a chance to play sports.
>
> —John R. Gerdy, "For True Reform,
> Athletics Scholarships Must Go"

Gerdy bases his refutation on statistics showing that for more than half of African American college athletes, the opportunity to earn a degree by playing a sport is an illusion.

427–29   When you incorporate differing viewpoints, be careful to avoid the **FALLACIES** of attacking the person making the argument or refuting a competing position that no one seriously entertains. It's also important that you not distort or exaggerate opposing viewpoints. If *your* argument is to be persuasive, other arguments should be represented fairly.

Appealing to Readers' Emotions

Logic and facts, even when presented by someone who seems reasonable and trustworthy, may not be enough to persuade readers. Many successful arguments include an emotional component that appeals to readers' hearts as well as to their minds. Advertising often works by appealing to its audience's emotions, as in this paragraph from a Volvo ad:

> Choosing a car is about the comfort and safety of your passengers, most especially your children. That's why we ensure Volvo's safety research

✳ academic literacies   ◆ fields   ● research
■ rhetorical situations   ⋮ processes   ⬮ media/design
▲ genres   ◆ strategies

examines how we can make our cars safer for everyone who travels in them—from adults to teenagers, children to babies. Even those who aren't even born yet.

—Volvo.com

This ad plays on the fear that children—or a pregnant mother—may be injured or killed in an automobile accident.

Keep in mind that emotional appeals, also known as *pathos*, can make readers feel as though they're being manipulated and, consequently, less likely to accept an argument. For most kinds of academic writing, use emotional appeals sparingly.

Checking for Fallacies

Fallacies are arguments that involve faulty reasoning. It's important to avoid fallacies in your writing because they often seem plausible but are usually unfair or inaccurate and make reasonable discussion difficult. Here are some of the most common fallacies:

- *Ad hominem* arguments attack someone's character rather than address the issues. ("Ad hominem" is Latin for "to the man.") It's an especially common fallacy in political discourse and elsewhere: "Jack Turner has no business talking about the way we run things in this city. He's just another liberal snowflake." Whether or not Turner is a "liberal snowflake" has no bearing on the worth of his argument about "the way we run things in this city"; insulting one's opponents isn't an argument against their positions. A variation, the "you too" or "whataboutism" fallacy, results when someone responds to criticism by accusing the attacker of hypocrisy but not answering the criticism itself: "You say I'm lying, but what about your use of a company car to take a family vacation?"

- *Bandwagon appeals* argue that because others think or do something, we should, too. For example, an advertisement for a breakfast cereal claims that it is "America's favorite cereal." It assumes that readers want to be part of the group and implies that an opinion that's popular must be correct.

- *Begging the question* is a circular argument. It assumes as a given what is trying to be proved, essentially asserting that A is true because A is true. Consider this statement: "Affirmative action can never be fair or just because you cannot remedy one injustice by committing another." This statement begs the question because in trying to prove that affirmative action is unjust, it assumes that it is an injustice.

- *Either-or* arguments, also called *false dilemmas*, are oversimplifications that assert there can be only two possible positions on a complex issue. For example, "Those who oppose our actions in this war are enemies of freedom" inaccurately assumes that if someone opposes the war in question, they oppose freedom. In fact, people might have many other reasons for opposing the war.

- *False analogies* compare things that resemble each other in some ways but not in the most important respects—for example, "Trees pollute the air just as much as cars and trucks do." Although it's true that plants emit hydrocarbons, and hydrocarbons are a component of smog, plants also produce oxygen, whereas motor vehicles emit gases that combine with hydrocarbons to form smog. Vehicles pollute the air; trees provide the air that vehicles' emissions pollute.

- *Faulty causality,* also known as *post hoc, ergo propter hoc* (Latin for "after this, therefore because of this"), assumes that because one event followed another, the first event caused the second—for example, "Legalizing same-sex marriage in Sweden led to a decline in the marriage rate of opposite-sex couples." The statement contains no evidence to show that the first event caused the second.

- *Straw man* arguments misrepresent an opposing position to make it sound ridiculous or extreme and thus easy to refute, rather than dealing with the actual position. For example, if someone argues that funding for supplemental nutrition assistance should be cut, a straw man response would be "You want the poor to starve," transforming a proposal to cut a specific program into an exaggerated argument that the proposer hasn't made.

- *Hasty generalizations* are conclusions based on insufficient or inappropriately qualified evidence. This summary of a research study is a

academic literacies   ● fields   ● research

■ rhetorical situations   ⁙ processes   ● media/design

▲ genres   ◆ strategies

good example: "Twenty randomly chosen residents of Brooklyn, New York, were asked whether they found graffiti tags offensive; fourteen said yes, five said no, and one had no opinion. Therefore, 70 percent of Brooklyn residents find tagging offensive." In Brooklyn, a part of New York City with a population of over two million, twenty residents is far too small a group from which to draw meaningful conclusions. To be able to generalize, the researcher would have had to survey a much greater percentage of Brooklyn's population.

- *Slippery slope* arguments assert that one event will inevitably lead to another, often cataclysmic event without presenting evidence that such a chain of causes and effects will in fact take place. Here's an example: "If the state legislature passes this 2 percent tax increase, it won't be long before all the corporations in the state move to other states and leave thousands unemployed." According to this argument, if taxes are raised, the state's economy will be ruined—not a likely scenario, given the size of the proposed increase.

Considering the Rhetorical Situation

To argue effectively, it's important to think about the message you want to articulate, the audience you want to persuade, the effect of your stance, and the larger context you are writing in.

PURPOSE	What do you want your audience to do? To think a certain way? To take a certain action? To change their minds? To consider alternative views to their current ones? To accept your position as plausible? To see that you have thought carefully about an issue and researched it appropriately?
AUDIENCE	Who is your intended audience? What do they likely know and believe about your topic? How personal is it for them? To what extent are they likely to agree or disagree with you? Why? What common ground can you find with them? How should you incorporate other viewpoints they might have? What kinds of evidence are they likely to accept?

59–60

61–64

65–71 ■ **GENRE** What genre will help you achieve your purpose? A position paper? An evaluation? A review? A proposal? An analysis?

72–74 ■ **STANCE** What's your attitude toward your topic, and why? What strategies will help you to convey that stance? How do you want your audience to perceive you? As an authority on your topic? As someone much like them? As calm? reasonable? impassioned or angry? something else?

75–77 ■ **MEDIA/DESIGN** What media will you use, and how will your choice of media affect your argument? If you're writing on paper, does your argument call for photos or charts? If you're giving an oral presentation, should you put your reasons and support on slides? If you're writing online, should you add links to sites representing other positions or containing evidence that supports your position?

If you need more help

164–95 ▲
79
325 ⸪ See also Chapter 13 for advice on writing an **ARGUMENT** essay. And see other appropriate **GENRE** chapters and all the **PROCESSES** chapters for guidelines on drafting, revising, and so on for help writing an essay that includes arguments.

✳ academic literacies   ● fields   ● research

■ rhetorical situations   ⸪ processes   ● media/design

▲ genres   ◆ strategies

38 Classifying and Dividing

Classification and division are ways of organizing information: various items may be classified according to their similarities, or a single topic may be divided into parts. We might classify different kinds of flowers as annuals or perennials, for example, and classify the perennials further as daylilies, irises, roses, and peonies. We might also divide a garden into distinct areas: for herbs, flowers, and vegetables.

Writers often use classification and division as ways of developing and organizing material. This book, for instance, classifies comparison, definition, description, and several other common ways of thinking and writing as strategies. It divides the information it provides about writing into eight parts: "Rhetorical Situations," "Genres," and so on. Each part further divides its material into various chapters. Even if you never write a book, you will have occasion to classify and divide material in **ANNOTATED BIBLIOGRAPHIES**, essays **ANALYZING TEXTS**, and other kinds of writing. This chapter offers advice for classifying and dividing information for various purposes—and in a way that suits your own rhetorical situation.

▲ 201–13
104–39

Classifying

When we classify something, we group it with similar things. A linguist would classify French, Spanish, and Italian as Romance languages, for example—and Russian, Polish, and Bulgarian as Slavic languages. In a phony news story from the *Onion* about a church bake sale, the writer classifies the activities observed there as examples of the seven deadly sins:

GADSDEN, AL—The seven deadly sins—avarice, sloth, envy, lust, gluttony, pride, and wrath—were all committed Sunday during the twice-annual bake sale at St. Mary's of the Immaculate Conception Church.

—"All Seven Deadly Sins Committed at Church Bake Sale,"
Onion

The article goes on to categorize the participants' behavior in terms of the sins, describing one parishioner who commits the sin of pride by bragging about her cookies and others who commit the sin of envy by resenting the popularity of the prideful parishioner's baked goods (the eating of which leads to the sin of gluttony). In all, the article humorously notes, "347 individual acts of sin were committed at the bake sale," and every one of them can be classified as one of the seven deadly sins.

Dividing

As a writing strategy, division is a way of breaking something into parts—and a way of making the information easy for readers to follow and understand. See how this example about children's ways of nagging divides their tactics into seven categories:

James U. McNeal, a professor of marketing at Texas A&M University, is considered America's leading authority on marketing to children. In his book *Kids as Customers* (1992), McNeal provides marketers with a thorough analysis of "children's requesting styles and appeals." He [divides] juvenile nagging tactics into seven major categories. A *pleading* nag is one accompanied by repetitions of words like "please" or "mom, mom, mom." A *persistent* nag involves constant requests for the coveted product and may include the phrase "I'm gonna ask just one more time." *Forceful* nags are extremely pushy and may include subtle threats, like "Well, then, I'll go and ask Dad." *Demonstrative* nags are the most high risk, often characterized by full-blown tantrums in public places, breath holding, tears, a refusal to leave the store. *Sugar-coated* nags promise affection in return for a purchase and may rely on seemingly heartfelt declarations, like "You're the best dad in the world." *Threatening* nags are youthful forms of blackmail, vows of eternal hatred and of running away if something isn't bought. *Pity* nags claim the child will be heartbroken, teased, or socially stunted if the parent refuses to buy a certain item. "All of these appeals and styles may be used in combination," McNeal's research has discovered, "but kids tend to stick to one or two of each that prove most effective . . . for their own parents."

—Eric Schlosser, *Fast Food Nation:*
The Dark Side of the All-American Meal

Here the writer announces the division scheme of "seven major categories." Then he names each tactic and describes how it works. Notice the italics: each tactic is italicized, making it easy to recognize and follow. Take away the italics, and the divisions would be less visible.

Creating Clear and Distinct Categories

When you classify or divide, it's important to create clear and distinct categories. If you're writing about music, you might divide it on the basis of the genre (rap, rock, classical, gospel), artist (male or female, group or solo), or instruments (violins, trumpets, bongos, guitars). These categories must be distinct so that no information overlaps or fits into more than one category, and they must include every member of the group you're discussing. The simpler the criteria for selecting the categories, the better. The nagging categories in the example from *Fast Food Nation* are based on only one criterion: a child's verbal behavior.

Sometimes you may want to highlight your categories visually to make them easier to follow. Eric Schlosser does that by italicizing each category: the *pleading* nag, the *persistent* nag, the *forceful* nag, and so on. Other **DESIGN** elements—bulleted lists, pie charts, tables, images—might also prove useful.

664–72

Sometimes you might show categories visually, as in the following chart. The differences among the six varieties pictured are visible at a glance, and the chart next to the photos shows the best uses for each variety—and its level of tartness.

	EATING	BAKING	COOKING	
Red Delicious	✔	✔		**LESS TART**
Honeycrisp	✔	✔	✔	
Red Rome		✔	✔	
Braeburn	✔		✔	
McIntosh	✔	✔	✔	**MORE TART**

All photos © New York Apple Association

The photographs allow us to see the differences among the varieties at a glance. Although the varieties shown here are arranged according to the tartness of their flavor, they could have been arranged in other ways, too—for example, alphabetically or by shape or size.

✷ academic literacies   ● fields   ● research
■ rhetorical situations   ⁝ processes   ● media/design
▲ genres   ◆ strategies

For another example, see how *The World of Caffeine* authors Bennett Alan Weinberg and Bonnie K. Bealer use a two-column list to show what they say are the differing cultural connotations of coffee and tea:

Coffee Aspect	Tea Aspect
Male	Female
Boisterous	Decorous
Indulgence	Temperance
Hardheaded	Romantic
Topology	Geometry
Heidegger	Carnap
Beethoven	Mozart
Libertarian	Statist
Promiscuous	Pure

—Bennett Alan Weinberg and Bonnie K. Bealer,
The World of Caffeine

Considering the Rhetorical Situation

As a writer or speaker, it's important to think about the message you want to articulate, the audience you want to reach, and the larger context you are writing in.

PURPOSE   Your purpose for writing will affect how you classify or divide information. Weinberg and Bealer classify coffee as "boisterous" and tea as "decorous" to help readers understand the cultural styles the two beverages represent, whereas J. Crew might divide sweaters into cashmere, wool, and cotton to help shoppers find and buy clothing from its website.

■ 59–60

61–64 ■   **AUDIENCE**   Who do you want to reach, and will classifying or dividing your material help them follow your discussion?

65–71 ■   **GENRE**   Does your genre call for you to categorize or divide information? A long report might need to be divided into sections, for instance.

72–74 ■   **STANCE**   Your stance may affect the way you classify information. Weinberg and Bealer's classification of coffee as "Beethoven" and tea as "Mozart" reflects a stance that focuses on cultural analysis (and assumes an audience familiar with the difference between the two composers). If the authors were botanists, they might categorize the two beverages in terms of their biological origins ("seed based" and "leaf based").

75–77 ■   **MEDIA / DESIGN**   You can classify or divide in paragraph form, but sometimes a pie chart or list will show the categories better.

If you need more help

334–36 ⁂
325

See also **CLUSTERING**, **CUBING**, and **LOOPING**, three methods of generating ideas discussed in Chapter 28 that can be especially helpful for classifying material. And see all the **PROCESSES** chapters for guidelines on drafting, revising, and so on if you need to write a classification essay.

✳ academic literacies   ● fields   ● research
■ rhetorical situations   ⁂ processes   ● media/design
▲ genres   ◆ strategies

39 Comparing and Contrasting

Comparing things looks at their similarities; contrasting them focuses on their differences. It's a kind of thinking that comes naturally and that we do constantly—for example, comparing Houston with Dallas, iPhones with Androids, or three paintings by Renoir. And once we start comparing, we generally find ourselves contrasting—Houston and Dallas have differences as well as similarities.

As a student, you'll often be asked to compare and contrast paintings or poems or other things. As a writer, you'll have cause to compare and contrast in most kinds of writing. In a **PROPOSAL**, for instance, you'll need to compare your solution with other possible solutions; or in an **EVALUATION**, such as a movie review, you might contrast the film you're reviewing with some other film. This chapter offers advice on ways of comparing and contrasting things for various writing purposes and for your own rhetorical situations.

▲ 258–68
214–22

Most of the time, we compare obviously similar things: laptops we might purchase, three competing political candidates, two versions of a film. Occasionally, however, we might compare things that are less obviously similar. See how John McMurtry, a former football player, compares football with war in an essay arguing that the attraction football holds for spectators is based in part on its potential for violence and injury:

> The family resemblance between football and war is, indeed, striking. Their languages are similar: "field general," "long bomb," "blitz," "take a shot," "front line," "pursuit," "good hit," "the draft," and so on. Their principles and practices are alike: mass hysteria, the art of intimidation, absolute command and total obedience, territorial aggression, censorship, inflated insignia and propaganda, blackboard maneuvers and strategies, drills, uniforms, marching bands, and training camps.

And the virtues they celebrate are almost identical: hyperaggressiveness, coolness under fire, and suicidal bravery.

—John McMurtry, "Kill 'Em! Crush 'Em! Eat 'Em Raw!"

McMurtry's comparison helps focus readers' attention on what he's arguing about football in part because it's somewhat unexpected. But the more unlikely the comparison, the more you might be accused of comparing apples and oranges. It's important, therefore, that the things we compare be *legitimately* compared—as is the case in the following comparison of the health of the world's richest and poorest people:

> World Health Organization (WHO) data indicate that roughly 1.2 billion people are undernourished, underweight, and often hungry. At the same time, roughly 1.2 billion people are overnourished and overweight, most of them suffering from excessive caloric intake and exercise deprivation. So while 1 billion people worry whether they will eat, another billion should worry about eating too much.
>
> Disease patterns also reflect the widening gap. The billion poorest suffer mostly from infectious diseases—malaria, tuberculosis, dysentery, and AIDS. Malnutrition leaves infants and small children even more vulnerable to such infectious diseases. Unsafe drinking water takes a heavier toll on those with hunger-weakened immune systems, resulting in millions of fatalities each year. In contrast, among the billion at the top of the global economic scale, it is diseases related to aging and lifestyle excesses, including obesity, smoking, diets rich in fat and sugar, and exercise deprivation, that cause most deaths.
>
> —Lester R. Brown, *Plan B 2.0: Rescuing a Planet under Stress and a Civilization in Trouble*

While the two groups of roughly a billion people each undoubtedly have similarities, this selection from a book arguing for global action on the environment focuses on the stark contrasts.

Two Ways of Comparing and Contrasting

Comparisons and contrasts may be organized in two basic ways: block and point by point.

* academic literacies   ● fields   ● research
■ rhetorical situations ° processes   ● media/design
▲ genres   ◆ strategies

The block method.   One way is to discuss separately each item you're comparing, giving all the information about one item and then all the information about the next item. A report on Seattle and Vancouver, for example, compares the firearm regulations in each city by using a paragraph about Seattle and then a paragraph about Vancouver:

> Although similar in many ways, Seattle and Vancouver differ markedly in their approaches to the regulation of firearms. In Seattle, handguns may be purchased legally for self-defense in the street or at home. After a thirty-day waiting period, a permit can be obtained to carry a handgun as a concealed weapon. The recreational use of handguns is minimally restricted.
>
> In Vancouver, self-defense is not considered a valid or legal reason to purchase a handgun. Concealed weapons are not permitted. Recreational uses of handguns (such as target shooting and collecting) are regulated by the province, and the purchase of a handgun requires a restricted-weapons permit. A permit to carry a weapon must also be obtained in order to transport a handgun, and these weapons can be discharged only at a licensed shooting club. Handguns can be transported by car, but only if they are stored in the trunk in a locked box.
>
> —John Henry Sloan et al., "Handgun Regulations, Crime,
> Assaults, and Homicide: A Tale of Two Cities"

The point-by-point method.   The other way to compare things is to focus on specific points of comparison. In this paragraph, humorist David Sedaris compares his childhood with his partner's, discussing corresponding aspects of the childhoods one at a time:

> Certain events are parallel, but compared with Hugh's, my childhood was unspeakably dull. When I was seven years old, my family moved to North Carolina. When he was seven years old, Hugh's family moved to the Congo. We had a collie and a house cat. They had a monkey and two horses named Charlie Brown and Satan. I threw stones at stop signs. Hugh threw stones at crocodiles. The verbs are the same, but he definitely wins the prize when it comes to nouns and objects. An eventful day for my mother might have involved a trip to the dry cleaner or a conversation with the potato-chip deliveryman. Asked one ordinary Congo afternoon what she'd done with her day, Hugh's mother

answered that she and a fellow member of the Ladies' Club had visited
a leper colony on the outskirts of Kinshasa.

—David Sedaris, "Remembering My Childhood
on the Continent of Africa"

Using Graphs and Images to Present Comparisons

674–80

Some comparisons can be easier to understand if they're presented visually, as a **CHART**, **GRAPH**, or **ILLUSTRATION**. For example, the following line
graph, from *Business Insider*, compares the incomes of Black and White
Americans between 2002 and 2018.

It would be possible to write out this information in a paragraph—but
it's much easier to understand it this way:

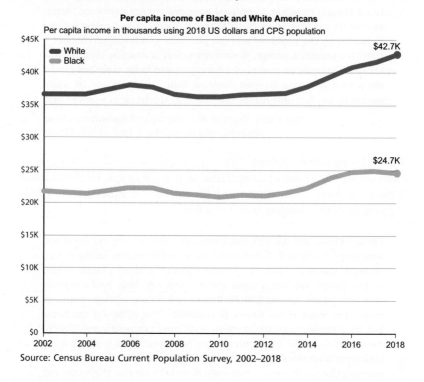

Per capita income of Black and White Americans
Per capita income in thousands using 2018 US dollars and CPS population

Source: Census Bureau Current Population Survey, 2002–2018

* academic literacies
■ rhetorical situations
▲ genres
● fields
∴ processes
◆ strategies
● research
● media/design

Roadway in Houston before the 2017 hurricane (left) and after (right).

Sometimes photographs can make a comparison. The two photos above show a street in Houston before and after Hurricane Harvey in 2017.

Using Figurative Language to Make Comparisons

Another way to make comparisons is with figurative language: words and phrases used in a nonliteral way to help readers see a point. Three kinds of figurative language that make comparisons are similes, metaphors, and analogies. When Robert Burns wrote that his love was "like a red, red rose," he was comparing his love with a rose and evoking an image—in this case, a simile—that helps us understand his feelings for her. A simile makes a comparison using "like" or "as." In the following example, from an article in the food section of the *New York Times*, a restaurant critic uses several similes (underlined) to help us visualize an unusual food dish:

> Once upon a time, possibly at a lodge in Wyoming, possibly at a butcher shop in Maurice, Louisiana, or maybe even at a plantation in South Carolina, an enterprising cook decided to take a boned chicken, a boned duck, and a boned turkey, stuff them one inside the other <u>like Russian dolls</u>, and roast them. He called his masterpiece turducken. . . .

A well-prepared turducken is a marvelous treat, a free-form poultry terrine layered with flavorful stuffing and moistened with duck fat. When it's assembled, it looks <u>like a turkey</u> and it roasts <u>like a turkey</u>, but when you go to carve it, you can slice through it <u>like a loaf of bread</u>. In each slice you get a little bit of everything: white meat from the breast, dark meat from the legs, duck, carrots, bits of sausage, bread, herbs, juices, and chicken, too.

—Amanda Hesser,
"Turkey Finds Its Inner Duck (and Chicken)"

Metaphors make comparisons without such connecting words as "like" or "as." See how desert ecologist Craig Childs uses a metaphor to help us understand the nature of water during a flood in the Grand Canyon:

Water splashed off the desert and ran all over the surface, looking for the quickest way down. It was too swift for the ground to absorb. When water flows like this, it will not be clean tap water. It will be <u>a gravy of debris</u>, snatching everything it finds.

—Craig Childs, *The Secret Knowledge of Water*

Calling the water "a gravy of debris" allows us to see the murky liquid as it streams through the canyon.

Analogies are extended similes or metaphors that compare something unfamiliar with something more familiar. Arguing that corporations should not patent parts of DNA whose function isn't yet clear, a genetics professor uses the familiar image of a library to explain an unfamiliar concept:

It's like having a library of books and randomly tearing pages out. You may know which books the pages came from but that doesn't tell you much about them.

—Peter Goodfellow, quoted in John Vidal and
John Carvel, "Lambs to the Gene Market"

Sometimes analogies are used for humorous effect as well as to make a point, as in this passage from a critique of history textbooks:

※ academic literacies   ● fields   ● research
■ rhetorical situations   ⁂ processes   ● media/design
▲ genres   ◆ strategies

Another history text—this one for fifth grade—begins with the story of how Henry B. Gonzalez, who is a member of Congress from Texas, learned about his own nationality. When he was ten years old, his teacher told him he was an American because he was born in the United States. His grandmother, however, said, "The cat was born in the oven. Does that make him bread?"

—Frances FitzGerald, *America Revised: History Schoolbooks in the Twentieth Century*

The grandmother's question shows how an intentionally ridiculous analogy can be a source of humor—and can make a point memorably.

Considering the Rhetorical Situation

As a writer or speaker, it's important to think about the message you want to articulate, the audience you want to reach, and the larger context you are writing in.

PURPOSE	Sometimes your main purpose for writing will be to compare two or more things. Other times, you may want to compare several things for some other purpose—to compare your views with those of others in an argument essay or to compare one text with another as you analyze them.	▉ 59–60
AUDIENCE	Who is your audience, and will comparing your topic with a more familiar one help them to follow your discussion?	▉ 61–64
GENRE	Does your genre require you to compare something? Evaluations often include comparisons—one book to another in a review, or ten different cell phones in *Consumer Reports*.	▉ 65–71
STANCE	Your stance may affect any comparisons you make. How you compare two things—evenhandedly, or clearly favoring one over the other, for example—will reflect your stance.	▉ 72–74

75–77 ■

MEDIA/DESIGN　Some things you'll want to compare with words alone (lines from two poems, for instance), but sometimes you may wish to make comparisons visually (two images juxtaposed on a page, or several numbers plotted on a line graph).

If you need more help

334
336
325

See **LOOPING** and **CUBING**, two methods of generating ideas discussed in Chapter 28 that can be especially helpful for comparing and contrasting. If you're writing an essay whose purpose is to compare two or more things, see also the **PROCESSES** chapters for help with drafting, revising, and so on.

※ academic literacies　● fields　● research
■ rhetorical situations　⁙ processes　● media/design
▲ genres　◆ strategies

40 Defining

Defining something says what it is—and what it is not. A terrier, for example, is a kind of dog. A fox terrier is a small dog now generally kept as a pet but once used by hunters to dig for foxes. Happiness is a pink frosted doughnut, at least according to Homer Simpson. All of those are definitions. As writers, we need to define any terms our readers may not know. And sometimes you'll want to stipulate your own definition of a word in order to set the terms of an **ARGUMENT**—as Homer Simpson does with a definition that's not found in any dictionary. This chapter details strategies for using definitions in your writing to suit your own rhetorical situations.

◆ 410–30

Formal Definitions

Sometimes to make sure readers understand you, you'll need to provide a formal definition. If you are using a technical term that readers are unlikely to know or if you are using a term in a specific way, you should say then and there what the word means. The word *mutual*, for example, has several meanings: it can mean *shared* or *reciprocal*, as when two people have mutual interests or have mutual respect. It can mean having the *same relationship toward one another*, as when two people are mutual enemies. And it can refer to a type of organization in which profits, losses, and expenses are shared by the organization's members—a common form of insurance in which policyholders pay into a common fund that is used to pay insurance claims. (Examples might include companies like Mutual of Omaha and Liberty Mutual Insurance.)

The first two meanings are commonly understood and probably require no definition. But if you were to use *mutual* in the third sense, it might need to be defined, depending on your audience. A general audience would probably need the definition; an audience from the insurance industry would not. A website that gives basic financial advice to an audience of nonspecialists, for instance, offers a specific definition of the term "mutual fund":

> *Mutual funds* are financial intermediaries. They are companies set up to receive your money and then, having received it, to make investments with the money.
>
> —Bill Barker, "A Grand, Comprehensive
> Overview to Mutual Funds Investing"

But even writers in specialized fields routinely provide formal definitions to make sure their readers understand the way they're using certain words. See how two writers define the word "stock" as it pertains to their respective (and very different) fields:

> Stocks are the basis for sauces and soups and important flavoring agents for braises. Admittedly, stock making is time consuming, but the extra effort yields great dividends.
>
> —Tom Colicchio, *Think Like a Chef*

> Want to own part of a business without having to show up at its office every day? Or ever? Stock is the vehicle of choice for those who do. Dating back to the Dutch mutual stock corporations of the sixteenth century, the modern stock market exists as a way for entrepreneurs to finance businesses using money collected from investors. In return for ponying up the dough to finance the company, the investor becomes a part owner of the company. That ownership is represented by stock—specialized financial "securities," or financial instruments, that are "secured" by a claim on the assets and profits of a company.
>
> —"Investing Basics: Stocks," *Motley Fool*

To write a formal definition

- Use words that readers are likely to be familiar with.
- Don't use the word being defined in the definition.
- Begin with the word being defined; include the general category to which the term belongs and the attributes that make it different from the others in that category.

* academic literacies
■ rhetorical situations
▲ genres

● fields
• processes
◆ strategies

● research
● media/design

For example:

Term	General Category	Distinguishing Attributes
"Stock" is	a specialized financial "security"	that is "secured" by a claim.
"Photosynthesis" is	a process	by which plants use sunlight to create energy.
"Astronomers" are	scientists	who study celestial objects and phenomena.
"Zach Galifianakis,"	an actor,	has been featured in several films, including *The Hangover* and *Birdman*.

Note that the category and distinguishing attributes cannot be stated too broadly; if they were, the definition would be too vague to be useful. It wouldn't be helpful in most circumstances, for example, to say, "Zach Galifianakis is a man who has acted" or "Photosynthesis is something having to do with plants."

Extended Definitions

Sometimes it's useful to provide a more detailed definition. Extended definitions may be several sentences long or several paragraphs long and may include pictures or diagrams. Sometimes an entire essay is devoted to defining a difficult or important concept. Here is one writer's extended definition of "soul food":

> I've been eating soul food all my life and cooking it my whole career. I don't just know soul food. Soul food is *in* my soul. . . .
>
> By definition, soul food refers to the dishes of the Cotton Belt of Georgia, Mississippi, and Alabama that traveled out to the rest of the country during the Great Migration. (The term itself came around the middle of the twentieth century.) You know what travels well? Fried chicken. Mac and cheese. Delicious, but not what anyone's meant to eat every day. I'm here to redefine soul food, to reclaim it.
>
> Soul food is the true food of African-Americans.

The roots of our cooking are in West Africa. And from there, the American South, from the slave ports along the eastern coast to the southern border. We relied on seasonal vegetables, beans, and grains, with meat on rare occasions. Let's be clear: those were horrible times of suffering under the most unspeakable evil. I don't want to romanticize any of it. Not even the food. Remember, we didn't get to choose what we ate. But we made the most delicious dishes from what little we had. And what we cooked for the slave owners effectively became what we know as "American" food today.

—Carla Hall, *Carla Hall's Soul Food*

That definition includes a description of the basic features of soul food, examples of it, and the origin of the term. We can assume that it's written for a general audience, one that doesn't know much about soul food.

Abstract concepts often require extended definitions because by nature they are more complicated to define. There are many ways of writing an extended definition, depending in part on the term being defined and on the writer's audience and purpose. The following examples show some of the methods that can be used for composing extended definitions of "democracy."

Explore the word's origins. Where did the word come from? When did it first come into use? In the following example, from an essay considering what democracy means in the twenty-first century, the writer started by looking at the word's first known use in English. Though it's from an essay written for a first-year writing course and thus for a fairly general audience, it's a definition that might pique any audience's interest:

According to the *Oxford English Dictionary*, the term *democracy* first appeared in English in a thirteenth-century translation of Aristotle's works—specifically, in his *Politics*, where he stated that the "underlying principle of democracy is freedom" and that "it is customary to say that only in democracies do men have a share in freedom, for that is what every democracy makes its aim." By the sixteenth century, the word was used much as it is now. One writer in 1586, for instance, defined it in this way: "where free and poore men being the greater number, are lords of the estate."

—Susanna Mejía, "What Does Democracy Mean Now?"

Norman Rockwell's 1943 painting *Freedom of Speech* presents a visual definition of democracy: a citizen stands to speak at a public meeting while his fellow citizens listen attentively.

Here's another example, this one written for a scholarly audience, from an essay about women, participation, democracy, and the information age:

> The very word *citizenship* carries with it a connotation of place, a "citizen" being, literally, the inhabitant of a city. Over the years the word has, of course, accumulated a number of associated meanings . . . and the word has come to stand in for such concepts as participation, equality, and democracy. The fact that the concept of locality is deeply embedded in the word *citizen* suggests that it is also fundamental to our current understanding of these other, more apparently abstract words.
>
> In Western thought, the concepts of citizenship, equality, and democracy are closely interlinked and can be traced back to a common source, in Athens in the fifth century BCE. Perhaps it is no accident that it was the same culture which also gave us, in its theater, the concept of the unity of time and space. The Greek city-state has been represented for centuries as the ideal model of democracy, with free and equal access for all citizens to decision making. Leaving aside, for the moment, the question of who was included, and who excluded from this notion of citizenship, we can see that the sense of place is fundamental to this model. Entitlement to participate in the democratic process is circum-scribed by geography; it is the inhabitants of the geographical entity of the city-state, precisely defined and bounded, who have the rights to citizenship. Those who are not defined as inhabitants of that specific city-state are explicitly excluded, although, of course, they may have the right to citizenship elsewhere.
>
> —Ursula Huws, "Women, Participation, and Democracy in the Information Society"

Provide details. What are its characteristics? What is it made of? See how a historian explores the basic characteristics of democracy in a book written for an audience of historians:

> As a historian I am naturally disposed to be satisfied with the meaning which, in the history of politics, men have commonly attributed to the word—a meaning, needless to say, which derives partly from the experience and partly from the aspirations of mankind. So regarded, the term *democracy* refers primarily to a form of government, and it

* academic literacies   ● fields   ● research
■ rhetorical situations   ⋮ processes   ● media/design
▲ genres   ◆ strategies

has always meant government by the many as opposed to government by the one—government by the people as opposed to government by a tyrant, a dictator, or an absolute monarch. . . . Since the Greeks first used the term, the essential test of democratic government has always been this: the source of political authority must be and remain in the people and not in the ruler. A democratic government has always meant one in which the citizens, or a sufficient number of them to represent more or less effectively the common will, freely act from time to time, and according to established forms, to appoint or recall the magistrates and to enact or revoke the laws by which the community is governed.

—Carl Becker, *Modern Democracy*

Compare it with other words. How is this concept like other similar things? How does it differ? What is it *not* like? **COMPARE AND CONTRAST** it. See how a political science textbook defines a *majoritarian democracy* by comparing its characteristics with those of a *consensual democracy*:

◆ 437–44

A majoritarian democracy is one

1. having only two major political parties, not many

2. having an electoral system that requires a bare majority to elect one clear winner in an election, as opposed to a proportional electoral system that distributes seats to political parties according to the rough share of votes received in the election

3. a strong executive (president or prime minister) and cabinet that together are largely independent of the legislature when it comes to exercising the executive's constitutional duties, in contrast to an executive and cabinet that are politically controlled by the parties in the legislature and therefore unable to exercise much influence when proposing policy initiatives.

—Benjamin Ginsberg, Theodore J. Lowi, and Margaret Weir,
We the People: An Introduction to American Politics

And here's an example in which democracy is contrasted with various other forms of governments of the past:

Caesar's power derived from a popular mandate, conveyed through established republican forms, but that did not make his government any the less a dictatorship. Napoleon called his government a democratic republic, but no one, least of all Napoleon himself, doubted that he had destroyed the last vestiges of the democratic republic.

—Carl Becker, *Modern Democracy*

Give examples. See how the essayist E. B. White defines democracy by giving some everyday examples of considerate behavior, humility, and civic participation—all things he suggests constitute democracy:

It is the line that forms on the right. It is the don't in "don't shove." It is the hole in the stuffed shirt through which the sawdust slowly trickles; it is the dent in the high hat. Democracy is the recurrent suspicion that more than half of the people are right more than half of the time. . . . Democracy is a letter to the editor.

—E. B. White, "Democracy"

White's definition is elegant because he uses examples that his readers will know. His characteristics—metaphors, really—define democracy not as a conceptual way of governing but as an everyday part of American life.

431–36 ◆ **Classify it.** Often it's useful to divide or **CLASSIFY** a term. The ways in which democracy unfolds are complex enough to warrant entire textbooks, of course; but the following definition, from a political science textbook, divides democracy into two kinds, representative and direct:

A system of government that gives citizens a regular opportunity to elect the top government officials is usually called a representative democracy or republic. A system that permits citizens to vote directly on laws and policies is often called a direct democracy. At the national level, America is a representative democracy in which citizens select government officials but do not vote on legislation. Some states, however, have provisions for direct legislation through popular referendum. For example, California voters in 1995 decided to bar undocumented immigrants from receiving some state services.

—Benjamin Ginsberg, Theodore J. Lowi, and Margaret Weir,
We the People: An Introduction to American Politics

✳ academic literacies   ● fields   ● research
■ rhetorical situations   ⁖ processes   ● media/design
▲ genres   ◆ strategies

Stipulative Definitions

Sometimes a writer will stipulate a certain definition, essentially saying, "This is how I'm defining x." Such definitions are not usually found in a dictionary—and at the same time are central to the argument the writer is making. Here is one example, from an essay by Toni Morrison. Describing a scene from a film in which a newly arrived Greek immigrant, working as a shoe shiner in Grand Central Terminal, chases away an African American competitor, Morrison calls the scene an example of "race talk," a concept she then goes on to define:

> This is race talk, the explicit insertion into everyday life of racial signs and symbols that have no meaning other than pressing African Americans to the lowest level of the racial hierarchy. Popular culture, shaped by film, theater, advertising, the press, television, and literature, is heavily engaged in race talk. It participates freely in this most enduring and efficient rite of passage into American culture: negative appraisals of the native-born black population. Only when the lesson of racial estrangement is learned is assimilation complete. Whatever the lived experience of immigrants with African Americans—pleasant, beneficial, or bruising—the rhetorical experience renders blacks as noncitizens, already discredited outlaws.
>
> All immigrants fight for jobs and space, and who is there to fight but those who have both? As in the fishing ground struggle between Texas and Vietnamese shrimpers, they displace what and whom they can. Although U.S. history is awash in labor battles, political fights and property wars among all religious and ethnic groups, their struggles are persistently framed as struggles between recent arrivals and blacks. In race talk the move into mainstream America always means buying into the notion of American blacks as the real aliens. Whatever the ethnicity or nationality of the immigrant, his nemesis is understood to be African American.
>
> —Toni Morrison, "On the Backs of Blacks"

The following example is from a book review of Nancy L. Rosenblum's *Membership and Morals: The Personal Uses of Pluralism in America*, published in the *American Prospect*, a magazine for readers interested in political analysis. In it a Stanford law professor outlines a definition of "the democracy of everyday life":

Democracy, in this understanding of it, means simply treating people as equals, disregarding social standing, avoiding attitudes of either deference or superiority, making allowances for others' weaknesses, and resisting the temptation to respond to perceived slights. It also means protesting everyday instances of arbitrariness and unfairness—from the rudeness of the bakery clerk to the sexism of the car dealer or the racism of those who vandalize the home of the first black neighbors on the block.

—Kathleen M. Sullivan, "Defining Democracy Down"

Considering the Rhetorical Situation

As a writer or speaker, it's important to think about the message you want to articulate, the audience you want to reach, and the larger context you are writing in.

59–60 ■	**PURPOSE**	Your purpose for writing will affect any definitions you include. Would writing an extended definition help you explain something? Would stipulating definitions of key terms help you shape an argument? Could an offbeat definition help you entertain your readers?
61–64 ■	**AUDIENCE**	What audience do you want to reach, and are there any terms your readers are unlikely to know (and therefore need to be defined)? Are there terms they might understand differently from the way you're defining them?
65–71 ■	**GENRE**	Does your genre require you to define terms? Chances are that if you're reporting information you'll need to define some terms, and some arguments rest on the way you define key terms.
72–74 ■	**STANCE**	What is your stance, and do you need to define key terms to show that stance clearly? How you define "fetus," for example, is likely to reveal your stance on abortion.

☀ academic literacies	⬢ fields	⬤ research
■ rhetorical situations	⁂ processes	⬤ media/design
▲ genres	◆ strategies	

MEDIA/DESIGN   Your medium will affect the form your definitions take. In a print text, you'll need to define terms in your text; if you're giving a speech or presentation, you might also provide images of important terms and their definitions. In an electronic text, you may be able to define terms by linking to an online dictionary definition.

75–77

If you need more help

See also the **PROCESSES** chapters for help with generating ideas, drafting, revising, and so on if you are writing a whole essay dedicated to defining a term or concept.

325

41 Describing

When we describe something, we indicate what it looks like—and sometimes how it sounds, feels, smells, and tastes. Descriptive details are a way of showing rather than telling, of helping readers see (or hear, smell, and so on) what we're writing about—that the sky is blue, that Miss Havisham is wearing an old yellowed wedding gown, that the chemicals in the beaker have reacted and smell like rotten eggs. You'll have occasion to describe things in most of the writing you do—from describing a favorite hat in a **MEMOIR** or **REFLECTION** to detailing a chemical reaction in a lab report. This chapter will help you work with description—and, in particular, help you think about the use of *detail*, about *objectivity and subjectivity*, about *vantage point*, about creating a clear *dominant impression*, and about using description to fit your rhetorical situation.

236–44 ▲
391–401 ⁖

Detail

The goal of using details is to be as specific as possible, providing information that will help your audience imagine the subject or make sense of it. See, for example, how Nancy Mairs, an author with multiple sclerosis, describes the disease in clear, specific terms:

> During its course, which is unpredictable and uncontrollable, one may lose vision, hearing, speech, the ability to walk, control of bladder and/or bowels, strength in any or all extremities, sensitivity to touch, vibration, and/or pain, potency, coordination of movements—the list of possibilities is lengthy and, yes, horrifying. One may also lose one's sense of humor. That's the easiest to lose and the hardest to survive without.
>
> In the past ten years, I have sustained some of these losses. Characteristic of MS are sudden attacks, called exacerbations, followed by remissions, and these I have not had. Instead, my disease has been slowly progressive. My left leg is now so weak that I walk with the aid of a brace and a cane, and for distances I use an Amigo, a variation on the

※ academic literacies   ● fields   ● research
■ rhetorical situations   ⁖ processes   ● media/design
▲ genres   ◆ strategies

electric wheelchair that looks rather like an electrified kiddie car. I no longer have much use of my left hand. Now my right side is weakening as well. I still have the blurred spot in my right eye. Overall, though, I've been lucky so far.

—Nancy Mairs, "On Being a Cripple"

Mairs's gruesome list demonstrates, through *specific details*, how the disease affects sufferers generally and her in particular. We know far more after reading this text than we do from the following more general description, from a National Multiple Sclerosis Society brochure:

Multiple sclerosis is a chronic, unpredictable disease of the central nervous system (the brain, optic nerves, and spinal cord). It is thought to be an autoimmune disorder. This means the immune system incorrectly attacks the person's healthy tissue.

MS can cause blurred vision, loss of balance, poor coordination, slurred speech, tremors, numbness, extreme fatigue, problems with memory and concentration, paralysis, and blindness. These problems may be permanent, or they may come and go.

—National Multiple Sclerosis Society, *Just the Facts*

Specific details are also more effective than labels, which give little meaningful information. Instead of saying that someone is a "loser" or "really smart," it's better to give details so that readers can understand the reasons behind the label: What does this person *do* or *say* that makes them deserve this label? See, for example, how the writer of a memoir focused on his pet snake describes the way his snake, Woohoo, and he interacted:

He wound around my wrist, hung in the air, pulled himself up and into the arm of my shirt, through which he slithered until he decided on another opening, the neck, from which his head emerged, and then his forked tongue, darting out, shaking, tasting and retreating into his mouth. I gave his cold blood my heat and flexed hello to his constrictions. My fingers followed the grain of his scales down his undulating length, which grew to four feet from ten inches as the years passed, its colors freshly radiant after every shedding.

—Paul McAdory, "Snakes"

The writer might simply have said, "The snake moved around under my shirt." Instead, he shows the snake as it moves from place to place ("He wound around my wrist, hung in the air, pulled himself up and into the arm of my shirt") and describes his own physical reaction ("I . . . flexed hello to his constrictions," "My fingers followed the grain of his scales")—all details that create a far more vivid description.

Sensory details help readers imagine sounds, odors, tastes, and physical sensations in addition to sights. In the following example, writer Scott Russell Sanders recalls sawing wood as a child. Note how visual details, odors, and even the physical sense of being picked up by his father mingle to form a vivid scene:

> As the saw teeth bit down, the wood released its smell, each kind with its own fragrance, oak or walnut or cherry or pine—usually pine because it was the softest, easiest for a child to work. No matter how weathered and gray the board, no matter how warped and cracked, inside there was this smell waiting, as of something freshly baked. I gathered every smidgen of sawdust and stored it away in coffee cans, which I kept in a drawer of the workbench. When I did not feel like hammering nails I would dump my sawdust on the concrete floor of the garage and landscape it into highways and farms and towns, running miniature cars and trucks along miniature roads. Looming as huge as a colossus, my father worked over and around me, now and again bending down to inspect my work, careful not to trample my creations. It was a landscape that smelled dizzyingly of wood. Even after a bath my skin would carry the smell, and so would my father's hair, when he lifted me for a bedtime hug.
>
> —Scott Russell Sanders, *The Paradise of Bombs*

Whenever you describe something, you'll select from many possible details you might use. Simply put, to exhaust all the details available to describe something is impossible—and would exhaust your readers as well. To focus your description, you'll need to determine the kinds of details appropriate for your subject. They will vary, depending on your **PURPOSE**. See, for example, how the details might differ in three different genres:

59–60 ■

236–44 ▲

- *For a* **MEMOIR** *about an event,* you might choose details that are significant for you, that evoke the sights, sounds, and other sensations that give personal meaning to the event.

✳ academic literacies   ● fields   ● research
■ rhetorical situations   ⁝ processes   ● media/design
▲ genres   ◆ strategies

- For a **PROFILE**, you're likely to select details that will reinforce the dominant impression you want to give, that portray the event from the perspective you want readers to see.

▲ 245–57

- For a lab report, you should give certain specifics—what equipment was used, what procedures were followed, what exactly were the results.

Deciding on a focus for your description can help you see it better, as you'll look for details that contribute to that focus.

Objectivity and Subjectivity

Descriptions can be written with objectivity, with subjectivity, or with a mixture of both. Objective descriptions attempt to be uncolored by personal opinion or emotion. Police reports and much news writing aim to describe events objectively; scientific writing strives for objectivity in describing laboratory procedures and results. See, for example, the following objective account of what happened at the World Trade Center on September 11, 2001:

World Trade Center Disaster—Tuesday, September 11, 2001

On Tuesday, September 11, 2001, at 8:45 a.m. New York local time, One World Trade Center, the north tower, was hit by a hijacked 767 commercial jet airplane loaded with fuel for a transcontinental flight. Two World Trade Center, the south tower, was hit by a similar hijacked jet eighteen minutes later, at 9:03 a.m. (In separate but related attacks, the Pentagon building near Washington, D.C., was hit by a hijacked 757 at 9:43 a.m., and at 10:10 a.m. a fourth hijacked jetliner crashed in Pennsylvania.) The south tower, WTC 2, which had been hit second, was the first to suffer a complete structural collapse, at 10:05 a.m., 62 minutes after being hit itself, 80 minutes after the first impact. The north tower, WTC 1, then also collapsed, at 10:29 a.m., 104 minutes after being hit. WTC 7, a substantial forty-seven-story office building in its own right, built in 1987, was damaged by the collapsing towers, caught fire, and later in the afternoon also totally collapsed.

— "World Trade Center," *GreatBuildings.com*

Subjective descriptions, in contrast, allow the writer's opinions and emotions to come through. A house can be described as comfortable, with a lived-in look, or as run-down and in need of a paint job and a new roof.

Here's a subjective description of the planes striking the World Trade Center, as told by a woman watching from a nearby building:

> Incredulously, while looking out [the] window at the damage and carnage the first plane had inflicted, I saw the second plane abruptly come into my right field of vision and deliberately, with shimmering intention, thunder full-force into the south tower. It was so close, so low, so huge and fast, so intent on its target that I swear to you, I swear to you, I felt the vengeance and rage emanating from the plane.
>
> —Debra Fontaine, "Witnessing"

Vantage Point

Sometimes you'll want or need to describe something from a certain vantage point. Where you locate yourself in relation to what you're describing will determine what you can perceive (and so describe) and what you can't. You may describe your subject from a *stationary vantage point*, from which you (and your readers) see your subject from one angle only, as if you were a camera. This description of one of three photographs that captured a woman's death records only what the camera saw from one angle at one particular moment:

> The first showed some people on a fire escape—a fireman, a woman and a child. The fireman had a nice strong jaw and looked very brave. The woman was holding the child. Smoke was pouring from the building behind them. A rescue ladder was approaching, just a few feet away, and the fireman had one arm around the woman and one arm reaching out toward the ladder.
>
> —Nora Ephron, "The Boston Photographs"

By contrast, this description of a drive to an Italian villa uses a *moving vantage point*; the writer recounts what he saw as he passed through a gate in a city wall, moving from city to country:

> La Pietra—"the stone"—is situated one mile from the Porta San Gallo, an entry to the Old City of Florence. You drive there along the Via Bolognese, twisting past modern apartment blocks, until you come to a gate, which swings open—and there you are, at the upper end of a long lane of cypresses facing a great ocher palazzo; with olive groves

academic literacies • fields • research
rhetorical situations •• processes • media/design
genres ◆ strategies

spreading out on both sides over an expanse of fifty-seven acres. There's something almost comically wonderful about the effect: here, the city, with its winding avenue; there, on the other side of a wall, the country, fertile and gray green.

—James Traub, "Italian Hours"

The description of quarries in the following section uses *multiple vantage points* to capture the quarries from many perspectives.

Dominant Impression

With any description, your aim is to create some dominant impression—the overall feeling that the individual details add up to. The dominant impression may be implied, growing out of the details themselves. For example, Scott Russell Sanders's memory of the smell of sawdust creates a dominant impression of warmth and comfort: the "fragrance . . . as of something freshly baked," sawdust "stored . . . away in coffee cans," a young boy "lifted . . . for a bedtime hug." Sometimes, though, a writer will state the dominant impression directly, in addition to creating it with details. In an essay about Indiana limestone quarries, Sanders makes the dominant impression clear from the start: "They are battlefields."

The quarries will not be domesticated. They are not backyard pools; they are battlefields. Each quarry is an arena where violent struggles have taken place between machines and planet, between human ingenuity and brute resisting stone, between mind and matter. Waste rock litters the floor and brim like rubble in a bombed city. The ragged pits might have been the basements of vanished skyscrapers. Stones weighing tens of tons lean against one another at precarious angles, as if they have been thrown there by some gigantic strength and have not yet finished falling. Wrecked machinery hulks in the weeds, grimly rusting, the cogs and wheels, twisted rails, battered engine housings, trackless bulldozers and burst boilers like junk from an armored regiment. Everywhere the ledges are scarred from drills, as if from an artillery barrage or machine-gun strafing. Stumbling onto one of these abandoned quarries and gazing at the ruins, you might be left wondering who had won the battle, men or stone.

—Scott Russell Sanders, *The Paradise of Bombs*

The rest of his description, full of more figurative language ("like rubble in a bombed city," "like junk from an armored regiment," "as if from an artillery barrage or machine-gun strafing") reinforces the direct "they are battlefields" statement.

The orange sunset and expanse of sky and water in this Michigan tourism ad create a dominant impression of spaciousness and warmth, while the text invites readers to visit a Michigan beach and enjoy watching the sun set, rather than watching television.

Organizing Descriptions

You can organize descriptions in many ways. When your description is primarily visual, you'll probably organize it spatially: from left to right, top to bottom, outside to inside. One variation on this approach is to begin with the most significant or noteworthy feature and move outward from that center, as Ephron does in describing a photo. Or you may create a chronological description of objects as you move past or through them in space, as Traub does in his description of his drive. You might even pile up details to create a dominant impression, as Sanders and Mairs do, especially if your description draws on senses besides vision.

* academic literacies   ● fields   ● research
■ rhetorical situations   ∴ processes   ● media/design
▲ genres   ◆ strategies

Considering the Rhetorical Situation

As a writer or speaker, it's important to think about the message you want to articulate, the audience you want to reach, and the larger context you are writing in.

PURPOSE	Your purpose may affect the way you use description. If you're arguing that a government should intervene in another country's civil war, for example, describing the anguish of refugees from that war could make your argument more persuasive. If you're analyzing a painting, you will likely need to describe it.	▪ 59–60
AUDIENCE	Who is your audience, and will they need detailed description to understand the points you wish to make?	▪ 61–64
GENRE	Does your genre require description? A lab report generally calls for you to describe materials and results; a memoir about Grandma should probably describe her— her smile, her favorite outfit, her apple pie.	▪ 65–71
STANCE	The way you describe things can help you convey your stance. For example, the details you choose can show you to be objective (or not), careful or casual.	▪ 72–74
MEDIA/DESIGN	Your medium will affect the form your description can take. In a print or spoken text, you'll likely rely on words, though you may also include visuals. In an electronic text, you can easily provide links to visuals as well as audio clips and so may need fewer words of your own.	▪ 75–77

If you need more help

See also **FREEWRITING**, **CUBING**, and **LISTING**, three methods of generating ideas that can be especially helpful for developing detailed descriptions. Sometimes you may be assigned to write a whole essay describing something: see the **PROCESSES** chapters for help with drafting, revising, and so on.

●● 333–34
336
334–35
325

42 Using Dialogue

236–44 ▲
245–57
223–35
164–95

Dialogue is a way of including people's own words in a text, letting readers hear those people's voices—not just what you say about them. **MEMOIRS** and **PROFILES** often include dialogue, and many other genres do as well: **LITERARY ANALYSES** often quote dialogue from the texts they analyze, and essays **ARGUING A POSITION** might quote an authoritative source as support for a claim. This chapter provides brief guidelines for the conventions of paragraphing and punctuating dialogue and offers some good examples of how you can use dialogue most effectively to suit your own rhetorical situations.

Why Add Dialogue?

Dialogue is a way of bringing in voices other than your own, of showing people and scenes rather than just telling about them. It can add color and texture to your writing, making it memorable. Most important, however, dialogue should be more than just colorful or interesting. It needs to contribute to your rhetorical purpose, to support the point you're making. See how dialogue is used in the following excerpt from a magazine profile of the Mall of America, how it gives us a sense of the place that the journalist's own words could not provide:

> Two pubescent girls in retainers and braces sat beside me sipping coffees topped with whipped cream and chocolate sprinkles, their shopping bags gathered tightly around their legs, their eyes fixed on the passing crowds. They came, they said, from Shakopee—"It's nowhere," one of them explained. The megamall, she added, was "a buzz at first, but now it seems pretty normal. 'Cept my parents are like Twenty Questions every time I want to come here. 'Specially since the shooting."
>
> On a Sunday night, she elaborated, three people had been wounded when shots were fired in a dispute over a San Jose Sharks

* academic literacies   ● fields   ● research
■ rhetorical situations ⁂ processes   ● media/design
▲ genres   ◆ strategies

jacket. "In the *mall*," her friend reminded me. "Right here at megamall. A shooting."

"It's like nowhere's safe," the first added.

—David Guterson, "Enclosed. Encyclopedic. Endured.
One Week at the Mall of America"

Of course, it was the writer who decided whom and what to quote, and Guterson deliberately chose words that capture the young shoppers' speech patterns, quoting fragments ("In the *mall*. . . . Right here at megamall. A shooting"), slang ("a buzz at first," "my parents are like Twenty Questions"), even contractions ("'Cept," "'Specially").

Integrating Dialogue into Your Writing

There are certain conventions for punctuating and paragraphing dialogue:

- *Punctuating.* Enclose each speaker's words in quotation marks, and put any end punctuation—periods, question marks, and exclamation marks—inside the closing quotation mark. Whether you're transcribing words you heard or making them up, you'll sometimes need to add punctuation to reflect the rhythm and sound of the speech. In the last sentence of the example below, see how Chang-Rae Lee adds a comma after "Well" and italicizes "practice" to show intonation—and attitude.

- *Paragraphing.* When you're writing dialogue that includes more than one speaker, start a new paragraph each time the speaker changes.

- *Signal phrases.* Sometimes you'll need to introduce dialogue with SIGNAL PHRASES —"I said," "she asked," and so on—to make clear who is speaking. At times, however, the speaker will be clear enough, and you won't need any signal phrases.

● 551–54

Here is a conversation between a mother and her son that illustrates each of the conventions for punctuating and paragraphing dialogue:

"Whom do I talk to?" she said. She would mostly speak to me in Korean, and I would answer back in English.

"The bank manager, who else?"

"What do I say?"

"Whatever you want to say."

"Don't speak to me like that!" she cried.

"It's just that you should be able to do it yourself," I said.

"You know how I feel about this!"

"Well, maybe then you should consider it *practice*," I answered lightly, using the Korean word to make sure she understood.

—Chang-Rae Lee, "Coming Home Again"

Interviews

Interviews are a kind of dialogue, with different conventions for punctuation. When you're transcribing an interview, give each speaker's name each time they speak, starting a new line but not indenting, and do not use quotation marks. Here's an excerpt from an interview that graduate student Emma Peters conducted with Brenda Ouattara, a recent two-year college graduate, while researching how the COVID-19 pandemic affected college education and online learning.

Emma Peters: What school did you go to, and what year were you in when the pandemic started?

Brenda Ouattara: I attended LaGuardia Community College in Queens, and it was during my first year there. I was only on campus for a few months before COVID, so I actually finished almost my whole two-year college experience online instead of in person.

Peters: Did you take online classes before the pandemic? How were they different?

Ouattara: I was in hybrid classes before, where we'd meet once a week in person and the rest was online. The online classes during the pandemic were more challenging—it felt like they had more work. Because, in my opinion, the professors felt like we were going to be missing out on the full experience of their class, so they would give us more work. And we also had to learn how to manage doing online courses, and how to figure out and navigate the websites.

Peters: What do you think is lost with an online learning experience that you might have had if you were in person?

Ouattara: The experience of meeting new students, meeting your actual professors, just being face to face to get the help that you need . . . and having the opportunities to have student fairs or any other events. All of those things were just not happening for us. I feel like it was hard for some students to really be motivated at home. I know a few of my friends actually just decided to take the semesters off. I kept going, but I wasn't as motivated to after a while because it's online, so it's not as exciting as walking in the buildings and meeting people and going straight to your professors for help.

Peters: What do you think are the benefits of online classes?

Ouattara: It's a little bit easier to manage with your personal life. You can have a regular work schedule and then come home and do assignments. But when you're in person you have to be physically in a classroom. It was definitely a benefit being able to set my own schedule.

Peters: How did being online affect your relationship with your professors?

Ouattara: The communication was different—you had to speak through email and online calls, and sometimes it was harder to get a fast response. Some professors were also struggling to use online resources, and sometimes I would ask them a question and they would ask me a question—and we were helping each other out. [Laughs]

Peters: Do you think anything will change permanently going forward after the pandemic?

Ouattara: I don't think it will go back to exactly how it was before, even though many colleges are trying. I feel like I've spent two years doing online learning and now it would almost be out of my comfort zone to go back to in-person classes—this is normal for me now, you know? But everyone is different.

In preparing the interview transcript for publication, Peters had to add punctuation, which of course was not part of the oral conversation, and probably deleted pauses and verbal expressions such as "um" and "uh." At the same time, she kept informal interjections ("you know?") and included expressions of emotion ("Laughs") to maintain the oral flavor of the interview and reflect Ouattara's voice. More tips on interviewing may be found in Chapter 47.

Considering the Rhetorical Situation

As a writer or speaker, it's important to think about the message you want to articulate, the audience you want to reach, and the larger context of your writing.

59–60   **PURPOSE**   Your purpose will affect any use of dialogue. Dialogue can help bring a profile to life and make it memorable. Interviews with experts or firsthand witnesses can add credibility to a report or argument.

61–64   **AUDIENCE**   Whom do you want to reach, and will dialogue help? Sometimes actual dialogue can help readers hear human voices behind facts or reason.

65–71   **GENRE**   Does your genre require dialogue? If you're evaluating or analyzing a literary work, for instance, you may wish to include dialogue from that work. If you're writing a profile of a person or event, dialogue can help you bring your subject to life. Similarly, an interview with an expert can add credibility to a report or argument.

72–74   **STANCE**   What is your stance, and can dialogue help you communicate that stance? For example, excerpts of an interview may enable you to challenge someone's views and make your own views clear.

75–77   **MEDIA/DESIGN**   Your medium will affect the way you present dialogue. In a print text, you'll present dialogue through written words. In an oral or electronic text, you might include actual recorded dialogue.

If you need more help

518–20
542–54.   See also the guidelines on **INTERVIEWING EXPERTS** for advice on setting up and recording interviews and those on **QUOTING, PARAPHRASING,** and **SUMMARIZING** for help with deciding how to integrate dialogue into your text.

* academic literacies   ● fields   ● research
■ rhetorical situations   ⁝ processes   ● media/design
▲ genres   ◆ strategies

43 Explaining Processes

When you explain a process, you tell how something is (or was) done—how a bill becomes a law, how an embryo develops; or you tell someone how to do something—how to throw a curve ball, how to write a memoir. This chapter focuses on those two kinds of explanations, offering examples and guidelines for explaining a process in a way that works for your rhetorical situation.

Explaining a Process Clearly

Whether the process is simple or complex, you'll need to identify its key stages or steps and explain them one by one, in order. The sequence matters because it enables readers to follow your explanation; it is especially important when you're explaining a process that others are going to follow. Most often you'll explain a process chronologically, from start to finish. **TRANSITIONS**—words like "first," "next," "then," and so on—are often necessary, therefore, to show readers how the stages of a process relate to one another and to indicate time sequences. Finally, you'll find that verbs matter; they indicate the actions that take place at each stage of the process.

361–62

Explaining How Something Is Done

All processes consist of steps, and when you explain how something is done, you describe each step, generally in order, from first to last. Here, for example, is an explanation of how french fries are made, from an essay published in the *New Yorker*:

> Fast-food French fries are made from a baking potato like an Idaho russet, or any other variety that is mealy, or starchy, rather than waxy. The potatoes are harvested, cured, washed, peeled, sliced, and then blanched—cooked enough so that the insides have a fluffy texture but not so much that the fry gets soft and breaks. Blanching is followed by drying, and drying by a thirty-second deep fry, to give the potatoes a crisp shell. Then the fries are frozen until the moment of service, when they are deep-fried again, this time for somewhere around three minutes. Depending on the fast-food chain involved, there are other steps interspersed in this process. McDonald's fries, for example, are briefly dipped in a sugar solution, which gives them their golden-brown color; Burger King fries are dipped in a starch batter, which is what gives those fries their distinctive hard shell and audible crunch. But the result is similar. The potato that is first harvested in the field is roughly 80 percent water. The process of creating a French fry consists, essentially, of removing as much of that water as possible—through blanching, drying, and deep-frying—and replacing it with fat.
>
> —Malcolm Gladwell, "The Trouble with Fries"

Gladwell clearly explains the process of making french fries, showing us the specific steps—how the potatoes "are harvested, cured, washed, peeled, sliced," and so on—and using clear transitions—"followed by," "then," "until," "when"—and action verbs to show the sequence. His last sentence makes his stance clear, pointing out that the process of creating a french fry consists of removing as much of a potato's water as possible "and replacing it with fat."

Explaining How to Do Something

In explaining how to do something, you are giving instruction so that others can follow the process themselves. See how cookbook author Amanda Hesser explains the process of making french fries. She starts by listing the ingredients and then describes the steps:

✳ academic literacies   ● fields   ● research

■ rhetorical situations   ⁖ processes   ● media/design

▲ genres   ◆ strategies

4 large long Idaho potatoes
Peanut oil
Kosher or coarse sea salt

1. Peel the potatoes. Place in a bowl, cover with water, and refrigerate for 8 hours.

2. Slice the potatoes lengthwise into ¼-inch-thick sticks. Place in a bowl, cover with water, and refrigerate for 8 hours more.

3. Drain the potato sticks and lay out on dish towels to dry. Be sure they are completely dry before frying.

4. Heat 2 inches of oil to 300 degrees in a large deep pot with a frying basket and a deep-frying thermometer clipped to the side. Add just enough potatoes to cover the bottom of the frying basket and cook until slightly limp, 1½ to 2 minutes; do not brown. Lift the basket and drain the fries, then transfer the potatoes to a wire rack set over a baking sheet and separate the sticks. Repeat with the remaining potatoes.

5. Increase the heat to 375 degrees. Again add the potatoes in batches to the oil and fry until chestnut brown on the edges and crisp. Drain and transfer to a bowl lined with paper towels. Immediately season with salt, tossing to coat.

—Amanda Hesser, "French Fries"

Hesser's explanation leaves out no details, giving a clear sequence of steps and descriptive verbs that tell us exactly what to do: "Peel," "Slice," "Heat," and so on. After she gives the recipe, she offers variations, including adding a slice of bacon to the oil "for a light pork flavor" or adding some herb leaves into the oil and then serving the fries "with the crisped herbs."

Explaining a Process Visually

Some processes are best explained **VISUALLY**, with diagrams or photographs. See, for example, how a blogger explains one process of shaping dough into a bagel—giving the details in words and then showing us in photos how to do it:

674–80

Gently press dough to deflate it a bit and divide into 6 equal portions.

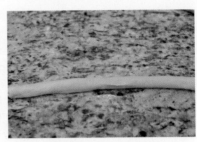

Roll each portion into a rope about 1/2-inch in diameter.

Wrap the dough around your hand like this.

Seal the ends together by rolling back and forth on the counter a few times.

Place bagels on a lined sheet pan. Allow to rise, uncovered.

—Patricia Reitz, *ButterYum*

Photos by Patricia Reitz (butteryum.org).

* academic literacies

● fields

● research

■ rhetorical situations

⁘ processes

● media/design

▲ genres

◆ strategies

Considering the Rhetorical Situation

As always, it's important to think about the message you want to articulate, the audience you want to reach, and the larger context you are writing in.

PURPOSE   Your purpose for writing will affect the way you explain a process. If you're arguing that we should avoid eating fast food, you might explain the process by which chicken nuggets are made. But to give information about how to fry chicken, you would explain the process quite differently.

59–60

AUDIENCE   Whom are you trying to reach, and will you need to provide any special background information or to interest them in the process before you explain it?

61–64

GENRE   Does your genre require you to explain a process? In a lab report, for example, you'll need to explain processes used in the experiment. You might want to explain a process in a profile of an activity or a proposal for a solution.

65–71

STANCE   If you're giving practical directions for doing something, you'll want to take a straightforward "do this, and then do that" perspective. If you're writing to entertain, try taking a clever or amusing stance.

72–74

MEDIA/DESIGN   Your medium will affect the way you explain a process. In a print text, you can use both words and images. On the web, you may have the option of showing a video of the process as well.

75–77

If you need more help

See also **PROFILES** if you are writing about an activity that needs to be explained. See **NARRATING** for more advice on organizing an explanation chronologically. Sometimes you may be assigned to write a whole essay or report that explains a process; see **PROCESSES** for help with drafting, revising, and so on.

245–57
474–82
325

44 Narrating

164–95 ▲

245–57 ▲

Narratives are stories. As a writing strategy, a good narrative can lend support to most kinds of writing—in a **POSITION PAPER** arguing for Title IX compliance, for example, you might include a brief narrative about an Olympic sprinter who might never have had an opportunity to compete on a track-and-field team without Title IX. Or you can bring a **PROFILE** of a favorite coach to life with an anecdote about a pep talk they once gave before a championship track meet. Whatever your larger writing purpose, it's important to make sure that any narratives you add support that purpose—they should not be inserted simply to tell an interesting story. You'll also need to compose them carefully—to put them in a clear *sequence*, include *pertinent detail*, and make sure they are appropriate to your particular rhetorical situation.

Sequencing

When we write a narrative, we arrange events in a particular sequence. Writers typically sequence narratives in chronological order, reverse chronological order, or as a flashback.

Use chronological order.   Often you may tell the story chronologically, starting at the beginning of an event and working through to the end, as Maya Angelou does in this brief narrative from an essay about her high school graduation:

> The school band struck up a march and all classes filed in as had been rehearsed. We stood in front of our seats, as assigned, and on a signal from the choir director, we sat. No sooner had this been accomplished than the band started to play the national anthem. We rose again and sang the song, after which we recited the pledge of allegiance. We

---

⁕ academic literacies   ● fields   ● research

■ rhetorical situations   ⁚ processes   ● media/design

▲ genres   ◆ strategies

remained standing for a brief minute before the choir director and the principal signaled to us, rather desperately I thought, to take our seats.

—Maya Angelou, "Graduation"

Use reverse chronological order.   You may also begin with the final action and work back to the first, as Aldo Leopold does in this narrative about cutting down a tree:

> Now our saw bites into the 1890s, called gay by those whose eyes turn cityward rather than landward. We cut 1899, when the last passenger pigeon collided with a charge of shot near Babcock, two counties to the north; we cut 1898, when a dry fall, followed by a snowless winter, froze the soil seven feet deep and killed the apple trees; 1897, another drouth year, when another forestry commission came into being; 1896, when 25,000 prairie chickens were shipped to market from the village of Spooner alone; 1895, another year of fires; 1894, another drouth year; and 1893, the year of "the Bluebird Storm," when a March blizzard reduced the migrating bluebirds to near zero.
>
> —Aldo Leopold, *A Sand County Almanac*

Glossary

RÉSUMÉS* are one genre where we generally use reverse chronological order, listing the most recent jobs or degrees first and then working backward. Notice, too, that we usually write these as narratives—telling what we have done rather than just naming positions we have held:

Sept. 2020–present	*Student worker*, Department of Information Management, Central State University, Wilberforce, OH. Compile data and format reports using Excel, Word, and university database.
June–Sept. 2020	*Intern*, QuestPro Corporation, West Louisville, KY. Assisted in development of software.
Sept. 2019–June 2020	*Bagger*, Ace Groceries, Elba, KY. Bagged customers' purchases.

*See the ebook at digital.wwnorton.com/fieldguide6 for a chapter on Résumés and Job Letters.

Use a flashback. You can sometimes put a flashback in the middle of a narrative, to tell about an incident that illuminates the larger narrative. Terry Tempest Williams does this in an essay about the startling incidence of breast cancer in her family: she recalls a dinnertime conversation with her father right after her mother's death from cancer, when she learned for the first time what caused all of the cancer in her family:

> Over dessert, I shared a recurring dream of mine. I told my father that for years, as long as I could remember, I saw this flash of light in the night in the desert. That this image had so permeated my being, I could not venture south without seeing it again, on the horizon, illuminating buttes and mesas.
>
> "You did see it," he said.
>
> "Saw what?" I asked, a bit tentative.
>
> "The bomb. The cloud. We were driving home from Riverside, California. You were sitting on your mother's lap. She was pregnant. In fact, I remember the date, September 7, 1957. We had just gotten out of the Service. We were driving north, past Las Vegas. It was an hour or so before dawn, when this explosion went off. We not only heard it, but felt it. I thought the oil tanker in front of us had blown up. We pulled over and suddenly, rising from the desert floor, we saw it, clearly, this golden-stemmed cloud, the mushroom. The sky seemed to vibrate with an eerie pink glow. Within a few minutes, a light ash was raining on the car."
>
> I stared at my father. This was new information to me.
>
> —Terry Tempest Williams,
> "The Clan of the One-Breasted Women"

Williams could have simply announced this information as a fact—but see how much more powerful it is when told in narrative form.

Use time markers. Time markers help readers follow a sequence of events. The most obvious time markers are those that simply label the time, as the narrative entries in a diary, journal, or log might. For example, here is the final part of the narrative kept in a diary by a doomed Antarctic explorer:

---

* academic literacies   ● fields   ● research
■ rhetorical situations   ⁖ processes   ● media/design
▲ genres   ◆ strategies

WEDNESDAY, MARCH 21: Got within eleven miles of depot. Monday night; had to lay up all yesterday in severe blizzard. Today forlorn hope, Wilson and Bowers going to depot for fuel.

MARCH 22 and 23: Blizzard bad as ever—Wilson and Bowers unable to start—tomorrow last chance—no fuel and only one or two [days] of food left—must be near the end. Have decided it shall be natural—we shall march for the depot with or without our effects and die in our tracks.

THURSDAY, MARCH 29: Since the 21st we have had a continuous gale from W.S.W. and S.W. We had fuel to make two cups of tea apiece and bare food for two days on the 20th. Every day we have been ready to start for our depot eleven miles away, but outside the door of the tent it remains a scene of whirling drift. I do not think we can hope for any better things now. We shall stick it out to the end, but we are getting weaker, of course, and the end cannot be far. It seems a pity, but I do not think I can write more. . . .

Last Entry: For God's sake look after our people.

—Robert F. Scott, *Scott's Last Expedition: The Journals*

More often you will integrate time markers into the prose itself, as is done in this narrative about a woman preparing and delivering meals to workers at a cotton gin:

She made her plans meticulously and in secret. <u>One early evening</u> to see if she was ready, she placed stones in two five-gallon pails and carried them three miles to the cotton gin. She rested a little, and then, discarding some rocks, she walked in the darkness to the sawmill five miles farther along the dirt road. <u>On her way back</u> to her little house and her babies, she dumped the remaining rocks along the path.

    <u>That same night</u> she worked into the early hours boiling chicken and frying ham. She made dough and filled the rolled-out pastry with meat. <u>At last</u> she went to sleep.

    <u>The next morning</u> she left her house carrying the meat pies, lard, an iron brazier, and coals for a fire. <u>Just before lunch</u> she appeared in an empty lot behind the cotton gin. <u>As the dinner noon bell rang</u>, she dropped the savors into boiling fat, and the aroma rose and floated

over to the workers who spilled out of the gin, covered with white lint, looking like specters.

—Maya Angelou,
Wouldn't Take Nothing for My Journey Now

361–62

Use transitions.   Another way to help readers follow a narrative is with TRANSITIONS , words like "first," "then," "meanwhile," "at last," and so on. See how the following paragraphs from Langston Hughes's classic essay about meeting Jesus use transitions (and time markers) to advance the action:

Suddenly the whole room broke into a sea of shouting, as they saw me rise. Waves of rejoicing swept the place. Women leaped in the air. My aunt threw her arms around me. The minister took me by the hand and led me to the platform.

When things quieted down, in a hushed silence, punctuated by a few ecstatic "Amens," all the new young lambs were blessed in the name of God. Then joyous singing filled the room. That night, for the last time in my life but one—for I was a big boy twelve years old—I cried.

—Langston Hughes, "Salvation"

Including Pertinent Detail

When you include a narrative in your writing, you must decide which details you need—and which ones you don't. For example, you don't want to include so much detail that the narrative distracts the reader from the larger text. You must also decide whether you should include any background, to set the stage for the narrative. The amount of detail you include depends on your audience and purpose: How much detail does your audience need? How much detail do you need to make your meaning clear? In an essay on the suspicion African American men often face when walking at night, a journalist deliberately presents a story without setting the stage at all:

My first victim was a woman—white, well dressed, probably in her late twenties. I came upon her late one evening on a deserted street

academic literacies   ● fields   ● research
■ rhetorical situations   ⁂ processes   ● media/design
▲ genres   ◆ strategies

in Hyde Park, a relatively affluent neighborhood in an otherwise mean, impoverished section of Chicago. As I swung onto the avenue behind her, there seemed to be a discreet, uninflammatory distance between us. Not so. She cast back a worried glance. To her, the youngish black man—a broad six feet two inches with a beard and billowing hair, both hands shoved into the pockets of a bulky military jacket—seemed menacingly close. After a few more quick glimpses, she picked up her pace and was soon running in earnest. Within seconds she disappeared into a cross street.

—Brent Staples, "Black Men and Public Space"

Words like "victim" and phrases like "came upon her" lead us to assume the narrator is scary and perhaps dangerous. We don't know why he is walking on the deserted street because he hasn't told us: he simply begins with the moment he and the woman encounter each other. For his purposes, that's all the audience needs to know at first, and details of his physical appearance that explain the woman's response come later, after he tells us about the encounter. Had he given us those details at the outset, the narrative wouldn't have been nearly so effective. In a way, Staples lets the story sneak up on us, as the woman apparently felt he had on her.

Other times you'll need to provide more background information, as an MIT professor does when she uses an anecdote to introduce an essay about young children's experiences with electronic toys. First the writer tells us a little about *Merlin*, the computer tic-tac-toe game that the children in her anecdote play with. As you'll see, the anecdote would be hard to follow without the introduction:

Among the first generation of computational objects was Merlin, which challenged children to games of tic-tac-toe. For children who had only played games with human opponents, reaction to this object was intense. For example, while Merlin followed an optimal strategy for winning tic-tac-toe most of the time, it was programmed to make a slip every once in a while. So when children discovered strategies that allowed them to win and then tried these strategies a second time, they usually would not work. The machine gave the impression of not being "dumb enough" to let down its defenses twice. Robert, seven, playing with his friends on the beach, watched his friend Craig perform the "winning trick," but when he tried it, Merlin did not slip up and the game ended in a draw. Robert, confused and frustrated, threw Merlin into the sand and said, "Cheater. I hope your brains break." He was overheard by Craig and Greg, aged six and eight, who salvaged the by-now very sandy toy and took it upon themselves to set Robert straight. "Merlin doesn't know if it cheats," says Craig. "It doesn't know if you break it, Robert. It's not alive." Greg adds, "It's smart enough to make the right kinds of noises. But it doesn't really know if it loses. And when it cheats, it don't even know it's cheating." Jenny, six, interrupts with disdain: "Greg, to cheat you have to know you are cheating. Knowing is part of cheating."

—Sherry Turkle, "Cuddling Up to Cyborg Babies"

Opening and Closing with Narratives

346–54
Narratives are often useful as **BEGINNINGS** to essays and other kinds of writing. Everyone likes a good story, so an interesting or pithy narrative can be a good way to get your audience's attention. In the following introductory paragraph, a historian tells a gruesome but gripping story to attract our attention to a subject that might not otherwise merit our interest—bubonic plague:

In October 1347, two months after the fall of Calais, Genoese trading ships put into the harbor of Messina in Sicily with dead and dying men at the oars. The ships had come from the Black Sea port of Caffa (now Feodosiya) in the Crimea, where the Genoese maintained a trading post. The diseased sailors showed strange black swellings about the size of an egg or an apple in the armpits and groin. The swellings oozed blood and pus and were followed by spreading boils and black blotches on the skin from internal bleeding. The sick suffered severe pain and died quickly, within five days of the first symptoms. As the disease spread, other symptoms of continuous fever and spitting of blood appeared instead of the swellings or buboes. These victims coughed and sweated heavily and died even more quickly, within three days or less, sometimes in twenty-four hours. In both types everything that issued from the body—breath, sweat, blood from the buboes and lungs, bloody urine,

* academic literacies   ● fields   ● research
■ rhetorical situations   ⁙ processes   ● media/design
▲ genres   ◆ strategies

and blood-blackened excrement—smelled foul. Depression and despair accompanied the physical symptoms, and before the end "death is seen seated on the face."

—Barbara Tuchman,
"This Is the End of the World: The Black Death"

Imagine how different the preceding paragraph would be if it weren't in the form of a narrative. Imagine, for example, that Tuchman had begun by defining bubonic plague. Would that have gotten your interest? The piece was written for a general audience; how might it have been different if it had been written for scientists? Would they need (or appreciate) the story told here?

Narrative can be a good way of **ENDING** a text, too, by winding up a discussion with an illustration of the main point. Here, for instance, is a concluding paragraph from an essay on American values and Las Vegas weddings:

354–58

> I sat next to one . . . wedding party in a Strip restaurant the last time I was in Las Vegas. The marriage had just taken place; the bride still wore her dress, the mother her corsage. A bored waiter poured out a few swallows of pink champagne ("on the house") for everyone but the bride, who was too young to be served. "You'll need something with more kick than that," the bride's father said with heavy jocularity to his new son-in-law; the ritual jokes about the wedding night had a certain Panglossian character, since the bride was clearly several months pregnant. Another round of pink champagne, this time not on the house, and the bride began to cry. "It was just as nice," she sobbed, "as I hoped and dreamed it would be."
>
> —Joan Didion, "Marrying Absurd"

No doubt Didion makes her points about American values clearly and cogently in the essay. But concluding with this story lets us *see* (and hear) what she is saying about Las Vegas wedding chapels, which sell "'niceness,' the facsimile of proper ritual, to children who do not know how else to find it, how to make the arrangements, how to do it 'right.'"

Considering the Rhetorical Situation

As a writer or speaker, it's important to think about the message you want to articulate, the audience you want to reach, and the larger context you are writing in.

59–60 **PURPOSE**   Your purpose will affect the way you use narrative. For example, in an essay about seat belt laws, you might tell about the painful rehabilitation of a teenager who wasn't wearing a seat belt and was injured in an accident in order to show readers why seat belt use is mandatory in all but one state.

61–64 **AUDIENCE**   Whom do you want to reach, and do you have an anecdote or other narrative that will help them understand your topic or persuade them that your argument has merit?

65–71 **GENRE**   Does your genre require you to include narrative? A memoir about an important event might be primarily narrative, whereas a reflection about an event might focus more on the significance of the event than on what happened.

72–74 **STANCE**   What is your stance, and do you have any stories that would help you convey that stance? A funny story, for example, can help create a humorous stance.

75–77 **MEDIA/DESIGN**   In a print or spoken text, you will likely be limited to brief narratives, perhaps illustrated with photos or other images. In an electronic text, you might have the option of linking to full-length narratives or videos available on the web.

If you need more help

325
322
Glossary

See also the **PROCESSES** chapters if you are assigned to write a narrative essay and need help with drafting, revising, and so on. Two special kinds of narratives are **LAB REPORTS** (which use narrative to describe the steps in an experiment from beginning to end) and **RÉSUMÉS** (which essentially tell the story of the work we've done, at school and on the job).

* academic literacies   ● fields   ● research
■ rhetorical situations   ∴ processes   ● media/design
▲ genres   ◆ strategies

45 Taking Essay Exams

Essay exams present writers with special challenges. You must write quickly, on a topic presented to you on the spot, to show your instructor what you know about a specific body of information. This chapter offers advice on how to take essay exams.

Considering the Rhetorical Situation

PURPOSE   In an essay exam, your purpose is to show that you have mastered certain material and that you can analyze and apply it in an essay. You may need to make an argument or simply convey information on a topic.   59–60

AUDIENCE   Will your course instructor be reading your exam, or will a teaching assistant? Sometimes standardized tests are read by groups of trained readers. What specific criteria will your audience use to evaluate your writing?   61–64

GENRE   Does the essay question specify or suggest a certain genre? In a literature course, you may need to write a compelling literary analysis of a passage. In a history course, you may need to write an argument for the significance of a key historical event. In an economics course, you may need to contrast the economies of the North and South before the Civil War. If the essay question doesn't specify a genre, look for keywords such as "argue," "evaluate," or "explain," which point to a certain genre.   65–71

72–74 ■
STANCE   In an essay exam, the most appropriate stance is usually unemotional, thoughtful, and critical.

75–77 ■
MEDIA/DESIGN   If you're taking a test online, write your answers in a word processor, edit there, and then paste them into the exam. If you're handwriting on lined paper or in an exam booklet, write as legibly as you can.

Analyzing Essay Questions

Essay questions usually include key verbs that specify the kind of writing you'll need to do—*argue* a position, *compare* two texts, and so on. Here are some of the most common kinds of writing you'll be asked to do on an essay exam:

104–39 ▲
- *Analyze.* Break an idea, theory, text, or event into its parts and examine them. For example, a world history exam might ask you to **ANALYZE** European imperialism's effect on Africa in the late nineteenth century and discuss how Africans responded.

- *Apply.* Consider how an idea or concept might work out in practice. For instance, a film studies exam might ask you to apply the concept of auteurism—a theory of film that sees the director as the primary creator, whose body of work reflects a distinct personal style—to two films by Clint Eastwood. An economics exam might ask you to apply the concept of opportunity costs to a certain supplied scenario.

410–30 ◆
- *Argue/prove/justify.* Offer reasons and evidence to support a position. A philosophy exam, for example, might ask you to **ARGUE** whether or not all stereotypes contain a "kernel of truth" and whether believing a stereotype is ever justified.

431–36 ◆
- *Classify.* Group something into categories. For example, a marketing exam might ask you to **CLASSIFY** shoppers in categories based on their purchasing behavior, motives, attitudes, or lifestyle patterns.

✳ academic literacies   ⬤ fields   ⬤ research
■ rhetorical situations   ⁘ processes   ⬤ media/design
▲ genres   ◆ strategies

- *Compare/contrast.* Explore the similarities and/or differences between two or more things. An economics exam, for example, might ask you to **COMPARE** the effectiveness of patents and tax incentives in encouraging technological advances.

  437–44

- *Critique.* **ANALYZE** and **EVALUATE** a text or argument, considering its strengths and weaknesses. For instance, an evolutionary biology exam might ask you to critique John Maynard Smith's assertion that "scientific theories say nothing about what is right but only about what is possible" in the context of the theory of evolution.

  104–39
  214–22

- *Define.* Explain what a word or phrase means. An art history exam, for example, might ask you to **DEFINE** negative space and discuss the way various artists use it in their work.

  445–55

- *Describe.* Tell about the important characteristics or features of something. For example, a sociology exam might ask you to **DESCRIBE** Erving Goffman's theory of the presentation of self in ordinary life, focusing on roles, props, and setting.

  456–63

- *Evaluate.* Determine something's significance or value. A drama exam, for example, might ask you to **EVALUATE** the setting, lighting, and costumes in a filmed production of *Macbeth*.

  214–22

- *Explain.* Provide reasons and examples to clarify an idea, argument, or event. For instance, a rhetoric exam might ask you to explain the structure of the African American sermon and discuss its use in writings of Frederick Douglass and Martin Luther King Jr.

- *Summarize/review.* Give the major points of a text or idea. A political science exam, for example, might ask you to **SUMMARIZE** John Stuart Mill's concept of utilitarianism and its relation to freedom of speech.

  550–51

- *Trace.* Explain a sequence of ideas or order of events. For instance, a geography exam might ask you to trace the patterns of international migration since 1970 and discuss how these patterns differ from those of the period between 1870 and World War I.

Some Guidelines for Taking Essay Exams

Before the exam

16–19
- *Read over* your class notes and course texts strategically, **ANNOTATING** them to keep track of details you'll want to remember.

- *Collaborate* by forming a study group to help one another master the course content.

535–39
- *Review* key ideas, events, terms, and themes. Look for common themes and **CONNECTIONS** in lecture notes, class discussions, and any readings—they'll lead you to important ideas.

- *Ask* your instructor about the form the exam will take: how long it will be, what kind of questions will be on it, how it will be evaluated, and so on. Working with a study group, write questions you think your instructor might ask, and then answer the questions together.

333–34
- *Warm up* just before the exam by **FREEWRITING** for 10 minutes or so to gather your thoughts.

During the exam

- *Scan the questions* to determine how much each part of the test counts and how much time you should spend on it. For example, if one essay is worth 50 points and two others are worth 25 points each, you'll want to spend half your time on the 50-point question.

- *Read over* the entire test before answering any questions. Start with the question you feel most confident answering, which may or may not be the first question on the test.

- *Don't panic.* Sometimes when students first read an essay question, their minds go blank, but after a few moments they start to recall the information they need.

- *Plan.* Although you won't have much time for revising or editing, you still need to plan and allow yourself time to make some last-minute changes before turning in the exam. So apportion your time. For a three-question essay test in a two-hour test period, you might divide your time like this:

✳ academic literacies	◆ fields	● research
■ rhetorical situations	⁝ processes	⬤ media/design
▲ genres	◆ strategies	

Total Exam Time—120 minutes
Generating ideas—20 minutes (6–7 minutes per question)
Drafting—85 minutes (45 for the 50-point question,
                    20 for each 25-point question)
Revising, editing, proofreading—15 minutes

Knowing that you have built in time at the end of the exam period can help you remain calm as you write, because you can use that time to fill in gaps or reconsider answers you feel unsure about.

- *Jot down the main ideas* you need to cover in answering the question on scratch paper or on the cover of your exam book, numbering those ideas in the order you think makes sense—and you have an outline for your essay. If you're worried about time, plan to write the most important parts of your answers early on. If you don't complete your answer, refer your instructor to your outline to show where you were headed.

- *Turn the essay question into your introduction,* like this:

    Question: How did the outcomes of World War II differ from those of World War I?

    Introduction: The outcomes of World War II differed from those of World War I in three major ways: World War II affected more of the world and its people than World War I did, distinctions between citizens and soldiers were eroded, and the war's brutality made it impossible for Europe to continue to claim cultural superiority over other cultures.

- *State your thesis explicitly,* provide **REASONS** and **EVIDENCE** to support your thesis, and use **TRANSITIONS** to move logically from one idea to the next. Restate your main point in your conclusion. You don't want to give what one professor calls a "garbage truck answer," dumping everything you know into your answer and expecting the instructor to sort it all out.

    413–14
    414–22
    361–62

- *Write on every other line* and only on one side of each page so that you'll have room to make additions or corrections. If you're typing on a computer, be sure to double-space.

- *If you have time left, go over your exam,* looking for ideas that need elaboration as well as for grammatical and punctuation errors.

After the exam.   Your instructor may not return your exam or may not provide comments on it. So consider asking for a conference to go over your work so you can learn what you did well and where you need to improve—important knowledge to take with you into your next exam.

Part 7
Doing Research

We do research all the time, for many different reasons. We search the web for information about a new computer, ask friends about the best place to get coffee, try on several pairs of jeans before deciding which ones to buy. You have no doubt done your share of library research before now, and you probably have visited a number of schools' websites before deciding which college you wanted to attend. Research, in other words, is something you do every day. The following chapters offer advice on the kind of research you'll need to do for your academic work and, in particular, for research projects.

Doing Research

46 Getting a Start on Research   491

47 Finding Sources   501

48 Evaluating Sources   524

49 Synthesizing Ideas   535

50 Quoting, Paraphrasing, and Summarizing   542

51 Acknowledging Sources,
Avoiding Plagiarism   555

52 Documentation   560

53 MLA Style   564

54 APA Style   615

46 Getting a Start on Research

When you need to do research, it's sometimes tempting to jump in and start looking for information right away. However, doing research is complex and time-consuming. Research-based writing projects usually require you to follow several steps. You need to come up with a topic (or to analyze the requirements of an assigned topic) and come up with a research question to guide your research efforts. Once you do some serious, focused research to find the information you need, you'll be ready to turn your research question into a tentative thesis and sketch out a rough outline. After doing whatever additional research you need to fill in your outline, you'll write a draft—and get some response to that draft. You may then need to do even more research before revising. Once you revise, you'll need to edit and proofread. In other words, there's a lot to do. You need a schedule.

Establishing a Schedule and Getting Started

A good way to start a research project is by creating a timeline for getting all this work done, perhaps using the form on the next page. Once you have a schedule, you can get started. The sections that follow offer advice on considering your rhetorical situation, coming up with a topic, and doing preliminary research; developing a research question, a tentative thesis, and a rough outline; and creating a working bibliography and keeping track of your sources. The chapters that follow offer guidelines for **FINDING SOURCES**, **EVALUATING SOURCES**, and **SYNTHESIZING IDEAS**.

501–23
524–34
535–41

Scheduling a Research Project

Complete by:

Analyze your rhetorical situation.	_____
Choose a possible topic or analyze the assignment.	_____
Plan a research strategy, and do preliminary research.	_____
Come up with a research question.	_____
Schedule interviews and other field research.	_____
Find and evaluate sources.	_____
Read sources, and take notes.	_____
Do any field research.	_____
Come up with a tentative thesis and outline.	_____
Write a draft.	_____
Get response.	_____
Do any additional research.	_____
Revise.	_____
Prepare a list of works cited.	_____
Edit.	_____
Proofread the final draft.	_____
Submit the final draft: your deadline.	_____

You may find it useful to start with your deadline—when the final project is due—and work backward from there, so you'll know how much time you have and can estimate how much time you'll need to do each task.

Considering the Rhetorical Situation

As with any writing task, you need to start by considering your purpose, your audience, and the rest of your rhetorical situation:

59–60 ■

PURPOSE   Is this project part of an assignment—and if so, does it specify any one purpose? If not, what is your broad purpose? To inform? argue? analyze? A combination?

※ academic literacies   ● fields   ● research

■ rhetorical situations   ⁂ processes   ● media/design

▲ genres   ◆ strategies

AUDIENCE	To whom are you writing? What does your audience likely know about your topic, and is there any background information you'll need to provide? What opinions or attitudes do your readers likely hold? What kinds of evidence will they find persuasive? How do you want them to respond to your writing?	▪ 61–64
GENRE	Are you writing to report on something? to compose a profile? to make a proposal? an argument? What are the requirements of your genre in terms of the number and kind of sources you must use?	▪ 65–71
STANCE	What is your attitude toward your topic? What accounts for your attitude? How do you want to come across? As curious? Critical? Positive? Something else?	▪ 72–74
MEDIA/DESIGN	What medium or media will you use? Print? Spoken? Electronic? Will you need to create any charts, photographs, video, presentation software slides, or other visuals?	▪ 75–77

Coming Up with a Topic

If you need to choose a topic, consider your interests as they relate to the course for which you're writing. What do you want to learn about? What do you have questions about? What topics from the course have you found intriguing? What community, national, or global issues do you care about? Once you've thought of a potential topic, use the questions in Chapter 27, **WRITING AS INQUIRY**, to explore it and find an angle on it that you can write about—and want to.

⁚▪ 329–32

If your topic is assigned, make sure you understand exactly what it asks you to do. Read the assignment carefully, looking for keywords: Does it ask you to **ANALYZE**, **COMPARE**, **EVALUATE**, **SUMMARIZE**, or **ARGUE**? If the assignment offers broad guidelines but allows you to choose within them, identify the requirements and the range of possible topics, and define your topic within those constraints.

▲ 104–39
◆ 437–44
▲ 214–22
● 550–51
◆ 410–30

For example, in an American history course, your instructor might ask you to "discuss social effects of the Civil War." Potential but broad topics might include poverty among Confederate soldiers or former slaveholders, the migration of members of those groups to Mexico or Northern cities, the establishment of independent African American churches, or the spread of the Ku Klux Klan—to name only a few of the possibilities.

Think about what you know about your topic.   Chances are you already know something about your topic, and articulating that knowledge can help you see possible ways to focus the topic or come up with potential sources of information. FREEWRITING, LISTING, CLUSTERING, and LOOPING are all good ways of tapping your knowledge of your topic. Consider where you might find information about it: Have you read about it in a textbook? heard stories about it on the news? visited websites focused on it? Do you know anyone who knows about this topic?

333–36

Narrow the topic.   As you consider possible topics, look for ways to narrow your topic's focus to make it specific enough to discuss in depth. For example:

> **Too general:** fracking
>
> **Still too general:** fracking and the environment
>
> **Better:** the potential environmental effects of extracting natural gas through the process of hydraulic fracturing, or fracking

If you limit your topic, you can address it with specific information that you'll be more easily able to find and manage. In addition, a limited topic will be more likely to interest your audience than a broad topic that forces you to use abstract, general statements. For example, it's much harder to write well about "the environment" than it is to address a topic that explores a single environmental issue.

Consulting with Librarians and Doing Preliminary Research

Consulting with a reference librarian at your school and doing some preliminary research in the library can save you time in the long run. Reference librarians can direct you to the best scholarly sources for your topic

academic literacies   ● fields   ● research
■ rhetorical situations   ⁙ processes   ● media/design
▲ genres   ◆ strategies

and help you focus the topic by determining appropriate search terms and **KEYWORDS** —significant words that appear in the title, abstract, or text of potential sources and that you can use to search for information on your topic in library catalogs, in databases, and on the web. These librarians can also help you choose the most appropriate reference works, sources that provide general overviews of the scholarship in a field. General internet searches can be time-consuming, as they often result in thousands of possible sites—too many to weed out efficiently, either by revising your search terms or by going through the sites themselves, many of which are unreliable. Library databases, in contrast, include only sources that already have been selected by experts, and searches in them usually present manageable numbers of results.

● 506–9

Reading a *Wikipedia* entry on your topic can help you understand background information, come up with new keywords to search, and discover related topics. A list of references—often with hyperlinks—at the bottom of each entry can lead to potential sources. *Google*, *Google Scholar*, and other free search tools can also be helpful as you begin to explore your topic. See pages 509–11 for advice on using these and other online search tools.

Coming Up with a Research Question

Once you've surveyed the territory of your topic, you'll likely find that your understanding of it has become broader and deeper. You may find that your interests have changed and your research has led to surprises and additional research. That's okay: as a result of exploring avenues you hadn't anticipated, you may well come up with a better topic than the one you'd started with. At some point, though, you need to develop a research question—a specific question that you will then work to answer through your research.

To write a research question, review your analysis of the **RHETORICAL SITUATION** to remind yourself of any time constraints or length considerations. Generate a list of questions beginning with "what," "when," "where," "who," "how," "why," "would," "could," and "should." Here, for example, are some questions about the tentative topic "the potential environmental

■ 57

effects of extracting natural gas through the process of hydraulic fracturing, or fracking":

> *What* are the environmental effects of fracking?
>
> *When* was fracking introduced as a way to produce natural gas?
>
> *Where* is fracking done, and *how* does this affect the surrounding people and environment?
>
> *Who* will benefit from increased fracking?
>
> *How* is fracking done, and *how much* energy does the process use?
>
> *Why* do some environmental groups oppose fracking?
>
> *Would* other methods of extracting natural gas be safer?
>
> *Could* fracking cause earthquakes?
>
> *Should* fracking be expanded, regulated, or banned?

Select one question from your list that you find interesting and that suits your rhetorical situation. Use the question to guide your research.

Drafting a Tentative Thesis

347–49

Once your research has led you to a possible answer to your research question, try formulating that answer as a tentative **THESIS**. You need not be committed to the thesis; in fact, you shouldn't be. The object of your research should be to learn about your topic, not to find information that simply supports what you already think you believe. Your tentative thesis may (and probably will) change as you learn more about your subject, consider the many points of view on it, and reconsider your topic and, perhaps, your goal: what you originally planned to be an argument for considering other points of view may become a call to action. However tentative, a thesis allows you to move forward by clarifying your purpose for doing research. Here are some tentative thesis statements on the topic of fracking:

> Fracking is a likely cause of earthquakes in otherwise seismically stable regions of the country.

---

* academic literacies   ● fields   ● research
* ■ rhetorical situations   ⁘ processes   ● media/design
* ▲ genres   ◆ strategies

The federal government should strictly regulate the production of natural gas by fracking.

Fracking can greatly increase our supplies of natural gas, but other methods of producing energy should still be pursued.

As with a research question, a tentative thesis should guide your research efforts—but you should be ready to revise it as you learn still more about your topic. Research should be a process of **INQUIRY** in which you approach your topic with an open mind, ready to learn and possibly change. If you hold too tightly to a tentative thesis, you risk focusing only on evidence that supports your own view—a tendency called **CONFIRMATION BIAS** that can make your writing biased and unconvincing.

329–32

Glossary

Creating a Rough Outline

After you've created a tentative thesis, write out a rough **OUTLINE** for your research project. This outline can be a simple list of topics you want to explore, something that will help you structure your research efforts and organize your notes and other materials. As you read your sources, you can use the outline to keep track of what you need to find and where the information you do find fits into your argument. Then you'll be able to see if you've covered all the ideas you intended to explore—or whether you need to rethink the categories on your outline.

340–42

Keeping a Working Bibliography

A working bibliography is a record of all the sources you consult. You should keep such a record so that you can find sources easily when you need them and then cite any that you actually use. Your library likely offers tools to store source information you find in its databases and catalog, and software such as *Zotero* or *EasyBib* can also help you save, manage, and cite your sources. You may find it helpful to print out bibliographical data you find useful or to keep your working bibliography on index cards or in a notebook. However you decide to compile your working bibliography, include all the information you'll need later to document any sources you use; follow the **DOCUMENTATION** style you'll use when you write so that you won't need to go back to your sources to find the information. Some

560–63

Information for a Working Bibliography

FOR A BOOK

Library call number
Author(s) or editor(s)
Title and subtitle
Publication information: city, publisher, year of publication
Other information: edition, volume number, translator, and so on
If your source is an essay in a collection, include its author, title, and page numbers.

FOR A SOURCE FROM A DATABASE

Publication information for the source, as listed above
Name of database
DOI (digital object identifier) or URL of original source, such as the periodical in which an article was published
Stable URL or permalink for database
Date you accessed source

FOR AN ARTICLE IN A PRINT PERIODICAL

Author(s)
Title and subtitle
Name of periodical
Volume number, issue number, date
Page numbers

FOR A WEB SOURCE

URL
Author(s) or editor(s) if available
Name of site
Sponsor of site
Date site was first posted or last updated
Date you accessed site
If the source is an article or book reprinted on the web, include its title, the title and publication information of the periodical or book, where it was first published, and any page numbers.

✳ academic literacies   ⬤ fields   ⬤ research
◼ rhetorical situations   ⦂ processes   ⬤ media/design
▲ genres   ◆ strategies

databases make this step easy by preparing rough-draft citations in several styles that you can copy, paste, and edit.

On the previous page is most of the basic information you'll want to include for each source in your working bibliography. Go to digital.wwnorton.com/fieldguide6 for templates you can use to keep track of this information.

Keeping Track of Your Sources

- *Staple together photocopies and printouts.* It's easy for individual pages to get shuffled or lost on a desk or in a backpack. Keep a stapler handy, and fasten pages together as soon as you copy them or print them out.

- *Bookmark web sources,* or save them using a free bookmark management tool available through several library databases. For database sources, use the *DOI* or *stable URL*, *permalink*, or *document URL* (the terms used by databases vary)—not the URL in the "Address" or "Location" box in your browser, which will expire after you end your online session.

- *Label everything.* Label your copies with the source's author and title.

- *Highlight sections you plan to use.* When you sit down to draft, your goal will be to find what you need quickly, so as soon as you decide you might use a source, highlight the paragraphs or sentences that you think you'll use. If your instructor wants copies of your sources to see how you used them, you've got them ready. If you're using PDF copies or websites, you can highlight or add notes using an online annotation tool like *Hypothesis* or *Diigo*.

- *Use your rough outline to keep track of what you've got.* In the margin of each highlighted section, write the number or letter of the outline division to which the section corresponds. (It's a good idea to write it in the same place consistently so you can flip through a stack of copies and easily see what you've got.) Alternatively, attach sticky notes to each copy, using a different color for each main heading in your outline.

- *Store all your research material in one place.* If you prefer to work digitally, create computer folders and subfolders that correspond to your rough outline. Or use web apps like *PowerNotes* or *Scrible* to collect, annotate, and organize your sources. If you prefer to work with paper, use an accordion file folder or a box. Having your material in one place will make writing a draft easier—and will serve you well if you're required to create a portfolio that includes your research notes, copies of sources, and drafts.

- *Use a reference manager.* Web-based reference or citation management software allows you to create and organize a personal database of resources. You can import references from databases to a personal account, organize them, and draft citations in various formats. *RefWorks, EndNote, Mendeley*, and *Zotero* are four such systems; check with your librarian to see what system your library supports, or search online, as several of them are available for free. Be aware, though, that the citations generated are often inaccurate and need to be checked carefully for content and format. So treat them as rough drafts, and plan to edit them.

If you need more help

501–23
524–34

See the guidelines on **FINDING SOURCES** once you're ready to move on to in-depth research and those on **EVALUATING SOURCES** for help thinking critically about the sources you find.

- ☀ academic literacies   ● fields   ● research
- ■ rhetorical situations   ⦂ processes   ● media/design
- ▲ genres   ◆ strategies

47 Finding Sources

To analyze media coverage of the 2020 Democratic National Convention, you examine news stories and blogs published at the time. To write an essay interpreting a poem by Maya Angelou, you study the poem and read several critical interpretations in literary journals. To write a report on career opportunities in psychology, you interview a graduate of your university who is working in a counseling center. In each of these cases, you go beyond your own knowledge to consult additional sources of information. Depending on your topic, then, you'll need to choose from many sources for your research—from reference works, books, periodicals, and websites to surveys, interviews, and other kinds of field research that you yourself conduct.

This chapter offers guidelines for locating a range of sources—print and online, general and specialized, published and firsthand. Keep in mind that as you do research, finding and **EVALUATING SOURCES** are two activities that usually take place simultaneously. So this chapter and the next one go hand in hand.

524–34

Kinds of Sources

Primary and secondary sources. Your research will likely lead you to both primary and secondary sources. *Primary sources* include historical documents, literary works, eyewitness accounts, field reports, diaries, letters, and lab studies, as well as any original research you do through interviews, observation, experiments, or surveys. *Secondary sources* include scholarly books and articles, reviews, biographies, textbooks, and other works that interpret or discuss primary sources. Novels and films are primary sources; articles interpreting them are secondary sources. The Declaration of Independence is a primary historical document; a historian's description of the events surrounding the Declaration's writing is secondary. A published report of scientific findings is primary; a critique of that report is secondary.

Whether a work is considered primary or secondary sometimes depends on your topic and purpose. If you're analyzing a poem, a critic's article interpreting the poem is a secondary source—but if you're investigating that critic's work, the article would be a primary source for your own study and interpretation.

Secondary sources are often useful because they can help you understand and evaluate primary source material. Whenever possible, however, you should find and use primary sources, because secondary sources can distort or misrepresent the information in primary sources. For example, a seemingly reputable secondary source describing the 1948 presidential election asserted that the *New York Times* ran a headline reading, "Thomas E. Dewey's Election as President Is a Foregone Conclusion." But the actual article was titled "Talk Is Now Turning to the Dewey Cabinet," and it began by noting "[the] *popular view that* Gov. Thomas E. Dewey's election as President is a foregone conclusion." Here the secondary source not only got the headline wrong but also distorted the source's intended meaning by leaving out an important phrase. Your research should be as accurate and reliable as possible; using primary sources whenever you can helps ensure that it is.

Scholarly and popular sources.   Scholarly sources are written by academic experts or scholars in a particular discipline and are *peer-reviewed*—evaluated by other experts in the same discipline for their factual accuracy and lack of bias. They are also written largely *for* experts in a discipline, as a means of sharing research, insights, and in-depth analysis with one another; that's why they must meet high standards of accuracy and objectivity and adhere to the discipline's accepted research methods, including its style for documenting sources. Scholarly articles are usually published in academic journals; scholarly books may be published by university presses or by other academically focused publishers.

Popular sources include just about all other online and print publications, from websites to magazines to books written for nonspecialists. These sources generally explain or provide opinion on current events or topics of general interest; when they discuss scholarly research, they tend

* academic literacies   ● fields   ● research
■ rhetorical situations   ∴ processes   ● media/design
▲ genres   ◆ strategies

to simplify the concepts and facts, providing definitions, narratives, and examples to make them understandable to nonspecialist audiences. They are often written by journalists or other professional writers who may specialize in a particular area but who report or comment on the scholarship of others rather than doing any themselves. Their most important difference from scholarly sources is that popular sources are not reviewed by other experts in the field being discussed, although editors or fact-checkers review the writing before it's published.

That said, the distinction can be blurry: many scholars write books for a general readership that are informed by those authors' own scholarship, and many writers of popular sources have extensive expertise in the subject. Even if it's not a requirement, citing scholarly sources often contributes to your own authority as a writer, demonstrating that you are familiar with important research and scholarship and that your own writing is informed by it.

In most of your college courses, you'll be expected to rely primarily on scholarly sources rather than popular ones. However, if you're writing about a very current topic or need to provide background information on a topic, a mix of scholarly and popular sources may be appropriate. To see how scholarly and popular sources differ in appearance, look at the Documentation Map for scholarly journals (p. 583) and at the illustrations on pages 504–5. Here's a guide to determining whether or not a potential source is scholarly:

Identifying scholarly sources: what to look for

- *The author:* Look for the author's credentials, including affiliations with academic or other research-oriented institutions. Make sure the author has expertise on the topic being discussed; an English professor may have academic credentials but not be an expert on the environment, while a journalist may have studied environmental issues for years and know a great deal.

- *The publisher:* Look for academic journals, university presses, and professional organizations such as the Modern Language Association or the American Psychological Association; popular sources are published in general-interest publications such as the *Atlantic* or *Slate* or trade publishers such as Penguin Random House or HarperCollins.

Scholarly Source

Published in an academic journal.

Includes an abstract.

Cites academic research with consistent documentation style.

Describes research methods; includes numerical data.

Lists multiple authors who are academics.

Includes complete references list.

Journal List › NIHPA Author Manuscripts › PMC2918908

NIH Public Access
Author Manuscript
Accepted for publication in a peer reviewed journal
About Author manuscripts   Submit a manuscript

J Res Pers. Author manuscript; available in PMC 2011 August 1.
Published in final edited form as:
J Res Pers. 2010 August 1; 44(4): 478–484.
doi: 10.1016/j.jrp.2010.06.001

PMCID: PMC2918908
NIHMSID: NIHMS216233

Sounds like a Narcissist: Behavioral Manifestations of Narcissism in Everyday Life

Nicholas S. Holtzman, Simine Vazire, and Matthias R. Mehl
Author information ► Copyright and License information ►

See other articles in PMC that cite the published article.

Abstract   Go to: ▼

Little is known about narcissists' everyday behavior. The goal of this study was to describe how narcissism is manifested in everyday life. Using the Electronically Activated Recorder (EAR), we obtained naturalistic behavior from participants' everyday lives. The results suggest that the defining characteristics of narcissism that have been established from questionnaire and laboratory-based studies are borne out in narcissists' day-to-day behaviors. Narcissists do indeed behave in more extraverted and less agreeable ways than non-narcissists, skip class more (among narcissists high in exploitativeness/entitlement only), and use more sexual language. Furthermore, we found that the link between narcissism and disagreeable behavior is strengthened when controlling for self-esteem, thus extending prior questionnaire-based findings (Paulhus, Robins, Trzesniewski, & Tracy, 2004) to observed, real-world behavior.

Keywords: narcissism, behavior, personality traits, sexual behavior, language use

Narcissists love attention. Lucky for them, they have recently received a considerable amount of it from academic psychologists, especially in laboratory settings (e.g., Back, Schmukle, & Egloff, 2010; Bushman & Baumeister, 1998; Campbell, Foster, & Finkel, 2002; Miller et al., 2009). This laboratory research has led to several wide-reaching theories about why narcissists do what they do (Holtzman & Strube, 2010a; Morf & Rhodewalt, 2001; Twenge & Campbell, 2009; Vazire & Funder, 2006). Despite all this attention from researchers, however, we still know little about what narcissists actually do in their everyday lives. The aim of this paper is to help create an empirical basis for a more complete understanding of narcissism by exploring behavioral manifestations of narcissism in everyday life. Thus, we intend to answer a simple, yet largely unanswered question: What do narcissists do on a day-to-day basis?

Method   Go to: ▼

Participants

Participants were 80 undergraduate students at the University of Texas at Austin (79 provided valid EAR data), recruited mainly from introductory psychology courses and by flyers in the psychology department. The sample was 54% female, and the ethnic composition of the sample was 65% White, 21% Asian, 11% Latino, and 3% of another ethnicity. Participants ranged from 18 to 24 years old (M = 18.7, SD = 1.4). Participants were compensated $50. Data from this sample were also reported in Vazire and Mehl (2008), where further information can be found about the study.[1]

Narcissistic Personality Inventory (NPI)

The NPI is a 40-item test of narcissism that is reliable and well-validated (Raskin & Terry, 1988). The items on this forced-choice test contain pairs of statements such as "Sometimes I tell good stories" (non-narcissistic) versus "Everybody likes to hear my stories" (narcissistic). In our study, the NPI exhibited good reliability (α = .83). As seen in Table 1, we also calculated means and reliabilities for four facets (Emmons, 1987).

Table 1
Means, Standard Deviations, Gender-Differences, and Reliabilities
for the NPI and NPI Facets

Contributor Information   Go to: ▼

Nicholas S. Holtzman, Washington University in St. Louis.

Simine Vazire, Washington University in St. Louis.

Matthias R. Mehl, University of Arizona.

References   Go to: ▼

1. Back MD, Schmukle SC, Egloff B. Why are narcissists so charming at first sight? Decoding the narcissism-popularity link at zero acquaintance. Journal of Personality and Social Psychology. 2010;98:132–145. [PubMed]
2. Baumeister RF, Vohs KD, Funder DC. Psychology as the science of self-reports and finger movements: Whatever happened to actual behavior? Perspectives on Psychological Science. 2007;2:396–403.

Formats:
Article | PubReader | ePub (beta) | PDF (338K)

PubReader format:
click here to try

Related citations in PubMed
Impulsivity and the self-defeating behavior of narcissists.
[Pers Soc Psychol Rev. 2006]
Why are narcissists so charming at first sight? Decoding the narcissism-popularity link at zero acqua[J Pers Soc Psychol. 2010]
The performance of narcissists rises and falls with perceived opportunity for glory.   [J Pers Soc Psychol. 2002]
An empirical typology of narcissism and mental health in late adolescence.   [J Adolesc. 2006]
Animal models of obsessive-compulsive disorder: rationale to understanding psychobiology and ; [Psychiatr Clin North Am. 2006]
See reviews...
See all...

Cited by other articles in PMC
Evidence for the criterion validity and clinical utility of the Pathological Narcissism Inventory   [Assessment. 2012]
See all...

Links
MedGen
PubMed

Recent activity   Turn Off Clear
Sounds like a Narcissist: Behavioral Manifestations of Narcissism in Everyday Li...   PMC
See more...

Does self-love lead to love for others? A story of narcissistic game playing   [J Pers Soc Psychol. 2002]
Interpersonal and intrapsychic adaptiveness of trait self-enhancement: a mixed blessing?   [J Pers Soc Psychol. 1998]

Knowing me, knowing you: the accuracy and unique predictive validity of self-ratings and other-ratin[J Pers Soc Psychol. 2008]

A principal-components analysis of the Narcissistic Personality Inventory and further evidence of its [J Pers Soc Psychol. 1988]
Narcissism: theory and measurement.
[J Pers Soc Psychol. 1987]

✳ academic literacies   ● fields   ● research
■ rhetorical situations   ◆◆ processes   ● media/design
▲ genres   ◆ strategies

Popular Source

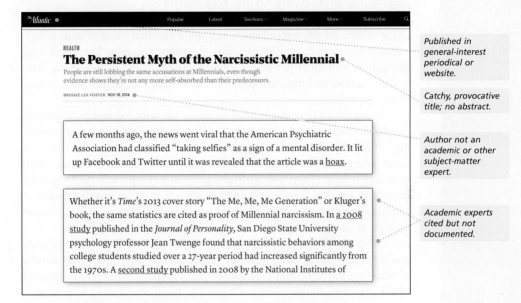

The Atlantic ● | Popular | Latest | Sections ⌄ | Magazine ⌄ | More ⌄ | Subscribe | Q

> **HEALTH**
> ### The Persistent Myth of the Narcissistic Millennial ●
> People are still lobbing the same accusations at Millennials, even though
> evidence shows they're not any more self-absorbed than their predecessors.
>
> BROOKE LEA FOSTER NOV 19, 2014 ● ⋯
>
> A few months ago, the news went viral that the American Psychiatric
> Association had classified "taking selfies" as a sign of a mental disorder. It lit
> up Facebook and Twitter until it was revealed that the article was a <u>hoax</u>.
>
> Whether it's *Time*'s 2013 cover story "The Me, Me, Me Generation" or Kluger's
> book, the same statistics are cited as proof of Millennial narcissism. In <u>a 2008
> study</u> published in the *Journal of Personality*, San Diego State University
> psychology professor Jean Twenge found that narcissistic behaviors among
> college students studied over a 27-year period had increased significantly from
> the 1970s. A <u>second study</u> published in 2008 by the National Institutes of

Published in general-interest periodical or website.

Catchy, provocative title; no abstract.

Author not an academic or other subject-matter expert.

Academic experts cited but not documented.

- *Peer review.* Look for a list of reviewers at the front of the journal or on the journal's or publisher's website. If you don't find one, the source is probably not peer-reviewed.

- *Source citations.* Look for a detailed list of works cited or references at the end of the source and citations either parenthetically within the text or in footnotes or endnotes. (Popular sources may include a reference list but seldom cite sources within the text, except in signal phrases.)

- *Language and content.* Look for abstracts (one-paragraph summaries of the contents) at the beginning of articles and for technical or specialized language and concepts that readers are assumed to be familiar with.

- *Other clues.* Look for little or no advertising on websites or within the journal; for a plain design with few or no illustrations, especially in print sources; and for listing in academic databases when you limit your search to *academic*, *peer-reviewed*, or *scholarly sources*.

Searching Effectively Using Keywords

Whether you're searching for books, articles in periodicals, or other material available on the web, chances are you'll conduct most of your search online. Most materials produced since the 1980s and most library catalogs are online, and most periodical articles can be found by searching electronic indexes and databases. In each case, you can search for authors, titles, or subjects.

To search online, you'll need to come up with keywords. Keywords are significant words that stand for an idea or concept. The key to searching efficiently is to use keywords and combinations of them that will focus your searches on the information you need—but not too much of it. Often you'll start out with one general keyword that will yield far too many results; then you'll need to switch to more specific terms or combinations (*homeopathy* instead of *medicine*, or *secondary education Japan* instead of *education Japan*).

Other times your keyword search won't yield enough sources; then you'll need to use broader terms or combinations (*education Japan* instead of *secondary education Japan*) or substitute synonyms (*home remedy* instead of *folk medicine*). Sometimes you'll need to learn terms used in academic disciplines or earlier in history for things you know by other names, such as *myocardial infarction* rather than *heart attack* or *the Great War* instead of *World War I*. Or look through the sources that turn up in response to other terms to see what keywords you might use in subsequent searches. Searching requires flexibility, in the words you use and the methods you try.

Finding keywords using word clouds.   One way to find keywords to help you narrow and focus your topic is to create a word cloud, a visual representation of words used in a text; the more often a word is used, the larger it looks in the word cloud. Several websites, including *Tagxedo*, *Wordle*, and *TagCrowd*, let you create word clouds. Examining a word cloud created from an article in a reference work may help you see what terms are used to discuss your topic—and may help you see new possible ways

to narrow it. Above, for example, is a word cloud derived from an article in *Scientific American* discussing fracking. Many of the terms—"fracking," "water," "gas," "wells," "drilling"—are just what you'd expect. However, some terms—"USGS," "DiGiulio," "coalfired"—may be unfamiliar and lead to additional possibilities for research. For instance, "DiGiulio" is the last name of an expert on fracking whose publications might be worth examining, while "USGS" is an acronym for the United States Geological Survey, a scientific government agency.

Finding keywords using databases. Once you've begun searching for and finding possible sources, you can expand your list of possible keywords by skimming the "detailed record" or "metadata" page for any scholarly articles you find, where full bibliographic information on the source may be found. A search for *fracking* resulted in this source:

Note the list of author-supplied keywords, which offers options for narrowing and focusing your topic. Each keyword is a link, so simply clicking on it will produce a new list of sources. Also look for "permalink," which will allow you to find the source again quickly.

Advanced keyword searching.   Most search sites have "advanced search" options that will help you focus your research. Some allow you to ask questions in conversational language: *What did Thomas Jefferson write about slavery?* Others allow you to focus your search by using specific words or symbols. Here are some of the most common ones:

- Type quotation marks around words to search for an exact phrase— "Thomas Jefferson."

- Type AND to specify that more than one keyword must appear in sources: Jefferson AND Adams. Some search engines require a plus sign instead: +Jefferson +Adams.

academic literacies   ● fields   ● research

■ rhetorical situations   ● processes   ● media/design

▲ genres   ◆ strategies

- Type OR if you're looking for sources that include any of several terms: Jefferson OR Adams OR Madison.

- Type NOT to find sources *without* a certain word: Jefferson NOT Adams. Some search engines call for a minus sign (actually, a hyphen) instead: +Jefferson –Adams.

- Type an asterisk to search for words in different form. For example, teach* will yield sources containing "teacher"/"teaching."

In addition, look for features that allow you to filter in order to limit results to a specific date range; only full-text articles (articles that are available in full online); and, in library databases, only scholarly, peer-reviewed sites.

If a search turns up too many sources, be more specific (*homeopathy* instead of *medicine*). If your original keywords don't generate good results, try synonyms (*home remedy* instead of *folk medicine*). Keep in mind that searching requires flexibility, both in the words you use and in the methods you try. And remember that the first items in a results list are not necessarily the best; scan what appears beyond page 1 of your results. Exercise "click restraint" by scanning through many items in the results and choosing only the ones that look most promising for your needs. Open each potential source in its own separate tab for evaluation.

Searching Using Popular Sites and Search Engines

When we need to find something out, most of us begin with *Google* or *Wikipedia*. If you aren't familiar with your research topic, these sites provide general information and a variety of perspectives. However, using general search engines can present challenges: paywalls limit access, it's easy to be overwhelmed by the number of sources, and determining what's trustworthy can be difficult. So you'll want to rely primarily on your library's resources to find accurate, up-to-date, scholarly sources; but the following sites can still serve as helpful starting points.

Wikipedia An open, online reference, *Wikipedia* often serves as a starting point for preliminary research. Reading a *Wikipedia* entry on a topic can help you understand background information, come up with new **KEYWORDS** to search, and discover related topics. A list of references—

● 506–9

often hyperlinked—at the bottom of each entry can lead to potential sources. Be sure to check information you find on *Wikipedia* for accuracy, since entries can be written or edited by anyone.

Google, Google Scholar, and other free search tools. To search *Google*, use simple and specific **KEYWORDS**. Googling "fracking environmental effects" will turn up more focused results than googling "what is fracking." Scan the list of results and open sources that look promising in a new tab instead of stopping to read the first result that catches your eye. Be sure to look beyond the first page of results; higher placement doesn't always mean most relevant to your topic.

506–9

Google Scholar limits your search results to scholarly literature such as researched articles, theses, books, abstracts, and court opinions. Do a keyword search in *Google Scholar*, and scan the results to get an initial idea of the scholarly authors, publications, and databases publishing on your topic. You can sort results by publication date—a good way to check if there's recent research. Some articles and books in *Google Scholar* are full-text, but many are behind paywalls so must be accessed through your campus library.

Here are several more tools for searching online, outside of the library, to get started:

- *Keyword search engines.* Search engines use algorithms to tailor results to you, so search engines—and the results they show you—are not all the same. Compare results from *Google*, *Microsoft Edge*, *DuckDuckGo*, and other search sites to get more varied results.

- *Nonlibrary, academic searches.* In addition to Google Scholar, for peer-reviewed academic writing in many disciplines, try *Microsoft Academic* or *BASE*. *Science.gov* offers results from more than 15 US federal agencies, and *CORE* collects open-access research papers.

- *Social media searches.* *Google Social Search*, *Social Searcher*, and *Talkwalker* let you search various social media platforms. Use **HASHTAGS** (#) or *Tagboard*, a hashtag-based search engine, to search the contents of posts.

Glossary

❋ academic literacies   ● fields   ● research

■ rhetorical situations   ⁙ processes   ● media/design

▲ genres   ◆ strategies

Image, video, and audio platforms.   *Google Images* and *TinEye* allow you to search for images by keyword or by uploading an image. *Google Video Search* lets you search for videos by keyword, and *YouTube*'s search function allows you to find videos by relevance, upload date, view count, or rating. *Audioburst Search* provides results from podcast and radio segments.

News sites.   Sites for newspapers, magazines, and radio and TV stations provide both up-to-the-minute information and also archives of older stories online. Through news-aggregating sites like *Google News* and *Apple News* you can sort through worldwide news from a wide range of sources. *Google News Archive* has news archives extending back to the 1700s. Beware that **MISINFORMATION** and lies are spread most often as news, so **FACT-CHECKING** sources that *appear* to be news is essential.

Glossary
● 526–32

Government sites.   Many government agencies and departments maintain websites where you can find government reports, statistics, legislative information, and other resources. *USA.gov* offers resources from the US government.

Digital archives.   You can find primary sources from the past, including drawings, maps, recordings, speeches, and historic documents, at sites maintained by the National Archives, the Library of Congress, the New York Public Library, and others.

Although many websites provide authoritative information, content found online varies greatly in stability and reliability: what you see on a site today may be different (or gone) tomorrow, so save copies of all pages you use. In addition, many reference and news sites are behind paywalls, their content unavailable unless you pay a fee or subscribe. If you find that a source you need is behind a paywall, check to see if it's available through your library or through interlibrary loan.

Searching in Academic Libraries

College and university libraries typically offer several ways to search their holdings. Their websites may look very different from one another, but most include search boxes like this one, from the Wright State University Libraries:

This box allows you to search through all the library's holdings at once, an option that may be a good way to get started. You may already know, though, that you need to focus your search on one type of source, such as scholarly articles, or search using a particular method. In that case, it's best to use a more advanced search box like this one:

This box lets you shape and limit your search in several ways: the drop-down menu on the left lets you choose to search by title, keyword, author, or several other identifiers; the drop-down menu on the right lets you choose to search the library's entire collection, journals, books, media, or even materials in a specific location, such as course reserves or archives; and "Advanced Search" gives even more options. When in doubt, take advantage of "Ask a Librarian" services, which may include texting, chat, email, and phone conversations with reference librarians, when you need help but aren't working in the library.

Reference Works

The reference section of your school's library is the place to find encyclopedias, dictionaries, atlases, almanacs, bibliographies, and other reference

works in print. Many of these sources are also online and can be accessed from any computer that is connected to the internet. Others are available only in the library. Remember, though, that whether in print or online, reference works are only a starting point, a place where you can get an overview of your topic.

General reference works. Consult encyclopedias for general background information on a subject, dictionaries for definitions of words, atlases for maps and geographic data, and almanacs for statistics and other data on current events. These are some works you might consult:

The New Encyclopaedia Britannica

The Columbia Encyclopedia

Webster's Third New International Dictionary

Oxford English Dictionary

National Geographic Atlas of the World

Statistical Abstract of the United States

The World Almanac and Book of Facts

Specialized reference works. You can also go to specialized reference works, which provide in-depth information on a single field or topic. These may also include authoritative bibliographies, leading you to more specific works. A reference librarian can refer you to specialized encyclopedias in particular fields, but good places to start are online collections of many topic-specific reference works that offer overviews of a topic, place it in a larger context, and sometimes provide links to potential academic sources. Collections that are available through libraries include the following:

CQ Researcher offers in-depth reports on topics in education, health, the environment, criminal justice, international affairs, technology, the economy, and social trends. Each report gives an overview of a particular topic, outlines of the differing positions on it, and a bibliography of resources on it.

Gale eBooks offers thousands of full-text specialized encyclopedias, almanacs, articles, and ebooks.

Oxford Reference contains hundreds of dictionaries, encyclopedias, and other reference works on a wide variety of subjects, as well as timelines with links to each item mentioned on each timeline.

SAGE Knowledge includes many encyclopedias and handbooks on topics in the social sciences.

Bibliographies.　Bibliographies provide an overview of what has been published on a topic, listing published works along with the information you'll need to find each work. Some are annotated with brief summaries of each work's contents. You'll find bibliographies at the end of scholarly articles and books, and you can also find book-length bibliographies, both in the reference section of your library and online. Check with a reference librarian for bibliographies on your research topic.

Books / Searching the Library Catalog

The library catalog is your primary source for finding books. Almost all library catalogs are computerized and can be accessed through the library's website. You can search by author, title, subject, or keyword. The image below shows the result of a keyword search for material on looted art in Nazi Germany. This search of the library's catalog revealed six items—print books

* academic literacies
* fields
* research
* rhetorical situations
* processes
* media / design
* genres
* strategies

and ebooks—on the topic; to access information on each one, the researcher must simply click on the title or thumbnail image. The image below shows detailed information for one source: bibliographic data about author, title, and publication; related subject headings (which may lead to other useful materials in the library)—and more. Library catalogs also supply a call number, which identifies the book's location on the library's shelves.

Ebooks / Finding Books Online

Many books in the library catalog are available online. Some may be downloaded to a tablet or mobile device. In addition, thousands of classic works that are in the public domain—no longer protected by copyright—may be read online. *Bartleby, Google Books, Open Library,* and *Project Gutenberg* are four collections of public-domain works. Here are some other sources of ebooks:

> *HathiTrust Digital Library* offers access to millions of ebooks, about a third of them in the public domain, contributed by university libraries.

> *Internet Archive* includes millions of ebooks as well as audio, video, music, software, images, and the Wayback Machine, which archives historical webpages.

> *Gale eBooks, Oxford Reference,* and *SAGE Knowledge* all contain large ebook collections.

Periodicals / Searching Indexes and Databases

To find journal, magazine, and newspaper articles, you will need to search periodical indexes and databases. Indexes provide listings of articles organized by topics; many databases provide the full texts. Some indexes are in print and can be found in the reference section of the library; most are online. Some databases are available for free; most of the more authoritative ones, however, are available only by subscription and so must be accessed through a library.

Many databases now include not only scholarly articles but also dissertations, theses, book chapters, book reviews, and conference proceedings. Dissertations and theses are formal works of scholarship done as requirements for graduate degrees; book reviews offer critical evaluations of scholarly and popular books; and conference proceedings are papers presented, usually orally, at scholarly meetings.

When you access a source through a database, the URL or link address is different each time you log in, so if you want to return to a source, look for a *stable URL*, *permalink*, or *DOI* option and choose it to copy and paste into your list of sources.

General indexes and databases. A reference librarian can help you determine which databases will be most helpful for your needs, but here are some useful ones:

> *Academic Search Complete* and *Academic Search Premier* are multidisciplinary indexes and databases containing the full text of articles in thousands of journals and indexing of even more, with abstracts of their articles.

> *InfoTrac* offers millions of full-text articles in a broad spectrum of disciplines and on a wide variety of topics from thousands of scholarly and popular periodicals, including the *New York Times*.

> *JSTOR* archives scanned copies of entire publication runs of scholarly journals in many disciplines, but it may not include current issues of the journals.

> *ProQuest Central* provides access to full-text articles from thousands of books, scholarly journals, conference papers, magazines, newspapers,

---

* academic literacies   ● fields   ● research
■ rhetorical situations   ⋮ processes   ● media/design
▲ genres   ◆ strategies

blogs, podcasts, and websites and a large collection of dissertations and theses.

Single-subject indexes and databases. The following are just a sample of what's available; check with a reference librarian for indexes and databases in the subject you're researching.

America: History and Life indexes scholarly literature on the history and culture of the United States and Canada.

BIOSIS Previews provides abstracts and indexes for thousands of sources on a wide variety of biological and medical topics.

ERIC is the US Department of Education's Educational Resource Information Center database. It includes hundreds of journal titles as well as conference papers, technical reports, and other resources on education.

Historical Abstracts includes abstracts of articles on the history of the world, excluding the United States and Canada, since 1450.

Humanities International Index contains bibliographic references to thousands of journals dealing with the humanities.

MLA International Bibliography indexes scholarly articles on modern languages, literature, folklore, and linguistics.

PsycINFO indexes scholarly literature in a number of disciplines relating to the behavioral and social sciences.

PubMed includes millions of citations for biomedical literature, many with links to full-text content.

Print indexes. You may need to consult print indexes to find articles published before the 1980s. Here are six useful ones:

The Readers' Guide to Periodical Literature (print, 1900–; online, 1983–)

InfoTrac Magazine Index (print, 1988–; online, 1973–)

The New York Times Index (print and online, 1851–)

Humanities Index (print, 1974–; online, 1984–)

Social Sciences Index (print, 1974–; online, 1983–)

General Science Index (print, 1978–; online, 1984–)

Images, Sound, and More

Your library likely subscribes to various databases that allow you to find and download video, audio, and image files. Here is a sampling:

AP Images provides access to photographs taken for the Associated Press, the cooperative agency of thousands of newspapers and radio and television stations worldwide.

ArtStor provides images in the arts, architecture, humanities, and sciences.

Dance Online: Dance in Video offers hundreds of videos of dance productions and documentaries on dance.

Bird Sounds from the Borror Laboratory of Bioacoustics includes digitized recordings of the sounds of over 1,000 species of animals.

Music Online: Smithsonian Global Sound for Libraries is a "virtual encyclopedia of the world's musical and aural traditions."

Naxos Music Library contains more than 130,000 classical, jazz, and world music recordings, as well as libretti and synopses of hundreds of operas and other background information.

Theatre in Video provides videos of hundreds of performances of plays and film documentaries.

Doing Field Research

Sometimes you'll need to do your own research, to go beyond the information you find in published sources and gather data by doing field research. Three kinds of field research you might want to consider are interviews, observations, and questionnaires.

Interviewing experts.   Some kinds of writing—a profile of a living person, for instance—almost require that you conduct an interview. And sometimes you may just need to find information that you haven't been able to find in published sources. To get firsthand information on the experience of serving as a soldier in Afghanistan, you might interview your cousin who served a tour of duty there; to find current research on pesticide residues in food, you might need to interview a toxicologist. Whatever your goal, you can conduct interviews in person, using video-calling software such as *Skype* or *FaceTime*, by telephone, through email, or by mail. In general, you will want to use interviews to find information you can't find elsewhere. Below is some advice on planning and conducting an interview.

BEFORE THE INTERVIEW

1. Once you identify someone you want to interview, email or phone to ask the person, stating your **PURPOSE** for the interview and what you hope to learn.

■ 59–60

2. Once you've set up an appointment, send a note or email confirming the time and place. If you wish to record the interview, be sure to ask for permission to do so. If you plan to conduct the interview by mail or email, state when you will send your questions.

3. Write out questions. Plan questions that invite extended response and supporting details: "What accounts for the recent spike in gasoline prices?" forces an explanation, whereas "Is the recent spike in gas prices a direct result of global politics?" is likely to elicit only a yes or a no.

AT THE INTERVIEW

4. Record the full name of the person you interview, along with the date, time, and place of the interview; you'll need this information to cite and document the interview accurately.

5. Take notes, even if you are recording the interview.

6. Keep track of time: don't take more than you agreed to beforehand unless both of you agree to keep talking. End by thanking your subject and offering to provide a copy of your final product.

AFTER THE INTERVIEW

7. Flesh out your notes with details as soon as possible after the interview, while you still remember them. What did you learn? What surprised you? Summarize both the interviewee's words and your impressions.

8. Make sure you've reproduced quotations from the interview accurately and fairly. Avoid editing quotations in ways that distort the speaker's intended meaning.

9. Be sure to send a thank-you note or email.

Observation. Some writing projects are based on information you get by observing something. For a sociology report, you may observe how students behave in large lectures. For an education course, you may observe one child's progress as a writer over a period of time. The following advice can help you conduct observations.

BEFORE OBSERVING

59–60

1. Think about your research **PURPOSE**: What are you looking for? What do you expect to find? How will your presence as an observer affect what you observe? What do you plan to do with what you find?

2. If necessary, set up an appointment. You may need to ask permission of the people you wish to observe and of your school as well. (Check with your instructor about your school's policy in this area.) Be honest and open about your goals and intentions; college students doing research assignments are often welcomed where others may not be.

WHILE OBSERVING

3. If you're taking notes on paper, you may want to divide each page down the middle vertically and write only on the left side of the page, reserving the right side for information you will fill in later. If you're using a laptop, you can set up two columns or a split screen.

4. Note descriptive details about the setting. What do you see? What do you hear? Do you smell anything? Get down details about color, shape, size, sound, and so on. Consider photographing or making a sketch of what you see.

456–63

5. Who is there, and what are they doing? **DESCRIBE** what they look like, and make notes about what they say. Note any significant demographic details—about gender, race, occupation, age, dress, and so on.

✴ academic literacies ● fields ● research
■ rhetorical situations ⦂ processes ● media/design
▲ genres ◆ strategies

6. What is happening? Who's doing what? What's being said? Make note of these kinds of **NARRATIVE** details.

◆ 474–82

AFTER OBSERVING

7. As soon as possible after you complete your observations, use the right side of your notes to fill in gaps and include additional details.

8. **ANALYZE** your notes, looking for patterns. Did some things appear or happen more than once? Did anything stand out? surprise or puzzle you? What did you learn?

▲ 104–39

Questionnaires and surveys. Various kinds of questionnaires and surveys can provide information or opinions from a large number of people. For a political science course, you might conduct a survey to ask students who they plan to vote for. Or, for a marketing course, you might distribute a questionnaire asking what they think about an advertising campaign. The advice in this section will help you create useful questionnaires and surveys.

Define your goal. The goal of a questionnaire or survey should be limited and focused, so that every question will contribute to your research question. Also, people are more likely to respond to a brief, focused survey.

Define your sample. A survey gets responses from a representative sample of the whole group. The answers to these questions will help you define that sample:

1. Who should answer the questions? The people you contact should represent the whole population. For example, if you want to survey undergraduate students at your school, your sample should reflect your school's enrollment in terms of gender, year, major, age, ethnicity, and so forth as closely as possible.

2. How many people make up a representative sample? In general, the larger your sample, the more the answers will reflect those of the whole group. But if your population is small—200 students in a history course, for example—your sample must include a large percentage of that group.

Decide on a medium.   Will you ask the questions face-to-face? over the phone? on a website such as *SurveyMonkey?* by mail? by email? Face-to-face questions work best for simple surveys or for gathering impersonal information. You're more likely to get responses to more personal questions with printed or online questionnaires, which should be neat and easy to read. Phone interviews may require well-thought-out scripts that anticipate possible answers and make it easy to record these answers.

Design good questions.   The way you ask questions will determine the usefulness of the answers you get, so take care to write questions that are clear and unambiguous. Here are some typical question types:

MULTIPLE-CHOICE
What is your current age?
_____ 15–20   _____ 21–25   _____ 26–30   _____ 31–35   _____ Other

RATING SCALE
How would you rate the service at the campus bookstore?
_____ Excellent   _____ Good   _____ Fair   _____ Poor

AGREEMENT SCALE
How much do you agree with the following statements?

	Strongly Agree	Agree	Disagree	Strongly Disagree
The bookstore has sufficient numbers of textbooks available.	❑	❑	❑	❑

	Strongly Agree	Agree	Disagree	Strongly Disagree
Staff at the bookstore are knowledgeable.	❑	❑	❑	❑
Staff at the bookstore are courteous.	❑	❑	❑	❑

OPEN-ENDED
How often do you visit the campus bookstore?
How can the campus bookstore improve its service?

※ academic literacies   ● fields   ● research
■ rhetorical situations   ⁖ processes   ● media/design
▲ genres   ◆ strategies

Include all potential alternatives when phrasing questions to avoid biasing the answers. And make sure each question addresses only one issue—for example, "Bookstore staff are knowledgeable and courteous" could lead to the response "knowledgeable, agree; courteous, disagree."

When arranging questions, place easier ones at the beginning and harder ones near the end (but if the questions seem to fall into a different natural order, follow it). Make sure each question asks for information you will need—if a question isn't absolutely necessary, omit it.

Include an introduction.　Start by stating your survey's purpose and how the results will be used. It's also a good idea to offer an estimate of the time needed to complete the questions. Remind participants of your deadline.

Test the survey or questionnaire.　Make sure your questions elicit the kinds of answers you need by asking three or four people who are part of your target population to answer them. They can help you find unclear instructions, questions that aren't clear or that lack sufficient alternatives, or other problems that you should correct to make sure your results are useful. But if you change the questionnaire as a result of their responses, don't include their answers in your total.

If you need more help

See **EVALUATING SOURCES** for help determining their usefulness. See also Chapter 50 for help **TAKING NOTES** on your sources.

524–34
542–44

48 Evaluating Sources

Searching the *Health Source* database for information on the incidence of meningitis among college students, you find thirty-three articles. A *Google* search on the same topic produces over 13 million hits. How do you decide which sources to read? This chapter presents advice on evaluating sources—first to determine whether a source might be useful for your purposes and is worth looking at more closely, and then to read with a critical eye the ones you choose.

Considering Whether a Source Might Be Useful

As you consider potential sources—sources you've found online or from library resources—keep your **PURPOSE** in mind. Are you trying to persuade readers to believe or do something? If so, look for sources representing various positions. Are you reporting on a topic? If so, you'll likely need sources that are factual or informative. Consider your **AUDIENCE**. What kinds of sources will they find persuasive? If you're writing for readers in a particular field, what counts as **EVIDENCE** in that field? Following are some questions that can help you judge whether a possible source you've found deserves your time and attention—but remember to consider most or all of the questions, rather than relying on a single criterion:

59–60
61–64
414–22

- *Is it relevant?* How well does the source relate to your purpose? What would it add to your work? To see what it covers, look at the title and at any introductory material (such as a preface or an abstract).

- *Is it reliable?* Is it scholarly? peer-reviewed? published in a reputable journal or magazine, or by a reputable publisher? Did you find it in a library database? on the web? Evaluating web-based texts may require more work than using results from library databases. Whatever kind of search you do, skim the results quickly to evaluate their reliability—and use the techniques described below to fact-check them. You might

academic literacies
rhetorical situations
genres
fields
processes
strategies
research
media/design

also check the *Media Bias/Fact Check* website, which ranks news organizations on their political slant and factual reporting.

- *What are the author's credentials?* How is the author qualified to write
  on the subject? Has the author written other works on this subject?
  Are they known for a particular position on it? As an expert? A scholar?
  A journalist? Will your audience find the author credible? If the credentials aren't stated, do a search to see what reliable sources say
  about the author.

- *What is the* STANCE? Does the source explain various points of view or
  advocate only one perspective? Does its title suggest a certain slant? If
  it's online, check to see whether it includes links to other sites—and
  if so, what their perspectives are. You'll want to consult sources with
  various viewpoints and understand the bias of each source you use.

■ 72–74

- *Who is the publisher or sponsor?* If it's a book, what kind of company
  published it; if an article, what kind of periodical did it appear in?
  Books published by university presses and articles in scholarly journals are reviewed by experts before they're published. Many books
  and articles written for the general public also undergo careful fact-
  checking, but some do not—and they may lack the kind of in-depth
  discussion that is useful for research.

- *At what level is it written?* Can you understand the material? Texts
  written for a general audience might be easier to understand but not
  authoritative enough for academic work. Scholarly texts will be more
  authoritative but may be hard to comprehend.

- *How current is it?* Check to see when books and articles were published
  and when websites were last updated. (If a site lists no date, see if
  links to other sites still work; if not, the site is probably too dated to
  use.) A recent publication date or update, however, doesn't necessarily
  mean that a potential source is good—some topics require current
  information; others call for older sources.

- *Is it cited in other works?* If so, you can probably assume that some
  other writers regard it as trustworthy.

- *Does it include other useful information?* Is there a bibliography that
  might lead you to other sources? How current or authoritative are the
  sources it cites?

- **Is it *available*?** If it's a book and your school's library doesn't have it, can you get it through interlibrary loan? If it's online and there's a paywall, can your library get you access?

Fact-Checking Popular Sources Online

Scholarly books are edited; scholarly articles are reviewed by experts; established news sources employ fact-checkers to verify information. But many websites and social media sites aren't checked by anyone. As a result, when you're using *Google* and other nonlibrary resources online to get started, you may find misleading information, data, images, and videos.

Sometimes such misleading information takes the form of satires, such as Jonathan Swift's "A Modest Proposal," stories in the *Onion*, or episodes of *The Daily Show*. Such satires offer humorous exaggerations to expose and criticize people and governments. Other misleading or false news stories are malicious, created usually for political ends. World War II Nazi propaganda and recent fraudulent stories such as "Pope Francis Endorses Donald Trump," a false story that went viral on *Facebook*, are intended to mislead readers. Further complicating things, some politicians and other public figures have taken to calling news reports with which they disagree "fake news"—even though the stories reported are verifiably true and the news outlets are considered trustworthy.

Although false news has been around at least since the invention of the printing press, the internet and social media have led to a huge increase in false news stories, seriously challenging and muddying "real" news. Each false story can rapidly multiply over sites such as *Facebook* and *Twitter* and through email. As a reader and researcher, you need to be able to determine whether a potential news source is false. As a writer, you risk harming your credibility if you cite a false news story as evidence. To conduct sound research—and to use good information to form our own ideas—we need to be able to determine what is true, what is false, and what is trying to manipulate us when reading popular online sources. Professional fact-checkers, people who investigate the truthfulness of assertions made in published work, use the following methods to evaluate their accuracy.

Fact-checkers begin not by immediately reading something they find online that looks relevant, but by first moving *outside* the source—

✳ academic literacies	● fields	● research
■ rhetorical situations	⁝ processes	● media/design
▲ genres	◆ strategies	

opening new tabs in the same browser—to search and see what other reliable sites say about it. Only after they've done some research to confirm a source's accuracy do they read the source itself. When you find something online that looks relevant, first stop and ask yourself if you know the website publishing the source and have reason to trust it. If not, take the following steps to assess the source before reading any further:

- *Look up the main* CLAIMS. Copy and paste the title or a few key words of the article, essay, or post into *Google* or another browser to see if a reliable fact-checking site—*Snopes, FactCheck, Politifact, Allsides,* or *mediabiasfactcheck*—has already evaluated it. If several reputable sources report the same information, it's probably true. If the information appears in only one source—even if many other people are quoting it—it's worth taking more steps to check whether it's reliable and even-handed enough for your academic writing.

  ◆ 411–13

- *Investigate the author's expertise and* STANCE. Use *Wikipedia, Google News,* or *Google Scholar* to see if the author is an expert on the topic they're weighing in on. Some signs that the author has expertise include: an academic position in a relevant field, other pieces published in reputable sources on the same topic, or considerable experience in the area being written about. If you can't find any evidence of an author's expertise on the topic, the source may still be useful to you, but don't depend on the information as authoritative. Also, the author's affiliations—the groups they're members of or the places they've published—can help you determine the author's stance.

  ■ 72–74

- *Check out who runs the site.* Don't rely on the site's About page alone. Instead, google the organization's name in quotation marks and add keywords like "who sponsors" or "funding." What do other reputable sites say about the publisher or sponsoring organization? Take note of information on controversy or a specific agenda attached to the organization. Do reliable sources say the organization has a good reputation? a lot of members? a long history? Those are all good signs the publication is trustworthy.

- *Check the date of the story and dates within the story.* Sometimes old stories resurface as "news." They aren't any truer now than they were then.

59–60 ■

- *Take stock, and use your judgment.* Consider your **PURPOSE** and what you've found about the source's main claims, author, and publisher. Does the source seem accurate and trustworthy, given what you know about the world and how it works? Do the claims seem designed to generate a strong emotional response, especially anger or fear, rather than appealing to logic or sound evidence? If taking these steps shows you that a source has a strong **STANCE** or bias, that doesn't automatically mean you should discard it, but it does mean you should keep that stance in mind as you work with the source.

72–74 ■

If even just one of these steps reveals troubling information, it's best to move on to find a different, more solidly reliable source. As you use these fact-checking moves, don't just click on the first item in a list of search results. Instead, scan the results to get a broad sense of what others are saying, and choose the most trustworthy ones to read.

The graphics on the following pages show a good example of how fact-checking a popular source found on the web works.

Fact-checking photos and video. Visual media—especially images and videos posted online—can also be manipulated to present misleading information. Hoax photos are images taken out of context or doctored in order to deceive using *Photoshop* or another photo manipulation program. For example, this misleading image of presidential candidate John Kerry and antiwar activist and actor Jane Fonda was widely distributed during the 2004 election campaign:

The image was created by combining two photos taken more than a year apart on two different occasions and was used to discredit Kerry's patriotism despite his service in Vietnam.

However, doctoring sometimes isn't even needed: the camera lenses used or the camera's position can lead to very different views. For example, during the coronavirus pandemic, the photo on the left purported to show people ignoring social distancing guidance to stay at least six feet apart on a beach in Florida:

The photo on the right, though, shows that the beachgoers were in fact maintaining a safe distance from one another.

To identify the source of most photographs, you can do a reverse image search using these tools:

- *Google Image.* Click on the small camera icon to the right of the search box, and paste in the image's web address. The results will show other uses of the image as well as similar images.

- *TinEye.* Upload the image or enter its URL in the search box to get a list of other places where the image has appeared online.

Hoax videos are altered or presented in misleading ways. The *Washington Post* identifies three ways hoax videos are made:

- *Missing context.* The video itself hasn't been altered, but it is misrepresented in order to mislead the viewer—using an incorrect date, location, or summary. Or it's a brief clip from a longer video taking an event out of context.

- *Deceptive editing.* Portions of the video have been edited out and the remaining parts spliced together to create a misleading narrative. Or videos shot on two different occasions have been spliced together to create a single false narrative.

Fact-Checking Popular Sources

Once you've got a source to fact-check, begin by looking outside the site itself following the steps below.

Look Up the Claim

Other reliable news organizations report similar claims from various sources.

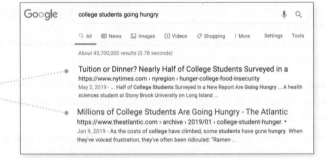

Check Out the Website

Wikipedia says the site began in 2008 and closed in 2019. Be skeptical of a new site or one that no longer exists.

A New York Times article confirms the site was funded by a well-established academic publisher and won two awards for quality, so it appears trustworthy.

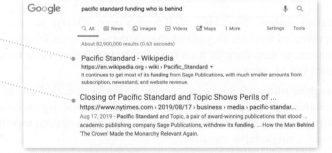

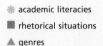 academic literacies   fields   research

■ rhetorical situations   ⦂ processes   media/design

▲ genres   ◆ strategies

Investigate the Author

The author has published several more pieces on the same site.

The author's bio from his book publisher appears at the bottom of the first search results page.

Opening the author's academic webpage shows he's a professor at Texas State University, teaching courses in American history and writing about the history of eating habits.

An Amazon page shows the author's published a book on food and eating. So he appears credible on this topic.

- *Malicious transformation.* The video itself has been altered to deceive the viewer, or artificial intelligence has been used to create fake images and audio.

In addition, videos may simply present lies as factual information. For example, during the coronavirus pandemic, online videos included false statements including "The pharmaceutical companies have a cure but won't sell it," "Coronavirus is caused by 5G mobile phone network signals," and "The coronavirus is being used for worldwide population control." Some of these videos are viewed by millions of people, so the popularity of a video may not reflect its accuracy or truthfulness, either.

To evaluate the accuracy of videos, type a brief summary of the video into *Google* to see if fact-checking sites like *Snopes* have reported on it. Also, do your own analysis: Does anything in the video seem doctored? Are the events depicted believable or unlikely? Is the language used inflammatory or demeaning? If the video appears on several websites, do its details change from site to site? Use *Youtube DataViewer*, available at citizen evidence.amnestyusa.org, to see where else a *YouTube* video has been posted, and do a reverse image search on stills from a video.

Reading Sources with a Critical Eye

Approach your sources with an open mind, but consider their arguments with a critical eye. Pay attention to what they say, to the reasons and evidence they offer to support what they say, and to whether they address viewpoints other than their own. Assume that each author is responding to some other argument. Ask some of these questions of each of your sources:

164–95 ▲

- *What* ARGUMENTS *does the author make?* Does the author present several different positions or argue for a particular position? What arguments is the author responding to?

413–14 ◆
414–22
526–28 ●

- *How persuasive do you find the argument to be?* What REASONS and EVIDENCE does the author provide to support their positions? Are there citations or links—and if so, are they CREDIBLE? Is any evidence presented without citations? Are any of the author's assumptions questionable? How thoroughly does the author consider alternative arguments?

※ academic literacies   ● fields   ● research
■ rhetorical situations   ∴ processes   ● media/design
▲ genres   ◆ strategies

- *What is the author's* STANCE? Does it seem objective, or does the content or language reveal a particular bias? Are opposing views considered and treated fairly? Do the headlines and text try to elicit an emotional reaction?

72–74

- *Do you recognize ideas you've run across in other sources?* Does the source leave out any information or perspective that other sources include—or does it include any that they leave out?

- *What can you tell about the intended* AUDIENCE *and* PURPOSE? Are you a member of the audience for which the source was written—and if not, does that affect the way you interpret what you read? Is the main purpose to inform readers about a topic or to argue a certain point?

61–64
59–60

- *Does this source support or challenge your own position—or does it do both?* Does it support your thesis? Does it support a different argument altogether? Does it represent a position you need to address? Don't reject a source just because it challenges your views; work to understand the various perspectives or positions taken on your topic to avoid CONFIRMATION BIAS, which is our tendency to believe things that match what we already believe and to discount information that doesn't. Be wary of assuming a story or article is trustworthy just because you agree with the author—you need to step back and make sure your own beliefs aren't clouding your judgment.

Glossary

Comparing Sources

You may find that two or more of your sources present similar information or arguments. How do you decide which one to use? Compare them, using these questions as a guide:

- *Which source is most current?* Generally, a more recent source is better than an older one, because the newer source includes information or data that is more up to date—and may include (or refute) the information in the earlier source. Be aware, though, that in some fields, such as literary criticism, decades-old sources may still be important.

- *Which argument is more persuasive?* Examine the CLAIMS, REASONS, and EVIDENCE presented in each source. Which source's argument is most logical? Which one has the best supporting reasons and

411–22

424–26
evidence? Which one best **ACKNOWLEDGES**, **ACCOMMODATES**, or **REFUTES** opposing arguments?

- *Which author or authors are most authoritative?* An expert in the subject is more authoritative than, say, a journalist writing on the subject. An article published in a scholarly journal is more authoritative than one published in a general-circulation magazine or website. The journalist's article may be easier to read and more interesting, but you're best off looking for the best information—not the best read.

72–74
- *Which source has the most appropriate* **STANCE**? In general, look for sources that strive for objectivity, rather than a particular bias. Also, be aware that we all tend to favor information that agrees with our views—and that may lead us to choose sources we agree with rather than sources that present all sides of an issue.

- *Which source best fits your needs?* All other things being equal, the best source to choose is the one that will give you the information you need, support the argument you're making, and perhaps provide useful quotations to add to your writing. The best source will show that you've done appropriate research and will enhance your own credibility as a thinker, reader, researcher, and writer.

If you need more help

542–54
555–59
See Chapter 50, **QUOTING, PARAPHRASING, AND SUMMARIZING**, for help in taking notes on your sources and deciding how to use them in your writing. See also Chapter 51, **ACKNOWLEDGING SOURCES, AVOIDING PLAGIARISM**, for advice on giving credit to the sources you use.

✳ academic literacies   ● fields   ● research
■ rhetorical situations   ⦂ processes   ● media/design
▲ genres   ◆ strategies

49 Synthesizing Ideas

To **ANALYZE** a collection of poetry, you show how the poet uses similar images in three different poems to explore a recurring concept. To solve a crime, a detective studies several eyewitness accounts to figure out who did it. To trace the history of photojournalism, a professor **COMPARES** the uses of photography during the Civil War and during the Vietnam War. These are all cases where someone synthesizes—brings together material from two or more sources in order to generate new information or to support a new perspective. When you do research, you need to go beyond what your sources say; you need to use what they say to inspire and support what you want to say. This chapter focuses on how to synthesize ideas you find in other sources as the basis for your own ideas.

▲ 104–39

◆ 437–44

Reading for Patterns and Connections

Your task as a writer is to find as much information as you can on your topic—and then to sift through all that you have found to determine and support what you yourself will write. In other words, you'll need to synthesize ideas and information from the sources you've consulted to figure out first what arguments *you* want to make and then to provide support for those arguments.

When you synthesize, you group similar bits of information together, looking for patterns or themes or trends and trying to identify the key points. In the brief report on the following page, writer Jude Stewart synthesizes several pieces of research on boredom. Stewart's report originally appeared in the *Atlantic*, which uses an abbreviated documentation style.

Boredom Is Good for You

Boredom has, paradoxically, become quite interesting to academics lately. The International Interdisciplinary Boredom Conference gathered humanities scholars in Warsaw for the fifth time in April. In early May, its less scholarly forerunner, London's Boring Conference, celebrated seven years of delighting in tedium. At this event, people flock to talks about toast, double yellow lines, sneezing, and vending-machine sounds, among other snooze-inducing topics.

What, exactly, is everybody studying? One widely accepted psychological definition of boredom is "the aversive experience of wanting, but being unable, to engage in satisfying activity." [1] But how can you quantify a person's boredom level and compare it with someone else's? In 1986, psychologists introduced the Boredom Proneness Scale, [2] designed to measure an individual's overall propensity to feel bored (what's known as "trait boredom"). By contrast, the Multidimensional State Boredom Scale, [3] developed in 2008, measures a person's feelings of boredom in a given situation ("state boredom"). A German-led team has since identified five types of state boredom: indifferent, calibrating, searching, reactant, and apathetic (indifferent boredom—characterized by low arousal—was the mellowest, least unpleasant kind; reactant—high arousal—was the most aggressive and unpleasant). [4] Boredom may be miserable, but let no one call it simple.

Boredom has been linked to behavior issues, including bad driving, [5] mindless snacking, [6] binge-drinking, [7] risky sex, [8] and problem gambling. [9] In fact, many of us would take pain over boredom. One team of psychologists discovered that two-thirds of men and a quarter of women would rather self-administer electric shocks than sit alone with their thoughts for 15 minutes. [10] Probing this phenomenon, another team asked volunteers to watch boring, sad, or neutral films, during which they could self-administer electric shocks. The bored volunteers shocked themselves more and harder than the sad or neutral ones did. [11]

But boredom isn't all bad. By encouraging contemplation and daydreaming, it can spur creativity. An early, much-cited study gave participants abundant time to complete problem-solving and word-association exercises. Once all the obvious answers were exhausted, participants gave more and more inventive answers to fend off boredom. [12] A British study took these findings one step further, asking subjects

---

This question allows Stewart to bring together four ways boredom can be measured.

Stewart synthesizes seven different studies under one category, "behavior issues."

One study builds on a previous study.

Again, Stewart creates a category that includes two different studies.

🌸 academic literacies   ♦ fields   ● research

■ rhetorical situations   ⁝ processes   ● media/design

▲ genres   ◆ strategies

to complete a creative challenge (coming up with a list of alternative uses for a household item). One group of subjects did a boring activity first, while the others went straight to the creative task. Those whose boredom pumps had been primed were more prolific. [13]

In our always-connected world, boredom may be an elusive state, but it is a fertile one. Watch paint dry or water boil, or at least put away your smartphone for a while. You might unlock your next big idea.

Stewart shows how one study relates to an earlier one's findings.

Conclusion brings together all the research, creating a synthesis of the findings of all 13 sources.

The Studies

[1] Eastwood et al., "The Unengaged Mind" (*Perspectives on Psychological Science*, Sept. 2012)

[2] Farmer and Sundberg, "Boredom Proneness" (*Journal of Personality Assessment*, Spring 1986)

[3] Fahlman et al., "Development and Validation of the Multidimensional State Boredom Scale" (*Assessment*, Feb. 2013)

[4] Goetz et al., "Types of Boredom" (*Motivation and Emotion*, June 2014)

[5] Steinberger et al., "The Antecedents, Experience, and Coping Strategies of Driver Boredom in Young Adult Males" (*Journal of Safety Research*, Dec. 2016)

[6] Havermans et al., "Eating and Inflicting Pain Out of Boredom" (*Appetite*, Feb. 2015)

[7] Biolcati et al., " 'I Cannot Stand the Boredom' " (*Addictive Behaviors Reports*, June 2016)

[8] Miller et al., "Was Bob Seger Right?" (*Leisure Sciences*, Jan. 2014)

[9] Mercer and Eastwood, "Is Boredom Associated with Problem Gambling Behaviour?" (*International Gambling Studies*, April 2010)

[10] Wilson et al., "Just Think: The Challenges of the Disengaged Mind" (*Science*, July 2014)

[11] Nederkoorn et al., "Self-Inflicted Pain Out of Boredom" (*Psychiatry Research*, March 2016)

[12] Schubert, "Boredom as an Antagonist of Creativity" (*Journal of Creative Behavior*, Dec. 1977)

[13] Mann and Cadman, "Does Being Bored Make Us More Creative?" (*Creativity Research Journal*, May 2014)

—Jude Stewart, "Boredom Is Good for You: The Surprising Benefits of Stultification"

Here are some tips for reading to identify patterns and connections:

- Read all your sources with an open mind. Withhold judgment, even of sources that seem wrong-headed or implausible. Don't jump to conclusions.

550–51
- Take notes, and write a brief **SUMMARY** of each source to help you see relationships, patterns, and connections among your sources. Take notes on your own thoughts, too.

333–36
340–42
- Pay attention to your first reactions. You'll likely have many ideas to work with, but your first thoughts can often lead somewhere that you'll find interesting. Try **FREEWRITING**, **CLUSTERING**, or **LISTING** to see where they lead. How do these thoughts and ideas relate to your topic? Where might they fit into your rough **OUTLINE**?

- Try to think creatively, and pay attention to thoughts that flicker at the edge of your consciousness, as they may well be productive.

- Be playful. Good ideas sometimes come when we let our guard down or take ideas to extremes just to see where they lead.

Ask yourself these questions about your sources:

- What sources make the strongest arguments? What makes them so strong?

- Do some arguments crop up in several sources?

424–25
- Which arguments do you agree with? disagree with? Of those you disagree with, which ones seem strong enough that you need to **ACKNOWLEDGE** them in your text?

- Are there any disagreements among your sources?

- Are there any themes you see in more than one source?

- Are any data—facts, statistics, examples—or experts cited in more than one source?

- Do several of your sources use the same terms? Do they use the terms similarly, or do they use them in different ways?

❊ academic literacies	⬤ fields	⬤ research
▪ rhetorical situations	⁙ processes	⬤ media/design
▲ genres	◆ strategies	

- What have you learned about the topic? How have your sources affected your thinking on the topic? Do you need to adjust your **THESIS**? If so, how?

347–49

- Have you discovered new questions you need to investigate?

- Keep in mind your **RHETORICAL SITUATION** —have you found the information you need that will achieve your purpose, appeal to your audience, and suit your genre and medium?

57

What is likely to emerge from this questioning is a combination of big ideas, including new ways of understanding your topic and insights into recent scholarship about it, and smaller ones, such as how two sources agree with each other but not completely and how the information in one source supports or undercuts the argument of another. These ideas and insights will become the basis for your own ideas and for what *you* have to say about the topic.

Synthesizing Ideas Using Notes

You may find that identifying connections among your sources is easier if you examine them together rather than reading them one by one. For example, taking notes on note cards and then laying the cards out on a desk or table (or on the floor) lets you see passages that seem related. Doing the same with photocopies or printouts of your sources can help you identify similarities as well.

In doing research for an essay arguing that the sale of assault weapons should be banned, you might find several sources that address the scope of US citizens' right to bear arms. On the next page are notes taken on three such sources: Joe Klein, a journalist writing in *Time.com*; Antonin Scalia, a former US Supreme Court justice, quoted in an online news article; and Drew Westen, a professor of psychology writing in a blog sponsored by the *New York Times*. Though the writers hold very different views, juxtaposing these notes and highlighting certain passages show a common thread running through the sources. In this example, all three sources might be used to support the thesis that restrictions on the owning of weapons—but not an outright ban—are both constitutional and necessary.

Source 1

Limits of gun ownership

Although the U.S. Constitution includes the right to bear arms, that right is not absolute. "No American has the right to own a stealth bomber or a nuclear weapon. Armor-piercing bullets are forbidden. The question is where you draw a reasonable bright line."
— Klein, "How the Gun Won" — quote

Source 4

Limits of gun ownership

Supreme Court justice Antonin M. Scalia has noted that when the Constitution was written and ratified, some weapons were barred. So limitations could be put on owning some weapons, as long as the limits are consistent with those in force in 1789.
— Scalia, quoted in Woods — paraphrase

Source 3

Limits of gun ownership

Westen's "message consulting" research has shown that Americans are ambivalent about guns but react very positively to a statement of principle that includes both the right to own guns and restrictions on their ownership, such as prohibiting large ammunition clips and requiring all gun purchasers to undergo background checks for criminal behavior or mental illness.
— Westen — paraphrase

Synthesizing Information to Support Your Own Ideas

If you're doing research to write a **REPORT**, your own ideas will be communicated primarily through which information you decide to include from the sources you cite and how you organize that information. If you're writing a **TEXTUAL ANALYSIS**, your synthesis may focus on the themes, techniques, or other patterns you find. If you're writing a research-based **ARGUMENT**, in contrast, your synthesis of sources must support the position you take in that argument. No matter what your genre, the challenge is to synthesize information from your research to develop ideas about your topic and then to support those ideas.

▲ 140–63

▲ 104–39

▲ 164–95

Entering the Conversation

As you read and think about your topic, you will come to an understanding of the concepts, interpretations, and controversies relating to the topic—and you'll become aware that there's a larger conversation going on. When you begin to find connections among your sources, you'll begin to see your own place in that conversation, to discover your own ideas and your own stance on the topic. This is the exciting part of a research project, for when you write out your own ideas on the topic, you will find yourself entering that conversation. Remember that your **STANCE** as an author needs to be clear: simply stringing together the words and ideas of others isn't enough. You need to show readers how your source materials relate to one another and to your thesis.

■ 72–74

If you need more help

See Chapter 50, QUOTING, PARAPHRASING, AND SUMMARIZING, for help in integrating source materials into your own text. See also Chapter 51 on ACKNOWLEDGING SOURCES, AVOIDING PLAGIARISM for advice on giving credit to the sources you cite.

● 542–54

555–59

50 Quoting, Paraphrasing, and Summarizing

In an oral presentation about the rhetoric of Abraham Lincoln, you quote a memorable line from the Gettysburg Address. For an essay on the Tet Offensive in the Vietnam War, you paraphrase arguments made by several commentators and summarize some key debates about that war. When you work with the ideas and words of others, you need to clearly distinguish those ideas and words from your own and give credit to their authors. This chapter will help you with the specifics of quoting, paraphrasing, and summarizing source materials that you use in your writing.

Taking Notes

When you find material you think will be useful, take careful notes. How do you determine how much to record? You need to write down enough information so that when you refer to it later, you will be reminded of its main points and have a precise record of where it comes from.

- *Use a computer file, note cards, or a notebook,* labeling each entry with the information that will enable you to keep track of where it comes from—author, title, and the pages or the URL (or DOI, the digital object identifier). You needn't write down full bibliographic information (you can abbreviate the author's name and title) since you'll include that information in your WORKING BIBLIOGRAPHY .

- *Take notes in your own words, and use your own sentence patterns.* If you make a note that is a detailed PARAPHRASE, label it as such so that you'll know to provide appropriate DOCUMENTATION if you use it.

- *If you find wording that you'd like to quote,* be sure to enclose it in quotation marks to distinguish your source's words from your own.

497–99

547–50
560–63

※ academic literacies   ● fields   ● research
■ rhetorical situations   ⦂ processes   ● media/design
▲ genres   ◆ strategies

Double-check your notes to be sure any quoted material is accurately quoted—and that you haven't accidentally **PLAGIARIZED** your sources.

555–59

- *Label each note with a number to identify the source and a subject heading* to relate the note to a subject, supporting point, or other element in your essay. Doing this will help you to sort your notes easily and match them up with your rough outline. Restrict each note to a single subject.

Here are a few examples of one writer's notes on a source discussing synthetic dyes, bladder cancer, and the use of animals to determine what causes cancers. Each note includes a subject heading and brief source information and identifies whether the source is quoted or paraphrased.

> **Source 3**
>
> Synthetic dyes
>
> The first synthetic dye was mauve, invented in 1854 and derived from coal. Like other coal-derived dyes, it contained aromatic amines.
> Steingraber, "Pesticides," 976 — paraphrase

> **Source 3**
>
> Synthetic dyes & cancer
>
> Bladder cancer was common among textile workers who used dyes. Steingraber: "By the beginning of the twentieth century, bladder cancer rates among this group of workers had skyrocketed."
> Steingraber, "Pesticides," 976 — paraphrase and quote

> **Source 3**
>
> Synthetic dyes & cancer
>
> In 1938, Wilhelm Hueper exposed dogs to aromatic amines
> and showed that the chemical caused bladder cancer.
> Steingraber, "Pesticides," 976 — paraphrase

Deciding Whether to Quote, Paraphrase, or Summarize

364–66
544–47

When it comes time to **DRAFT**, you'll need to decide *how* to use any source you want to include—in other words, whether to quote, paraphrase, or summarize it. You might follow this rule of thumb: **QUOTE** texts when the wording is worth repeating or makes a point so well that no rewording will do it justice, when you want to cite the exact words of a known authority on your topic, when an authority's opinions challenge or disagree with those of others, or when the source is one you want to emphasize.

547–50
550–51

PARAPHRASE sources that are not worth quoting but contain details you need to include. **SUMMARIZE** longer passages whose main points are impor-

551–54

tant but whose details are not. Whatever your choice, you'll need to introduce any words or ideas that aren't your own with a **SIGNAL PHRASE** in order to clearly distinguish what your sources say from what *you* have to say.

Quoting

Quoting a source is a way of weaving someone else's exact words into your text. You need to reproduce the source exactly, though you can modify it to omit unnecessary details (with ellipses) or to make it fit smoothly into your text (with brackets). You also need to distinguish quoted material from your own by enclosing short quotations in quotation marks, setting

551–54

off longer quotes as a block, and using appropriate **SIGNAL PHRASES**.

Incorporate short quotations into your text, enclosed in quotation marks.

MLA 606–7

If you are following **MLA STYLE**, short quotations are defined as four typed

☀ academic literacies   ● fields   ● research
■ rhetorical situations   ⋮ processes   ● media/design
▲ genres   ◆ strategies

lines or fewer; if using **APA STYLE**, as below, short means fewer than forty words.

APA 646

> Gerald Graff (2003) has argued that colleges make the intellectual life seem more opaque than it needs to be, leaving many students with "the misconception that the life of the mind is a secret society for which only an elite few qualify" (p. 1).

If you are quoting three lines or fewer of poetry, run them in with your text, enclosed in quotation marks. Separate lines with slashes, leaving one space on each side of the slashes.

> Emma Lazarus almost speaks for the Statue of Liberty with the words inscribed on its pedestal: "Give me your tired, your poor, / Your huddled masses yearning to breathe free, / The wretched refuse of your teeming shore" (lines 10–12).

Set off long quotations block style. If you are using MLA style, set off quotations of five or more typed lines by indenting the quote one-half inch from the left margin. If you are using APA style, indent quotations of forty or more words one-half inch (or five to seven spaces) from the left margin. In either case, do not use quotation marks, and put any parenthetical documentation *after* any end punctuation.

> Nonprofit organizations such as Oxfam and Habitat for Humanity rely on visual representations of the poor. What better way to get our attention, asks rhetorician Diana George:
>
> > In a culture saturated by the image, how else do we convince Americans that—despite the prosperity they see all around them—there is real need out there? The solution for most nonprofits has been to show the despair. To do that they must represent poverty as something that can be seen and easily recognized: fallen-down shacks and trashed-out public housing, broken windows, dilapidated porches, barefoot kids with stringy hair, emaciated old women and men staring out at the camera with empty eyes. (210)

If you are quoting four or more lines of poetry, they need to be set off block style in the same way.

Indicate any omissions with ellipses.   You may sometimes delete words from a quotation that are unnecessary for your point. Insert three ellipsis marks (leaving a space before the first and after the last one) to indicate the deletion. If you omit a sentence or more in the middle of a quotation, put a period before the three ellipsis dots. Be careful not to distort the source's meaning, however.

> Faigley points out that Gore's "Information Superhighway" metaphor "associated the economic prosperity of the 1950s and . . . 1960s facilitated by new highways with the potential for vast . . . commerce to be conducted over the Internet" (253).

> According to Welch, "Television is more acoustic than visual. . . . One can turn one's gaze away from the television, but one cannot turn one's ears from it without leaving the area where the monitor leaks its aural signals into every corner" (102).

Indicate additions or changes with brackets.   Sometimes you'll need to change or add words in a quotation—to make the quotation fit grammatically within your sentence, for example, or to add a comment. In the following example, the writer changes the passage "one of our goals" to clarify the meaning of "our."

> Writing about the dwindling attention among some composition scholars to the actual teaching of writing, Susan Miller notes that "few discussions of writing pedagogy take it for granted that one of [writing teachers'] goals is to teach how to write" (480).

Here's an example of brackets used to add explanatory words to a quotation:

> Barbosa observes that Buarque's lyrics have long included "many a metaphor of *saudades* [yearning] so characteristic of *fado* music" (207).

Use punctuation correctly with quotations.   When incorporating a quotation into your text, be sure to think about the end punctuation in the quoted material and also about any punctuation you need to add when inserting the quote into your own sentence.

---

* academic literacies   ● fields   ● research
■ rhetorical situations   ⁞ processes   ● media/design
▲ genres   ◆ strategies

Periods and commas. Put periods or commas *inside* closing quotation marks, except when you have parenthetical documentation at the end, in which case you put the period or comma after the parentheses.

> "Country music," Tichi says, "is a crucial and vital part of the American identity" (23).

After long quotations set off block style with no quotation marks, however, the period goes *before* the documentation, as in the example on page 545.

Question marks and exclamation points. These go *inside* closing quotation marks if they are part of the quoted material but *outside* when they are not. If there's parenthetical documentation at the end of the quotation, any punctuation that's part of your sentence comes after it.

> Speaking at a Fourth of July celebration in 1852, Frederick Douglass asked, "What have I, or those I represent, to do with your national independence?" (35).

> Who can argue with W. Charisse Goodman's observation that media images persuade women that "thinness equals happiness and fulfillment" (53)?

Colons and semicolons. These always go *outside* closing quotation marks.

> It's hard to argue with W. Charisse Goodman's observation that media images persuade women that "thinness equals happiness and fulfillment"; nevertheless, American women today are more overweight than ever (53).

Paraphrasing

When you paraphrase, you restate information from a source in your own words, using your own sentence structures. Paraphrase when the source material is important but the original wording is not. Because it includes all the main points of the source, a paraphrase is usually about the same length as the original.

Here is a paragraph about synthetic dyes and cancer, followed by two paraphrases of it that demonstrate some of the challenges of paraphrasing:

ORIGINAL SOURCE

In 1938, in a series of now-classic experiments, exposure to synthetic dyes derived from coal and belonging to a class of chemicals called aromatic amines was shown to cause bladder cancer in dogs. These results helped explain why bladder cancers had become so prevalent among dyestuffs workers. With the invention of mauve in 1854, synthetic dyes began replacing natural plant-based dyes in the coloring of cloth and leather. By the beginning of the twentieth century, bladder cancer rates among this group of workers had skyrocketed, and the dog experiments helped unravel this mystery. The International Labor Organization did not wait for the results of these animal tests, however, and in 1921 declared certain aromatic amines to be human carcinogens. Decades later, these dogs provided a lead in understanding why tire-industry workers, as well as machinists and metalworkers, also began falling victim to bladder cancer: aromatic amines had been added to rubbers and cutting oils to serve as accelerants and antirust agents.

— Sandra Steingraber, "Pesticides, Animals, and Humans"

The following paraphrase borrows too much of the language of the original or changes it only slightly, as the highlighted words and phrases show:

UNACCEPTABLE PARAPHRASE: WORDING TOO CLOSE

Now-classic experiments in 1938 showed that when dogs were exposed to aromatic amines, chemicals used in synthetic dyes derived from coal, they developed bladder cancer. Similar cancers were prevalent among dyestuffs workers, and these experiments helped to explain why. Mauve, a synthetic dye, was invented in 1854, after which cloth and leather manufacturers replaced most of the natural plant-based dyes with synthetic dyes. By the early twentieth century, this group of workers had skyrocketing rates of bladder cancer, a mystery the dog experiments helped to unravel. As early as 1921, though, before the test results proved the connection, the International Labor Organization had labeled certain aromatic amines carcinogenic. Even so, decades later many metalworkers, machinists, and tire-industry workers began developing bladder cancer. The animal tests helped researchers understand that rubbers and cutting oils contained aromatic amines as accelerants and antirust agents (Steingraber 976).

✳ academic literacies   ◆ fields   ● research
■ rhetorical situations   ⁘ processes   ● media/design
▲ genres   ◆ strategies

The next paraphrase uses original language but follows the sentence structure of Steingraber's text too closely:

UNACCEPTABLE PARAPHRASE: SENTENCE STRUCTURE TOO CLOSE

In 1938, several pathbreaking experiments showed that being exposed to synthetic dyes that are made from coal and belong to a type of chemicals called aromatic amines caused dogs to get bladder cancer. These results helped researchers identify why cancers of the bladder had become so common among textile workers who worked with dyes. With the development of mauve in 1854, synthetic dyes began to be used instead of dyes based on plants in the dyeing of leather and cloth. By the end of the nineteenth century, rates of bladder cancer among these workers had increased dramatically, and the experiments using dogs helped clear up this oddity. The International Labor Organization anticipated the results of these tests on animals, though, and in 1921 labeled some aromatic amines carcinogenic. Years later these experiments with dogs helped researchers explain why workers in the tire industry, as well as metalworkers and machinists, also started dying of bladder cancer: aromatic amines had been put into rubbers and cutting oils as rust inhibitors and accelerants (Steingraber 976).

Patchwriting, a third form of unacceptable paraphrase, combines the other two. Composition researcher Rebecca Moore Howard defines it as "copying from a source text and then deleting some words, altering grammatical structures, or plugging in one-for-one synonym-substitutes." Here is a patchwrite of the first two sentences of the original source: (The source's exact words are shaded in yellow; paraphrases are in blue.)

PATCHWRITE

Scientists have known for a long time that chemicals in the environment can cause cancer. For example, in 1938, in a series of important experiments, being exposed to synthetic dyes made out of coal and belonging to a kind of chemicals called aromatic amines was shown to cause dogs to develop bladder cancer. These experiments explain why this type of cancer had become so common among workers who handled dyes.

Here is an acceptable paraphrase of the entire passage:

ACCEPTABLE PARAPHRASE

Biologist Sandra Steingraber explains that pathbreaking experiments in 1938 demonstrated that dogs exposed to aromatic amines (chemicals used in coal-based synthetic dyes) developed cancers of the bladder that were similar to cancers common among dyers in the textile industry. After mauve, the first synthetic dye, was invented in 1854, leather and cloth manufacturers replaced most natural dyes made from plants with synthetic dyes, and by the early 1900s textile workers had very high rates of bladder cancer. The experiments with dogs proved the connection, but years before, in 1921, the International Labor Organization had labeled some aromatic amines carcinogenic. Even so, years later many metalworkers, machinists, and workers in the tire industry started to develop unusually high rates of bladder cancer. The experiments with dogs helped researchers understand that the cancers were caused by aromatic amines used in cutting oils to inhibit rust and in rubbers to speed up the manufacturing process (976).

SOME GUIDELINES FOR PARAPHRASING

- *Use your own words and sentence structure.* It's acceptable to use some words from the original; but as much as possible, the phrasing and sentence structures should be your own.

551–54

- *Introduce paraphrased text with* SIGNAL PHRASES.

- *Put in quotation marks any of the source's original phrasing that you use.*

- *Indicate the source.* Although the wording may be yours, the ideas and information come from another source; be sure to name the author, and include DOCUMENTATION to avoid the possibility of PLAGIARISM.

MLA 567–74
APA 618–22
551–54

Summarizing

A summary states the main ideas in a source concisely and in your own words. Unlike a paraphrase, a summary does *not* present all the details, and it is generally as brief as possible. Summaries may boil down an entire

---

✳ academic literacies   ◆ fields   ● research
◼ rhetorical situations   ⁝ processes   ● media/design
▲ genres   ◆ strategies

book or essay into a single sentence, or they may take a paragraph or more to present the main ideas. Here, for example, is a one-sentence summary of the Steingraber paragraph:

> Steingraber explains that experiments with dogs demonstrated that aromatic amines, chemicals used in synthetic dyes, cutting oils, and rubber, cause bladder cancer (976).

In the context of an essay, the summary might take this form:

> Medical researchers have long relied on experiments using animals to expand understanding of the causes of disease. For example, biologist and ecologist Sandra Steingraber notes that in the second half of the nineteenth century, the rate of bladder cancer soared among textile workers. According to Steingraber, experiments with dogs demonstrated that synthetic chemicals in dyes used to color the textiles caused the cancer (976).

SOME GUIDELINES FOR SUMMARIZING

- *Include only the main ideas; leave out the details.* A summary should include just enough information to give the reader the gist of the original. It is always much shorter than the original, sometimes even as brief as one sentence.

- *Use your own words.* If you quote phrasing from the original, enclose the phrase in quotation marks.

- *Indicate the source.* Although the wording may be yours, the ideas and information come from another source. Name the author, either in a signal phrase or in parentheses, and include an appropriate **IN-TEXT CITATION** to avoid the possibility of **PLAGIARISM**.

MLA 567–74
APA 618–22
551–54

Introducing Source Materials Using Signal Phrases

You need to introduce quotations, paraphrases, and summaries clearly, usually letting readers know who the author is—and, if need be, something about their credentials. Consider this sentence:

> Professor and textbook author Elaine Tyler May argues that many high school history books are too bland to interest young readers (531).

The beginning ("Professor and textbook author Elaine Tyler May argues") functions as a *signal phrase*, telling readers who is making the assertion and why she has the authority to speak on the topic—and making clear that everything between the signal phrase and the parenthetical citation comes from that source. Since the signal phrase names the author, the parenthetical citation includes only the page number; had the author not been identified in the signal phrase, she would have been named in the parentheses:

> Even some textbook authors believe that many high school history books are too bland to interest young readers (May 531).

MLA and APA have different conventions for constructing signal phrases. In MLA, the language you use in a signal phrase can be neutral—like "X says"/"Y thinks"/"according to Z." Or it can suggest something about the **STANCE** —the source's or your own. The example above referring to the textbook author uses the verb "argues," suggesting that what she says is open to dispute (or that the writer believes it is). How would it change your understanding if the signal verb were "observes"/"suggests"?

In addition to the names of sources' authors, signal phrases often give readers information about institutional affiliations and positions authors have, their academic or professional specialties, and any other information that lets readers judge the credibility of the sources. You should craft each signal phrase you use so as to highlight the credentials of the author. Here are some examples:

> A study done by Keenan Johnson, professor of psychology at Duke University, showed that . . .

The signal phrase identifies the source's author, his professional position, and his university affiliation, emphasizing his title.

> Science writer Isaac McDougal argues that . . .

72–74

✳ academic literacies   ● fields   ● research
■ rhetorical situations   ⦂ processes   ● media/design
▲ genres   ◆ strategies

This phrase acknowledges that the source's author may not have scholarly credentials but is a published writer; it's a useful construction if the source doesn't provide much information about the writer.

> Writing in *Psychology Today,* Amanda Chao-Fitz notes that . . .

This is the sort of signal phrase to use if you have no information on the author; you establish credibility on the basis of the publication in which the source appears.

If you're writing using APA style, signal phrases are typically briefer, giving only the author's last name and the date of publication:

> According to Benzinger (2010), . . .
> Quartucci (2011) observed that . . .

Signal verbs. The verbs used in signal phrases do more than simply introduce a quote, paraphrase, or reference; they also provide information on the author's intended meaning and give your reader a clue as to how the source should be read. They also can give your writing variety and interest.

SOME COMMON SIGNAL VERBS

acknowledge	comment	dispute	point out
admit	conclude	emphasize	reason
advise	concur	grant	reject
agree	confirm	illustrate	report
argue	contend	imply	respond
assert	declare	insist	state
believe	deny	note	suggest
charge	disagree	observe	think
claim			

Verb tenses. MLA and APA also have different conventions regarding the tenses of verbs in signal phrases. MLA requires present-tense verbs ("writes," "asserts," " notes") in signal phrases to introduce a work you are quoting, paraphrasing, or summarizing.

In *Poor Richard's Almanack*, Benjamin Franklin <u>notes</u>, "He that cannot obey, cannot command" (739).

If, however, you are referring to the act of writing or saying something rather than simply quoting someone's words, you might not use the present tense. The writer of the following sentence focuses on the year in which the source was written — therefore, the verb is necessarily in the past tense:

Back in 1941, Kenneth Burke <u>wrote</u> that "the ethical values of work are in its application of the competitive equipment to cooperative ends" (316).

If you are following APA style, use the past tense to introduce sources composed in the past. If you are referring to a past action that didn't occur at a specific time or that continues into the present, you should use the present perfect.

Dowdall et al. (2020) <u>observed</u> that women attending women's colleges are less likely to engage in binge drinking than are women who attend coeducational colleges (p. 713).

Many researchers <u>have studied</u> drinking habits on college campuses.

APA requires the present tense, however, to discuss the results of an experiment or to explain conclusions that are generally agreed on.

The findings of this study <u>suggest</u> that excessive drinking has serious consequences for college students and their institutions.

The authors of numerous studies <u>agree</u> that smoking and drinking among adolescents are associated with lower academic achievement.

If you need more help

555–59
MLA 608–14
APA 648–55
33–45

See Chapter 51 for help **ACKNOWLEDGING SOURCES** and giving credit to the sources you use. See also the **SAMPLE RESEARCH PAPERS** to see how sources are cited in MLA and APA styles. And see Chapter 3 if you're writing a **SUMMARY/RESPONSE** essay.

* academic literacies   ● fields   ● research
■ rhetorical situations   ⁘ processes   ● media/design
▲ genres   ◆ strategies

51 Acknowledging Sources, Avoiding Plagiarism

Whenever you do research-based writing, you find yourself entering a conversation—reading what many others have had to say about your topic, figuring out what you yourself think, and then putting what you think in writing—"putting in your oar," as the rhetorician Kenneth Burke once wrote. As a writer, you need to *acknowledge* any words and ideas that come from others—to give credit where credit is due, to recognize the various authorities and many perspectives you have considered, to show readers where they can find your sources, and to situate your own arguments in the ongoing conversation. Using other people's words and ideas without acknowledgment is *plagiarism*, a serious academic and ethical offense. This chapter will show you how to acknowledge the materials you use and avoid plagiarism.

Acknowledging Sources

When you insert in your text information that you've obtained from others, your readers need to know where your source's words or ideas begin and end. Therefore, you should usually introduce a source by naming the author in a **SIGNAL PHRASE** and then provide brief **DOCUMENTATION** of the specific material from the source in a parenthetical reference following the material. (Sometimes you can put the author's name in the parenthetical reference as well.) You need only brief documentation of the source here, since your readers will find full bibliographic information about it in your list of **WORKS CITED** or **REFERENCES**.

551–54
MLA 567–74
APA 618–22

MLA 574–605
APA 623–44

Sources that need acknowledgment. You almost always need to acknowledge any information that you get from a specific source. Material you should acknowledge includes the following:

- *Direct quotations.* Unless they are well known (see p. 558 for some examples), any quotations from another source must be enclosed in quotation marks, cited with brief bibliographic information in parentheses, and usually introduced with a signal phrase that tells who wrote or said it and provides necessary contextual information, as in the following sentence:

  In a dissenting opinion on the issue of racial preferences in college admissions, Supreme Court justice Ruth Bader Ginsburg argues, "The stain of generations of racial oppression is still visible in our society, and the determination to hasten its removal remains vital" (*Gratz v. Bollinger*).

- *Arguable statements and information that may not be common knowledge.* If you state something about which there is disagreement or for which arguments can be made, cite the source of your statement. If in doubt about whether you need to give the source of an assertion, provide it. As part of an essay on "fake news" programs, for example, you might make the following assertion:

  The satire of *The Daily Show* complements the conservative bias of Fox News, since both have abandoned the stance of objectivity maintained by mainstream news sources, contends Michael Hoyt, executive editor of the *Columbia Journalism Review* (43).

  Others might argue with the contention that the Fox News Channel offers biased reports of the news, so the source of this assertion needs to be acknowledged. In the same essay, you might present information that should be cited because it's not widely known, as in this example:

  According to a report by the Pew Research Center, 25 percent of Americans got information about the 2016 presidential campaign from comedy shows like *The Late Show with Stephen Colbert* and *Saturday Night Live* (2).

- *The opinions and assertions of others.* When you present the ideas, opinions, and assertions of others, cite the source. You may have rewritten

✳ academic literacies ● fields ● research
◼ rhetorical situations ⁚• processes ● media/design
▲ genres ◆ strategies

the concept in your own words, but the ideas were generated by someone else and must be acknowledged, as they are here:

David Boonin, writing in the *Journal of Social Philosophy*, asserts that, logically, laws banning marriage between people of different races are not discriminatory since everyone of each race is affected equally by them. Laws banning same-sex unions are discriminatory, however, since they apply only to people with a certain sexual orientation (256).

- *Photographs, visual images, or video.* If you didn't create a photo, image, or video yourself, cite the source. If possible, use the original source, not a version that appears in another source, to ensure that the version you're using hasn't been altered.

- *Any information that you didn't generate yourself.* If you didn't do the research or compile the data yourself, cite your source. This goes for interviews, statistics, graphs, charts, visuals, photographs—anything you use that you didn't create. If you create a chart using data from another source, you need to cite that source.

- *Collaboration with and help from others.* In many of your courses and in work situations, you'll be called on to work with others. You may get help with your writing at your school's writing center or from fellow students in your writing courses. Acknowledging such collaboration or assistance, in a brief informational note, is a way of giving credit—and saying thank you. See guidelines for writing notes in the **MLA** and **APA** sections of this book.

● MLA 574
APA 622–23

Sources that don't need acknowledgment.   Widely available information and common knowledge do not require acknowledgment. What constitutes common knowledge may not be clear, however. When in doubt, provide a citation, or ask your instructor whether the information needs to be cited. You generally do not need to cite the following:

- *Information that most readers are likely to know.* You don't need to acknowledge information that is widely known or commonly accepted as fact. For example, in a literary analysis, you wouldn't cite a source saying that Harriet Beecher Stowe wrote *Uncle Tom's Cabin*; you can assume your readers already know that. However, you should cite the source from which you got the information that the book was first published in installments in a magazine and then, with revisions, in book form, because that information isn't common knowledge. As you do research in areas you're not familiar with, be aware that what constitutes common knowledge isn't always clear; the history of the novel's publication would be known to Stowe scholars and would likely need no acknowledgment in an essay written for them. In this case, too, if you aren't sure whether to acknowledge information, it's best to do so.

- *Information and documents that are widely available.* If a piece of information appears in several sources or reference works or if a document has been published widely, you needn't cite a source for it. For example, the date when astronauts Neil Armstrong and Buzz Aldrin landed a spacecraft on the moon can be found in any number of reference works. Similarly, the Declaration of Independence and the Gettysburg Address are reprinted in thousands of sources, so the ones where you found them need no citation.

- *Well-known quotations.* These include such famous quotations as Lady Macbeth's "Out, damned spot!" and John F. Kennedy's "Ask not what your country can do for you; ask what you can do for your country." Be sure, however, that the quotation is correct. Winston Churchill is said to have told a class of schoolchildren, "Never, ever, ever, ever, ever, ever, ever give up. Never give up. Never give up. Never give up." His actual words, however, are much different and begin "Never give in."

- *Material that you created or gathered yourself.* You need not cite photographs that you took, graphs that you composed based on your own findings, or data from an experiment or survey that you conducted—though you should make sure readers know that the work is yours.

A good rule of thumb: *when in doubt, cite your source.* You're unlikely to be criticized for citing too much—but you may invite charges of plagiarism by citing too little.

Avoiding Plagiarism

In North America, authors' words and ideas are considered to belong to them, so using others' words or ideas without acknowledging the source is considered to be a serious offense called plagiarism. In fact, plagiarism is often committed unintentionally—as when a writer paraphrases someone else's ideas in language that is too close to the original. It is essential, therefore, to know what constitutes plagiarism: (1) using another writer's words or ideas without acknowledging the source, (2) using another writer's exact words without quotation marks, and (3) paraphrasing or summarizing someone else's ideas using language or sentence structures that are too close to theirs.

To avoid plagiarizing, take careful **NOTES** as you do your research, clearly labeling as quotations any words you quote directly and being careful to use your own phrasing and sentence structures in paraphrases and summaries. Be sure you know what source material you must **DOCUMENT**, and give credit to your sources, both in the text and in a list of **REFERENCES** or **WORKS CITED**.

● 542–44

● 560–63
APA 623–44
MLA 574–605

Be aware that it's easy to plagiarize inadvertently when working with online sources, such as full-text articles, that you've downloaded or cut and pasted into your notes. Keep careful track of these materials, since saving copies of your sources is so easy. Later, be sure to check your draft against the original sources to make sure your quotations are accurately worded—and take care, too, to include quotation marks and document the source correctly. Copying online material right into a document you are writing and forgetting to put quotation marks around it or to document it (or both) is all too easy to do. You must acknowledge information you find on the web just as you must acknowledge all other source materials.

And you must recognize that plagiarism has consequences. Scholars' work will be discredited if it too closely resembles another's. Journalists who are found to have plagiarized lose their jobs, and students routinely fail courses or are dismissed from their school when they are caught cheating—all too often by submitting as their own essays that they have purchased from online "research" sites. If you're having trouble completing an assignment, seek assistance. Talk with your instructor; or if your school has a writing center, go there for advice on all aspects of your writing, including acknowledging sources and avoiding plagiarism.

52 Documentation

In everyday life, we are generally aware of our sources: "I read it on Megan McArdle's blog." "Amber told me it's your birthday." "If you don't believe me, ask Mom." Saying how we know what we know and where we got our information is part of establishing our credibility and persuading others to take what we say seriously.

The goal of a research project is to study a topic, combining what we learn from sources with our own thinking and then composing a written text. When we write up the results of a research project, we cite the sources we use, usually by quoting, paraphrasing, or summarizing, and we acknowledge those sources, telling readers where the ideas came from. The information we give about sources is called documentation, and we provide it not only to establish our credibility as researchers and writers but also so that our readers, if they wish to, can find the sources themselves.

Understanding Documentation Styles

The Norton Field Guide covers the documentation styles of the Modern Language Association (MLA) and the American Psychological Association (APA). MLA style is used chiefly in the humanities; APA is used in the social sciences, sciences, education, and nursing. Both are two-part systems, consisting of (1) brief in-text parenthetical documentation for quotations, paraphrases, or summaries and (2) more-detailed documentation in a list of sources at the end of the text. MLA and APA require that the end-of-text documentation provide the following basic information about each source you cite:

TITLE   AUTHOR   PUBLICATION

- author, editor, or creator of the source
- title of source (and of publication or site where it appears)
- version or edition of source
- name of publisher
- date of publication
- retrieval information (for online sources)

MLA and APA are by no means the only documentation styles. Many other publishers and organizations have their own style, among them the University of Chicago Press and the Council of Science Editors. We focus on MLA and APA here because those are styles that college students are often required to use. On the following page are examples of how the two parts—the brief parenthetical documentation in your text and the more detailed information at the end—correspond in each of these systems.

The examples here and throughout this book are color-coded to help you see the crucial parts of each citation: tan for author and editor, yellow for titles, and gray for publication information: name of publisher, date of publication, page number(s), DOI or URL, and so on.

As the examples of in-text documentation show, in either MLA or APA style you should name the author either in a signal phrase or in parentheses following the source information. But there are several differences between the two styles in the details of the documentation. In MLA, the author's first and last names are used in a signal phrase at first mention; in APA, only the last name is used. In APA, the abbreviation "p." is used with the page number; in MLA, there is no abbreviation before a page number. Finally, in APA the date of publication always appears just after the author's name.

Comparing the MLA and APA styles of listing works cited or references also reveals some differences: MLA includes an author's first name while APA gives only initials; MLA puts the date near the end while APA places it right after the author's name; MLA capitalizes most of the words in a book's title and subtitle while APA capitalizes only the first words and proper nouns and proper adjectives in each.

MLA Style

IN-TEXT DOCUMENTATION

As Lester Faigley puts it, "The world has become a bazaar from which to shop for an individual 'lifestyle'" (12).

As one observer suggests, "The world has become a bazaar from which to shop for an individual 'lifestyle'" (Faigley 12).

WORKS-CITED DOCUMENTATION

Faigley, Lester. *Fragments of Rationality: Postmodernity and the Subject of Composition*. U of Pittsburgh P, 1992.

APA Style

IN-TEXT DOCUMENTATION

As Faigley (1992) suggested, "The world has become a bazaar from which to shop for an individual 'lifestyle'" (p. 12).

As one observer has noted, "The world has become a bazaar from which to shop for an individual 'lifestyle'" (Faigley, 1992, p. 12).

REFERENCE-LIST DOCUMENTATION

Faigley, L. (1992). *Fragments of rationality: Postmodernity and the subject of composition*. University of Pittsburgh Press.

Some of these differences are related to the nature of the academic fields in which the two styles are used. In humanities disciplines, the authorship of a text is emphasized, so both first and last names are included in MLA documentation. Scholarship in those fields may be several years old but still current, so the publication date doesn't appear in the in-text citation. In APA style, as in many documentation styles used in the sciences, education, and engineering, emphasis is placed on the date of publication because in these fields, more recent research is usually preferred over older studies. However, although the elements are arranged differently, both MLA and APA—and other documentation styles as well—require similar information about author, title, and publication.

53 MLA Style

MLA style calls for (1) brief in-text documentation and (2) complete bibliographic information in a list of works cited at the end of your text. The models and examples in this guide draw on the ninth edition of the *MLA Handbook*, published by the Modern Language Association of America in 2021. For additional information, or if you're citing a source that isn't covered in this guide, visit style.mla.org.

A DIRECTORY TO MLA STYLE

In-Text Documentation   567

1. Author named in a signal phrase   568
2. Author named in parentheses   568
3. Two or more works by the same author   568
4. Authors with the same last name   569
5. Two or more authors   569
6. Organization or government as author 570
7. Author unknown   570
8. Literary works   570
9. Work in an anthology   571
10. Encyclopedia or dictionary   571
11. Legal documents   571
12. Sacred text   572
13. Multivolume work   572
14. Two or more works cited together   572
15. Source quoted in another source   573
16. Work without page numbers   573
17. An entire work or a one-page article   574

Notes   574

List of Works Cited   574

CORE ELEMENTS   574

AUTHORS AND CONTRIBUTORS   580

1. One author   580

2. Two authors   580

3. Three or more authors   580

4. Two or more works by the same author   580

5. Author and editor or translator   581

6. No author or editor   581

7. Organization or government as author   582

ARTICLES AND OTHER SHORT WORKS   582

Documentation Map: Article in a Print Journal   583

Documentation Map: Article in an Online Magazine   584

Documentation Map: Journal Article Accessed through a Database   587

8. Article in a journal   582

9. Article in a magazine   585

10. Article in a news publication   585

11. Article accessed through a database   586

12. Entry in a reference work   586

13. Editorial or op-ed   588

14. Letter to the editor   588

15. Review   589

16. Comment on an online article   589

BOOKS AND PARTS OF BOOKS   590

Documentation Map: Print Book   591

17. Basic entries for a book   590

18. Anthology or edited collection   590

19. Work in an anthology   592

20. Multivolume work   592

21. Book in a series   593

22. Graphic narrative or comic book   593

23. Sacred text   593

24. Edition other than the first   594

25. Republished work   594

26. Foreword, introduction, preface, or afterword   594

27. Published letter   594

28. Paper heard at a conference   594

29. Dissertation   595

WEBSITES   595

Documentation Map: Work on a Website   596

30. Entire website   595

31. Work on a website   597

32. Blog entry   597

33. Wiki   597

PERSONAL COMMUNICATION AND SOCIAL MEDIA   598

34. Personal letter   598

35. Email or text message   598

36. Post to *Twitter*, *Instagram*, or other social media   598

AUDIO, VISUAL, AND OTHER SOURCES   599

37. Advertisement   599

38. Art   599

39. Cartoon   600

40. Supreme Court case   600

41. Film   600

42. TV show episode   601

43. Online video   602

44. Presentation on *Zoom* or other virtual platform   602

45. Interview   602

46. Map   603

47. Musical score   603

48. Oral presentation   603

49. Podcast   604

50. Radio program   604

51. Sound recording   604

52. Video game   605

Formatting a Research Paper   605

Sample Research Paper   607

Throughout this chapter, you'll find color-coded templates and examples to help you see how writers include source information in their texts and in their lists of works cited: tan for author, editor, translator, and other contributors; yellow for titles; blue for publication information—date of publication, page number(s), DOIs, and other location information.

IN-TEXT DOCUMENTATION

Whenever you **QUOTE**, **PARAPHRASE**, or **SUMMARIZE** a source in your writing, you need to provide brief documentation that tells readers what you took from the source and where in the source you found that information. This brief documentation also refers readers to the full entry in your works-cited list, so begin with whatever comes first there: the author, the title, or a description of the source.

544–47

You can mention the author or title either in a signal phrase—"Toni Morrison writes," "In *Beowulf*," "According to the article 'Every Patient's Nightmare'"—or in parentheses—(Morrison). If relevant, include pages or other details about where you found the information in the parenthetical reference: (Morrison 67).

Shorten any lengthy titles or descriptions in parentheses by including the first noun with any preceding adjectives and omitting any initial articles (*Norton Field Guide* for *The Norton Field Guide to Writing*). If the title doesn't start with a noun, use the first phrase or clause (*How to Be* for *How to Be an Antiracist*). Use the full title if it's short.

The first two examples below show basic in-text documentation of a work by one author. Variations on those examples follow. The examples illustrate the MLA style of using quotation marks around titles of short works and italicizing titles of long works.

1. AUTHOR NAMED IN A SIGNAL PHRASE

551–54

If you mention the author in a **SIGNAL PHRASE**, put only the page number(s) in parentheses. Do not write "page" or "p." The first time you mention the author, use their first and last names. You can usually omit any middle initials.

> David McCullough describes John Adams's hands as those of someone used to manual labor (18).

2. AUTHOR NAMED IN PARENTHESES

If you do not mention the author in a signal phrase, put the author's last name in parentheses along with any page number(s). Do not use punctuation between the name and the page number(s).

> Adams is said to have had "the hands of a man accustomed to pruning his own trees, cutting his own hay, and splitting his own firewood" (McCullough 18).

Whether you use a signal phrase and parentheses or parentheses only, try to put the parenthetical documentation at the end of the sentence or as close as possible to the material you've cited—without awkwardly interrupting the sentence. When the parenthetical reference comes at the end of the sentence, the period follows it.

3. TWO OR MORE WORKS BY THE SAME AUTHOR

If you cite multiple works by one author, include the title of the work you are citing either in the signal phrase or in parentheses.

Robert Kaplan insists that understanding power in the Near East requires "Western leaders who know when to intervene, and do so without illusions" (*Eastward to Tartary* 330).

Put a comma between author and title if both are in the parentheses.

Understanding power in the Near East requires "Western leaders who know when to intervene, and do so without illusions" (Kaplan, *Eastward to Tartary* 330).

4. AUTHORS WITH THE SAME LAST NAME

Give each author's first and last names in any signal phrase, or add the author's first initial in the parenthetical reference.

"Imaginative" applies not only to modern literature but also to writing of all periods, whereas "magical" is often used in writing about Arthurian romances (A. Wilson 25).

5. TWO OR MORE AUTHORS

For a work with two authors, name both. If you first mention them in a signal phrase, give their first and last names.

Lori Carlson and Cynthia Ventura's stated goal is to introduce Julio Cortázar, Marjorie Agosín, and other Latin American writers to an audience of English-speaking adolescents (v).

For a work by three or more authors that you mention in a signal phrase, you can either name them all or name the first author followed by "and others" or "and colleagues." If you mention them in a parenthetical reference, name the first author followed by "et al."

Phyllis Anderson and colleagues describe British literature thematically (A54-A67).

One survey of British literature breaks the contents into thematic groupings (Anderson et al. A54-A67).

6. ORGANIZATION OR GOVERNMENT AS AUTHOR

In a signal phrase, use the full name of the organization: American Academy of Arts and Sciences. In parentheses, use the shortest noun phrase, omitting any initial articles: American Academy.

> The US government can be direct when it wants to be. For example, it sternly warns, "If you are overpaid, we will recover any payments not due you" (Social Security Administration 12).

7. AUTHOR UNKNOWN

If you don't know the author, use the work's title in a signal phrase or in a parenthetical reference.

> A powerful editorial in *The New York Times* asserts that healthy liver donor Mike Hurewitz died because of "frightening" faulty postoperative care ("Every Patient's Nightmare").

8. LITERARY WORKS

When referring to common literary works that are available in many different editions, give the page numbers from the edition you are using, followed by information that will let readers of any edition locate the text you are citing.

NOVELS AND PROSE PLAYS. Give the page number followed by a semicolon and any chapter, section, or act numbers, separated by commas.

> In *Pride and Prejudice,* Mrs. Bennet shows no warmth toward Jane when she returns from Netherfield (Austen 105; ch. 12).

VERSE PLAYS. Give act, scene, and line numbers, separated with periods.

> Shakespeare continues the vision theme when Macbeth says, "Thou hast no speculation in those eyes / Which thou dost glare with" (*Macbeth* 3.3.96-97).

POEMS. Give the part and the line numbers, separated by periods. If a poem has only line numbers, use the word "line" or "lines" in the first reference; after that, give only numbers.

> Walt Whitman sets up not only opposing adjectives but also opposing nouns in "Song of Myself" when he says, "I am of old and young, of the foolish as much as the wise, / . . . a child as well as a man" (16.330-32).

> One description of the mere in *Beowulf* is "not a pleasant place" (line 1372). Later, it is labeled "the awful place" (1378).

9. WORK IN AN ANTHOLOGY

Name the author(s) of the work, not the editor of the anthology.

> "It is the teapots that truly shock," according to Cynthia Ozick in her essay on teapots as metaphor (70).

> In *In Short: A Collection of Creative Nonfiction,* readers will find both an essay on Scottish tea (Hiestand) and a piece on teapots as metaphors (Ozick).

10. ENCYCLOPEDIA OR DICTIONARY

Acknowledge an entry in an encyclopedia or dictionary by giving the author's name, if available. For an entry without an author, give the entry's title.

> According to *Funk and Wagnall's New World Encyclopedia*, early in his career, most of Kubrick's income came from "hustling chess games in Washington Square Park" ("Kubrick, Stanley").

11. LEGAL DOCUMENTS

For legal cases, give whatever comes first in the works-cited entry. If you're citing a government document in parentheses and multiple entries in your works-cited list start with the same government author, give as much of the name as you need to differentiate the sources.

> In 2015, for the first time, all states were required to license and recognize the marriages of same-sex couples (United States, Supreme Court).

12. SACRED TEXT

When citing a sacred text such as the Bible or the Qur'an for the first time, give the title of the edition as well as the book, chapter, and verse (or their equivalent), separated by periods. MLA recommends abbreviating the names of the books of the Bible in parenthetical references. Later citations from the same edition do not have to repeat its title.

> The wording from *The New English Bible* follows: "In the beginning of creation, when God made heaven and earth, the earth was without form and void . . ." (Gen. 1.1-2).

13. MULTIVOLUME WORK

If you cite more than one volume of a multivolume work, each time you cite one of the volumes, give the volume *and* the page number(s) in parentheses, separated by a colon and a space.

> Carl Sandburg concludes with the following sentence about those paying last respects to Lincoln: "All day long and through the night the unbroken line moved, the home town having its farewell" (4: 413).

If you cite an entire volume of a multivolume work in parentheses, give the author's last name followed by a comma and "vol." before the volume number: (Sandburg, vol. 4). If your works-cited list includes only a single volume of a multivolume work, give just the page number in parentheses: (413).

14. TWO OR MORE WORKS CITED TOGETHER

If you're citing two or more works closely together, you will sometimes need to provide a parenthetical reference for each one.

> Dennis Baron describes singular "they" as "the missing word that's been hiding in plain sight" (182), while Benjamin Dreyer believes that "singular 'they' is not the wave of the future; it's the wave of the present" (93).

If you are citing multiple sources for the same idea in parentheses, separate the references with a semicolon.

> Many critics have examined great works of literature from a cultural perspective (Tanner 7; Smith viii).

15. SOURCE QUOTED IN ANOTHER SOURCE

When you are quoting text that you found quoted in another source, use the abbreviation "qtd. in" in the parenthetical reference.

> Charlotte Brontë wrote to G. H. Lewes, "Why do you like Miss Austen so very much? I am puzzled on that point" (qtd. in Tanner 7).

16. WORK WITHOUT PAGE NUMBERS

For works without page or part numbers, including many online sources, no number is needed in a parenthetical reference.

> Studies show that music training helps children to be better at multitasking later in life ("Hearing the Music").

If you mention the author in a signal phrase, or if you mention the title of a work with no author, no parenthetical reference is needed.

> Arthur Brooks argues that a switch to fully remote work would have a negative effect on mental and physical health.

If the source has chapter, paragraph, or section numbers, use them with the abbreviations "ch.," "par.," or "sec.": ("Hearing the Music," par. 2). Don't count lines or paragraphs on your own if they aren't numbered in the source. For an ebook, use chapter numbers. For an audio or video recording, give the hours, minutes, and seconds (separated by colons) as shown on the player: (00:05:21-31).

17. AN ENTIRE WORK OR A ONE-PAGE ARTICLE

If you cite an entire work rather than a part of it, or if you cite a single-page article, there's no need to include page numbers.

> Throughout life, John Adams strove to succeed (McCullough).

NOTES

Sometimes you may need to give information that doesn't fit into the text itself—to thank people who helped you, to provide additional details, to refer readers to other sources, or to add comments about sources. Such information can be given in a footnote (at the bottom of the page) or an endnote (on a separate page with the heading "Notes" or "Endnotes" just before your works-cited list). Put a superscript number at the appropriate point in your text, signaling to readers to look for the note with the corresponding number. If you have multiple notes, number them consecutively throughout your paper.

TEXT

This essay will argue that giving student athletes preferential treatment undermines educational goals.[1]

NOTE

[1] I want to thank those who contributed to my thinking on this topic, especially my teacher Vincent Yu.

LIST OF WORKS CITED

A works-cited list provides full bibliographic information for every source cited in your text. See page 607 for guidelines on formatting this list and page 613 for a sample works-cited list.

Core Elements

MLA style provides a list of core elements for documenting sources in a works-cited list. Not all sources will include each of these elements; include as much information as is available for any title you cite. For guidance about specific sources you need to document, see the templates and examples on pages 580–605, but here are some general guidelines for how to treat each of the core elements.

CORE ELEMENTS FOR ENTRIES IN A WORKS-CITED LIST

- Author
- Title of the source
- Title of any "container," a larger work in which the source is found—an anthology, a website, a journal or magazine, a database, a streaming service like *Netflix*, or a learning management system, among others
- Editor, translator, director, or other contributors
- Version
- Number of volume and issue, episode and season
- Publisher
- Date of publication
- Location of the source: page numbers, DOI, permalink, URL, etc.

The above order is the general order MLA recommends, but there will be exceptions. To document a translated essay that you found in an anthology, for instance, you'd identify the translator after the title of the essay rather than after that of the anthology. You may sometimes need additional elements as well, either at the end of an entry or in the middle—for instance, a label to indicate that your source is a map, or an original year of publication. Remember that your goal is to tell readers what sources you've consulted and where they can find them. Providing this information is one way you can engage with readers—and enable them to join in the conversation with you and your sources.

AUTHORS AND CONTRIBUTORS

- An author can be any kind of creator—a writer, a musician, an artist, and so on.
- If there is one author, put the last name first, followed by a comma and the first name: Morrison, Toni.

- If there are two authors, list the first author last name first and the second one first name first: Lunsford, Andrea, and Lisa Ede. Put their names in the order given in the work. For three or more authors, give the first author's name followed by "et al.": Greenblatt, Stephen, et al.

- Include any middle names or initials: Toklas, Alice B.

- If the author is a group or organization, use the full name, omitting any initial article: United Nations.

- If an author uses a handle that is significantly different from their name, include the handle in square brackets after the name: Ocasio-Cortez, Alexandria [@AOC].

- If there's no known author, start the entry with the title.

- If there's an editor but no author, put the editor's name in the author position and specify their role: Lunsford, Andrea, editor.

- If you're citing someone in addition to an author—an editor, translator, director, or other contributors—specify their role. If there are multiple contributors, put the one whose work you wish to highlight before the title, and list any others you want to mention after the title. If you don't want to highlight one particular contributor, start with the title and include any contributors after the title. For contributors named before the title, specify their role after the name: Fincher, David, director. For those named after the title, specify their role first: Directed by David Fincher.

TITLES

- Include any subtitles, and capitalize all the words except for articles ("a," "an," "the"), prepositions ("to," "at," "from," and so on), and coordinating conjunctions ("and," "but," "for," "or," "nor," "so," "yet")—unless they are the first or last word of a title or subtitle.

- Italicize the titles of books, periodicals, websites, and other long works: *Pride and Prejudice*, *Wired*.

- Put quotation marks around the titles of articles and other short works: "Letter from Birmingham Jail."

- To document a source that has no title, describe it without italics or quotation marks: Letter to the author, Photograph of a tree. For a short, untitled email, text message, tweet, or poem, you may want to include the text itself instead: Dickinson, Emily. "Immortal is an ample word." *American Poems*, www.americanpoems.com/poets/emilydickinson /immortal-is-an-ample-word.

VERSIONS

- If you cite a source that's available in more than one version, specify the one you consulted in your works-cited entry. Write ordinal numbers with numerals, and abbreviate "edition": 2nd ed. Write out names of specific versions, and capitalize following a period or if the name is a proper noun: King James Version, unabridged version, director's cut.

NUMBERS

- If you cite a book that's published in multiple volumes, indicate the volume number. Abbreviate "volume," and write the number as a numeral: vol. 2.

- Indicate volume and issue numbers (if any) of journals, abbreviating both "volume" and "number": vol. 123, no. 4.

- If you cite a TV show or podcast episode, indicate the season and episode numbers: season 1, episode 4.

PUBLISHERS

- Write publishers', studios', and networks' names in full, but omit initial articles and business words like "Inc." or "Company."

- For academic presses, use "U" for "University" and "P" for "Press": Princeton UP, U of California P. Spell out "Press" if the name doesn't include "University": MIT Press.

- Many publishers use "&" in their name: Simon & Schuster. MLA says to use "and" instead: Simon and Schuster.

- If the publisher is a division of an organization, list the organization and any divisions from largest to smallest: Stanford U, Center for the Study of Language and Information, Metaphysics Research Lab.

DATES

- Whether to give just the year or to include the month and day depends on the source. In general, give the full date that you find there. If the date is unknown, simply omit it.
- Abbreviate the months except for May, June, and July: Jan., Feb., Mar., Apr., Aug., Sept., Oct., Nov., Dec.
- For books, give the publication date on the copyright page: 1948. If a book lists more than one date, use the most recent one.
- Periodicals may be published annually, monthly, seasonally, weekly, or daily. Give the full date that you find there: 2019, Apr. 2019, 16 Apr. 2019. Do not capitalize the names of seasons: spring 2021.
- For online sources, use the copyright date or the full publication date that you find there, or a date of revision. If the source does not give a date, use the date of access: Accessed 6 June 2020. Give a date of access as well for online sources you think are likely to change, or for websites that have disappeared.

LOCATION

- For most print articles and other short works, give a page number or range of pages: p. 24, pp. 24-35. For articles that are not on consecutive pages, give the first page number with a plus sign: pp. 24+.
- If it's necessary to specify a section of a source, give the section name before the page numbers: Sunday Review sec., p. 3.
- Indicate the location of an online source by giving a DOI if one is available; if not, give a URL—and use a permalink if one is available. MLA notes that URLs are not always reliable, so ask your instructor if you should include them. DOIs should start with "https://doi.org/"—but no need to include "https://" for a URL, unless you want the URL to be a hyperlink.

- For a geographical location, give enough information to identify it: a city (Houston), a city and state (Portland, Maine), or a city and country (Manaus, Brazil).
- For something seen in a museum, archive, or elsewhere, name the institution and its location: Maine Jewish Museum, Portland, Maine.
- For performances or other live presentations, name the venue and its location: Mark Taper Forum, Los Angeles.

PUNCTUATION
- Use a period after the author name(s) that start an entry (Morrison, Toni.) and the title of the source you're documenting (*Beloved*.).
- Use a comma between the author's last and first names: Ede, Lisa.
- Some URLs will not fit on one line. MLA does not specify where to break a URL, but we recommend breaking it before a punctuation mark. Do *not* add a hyphen or a space.
- Sometimes you'll need to provide information about more than one work for a single source—for instance, when you cite an article from a periodical that you access through a database. MLA refers to the periodical and database (or any other entity that holds a source) as "containers" and specifies certain punctuation. Use commas between elements within each container, and put a period at the end of each container. For example:

Semuels, Alana. "The Future Will Be Quiet." *The Atlantic,* Apr. 2016,
pp. 19-20. *ProQuest,* search.proquest.com/docview
/1777443553?accountid+42654.

The guidelines that follow will help you document the kinds of sources you're likely to use. The first section shows how to acknowledge authors and other contributors and applies to all kinds of sources—print, online, or others. Later sections show how to treat titles, publication information, location, and access information for many specific kinds of sources. In general, provide as much information as possible for each source—enough to tell readers how to find a source if they wish to access it themselves.

SOURCES NOT COVERED

These guidelines will help you cite a variety of sources, but there may be sources you want to use that aren't mentioned here. If you're citing a source that isn't covered, consult the MLA style blog at style.mla.org, or ask them a question at style.mla.org/ask-a-question.

Authors and Contributors

When you name authors and other contributors in your citations, you are crediting them for their work and letting readers know who's in on the conversation. The following guidelines for citing authors and contributors apply to all sources you cite: in print, online, or in some other media.

1. ONE AUTHOR

> Author's Last Name, First Name. *Title.* Publisher, Date.

> Anderson, Chris. *The Long Tail: Why the Future of Business Is Selling Less of More.* Hyperion, 2006.

2. TWO AUTHORS

> 1st Author's Last Name, First Name, and 2nd Author's First and Last Names. *Title.* Publisher, Date.

> Lunsford, Andrea, and Lisa Ede. *Singular Texts/Plural Authors: Perspectives on Collaborative Writing.* Southern Illinois UP, 1990.

3. THREE OR MORE AUTHORS

> 1st Author's Last Name, First Name, et al. *Title.* Publisher, Date.

> Sebranek, Patrick, et al. *Writers INC: A Guide to Writing, Thinking, and Learning.* Write Source, 1990.

4. TWO OR MORE WORKS BY THE SAME AUTHOR

Give the author's name in the first entry, and then use three hyphens in the author slot for each of the subsequent works, listing them alphabetically by the first word of each title and ignoring any initial articles.

TITLE   AUTHOR   PUBLICATION

Author's Last Name, First Name. *Title That Comes First*
    Alphabetically. Publisher, Date.

---. *Title That Comes Next Alphabetically.* Publisher, Date.

Kaplan, Robert D. *The Coming Anarchy: Shattering the Dreams of the*
    Post Cold War. Random House, 2000.

---. *Eastward to Tartary: Travels in the Balkans, the Middle East, and the*
    Caucasus. Random House, 2000.

5. AUTHOR AND EDITOR OR TRANSLATOR

Author's Last Name, First Name. *Title.* Role by First and Last
    Names, Publisher, Date.

Austen, Jane. *Emma.* Edited by Stephen M. Parrish, W. W. Norton, 2000.

Dostoevsky, Fyodor. *Crime and Punishment.* Translated by Richard Pevear
    and Larissa Volokhonsky, Vintage Books, 1993.

Start with the editor or translator, followed by their role, if you are focusing on that contribution rather than the author's. If there is a translator
but no author, start with the title.

Pevear, Richard, and Larissa Volokhonsky, translators. *Crime and*
    Punishment. By Fyodor Dostoevsky, Vintage Books, 1993.

Beowulf. Translated by Kevin Crossley-Holland, Macmillan, 1968.

6. NO AUTHOR OR EDITOR

When there's no known author or editor, start with the title.

The Turner Collection in the Clore Gallery. Tate Publications, 1987.

"Being Invisible Closer to Reality." *The Atlanta Journal-Constitution,* 11
    Aug. 2008, p. A3.

7. ORGANIZATION OR GOVERNMENT AS AUTHOR

> Organization Name. *Title.* Publisher, Date.

> Diagram Group. *The Macmillan Visual Desk Reference.* Macmillan, 1993.

For a government publication, give the name that is shown in the source.

> United States, Department of Health and Human Services, National
> Institute of Mental Health. *Autism Spectrum Disorders.* Government
> Printing Office, 2004.

When a nongovernment organization is both author and publisher, start with the title and list the organization only as the publisher.

> *Stylebook on Religion 2000: A Reference Guide and Usage Manual.*
> Catholic News Service, 2002.

If a division of an organization is listed as the author, give the division as the author and the organization as the publisher.

> Center for Workforce Studies. *2005-13: Demographics of the U.S.*
> *Psychology Workforce.* American Psychological Association, July 2015.

Articles and Other Short Works

Articles, essays, reviews, and other shorts works are found in journals, magazines, newspapers, other periodicals, and also in books—all of which you may find in print, online, or in a database. For most short works, you'll need to provide information about the author, the titles of both the short work and the longer work where it's found, any page numbers, and various kinds of publication information, all explained below.

8. ARTICLE IN A JOURNAL

PRINT

> Author's Last Name, First Name. "Title of Article." *Name*
> *of Journal,* Volume, Issue, Date, Pages.

> Cooney, Brian C. "Considering *Robinson Crusoe's* 'Liberty of Conscience' in an
> Age of Terror." *College English,* vol. 69, no. 3, Jan. 2007, pp. 197-215.

TITLE   AUTHOR   PUBLICATION

Documentation Map (MLA)
Article in a Print Journal

Marge Simpson, Blue-Haired Housewife: •·············· TITLE OF ARTICLE
Defining Domesticity on *The Simpsons*

JESSAMYN NEUHAUS   •·············· AUTHOR

MORE THAN TWENTY SEASONS AFTER ITS DEBUT AS A SHORT ON *THE Tracy Ullman Show* in 1989, pundits, politicians, scholars, journalists, and critics continue to discuss and debate the meaning and relevance of *The Simpsons* to American society. For academics and educators, the show offers an especially dense pop culture text, inspiring articles and anthologies examining *The Simpsons* in light of American religious life, the representation of homosexuality in cartoons, and the use of pop culture in the classroom, among many other topics (Dennis; Frank; Henry "The Whole World's Gone Gay"; Hobbs; Kristiansen). Philosophers and literary theorists in particular are intrigued by the quintessentially postmodern self-aware form and content of *The Simpsons* and the questions about identity, spectatorship, and consumer culture it raises (Alberti; Bybee and Overbeck; Glynn; Henry "The Triumph of Popular Culture"; Herron; Hull; Irwin et al.; Ott; Parisi).

Simpsons observers frequently note that this TV show begs one of the fundamental questions in cultural studies: can pop culture ever provide a site of individual or collective resistance or must it always ultimately function in the interests of the capitalist dominant ideology? Is *The Simpsons* a brilliant satire of virtually every cherished American myth about public and private life, offering dissatisfied Americans the opportunity to critically reflect on contemporary issues (Turner 435)? Or is it simply another TV show making money for the Fox Network? Is *The Simpsons* an empty, cynical, even nihilistic view of the world, lulling its viewers into laughing hopelessly at the pointless futility of

NAME OF JOURNAL
VOLUME
ISSUE
PAGES
YEAR

The Journal of Popular Culture, Vol. 43, No. 4, 2010, pp.761-81 •··········
© 2010, Wiley Periodicals, Inc.

Neuhaus, Jessamyn. "Marge Simpson, Blue-Haired Housewife:
   Defining Domesticity on *The Simpsons*." *The Journal of
   Popular Culture*, vol. 43, no. 4, 2010, pp. 761-81.

● 582–89
for more
on citing
articles
MLA style

Documentation Map (MLA)
Article in an Online Magazine

URL

NAME OF MAGAZINE

TITLE OF
ARTICLE

AUTHOR

DATE

595–98
for more
on citing
websites
MLA style

Segal, Michael. "The Hit Book That Came from Mars." *Nautilus*,
8 Jan. 2015, nautil.us/issue/20/creativity/the-hit-book-that
-came-from-mars.

TITLE   AUTHOR   PUBLICATION

ONLINE

Author's Last Name, First Name. "Title of Article." *Name of
Journal*, Volume, Issue, Date, DOI *or* URL.

Schmidt, Desmond. "A Model of Versions and Layers." Digital Humanities
Quarterly, vol. 13, no. 3, 2019, www.digitalhumanities.org/dhq
/vol/13/3/000430/000430.html.

9. ARTICLE IN A MAGAZINE

PRINT

Author's Last Name, First Name. "Title of Article." *Name
of Magazine*, Volume (if any), Issue (if any), Date, Pages.

Burt, Tequia. "Legacy of Activism: Concerned Black Students' 50-Year
History at Grinnell College." *Grinnell Magazine*, vol. 48, no. 4,
summer 2016, pp. 32-38.

ONLINE

Author's Last Name, First Name. "Title of Article." *Name
of Magazine*, Volume (if any), Issue (if any), Date, DOI *or* URL.

Brooks, Arthur C. "The Hidden Toll of Remote Work." *The Atlantic*,
1 Apr. 2021, www.theatlantic.com/family/archive/2021/04/zoom
-remote-work-loneliness-happiness/618473.

10. ARTICLE IN A NEWS PUBLICATION

PRINT

Author's Last Name, First Name. "Title of Article." *Name
of Publication*, Date, Pages.

Saulny, Susan, and Jacques Steinberg. "On College Forms, a Question of
Race Can Perplex." *The New York Times*, 14 June 2011, p. A1.

To document a particular edition of a newspaper, list the edition before
the date. If a section name or number is needed to locate the article,
put that detail after the date.

Burns, John F., and Miguel Helft. "Under Pressure, YouTube Withdraws Muslim Cleric's Videos." *The New York Times*, late ed., 4 Nov. 2010, sec. 1, p. 13.

ONLINE

Author's Last Name, First Name. "Title of Article." *Name of Publication*, Date, URL.

Banerjee, Neela. "Proposed Religion-Based Program for Federal Inmates Is Canceled." *The New York Times,* 28 Oct. 2006, www.nytimes.com/2006/10/28/us/28prison.html.

11. ARTICLE ACCESSED THROUGH A DATABASE

Author's Last Name, First Name. "Title of Article." *Name of Periodical*, Volume, Issue, Date, Pages. *Name of Database*, DOI or URL.

Stalter, Sunny. "Subway Ride and Subway System in Hart Crane's 'The Tunnel.'" *Journal of Modern Literature*, vol. 33, no. 2, Jan. 2010, pp. 70-91. *JSTOR*, https://doi.org/10.2979/jml.2010.33.2.70.

12. ENTRY IN A REFERENCE WORK

PRINT

Author's Last Name, First Name (if any). "Title of Entry." *Title of Reference Book*, edited by First and Last Names (if any), Edition number, Volume (if any), Publisher, Date, Pages.

Fritz, Jan Marie. "Clinical Sociology." *Encyclopedia of Sociology*, edited by Edgar F. Borgatta and Rhonda J. V. Montgomery, 2nd ed., vol. 1, Macmillan Reference USA, 2000, pp. 323-29.

"California." *The New Columbia Encyclopedia*, edited by William H. Harris and Judith S. Levey, 4th ed., Columbia UP, 1975, pp. 423-24.

Documentation Map (MLA)
Journal Article Accessed through a Database

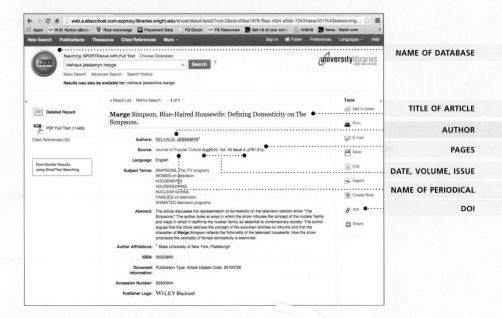

Neuhaus, Jessamyn. "Marge Simpson, Blue-Haired Housewife:
    Defining Domesticity on *The Simpsons*." *Journal of Popular
    Culture*, vol. 43, no. 4, Aug. 2010, pp. 761-81. *EBSCOhost*,
    https://doi.org/10.1111/j.1540-5931.2010.00769.x.

ONLINE

Document online reference works the same as print ones, adding the URL after the date of publication.

> "Baseball." *The Columbia Electronic Encyclopedia*, edited by Paul Lagassé, 6th ed., Columbia UP, 2012, www.infoplease.com/encyclopedia.

13. EDITORIAL OR OP-ED

EDITORIAL

> Editorial Board. "Title." *Name of Periodical*, Date, Page *or* URL.

> Editorial Board. "A New Look for Local News Coverage." *The Lakeville Journal*, 13 Feb. 2020, p. A8.

> Editorial Board. "Editorial: Protect Reporters at Protest Scenes." *Los Angeles Times*, 11 Mar. 2021, www.latimes.com/opinion/story/2021 -03-11/reporters-protest-scenes.

OP-ED

> Author's Last Name, First Name. "Title." *Name of Periodical*, Date, Page *or* URL.

> Okafor, Kingsley. "Opinion: The First Step to COVID Vaccine Equity Is Overall Health Equity." *The Denver Post*, 15 Apr. 2021, www.denverpost.com/2021/04/15/covid-vaccine-equity-kaiser.

If it's not clear that it's an op-ed, add a label at the end.

> Balf, Todd. "Falling in Love with Swimming." *The New York Times*, 17 Apr. 2021, p. A21. Op-ed.

14. LETTER TO THE EDITOR

> Author's Last Name, First Name. "Title of Letter (if any)." *Name of Periodical*, Date, Page *or* URL.

> Pinker, Steven. "Language Arts." *The New Yorker*, 4 June 2012, p. 10.

If the letter has no title, include "Letter" after the author's name.

> Fleischmann, W. B. Letter. *The New York Review of Books*, 1 June 1963,
> www.nybooks.com/articles/1963/06/01/letter-21.

15. REVIEW

PRINT

> Reviewer's Last Name, First Name. "Title of Review." *Name
> of Periodical*, Date, Pages.

> Frank, Jeffrey. "Body Count." *The New Yorker*, 30 July 2007, pp. 86-87.

ONLINE

> Reviewer's Last Name, First Name. "Title of Review." *Name of
> Periodical*, Date, URL.

> Donadio, Rachel. "Italy's Great, Mysterious Storyteller." *The New York
> Review of Books*, 18 Dec. 2014, www.nybooks.com/articles/2014/12
> /18/italys-great-mysterious-storyteller.

If a review has no title, include the title and author of the work being reviewed after the reviewer's name.

> Lohier, Patrick. Review of *Exhalation*, by Ted Chiang. *Harvard Review
> Online*, 4 Oct. 2019, www.harvardreview.org/book-review
> /exhalation.

16. COMMENT ON AN ONLINE ARTICLE

> Commenter's Last Name, First Name *or* Username. Comment on "Title of
> Article." *Name of Periodical*, Date posted, Time posted, URL.

> ZeikJT. Comment on "The Post-Disaster Artist." *Polygon*, 6 May 2020,
> 4:33 a.m., www.polygon.com/2020/5/5/21246679/josh-trank-capone
> -interview-fantastic-four-chronicle.

Books and Parts of Books

For most books, you'll need to provide information about the author, the title, the publisher, and the year of publication. If you found the book inside a larger volume, a database, or some other work, be sure to specify that as well.

17. BASIC ENTRIES FOR A BOOK

PRINT

Author's Last Name, First Name. *Title.* Publisher, Year of publication.

Watson, Brad. *Miss Jane.* W. W. Norton, 2016.

EBOOK

Author's Last Name, First Name. *Title.* Ebook ed., Publisher, Year of Publication.

Watson, Brad. *Miss Jane.* Ebook ed., W. W. Norton, 2016.

ON A WEBSITE

Author's Last Name, First Name. *Title.* Publisher, Year of publication, DOI *or* URL.

Ball, Cheryl E., and Drew M. Loewe, editors. *Bad Ideas about Writing.* West Virginia U Libraries, 2017, textbooks.lib.wvu.edu/badideas /badideasaboutwriting-book.pdf.

WHEN THE PUBLISHER IS THE AUTHOR

Title. Edition number (if any), Publisher, Year of publication.

MLA Handbook. 9th ed., Modern Language Association of America, 2021.

18. ANTHOLOGY OR EDITED COLLECTION

Last Name, First Name, editor. *Title.* Publisher, Year of publication.

Kitchen, Judith, and Mary Paumier Jones, editors. *In Short: A Collection of Brief Nonfiction.* W. W. Norton, 1996.

Documentation Map (MLA)
Print Book

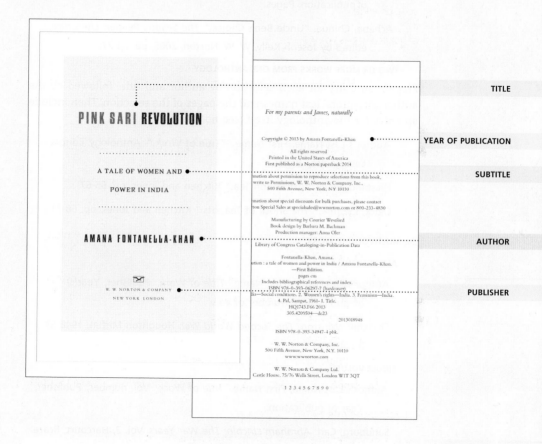

TITLE

YEAR OF PUBLICATION

SUBTITLE

AUTHOR

PUBLISHER

Fontanella-Khan, Amana. *Pink Sari Revolution: A Tale of Women and Power in India.* W. W. Norton, 2013.

590–95 for more on citing books MLA style

19. WORK IN AN ANTHOLOGY

Author's Last Name, First Name. "Title of Work." *Title of Anthology*, edited by First and Last Names, Publisher, Year of publication, Pages.

Achebe, Chinua. "Uncle Ben's Choice." *The Seagull Reader: Literature*, edited by Joseph Kelly, W. W. Norton, 2005, pp. 23-27.

TWO OR MORE WORKS FROM ONE ANTHOLOGY

Prepare an entry for each selection by author and title, followed by the anthology editors' last names and the pages of the selection. Then include an entry for the anthology itself (see no. 18).

Author's Last Name, First Name. "Title of Work." Anthology Editors' Last Names, Pages.

Hiestand, Emily. "Afternoon Tea." Kitchen and Jones, pp. 65-67.

Ozick, Cynthia. "The Shock of Teapots." Kitchen and Jones, pp. 68-71.

20. MULTIVOLUME WORK

ALL VOLUMES

Author's Last Name, First Name. *Title of Work.* Publisher, Year(s) of publication. Number of vols.

Churchill, Winston. *The Second World War.* Houghton Mifflin, 1948-53. 6 vols.

SINGLE VOLUME

Author's Last Name, First Name. *Title of Work.* Vol. number, Publisher, Year of publication.

Sandburg, Carl. *Abraham Lincoln: The War Years.* Vol. 2, Harcourt, Brace and World, 1939.

If the volume has its own title, include it after the author's name, and indicate the volume number and series title after the year.

Caro, Robert A. *Means of Ascent*. Vintage Books, 1990. Vol. 2 of *The Years of Lyndon Johnson*.

21. BOOK IN A SERIES

Author's Last Name, First Name. *Title of Book*. Edited by First and Last Names, Publisher, Year of publication. Series Title.

Walker, Alice. *Everyday Use*. Edited by Barbara T. Christian, Rutgers UP, 1994. Women Writers: Texts and Contexts.

22. GRAPHIC NARRATIVE OR COMIC BOOK

Author's Last Name, First Name. *Title*. Publisher, Year of publication.

Barry, Lynda. *One! Hundred! Demons!* Drawn and Quarterly, 2005.

If the work has both an author and an illustrator, start with the one you want to highlight, and label the role of anyone who's not an author.

Pekar, Harvey. *Bob and Harv's Comics*. Illustrated by R. Crumb, Running Press, 1996.

Crumb, R., illustrator. *Bob and Harv's Comics*. By Harvey Pekar, Running Press, 1996.

To cite several contributors, you can also start with the title.

Secret Invasion. By Brian Michael Bendis, illustrated by Leinil Yu, inked by Mark Morales, Marvel, 2009.

23. SACRED TEXT

If you cite a specific edition of a religious text, you need to include it in your works-cited list.

The New English Bible with the Apocrypha. Oxford UP, 1971.

The Torah: A Modern Commentary. W. Gunther Plaut, general editor, Union of American Hebrew Congregations, 1981.

24. EDITION OTHER THAN THE FIRST

> Author's Last Name, First Name. *Title.* Edition name *or* number, Publisher, Year of publication.

> Smart, Ninian. *The World's Religions.* 2nd ed., Cambridge UP, 1998.

25. REPUBLISHED WORK

> Author's Last Name, First Name. *Title.* Year of original publication. Current publisher, Year of republication.

> Bierce, Ambrose. *Civil War Stories.* 1909. Dover, 1994.

26. FOREWORD, INTRODUCTION, PREFACE, OR AFTERWORD

> Part Author's Last Name, First Name. Name of Part. *Title of Book,* by Author's First and Last Names, Publisher, Year of publication, Pages.

> Tanner, Tony. Introduction. *Pride and Prejudice,* by Jane Austen, Penguin, 1972, pp. 7-46.

27. PUBLISHED LETTER

> Letter Writer's Last Name, First Name. "Title of letter." Day Month Year. *Title of Book,* edited by First and Last Names, Publisher, Year of publication, Pages.

> White, E. B. "To Carol Angell." 28 May 1970. *Letters of E. B. White,* edited by Dorothy Lobrano Guth, Harper and Row, 1976, p. 600.

28. PAPER HEARD AT A CONFERENCE

> Author's Last Name, First Name. "Title of Paper." Conference, Day Month Year, Location.

> Hern, Katie. "Inside an Accelerated Reading and Writing Classroom." Conference on Acceleration in Developmental Education, 15 June 2016, Sheraton Inner Harbor Hotel, Baltimore.

29. DISSERTATION

> Author's Last Name, First Name. *Title.* Year. Institution, PhD
>   dissertation. *Name of Database*, URL.

> Simington, Maire Orav. *Chasing the American Dream Post World War II:*
>   *Perspectives from Literature and Advertising.* 2003. Arizona State U,
>   PhD dissertation. *ProQuest*, search.proquest.com/docview/305340098.

For an unpublished dissertation, end with the institution and a description of the work.

> Kim, Loel. *Students Respond to Teacher Comments: A Comparison of*
>   *Online Written and Voice Modalities.* 1998. Carnegie Mellon U, PhD
>   dissertation.

Websites

Many sources are available in multiple media—for example, a print periodical that is also on the web and contained in digital databases—but some are published only on websites. A website can have an author, an editor, or neither. Some sites have a publisher, and some do not. Include whatever information is available. If the publisher and title of the site are essentially the same, omit the name of the publisher.

30. ENTIRE WEBSITE

> Editor's Last Name, First Name, role. *Title of Site.* Publisher, Date, URL.

> Proffitt, Michael, chief editor. *The Oxford English Dictionary.* Oxford UP,
>   2021, www.oed.com.

PERSONAL WEBSITE

> Author's Last Name, First Name. *Title of Site.* Date, URL.

> Park, Linda Sue. *Linda Sue Park: Author and Educator.* 2021,
>   lindasuepark.com.

Documentation Map (MLA)
Work on a Website

URL

TITLE OF SITE

TITLE OF WORK

DATE

AUTHOR

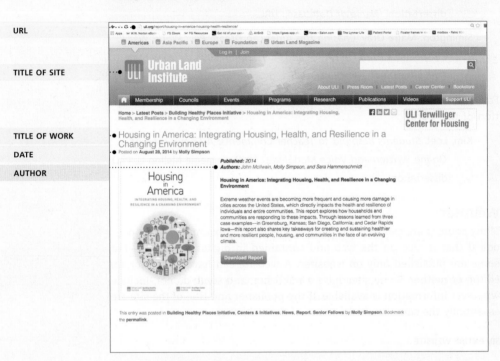

595–97
for more
on citing
websites
MLA style

McIlwain, John, et al. "Housing in America: Integrating Housing, Health, and Resilience in a Changing Environment." *Urban Land Institute*, 28 Aug. 2014, uli.org/report/housing-in -america-housing-health-resilience.

TITLE   AUTHOR   PUBLICATION

If the site is likely to change, if it has no date, or if it no longer exists, include a date of access.

> *Archive of Our Own*. Organization for Transformative Works,
>   archiveofourown.org. Accessed 23 Apr. 2021.

31. WORK ON A WEBSITE

> Author's Last Name, First Name (if any). "Title of Work." *Title
>   of Site*, Publisher (if any), Date, URL.

> Cesareo, Kerry. "Moving Closer to Tackling Deforestation at Scale."
>   *World Wildlife Fund*, 20 Oct. 2020, www.worldwildlife.org/blogs
>   /sustainability-works/posts/moving-closer-to-tackling-deforestation
>   -at-scale.

32. BLOG ENTRY

> Author's Last Name, First Name. "Title of Blog Entry." *Title
>   of Blog*, Date, URL.

> Hollmichel, Stefanie. "Bring Up the Bodies." *So Many Books*, 10 Feb.
>   2014, somanybooksblog.com/2014/02/10/bring-up-the-bodies.

Document a whole blog as you would an entire website (no. 30) and a comment on a blog as you would a comment on an online article (no. 16).

33. WIKI

> "Title of Entry." *Title of Wiki*, Publisher, Date, URL.

> "Pi." *Wikipedia*, Wikimedia Foundation, 28 Aug. 2013, en.wikipedia.org
>   /wiki/Pi.

Personal Communication and Social Media

34. PERSONAL LETTER

Sender's Last Name, First Name. Letter to the author. Day Month Year.

Quindlen, Anna. Letter to the author. 11 Apr. 2013.

35. EMAIL OR TEXT MESSAGE

Sender's Last Name, First Name. Email *or* Text message to First Name Last Name *or* to the author. Day Month Year.

Smith, William. Email to Richard Bullock. 19 Nov. 2013.

Rombes, Maddy. Text message to Isaac Cohen. 4 May 2021.

O'Malley, Kit. Text message to the author. 2 June 2020.

You can also include the text of a short email or text message, with a label at the end.

Rust, Max. "Trip to see the cows tomorrow?" 27 Apr. 2021. Email.

36. POST TO *TWITTER*, *INSTAGRAM*, OR OTHER SOCIAL MEDIA

Author. "Title." *Title of Site*, Day Month Year, URL.

Oregon Zoo. "Winter Wildlife Wonderland." *Facebook*, 8 Feb. 2019, www.facebook.com/80229441108/videos/2399570506799549.

If there's no title, you can use a concise description or the text of a short post.

Millman, Debbie. Photos of Roxane Gay. *Instagram*, 18 Feb. 2021, www .instagram.com/p/CLcT_EnhnWT.

Obama, Barack [@POTUS44]. "It's been the honor of my life to serve you. You made me a better leader and a better man." *Twitter*, 20 Jan. 2017, twitter.com/POTUS44/status/822445882247413761.

Audio, Visual, and Other Sources

37. ADVERTISEMENT

PRINT

Description of ad. *Title of Periodical*, Date, Page.

Advertisement for Grey Goose. *Wine Spectator*, 18 Dec. 2020, p. 22.

VIDEO

"Title." *Title of Site*, uploaded by Company, Date, URL.

"First Visitors." *YouTube*, uploaded by Snickers, 20 Aug. 2020,
www.youtube.com/watch?v=negeco0b1L0.

38. ART

ORIGINAL

Artist's Last Name, First Name. *Title of Art.* Year created, Location.

Van Gogh, Vincent. *The Potato Eaters.* 1885, Van Gogh Museum,
Amsterdam.

IN A BOOK

Artist's Last Name, First Name. *Title of Art.* Year created, Location. *Title of
Book*, by First and Last Names, Publisher, Year of publication, Page.

Van Gogh, Vincent. *The Potato Eaters.* 1885, Scottish National Gallery.
*History of Art: A Survey of the Major Visual Arts from the Dawn of
History to the Present Day*, by H. W. Janson, Prentice Hall / Harry N.
Abrams, 1969, p. 508.

ONLINE

Artist's Last Name, First Name. *Title of Art.* Year created. *Title
of Site*, URL.

Warhol, Andy. *Self-portrait.* 1979. *J. Paul Getty Museum*, www.getty
.edu/art/collection/objects/106971/andy-warhol-self-portrait
-american-1979.

39. CARTOON

PRINT

> Author's Last Name, First Name. Cartoon *or* "Title of Cartoon." *Name of Periodical*, Date, Page.

> Mankoff, Robert. Cartoon. *The New Yorker*, 3 May 1993, p. 50.

ONLINE

> Author's Last Name, First Name. Cartoon *or* "Title of Cartoon." *Title of Site*, Date, URL.

> Munroe, Randall. "Up Goer Five." *xkcd*, 12 Nov. 2012, xkcd.com/1133.

40. SUPREME COURT CASE

> United States, Supreme Court. *First Defendant v. Second Defendant.* Date of decision. *Title of Source Site*, Publisher, URL.

> United States, Supreme Court. *District of Columbia v. Heller.* 26 June 2008. *Legal Information Institute*, Cornell Law School, www.law.cornell.edu/supremecourt/text/07-290.

41. FILM

Name individuals based on the focus of your project—the director, the screenwriter, or someone else.

> *Title of Film.* Role by First and Last Names, Production Company, Date.

> *Breakfast at Tiffany's.* Directed by Blake Edwards, Paramount, 1961.

ONLINE

> *Title of Film.* Role by First and Last Names, Production Company, Date. *Title of Site*, URL.

> *Interstellar.* Directed by Christopher Nolan, Paramount, 2014. *Amazon Prime Video*, www.amazon.com/Interstellar-Matthew-McConaughey/dp/B00TU9UFTS.

If your essay focuses on one contributor, you may put their name before the title.

> Edwards, Blake, director. *Breakfast at Tiffany's*. Paramount, 1961.

42. TV SHOW EPISODE

Name contributors based on the focus of your project—director, creator, actors, or others. If you don't want to highlight anyone in particular, don't include any contributors.

BROADCAST

> "Title of Episode." *Title of Program*, role by First and Last Names (if any), season, episode, Production Company, Date.

> "The Storm." *Avatar: The Last Airbender*, created by Michael Dante DiMartino and Bryan Konietzko, season 1, episode 12, Nickelodeon Animation Studios, 3 June 2005.

DVD

> "Title of Episode." Broadcast Date. *Title of DVD*, role by First and Last Names (if any), season, episode, Production Company, Release Date, disc number. DVD.

> "The Storm." 2005. *Avatar: The Last Airbender: The Complete Book 1 Collection*, created by Michael Dante DiMartino and Bryan Konietzko, episode 12, Nickelodeon Animation Studios, 2006, disc 3. DVD.

STREAMING ONLINE

> "Title of Episode." *Title of Program*, role by First and Last Names (if any), season, episode, Production Company, Date. *Title of Site*, URL.

> "The Storm." *Avatar: The Last Airbender*, season 1, episode 12, Nickelodeon Animation Studios, 2005. *Netflix*, www.netflix.com.

STREAMING ON AN APP

"Title of Episode." *Title of Program*, role by First and Last Names (if
any), season, episode, Production Company, Date. *Name of* app.

"The Storm." *Avatar: The Last Airbender*, season 1, episode 12,
Nickelodeon Animation Studios, 2005. *Netflix* app.

If you're focusing on a contributor who's relevant specifically to the
episode you're citing, include their name after the episode title.

"The Storm." Directed by Lauren MacMullan. *Avatar: The Last Airbender*,
season 1, episode 12, Nickelodeon Animation Studios, 3 June 2005.

43. ONLINE VIDEO

"Title of Video." *Title of Site*, uploaded by Uploader's Name, Day
Month Year, URL.

"Everything Wrong with *National Treasure* in 13 Minutes or Less."
YouTube, uploaded by CinemaSins, 21 Aug. 2014, www.youtube
.com/watch?v=1ul-_ZWvXTs.

44. PRESENTATION ON *ZOOM* OR OTHER VIRTUAL PLATFORM

MLA doesn't give specific guidance on how to cite a virtual presentation,
but this is what we recommend. See style.mla.org for more information.

Author's Last Name, First Name. "Title." Sponsoring Institution, Day
Month Year. *Name of Platform*.

Budhathoki, Thir. "Cross-Cultural Perceptions of Literacies in Student
Writing." Conference on College Composition and Communication,
9 Apr. 2021. *Zoom*.

45. INTERVIEW

If it's not clear that it's an interview, add a label at the end. If you are citing
a transcript of an interview, indicate that at the end as well.

PUBLISHED

Subject's Last Name, First Name. *"Title of Interview."* Interview by First Name Last Name (if given). *Name of Publication,* Date, Pages *or* URL.

Whitehead, Colson. "Colson Whitehead: By the Book." *The New York Times,* 15 May 2014, www.nytimes.com/2014/05/18/books/review /colson-whitehead-by-the-book.html. Interview.

PERSONAL

Subject's Last Name, First Name. Concise description. Day Month Year.

Bazelon, L. S. Telephone interview with the author. 4 Oct. 2020.

46. MAP

If the title doesn't make clear it's a map, add a label at the end.

Title of Map. Publisher, Date.

Brooklyn. J. B. Beers, 1874. Map.

47. MUSICAL SCORE

Composer's Last Name, First Name. *Title of Composition.* Publisher, Year of publication.

Frank, Gabriela Lena. *Compadrazgo.* G. Schirmer, 2007.

48. ORAL PRESENTATION

Presenter's Last Name, First Name. "Title of Presentation." Sponsoring Institution, Date, Location.

Cassin, Michael. "Nature in the Raw—The Art of Landscape Painting." Berkshire Institute for Lifelong Learning, 24 Mar. 2005, Clark Art Institute, Williamstown, Massachusetts.

49. PODCAST

If you accessed a podcast on the web, give the URL.

> "Title of Episode." *Title of Podcast*, hosted by First Name Last
> Name, season, episode, Production Company, Date, URL.

> "DUSTWUN." *Serial*, hosted by Sarah Koenig, season 2, episode 1, WBEZ /
> Serial Productions, 10 Dec. 2015, serialpodcast.org/season-two/1
> /dustwun.

THROUGH AN APP

> "DUSTWUN." *Serial*, hosted by Sarah Koenig, season 2, episode 1, WBEZ /
> Serial Productions, 10 Dec. 2015. *Spotify* app.

50. RADIO PROGRAM

> "Title of Episode." *Title of Program*, hosted by First Name Last
> Name, Station, Day Month Year.

> "In Defense of Ignorance." *This American Life*, hosted by Ira Glass, WBEZ,
> 22 Apr. 2016.

51. SOUND RECORDING

If you accessed a recording on the web, give the URL.

> Artist's Last Name, First Name. "Title of Work." *Title of Album*, Label,
> Date, URL.

> Beyoncé. "Pray You Catch Me." *Lemonade*, Parkwood Entertainment /
> Columbia Records, 2016, www.beyonce.com/album/lemonade
> -visual-album/songs.

THROUGH AN APP

> Simone, Nina. "To Be Young, Gifted and Black." *Black Gold*, RCA Records,
> 1969. *Spotify* app.

ON A CD

Artist's Last Name, First Name. "Title of Work." *Title of Album*, Label, Date. CD.

Brown, Greg. "Canned Goods." *The Live One*, Red House, 1995. CD.

52. VIDEO GAME

Title of Game. Version, Distributor, Date of release.

Animal Crossing: New Horizons. Version 1.1.4, Nintendo, 6 Apr. 2020.

FORMATTING A RESEARCH PAPER

Name, course, title. MLA does not require a separate title page, unless your paper is a group project. In the upper left-hand corner of your first page, include your name, your instructor's name, the course name and number, and the date. Center the title of your paper on the line after the date; capitalize it as you would a book title. If your paper is a group project, include all of that information on a title page instead, listing all the authors.

Page numbers. In the upper right-hand corner of each page, one-half inch below the top of the page, include your last name and the page number. If it's a group project and all the names don't fit, include only the page number. Number pages consecutively throughout your paper.

Font, spacing, margins, and indents. Choose a font that is easy to read (such as Times New Roman) and that provides a clear contrast between regular text and italic text. Set the font size between 11 and 13 points. Double-space the entire paper, including your works-cited list and any notes. Set one-inch margins at the top, bottom, and sides of your text; do not justify your text. The first line of each paragraph should be indented one-half inch from the left margin. End punctuation should be followed by one space.

Headings. Short essays do not generally need headings, but they can be useful in longer works. Use a large, bold font for the first level of heading, and smaller fonts and italics to signal lower-level headings. MLA requires that headings all be flush with the left margin.

First-Level Heading

Second-Level Heading

Third-Level Heading

Long quotations. When quoting more than three lines of poetry, more than four lines of prose, or dialogue between characters in a drama, set off the quotation from the rest of your text, indenting it one-half inch (or five spaces) from the left margin. Do not use quotation marks, and put any parenthetical documentation *after* the final punctuation.

> In *Eastward to Tartary*, Robert Kaplan captures ancient and contemporary Antioch for us:
>
> > At the height of its glory in the Roman-Byzantine age, when it had an amphitheater, public baths, aqueducts, and sewage pipes, half a million people lived in Antioch. Today the population is only 125,000. With sour relations between Turkey and Syria, and unstable politics throughout the Middle East, Antioch is now a backwater—seedy and tumbledown, with relatively few tourists. I found it altogether charming. (123)

> In the first stanza of Matthew Arnold's "Dover Beach," the exclamations make clear that the speaker is addressing someone who is also present in the scene:
>
> > Come to the window, sweet is the night air!
> > Only, from the long line of spray
> > Where the sea meets the moon-blanched land,
> > Listen! You hear the grating roar
> > Of pebbles which the waves draw back, and fling. (lines 6-10)

Be careful to maintain the poet's line breaks. If a line does not fit on one line of your paper, put the extra words on the next line. Indent that line an additional quarter inch (or two spaces). If a citation doesn't fit, put it on the next line, flush with the right margin.

Tables and illustrations. Insert illustrations and tables close to the text that discusses them, and be sure to make clear how they relate to your point. For tables, provide a number (Table 1) and a title on separate lines above the table. Below the table, provide a caption with source information and any notes. Notes should be indicated with lowercase letters. For graphs, photos, and other figures, provide a figure number (Fig. 1) and caption with source information below the figure. Use a lowercase "f" when referring to a figure in your text: (fig. 1). If you give only brief source information, use commas between elements—Zhu Wei, *New Pictures of the Strikingly Bizarre #9*, print, 2004—and include full source information in your list of works cited. If you give full source information in the caption, don't include the source in your list of works cited. Punctuate as you would in the works-cited list, but don't invert the author's name: Berenice Sydney. *Fast Rhythm*. 1972, Tate Britain, London.

List of works cited. Start your list on a new page, following any notes (see p. 574). Center the title, Works Cited, and double-space the entire list. Begin each entry at the left margin, and indent subsequent lines one-half inch (or five spaces). Alphabetize the list by authors' last names (or by editors' or translators' names, if appropriate). Alphabetize works with no author or editor by title, disregarding "A," "An," and "The." To cite more than one work by a single author, list them as in number 4 on page 580.

SAMPLE RESEARCH PAPER

The following report was written by Dylan Borchers for a first-year writing course. It's formatted according to the guidelines of the MLA (style.mla.org).

Sample Research Paper, MLA Style

$\frac{1}{2}$"

1"

Borchers   1

Dylan Borchers

Professor Bullock

English 102, Section 4

4 May 2019

Against the Odds:

Harry S. Truman and the Election of 1948

Just over a week before Election Day in 1948, a *New York Times* article noted "[t]he popular view that Gov. Thomas E. Dewey's election as President is a foregone conclusion" (Egan). This assessment of the race between incumbent Democrat Harry S. Truman and Dewey, his Republican challenger, was echoed a week later when *Life* magazine published a photograph whose caption labeled Dewey "The Next President" (Photograph). In a *Newsweek* survey of fifty prominent political writers, each predicted Truman's defeat, and *Time* correspondents declared Dewey would carry 39 of the 48 states (Donaldson 210). Nearly every major US media outlet endorsed Dewey. As historian Robert Ferrell observes, even Truman's wife, Bess, thought he would lose (270).

The results of an election are not easily predicted, as is shown in the famous photograph in which Truman holds up a newspaper proclaiming Dewey the victor (fig. 1). Not only did Truman win, but he won by a significant margin: 303 electoral votes and 24,179,259 popular votes to Dewey's 189 electoral votes and 21,991,291 popular votes (Donaldson 204-07). In fact, many historians and political analysts argue that Truman would have won by an even greater margin had third-party candidates Henry A. Wallace and Strom Thurmond not won votes (McCullough 711). Although Truman's defeat was predicted, those predictions themselves, Dewey's passiveness as a campaigner, and Truman's zeal turned the tide for a Truman victory.

1"

1"

1"

Illustration is positioned close to the text to which it relates, with figure number, caption, and parenthetical documentation.

Fig. 1. President Harry S. Truman holds up an edition of the *Chicago Daily Tribune* that mistakenly announced "Dewey Defeats Truman." Byron Rollins, *Dewey Defeats Truman*, photograph, 1948.

In the months preceding the election, public opinion polls predicted that Dewey would win by a large margin. Pollster Elmo Roper stopped polling in September, believing there was no reason to continue, given a seemingly inevitable Dewey landslide. Although the margin narrowed as the election drew near, other pollsters predicted a Dewey win by at least 5 percent (Donaldson 209). Many historians believe that these predictions aided the president. First, surveys showing Dewey in the lead may have prompted some Dewey supporters to feel overconfident and therefore to stay home from the polls. Second, the same surveys may have energized Democrats to mount late get-out-the-vote efforts (Lester). Other analysts believe that the overwhelming predictions of a Truman loss kept home some Democrats who saw a Truman loss as inevitable. According to

No signal phrase; author and page number in parentheses.

political analyst Samuel Lubell, those Democrats may have saved Dewey from an even greater defeat (Hamby, *Man* 465). Whatever the impact on the voters, the polls had a decided effect on Dewey.

Historians and political analysts alike cite Dewey's overly cautious campaign as a main reason Truman was able to win. Dewey firmly believed in public opinion polls. With all signs pointing to an easy victory, Dewey and his staff believed that all he had to do was bide his time and make no foolish mistakes. Dewey himself said, "When you're leading, don't talk" (Smith 30). As the leader in the race, Dewey kept his remarks faultlessly positive, with the result that he failed to deliver a solid message or even mention Truman. Eventually, Dewey began to be perceived as aloof, stuffy, and out of touch with the public. One observer compared him to the plastic groom on top of a wedding cake (Hamby, "Harry S. Truman"), and others noted his stiff, cold demeanor (McCullough 671–74).

Through the autumn of 1948, Dewey's speeches failed to address the issues, with the candidate declaring that he did not want to "get down in the gutter" (Smith 515). When fellow Republicans said he was losing ground, Dewey insisted that his campaign stay the course. Even *Time* magazine, though it endorsed and praised him, conceded that his speeches were dull (McCullough 696). According to historian Zachary Karabell, they were "notable only for taking place, not for any specific message" (244). Dewey's poll numbers slipped before the election, but he still held a comfortable lead. Truman's famous whistle-stop campaign would make the difference.

Few candidates in US history have campaigned for the presidency with more passion and faith than Harry Truman. In the autumn of 1948, Truman wrote to his sister, "It will be the greatest campaign any President

Borchers   4

ever made. Win, lose, or draw, people will know where I stand." For thirty-

three days, he traveled the nation, giving hundreds of speeches from the

back of the *Ferdinand Magellan* railroad car. In the same letter, Truman

described the pace: "We made about 140 stops and I spoke over 147 times,

shook hands with at least 30,000 and am in good condition to start out

again tomorrow." David McCullough writes of Truman's campaign:

> No President in history had ever gone so far in quest of support from
>
> the people, or with less cause for the effort, to judge by informed
>
> opinion. . . . As a test of his skills and judgment as a professional
>
> politician, not to say his stamina and disposition at age sixty-four, it
>
> would be like no other experience in his long, often difficult career, as
>
> he himself understood perfectly. (655)

Quotations of more than 4 lines indented ½ inch (5 spaces) and double-spaced.

Parenthetical reference after final punctuation.

He spoke in large cities and small towns, defending his policies and

attacking Republicans. As a former farmer, Truman was able to connect

with the public. He developed an energetic style, usually speaking from

notes rather than from a prepared speech, and often mingled with the

crowds, which grew larger as the campaign progressed. In Chicago, over

half a million people lined the streets as he passed, and in St. Paul the

crowd numbered over 25,000. When Dewey entered St. Paul two days later,

only 7,000 supporters greeted him (McCullough 842). Reporters brushed

off the large crowds as mere curiosity seekers wanting to see a president

(682). Yet Truman persisted, even if he often seemed to be the only one

who thought he could win. By connecting directly with the American peo-

ple, Truman built the momentum to surpass Dewey and win the election.

The legacy and lessons of Truman's whistle-stop campaign con-

tinue to be studied, and politicians still mimic his campaign methods by

scheduling multiple visits to key states, as Truman did. He visited Cali-

fornia, Illinois, and Ohio 48 times, compared with 6 visits to those states by Dewey. Political scientist Thomas Holbrook concludes that his strategic campaigning in those states and others gave Truman the electoral votes he needed to win (61, 65).

The 1948 election also had an effect on pollsters, who, as Roper admitted, "couldn't have been more wrong." *Life* magazine's editors concluded that pollsters as well as reporters and commentators were too convinced of a Dewey victory to analyze the polls seriously, especially the opinions of undecided voters (Karabell 256). Pollsters assumed that undecided voters would vote in the same proportion as decided voters—and that turned out to be a false assumption (257). In fact, the lopsidedness of the polls might have led voters who supported Truman to call themselves undecided out of an unwillingness to associate themselves with the losing side, further skewing the polls' results (McDonald et al. 152). Such errors led pollsters to change their methods significantly after the 1948 election.

Many political analysts, journalists, and historians concluded that the Truman upset was in fact a victory for the American people. And Truman biographer Alonzo Hamby notes that "polls of scholars consistently rank Truman among the top eight presidents in American history" (*Man* 641). But despite Truman's high standing, and despite the fact that the whistle-stop campaign remains in our political landscape, politicians have increasingly imitated the style of the Dewey campaign, with its "packaged candidate who ran so as not to lose, who steered clear of controversy, and who made a good show of appearing presidential" (Karabell 266). The election of 1948 shows that voters are not necessarily swayed by polls, but it may have presaged the packaging of candidates by public relations experts, to the detriment of public debate on the issues in future presidential elections.

Work by 3 or more authors is shortened using "et al."

Borchers   6

Works Cited

Donaldson, Gary A. *Truman Defeats Dewey*. UP of Kentucky, 1999.

Egan, Leo. "Talk Is Now Turning to the Dewey Cabinet." *The New York Times*, 20 Oct. 1948, p. E8.

Ferrell, Robert H. *Harry S. Truman: A Life*. U of Missouri P, 1994.

Hamby, Alonzo L. "Harry S. Truman: Campaigns and Elections." *Miller Center*, U of Virginia, millercenter.org/president/biography/truman-campaigns-and-elections. Accessed 17 Mar. 2019.

---. *Man of the People: A Life of Harry S. Truman*. Oxford UP, 1995.

Holbrook, Thomas M. "Did the Whistle-Stop Campaign Matter?" *PS: Political Science and Politics*, vol. 35, no. 1, Mar. 2002, pp. 59-66.

Karabell, Zachary. *The Last Campaign: How Harry Truman Won the 1948 Election*. Alfred A. Knopf, 2000.

Lester, Will. "'Dewey Defeats Truman' Disaster Haunts Pollsters." *Los Angeles Times*, 1 Nov. 1998, www.latimes.com/archives/la-xpm-1998-nov-01-mn-38174-story.html.

McCullough, David. *Truman*. Simon and Schuster, 1992.

McDonald, Daniel G., et al. "The Spiral of Silence in the 1948 Presidential Election." *Communication Research*, vol. 28, no. 2, Apr. 2001, pp. 139-55.

Photograph of Truman. *Life*, 1 Nov. 1948, p. 37. *Google Books*, books.google.com/books?id=ekoEAAAAMBAJ&printsec=frontcover#v=onepage&q&f=false.

Rollins, Byron. *Dewey Defeats Truman*. 1948. *Harry S. Truman Library and Museum*, National Archives and Records Administration, www.trumanlibrary.gov/photograph-records/95-187.

Borchers   7

Roper, Elmo. "Roper Eats Crow; Seeks Reason for Vote Upset." *Evening Independent*, 6 Nov. 1948, p. 10. *Google News*, news.google.com /newspapers?nid=PZE8UkGerEcC&dat=19481106&printsec =frontpage&hl=en.

Smith, Richard Norton. *Thomas E. Dewey and His Times*. Simon and Schuster, 1982.

Truman, Harry S. "Campaigning, Letter, October 5, 1948." *Harry S. Truman*, edited by Robert H. Ferrell, CQ Press, 2003, p. 91. American Presidents Reference Series.

Every source used is in the list of works cited.

54 APA Style

American Psychological Association (APA) style calls for (1) brief documentation in parentheses near each in-text citation and (2) complete documentation in a list of references at the end of your text. The models in this chapter draw on the *Publication Manual of the American Psychological Association*, 7th edition (2020). Additional information is available at www.apastyle.org.

A DIRECTORY TO APA STYLE

In-Text Documentation   618

1. Author named in a signal phrase 618
2. Author named in parentheses   619
3. Authors with the same last name   619
4. Two authors   619
5. Three or more authors   620
6. Organization or government as author   620
7. Author unknown   620
8. Two or more works together   621
9. Two or more works by one author in the same year   621
10. Source quoted in another source   621
11. Work without page numbers   621
12. An entire work   622
13. Personal communications   622

Notes   622

Reference List   623

KEY ELEMENTS FOR DOCUMENTING SOURCES   623

AUTHORS AND OTHER CONTRIBUTORS   626

1. One author   626

2. Two authors   626

3. Three or more authors   626

4. Two or more works by the same author   627

5. Author and editor   628

6. Author and translator   628

7. Editor   628

8. Unknown or no author or editor   628

9. Organization or government as author   629

ARTICLES AND OTHER SHORT WORKS   629
Documentation Map: Article in a Journal with a DOI   631
Documentation Map: Webpage   633

10. Article in a journal   629

11. Article in a magazine   629

12. Article in a newspaper   630

13. Article on a news website   630

14. Journal article from a database   630

15. Editorial   630

16. Review   632

17. Comment on an online periodical article or blog post   632

18. Webpage   632

BOOKS, PARTS OF BOOKS, AND REPORTS   634
Documentation Map: Book   635

19. Basic entry for a book   634

20. Edition other than the first   634

21. Edited collection or anthology   636

22. Work in an edited collection or anthology   636

23. Chapter in an edited book   636

24. Entry in a reference work 636

25. Book in a language other than English 637

26. One volume of a multivolume work 637

27. Religious work 637

28. Report by a government agency or other organization 638

29. Dissertation 638

30. Paper or poster presented at a conference 638

AUDIO, VISUAL, AND OTHER SOURCES 639

31. *Wikipedia* entry 639

32. Online forum post 639

33. Blog post 639

34. Online streaming video 640

35. Podcast 640

36. Podcast episode 640

37. Film 640

38. Television series 641

39. Television series episode 641

40. Music album 641

41. Song 642

42. *PowerPoint* slides 642

43. Recording of a speech or webinar 642

44. Photograph 642

45. Map 643

46. Social media posts 643

47. Data set 644

48. Supreme Court case 644

SOURCES NOT COVERED BY APA 644

Formatting a Paper 645

Sample Research Paper 647

Throughout this chapter, you'll find models and examples that are color-coded to help you see how writers include source information in their texts and reference lists: tan for author or editor, yellow for title, blue for publication information—publisher, date of publication, page number(s), DOI or URL, and so on.

IN-TEXT DOCUMENTATION

Brief documentation in your text makes clear to your readers precisely what you took from a source. If you are quoting, provide the page number(s) or other information that will help readers find the quotation in the source. You're not required to give the page number(s) with a paraphrase or summary, but you may want to do so if you are citing a long or complex work.

542–54   PARAPHRASES and SUMMARIES are more common than QUOTATIONS in APA-style projects. As you cite each source, you will need to decide whether to name the author in a signal phrase—"as McCullough (2020) wrote"—or in parentheses—"(McCullough, 2020)." Note that APA requires 551–54 you to use the past tense for verbs in SIGNAL PHRASES, or the present perfect if you are referring to a past action that didn't occur at a specific time or that continues into the present: "Moss (2019) argued," "Many authors have argued."

1. AUTHOR NAMED IN A SIGNAL PHRASE

Put the date in parentheses after the author's last name, unless the year is mentioned in the sentence. Put any page number(s) you're including in parentheses after the quotation, paraphrase, or summary. Parenthetical documentation should come *before* the period at the end of the sentence and *after* any quotation marks.

> McCullough (2001) described John Adams as having "the hands of a man accustomed to pruning his own trees, cutting his own hay, and splitting his own firewood" (p. 18).

In 2001, McCullough noted that John Adams's hands were those of a laborer (p. 18).

John Adams had "the hands of a man accustomed to pruning his own trees," according to McCullough (2001, p. 18).

If the author is named after a quotation, as in this last example, put the page number(s) after the date within the parentheses.

2. AUTHOR NAMED IN PARENTHESES

If you do not mention an author in a signal phrase, put the name, the year of publication, and any page number(s) in parentheses at the end of the sentence or right after the quotation, paraphrase, or summary.

John Adams had "the hands of a man accustomed to pruning his own trees, cutting his own hay, and splitting his own firewood" (McCullough, 2001, p. 18).

3. AUTHORS WITH THE SAME LAST NAME

If your reference list includes more than one first author with the same last name, include initials in all documentation to distinguish the authors from one another.

Eclecticism is common in modern criticism (J. M. Smith, 1992, p. vii).

4. TWO AUTHORS

Always mention both authors. Use "and" in a signal phrase, but use an ampersand (&) in parentheses.

Carlson and Ventura (1990) wanted to introduce Julio Cortázar, Marjorie Agosín, and other Latin American writers to an audience of English-speaking adolescents (p. v).

According to the Peter Principle, "In a hierarchy, every employee tends to rise to his level of incompetence" (Peter & Hull, 1969, p. 26).

5. THREE OR MORE AUTHORS

When you refer to a work by three or more contributors, name only the first author followed by "et al.," Latin for "and others."

> Peilen et al. (1990) supported their claims about corporate corruption with startling anecdotal evidence (p. 75).

6. ORGANIZATION OR GOVERNMENT AS AUTHOR

If an organization name has a familiar abbreviation, give the full name and the abbreviation the first time you cite the source. In subsequent references, use only the abbreviation. If the organization does not have a familiar abbreviation, always use its full name.

FIRST REFERENCE

> The American Psychological Association (APA, 2020)

> (American Psychological Association [APA], 2020)

SUBSEQUENT REFERENCES

> The APA (2020)

> (APA, 2020)

7. AUTHOR UNKNOWN

Use the complete title if it's short; if it's long, use the first few words of the title under which the work appears in the reference list. Italicize the title if it's italicized in the reference list; if it isn't italicized there, enclose the title in quotation marks.

> According to Feeding Habits of Rams (2000), a ram's diet often changes from one season to the next (p. 29).

> The article noted that one donor died because of "frightening" postoperative care ("Every Patient's Nightmare," 2007).

8. TWO OR MORE WORKS TOGETHER

If you document multiple works in the same parentheses, place the source information in alphabetical order, separated by semicolons.

> Many researchers have argued that what counts as "literacy" is not necessarily learned at school (Heath, 1983; Moss, 2003).

Multiple authors in a signal phrase can be named in any order.

9. TWO OR MORE WORKS BY ONE AUTHOR IN THE SAME YEAR

If your list of references includes more than one work by the same author published in the same year, order them alphabetically by title, adding lowercase letters ("a," "b," and so on) to the year.

> Kaplan (2000a) described orderly shantytowns in Turkey that did not resemble the other slums he visited.

10. SOURCE QUOTED IN ANOTHER SOURCE

When you cite a source that was quoted in another source, add the words "as cited in." If possible, cite the original source instead.

> Thus, Modern Standard Arabic was expected to serve as the "moral glue" holding the Arab world together (Choueri, 2000, as cited in Walters, 2019, p. 475).

11. WORK WITHOUT PAGE NUMBERS

Instead of page numbers, some works have paragraph numbers, which you should include (preceded by the abbreviation "para.") if you are referring to a specific part of such a source.

> Russell's dismissals from Trinity College at Cambridge and from City College in New York City have been seen as examples of the controversy that marked his life (Irvine, 2006, para. 2).

In sources with neither page nor paragraph numbers, point to a particular part of the source if possible: (Brody, 2020, Introduction, para. 2).

12. AN ENTIRE WORK

You do not need to give a page number if you are directing readers' attention to an entire work.

> Kaplan (2000) considered Turkey and Central Asia explosive.

When you're citing an entire website, give the URL in the text. You do not need to include the website in your reference list. To document a webpage, see number 18 on page 632.

> Beyond providing diagnostic information, the website for the Alzheimer's Association (http://www.alz.org) includes a variety of resources for the families of patients.

13. PERSONAL COMMUNICATIONS

Document emails, telephone conversations, personal interviews, personal letters, messages from nonarchived online discussion sources, and other personal texts as "personal communication," along with the person's initial(s), last name, and the date. You do not need to include such personal communications in your reference list.

> L. Strauss (personal communication, December 6, 2013) told about visiting Yogi Berra when they both lived in Montclair, New Jersey.

NOTES

You may need to use footnotes to give an explanation or information that doesn't fit into your text. To signal a content footnote, place a superscript numeral at the appropriate point in your text. Include this information in a footnote, either at the bottom of that page or on a separate page with the heading "Footnotes" centered and in bold, after your reference list. If you have multiple notes, number them consecutively throughout your text. Here is an example from *In Search of Solutions: A New Direction in Psychotherapy* (2003).

TEXT WITH SUPERSCRIPT

An important part of working with teams and one-way mirrors is taking the consultation break, as at Milan, BFTC, and MRI.[1]

FOOTNOTE

[1]It is crucial to note here that while working within a team is fun, stimulating, and revitalizing, it is not necessary for successful outcomes. Solution-oriented therapy works equally well when working solo.

REFERENCE LIST

A reference list provides full bibliographic information for every source cited in your text with the exception of entire websites, common computer software and mobile apps, and personal communications. See page 646 for guidelines on preparing such a list; for a sample reference list, see page 654.

Key Elements for Documenting Sources

To document a source in APA style, you need to provide information about the author, the date, the title of the work you're citing, and the source itself (who published it; volume, issue, and page numbers; any DOI or URL). The following guidelines explain how to handle each of these elements generally, but there will be exceptions. For that reason, you'll want to consult the entries for the specific kinds of sources you're documenting; these entries provide templates showing which details you need to include. Be aware, though, that sometimes the templates will show elements that your source doesn't have; if that's the case, just omit those elements.

AUTHORS

Most entries begin with the author's last name, followed by the first and any middle initials: Smith, Z. for Zadie Smith; Kinder, D. R. for Donald R. Kinder.

- If the author is a group or organization, use its full name: Black Lives Matter, American Historical Association.
- If there is no author, put the title of the work first, followed by the date.
- If the author uses a screen name, first give their real name, followed by the screen name in brackets: Scott, B. [@BostonScott2]. If only the screen name is known, leave off the brackets: AvalonGirl1990.

DATES

Include the date of publication, in parentheses right after the author. Some sources require only the year; others require the year, month, and day; and still others require something else. Consult the entry in this chapter for the specific source you're documenting.

- For a book, use the copyright year, which you'll find on the copyright page. If more than one year is given, use the most recent one.
- For most magazine or newspaper articles, use the full date that appears on the work, usually the year followed by the month and day.
- For a journal article, use the year of the volume.
- For a work on a website, use the date when the work was last updated. If that information is not available, use the date when the work was published.
- If a work has no date, use "n.d." for "no date."
- For online content that is likely to change, include the month, day, and year when you retrieved it. No need to include a retrieval date for materials that are unlikely to change.

TITLES

Capitalize only the first word and any proper nouns and adjectives in the title and subtitle of a work. But sometimes you'll also need to provide the title of a periodical or website where a source was found, and those are

TITLE   AUTHOR   PUBLICATION

treated differently: capitalize all the principal words (excluding articles and prepositions).

- For books, reports, webpages, podcasts, and any other works that stand on their own, italicize the title: *White fragility, Radiolab, The 9/11 report*. Do not italicize the titles of the sources where you found them, however: NPR, ProQuest.

- For journal articles, book chapters, TV series episodes, and other works that are part of a larger work, do not italicize the title: The snowball effect, Not your average Joe. But do italicize the title of the larger work: *The Atlantic, Game of thrones*.

- If a work has no title, include a description in square brackets after the date: [Painting of sheep on a hill].

- If the title of a work you're documenting includes another title, italicize it: *Frog and Toad and the self*. If the title you're documenting is itself in italics, do not italicize the title within it: *Stay, illusion!: The* Hamlet *doctrine*.

- For untitled social media posts or comments, include the first twenty words as the title, in italics, followed by a bracketed description: *TIL pigeons can fly up to 700 miles in one day* [Tweet].

SOURCE INFORMATION

This indicates where the work can be found (in a database or on a website, for example, or in a magazine or on a podcast) and includes information about the publisher; any volume, issue, and page numbers; and, for some sources, a DOI or URL. DOIs and URLs are included in all the templates; if the work you are documenting doesn't have one, just leave it off.

- For a work that stands on its own (a book, a report, a webpage), the source might be the publisher, a database, or a website.

- For a work that's part of a larger work (an article, an episode in a TV series, an essay in a collection), the source might be a magazine, a TV series, or an anthology.

- Give the volume and issue for journals and magazines that include that information. No need to give them for newspapers.

- Include a DOI for any work that has one, whether you accessed the source in print or online. For an online work with no DOI, include a working URL unless the work is from an academic database. You can use a shortDOI (https://shortdoi.org/) or a URL shortened using an online URL shortener, as long as the shorter DOI or URL leads to the correct work. No need to include a URL for a print work with no DOI.

Authors and Other Contributors

Most entries begin with authors—one author, two authors, or twenty-five. And some include editors, translators, or others who've contributed. The following templates show you how to document the various kinds of authors and other contributors.

1. ONE AUTHOR

> Author's Last Name, Initials. (Year of publication). *Title*. Publisher. DOI
> *or* URL

> Lewis, M. (2003). *Moneyball: The art of winning an unfair game*.
> W. W. Norton.

2. TWO AUTHORS

> First Author's Last Name, Initials, & Second Author's Last Name,
> Initials. (Year of publication). *Title*. Publisher. DOI *or* URL

> Montefiore, S., & Montefiore, S. S. (2016). *The royal rabbits of London*.
> Aladdin.

3. THREE OR MORE AUTHORS

For three to twenty authors, include all names.

> First Author's Last Name, Initials, Next Author's Last Name, Initials, &
> Final Author's Last Name, Initials. (Year of publication).
> *Title*. Publisher. DOI *or* URL

Greig, A., Taylor, J., & MacKay, T. (2013). *Doing research with children: A practical guide* (3rd ed.). Sage.

For a work by twenty-one or more authors, name the first nineteen authors, followed by three ellipsis points, and end with the final author.

Gao, R., Asano, S. M., Upadhyayula, S., Pisarev, I., Milkie, D. E., Liu, T.-L., Singh, V., Graves, A., Huynh, G. H., Zhao, Y., Bogovic, J., Colonell, J., Ott, C. M., Zugates, C., Tappan, S., Rodriguez, A., Mosaliganti, K. R., Sheu, S.-H., Pasolli, H. A., . . . Betzig, E. (2019, January 18). Cortical column and whole-brain imaging with molecular contrast and nanoscale resolution. *Science, 363*(6424). https://doi.org/10.1126/science.aau8302

4. TWO OR MORE WORKS BY THE SAME AUTHOR

If the works were published in different years, list them chronologically.

Lewis, B. (1995). *The Middle East: A brief history of the last 2,000 years.* Scribner.

Lewis, B. (2003). *The crisis of Islam: Holy war and unholy terror.* Modern Library.

If the works were published in the same year, list them alphabetically by title (ignoring "A," "An," and "The"), adding "a," "b," and so on to the year.

Kaplan, R. D. (2000a). *The coming anarchy: Shattering the dreams of the post Cold War.* Random House.

Kaplan, R. D. (2000b). *Eastward to Tartary: Travels in the Balkans, the Middle East, and the Caucasus.* Random House.

5. AUTHOR AND EDITOR

If a book has an author and an editor who is credited on the cover, include the editor in parentheses after the title.

> Author's Last Name, Initials. (Year of publication). *Title* (Editor's Initials Last Name, Ed.). Publisher. DOI *or* URL (Original work published Year)

> Dick, P. F. (2008). *Five novels of the 1960s and 70s* (J. Lethem, Ed.). Library of America. (Original works published 1964–1977)

6. AUTHOR AND TRANSLATOR

> Author's Last Name, Initials. (Year of publication). *Title* (Translator's Initials Last Name, Trans.). Publisher. DOI *or* URL (Original work published Year)

> Hugo, V. (2008). *Les misérables* (J. Rose, Trans.). Modern Library. (Original work published 1862)

7. EDITOR

> Editor's Last Name, Initials (Ed.). (Year of publication). *Title*. Publisher. DOI *or* URL

> Jones, D. (Ed.). (2007). *Modern love: 50 true and extraordinary tales of desire, deceit, and devotion*. Three Rivers Press.

8. UNKNOWN OR NO AUTHOR OR EDITOR

> *Title.* (Year of Publication). Publisher. DOI *or* URL

> *Feeding habits of rams.* (2000). Land's Point Press.

> Clues in salmonella outbreak. (2008, June 21). *The New York Times*, A13.

If the author is listed as "Anonymous," use that as the author's name in the reference list.

9. ORGANIZATION OR GOVERNMENT AS AUTHOR

Sometimes an organization or a government agency is both author and publisher. If so, omit the publisher.

> Organization Name *or* Government Agency. (Year of publication). *Title.* DOI *or* URL

> Catholic News Service. (2002). *Stylebook on religion 2000: A reference guide.*

Articles and Other Short Works

Articles, essays, reviews, and other short works are found in periodicals and books—in print, online, or in a database. For most short works, provide information about the author, the date, the titles of both the short work and the longer work, plus any volume and issue numbers, page numbers, and a DOI or URL if there is one.

10. ARTICLE IN A JOURNAL

> Author's Last Name, Initials. (Year). Title of article. *Title of Journal, volume*(issue), page(s). DOI *or* URL

> Gremer, J. R., Sala, A., & Crone, E. E. (2010). Disappearing plants: Why they hide and how they return. *Ecology, 91*(11), 3407–3413. https://doi.org/10.1890/09-1864.1

11. ARTICLE IN A MAGAZINE

If a magazine is published weekly, include the year, month, and day. Put any volume number and issue number after the title.

> Author's Last Name, Initials. (Year, Month Day). Title of article. *Title of Magazine, volume*(issue), page(s). DOI *or* URL

> Klump, B. (2019, November 22). Of crows and tools. *Science, 366*(6468), 965. https://doi.org/10.1126/science.aaz7775

12. ARTICLE IN A NEWSPAPER

If page numbers are consecutive, separate them with an en dash. If not, separate them with a comma.

> Author's Last Name, Initials. (Year, Month Day). Title of article. *Title of Newspaper*, page(s). URL

> Schneider, G. (2005, March 13). Fashion sense on wheels. *The Washington Post*, F1, F6.

13. ARTICLE ON A NEWS WEBSITE

Italicize the titles of articles on CNN and other news websites. Do not italicize the name of the website.

> Author's Last Name, Initials. (Year, Month Day). *Title of article.* Name of Site. URL

> Travers, C. (2019, December 3). *Here's why you keep waking up at the same time every night.* HuffPost. https://bit.ly/3drSwAR

14. JOURNAL ARTICLE FROM A DATABASE

> Author's Last Name, Initials. (Year). Title of article. *Title of Journal*, *volume*(issue), pages. DOI

> Simpson, M. (1972). Authoritarianism and education: A comparative approach. *Sociometry, 35*(2), 223–234. https://doi.org/10.2307/2786619

15. EDITORIAL

Editorials can appear in journals, magazines, and newspapers. If the editorial is unsigned, put the title in the author position.

> Author's Last Name, Initials. (Year, Month Day). Title of editorial [Editorial]. *Title of Periodical.* DOI or URL

> *The Guardian* view on local theatres: The shows must go on [Editorial]. (2019, December 6). *The Guardian.* https://bit.ly/2VZHIUg

Documentation Map (APA)
Article in a Journal with a DOI

TITLE OF JOURNAL

VOLUME AND ISSUE

PAGES

ETHICS & BEHAVIOR, *23*(4), 324–337
Copyright © 2013 Taylor & Francis Group, LLC
ISSN: 1050-8422 print / 1532-7019 online
DOI: 10.1080/10508422.2013.787359

Routledge
Taylor & Francis Group

PUBLISHER

DOI

TITLE OF ARTICLE

AUTHOR

Smart Technology and the Moral Life

Clifton F. Guthrie

Department of Science and Humanities
Husson University

Smart technology is recording and nudging our intuitive and behavioral reactions in ways that are not fully shaped by our conscious ethical reasoning and so are altering our social and moral worlds. Beyond reasons to worry, there are also reasons to embrace this technology for nudging human behavior toward prosocial activity. This article inquires about four ways that smart technology is shaping the individual moral life: the persuasive effect of promptware, our newly evolving experiences of embodiment, our negotiations with privacy, and our experiences of risk and serendipity.

Keywords: persuasive technology, morality, ethics, virtue

PERSUASIVE TECHNOLOGY

For some time, cars have worked to shape our behaviors, beeping to warn us when a door is unlocked or a seat belt unfastened, or giving us fuel efficiency feedback. These straightforward but persuasive sensor systems nudge us toward a repertoire of safe driving behaviors, and we often cannot override them even if we want to. Newer cars include an increasing number of smart technologies that interact with us more intelligently. Some detect the presence of electronic keys and make it impossible for drivers to lock themselves out. Others use sensors to monitor approaching obstacles or lane boundaries and give warnings or even apply the brakes. We are seeing the emergence of street intersections that communicate directly with cars and cars that can communicate with one another (Dean, Fletcher, Porges, & Ulrich, 2012). These are so-called smart technologies because they draw data from the environment and from us, and often make decisions on our behalf. A leading researcher in automated driving noted, "The driver is still in control. But if the driver is not doing the right thing, the technology takes over" (Markoff & Sengupta, 2013).

As cars become smarter they are helping to lead us into what technologists describe as a pervasive, ambient, or calm computing environment. In 1991, Mark Weiser of the Palo Alto Research Center presciently called it "ubiquitous computing" or "ubicomp" in a much-quoted article from *Scientific American*, in which he outlined what has come to be accepted as a standard interpretation of the history of human interaction with computers. This is the age in which computers are increasingly liberated from manual input devices like laptops and cell phones to become an invisible, interactive, computational sensorium. Early examples include motion sensors, smart

Correspondence should be addressed to Clifton F. Guthrie, Department of Science and Humanities, Husson University, 1 College Circle, Bangor, ME 04401. E-mail: cfguthrie@gmail.com

Guthrie, C. F. (2013). Smart technology and the moral life.
Ethics & Behavior, 23(4), 324–337. https://doi.org/10.1080
/10508422.2013.787359

629-34
for more
on citing
articles
APA style

16. REVIEW

Use this general format to document a review that appears in a periodical or on a blog.

> Reviewer's Last Name, Initials. (Year, Month Day). Title of review
> [Review of the work *Title*, by Author's Initials Last Name]. *Title of*
> *Periodical or Name of Blog.* DOI *or* URL

> Joinson, S. (2017, December 15). Mysteries unfold in a land of minarets
> and magic carpets [Review of the book *The city of brass*, by S. A.
> Chakraborty]. *The New York Times.* https://nyti.ms/2kvwHFP

For a review published on a website that is not associated with a periodical or a blog, italicize the title of the review and do not italicize the website name.

17. COMMENT ON AN ONLINE PERIODICAL ARTICLE OR BLOG POST

> Writer's Last Name, Initials [username]. (Year, Month Day). Text of
> comment up to 20 words [Comment on the article "Title of work"].
> Title of Publication. DOI *or* URL

> PhyllisSpecial. (2020, May 10). How about we go all the way again? It's
> about time . . . [Comment on the article "2020 Eagles schedule:
> Picking wins and losses for all 16 games"]. *The Philadelphia*
> *Inquirer.* https://rb.gy/iduabz

Link to the comment if possible; if not, include the URL of the article.

18. WEBPAGE

> Author's Last Name, Initials. (Year, Month Day). *Title of work.* Title of
> Site. URL

> Pleasant, B. (n.d.). *Annual bluegrass.* The National Gardening Association.
> https://garden.org/learn/articles/view/2936/

Documentation Map (APA)
Webpage

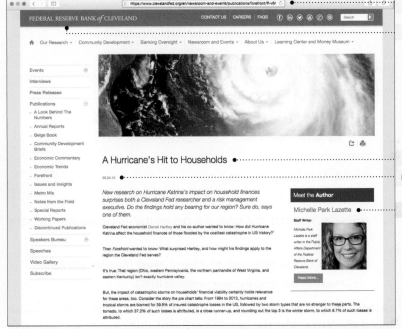

URL

TITLE OF SITE

TITLE OF WORK

DATE OF PUBLICATION

AUTHOR

Lazette, M. P. (2015, February 24). *A hurricane's hit to households.*
Federal Reserve Bank of Cleveland. https://www.clevelandfed.org
/en/newsroom-and-events/publications/forefront/ff-v6n01
/ff-20150224-v6n0107-a-hurricanes-hit-to-households.aspx

632–34
for more
on citing
webpages
APA style

If the author and the website name are the same, use the website name as the author. If the content of the webpage is likely to change and no archived version exists, use "n.d." as the date and include a retrieval date.

> Worldometer. (n.d.). *World population*. Retrieved February 2, 2020, from
> https://www.worldometers.info/world-population/

Books, Parts of Books, and Reports

19. BASIC ENTRY FOR A BOOK

> Author's Last Name, Initials. (Year of publication). *Title*.
> Publisher. DOI *or* URL

PRINT BOOK

> Schwab, V. E. (2018). *Vengeful*. Tor.

EBOOK

> Jemisin, N. K. (2017). *The stone sky*. Orbit. https://amzn.com/B01N7EQOFA

AUDIOBOOK

> Obama, M. (2018). *Becoming* (M. Obama, Narr.) [Audiobook]. Random
> House Audio. http://amzn.com/B07B3JQZCL

Include the word "Audiobook" in brackets and the name of the narrator only if the format and the narrator are something you've mentioned in what you've written.

20. EDITION OTHER THAN THE FIRST

> Author's Last Name, Initials. (Year). *Title* (Name *or* number ed.).
> Publisher. DOI *or* URL

> Burch, D. (2008). *Emergency navigation: Find your position and shape
> your course at sea even if your instruments fail* (2nd ed.).
> International Marine/McGraw-Hill.

Documentation Map (APA)

Book

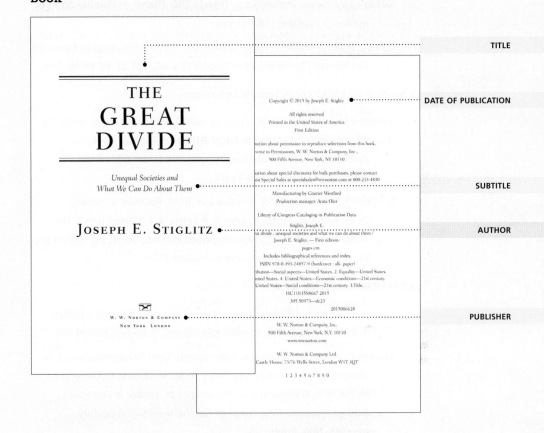

	TITLE
	DATE OF PUBLICATION
	SUBTITLE
	AUTHOR
	PUBLISHER

Stiglitz, J. E. (2015). *The great divide: Unequal societies and what we can do about them.* W. W. Norton.

634–37
for more
on citing
books APA
style

21. EDITED COLLECTION OR ANTHOLOGY

Editor's Last Name, Initials (Ed.). (Year). *Title* (Name *or* number ed., Vol. number). Publisher. DOI *or* URL

Gilbert, S. M., & Gubar, S. (Eds.). (2003). *The Norton anthology of literature by women: The traditions in English* (3rd ed., Vol. 2). W. W. Norton.

22. WORK IN AN EDITED COLLECTION OR ANTHOLOGY

Author's Last Name, Initials. (Year of edited edition). Title of work. In Editor's Initials Last Name (Ed.), *Title of collection* (Name *or* number ed., Vol. number, pp. pages). Publisher. DOI *or* URL (Original work published Year)

Baldwin, J. (2018). Notes of a native son. In M. Puchner, S. Akbari, W. Denecke, B. Fuchs, C. Levine, P. Lewis, & E. Wilson (Eds.), *The Norton anthology of world literature* (4th ed., Vol. F, pp. 728–743). W. W. Norton. (Original work published 1955)

23. CHAPTER IN AN EDITED BOOK

Author's Last Name, Initials. (Year). Title of chapter. In Editor's Initials Last Name (Ed.), *Title of book* (pp. pages). Publisher. DOI *or* URL

Amarnick, S. (2009). Trollope at fuller length: Lord Silverbridge and the manuscript of *The duke's children*. In M. Markwick, D. Denenholz Morse, & R. Gagnier (Eds.), *The politics of gender in Anthony Trollope's novels: New readings for the twenty-first century* (pp. 193–206). Routledge.

24. ENTRY IN A REFERENCE WORK (DICTIONARY, THESAURUS, OR ENCYCLOPEDIA)

If the entry has no author, use the name of the publisher as the author. If the reference work has an editor, include their name after the title of the entry. If the entry is archived or is not likely to change, use the publication date and do not include a retrieval date.

Author's Last Name, Initials. (Year). Title of entry. In Editor's Initials
    Last Name (Ed.), *Title of reference work* (Name *or* number ed., Vol.
    number, pp. pages). Publisher. URL

Merriam-Webster. (n.d.). Epoxy. In *Merriam-Webster.com dictionary*.
    Retrieved January 29, 2020, from https://www.merriam-webster
    .com/dictionary/epoxy

25. BOOK IN A LANGUAGE OTHER THAN ENGLISH

Author's Last Name, Initials. (Year). *Title of book* [English translation of
    title]. Publisher. DOI *or* URL

Ferrante, E. (2011). *L'amica geniale* [My brilliant friend]. Edizione E/O.

26. ONE VOLUME OF A MULTIVOLUME WORK

Author's Last Name, Initials. (Year). *Title of entire work* (Vol. number).
    Publisher. DOI *or* URL

Spiegelman, A. (1986). *Maus* (Vol. 1). Random House.

If the volume has a separate title, include the volume number and title
in italics after the main title.

Ramazani, J., Ellmann, R., & O'Clair, R. (Eds.). (2003). *The Norton
    anthology of modern and contemporary poetry: Vol. 1. Modern
    poetry* (3rd ed.). W. W. Norton.

27. RELIGIOUS WORK

Do not include an author for most religious works. If the date of original
publication is known, include it at the end.

Title. (Year of publication). Publisher. URL (Original work published Year)

New American Bible. (2002). United States Conference of Catholic
    Bishops. http://www.vatican.va/archive/ENG0839/_INDEX.HTM
    (Original work published 1970)

28. REPORT BY A GOVERNMENT AGENCY OR OTHER ORGANIZATION

> Author's Last Name, Initials. (Year). Title (Report No. number). Publisher. DOI *or* URL

> Centers for Disease Control and Prevention. (2009). *Fourth national report on human exposure to environmental chemicals.* US Department of Health and Human Services. https://www.cdc.gov/exposurereport/pdf/fourthreport.pdf

Include the year, month, and day if the report you're documenting includes that information. Omit the report number if one is not given. If more than one government department is listed as the publisher, list the most specific department as the author and the larger department as the publisher.

29. DISSERTATION

> Author's Last Name, Initials. (Year). Title (Publication No. number) [Doctoral dissertation, Name of School]. Database *or* Archive Name. URL

> Solomon, M. (2016). *Social media and self-examination: The examination of social media use on identity, social comparison, and self-esteem in young female adults* (Publication No. 10188962) [Doctoral dissertation, William James College]. ProQuest Dissertations and Theses Global.

If the dissertation is in a database, do not include a URL. Include a URL if it is published elsewhere online. If it is unpublished, write "Unpublished doctoral dissertation" in brackets, and use the name of the school in place of the database.

30. PAPER OR POSTER PRESENTED AT A CONFERENCE

> Presenter's Last Name, Initials. (Year, Month First Day–Last Day). *Title* [Paper or Poster presentation]. Name of Conference, City, State, Country. URL

Dolatian, H., & Heinz, J. (2018, May 25–27). *Reduplication and finite-state technology* [Paper presentation]. The 53rd Annual Meeting of the Chicago Linguistic Society, Chicago, IL, United States. http://shorturl.at/msuB2

Audio, Visual, and Other Sources

If you are referring to an entire website, do not include it in your reference list; simply mention the website's name in the body of your paper and include the URL in parentheses. Do not include email, personal communication, or other unarchived discussions in your list of references.

31. *WIKIPEDIA* ENTRY

Wikipedia has archived versions of its pages, so give the date when you accessed the page and the permanent URL of the archived page, which is found by clicking "View history."

Title of entry. (Year, Month Day). In *Wikipedia.* URL

List of sheep breeds. (2019, September 9). In *Wikipedia.* https://en.wikipedia .org/w/index.php?title=List_of_sheep_breeds&oldid=914884262

32. ONLINE FORUM POST

Author's Last Name, Initials [username]. (Year, Month Day). *Content of the post up to 20 words* [Online forum post]. Name of Site. URL

Hanzus, D. [DanHanzus]. (2019, October 23). *GETCHA DAN HANZUS. ASK ME ANYTHING!* [Online forum post]. Reddit. https://bit.ly/38WgmSF

33. BLOG POST

Author's Last Name, Initials [username]. (Year, Month Day). Title of post. Name of Blog. URL

gcrepps. (2017, March 28). Shania Sanders. *Women@NASA.* https://blogs .nasa.gov/womenatnasa/2017/03/28/shania-sanders/

If only the username is known, use it without brackets.

34. ONLINE STREAMING VIDEO

> Uploader's Last Name, Initials [username]. (Year, Month Day). *Title* [Video]. Name of Video Platform. URL

> CinemaSins. (2014, August 21). *Everything wrong with* National treasure *in 13 minutes or less* [Video]. YouTube. https://www.youtube.com /watch?v=1ul-_ZWvXTs

Whoever uploaded the video is considered the author, even if someone else created the content. If only the username is known, use it without brackets.

35. PODCAST

> Host's Last Name, Initials (Host). (First Year–Last Year). *Podcast name* [Audio podcast]. Production Company. URL

> Poor, N., Woods, E., & Thomas, R. (Hosts). (2017–present). *Ear hustle* [Audio podcast]. PRX. https://www.earhustlesq.com/

36. PODCAST EPISODE

> Host's Last Name, Initials (Host). (Year, Month Day). Episode title (No. number) [Audio podcast episode]. *In Podcast name.* Production Company. URL

> Tamposi, E., & Samocki, E. (Hosts). (2020, January 8). The year of the broads [Audio podcast episode]. In *The broadcast podcast*. Podcast One. https://podcastone.com/episode/the-year-of-the-broads

Omit the episode number if one is not given.

37. FILM

> Director's Last Name, Initials (Director). (Year). *Title* [Film]. Production Company. URL

> Jenkins, B. (Director). (2016). *Moonlight* [Film]. A24; Plan B; PASTEL.

Cuarón, A. (Director). (2016). *Harry Potter and the prisoner of Azkaban* [Film; two-disc special ed. on DVD]. Warner Brothers.

List the director as the author of the film. Indicate how you watched the film only if the format is relevant to what you've written.

38. TELEVISION SERIES

Executive Producer's Last Name, Initials (Executive Producer). (First Year–
Last Year). *Title of series* [TV series]. Production Company. URL

Iungerich, L., Gonzalez, E., & Haft, J. (Executive Producers).
(2018–present). *On my block* [TV series]. Crazy Cat Lady Productions.

Indicate how you watched the TV series (two-disc DVD set, for example) only if the format is relevant to your essay.

39. TELEVISION SERIES EPISODE

Writer's Last Name, Initials (Writer), & Director's Last Name, Initials
(Director). (Year, Month Day). Title of episode (Season number,
Episode number) [TV series episode]. In Executive Producer's
Initials Last Name (Executive Producer), *Title of series.* Production
Company. URL

Siegal, J. (Writer), Morgan, D. (Writer), & Sackett, M. (Director). (2018,
December 6). Janet(s) (Season 3, Episode 10) [TV series episode]. In
M. Schur, D. Miner, M. Sackett, & D. Goddard (Executive Producers),
The good place. Fremulon; 3 Arts Entertainment; Universal
Television.

40. MUSIC ALBUM

Artist's Last Name, Initials. (Year). *Title of album* [Album]. Label. URL

Jonas Brothers. (2019). *Happiness begins* [Album]. Republic.

41. SONG

> Artist's Last Name, Initials. (Year). Name of song [Song]. *On Title of album.* Label. URL

> Giddens, R. (2015). Waterboy [Song]. On *Tomorrow is my turn.* Nonesuch.

42. *POWERPOINT* SLIDES

> Author's Last Name, Initials. (Year, Month Day). *Title of presentation* [PowerPoint slides]. Publisher. URL

> Pavliscak, P. (2016, February 21). *Finding our happy place in the internet of things* [PowerPoint slides]. Slideshare. https://bit.ly/3aOcfs7

43. RECORDING OF A SPEECH OR WEBINAR

> Author's Last Name, Initials. (Year, Month Day *or* Year). *Title* [Speech audio recording or Webinar]. Publisher. URL

> Kennedy, J. F. (1961, January 20). *Inaugural address* [Speech audio recording]. American Rhetoric. https://bit.ly/339Gc3e

For a speech, include the year, month, and day. For a webinar, include only the year.

44. PHOTOGRAPH

> Photographer's Last Name, Initials. (Year). *Title of photograph* [Photograph]. Name of Site. URL

> Kudacki, P. (2013). [Photograph of Benedict Cumberbatch]. Time. http://content.time.com/time/covers/asia/0,16641,20131028,00.html

Use this format to document a photograph that is not in a museum or on a museum website. For a photograph with no title, include a description of the photograph in brackets after the date.

45. MAP

> Mapmaker's Last Name, Initials. (Year). *Title of map* [Map].
> Publisher. URL

> Daniels, M. (2018). *Human terrain: Visualizing the world's population, in*
> *3D* [Map]. The Pudding. https://pudding.cool/2018/10/city_3d/

46. SOCIAL MEDIA POSTS

If only the username is known, do not use brackets. List any audiovisual content (e.g., videos, images, or links) in brackets. Replicate emoji or include a bracketed description. Follow the spelling and capitalization of the post.

> Author's Last Name, Initials [@username]. (Year, Month Day).
> *Content of post up to 20 words* [Description of any audiovisual
> content] [Type of post]. Platform. URL

TWEET

> Baron, D. [@DrGrammar]. (2021, March 12). *Got vaxxed and now I'm*
> *coming to you in 5g.* [Image attached] [Tweet]. Twitter. https://bit
> .ly/3sxEELx

***INSTAGRAM* PHOTOGRAPH OR VIDEO**

> Jamil, J. [@jameelajamilofficial]. (2018, July 18). *Happy Birthday to our*
> *leader. I steal all my acting faces from you.* @kristenanniebell [Face
> with smile and sunglasses emoji] [Photograph]. Instagram.
> https://www.instagram.com/p/BlYX5F9FuGL/

***FACEBOOK* POST**

> Raptor Resource Project. (2020, May 8). *Happy Fri-yay, everyone! We'll*
> *keep the news short and sweet: today Decorah eaglets D34 and*
> *D35 turn 33 days* [Images attached]. Facebook. https://bit.ly/3icwFzN

47. DATA SET

> Author's Last Name, Initials. (Year). *Title of data set* (Version number) [Data set]. Publisher. DOI *or* URL

> Pew Research Center. (2019). *Core trends survey* [Data set]. https://www .pewresearch.org/internet/dataset/core-trends-survey/

Omit the version number if one is not given. If the publisher is the author, no need to list it twice; omit the publisher.

48. SUPREME COURT CASE

> Name of Case, volume US pages (Year). URL

> Plessy v. Ferguson, 163 US 537 (1896). https://www.oyez.org/cases /1850-1900/163us537

> Obergefell v. Hodges, 576 US ___ (2015). https://www.oyez.org /cases/2014/14-556

The source for most Supreme Court cases is the *United States Reports*, which is abbreviated "US" in the reference list entry. If the case does not yet have a page number, use three underscores instead.

Sources Not Covered by APA

To document a source for which APA does not provide guidelines, look at models similar to the source you have cited. Give any information readers will need in order to find the source themselves—author; date of publication; title; and information about the source itself (including who published it; volume, issue, and page numbers; and a DOI or URL). You might want to check your reference note to be sure it will lead others to your source.

FORMATTING A PAPER

Title page. APA generally requires a title page. The page number should go in the upper right-hand corner. Center the full title of the paper in bold in the top half of the page. Center your name, the name of your department and school, the course number and name, the instructor's name, and the due date on separate lines below the title. Leave one line between the title and your name.

Page numbers. Place the page number in the upper right-hand corner. Number pages consecutively throughout.

Fonts, spacing, margins, and indents. Use a legible font that will be accessible to everyone, either a serif font (such as Times New Roman or Bookman) or a sans serif font (such as Calibri or Verdana). Use a sans serif font within figure images. Double-space the entire paper, including any notes and your list of references; the only exception is footnotes at the bottom of a page, which should be single-spaced, and text within tables and images, the spacing of which will vary. Leave one-inch margins at the top, bottom, and sides of your text; do not justify the text. The first line of each paragraph should be indented one-half inch (or five to seven spaces) from the left margin. APA recommends using one space after end-of-sentence punctuation.

Headings. Though they are not required in APA style, headings can help readers follow your text. The first level of heading should be bold and centered; the second level of heading should be bold and flush with the left margin; the third level should be bold, italicized, and flush left. Capitalize all headings as you would any other title within the text.

First-Level Heading

Second-Level Heading

Third-Level Heading

Abstract. An abstract is a concise summary of your paper that introduces readers to your topic and main points. Most scholarly journals require an abstract; an abstract is not typically required for student papers, so check your instructor's preference. Put your abstract on the second page, with the word "Abstract" centered and in bold at the top. Unless your instructor specifies a length, limit your abstract to 250 words or fewer.

Long quotations. Indent quotations of forty or more words one-half inch (or five to seven spaces) from the left margin. Do not use quotation marks, and place the page number(s) or documentation information in parentheses *after* the end punctuation. If there are paragraphs in the quotation, indent the first line of each paragraph another one-half inch.

> Kaplan (2000) captured ancient and contemporary Antioch:
>> At the height of its glory in the Roman-Byzantine age, when it had an amphitheater, public baths, aqueducts, and sewage pipes, half a million people lived in Antioch. Today the population is only 125,000. With sour relations between Turkey and Syria, and unstable politics throughout the Middle East, Antioch is now a backwater—seedy and tumbledown, with relatively few tourists. (p. 123)
> Antioch's decline serves as a reminder that the fortunes of cities can change drastically over time.

List of references. Start your list on a new page after the text but before any notes. Title the page "References," centered and in bold, and double-space the entire list. Each entry should begin at the left margin, and subsequent lines should be indented one-half inch (or five to seven spaces). Alphabetize the list by authors' last names (or by editors' names, if appropriate). Alphabetize works that have no author or editor by title, disregarding "A," "An," and "The." Be sure every source listed is cited in the text; do not include sources that you consulted but did not cite.

Tables and figures. Above each table or figure (charts, diagrams, graphs, photos, and so on), provide the word "Table" or "Figure" and a number, flush left and in bold (e.g., **Table 1**). On the following line, give a descriptive title, flush left and italicized. Below the table or figure, include a note with any necessary explanation and source information. Number tables and figures separately, and be sure to discuss them in your text so that readers know how they relate.

TABLE 1
Hours of Instruction Delivered per Week

	American classrooms	Japanese classrooms	Chinese classrooms
First grade			
Language arts	10.5	8.7	10.4
Mathematics	2.7	5.8	4.0
Fifth grade			
Language arts	7.9	8.0	11.1
Mathematics	3.4	7.8	11.7

Note. Adapted from *Peeking Out from under the Blinders: Some Factors We Shouldn't Forget in Studying Writing* (Occasional Paper No. 25), by J. R. Hayes, 1991, National Center for the Study of Writing and Literacy (https://archive.nwp.org/cs/public/print/resource/720). Copyright 1991 by the Office of Educational Research and Improvement.

SAMPLE RESEARCH PAPER

The following sample pages are from "The Benefits of Prison Nursery Programs," a paper written by Analisa Johnson for a first-year writing course. It is formatted according to the guidelines of the *Publication Manual of the American Psychological Association*, 7th edition (2020). While APA guidelines are used widely in linguistics and the social sciences, exact requirements may vary from discipline to discipline and course to course. If you're unsure about what your instructor wants, ask for clarification.

Title bold and centered.

The Benefits of Prison Nursery Programs

Author's name, school name and department, course number and name, instructor's name, and due date.

Analisa Johnson

Writing Program, Boston University

WR 150: Burning Questions: Human Expression

Samantha Myers

May 1, 2017

2

Abstract •·······························

The rising population of women in prisons has resulted in the births

of some 2,000 babies per year to women behind bars. Female prisoners

suffer from a number of inadequacies in their health care, but changes

in birthing practices and the provision of nursery programs in prisons

could yield important benefits. Currently, nine states offer such programs,

and research conducted in these states has shown a number of positive

effects. Fully 86.3% of women who have come through these programs

remain in their communities after 3 years. Likewise, preschool perfor-

mance of their children shows better emotional / behavioral adjustment

than that of children who have been sent to foster care. Finally, estimates

show that the annual costs of such programs are approximately 40% less

than those of foster care.

Keywords: birthing practices, correctional, foster care, health care,

incarceration, nursery program, prenatal care, preschool, prison, recidi-

vism, sentencing project, shackles

Heading bold and centered.

Limited to 250 words or fewer.

"Keywords:" in italics, indented.

3

Title bold and centered.

The Benefits of Prison Nursery Programs

Double-spaced throughout.

Over the past 40 years or so, the United States has seen a steady increase in incarcerated individuals, with 2.2 million people currently in prisons and jails nationwide, according to statistics on prisons and the criminal justice system provided by the Sentencing Project (2017, p. 2). In particular, the number of incarcerated females has risen dramatically, at a rate 50% higher than that of men since the early 1980s. As recently as 2015, there were nearly 112,000 incarcerated women across the nation (Sentencing Project, 2017, p. 4). While there is a plethora of health care issues that women face when locked up, one of the most concerning is that of reproductive health, specifically pregnancy and birth in prison. Roughly 1 in 25 women entering prison or jail is pregnant (Yager, 2015). As a result, the number of babies born behind bars has also grown at an alarming rate.

It is estimated that up to 2,000 infants are born to incarcerated mothers each year, only to be taken from them a scant 24 hours after birth and placed either with a family member or, more often, in the foster care system (Sufrin, 2012). Current scholarly sources have proven prison nursery programs—which allow mothers to keep their infants with them while they serve out their sentences—to be a very effective method in dealing with the issue of incarcerated mothers. Despite this fact, there are only nine nursery programs currently operational in America. In order to make prison nursery programs more prevalent, better education is needed for correctional administrators about the effectiveness of nursery programs.

First-level headings bold and centered.

Inadequacies of Prison Health Care for Pregnant Women

Paragraphs indented $\frac{1}{2}$ inch or 5–7 spaces.

When it comes to women's health care in the prison system, there are many inadequate areas, but two that are of great importance are prenatal care and birthing practices.

4

Prenatal Care

Hotelling (2008) discussed the lack of quality health care provided to
expectant mothers behind bars. Despite adequate health care being man-
dated to all inmates through the Eighth Amendment to the Constitution,
women still make up a lesser percentage of total incarcerated individuals
than men—a fact that is used by correctional staff to justify providing
scarcer health care and rehabilitative programs for incarcerated women.
In addition, prisons are not subject to any sort of external review of their
standards of inmate care, so they are not encouraged to improve health
care services. As a result, many incarcerated women face unnecessarily
high-risk pregnancies.

Author named in a signal phrase, publication date in parentheses after the name.

Birthing Practices

Second-level headings bold and flush with left margin.

Another practice that increases the risk of complications in pregnancy
in prison is the custom of shackling female inmates during labor, delivery,
and postpartum. This practice is both degrading and inhumane and can
pose a problem for health care providers in case of an emergency. In an official position statement, the Association of Women's Health, Obstetric and
Neonatal Nurses (2011) noted that the unnecessary practice can interfere
with the ability of nurses and health care providers to deliver the proper
care and treatment (p. 817). Only 18 states in the United States currently
ban the shackling of expectant mothers in prison while they give birth
(American Civil Liberties Union Foundation, 2012). The remaining 32 states
are left to their own devices, in some cases shackling mothers with no
regard to the recommendations of nurses and other health care providers.

Prison Nursery Programs

In order to effectively spread awareness of prison nursery programs,
it must be clear exactly what they are and how they serve incarcerated

5

mothers. Prison nursery programs offer women who become incarcerated while pregnant the option to keep and parent their child while they serve their sentences. Getting into these programs can be a rigorous process; with limited spots available, prospective mothers must have a nonviolent conviction, no record of child abuse, and be roughly within 18 months of completing their sentence—which is the maximum amount of time a child can stay with their mother behind bars (Stein, 2010, p. 11).

Author name in parentheses when no signal phrase is used.

Benefits

When mothers do get into these programs, there are many benefits to be had for both themselves and their children. For starters, mothers are provided with parenting classes, support groups, substance abuse counseling, and complementary day-care services to attend these classes. Many prisons also provide high school and college courses for those mothers who have not yet completed their education (Wertheimer, 2005). Last, vocational programs are also offered, which aid in the job search once the women are released from prison.

Recidivism

As a result of the programs, many of the mothers have been shown to have a reduced recidivism rate. An astounding 86.3% of women exiting a prison nursery program remained in the community 3 years following their release (Goshin et al., 2013, Results section, para. 3). This is a proven positive for both the mothers and their children.

In-text citation of journal article without pagination.

Cost of Prison Nursery Programs

While it may seem as if implementing prison nursery programs across the country would be an expensive endeavor, it is important to consider by comparison the costs of putting children in foster care. On average, the total financial cost for one child to remain in foster care per

6

year in Oregon is about $26,600 (Fixsen, 2011, p. 3). Conversely, based on an evaluation of Nebraska's prison nursery program, expenses for the nursery program would be roughly 40% less per year than foster care expenses would be for the same babies, and even more money would be saved if the nursery program reduced recidivism (Carlson, 1998, as cited in Yager, 2015, para. 34). Rapidly increasing the number of prison nursery programs across the country may result in some extra money spent in the short run, but it will provide benefits in the long run, both financially and socially.

Source quoted in another source identified with "as cited in."

7

Heading bold and centered.

Alphabetized by authors' last names or first word of organization.

All lines after the first line of each entry indented.

References

American Civil Liberties Union Foundation. (2012). *The shackling of pregnant women & girls in U.S. prisons, jails & youth detention centers* [Briefing paper]. https://www.aclu.org/files/assets/anti-shackling _briefing_paper_stand_alone.pdf

Association of Women's Health, Obstetric and Neonatal Nurses. (2011). *Shackling incarcerated pregnant women* [Position statement]. http://www.jognn.org/article/S0884-2175(15)30763-2/pdf

Fixsen, A. (2011). *Children in foster care.* A Family for Every Child. http://www.afamilyforeverychild.org/wp=content/uploads/2018/04 /children_in_foster_care.pdf

Goshin, L. S., Byrne, M. W., & Henninger, A. M. (2013). Recidivism after release from a prison nursery program. *Public Health Nursing, 33*(2), 109–117. https://doi.org/10.1111/phn.12072

Hotelling, B. A. (2008). Perinatal needs of pregnant incarcerated women. *The Journal of Perinatal Education, 17*(2), 37–44. https://doi .org/10.1624/105812408X298372

Sentencing Project. (2017). *Trends in U.S. corrections* [Fact sheet]. http://sentencingproject.org/wp-content/uploads/2016/01 /Trends-in-US-Corrections.pdf

Stein, D. J. (2010, July/August). Babies behind bars: Nurseries for incarcerated mothers and their children. *Children's Voice, 19*(4), 10–13.

Sufrin, C. (2012, July 1). *Incarcerated women and reproductive health care* [Video]. YouTube. https://www.youtube.com /watch?v=WNx1ntLyI2Q

8

Wertheimer, L. (2005, November 5). *Prenatal care behind bars* [Radio broadcast]. NPR. http://www.npr.org/templates/story/story .php?storyId=4990886

Yager, S. (2015, July/August). Prison born. *The Atlantic.* https://www .theatlantic.com/magazine/archive/2015/07/prison-born/395297/

All sources cited in
the text are listed.

Part 8

Media / Design

Consciously or not, we design all the texts we write, choosing typefaces, setting up text as lists or charts, deciding whether to add headings—and then whether to center them or align them on the left. Sometimes our genre calls for certain design elements—essays begin with titles, letters begin with salutations ("Dear Auntie Em"). Other times we design texts to meet the demands of particular audiences, formatting documentation in MLA or APA or some other style, setting type larger for young children, and so on. And our designs always depend on our medium. A memoir might take the form of an essay in a book, be turned into a bulleted list for a slide presentation, or include links to images or other pages if presented on a website. The chapters in this part offer advice for **CHOOSING MEDIA**; working with **DESIGN**, **IMAGES**, and **SOUND**; **WRITING AND LEARNING ONLINE**; and **GIVING PRESENTATIONS**.

Media/Design

55 Choosing Media   659

56 Designing Text   664

57 Using Visuals, Incorporating Sound   673

58 Writing and Learning Online   684

59 Giving Presentations   694

55 Choosing Media

USA Today reports on contract negotiations between automakers and auto-workers with an article that includes a large photo and a colorful graph; the article on the same story on the *New York Times* website includes a video of striking workers. In your economics class, you give a presentation about the issue that includes *Prezi* slides.

These examples show how information about the same events can be delivered using three different media: print (*USA Today*), digital (nytimes.com), and spoken (the main medium for your class presentation). They also show how different media offer writers different modes of expressing meaning, ranging from words to images to sounds and hyperlinks. A print text can include written words and still visuals; online, the same text can also incorporate links to moving images and sound as well as to other written materials. A presentation with slides can include both spoken and written words, can incorporate video and audio elements—and can also include print handouts.

In college writing, the choice of medium often isn't up to you: your instructor may require a printed essay or a classroom talk, a website, or some combination of media. Sometimes, though, you'll be the one deciding. Because your medium will play a big part in the way your audience receives and reacts to your message, you'll need to think hard about what media best suit your audience, purpose, and message. This chapter will help you choose media when the choice is yours.

Print

When you have a choice of medium, print has certain advantages over spoken and digital text in that it's more permanent and doesn't depend on audience access to technology. Depending on your own access to technology, you can usually insert photos or other visuals and can present data and other information as graphs or charts. Obviously, though, print documents are more work than digital ones to update or change, and they don't allow for sound, moving images, or links to other materials.

Digital

Online writing is everywhere: on course learning management systems and class websites; in virtual discussion groups and wikis; in emails, text messages, tweets, and other social media. And when you're taking an online course, you are, by definition, always using a digital medium. Remember that this medium has advantages as well as limitations and potential pitfalls. You can add audio, video, and links—but your audience may not have the same access to technology that you do. These are just some of the things you'll need to keep in mind when deciding, say, whether to include or link to videos or a site that has restricted access. Also, digital texts that circulate online through blogs, websites, email, or social media can take on a life of their own; other viewers may forward, like, retweet, or repost your text to much larger audiences than you originally considered.

Spoken

If you deliver your text orally, as a speech or presentation, you have the opportunity to use your tone of voice, gestures, and physical bearing to establish credibility. But you must write your text so that it's easy to understand when it is heard rather than read. Speaking from memory or from notecards, rather than reading a script or essay, often makes it easier for the audience to follow your talk. The spoken medium can be used alone with a live, face-to-face audience, but it's often combined with print in the form of handouts, or with digital media in the form of presentation

academic literacies   ● fields   ● research
■ rhetorical situations   ∴ processes   ● media/design
▲ genres   ◆ strategies

software like *PowerPoint* or *Prezi*, or designed for remote audiences in formats like webcasts, webinars, podcasts, or videoconferencing platforms such as *Zoom*.

Multimedia

It's increasingly likely that you'll be assigned to create a multimedia text, one that includes some combination of print, oral, and digital elements. It's also possible that you'll have occasion to write a multimodal text, one that uses more than one mode of expression: words, images, audio, video, links, and so on. The words "multimedia" and "multimodal" are often used interchangeably, but "multimodal" is the term that's used most often in composition classes, whereas "multimedia" is the one used in other disciplines and in industry. In composition classes, the word generally refers to writing that includes more than just words.

For example, let's say that in a US history class you're assigned to do a project about the effects of the Vietnam War on American society. You might write an essay using words alone to discuss such effects as increased hostility toward the military and government, generational conflict within families and society at large, and increased use of recreational drugs. But you could also weave such a text together with many other materials to create a multimodal composition.

If you're using print, for example, you could include photographs from the Vietnam era, such as of antiwar protests or military funerals. Another possibility might be a timeline that puts developments in the war in the context of events going on simultaneously elsewhere in American life, such as in fashion and entertainment or in the feminist and civil rights movements. If you're posting your project online, you might also incorporate video clips of TV news coverage of the war and clips from films focusing on it or its social effects, such as *Apocalypse Now* or *Easy Rider*. Audio elements could include recorded interviews with veterans who fought in the war, people who protested against it, or government officials who were involved in planning or overseeing it. Many of these elements could be inserted into your document as links.

If your assignment specifies that you give an oral presentation, you could play some of the music of the Vietnam era, show videos of government officials defending the war and demonstrators protesting it, maybe hang some psychedelic posters from the era.

You might do something similar with your own work by creating an electronic portfolio, or e-portfolio. Tips for compiling an **E-PORTFOLIO** may be found in Chapter 34.

388

Considering the Rhetorical Situation

PURPOSE What's your purpose, and what media will best suit that purpose? A text message or email may be appropriate for inviting a friend to lunch, but neither would be ideal for demonstrating to a professor that you understand a complex historical event; for that, you'd likely write a report, either in print or online—and you might include photos, maps, or other such texts to provide visual context.

59–60

AUDIENCE What media are your audience likely to expect—and be able to access? A blog may be a good way to reach people who share your interest in basketball or cupcakes, but to reach your grandparents you may want to send them an email message—or a handwritten note in the mail. Some employers and graduate school admissions officers require applicants to submit résumés and applications online, while others prefer to receive them in print form.

61–64

GENRE Does your genre require a particular medium? If you're giving an oral presentation, you'll often be expected to include slides. Academic essays are usually formatted to be printed out, even if they are submitted electronically. An online essay based on field research might include audio files of those you've interviewed, but if your essay

65–71

academic literacies • fields • research
rhetorical situations • processes • media/design
genres • strategies

were in print, you'd need to quote (or paraphrase or summarize) what they said.

STANCE

If you have a choice of media, think about whether a particular medium will help you convey your stance. A print document in MLA format, for instance, will make you seem scholarly and serious. Tweeting or blogging, however, might work better for a more informal stance. Presenting data in charts will sometimes help you establish your credibility as a knowledgeable researcher.

■ 72–74

Once you decide on the media and modes of expression you're using, you'll need to design your text to take advantage of their possibilities and to deal with their limitations. The next chapters will help you do that.

56 Designing Text

You're trying to figure out why a magazine ad you're looking at is so funny, and you realize that the text's font is deliberately intended to make you laugh. An assignment for a research paper in psychology specifies that you are to follow APA format. Your classmates complain that the *PowerPoint* slides you use for a presentation are hard to read because there's not enough contrast between the words and the background. Another student says you include too many words on each slide. Whether you're putting together your résumé, creating a website for your intramural soccer league, or writing an essay for a class, you need to think about how you design what you write.

Sometimes you can rely on established conventions: in MLA and APA styles, for example, there are specific guidelines for margins, headings, and the use of single-, double-, or triple-spaced lines of text. But often you'll have to make design decisions on your own—and not just about words and spacing. If what you're writing includes photos, charts, tables, graphs, or other visuals, you'll need to integrate these with your written text in the most attractive and effective way; online, you may also need to decide where and how to include video clips and links. You might even use scissors, glue, and staples to attach objects to a poster or create pop-ups in a brochure.

No matter what your text includes, its design will influence how your audience responds to it and therefore how well it achieves your purpose. This chapter offers general advice on designing print and online texts.

Considering the Rhetorical Situation

As with all writing tasks, your rhetorical situation should affect the way you design a text. Here are some points to consider:

* academic literacies
■ rhetorical situations
▲ genres

● fields
⁂ processes
◆ strategies

● research
● media/design

59–60

PURPOSE How can you design your text to help achieve your purpose? If you're reporting information, for instance, you may want to present statistical data in a chart or table rather than in the main text to help readers grasp it more quickly. If you're trying to get readers to care about an issue, a photo or **PULL QUOTE**—a brief selection of text "pulled out" and featured in a larger font—might help you do so.

Glossary

AUDIENCE How can you make your design appeal to your intended audience? By using a certain font style or size to make your text look stylish, serious, or easy to read? What kind of headings—big and bold, simple and restrained?—would your readers expect or find helpful? What colors would appeal to them?

61–64

GENRE Are you writing in a genre that has design conventions, such as an abstract, an annotated bibliography, or a résumé? Do you need to follow a format such as those prescribed in MLA or APA style?

65–71

STANCE How can your design reflect your attitude toward your audience and subject? Do you need a businesslike font or a playful one? Would tables and graphs help you establish your credibility? How can illustrations help you convey a certain tone?

72–74

Some Basic Principles of Design

Be consistent. To keep readers oriented while reading documents or browsing multiple webpages, any design elements should be used consistently. In a print academic essay, that task may be as simple as using the same font throughout for your main text and using boldface or italics for headings. If you're writing for the web, navigation buttons and other major elements should be in the same place on every page. In a presentation, each slide should use the same background and the same font unless there's a good reason to introduce differences.

Keep it simple. One of your main design goals should be to help readers see quickly—even intuitively—what's in your text and how to find specific information. Adding headings to help readers see the parts, using consistent colors and fonts to help them recognize key elements, setting off steps in lists, using white space to set off blocks of text or to call attention to certain elements, and (especially) resisting the temptation to fill pages with fancy graphics or unnecessary animations—these are all ways of making your text simple to read.

Look, for example, at a furniture store's simple, easy-to-understand webpage design on the next page. This webpage contains considerable information: a row of links across the top, directing readers to various products; a search option; a column down the right side that provides details about the chair shown in the wide left-hand column; thumbnail photos below the chair and ordering information; and more details across the bottom. Despite the wealth of content, the site's design is both easy to figure out and, with the generous amount of white space, easy on the eyes.

Aim for balance. On the webpage on the next page, the photo takes up about a quarter of the screen and is balanced by a narrower column of text, and the product information tabs and text across the page bottom balance the company logo and search box across the top. For a page without images, balance can be created through the use of margins, headings, and spacing. In the journal page shown on page 583, notice how using white space around the article title and the author's name, as well as setting both in larger type and the author's name in all capital letters, helps to balance them vertically against the large block of text below. The large initial letter of the text also helps to balance the mass of smaller type that follows. MLA and APA styles have specific design guidelines for academic research papers that cover these elements. A magazine page might create a sense of balance by using **PULL QUOTES** and illustrations to break up dense vertical columns of text.

Glossary

Use color and contrast carefully. Academic readers usually expect black text on a white background, with perhaps one other color for headings. Presentation slides and webpages are most readable with a plain, light-colored

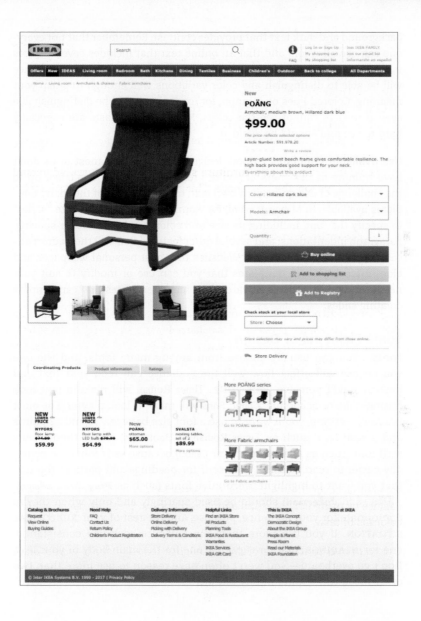

background and dark text that provides contrast. Remember that not everyone can see all colors and that an online text that includes several colors might be printed out and read in black and white; make sure your audience will be able to distinguish any color variations well enough to grasp your meaning. Colored lines on a graph, for example, should be distinguishable even if readers cannot see the colors. Red-green contrasts are especially hard to see and should be avoided.

Use available templates.   Good design takes time, and most of us don't have training as designers. If you're pressed for time or don't feel up to the challenge of designing your own text, take advantage of the many templates available. In *Microsoft Word*, for example, you can customize "styles" to specify the font, including its size and color; single- or double-spacing; paragraph indentations; and several other features that will then automatically apply to your document. Websites that host personal webpages and blogs offer dozens of templates that you can use or modify to suit your needs. And presentation software offers many templates that can simplify creating slides.

Some Elements of Design

Fonts.   You can usually choose from among many fonts, and the one you choose will affect how well the audience can read your text and how they will perceive your **TONE**. Times Roman will make a text look businesslike or academic; *Comic Sans* will make it look playful. For most academic writing, you'll want to use a font size between 10 and 12 points and a serif font (such as Times Roman or Bookman) rather than a sans serif font (such as Arial, **Verdana**, or Calibri) because serif fonts are generally easier to read. Reserve sans serif for headings and parts of the text that you want to highlight. Decorative fonts (such as *Magneto*, *Amaze*, Chiller, and **Jokerman**) should be used sparingly and only when they're appropriate for your audience, purpose, and the rest of your **RHETORICAL SITUATION**. If you use more than one font, use each one consistently: one for **HEADINGS**, one for captions, one for the main body of your text. Don't go overboard—you won't often have reason to use more than two or, at most, three fonts in any one text.

73–74 ■

57 ■

670–72 ●

☀ academic literacies   ● fields   ● research
■ rhetorical situations   ⁑ processes   ● media/design
▲ genres   ◆ strategies

Every font has regular, **bold**, and *italic* forms. In general, choose regular for the main text and lower-level headings, bold for major headings, and italic within the main text to indicate titles of books and other long works and, occasionally, to emphasize words or brief phrases. Avoid italicizing or boldfacing entire sentences or paragraphs, especially in academic writing. If you are following **MLA**, **APA**, or some other style format, be sure your use of fonts conforms to its requirements.

● MLA 564–614
    APA 614–55

Finally, consider the line spacing of your text. Generally, academic writing is double-spaced, whereas job application letters and **RÉSUMÉS*** are usually single-spaced. Some kinds of **REPORTS** may call for single-spacing; check with your instructor if you're not sure. You'll often need to add extra space to set off parts of a text—items in a list, for instance, or headings.

▲ 140–63

Layout.   Layout is the way text is arranged on a page. An academic essay, for example, will usually have a title centered at the top, one-inch margins all around, and double-spacing. A text can be presented in paragraphs— or in the form of **LISTS**, **TABLES**, **CHARTS**, **GRAPHS**, and so on. Sometimes you'll need to include other elements as well: headings, images and other graphics, captions, lists of works cited.

● 669–70
    676

Paragraphs.   Dividing text into paragraphs focuses information for readers and helps them process it by dividing it into manageable chunks. If you're writing a story for a print newspaper with narrow columns, for example, you'll divide your text into shorter paragraphs than you would if you were writing an academic essay. In general, indent paragraphs five to seven spaces (one-half inch) when your text is double-spaced; either indent or skip a line between single-spaced paragraphs.

Lists.   Put into list form information that you want to set off and make easily accessible. Number the items in a list when the sequence matters (in instructions, for example); use bullets when the order is not important. Set off lists with an extra line of space above and below, and add extra space between the items if necessary for legibility. Here's an example:

---

*See the ebook at digital.wwnorton.com/fieldguide6 for a chapter on Résumés and Job Letters.

Darwin's theory of how species change through time derives from three postulates, each of which builds on the previous one:

1. The ability of a population to expand is infinite, but the ability of any environment to support populations is always finite.
2. Organisms within populations vary, and this variation affects the ability of individuals to survive and reproduce.
3. The variations are transmitted from parents to offspring.

—Robert Boyd and Joan B. Silk, *How Humans Evolved*

Do not set off text as a list unless there's a good reason to do so, however. Some lists are more appropriately presented in paragraph form, especially when they give information that isn't meant to be referred to more than once. In the following example, there's no reason to highlight the information by setting it off in a list—and bad news is softened by putting it in paragraph form:

I regret to inform you that the Scholarship Review Committee did not approve your application for a Board of Rectors scholarship for the following reasons: your grade-point average did not meet the minimum requirements; your major is not among those eligible for consideration; and the required letter of recommendation was not received before the deadline.

Presented as a list, that information would be needlessly emphatic.

Headings. Headings make the structure of a text easier to follow and help readers find specific information. Some genres require standard headings—announcing an **ABSTRACT**, for example, or a list of **WORKS CITED**.

196–200
607

Other times you'll want to use headings to provide an overview of a section of text. You may not need any headings in brief texts, but when you do, you'll probably want to use one level at most, just to announce major topics. Longer texts, information-rich genres such as brochures or detailed

140–63

REPORTS, and websites may require several levels of headings. If you decide to include headings, you will need to decide how to phrase them, what fonts to use, and where to position them.

Phrase headings concisely. Make your headings succinct and parallel in

☀ academic literacies   ● fields   ● research
■ rhetorical situations   ⁘ processes   ● media/design
▲ genres   ◆ strategies

structure. You might make all the headings nouns **(Mushrooms)**, noun phrases **(Kinds of Mushrooms)**, gerund phrases **(Recognizing Kinds of Mushrooms)**, or questions **(How Do I Identify Mushrooms?)**. Whatever form you decide on, use it consistently for each heading. Sometimes your phrasing will depend on your purpose. If you're simply helping readers find information, use brief phrases:

Head	**Forms of Social Groups among Primates**
Subhead	*Solitary Social Groups*
Subhead	*Monogamous Social Groups*

If you want to address readers directly with the information in your text, consider writing your headings as questions:

How can you identify edible mushrooms?
Where can you find edible mushrooms?
How can you cook edible mushrooms?

Make headings visible. Headings need to be visible, so if you aren't following an academic style like MLA or APA, consider making them larger than the regular text, putting them in **bold** or *italics*, or using underlining—or a different font. For example, you could use a serif font like Times Roman for your main text and a sans serif font like Arial for your headings. On the web, consider making headings a different color from the body text. When you have several levels of headings, use capitalization, bold, and italics to distinguish among the various levels:

First-Level Head
Second-Level Head
Third-level head

APA format requires that each level of heading appear in a specific style: centered bold uppercase and lowercase for the first level, flush-left bold uppercase and lowercase for the second level, and so on.

● APA 645

Position headings appropriately. If you're following APA format, center first-level headings. If you aren't following a prescribed format, you get to decide where to position your headings: centered, flush with the left margin, or even alongside the text in a wide left-hand margin. Position each level of head consistently throughout your text. Generally, online headings are positioned flush left.

White space. Use white space to separate the various parts of a text. In general, use one-inch margins for the text of an essay or report. Unless you're following MLA or APA format, include space above headings, above and below lists, and around photos, graphs, and other visuals. See the two sample research papers in this book for examples of the formats required by **MLA** and **APA**.

MLA 606–14 ●
APA 648–55

Evaluating a Design

59–60 ■

Does the design suit your PURPOSE? Does the overall look of the design help convey the text's message, support its argument, or present information?

61–64 ■

How well does the design meet the needs of your AUDIENCE? Will the overall appearance of the text appeal to the intended readers? Is the font large enough for them to read? Are there headings to help them find their way through the text? Does the design help readers find the information they need?

65–71 ■

How well does the text meet any GENRE REQUIREMENTS? Can you tell by looking at the text that it is an academic essay, a lab report, a résumé, a blog? Do its fonts, margins, headings, and page layout meet the requirements of **MLA**, **APA**, or whatever style you're using?

MLA 605–7 ●
APA 645–47

72–74 ■

How well does the design reflect your STANCE? Do the page layout and fonts convey the appropriate tone—serious, playful, adventuresome, conservative, or whatever other tone you intended?

☀ academic literacies   ● fields   ● research
■ rhetorical situations   ⁝ processes   ● media/design
▲ genres   ◆ strategies

57 Using Visuals, Incorporating Sound

For an art history class, you write an essay comparing two paintings by Willem de Kooning. For a business class, you create a proposal to improve department communication in a small local firm and incorporate diagrams to illustrate the new procedure. For a visual rhetoric class, you take a photograph of yourself and include a two-page analysis of how the picture distills something essential about you. For an engineering class project, you design a model of a bridge and give an in-class presentation explaining the structures and forces involved, which you illustrate with slides. For a psychology assignment, you interview several people who've suffered foreclosures on their homes in recent years about how the experience affected them—and then create an online text weaving together a slideshow of photos of the people outside their former homes, a graph of foreclosure rates, video and audio clips from the interviews, and your own insights.

All of these writing tasks require you to incorporate and sometimes to create visuals and sound. Many kinds of visuals can be included in print documents: photos, drawings, diagrams, graphs, charts, and more. And with writing that's delivered online or as a spoken presentation, your choices expand to include audio and video, voice-over narration, and links to other materials.

Visuals and sound aren't always appropriate, however, or even possible—so think carefully before you set out to include them. But they can help you make a point in ways that words alone cannot. Election polling results are easier to see in a bar graph than in a paragraph; photos of an event may convey its impact more powerfully than words alone; an audio clip can make a written analysis of an opera easier to understand. This chapter provides some tips for using visuals and incorporating sound in your writing.

Considering the Rhetorical Situation

57 ■

Use visuals and sounds that are appropriate for your audience, purpose, and the rest of your **RHETORICAL SITUATION**. If you're trying to persuade voters in your town to back a proposal on an issue they don't know much about, for example, you might use dramatic pictures just to get their attention. But when it's important to come across as thoughtful and objective, maybe you need a more subdued look—or to make your points with written words alone. A newspaper article on housing prices might include a bar or line graph and also some photos. A report on that topic for an economics class would probably have graphs with no photos; a spoken presentation for a business class might use a dynamic graph that shows prices changing over time and an audio voice-over for pictures of a neighborhood; a community website might have graphs, links to related sites, and a video interview with a home owner.

In your academic writing, especially, be careful that any visuals you use support your main point—and don't just serve to decorate the text. (Therefore, avoid clip art, which is primarily intended as decoration and comes off as unsophisticated and childish.) Images should validate or exemplify what you say elsewhere with written words and add information that words alone can't provide as clearly or easily.

Using Visuals

Photos, drawings, diagrams, videos, tables, pie charts, bar graphs—these are many kinds of visuals you could use. Visuals can offer support, illustration, evidence, and comparison and contrast in your document.

410–30 ◆
474–82
469–73

Photographs.   Photos can support an **ARGUMENT**, illustrate **NARRATIVES** and **PROCESSES**, present other points of view, and help readers "place" your information in time and space. You may use photos you take yourself, or you can download photos and other images from the internet—within limits. Most downloadable photos are copyrighted, meaning that you can use

An essay discussing the theme of mother and child might compare this painting from the Italian Renaissance (left) with a modern photograph such as Dorothea Lange's *Migrant Mother* (right).

them without obtaining permission from the copyright owner only if you're doing so for academic purposes, to fulfill an assignment. If you're going to publish your text, either in print or on the web, you must have permission. You can usually gain permission by emailing the copyright holder, but that often entails a fee, so think carefully about whether you need the image. Consider, too, the file size of digital images; large files can clog readers' email in-boxes, take a long time to display on their screens, or be hard for you to upload in the first place, so you may have to compress an image in a zip file or reduce its resolution (which can diminish its sharpness).

Videos.   If you're writing online, you can include video clips for readers to play. If you're using a video already available online, such as on *YouTube*, you can show the opening image with an arrow for readers to click on to start the video, or you can simply copy the video's URL and paste it into your text as a **LINK**. In either case, be sure to introduce the video in your text with a **SIGNAL PHRASE**. As with any other source, be sure to provide an in-text citation and full documentation.

681–82

551–54

If you want to include a video you made yourself, you can edit it using such programs as *iMovie* or *Shotcut*. Once you're ready to insert it into your online document, the easiest way is to first upload it to *YouTube*, choosing the Private setting so only those you authorize may view it, and then create a link in your document.

Graphs, charts, and tables.   Statistical and other numerical information is often best presented in graphs, charts, and tables. If you can't find the right one for your purpose, you can create your own, as long as it's based on sound data from reliable sources. To do so, you can use various spreadsheet programs such as *Excel* or online chart and graph generators such as *Plotly* or *Venngage*.

665
666

In any case, remember to follow basic design principles: be **CONSISTENT**, label all parts clearly, and **KEEP THE DESIGN SIMPLE** so readers can focus on the information and not be distracted by a needlessly complex design. In particular, use color and contrast wisely to emphasize what's most signifi-

666–68

cant. Choose **COLORS** that are easy to distinguish from one another—and that remain so if the graph or chart is printed out in black and white. (Using distinct gradations of color from light to dark will show well in black and white.) Some common kinds of graphs, charts, and tables are shown on the next pages.

Diagrams, maps, flowcharts, and timelines.   Information about place and time is often presented in diagrams, maps, flowcharts, and timelines. If you're using one of these visuals from the web or elsewhere, be sure to

560–63

DOCUMENT it. Otherwise you can create one of these yourself using online tools like *Canva* or the Shape and Chart tabs in your word processing program. Make diagrams and maps as simple as possible for the point you're emphasizing. Unnecessarily complex maps can be more of a distraction than a help. For timelines, make sure the scale accurately depicts the passage of time you're writing about and avoids gaps and bunches.

※ academic literacies   ● fields   ● research
■ rhetorical situations   ∴ processes   ● media/design
▲ genres   ◆ strategies

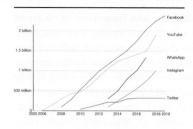

Line graphs are a good way of showing changes in data over time. Each line here represents the number of users logging on to a different social media platform. Plotting the lines together allows readers to compare the data at different points in time. Be sure to label the *x* and *y* axes, and limit the number of lines to avoid confusion.

China's expanding auto market

Number of vehicles sold in China and the U.S., in millions:

■ Sold in U.S.   ■ Sold in China

16.6   18.5   12.8   7.2

'06 '07 '08 '09 '10 '11

Source: China Association of Automobile Manufacturers, Automotive News
Graphic: Los Angeles Times   © 2012 MCT

Bar graphs are useful for comparing quantitative data, measurements of how much or how many. The bars can be horizontal or vertical. This graph compares the number of cars sold in China and the United States over a period of five years. Some software offers 3-D and other special effects, but simple graphs are often easier to read.

Costly walk down the aisle

According to The Wedding Report, the average cost of a wedding in the U.S. is about $25,300. Here's a breakdown of spending:

Venue, catering and rentals: **$11,230**

Beauty and spa **$124**

Gifts and favors **$641**

Invitations **$817**

Entertainment **$1,230**

Flowers and decorations **$1,510**

Planner/consultant **$1,540**

Jewelry **$3,920**

Photography and video **$2,670**

Attire and accessories **$1,610**

Source: The Wedding Report
Graphic: Dallas Morning News   © 2014 MCT

Pie charts can be used to show how a whole is divided into parts or how parts of a whole relate to one another. This pie chart shows the average cost of a traditional wedding in the United States. The segments in a pie should always add up to 100 percent, and each segment should be clearly labeled.

The wage gap in numbers

Year	Percent of men's income earned by women	Wage gap in dollars	Year	Percent of men's income earned by women	Wage gap in dollars
2015	80%	$10,470	1985	65%	$18,011
2010	77%	$12,027	1980	60%	$20,314
2005	77%	$11,564	1975	59%	$21,052
2000	74%	$13,474	1970	59%	$19,851
1995	71%	$13,908	1965	60%	$16,851
1990	72%	$13,822	1960	61%	$14,790

Source: U.S. Census Bureau   Graphic: Tribune News Service

Tables are useful for displaying numerical information concisely, especially when several items are being compared. This table shows the gap between men's and women's incomes over a fifty-five-year period. Presenting information in columns and rows permits readers to find data and identify relationships among them.

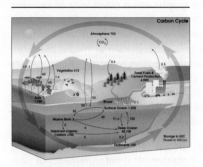

Diagrams and flowcharts are ways of showing relationships and processes. This diagram shows how carbon moves between the Earth and its atmosphere. Flowcharts can be made using widely available templates; diagrams, in contrast, can range from simple drawings to works of art. Some simple flowcharts may be found in the genres chapters.

Maps show physical locations. This map shows the annual average direct solar resources for each of the US states. Maps can be drawn to scale or purposefully out of scale to emphasize a point.

405–9 ◆

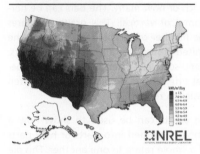

Figure 12.5
HOW THE PARTY SYSTEM EVOLVED

Timelines show change over time. These are useful to demonstrate **CAUSE** and **EFFECT** relationships or evolution. This timeline depicts how the American party system has evolved from 1788 to 2016. Timelines can be drawn horizontally or vertically.

* academic literacies   ◆ fields   ● research
■ rhetorical situations   ⁝ processes   ● media/design
▲ genres   ◆ strategies

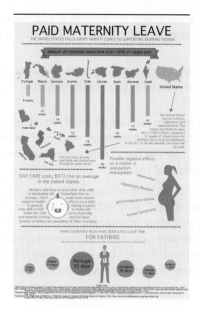

Infographics are eye-catching visual representations of information that help simplify a complicated subject. Infographics typically include an engaging title; a design that reflects the content being displayed; and a balance of charts, graphs, and other elements; readable fonts; and the sources of your information. Several websites offer templates to help you design and execute infographics, including *Piktochart*, *Infogram*, and several others.

SOME TIPS FOR USING VISUALS

- Position images as close as possible to the discussion to which they relate. In *Microsoft Word*, simply position your cursor where you want to insert an image; click the appropriate type of visual from the menu on the Insert tab; choose the appropriate image from your files; and click Insert. You may then need to adjust the way the text flows or wraps around the image: in the Page Layout tab, choose the appropriate option in Wrap Text.

- In academic writing, number all images, using separate sequences of numbers for figures (photos, graphs, diagrams, video clips, and drawings) and tables: Fig. 1, Fig. 2; Table 1, Table 2. Follow style guidelines (e.g., **MLA** or **APA**) for where to place the figure or table number and caption.

  ● MLA 607

  APA 646–47

- Explain in your written text whatever information you present in an image—don't expect it to speak for itself. Refer to the image before it appears, identifying it and summarizing its point. For example: "As Table 1 shows, Italy's economic growth rate has been declining for thirty years."

- Provide a title or caption for each image to identify it and explain its significance for your text. For example: "Table 1: Italy's Economic Growth Rate, 1990–2020."

- Label the parts of visuals clearly to ensure that your audience will understand what they show. For example, label each section of a pie chart to show what it represents.

- Cite the source of any images you don't create yourself. You need not document visuals you create, based on data from your own experimental or field research; but if you use data from a source to create a graph or chart, **CITE THE SOURCE** of the data.

555–58

- In general, you may use visuals created by someone else in your academic writing as long as you include full **DOCUMENTATION**. If you post your writing online, however, you must first obtain permission from the copyright owner and include permission information—for example: "Photo courtesy of Victoria and Albert Museum, London." Copyright holders will often tell you how they want the permission sentence to read.

560–63

Incorporating Sound

Audio clips, podcasts, and other sound files can serve various useful purposes in online writing and spoken presentation. Music, for example, can create a mood for your text, giving your audience hints about how to interpret the meaning of your words and images or what emotional response you're evoking. Other types of sound effects—such as background conversations, passing traffic, birdsongs, crowd noise at sports events—can provide a sense of immediacy, of being part of the scene or event you're describing. Spoken words can serve as the primary way you present an online text or as an enhancement of or even a counterpoint to a written text. (And if your audience includes visually impaired people, an audio track can allow or help them to follow the text.)

You can download or link to various spoken texts online, or you can record voice and music as podcasts using programs such as *GarageBand* and *Audacity*. Remember to provide an **IN-TEXT CITATION** and full **DOCUMENTATION** of any sound material you obtain from another source.

MLA 567–74
APA 618–22
560–63

* academic literacies   ● fields   ● research
■ rhetorical situations   ∴ processes   ● media / design
▲ genres   ◆ strategies

Adding Links

If you're writing an online text in which you want to include images, video, or sound material available on the web, it's often easier and more effective to create links to them within the text than to embed them by copying and pasting. Rather than provide the URL for the link, use relevant words to make it easier for a reader to decide to click on the link. (See the example below where the links are marked by blue color and words such as "Francis Davis Millet and Millet family papers.") Such links enable readers to see the materials' original context and to explore it if they wish. Be selective in the number of links you include: too many links can dilute a text.

The example below shows a blog post from the Archives of American Art with links to additional detail and documentation.

John Singer Sargent

This lively caricature from the Francis Davis Millet and Millet family papers features an artist fervently painting his subject, just in the background. Most likely it is John Singer Sargent at work on his painting *Carnation, Lily, Lily, Rose*. His posture and the expression on his face suggest an exuberance that matches the action of the paint dripping and splashing as it prepares to meet the canvas with energetic strokes.

Caricature of an artist painting vigorously, ca. 1885-1886. Francis Davis Millet and Millet family papers. Archives of American Art, Smithsonian Institution.

551–54

SOME TIPS FOR CREATING LINKS

- Indicate links with underlining and color (most often blue), and introduce them with a **SIGNAL PHRASE**.

- Don't include your own punctuation in a link. In the example on page 681, the period is not part of the link.

- Try to avoid having a link open in a new browser window. Readers expect links to open in the same window.

Editing Carefully—and Ethically

You may want to edit a photograph, cropping to show only part of it or using *Photoshop* or similar programs to enhance the colors or otherwise alter it. Similarly, you may want to edit a video, podcast, or other audio file to shorten it or remove irrelevant parts. If you are considering making a change of this kind, however, be sure not to do so in a way that misrepresents the content. If you alter a photo, be sure the image still represents the subject accurately; if you alter a recording of a speech or interview, be sure the edited version maintains the speaker's intent. Whenever you alter an image, a video, or a sound recording, tell your readers how you have changed it.

The same goes for editing charts and graphs. Changing the scale on a bar graph, for example, can change the effect of the comparison, making the quantities being compared seem very similar or very different, as shown in the two bar graphs of identical data in Figures 1 and 2.

Both charts show the increase in average housing costs in the United States between 2000 and 2020. However, by making the baseline in Figure 1 $200,000 instead of zero, the increase appears to be far greater than it was in reality. Just as you shouldn't edit a quotation or a photograph in a way that might misrepresent its meaning, you should not present statistical data in a way that could mislead readers.

✳ academic literacies   ● fields   ● research

■ rhetorical situations   ⁘ processes   ● media/design

▲ genres   ◆ strategies

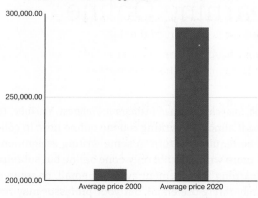

Figure 1. Average housing prices in the United States, 2000–2020 (exaggerated).

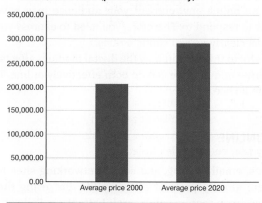

Figure 2. Average housing prices in the United States, 2000–2020 (presented accurately).

58 Writing and Learning Online

Email. *Facebook*. *Snapchat, Twitter, Instagram, Pinterest, YouTube*. Texts. Tweets. It may seem as if almost all writing is done online now. In college courses, you may still be required to turn in some writing assignments on paper, but more and more writing is not only done online but submitted that way too through learning management systems, email, or some other online system. You may rarely use email, but your professor may require you to do so. And many classes are being taught online, with little or no face-to-face communication between instructors and students.

Online, your instructor and classmates often cannot see or hear you—and that matters more than you might think. A puzzled look or a smile of recognition can start an important conversation in a face-to-face class, but in an online environment your audience may have only your written words to respond to. Therefore, you need to express your thoughts and feelings as clearly as you can *in writing*.

So it's useful to think about how the digital medium affects the way we write and learn—and how we can do both effectively online. This chapter provides some advice.

WRITING ONLINE

For most of us, email, texting, and social networking sites like *Facebook* and *Twitter* are already parts of everyday life. But using them for academic purposes may require some careful attention. Following are some guidelines.

⁂ academic literacies   ● fields   ● research

■ rhetorical situations   ⁙ processes   ● media/design

▲ genres   ◆ strategies

Email and Texts

When you're sending emails or texts to friends, you can be informal, using abbreviations, acronyms, emojis, and other shorthand ways of communicating. When you're texting or emailing your instructors, bosses, or colleagues, though, you need to write more formally: in emails, use an appropriate salutation ("Dear Professor McWilliams") and craft a specific subject line; instead of writing "Question about paper," be specific: "Profile organization question." In both email messages and texts, write clearly and concisely in complete sentences; use standard capitalization and punctuation; and proofread. If you're writing about group work or a specific course, identify the course or group explicitly. If you're writing to request something—for example, to read a draft or to write a letter of recommendation—be sure to give your readers adequate time to do what you ask before any deadlines. And be careful before you hit Send—you want to be good and sure that your email neither says something you'll regret later (don't send an email when you're angry—cool down and reread it!) nor includes anything you don't want the whole world reading (don't put confidential or sensitive information in an email).

Social Media

You may take courses that use social media or a **LEARNING MANAGEMENT SYSTEM** as a way for class members to communicate with the instructors or one another. When you do, be sure to consider your online rhetorical situation to make sure your course postings represent you as a respectful (and respectable) member of the class. Also, remember that many employers and graduate school administrators routinely check job applicants' social media pages, so don't post writing or photos on social media that you wouldn't want a potential employer to see.

689–91

Websites

You may need or want to create a website for school, a business you've started, or a hobby. While it's possible to create your own websites from

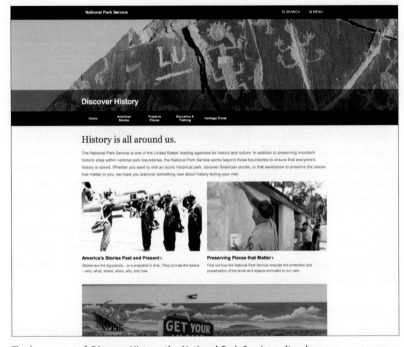

The homepage of *Discover History*, the National Park Service cultural resource program, provides a navigation menu that leads to various sections of the site. Links connect to pages describing Park Service programs.

scratch, free website builders such as *Wix*, *Weebly*, or *Duda* make it easy to create a site by providing templates for homepages, page designs, and navigation systems.

One key element in a website is the use of links to bring material from other sources into your text. You can link to the definition of a key term, for instance, rather than defining it yourself, or you can summarize a source and link to the full text rather than quoting or paraphrasing it. Providing links lets readers decide whether they need or want to see more detailed information—or not.

* academic literacies   ● fields   ● research
■ rhetorical situations   ⁂ processes   ● media/design
▲ genres   ◆ strategies

This blog, hosted by the Smithsonian Institution, focuses on marine biology and includes video, audio, slideshows, and written narratives.

Blogs

Blogs are websites that are maintained and updated regularly by individuals or groups who post opinions, reflections, information, and more—with writing, photos, video and audio files, and links to other sites. Blogs are an easy way to share your writing with others—and to invite response. Free blog hosting sites such as *WordPress*, *Wix*, or *Blogger* offer templates that let you create a blog and post to it easily, and some learning management systems include blogging capability as well.

If your blog is public, anyone can read it, including potential employers; so just as with *Facebook* and other social media, you'll want to be careful about how you present yourself and avoid posting anything that others could see as offensive. (Think twice before posting when you're angry or upset.) You may want to activate privacy settings that let you restrict access to some of the content or that make your blog unsearchable by *Google* and other search tools. Also, assume that what you post in a blog is permanent: your friends, family, employer—anyone—may read a posting years in the future, even if the blog is no longer active.

LEARNING ONLINE

It's likely that much of your learning in college will happen online. At the very least, you'll access course material through an online learning platform. But you might also take fully online courses—or hybrid courses that combine in-person and online learning. Following is advice for managing such learning effectively.

Keeping Track of Files

You'll create lots of documents as a college student. In a single writing course, for example, you may write three or four drafts of four essays—that's twelve to sixteen documents. To keep track of your files, you'll need to create folders, establish consistent file names, and back up your work.

Creating folders.   Create a folder for each course, and name it with the course title or number and the academic term: ENG 101 Fall 2021. Within each course folder, create a folder for each major assignment. Save your work in the appropriate folder, so you can always find it.

Naming and saving files.   If you're expected to submit files electronically, your instructor may ask you to name them in a certain way. If not, devise a system that will let you easily find the files, including multiple drafts of your writing. For example, you might name your files using *Your last name + Assignment + Draft number + Date:* Jones Evaluation Draft 2 10-5-2021.docx. You'll then be able to find a particular file by looking for the assignment, the draft number, or the date. Saving all your drafts as separate files will make it easy to include them in a portfolio; also, if you lose a draft, you'll be able to use the previous one to reconstruct it.

Backing up your work.   Hard drives fail, laptops and tablets get dropped, flash drives are left in public computers. Because files stored in computers can be damaged or lost, you should save your work in several places: on your computer, on a flash drive or portable hard drive, in space supplied by your school, or online. You can also ensure that an extra copy of your work exists by emailing a copy to yourself.

✳ academic literacies ● fields ● research
■ rhetorical situations ⦂ processes ● media/design
▲ genres ◆ strategies

Finding Basic Course Information

You'll need to learn some essential information about any online courses you take:

- *The phone number for the campus help desk* or technology center. Check the hours of operation, and keep the number handy.

- *The syllabus,* list of assignments, and calendar with deadlines.

- *Where to find tutorials* for your school's learning management system and other programs you may need help with.

- *Whether the course is synchronous or asynchronous.* In a *synchronous* class, you'll spend at least some of your course time in live virtual meetings with your classmates and teacher. In an *asynchronous* class, you'll interact with your peers and instructor through discussion boards, blogs, or other tools that don't require you to be logged in at a certain time. In both formats, course materials like videos, presentation slides, lecture notes, and assignments are usually available at any time through a learning management system.

- *How and when you can contact your instructor*—in person during office hours? by phone or email? through a videoconferencing platform like *Zoom?*—and how soon you can expect a response.

- *What file format you should use* to submit assignments—.doc, .docx, .rtf, .pdf, something else?—and how to submit them.

- *How to use the spell-check function* on your word processor or learning management system.

- *How to participate in online discussions*—will you use a discussion board? a chat function in a learning management system? a video-conferencing platform? something else?

Using Learning Management Systems

Whether you're in a face-to-face, hybrid, or online class, you may be asked to do some or all of your classwork online using a learning management system (LMS) such as *Blackboard, D2L, Moodle,* or *Canvas.* An LMS is a web-based educational tool that brings together all the course information your instructor wants you to have, along with features that allow you to

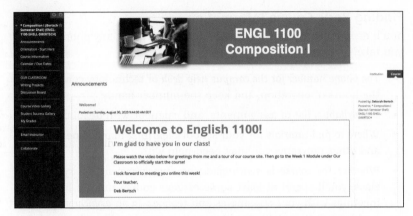

A course homepage from Columbus State Community College's LMS, *Blackboard*.

participate in the class in various ways. Your school's LMS likely includes the following features that you'll be expected to use:

A course homepage contains posts from your instructor; a calendar with due dates for assignments; and links to the course syllabus, other course content, and additional features available on the site.

A discussion board enables you to communicate with classmates even if everyone isn't logged in to the board at the same time. These conversations may be organized in "threads" so that posts on a particular topic appear together and may be read in order. When you contribute to a threaded discussion, treat it as an ongoing conversation: you need not introduce the topic but can simply add your comments.

A chat tool allows you to engage in written conversations in real time, with all participants logged in simultaneously. In a classroom, doing this may be like texting with many others at once, so the rules for class discussion apply: be patient while waiting for a response; focus on the topic being discussed; avoid sarcasm or personal attacks.

✳ academic literacies	◗ fields	● research
■ rhetorical situations	⁞ processes	◖ media/design
▲ genres	◆ strategies	

A dropbox is a place where you submit assignments online. If your course dropbox has folders for each assignment, be sure to upload your assignment into the correct folder. Keep in mind that systems go down, so don't wait until the last minute to submit a file. It's a good idea to double-check that the file you've submitted has been uploaded; often you can simply exit the dropbox and then return to it to see that your file is where it should be.

A web conferencing platform. If your course meets partly or completely online, you may attend class through a conferencing tool built into your LMS.

Online portfolios. Many LMSs allow you to create an online portfolio where you may post your coursework as well as photos, personal information, and links to other websites.

Additional features. An LMS may also include email; a space to keep a journal; a whiteboard for posting images, graphics, and presentations; a web conferencing tool; video and audio uploading capabilities; a gradebook; a social network (sometimes called a Ning) for class members only; and other features that can help you keep track of your work in a class.

Managing Challenges of Online Learning

Online classes offer a great deal of freedom and flexibility. You can work on your class almost anywhere—and often at your own pace (while still meeting deadlines, of course). Even so, online classes can present challenges, like managing your time effectively and keeping yourself motivated, disciplined, and engaged. Here are some tips for addressing those challenges and succeeding as an online learner.

- *Schedule your own "do dates."* Online classes may have only one or two due dates per week, but successful students create their own "do dates"—dates when they'll do the work. Try breaking the work into chunks each week and assigning yourself a specific day and time for each chunk: one day for reading the assigned texts, another day for generating ideas for a writing project, and so on. Put reminders in your phone, or ask friends or family to hold you accountable. The sense of accomplishment you get in completing one task can motivate you to move on to the next.

- *Find a good place to work, and avoid multitasking.* Having a dedicated work space can help you stay focused. Find a place that suits you best—a quiet corner in your home, a favorite booth in a cafe, a desk at your school library. Turn off notifications on your phone, and consider using a website blocker like *Freedom* or *Cold Turkey* to minimize distractions further.

- *Take breaks to increase productivity.* Working long stretches online can be exhausting. Be sure to take breaks from the work—and from the screen time. If you can, take a full day off from your course each week. And when you're in the midst of a work session, take micro breaks to help you recharge. Consider setting a timer on your phone—say twenty-five minutes of focused work, followed by a five-minute break. Then repeat the cycle, with a longer break after several work sessions. Or use a productivity app like *TomatoTimer* to schedule your focus times and your break times.

- *Connect with your classmates—and your teacher.* You might not see your online classmates in person, but you can still get to know them and draw on them for support. In online writing courses, you'll typically have lots of opportunities to interact via discussion boards, peer review, and maybe web-based meetings or break-out rooms. As you get acquainted with your peers, try to identify at least one who can be your go-to person for reminders, tips, and general help. Then check in with each other via email, text, *FaceTime*, or other tools. Take advantage of opportunities to connect with your teacher, too. Use the email, chat, or videoconferencing tools available in your learning management system to reach out to your instructor whenever you need help.

- *Participate actively in online class meetings.* If your class requires real-time meetings via *Zoom*, *Google Meet*, or another platform, try to approach the online session as you would an in-person one: do your homework, write down questions for your teacher or classmates, and show up on time. During the session, keep yourself engaged

---

* academic literacies   ● fields   ● research
■ rhetorical situations   ⁙ processes   ● media/design
▲ genres   ◆ strategies

and focused by taking notes, speaking during discussions, or making comments in the chat box. You might also volunteer to moderate the chat conversation and alert your teacher to important questions or comments.

Using Web Conferencing Tools

Zoom, Skype, Microsoft Teams, and *Google Hangouts* are all online platforms that enable groups of people to see and talk with one another. You may be in a class that meets partly or solely in a web conference session, or you may use one of these programs to meet with friends or coworkers. Since you're on camera, consider both your own appearance and the background. Here are some additional hints for participating in an online video conference:

- Consider adding a virtual background instead of the room behind you. *Zoom,* for example, offers several; or you can download photos of your own.

- Keep your microphone muted when you aren't speaking. Background noise, coughing, even setting drink glasses on the desk during a session can distract everyone.

- Consider recording online class sessions and meetings so you can review them later.

- Remember that online video discussions are different from face-to-face meetings or even conference calls. In *Zoom* and other programs, only one person can speak at a time, and people who are quick to respond can sometimes drown out and silence those who need more time before responding. So it's important to make sure that everyone gets the opportunity to speak.

- Also, it's harder to "read the room" by gauging others' reactions (and in large online classes, figuring out who's talking may be difficult). So you need to monitor yourself, making sure you're not holding the floor too long, being repetitive, or going off topic.

59 Giving Presentations

In a marketing class, you give a formal presentation that includes slides and handouts as part of a research project on developing brand loyalty to clothing labels among college students. As a candidate for student government, you deliver several speeches to various campus groups that are simultaneously broadcast over the web. At a good friend's wedding, after you make a toast to the married couple, another friend who couldn't attend in person toasts them remotely using *Zoom*; a third guest records both toasts on his cell phone and uploads them to *Facebook*.

Whether or not you include digital and print media, whenever you are called on to give a spoken presentation, you need to make your points clear and memorable. This chapter offers guidelines to help you prepare and deliver effective presentations. We'll start with two good examples.

ABRAHAM LINCOLN
Gettysburg Address

Given by the sixteenth president of the United States, at the dedication of the Gettysburg battlefield as a memorial to those who died in the Civil War, this is one of the most famous speeches ever delivered in the United States.

Four score and seven years ago our fathers brought forth on this continent, a new nation, conceived in Liberty, and dedicated to the proposition that all men are created equal.

Now we are engaged in a great civil war, testing whether that nation, or any nation so conceived and so dedicated, can long endure. We are met on a great battle-field of that war. We have come to

✺ academic literacies	● fields	● research
■ rhetorical situations	⸪ processes	● media/design
▲ genres	◆ strategies	

dedicate a portion of that field, as a final resting place for those who here gave their lives that that nation might live. It is altogether fitting and proper that we should do this.

But, in a larger sense, we can not dedicate—we can not consecrate—we can not hallow—this ground. The brave men, living and dead, who struggled here, have consecrated it, far above our poor power to add or detract. The world will little note, nor long remember what we say here, but it can never forget what they did here. It is for us the living, rather, to be dedicated here to the unfinished work which they who fought here have thus far so nobly advanced. It is rather for us to be here dedicated to the great task remaining before us—that from these honored dead we take increased devotion to that cause for which they gave the last full measure of devotion—that we here highly resolve that these dead shall not have died in vain—that this nation, under God, shall have a new birth of freedom—and that government of the people, by the people, for the people, shall not perish from the earth.

You won't likely be called on to deliver such an address, but the techniques Lincoln used—brevity, rhythm, recurring themes—are ones you can use in your own spoken texts. The next example represents the type of spoken text we are sometimes called on to deliver at important occasions in the lives of our families.

JUDY DAVIS

Ours Was a Dad . . .

This short eulogy was given at the funeral of the writer's father, Walter Boock. Judy Davis lives in Davis, California, where she was for many years the principal of North Davis Elementary School.

Elsa, Peggy, David, and I were lucky to have such a dad. Ours was a dad who created the childhood for us that he did not have for himself. The dad who sent us airborne on the soles of his feet, squealing with delight. The dad who built a platform in the peach tree so we could eat ourselves comfortably into peachy oblivion. The dad who assigned us chores and then did them with us. The dad who felt our pain when we skinned our knees.

Ours was the dad who took us camping, all over the U.S. and Canada, but most of all in our beloved Yosemite. The one who awed us with his ability to swing around a full pail of water without spilling a drop and let us hold sticks in the fire and draw designs in the night air with hot orange coals.

Our dad wanted us to feel safe and secure. On Elsa's eighth birthday, we acquired a small camping trailer. One very blustery night in Minnesota, Mom and Dad asleep in the main bed, David suspended in the hammock over them, Peggy and Elsa snuggled in the little dinette bed, and me on an air mattress on the floor, I remember the most incredible sense of well-being: our family all together, so snug, in that little trailer as the storm rocked us back and forth. It was only in the morning that I learned about the tornado warnings. Mom and Dad weren't sleeping: they were praying that when morning came we wouldn't find ourselves in the next state.

Ours was the dad who helped us with homework at the round oak table. He listened to our oral reports, taught us to add by looking for combinations of 10, quizzed us on spelling words, and when our written reports sounded a little too much like the *World Book* encyclopedia, he told us so.

Ours was a dad who believed our round oak table that seated twelve when fully extended should be full at Thanksgiving. Dad called the chaplain at the airbase, asked about homesick boys, and invited them to join our family. Or he'd call International House in Berkeley to see if someone from another country would like to experience an American Thanksgiving. We're still friends with the Swedish couple who came for turkey forty-five years ago. Many people became a part of our extended family around that table. And if twelve around the table was good, then certainly fourteen would be better. Just last fall, Dad commissioned our neighbor Randy to make yet another leaf for the table. There were fourteen around the table for Dad's last Thanksgiving.

Ours was a dad who had a lifelong desire to serve. He delivered Meals on Wheels until he was eighty-three. He delighted in picking up the day-old doughnuts from Mr. Rollen's shop to give those on his route an extra treat. We teased him that he should be receiving those meals

5

* academic literacies
■ rhetorical situations
▲ genres

● fields
•.• processes
◆ strategies

● research
● media/design

himself! Even after walking became difficult for him, he continued to drive and took along an able friend to carry the meals to the door.

Our family, like most, had its ups and downs. But ours was a dad who forgave us our human failings as we forgave him his. He died in peace, surrounded by love. Elsa, Peggy, David, and I were so lucky to have such a dad.

This eulogy, in honor of the writer's father, provides concrete and memorable details that give the audience a clear image of the kind of man he was. The repetition of the phrase "ours was a dad" provides a rhythm and unity that moves the text forward, and the use of short, conventional sentences makes the text easy to understand—and deliver.

Key Features / Spoken Presentations

A clear structure. Spoken texts need to be clearly organized so that your audience can follow what you're saying. The **BEGINNING** needs to engage their interest, make clear what you will be talking about, and perhaps forecast the central parts of your talk. The main part of the text should focus on a few main points—only as many as your listeners can be expected to absorb and retain. (Remember, they can't go back to reread!) The **ENDING** is especially important: it should leave your audience with something to remember, think about, or do. Davis ends as she begins, saying that she and her sisters and brother "were so lucky to have such a dad." Lincoln ends with a dramatic resolution: "that government of the people, by the people, for the people, shall not perish from the earth."

346–54

354–358

Signpost language to keep your audience on track. You may need to provide cues—signposts—to help listeners follow your text, especially **TRANSITIONS** that lead them from one point to the next. Sometimes you'll also want to stop and **SUMMARIZE** a complex point to help your audience keep track of your ideas and follow your development of them.

361–62
550–51

A tone to suit the occasion. Lincoln spoke at a serious, formal event, the dedication of a national cemetery, and his address is formal and even solemn. Davis's eulogy is more informal in **TONE**, as befits a speech given

73–74

for friends and loved ones. In a presentation to a panel of professors, you probably would want to take an academic tone, avoiding too much slang and speaking in complete sentences. If you had occasion to speak on the very same topic to a neighborhood group, however, you would likely want to speak more casually.

Repetition and parallel structure. Even if you're never called on to deliver a Gettysburg Address, you will find that repetition and parallel structure can lend power to a presentation, making it easier to follow—and more likely to be remembered. "We can not dedicate—we can not consecrate—we can not hallow": the repetition of "we can not" and the parallel forms of the three verbs are one reason these words stay with us more than 150 years after they were written and delivered. These are structures any writer can use. See how the repetition of "ours was a dad" in Davis's eulogy creates a rhythm that engages listeners and at the same time unifies the text.

Slides and other media. Depending on the way you deliver your presentation, you will often want or need to use other media—*PowerPoint*, *Prezi*, or other presentation slides, video and audio clips, handouts, flip charts, whiteboards, and so on—to present certain information and to highlight key points.

Considering the Rhetorical Situation

As with any writing, you need to consider your rhetorical situation when preparing a presentation:

58–60 ■   **PURPOSE**   Consider what your primary purpose is. To inform? persuade? entertain? evoke another kind of emotional response?

61–64 ■   **AUDIENCE**   Think about whom you'll be addressing and how well you know them. Will they be interested, or will you need to get them interested? Are they likely to be friendly? How can you get and maintain their attention, and how can you establish common ground with them?

※ academic literacies   ● fields   ● research
■ rhetorical situations   ∴ processes   ● media/design
▲ genres   ◆ strategies

How much will they know about your subject—will you need to provide background or define any terms?

GENRE　　　The genre of your text will affect the way you structure and present it. If you're making an argument, for instance, you'll need to consider counterarguments—and, depending on the way you're giving the presentation, perhaps to allow for questions and comments from members of the audience who hold other opinions. If you're giving a report, you may have reasons to prepare handouts with detailed information you don't have time to cover in your spoken text, or links to online documents or websites.

■ 65–71

STANCE　　　Consider the attitude you want to express. Is it serious? thoughtful? passionate? well informed? humorous? something else? Choose your words and any other elements of your presentation accordingly. Whatever your attitude, your presentation will be received better by your listeners if they perceive you as comfortable and sincere.

■ 72–74

A Brief Guide to Writing Presentations

Whether you're giving a poster presentation at a conference or an oral report in class, what you say will differ in important ways from what you might write for others to read. Here are some tips for composing an effective presentation.

Budget your time. A five-minute presentation calls for about two and a half double-spaced pages of writing, and ten minutes means only four or five pages. Your introduction and conclusion should each take about one-tenth of the total time available; time for questions (if the format allows for them) should take about one-fifth; and the body of the talk, the rest. In a ten-minute presentation, then, allot one minute for your introduction, one minute for your conclusion, and two minutes for questions, leaving six minutes for the body of your talk.

Organize and draft your presentation. Readers can go back and reread if they don't understand or remember something the first time through a text. Listeners can't. Therefore, it's important that you structure your presentation so that your audience can follow your text—and remember what you say.

346–54 ◆

- *Craft an introduction* that engages your audience's interest and tells them what to expect. Depending on your rhetorical situation, you may want to **BEGIN** with humor, with an anecdote, or with something that reminds them of the occasion for your talk or helps them see the reason for it. In any case, you always need to summarize your main points, provide any needed background information, and outline how you'll proceed.

413–14 ◆
414–22

- *In the body of your presentation,* present your main points in more detail and support them with **REASONS** and **EVIDENCE**. As you draft, you may well find that you have more material than you can present in the time available, so you'll need to choose the most important points to focus on and leave out the rest.

- *Let your readers know you're concluding* (but try to avoid saying "in conclusion"), and then use your remaining time to restate your main points and to explain why they're important. End by saying "thank you" and offering to answer questions or take comments if the format allows for them.

Consider whether to use visuals. You may want or need to include some visuals to help listeners follow what you're saying. Especially when you're presenting complex information, it helps to let them see it as well as hear it. Remember, though, that visuals should be a means of conveying information, not mere decoration.

DECIDING ON THE APPROPRIATE VISUALS

- *Slides* are useful for listing main points and for projecting illustrations, tables, and graphs.

- *Videos, animations, and sounds* can add additional information to your presentations.

※ academic literacies   ● fields   ● research
■ rhetorical situations   ⁘ processes   ● media/design
▲ genres   ◆ strategies

- *Flip charts, whiteboards, or chalkboards* allow you to create visuals as you speak or to keep track of comments from your audience.

- *Posters* sometimes serve as the main part of a presentation, providing a summary of your points. You then offer only a brief introduction and answer any questions. You should be prepared to answer questions from any portion of your poster.

- *Handouts* can provide additional information, lists of works cited, or copies of any slides you show.

What visual tools (if any) you decide to use is partly determined by how your presentation will be delivered. Will you be speaking to a crowd or a class, delivering your presentation through a podcast, or creating an interactive presentation for a web conference? Make sure that any necessary equipment and programs are available—and that they work. If at all possible, check out any equipment in the place where you'll deliver your presentation before you go live. If you bring your own equipment for a live presentation, make sure you can connect to the internet if you need to and that electrical outlets are in reach of your power cords. Also, make sure that your visuals can be seen. You may have to rearrange the furniture or the screen to make sure everyone can see.

And finally, have a backup plan. Computers fail; projector bulbs burn out; marking pens run dry. Whatever your plan is, have an alternative in case any problems occur.

Presentation software.   *PowerPoint, Keynote,* and other presentation software can include images, video, and sound in addition to displaying written text. They are most useful for linear presentations that move audiences along one slide at a time. Cloud-based programs like *Prezi* also allow you to arrange words or slides in various designs, group related content together, and zoom in and out. Here are some tips for writing and designing slides:

- *Use* LISTS *or images, not paragraphs.* Use slides to emphasize your main points, not to reproduce your talk onscreen: keep your audience's attention focused on what you're saying. A list of brief points, 669–70 presented one by one, reinforces your words. An image can provide additional information that your audience can take in quickly.

668–69

- *Make your text easy for your audience to read.* **FONTS** should be at least 18 points, and larger than that for headings. Projected slides are easier to read in sans serif fonts like Arial, Helvetica, and Tahoma than in serif fonts like Times New Roman. And avoid using all capital letters, which can be hard to read.

- *Choose colors carefully.* Your text and any illustrations must contrast with the background. Dark content on a light background is easier to read than the reverse. And remember that not everyone sees all colors; be sure your audience doesn't need to be able to see particular colors or contrasts in order to get your meaning. Red-green and blue-yellow contrasts are especially hard for some people to see and should be avoided.

This *Prezi* presentation rotates, includes audio and video, and zooms in and out to let viewers take a closer look.

☀ academic literacies	● fields	● research
■ rhetorical situations	⋮ processes	● media/design
▲ genres	◆ strategies	

Truman

- Conducted whistle-stop campaign
- Made hundreds of speeches
- Spoke energetically
- Connected personally with voters
- Focused on key states

Truman's Whistle-Stop Campaign

Two *PowerPoint* slides on the US presidential election of 1948. The slide on the left outlines the main points; the one on the right shows a map of Truman's whistle-stop campaign, providing a graphic illustration of the miles he traveled as he campaigned to be president.

- *Use bells and whistles sparingly, if at all.* Presentation software offers lots of decorative backgrounds, letters that fade in and out or dance across the screen, and sound effects. These features can be more distracting than helpful; use them only if they help to make your point.

- *Mark your text.* In your notes or prepared text, mark each place where you need to click a mouse to call up the next slide.

Handouts. When you want to give your audience information they can refer to later—reproductions of your visuals, bibliographic information about your sources, printouts of your slides—do so in the form of handouts. Refer to the handouts in your presentation, but unless they include material your audience needs to consult before or as you talk, wait until you are finished to distribute them so as not to distract listeners. Clearly label everything you give out, including your name and the date and title of the presentation. You might even upload your handouts to a blog or website and give its URL, share them using a program such as *Canva*, or provide your email address and invite interested audience members to request your handouts.

Delivering a Presentation

The success of a presentation often hinges on how it's delivered. As you work on your spoken texts, bear in mind the following points:

Practice.   Practice, practice, and then practice some more. The better you know your talk, the more confident you will be, and your audience will respond positively to that confidence. If you're reading a prepared text, try to write it as if you were talking. Then practice by recording it as you read it; listen for spots that sound as if you're reading, and work on your delivery to sound more relaxed. As you practice, pay attention to keeping within your time limit. If possible, rehearse your talk with a small group of friends to test their response and to get used to speaking in front of an audience.

Speak clearly.   When you're giving a spoken presentation, your first goal is to be understood by your audience. If listeners miss important words or phrases because you don't pronounce them distinctly, your talk will not succeed. Make sure, too, that your pace matches your audience's needs. Often you'll need to speak more slowly than usual to explain complex material (or to compensate for nerves); sometimes you may need to speed up to keep your audience's attention. In general, though, strive for a consistent pace throughout, one that ensures you don't have to rush at the end.

Pause for emphasis.   In writing, you have white space and punctuation to show readers where an idea or discussion ends. When speaking, you need to pause to signal the end of a thought, to give listeners a moment to consider something you've said, or to get them ready for a surprising or amusing statement.

Stand up (or sit up) straight, and look at your audience.   If you're in the same physical space as your audience, try to maintain some eye contact with them. If that's uncomfortable, fake it: pick a spot on the wall just above the head of a person in the back of the room, and focus on it. You'll appear as if you're looking at your audience even if you're not looking them in the eye. And if you stand or sit up straight, you'll project the sense that you have confidence in what you're saying. If you appear to believe in your words,

* academic literacies   ● fields   ● research
■ rhetorical situations   ⋮ processes   ● media/design
▲ genres   ◆ strategies

others will, too. If you're speaking via an online forum like *Zoom*, look at the computer's camera—not at the screen. Also, make sure the camera is positioned at your eye level, so you aren't looking down at it (and showing your viewers the ceiling behind you!).

Use gestures for emphasis. If you're not used to speaking in front of a group, you may let your nervousness show by holding yourself stiffly, elbows tucked in. To overcome some of that nervousness, take some deep breaths, try to relax, and move your arms and the rest of your body as you would if you were talking to a friend. Use your hands for emphasis: most public speakers use one hand to emphasize specific points and both hands to make larger gestures. Watch politicians on C-SPAN to see how people who speak on a regular basis use gestures as part of their overall delivery.

Credits

PHOTOGRAPHS

Everyday Life." *Journal of Research in Personality* 2010 Aug 1, 44(4):478–484. doi: 10.1016/j.jrp.2010.06.001; **pp. 508, 512, 514, 515**: Wright State University. **Chapter 48: p. 528** (Fonda): Owen Franken/Corbis via Getty Images, (Kerry): ©Ken Light; **p. 529** (left): David Rosenblum/Icon Sportswire via Getty Images, (right): Courtesy WJXT-TV/Jacksonville, FL; **p. 530** (top): Pacific Standard, (center and bottom): google.com; **p. 531**(top to bottom): google.com. **Chapter 53: p. 583**: Jessamyn Neuhasus "Marge Simpson Blue-Haired Housewife Defining Domesticity on *The Simpsons*." *Journal of Popular Culture* 43.4 (2010): 761–81. Print; **p. 584**: Segal, Michael. "The Hit Book That Came from Mars." *Nautilus*. NautilusThink. 8 January 2015. Web. 10 October 2016. Permission by Nautilus, (inset art): Matt Taylor; **p. 587**: ©2015 Ebsco Industries, Inc. All rights reserved; **p. 591**: from *Pink Sari Revolution: A Tale of Women and Power in India* by Amana Fontanella-Khan. New York: Norton 2013. Used by permission of W. W. Norton & Company, Inc; **p. 596**: John McIlwain, Molly Simpson, and Sara Hammerschmidt. "Housing in America: Integrating Housing Health and Resilience in a Changing Environment." *Urban Land Institute*. Urban Land Institute 2014. Web. 17 Sept. 2016; **p. 609**: Bettmann/Getty Images. **Chapter 54: p. 631**: Copyright 2013. From *Smart Technology and the Moral Life* by Guthrie, C. F. *Ethics & Behavior* Volume 23, 2013—Issue 4 Reproduced by permission of Taylor & Francis LLC (http://www.tandfonline.com); **p. 633**: Lazette, M. P. (2015, February 25). A hurricane's hit to households. © 2015 Federal Reserve Bank of Cleveland; **p. 635**: From *The Great Divide: Unequal Societies and What We Can Do about Them* by Joseph E. Stiglitz. Copyright © 2015 by Joseph E. Stiglitz. Used by permission of W. W. Norton & Company, Inc. **Chapter 56: p. 667**: Used with the permission of Inter IKEA Systems B.V. **Chapter 57: p. 675** (left): National Gallery of Art, (right): Dorothea Lange/Farm Security Administration—Office of War Information Photograph Collection (Library of Congress) LC-USF34-T01-009093-C (b&w film dup. neg.); **p. 677** (bar chart): Staff/MCT/Newscom, (pie chart): Staff/MCT/Newscom, (table): Staff/TNS/Newscom; **p. 678** (diagram): NASA Image Collection/Alamy Stock Photo, (map): This map was created by the National Renewable Energy Laboratory for the U.S. Department of Energy; **p. 681**: Caricature of an artist painting vigorously ca. 1885–1886. Francis Davis Millet and Millet family papers 1858–1984 bulk 1858–1955. Archives of American Art Smithsonian Institution. **Chapter 58: p. 686**: Courtesy of National Park Service; **p. 687**: NMNH, Smithsonian Institution. **Chapter 59: p. 694**: Library of Congress; **p. 695**: Courtesy of Judy Davis.

TEXT

Chapter 2: Michael J. Sandel: Excerpt from "What Wounds Deserve the Purple Heart?" from "Doing the Right Thing" from *Justice: What's the Right Thing to Do?* by Michael J. Sandel. Copyright © 2009 by Michael J. Sandel. Reprinted by permission of Farrar, Straus, and Giroux. **William Safire**: "A Spirit Reborn" by William Safire. Copyright © 2002 by The Cobbett Corporation. Originally appeared in *The New York Times Magazine*. Reprinted by permission of the author's estate. **Chapter 3: Jacob MacLeod**: "Guns and Cars Are Different." Copyright © Jacob MacLeod. Reprinted by permission of the author. **Chapter 10: Karla Mariana Herrera Gutierrez**: "Reading, Writing, and Riding."

Glossary/Index

A

abstract, 196–200 A writing GENRE that summarizes a book, an article, or a paper, usually in 100–200 words. Authors in some academic fields must provide, at the top of a report submitted for publication, an abstract of its content. The abstract may then appear in a journal of abstracts, such as *Psychological Abstracts*. An *informative abstract* summarizes a complete report; a briefer *descriptive abstract* provides only a brief overview; a *proposal abstract* (also called a TOPIC PROPOSAL) requests permission to conduct research, write on a topic, or present a report at a scholarly conference. Key Features: SUMMARY of basic information • objective description • brevity
  key features, 198
  reading: "Boredom Proneness," 196–97
  types and examples
    informative, 196–97
    proposal, 197
    science fields, 307
  writing guide, 198–99
academic fields. *See* field of study
academic habits of mind, 46–56
Academic Search Complete, 516
Academic Search Premier, 516
academic searches, nonlibrary, 505

academic writing, 3–10 Writing done in an academic or scholarly context, such as for course assignments. Key Features: evidence that you've carefully considered the subject • clear, appropriately qualified THESIS • response to what others have said • good reasons supported by evidence • acknowledgment of multiple perspectives • carefully documented sources • confident, authoritative STANCE • indication of why your topic matters • careful attention to correctness.
  in arts and humanities, 311–13
  in business, 317–18
  in education, 319–20
  in engineering and technology, 320–22
  in health sciences and nursing, 322–24
  rhetorical situation, 309–10
  in science and mathematics, 313–15
  in social sciences, 315–17

accommodating other viewpoints, 54, 425, 554
acknowledging other viewpoints. *See* multiple perspectives, incorporating
acknowledging sources, 555–58

action verb, 471 A VERB that expresses a physical or mental action (jump, consider).

active voice, 381 When a VERB is in the active voice, the SUBJECT performs the action: He sent a gift. *See also* passive voice

ad hominem argument A logical FALLACY that attacks someone's character rather than address the issues. ("Ad hominem" is Latin for "to the man.")
   defined, 427
   in position papers, 189

adjective A MODIFIER that describes a NOUN or PRONOUN (a <u>challenging</u> task, a <u>cloudless</u> <u>blue</u> sky).

adverb A MODIFIER that tell more about a VERB (speak <u>loudly</u>), an ADJECTIVE (<u>very</u> loud), another adverb (<u>very</u> loudly), or a whole CLAUSE (<u>Sometimes</u> speaking loudly is counterproductive).

"Against the Odds: Harry S. Truman and the Election of 1948" (Borchers), 341–42

agreement The correspondence between a SUBJECT and VERB in person and number (the dog chases the children down the street) or between a PRONOUN and its ANTECEDENT in gender and number (the cat nursed her kittens; the children flee because they are afraid).

"Airport Security: What Price Safety?" (McDonie), 353
Aitken, M., 321
"All Over but the Shoutin'" (Bragg), 236–40
"All Seven Deadly Sins Committed at Church Bake Sale" (*The Onion*), 431–32
"All Words Matter: The Manipulation behind 'All Lives Matter'" (Coryell), 164–70

Allen, Danielle, 35, 111–16

allusion An indirect reference to something. (When Lisa Simpson says to Bart, "A rose by any other name would smell as sweet," she is alluding to *Romeo and Juliet*.)

almanacs, 513
America: History and Life, 517
America Revised: History Schoolbooks in the Twentieth Century (FitzGerald), 443

analogy A STRATEGY for COMPARISON that explains something unfamiliar in terms of something familiar. *See also* figurative language
   comparison and contrast with, 442–43
   false, 428

analysis A writing GENRE that methodically examines something by breaking it into its parts and noting how they work in relation to one another. *See also* literary analysis; textual analysis

"Analysis of All Terrain Vehicle Crash Mechanisms" (Tanner et al.), 321
analyzing
   cubing and, 336
   in inquiry, 331

anecdote A brief NARRATIVE used to illustrate a point.
   beginning with, 159, 353
   ending with, 356
   in exploratory essays, 278
   reflection on, 396

Angelou, Maya, 474–75, 477–78
angle, in profiles, 252, 255, 256

annotated bibliography, 201–9 A writing GENRE that gives an overview of published research and scholarship on a topic. Each entry includes complete publication information and a **SUMMARY** or an **ABSTRACT**. A *descriptive annotation* summarizes the content of a source without commenting on its value; an *evaluative annotation* gives an opinion about the source along with a description of it. Key Features: statement of the scope • complete bibliographic information • relevant commentary • consistent presentation • brevity

    key features, 204–5
    types and examples
        descriptive: "Teen Film$," 202–3
        evaluative: "Researching Hunger and Poverty," 203–4
    writing guide, 205–8

annotating The process of marking up a text in order to better understand it by underlining or highlighting key words and phrases, connecting ideas with lines and symbols, and writing comments and questions in the margins.

    as reading strategy, 16–19
    textual analyses and, 125

antecedent, 382 The **NOUN** or **PRONOUN** to which a pronoun refers. In "<u>Maya</u> lost <u>her</u> wallet," "Maya" is the antecedent of "her." *See also* pronoun

AP Images, 518

APA style, 615–55 A system of **DOCUMENTATION** used in the social sciences. APA stands for the American Psychological Association.

    comparison with MLA style, 561–63
    directory, 615–17
    fields of study
        business, 317
        education, 319–20
        engineering and technology, 321
        health sciences and nursing, 322
        science and mathematics, 314
        social sciences, 314
    formatting
        headings, 645
        notes, 622–23
        papers, 645–47
        quotations, 545
    in-text documentation, 618–22
    reference list
        articles and other short works, 629–34
        audio, visual, and other sources, 639–44
        authors and other contributors, 626–29
        books, parts of books, and reports, 634–39
        sources not covered by APA, 644
    sample research paper, 647–55
    verb tense, 554

Apple News, 511

appropriate sources, 206

"The Architecture of Inequality: On Bong Joon-ho's *Parasite*" (Finn), 105–11

arguable positions. *See also* claim

    in literary analyses, 228
    in position papers, 180–81, 186

arguing, 410–30 A **STRATEGY** that can be used in any kind of writing to support a claim with **REASONS** and **EVIDENCE**.

    building blocks
        claims, 411–13
        evidence, 414–22
        reasons, 413–14
    establishing credibility
        accommodating other viewpoints, 425

arguing (cont.)
  acknowledging other viewpoints, 424–25
  common ground, 424
  refuting other viewpoints, 426
  genres
    essay questions, 484
    literary analyses, 233, 410
    profiles, 410
    proposals, 262, 410
    textual analyses, 127–28
  guidelines
    emotional appeals, 426–27
    logical fallacies, 427–29
    reasons for arguing, 410
    rhetorical situation, 429–30
  Rogerian argument, 422–23

arguing a position, 164–95 A writing GENRE that uses REASONS and EVIDENCE to support a CLAIM or POSITION and, sometimes, to persuade an AUDIENCE to accept that position. Key Features: clear and arguable position • necessary background • good reasons • convincing support for each reason • appeal to readers' values • trustworthy TONE • careful consideration of other positions
  choosing, 67
  cubing and, 336
  key features, 180–82
  with other genres, 288
  readings
    "All Words Matter: The Manipulation behind 'All Lives Matter,'" 164–70
    "Come Look at the Freaks: Examining and Advocating for Disability Theatre," 171–77
    "Our Blind Spot about Guns," 177–80
  revising to strengthen, 376
  in rhetorical reading, 26–27
  strategies for
    dialogue, 464
    narration, 474
  writing guide
    choosing a topic, 182–84
    considering a rhetorical situation, 184–85
    design, 192–93
    drafting, 190–92
    editing and proofreading, 194
    generating ideas and text, 185–89
    organizing, 189–90
    responses and revision, 193–94
    taking stock, 194–95
    ways of rewriting, 379

article The word "a," "an," or "the," used to indicate that a NOUN is indefinite (a writer, an author) or definite (the author).

articles. *See* periodical articles
arts, academic writing for, 311–13
ArtStor, 518
assessing own writing, 367–71
  in body of work, 371
  clarity, 370–71
  focus, 368–69
  organization, 370–71
  portfolios and, 388–89
  rhetorical situation and, 367–68
  support provided, 369
assigned topics, 155
At Day's Close: Night in Times Past (Ekirch), 415–16

atlases, 513

audience, 61–64, 378 Those to whom a text is directed—the people who read, listen to, or view the text. Audience is a key part of every text's RHETORICAL SITUATION. *See also* rhetorical situation

audience awareness, 395
audio platforms, research using, 511
Audioburst Search, 511

authorities, 416 People or texts that are cited as support for a writer's ARGUMENT. A structural engineer may be quoted as an authority on bridge construction, for example. "Authority" also refers to a quality conveyed by a writer who is knowledgeable about their subject.

"Automotive Literacy" (Kassfy), 91–93

B

background information. *See* context
balance of sources, 206
balanced assessment, 218

bandwagon appeal, 427 A logical FALLACY that argues for thinking or acting a certain way just because others do.

bar graph, 677
Barker, Bill, 445–46
Baron, Dennis, 360
Bartleby, 515
Bass, Cynthia, 347
Bealer, Bonnie K., 435
"because," with reasons for claims, 413–14
Becker, Carl, 450–51, 451–52

"Becoming an American Girl" (Karim), 81–85

begging the question, 428 A logical FALLACY that involves arguing in a circle, assuming as a given what the writer is trying to prove.

beginnings
    editing, 381
    endings that reference, 356–57
    genres
        literacy narratives, 99
        narration, 480–81
        position papers, 191
        reports, 158–59
        textual analyses, 136
    rhetorical situation and, 346–47
    strategies
        anecdotes, 353
        asking questions, 354
        background information, 351–52
        connecting to readers' interests, 353
        defining key concepts, 352
        explaining context, 350
        forecasting organization, 350–51
        jumping right in, 354
        provoking interest, 353
        stating thesis, 347–49
believing and doubting game, 20–21
Benton, Michael, 202–3
bibliography. *See also* annotated bibliography
    as research source, 514
    working, 497–99
biology, proposal in, 314
BIOSIS Previews, 517
Bird Sounds from the Borror Laboratory of Bioacoustics, 518

Bittman, Mark, 415
"Black Men and Public Space" (Staples), 478–79
block method of comparing and contrasting, 439

block quotation, 545 In a written work, a long quotation that is set off, or indented, from the main text and presented without quotation marks. In **MLA STYLE**: set off text more than four typed lines, indented five spaces (or one-half inch) from the left margin; in **APA STYLE**, set off quotes of forty or more words, indented five to seven spaces (or one-half inch) from the left margin. *See also* quotation

blogs
    as genre, 687
    for writing ideas, 332

"The Blues Merchant" (Washington), 354
book reviews, 516
books
    documenting, APA style
        electronic, 634
        print, 634–37
    documenting, MLA style, 590–95
    finding, as research source
        ebooks, 515
        library catalog, 514–15

Borchers, Dylan, 341–42
"Boredom Is Good for You" (Stewart), 535–37
"Boredom Proneness" (Sommers and Vodanovich; abstract), 196–97
"The Boston Photographs" (Ephron), 460
brackets, 546
Bragg, Rick, 236–40

brainstorming, 13, 156, 397 A **PROCESS** for **GENERATING IDEAS AND TEXT** by writing down everything that comes to mind about a topic, then looking for patterns or connections among the ideas.

brevity, of abstracts, 198
Brinkley, Rachel, 323
Brown, Lester R., 416, 438
bulletin boards, digital, 341–42
business, writing for, 317–18
Business Insider, 440
"Business Plan Executive Summary Sample" (Ward), 318
business plans, 318

C

calls for action
    in endings, 357–58
    in position papers, 192
    in proposals, 262, 263
career-focused fields of study, 308
"Carla Hall's Soul Food" (Hall), 447–48
Carroll, Cameron, 210–12
Carvel, John, 442
"The Case for Torture" (Levin), 425
case studies, 323–24, 419–20
catalog, library, 514–15
categories, clear and distinct, 433–35

cause and effect, 330, 405–9 A **STRATEGY** of analyzing why something occurred or speculating about what its consequences will be. Cause and effect can serve as the **ORGANIZING** principle for a whole text.
    arguing for causes or effects, 406–7
    determining plausible causes and effects, 405–6

organizing an analysis, 407–8
in reports, 158
rhetorical situation, 408–9
transitions used with, 361

changes in direction or expectations, transitions for, 361
charts, 30–31, 676, 677
Chicago documentation style, 561
Childs, Craig, 419–20, 442

chronological order A way of ORGANIZING text that proceeds from the beginning of an event to the end. Reverse chronological order proceeds in the other direction, from the end to the beginning.
in literacy narratives, 98
in narratives, 474–75

citation, 126, 233, 555–58 In a text, the act of giving information from a source. A citation and its corresponding parenthetical DOCUMENTATION, footnote, or endnote provide minimal information about the source; complete bibliographic information appears in a list of WORKS CITED or REFERENCES at the end of the text.

claim, 180–82, 185–89, 411–13 A statement that asserts a belief or position. In an ARGUMENT, a claim needs to be stated in a THESIS or clearly implied, and requires support by REASONS and EVIDENCE.

"The Clan of the One-Breasted Women" (Williams), 476
clarity
assessing own writing, 370–71
explaining processes, 469
revising for, 376–77
Clark, Roy Peter, 116–22

classifying and dividing, 330, 431–36 A STRATEGY that either groups (classifies) numerous individual items into categories by their similarities (for example, classifying cereal, bread, butter, chicken, cheese, cream, eggs, and oil as carbohydrates, proteins, and fats) or breaks (divides) one large category into small categories (for example, dividing food into carbohydrates, proteins, and fats). Classification and/or division can serve as the ORGANIZING principle for a whole text.
characteristics
clear and distinct categories, 433–35
rhetorical situation, 435–36
cubing and, 336
essay questions on, 484
guidelines
classifying, 431–32
dividing, 432–33

clause A group of words that consists of at least a SUBJECT and a PREDICATE; a clause may be either INDEPENDENT or SUBORDINATE. *See also* independent clause; subordinate clause

cliché, 382–83 An expression used so frequently that it is no longer fresh: busy as a bee.

clustering, 335–36 A PROCESS for GENERATING IDEAS AND TEXT, in which a writer visually connects thoughts by jotting them down and drawing lines between related items.

coding, 17 The process of developing and using a system of codes—like stars or other symbols—to track one's thoughts about a text.

Colicchio, Tom, 446

collaboration, 52–55, 557 The PROCESS of working with others.

collective noun A NOUN—such as "committee," "crowd," "family," "herd," or "team"—that refers to a group.

colons, 547
color, in design, 666–68
The Columbia Encyclopedia, 513
"Come Look at the Freaks: Examining and Advocating for Disability Theatre" (Schunk), 171–77
comfortable, getting, 364
"Coming Home Again" (Lee), 465–66

comma splice Two or more INDEPENDENT CLAUSES joined with only a comma: I came, I saw, I conquered.

commas, 382, 465, 547
commentary, 205

common ground, 424 Shared values. Writers build common ground with AUDIENCES by acknowledging others' POINTS OF VIEW, seeking areas of compromise, and using language that includes, rather than excludes, those they aim to reach.

comparing and contrasting, 330, 437–44 A STRATEGY that highlights the similarities and differences between items. Using the *block method* of comparison-contrast, a writer discusses all the points about one item and then all the same points about the other item; using the *point-by-point method*, a writer discusses one point for both items before going on to discuss the next point for both items, and so on. Sometimes comparison and/or contrast serves as the ORGANIZING principle for a whole text.
　　block method, 439
　　cubing and, 336
　　in evaluations, 220

figurative language, 441–43
methods and organization, 438–40
point-by-point method, 439–40
reading across fields of study, 301
in reports, 158
research sources, 533–34
transitions, 361
visuals, 440–41

complement A NOUN, NOUN PHRASE, PRONOUN, or ADJECTIVE that modifies either the SUBJECT or the direct OBJECT of a sentence. A subject complement follows a LINKING VERB and tells more about the subject: She is a good speaker. She is eloquent. An object complement describes or renames the direct object: Critics called the movie a masterpiece. We found the movie enjoyable.

complete sentences, 381
compound sentences, 382
conclusions. *See* endings
conference proceedings, 516
conferencing software, 52, 693

confirmation bias, 533 The tendency to look for information that supports what you already believe and to ignore information that doesn't.

connections, 287

consensus, 54 A position or opinion generally accepted by a group of people.

consistency, 206, 665

context Part of any RHETORICAL SITUATION, conditions affecting the text such as what else has been said about a topic; social, economic, and other factors; and constraints such as due date and length.
　　beginning with, 351–52
　　in literacy narratives, 99

in literary analyses, 231, 232
in position papers, 181, 191
in profiles, 250
in reports, 159
in rhetorical reading, 27–28
in textual analyses, 123, 125–26,
    130, 136

contrast, in design, 666–68
contrasting. See comparing and
    contrasting
conversation among researchers approach,
    303–4
Cooney, Nathaniel J., 399–401

coordinating conjunction One of these words—"and," "but," "or," "nor," "so," "for," or "yet"—used to join two elements in a way that gives equal weight to each one (bacon <u>and</u> eggs; pay up <u>or</u> get out).

correlative conjunction A pair of words used to connect two equal elements: "either . . . or," "neither . . . nor," "not only . . . but also," "just as . . . so," and "whether . . . or."

Coryell, Kelly, 164–70
Council of Science Editors documentation
    style, 561

count noun A word that names something that can be counted (one book, two books). *See also* noncount noun

counterargument, 182, 189, 424–26 In ARGUMENT, an alternative POSITION or objection to the writer's position. The writer of an argument should not only acknowledge counterarguments but also, if at all possible, accept, accommodate, or refute each one.

course management system (CMS). See
    learning management system.

CQ Researcher, 513
credentials
    researching, for annotated
        bibliographies, 207
    textual analyses and, 126–27

credibility The sense of trustworthiness that a writer conveys in their text.
    accommodating other viewpoints and,
        425
    acknowledging other viewpoints and,
        424–25
    common ground and, 424
    emotional appeals and, 426–27
    refuting other viewpoints, 426
    of sources, 206, 526–32

criteria, 207, 218, 220, 221 In EVALUATION, the standards against which something is judged.

cubing, 336 A PROCESS for GENERATING IDEAS AND TEXT in which a writer looks at a topic in six ways—to DESCRIBE it, to COMPARE it to something else, to associate it with other things or CLASSIFY it, to ANALYZE it, to apply it, and to ARGUE for or against it.

"Cuddling Up to Cyborg Babies" (Turkle),
    479–80
cueing devices
    beginning, 346–54
    ending, 354–58
    in presentations, 697–98
    thesis statements, 347–49
    titles, 363
    topic sentences, 358–60
    transitions, 361–62
"Cyberloafing: Distraction or Motivation?"
    (Mejia Avila), 346

D

Dance Online: Dance in Video, 518

databases, library
    vs. internet searches, 494–95
    keyword searching, 507–8
    subject coverage of, 516–17

Davis, Judy, 695–97

deadlines, 364, 492

"Defining Democracy Down" (Sullivan),
    453–54

defining key terms
    in beginnings, 191
    in literary analyses, 230
    in reports, 153

definition, 330, 445–55 A STRATEGY that says
what something is. *Formal definitions* identify
the category that something belongs to and
tell what distinguishes it from other things
in that category: a worm as an invertebrate (a
category) with a long, rounded body and no
appendages (distinguishing features). *Extended
definitions* go into more detail: a paragraph or
even an essay explaining why a character in
a story is tragic. *Stipulative definitions* explain
a writer's distinctive use of a term, one not
found in a dictionary. Definition can serve as
the **ORGANIZING** principle for a whole text.
    rhetorical situation, 454–55
    types of definitions
        extended, 447–52
        formal, 445–47
        stipulative, 453

"Democracy" (White), 452

"Democracy and Things Like That" (Vowell),
    356

description, 330, 456–63 A STRATEGY that tells
how something looks, sounds, smells, feels,
or tastes. Effective description creates a clear
DOMINANT IMPRESSION built from specific
details. Description can be *objective*, *subjective*, or both. Description can serve as the
ORGANIZING principle for a whole text.
    beginning with, 136
    cubing and, 336
    features of
        detail, 456–59
        dominant impression, 461–62
        objectivity and subjectivity,
            459–60
        vantage point, 460–61
    genres
        abstracts, 198
        annotated bibliographies,
            204–5
        essay questions, 485
        evaluations, 217
        explorations, 277
        literacy narratives, 96, 97
        literary analyses, 230
        memoirs, 242
        profiles, 256
        textual analysis, 123, 128–29
    organization and, 462
    rhetorical situation, 463

descriptive annotations, 202–3

design, 664–73 The way a text is arranged
and presented visually. Elements of design
include font, color, illustration, layout, and
white space. One component of a **RHETORI-
CAL SITUATION**, design plays an important

part in how well a text reaches its AUDIENCE and achieves its PURPOSE.
> elements of
>> colors, 666–68
>> contrast, 666–68
>> fonts, 668–69
>> headings, 670–71
>> layout, 669
>> white space, 672
> evaluating designs, 672
> genres and
>> literacy narratives, 100
>> literary analyses, 233
>> position papers, 192–93
>> remixes, 287
>> reports, 153–54, 160
>> textual analyses, 137
> principles of, 665–68
> rhetorical situation and, 75–77, 664–65

details
> engaging, 253
> in extended definitions, 450–51
> genres and
>> explorations, 275
>> literacy narratives, 93
>> memoirs, 240, 242–43
>> profiles, 253
> processes and
>> description, 456–59
>> narration, 478–80
> supporting, 256
> vivid, 93, 240
Devlin, Keith, 418–19
diagrams, 676, 678

dialogue, 454–68 A STRATEGY for including other people's spoken words to a text.
> function of, 464–65
> genres
>> literacy narratives, 97
>> memoirs, 242–43
>> profiles, 253, 256
> integrating, 465–66
> in interviews, 465–66
> punctuation with, 102
> rewriting narratives with, 378
> rhetorical situation and, 468

dictionaries, 513
Didion, Joan, 481
Diehl, Brian, 269–74
"Difficult-to-Follow Narrative Redeemed by Well-Executed Comedy in The Lovebirds" (Mazzucato), 215–17
digital archives, 511
digital bulletin boards, 341–42
Diigo, 499
discipline, 295, 302–4. See also field of study

discovery drafting, 344 A PROCESS of DRAFTING something quickly, mostly for the purpose of discovering what one wants to say.

discussion, in proposals, 267
dissertations, 516
dividing, 432–33. See also classifying and dividing
"do," forms of, 383
document maps
> APA style, 631, 633, 635
> MLA style, 583, 584, 587, 591, 596

documentation, 560–63 Publication information about the sources cited in a text. The documentation usually appears in an abbreviated form in parentheses at the point of CITATION or in an endnote or a footnote. Complete documentation usually appears as a list of WORKS CITED or REFERENCES at the end of the text. Documentation styles vary by discipline. For example, Modern Language Association (MLA) style requires an author's complete first name if it appears in a source, whereas American Psychological Association (APA) style requires only the initial of an author's first name.
    in academic writing, 7
    in annotated bibliographies, 204
    in literary analyses, 233
    styles of, 560–63 (*see also* APA style; MLA style)
    in summary and response essays, 35

DOI A digital object identifier, a stable number identifying the location of a source accessed through a database.
    APA style, 623, 626, 631
    documenting, 516
    MLA style, 575, 578

Dolan, Mark, 202–3

dominant impression The overall effect created through specific details when a writer DESCRIBES something.
    description and, 461–62
    in profiles, 253

Dorsten, E., 314

drafting, 364–66 The PROCESS of putting words on paper or screen. Writers often write several drafts, REVISING each until they achieve their goal or reach a deadline. At that point, they submit a finished final draft.
    writer's block, 366
    writing techniques, 365

"Dreams from My President" (Powers), 350
Dzubay, Sarah, 349

E

EasyBib, 497
ebooks, 515
"Edible Magic" (Schembri), 146–49

editing The PROCESS of fine-tuning a text by examining each word, PHRASE, sentence, and paragraph to be sure that the text is correct and precise and says exactly what the writer intends. *See also* proofreading; revision
    paragraphs, 380–81
    sentences, 381–82
    visuals, 682–83
    words, 382–83

education field, writing for, 319–20
effect. *See* cause and effect
"The Effect of Minimum Wages on Happiness" (Nizamoff), 316

either-or argument, 428 A logical FALLACY, also known as a FALSE DILEMMA, that oversimplifies by suggesting that only two possible POSITIONS exist on a complex issue.

Ekirch, A. Roger, 415–16
email, 685

emotional appeal, 427 In ARGUMENT, an appeal to readers' feelings. Emotional appeals should be used carefully in academic writing, where arguments are often expected to emphasize logical reasons and evidence more than emotion.

emotional responses, 129

"Enclosed. Encyclopedic. Endured. One Week at the Mall of America" (Guterson), 351, 464–65

encyclopedias, 513

end punctuation, 465, 547

endings
    editing, 381
    genres
        literacy narratives, 99
        position papers, 191–92
        reports, 159
        textual analyses, 137
    rhetorical situation and, 354–55
    strategies for
        anecdotes, 356
        discussing implications, 355–56
        narration, 481
        proposing an action, 357–58
        referring to beginning, 356–57
        restating main point, 355
    transitions used with, 362

EndNote, 500

engineering, writing for, 320–22

Ephron, Nora, 460

e-portfolio, 388 An electronic collection of writing and other evidence selected by a writer to show their work, including a statement assessing the work and explaining what it demonstrates.

ERIC, 517

essay exams, 483–88
    guidelines, 486–88
    patterns and strategies, 484–85
    rhetorical situation, 483–84

essential element, A word, PHRASE, or CLAUSE with information that is necessary for understanding the meaning of a sentence: French is the only language that I can speak.

"Esthetic Knowing with a Hospitalized Morbidly Obese Patient" (Brinkley et al.), 323

ethical appeal, 423–26 In ARGUMENT, a way a writer establishes credibility with readers, such as by demonstrating knowledge of the topic; pointing out common ground between the writer's values and those of readers; or incorporating the views of others, including opposing views, into the argument.

ethos. *See* ethical appeal

evaluation, 214–22 A writing GENRE that makes a judgment about something (for example, a source, poem, film, restaurant) based on certain CRITERIA. Key Features: description of the subject • clearly defined criteria • knowledgeable discussion of the subject • balanced and fair assessment
    choosing, 67
    combining genres in, 70
    comparison and contrast, 437
    essay questions on, 485
    key features, 217–18
    in literature reviews, 212
    reading: "Difficult-to-Follow Narrative Redeemed by Well-Executed Comedy in *The Lovebirds*," 215–17
    of sources, 524–34
    writing guide, 219–22

evaluative annotations, 203–4

events, reports about, 157

evidence, 414–22 In ARGUMENT, the data you present to support your REASONS. Such data may include statistics, calculations, examples, ANECDOTES, QUOTATIONS, case studies, or anything else that will convince your reader that your reasons are compelling. Evidence should be sufficient (enough to show that the reasons have merit) and relevant (appropriate to the argument you're making).
    in academic writing, 5
    assessing own writing, 369
    choosing appropriate, 422
    genres and
        evaluations, 218, 220
        literary analyses, 233
        position papers, 181, 187–89
    in paragraphs, 360
    reflection on, 396
    types of
        anecdotes, 416–18
        authorities, 416
        case studies and observations,
          419–20
        examples, 415–16
        facts, 414–15
        scenarios, 418–19
        statistics, 415
        textual evidence, 420–21
        visuals, 420–21
examples
    beginning with, 159
    in extended definitions, 452
    reflection on, 396
    as type of evidence, 415–16
exclamation points, 547
executive summary, business plan, 318
expectations, 331
explainer videos, 286

explaining a process, 469–73 A STRATEGY for telling how something is done or how to do something. An explanation of a process can serve as the ORGANIZING principle for a whole text.
    rhetorical situation, 473
    types of
        explaining visually, 471–72
        how something is done,
          469–70
        how to do something, 470–71

explanation, 330

expletive A word such as "it" or "there" used to introduce information provided later in a sentence: It was difficult to drive on the icy road. There is plenty of food in the refrigerator.

exploration, 269–79 A writing genre that presents a writer's thoughtful, personal consideration of a subject. Key Features: topic intriguing to the writer • some kind of structure • specific details • speculative tone.
    choosing, 68
    genres
        evaluations, 219
        literacy narratives, 96
        position papers, 185–86
        profiles, 254
        textual analyses, 129
    key features, 274–76
    reading: "Talking with Granddad,"
        269–74
    writing guide, 276–79

exploratory essay
    choosing, 68
    key features, 274–76

reading: "Talking with Granddad,"
269–74
writing guide, 276–79
extended definitions, 447–52

F
___

fact-checking, 511, 526–32 The act of verifying the accuracy of facts and claims presented in a piece of writing, a speech, media such as images or videos, or a social media post.

online sources, 526–28, 530–31
photos and video, 528–29, 532

facts
vs. arguable positions, 411
as type of evidence, 414–15

fallacy, logical, 189, 427–29 Faulty reasoning that can mislead an AUDIENCE. Fallacies include AD HOMINEM, BANDWAGON APPEAL, BEGGING THE QUESTION, EITHER-OR ARGUMENT (also called "false dilemma"), FALSE ANALOGY, FAULTY CAUSALITY (also called "post hoc, ergo propter hoc"), HASTY GENERALIZATION, SLIPPERY SLOPE, and WHATABOUTISM (also called "you too").

false analogy, 428 A FALLACY comparing things that resemble each other but are not alike in the most important respects.

false dilemma. *See* either-or argument

false news, 526–32 Propaganda, hoaxes, misinformation, and lies, including satires and counterfeit news stories.

Fast Food Nation: The Dark Side of the All-American Meal (Schlosser), 432–33

faulty causality, 428 A FALLACY, also called "post hoc, ergo propter hoc" (Latin for "after this, therefore because of this"), that mistakenly assumes the first of two events causes the second.

feedback. *See* response
feelings, 331

field of study, 293–324 A branch of learning that is taught and researched in a higher education setting. Fields of study generally belong to the following categories: humanities, social sciences, natural sciences and mathematics, and applied or career-focused fields. Also called "discipline."

and general education, 295–96
reading in fields of study,
296–308
advice, 299–304
career-focused fields, 308
humanities, 304–5
rhetorical situation, 298–99
sciences, 306–7
social studies, 305–6
readings
"Analysis of All Terrain Vehicle
Crash Mechanisms," 321
"Business Plan Executive Summary
Sample," 318
"The Effect of Minimum Wages on
Happiness," 316
"Esthetic Knowing with a Hospitalized Morbidly Obese Patient,"
323
"Identifying Genes Involved in
Suppression of Tumor Formation in the Planarian *Schmidtea
mediterranea*," 314

field of study (cont.)
    "Letting the Unspoken Speak: A Reexamination of the Pueblo Revolt of 1680," 312–13
    "Statement of Teaching Philosophy," 319–20
  studying, 296–97
  writing in, 296–97
    arts and humanities, 311–13
    business, 317–18
    education, 319–20
    engineering and technology, 320–22
    health sciences and nursing, 322–24
    rhetorical situation, 309–10
    science and mathematics, 313–15
    social sciences, 315–17

field research, 518–23 The collection of first-hand data through observation, interviews, and questionnaires or surveys.
  interviewing experts, 518–20
  observation, 520–21
  questionnaires and surveys, 521–23

"A Fighter's Chance" (Jones), 245–52
figurative language
  with comparison and contrast, 441–43
  in profiles, 253
findings, profile, 255
Finn, Pat, 105–11
firsthand account, 252–53
FitzGerald, Frances, 443

flashback, 476 In NARRATION, an interruption of the main story to tell about an earlier incident.

flowcharts, 394, 676, 678

focus
  assessing own writing, 368–69
  genres
    proposals, 267
    review of scholarly literature, 213
    textual analysis, 131–34
  revising to sharpen, 376
  in summary and response essays, 37–38

font, 668–69 A typeface, such as Arial or Times New Roman.

Fontaine, Debra, 459–60
"For True Reform, Athletics Scholarships Must Go" (Gerdy), 426
forecasting organization, 350–51
forecasting statement. *See* thesis
formal definitions, 445–47
formal outlines, 340–41, 345

formal writing Writing intended to be evaluated by someone such as an instructor or read by an AUDIENCE expecting academic or businesslike argument and presentation. Formal writing should be REVISED, EDITED, and PROOFREAD especially carefully. *See also* informal writing

fragment, sentence. *See* sentence fragment
"Fragrances" (*Health Care without Harm*), 352
Freedom of Speech (Rockwell), 449

freewriting, 333–34 A PROCESS FOR GENERATING IDEAS AND TEXT by writing continuously for several minutes without pausing to read what has been written.

"French Fries" (Hesser), 470–71
"Frost's Broken Roads" (Miller), 224–27

fused sentence Two or more INDEPENDENT CLAUSES with no punctuation between them: I came I saw I conquered.

G

Gale eBooks, 513, 515
Gaylin, Willard, 355
general education field, 295–96
general indexes and databases, 516–17
general language, editing, 382
general reference works, 513
General Science Index, 517

generating ideas and text, 333–44 A set of PROCESSES that help writers develop a topic, examples, REASONS, EVIDENCE, and other parts of a text.
 clustering or mapping ideas, 335–36
 cubing, 336
 discovery drafting, 344
 freewriting, 333–34
 journaling, 343–44
 letter writing, 342–43
 listing, 334–35
 looping, 334
 outlining, 340–42
 questioning, 337
 talking, 336
 using genre features, 340
 using visuals, 337–39

genre, 65–71, 79–292 A kind of writing marked by and expected to have certain key features and to follow certain conventions of style and presentation. In literary texts, readers recognize such genres as short stories and novels and poems; in academic and work-place settings, readers and writers focus on such genres as ABSTRACTS, ANNOTATED BIBLIOGRAPHIES, ARGUMENTS, EVALUATIONS, LAB REPORTS, LITERACY NARRATIVES, LITERARY ANALYSES, PROFILES, PROPOSALS, REFLECTIONS, RÉSUMÉS, REPORTS, and TEXTUAL ANALYSES.
 for ambiguous assignments, 68–69
 combining, 69–70
 definition, 65–66
 list of genres, 66–68
 in remixes, 287, 290

Gerdy, John R., 426

gerund A VERB form ending in "-ing" that functions as a NOUN: <u>Swimming</u> improves muscle tone and circulation.

"Gettysburg Address" (Lincoln), 694–95
"Gettysburg Address: Two Versions" (Bass), 347
Ginsberg, Benjamin, 451, 452
Gladwell, Malcolm, 470
Goodfellow, Peter, 442
Google, research using, 510
Google Books, 515
Google Hangouts, 693
Google Images, 511, 529
Google News, 511
Google News Archive, 511
Google Scholar, 510
Google Video Search, 511
government sites, research with, 511
"Graduation" (Angelou), 474–75
"A Grand, Comprehensive Overview to Mutual Funds Investing" (Barker), 445–46
graphs
 for comparing, 440–41
 design of, 676, 677
 reading, 30–31

GreatBuildings.com, 459

Green, Kelly, 203–4

Greenblatt, Stephen, 300

Grison, Sarah, 29

guiding your reader. *See* cueing devices

"Guns and Cars Are Different" (MacLeod), 40–42

Guterson, David, 351, 464–65

H

habits of mind, academic, 46–56

Hall, Carla, 447–48

"Handgun Regulations, Crime, Assaults, and Homicide: A Tale of Two Cities" (Sloan), 439

handouts for presentations, 703

Harjo, Suzan Shown, 413

hashtag, 510 A number sign (#) in front of a word or unspaced phrase (#BlackLivesMatter), used in social media to mark posts by **KEYWORD** or theme and make them searchable by these tags. Also used to add commentary to texts.

hasty generalization, 428–29 A **FALLACY** that reaches a conclusion based on insufficient or inappropriately qualified **EVIDENCE**.

HathiTrust Digital Library, 515

headings

    as design element, 670–72

    in literary analyses, 233

    reading, 14

"Health and Behavioral Consequences of Binge Drinking in College" (Wechsler et al.), 357–58

Health Care without Harm (website), 352

health sciences, writing for, 322–24

Help Wanted: Tales from the First Job Front (Lewis), 359

helping verb A **VERB** that works with a main verb to express a **TENSE** or **MOOD**. Helping verbs include "do," "have," "be," and **MODALS**: Elvis has left the building. Pigs can fly.

Herrera Gutierrez, Karla Mariana, 85–90

Hesser, Amanda, 441–42, 470–71

Historical Abstracts, 517

history, researched essay for, 312–13

hoax videos, 529, 532

Hughes, Langston, 478

humanities

    academic writing, 311–13

    reading texts in, 304–5

Humanities Index, 517

Humanities International Index, 517

Huws, Ursula, 450

Hypothesis, 499

I

idea mapping. *See* clustering

"Identifying Genes Involved in Suppression of Tumor Formation in the Planarian *Schmidtea mediterranea*" (Dorsten), 314

identity-first language A way of referring to individuals (or groups) with specific characteristics by stating the characteristic, either exclusively or as the first word in a description. "Blind musicians" rather than "musicians who are blind." Some people may prefer to be described using identity-first language; if you don't know or can't confirm this preference, use **PERSON-FIRST LANGUAGE**.

illustration. *See* visual

image platforms, research using, 511

"Immigrant Workers in the U.S. Labor Force" (Singer), 350–51

implications, discussing, 355–56

IMRaD, 307, 315, 322 An acronym representing sections of scientific reports: Introduction (asks a question), methods (tells about experiments), results (states findings), and discussion (tries to make sense of findings in light of what was already known). In some fields, an abstract, literature review, and list of references may also be required.

incident, account of, 242

indefinite pronoun A PRONOUN—such as "all," "anyone," "anything," "everyone," "everything," "few," "many," "nobody," "nothing," "one," "some," and "something"—that does not refer to a specific person or thing.

independent clause A CLAUSE, containing a SUBJECT and a VERB, that can stand alone as a sentence: She sang. The world-famous soprano sang several popular arias.

indexes, library, 516–17

infinitive "To" plus the base form of the verb: "to come," "to go." An infinitive can function as a NOUN (He likes to run first thing in the morning); an ADJECTIVE (She needs a campaign to run); or an ADVERB (He registered to run in the marathon).

infographics, 679–80

informal outlines, 340, 345

informal writing Writing not intended to be evaluated, sometimes not even to be read by others. Informal writing is produced primarily to explore ideas or to communicate casually with friends and acquaintances. See also formal writing

informative abstracts, 196–97, 199, 200

InfoTrac, 516

InfoTrac Magazine Index, 517

inquiry, writing as, 329–32 A PROCESS for investigating a topic by posing questions, searching for multiple answers, and keeping an open mind.

blogs, 332

journals, 332

starting with questions, 329–32

integrating dialogue, 465–66

integrating sources

deciding whether to quote, paraphrase, or summarize, 544

paraphrasing, 547–50

quoting

incorporating short quotations, 544–45

indicating additions or changes, 546

indicating omissions, 546

punctuation, 546–47

setting off long quotations, 545

signal phrases, 551–54

summarizing, 550–51

taking notes, 542–44

interjection A word expressing surprise, resignation, agreement, and other emotions. It can be attached to a sentence or stand on its own: Well, if you insist. Ouch!

Internet Archive, 515

internet research

ebooks, 515

vs. library databases, 494–95

popular sites and search engines, 509–11

interpretation, 123, 228, 233, 331 The act of making sense of something or explaining what one thinks it means. Interpretation is the goal of writing a LITERARY ANALYSIS or TEXTUAL ANALYSIS.

interviewing
    dialogue and, 466–67
    genres and
        literacy narratives, 96
        position papers, 185
        profiles, 255
    as research source, 518–20
in-text documentation
    APA style, 618–22
    MLA style, 567–74
introduction, Rogerian argument, 423
introductory elements, commas with, 382
inventory of writing, 394
"Investing Basics: Stocks" (*Motley Fool*), 446

irregular verb A VERB that does not form its past tense and past participle by adding "-ed" or "-d" to the base form (as in "eat," "ate," "eaten").

"Italian Hours" (Traub), 460–61

J

Jones, Ryan, 245–52
Jones, Todd, 281–86
journal articles. *See* periodical articles

journal keeping, 332, 343–44 A PROCESS for GENERATING IDEAS AND TEXT that involves recording ideas, experiences, and REFLECTIONS on a regular basis. Journals may be written or recorded, in print or online, and may include materials in more than one MEDIUM.

journalist's questions, 332, 337
JSTOR, 516

judgments, 123
jumping right in, 354
"Just How Dishonest Are Most Students?" (Miller), 59–60, 258–62
Just the Facts (National Multiple Sclerosis Society), 457

K

Karim, Rea, 81–85
Kassfy, Ana-Jamileh, 91–93
Keller, Evelyn Fox, 354
key terms, defining
    in beginning, 191, 352
    in literary analyses, 230
    in reports, 153

keyword A word or phrase that a researcher inputs when searching RÉSUMÉS, databases, and the internet for information.
    defined, 495
    searching with
        advanced searches, 508–9
        databases, 507–8
        online, 510
        word clouds, 506–7

"Kill 'Em! Crush 'Em! Eat 'Em Raw!" (McMurtry), 437–38
knowledgeable discussion, 218
Kristof, Nicholas, 177–80, 354–55

L

lab report, 322, 459 A writing GENRE that covers the process of conducting an experiment in a controlled setting. Key Features: explicit title • ABSTRACT • PURPOSE • methods • results and discussion • REFERENCES • APPENDIX • appropriate format

"Lambs to the Gene Market" (Vidal and Carvel), 442

"Last Rites for Indian Dead: Treating Remains Like Artifacts Is Intolerable" (Harjo), 413

layout, 669 The way text is arranged on a page or screen—for example, in paragraphs, in lists, on charts, with headings.

learning management system, 689–91 A web-based educational tool that brings together all the course information your instructor wants you to have, along with communication tools, dropboxes, and other features.

learning online, 688–93

Lee, Chang-Rae, 465–66

Lehman, Charles Fain, 353

Leopold, Aldo, 475

"Less All Be Friends: Rafts as Negotiating Platforms in Twain's *Huckleberry Finn*" (Nichols), 420

lesson plans, 320

letter writing, 342–43 A PROCESS of GENERATING IDEAS AND TEXT by going through the motions of writing to someone to explain a topic.

"Letting the Unspoken Speak: A Reexamination of the Pueblo Revolt of 1680" (McHugh), 312–13

Levin, Michael, 425

Lewis, Sydney, 359

library research. *See* sources, research

Lincoln, Abraham, 694–95

line graphs, 677

linking verb A VERB that expresses a state of being (appear, be, feel, seem).

links, guidelines for adding, 681–82

listing, 334–35 A PROCESS for GENERATING IDEAS AND TEXT by making lists while thinking about a topic, finding relationships among the notes, and arranging the notes as an OUTLINE.

lists, design of, 669–70

literacy narrative, 81–103 A writing GENRE that explores the writer's experiences with reading and writing. Key Features: well-told story • vivid detail • indication of the narrative's significance

    choosing, 66

    key features, 93–94

    readings

        "Automotive Literacy," 91–93

        "Becoming an American Girl," 81–85

        "Reading, Writing, and Riding: A Literacy Narrative," 85–90

    writing guide

        choosing a topic, 94–95

        considering rhetorical situation, 95

        design, 100

        drafting, 99–100

        generating ideas and text, 96–97

        organizing, 98

        responses and revision, 100–101

literacy portfolio

    organizing, 390

    reflecting on, 390

    what to include, 389–90

literary analysis, 223–35 A writing GENRE that examines a literary text (most often fiction, poetry, or drama) and argues for a particular INTERPRETATION of the text. Key Features: arguable THESIS • careful attention to the language of the text • attention to patterns or themes • clear interpretation • MLA STYLE. *See also* analysis; textual analysis

literary analysis (cont.)
    choosing, 66–67
    dialogue in, 464
    key features, 228
    literature for analysis: "The Road Not
        Taken," 223–24
    reading: "Frost's Broken Roads," 224–27
    strategies for, 410, 464
    writing guide, 229–35

literature Literary works—including fiction, poetry, drama, and some nonfiction; also, the body of written work produced in a given field.

literature review, 209–13, 306 A GENRE of writing that surveys and synthesizes the prior research on a TOPIC. In the sciences, a literature review is a required part of the introduction to an IMRAD report; in all disciplines, scholars write article-length literature reviews devoted to specific topics. Key Features: careful, thorough research • accurate, objective SUMMARIES of the relevant LITERATURE • synthesis of the scholarship • critical EVALUATION of the literature • a clear focus
    key features, 212–13
    sample review: "Zombie Film Scholar-
        ship: A Review of the Literature,"
        210–12
    taking stock, 213

"Little Things Can Mean a Lot" (Petroski), 355–56

logical appeal, 411–22 In ARGUMENT, an appeal to readers based on the use of logical reasoning and of evidence such as facts, statistics, statements from authorities on the subject, and so on.

logical fallacy. *See* fallacy, logical
logos. *See* logical appeal

looping, 334 A PROCESS for GENERATING IDEAS AND TEXT in which a writer writes about a topic quickly for several minutes and then reads the results and writes a one-sentence summary of the most important or interesting idea. The summary becomes the beginning of another round of writing and summarizing, and so on, until the writer finds a tentative focus for writing.

Lowi, Theodore J., 451, 452

M

MacLeod, Jacob, 40–42
Mairs, Nancy, 456–57
mapping ideas, 335–36
maps, 676, 678
Marcus, Jon, 35, 37–39, 149–52
"Marrying Absurd" (Didion), 481
mathematics, academic writing for, 313–15
"The Mathematics of Christmas" (Devlin),
    418–19
Mazzucato, Olivia, 215–17
McAdory, Paul, 457–58
McDonie, Andy, 353
McHugh, Erin, 312–13
McMurtry, John, 437–38

medium, 659–63 A way that a text is delivered. Some examples include in print, with speech, or online.
    multimedia, 661
    for presentations, 698
    print, electronic, spoken, 660–61
    in remixes, 287, 291
    rhetorical situation, 75–77, 662–63

Mejía, Susanna, 448
Mejia Avila, Rocio Celeste, 346

memoir, 236–44 A GENRE that focuses on something significant from the writer's past. Key Features: good story • vivid details • clear significance
>choosing, 67
>combining genres in, 69
>key features, 240–41
>with other genres, 287–88
>reading: "All Over but the Shoutin'," 236–40
>strategies for, 405, 456, 458, 464
>writing guide, 241–44

Mendeley, 500

metacognition, 52, 391 Awareness and understanding of one's own thought processes.

metaphor, 442 A figure of speech that makes a comparison without using the word "like" or "as": "All the world's a stage / And all the men and women merely players" (Shakespeare, *As You Like It* 2.7.138–39). *See also* figurative language; simile

Microsoft Teams, 693
Miller, Christian B., 59–60, 258–62
Miller, Matthew, 224–27
MLA International Bibliography, 517

MLA style, 564–614 A system of DOCUMENTATION used in the humanities. MLA stands for the Modern Language Association.
>comparison with APA style, 561–63
>directory, 564–67
>formatting
>>notes, 574
>>quotations, 544–45
>>research papers, 605–7
>in-text documentation, 567–74
>in literary analysis, 228
>sample research paper, 607–14
>verb tense in, 553–54
>works-cited list
>>articles and other short works, 582–89
>>audio, visual, and other sources, 599–605
>>authors and contributors, 580–82
>>books and parts of books, 590–95
>>personal communication and social media, 598
>>websites, 595–97

modal A HELPING VERB—such as "can," "could," "may," "might," "must," "ought to," "should," "will," or "would"—that does not change form for person or number and indicates probability or necessity.

Modern Democracy (Becker), 450–51, 451–52
modification, in remixes, 287

modifier A word, PHRASE, or CLAUSE that describes or specifies something about another word, phrase, or clause (a <u>long, informative</u> speech; the actors spoke <u>in unison</u>; the <u>man who would be king</u>).

Moller, William, 416–18

mood A characteristic of VERBS that indicates a writer's attitude toward the action or condition the verb expresses. The *indicative mood* is used to state fact or opinion: I'm waiting to buy tickets. The *imperative mood* is used to give commands or directions: Sit down, and take off your shoes. The *subjunctive mood* is used to express wishes, requests, or requirements or to indicate unlikely conditions: I wish the ticket line were shorter. I suggest that you be ready for a long wait.

Morrison, Toni, 453

"Mother Tongue" (Tan), 356–57

Motley Fool, 446

moving vantage points, 460–61

multimedia, 518 Using more than one medium of delivery, such as print, speech, or electronic. Often used interchangeably with MULTIMODAL.

multimodal, 518 Using more than one mode of expression, such as words, images, sound, links, and so on. Often used interchangeably with MULTIMEDIA.

multiple perspectives, incorporating, 6,
    331–32
    genres and
        arguments, 424–25
        evaluations, 220
        position papers, 188
        Rogerian argument, 423

multiple vantage points, 461–62

Murray, Donald, 377

*Music Online: Smithsonian Global Sound for
    Libraries*, 518

"My Freshman Year" (Nathan), 362

N

narration, 81–103, 474–82 A STRATEGY for presenting information as a story, for telling "what happened." It is a pattern most often associated with fiction, but it shows up in all kinds of writing. When used in an essay, a REPORT, or another academic GENRE, narration is used to support a point—not merely tell an interesting story for its own sake. It must also present events in some kind of sequence and include only pertinent detail. Narration can serve as the ORGANIZING principle for a whole text. *See also* literacy narrative

    in beginnings and endings, 480–81
    detail and, 478–80
    genres and
        literacy narratives, 101
        literary analyses, 230
        profiles, 256
    rhetorical situation and, 482
    sequencing
        chronological order, 474–75
        flashbacks, 476
        reverse chronological order, 475
        time markers, 476–78
        transitions, 478

narratives
    anecdotes as, 416–18
    rewriting, 378

narrowing a topic, 156

narrowing your thesis, 348

Nathan, Rebekah, 362

National Geographic Atlas of the World, 513

National Multiple Sclerosis Society, 457

Naxos Music Library, 518

New Encyclopedia Britannica, 513

The New York Times Index, 517

news sites, research using, 511

Nichols, Dave, 420

Nizamoff, Jenna, 316

noncount noun A word that names something that cannot be counted or made plural: "information," "rice."

nonessential element, 382 A word, PHRASE, or CLAUSE that gives additional information but that is not necessary for understanding the basic meaning of a sentence: I learned French, <u>which is a Romance language</u>, online.

Nonessential elements should be set off by commas.

nonrestrictive element. *See* nonessential element

notes
    in documentation
        APA style, 622–23
        MLA style, 574
    taking
        guidelines, 542–44
        plagiarism and, 559
        synthesizing ideas using, 539–40

noun A word that names a person, place, thing, or idea (teacher, Zadie Smith, forest, Amazon River, notebook, democracy).

nursing, academic writing for, 322–24

O

object A word or phrase that follows a PREPOSITION or that receives the action of a VERB. In the sentence "I handed him the mail on the table," "him" is an indirect object and "mail" is a direct object of the verb "handed"; "table" is an object of the preposition "on."

objective description, 198, 459–60
observational research, 520–21
observations, 419–20
"On Being a Cripple" (Mairs), 456–57
"On the Backs of Blacks" (Morrison), 453
The Onion, 431–32
online learning
    course information, 689
    keeping track of files, 688
    learning management systems, 689–91

    tips, 691–93
    web conferencing tools, 693
online sources
    APA style, 618–44
    fact-checking, 526–28, 530–31
    MLA style, 595–97
online writing
    blogs, 687
    email and texts, 685
    social media, 685
    websites, 685–86
onscreen reading, 31–32
Open Library, 515
openings. *See* beginnings

organizing Arranging parts of a text so that the text as a whole has COHERENCE. The text may use one STRATEGY throughout or may combine several strategies to create a suitable organization.
    assessing for organization, 370
    cause-and-effect analysis, 407–8
    comparison and contrast, 438–40
    cues to, 14
    description, 462
    fields of study
        arts and humanities, 313
        business, 318
        education, 320
        engineering, 322
        health sciences and nursing, 324
        sciences, 315
        social sciences, 316–17
    forecasting organization, 350–51
    genres
        abstracts, 199–200
        annotated bibliographies, 208–9
        evaluations, 221
        explorations, 278

organizing (cont.)
    literacy narratives, 98
    literacy portfolios, 390
    literary analyses, 234
    memoirs, 243
    position papers, 189–90
    profiles, 256
    proposals, 264–65
    reflections, 398–400
    remixes, 291
    reports, 157–58
    summary and response essay,
        44–45
    textual analyses, 134–35
    writing portfolios, 387–88
  revising for organization, 376
  of writing, 345–63
    beginnings, 346–54
    endings, 354–58
    outlining, 345
    paragraphs, 358–61
    thesis statements, 347–49
    titles, 363
    topic sentences, 358–60
    transitions, 361–62
Ouattara, Brenda, 466–67
"Our Blind Spot about Guns" (Kristof),
    177–80, 354–55
"Our Declaration" (Allen), 34, 111–16
"Ours Was a Dad . . ." (Davis), 695–97
"An Outbreak of the Irrational" (Dzubay), 349

outlining, 345 A PROCESS for GENERATING IDEAS AND TEXT or for organizing or examining a text. An *informal outline* simply lists ideas and then numbers them in the order that they will appear; a *working outline* distinguishes supporting from main ideas by indenting the former; a *formal outline* is arranged as a series of headings and indented subheadings, each on a separate line, with letters and numerals indicating relative levels of importance.

    generating ideas with, 340–42
    research and, 497
    textual analyses and, 125

Oxford English Dictionary, 513
Oxford Reference, 514, 515

P

paper portfolios, 387–88
The Paradise of Bombs (Sanders), 458, 461–62
paragraphs, 358–61
    design of, 669
    with dialogue, 465
    editing, 380–81
    length and number, 360–61
    topic sentences, 358–60

parallelism A writing technique that puts similar items into the same grammatical structure. For example, every item on a to-do list might begin with a command: "clean," "wash," "buy"; or a discussion of favorite hobbies might name each as a GERUND: running, playing basketball, writing poetry.

    editing and, 381
    in presentations, 698

paraphrasing Rewording someone else's text using about the same number of words but not the phrasing or sentence structure of the original. Paraphrasing is generally called for when a writer wants to include the details of a passage but does not need to quote it word for word. Like a QUOTATION or SUMMARY, a paraphrase requires DOCUMENTATION.

    deciding whether to quote, paraphrase,
        or summarize, 544

guidelines, 547–50
signal phrases and, 550, 551–53
as textual evidence, 420

Parsons, Joel, 131–34
part-by-part organization, 135

passive voice, 381 When a VERB is in the passive voice, the subject is acted upon: A gift was given to José. See also active voice

past participle A VERB form used with a HELPING VERB to create perfect tenses (have <u>walked</u>) or used alone as an ADJECTIVE (<u>processed</u> food). The past participle of most verbs is formed by adding "-ed" or "-d" to the base form; some past participles, though, are irregular (the <u>written</u> word).

past tense
in literary analyses, 233
for signal phrases, 554

patchwriting, 549 PARAPHRASES that lean too heavily on the words or sentence structure of the source, adding or deleting some words, replacing words with synonyms, altering the syntax slightly — in other words, not restating the passage in fresh language and structure.

pathos. See emotional appeal
patterns, 23–25, 228
peer-reviewed scholarly sources, 502, 505.
See also scholarly research sources

periodical articles Magazines, newspapers, and journals that are published regularly.
APA documentation style, 629–34
finding
general indexes and databases, 516–17
print indexes, 517
single-subject indexes and databases, 517
MLA documentation style, 582–89

periods, 547

permalink, 204, 516 A URL that permanently links to a specific web page or blog post.

personal attack. See ad hominem argument

person-first language A way of referring to individuals (or groups) with specific characteristics without defining them by those characteristics. "An enslaved person" rather than a "slave." Some people may prefer to be described using IDENTITY-FIRST LANGUAGE; if you don't know their preference, use person-first language.

Peters, Emma, 466–67
Petroski, Henry, 355–56
photographs, 528–29, 557

phrase A group of words that lacks a SUBJECT, a VERB, or BOTH.

pie charts, 677

plagiarism, 558–59 The use of another person's words, ideas, or sentence structures without appropriate credit and DOCUMENTATION. Plagiarism is a serious breach of ethics.

Plan B 2.0: Rescuing a Planet under Stress and a Civilization in Trouble (Brown), 416, 438
poetry, quoting, 545

point of view The choice a writer makes of whether to use the first person (I, we), the second person (you), or the third person (he, she, it, they, a student, the students).

point-by-point method of comparing and contrasting, 439–40

popular research sources, 502–3, 505

portfolio, 385–90 A collection of writing selected by a writer to show their work, including a statement assessing the work and explaining what it demonstrates.
    rhetorical situation, 385–86
    writing portfolios
        assessing, 388–89
        organizing, 387–88
        what to include, 386–87

position, 331, 411–13 A statement that asserts a belief or CLAIM. In an ARGUMENT, a position needs to be stated in a THESIS or clearly implied, and it requires support with REASONS and EVIDENCE. *See also* arguing a position

position paper
    choosing, 67
    key features, 180–82
    with other genres, 288
    readings
        "All Words Matter: The Manipulation behind 'All Lives Matter,'" 164–70
        "Come Look at the Freaks: Examining and Advocating for Disability Theatre," 171–77
        "Our Blind Spot about Guns," 177–80
    strategies for
        dialogue, 464
        narration, 474
    writing guide
        choosing a topic, 182–84
        considering a rhetorical situation, 184–85
        design, 192–93
        drafting, 190–92
        editing and proofreading, 194

        generating ideas and text, 185–89
        organizing, 189–90
        responses and revision, 193–94
        taking stock, 194–95
        ways of rewriting, 379
"post hoc, ergo propter hoc." *See* faulty causality
PowerNotes, 500
Powers, John, 350

predicate In a sentence or CLAUSE, the VERB and the words that tell more about the verb—MODIFIERS, COMPLEMENTS, and OBJECTS. In the sentence "Mario forcefully stated his opinion," the predicate is "forcefully stated his opinion."

premise A statement that assumes something is true and serves as the basis for an argument.

preposition A word or group of words that tells about the relationship of a NOUN or PRONOUN to another word in the sentence. Some common prepositions are "after," "at," "before," "behind," "between," "by," "for," "from," "in," "of," "on," "to," "under," "until," "with," and "without."

present participle A VERB form used with a HELPING VERB to create progressive TENSES (is <u>writing</u>) or used alone as an ADJECTIVE (a <u>living</u> organism). The present participle of a verb always ends in "-ing."

present perfect A TENSE used to indicate actions that took place at no specific time in the past or that began in the past and continue into the present: I <u>have</u> often <u>wondered</u> how I can make my love of language into a career. He <u>has cried</u> every day since his companion of fifty years died.

present tense, 233, 554
presentation slides, 698
presentations, 694–705
    annotated bibliographies, 205
    delivering, 704–5
    examples
        "Gettysburg Address," 694–95
        "Ours Was a Dad . . . ," 695–97
    guide to writing
        handouts, 703
        organizing and drafting, 700
        presentation software, 701–3
        time budgeting, 699
        visuals, 700–701
    key features, 697–98
    rhetorical situation, 698–99
previewing texts, 13, 125

primary source, 304–5, 501–2 A source such as a literary work, historical document, work of art, or performance that a researcher examines firsthand. Primary sources also include experiments and FIELD RESEARCH. A researcher would likely consider the Declaration of Independence a primary source and a textbook's description of how the document was written a SECONDARY SOURCE.

print indexes, 517
problem, well-defined, 262
procedures, reports about, 157
proceedings, conference, 516

process, 325–401 In writing, a series of actions that may include GENERATING IDEAS AND TEXT, ORGANIZING, DRAFTING, REVISING, EDITING, and PROOFREADING. See also explaining a process and specific processes

profile, 245–57 A GENRE that presents an engaging portrait of a person, place, or event based on firsthand FIELD RESEARCH. Key Features: interesting subject • necessary background • interesting angle • firsthand account • engaging details

    choosing, 67
    combining genres in, 69–70
    key features, 252–53
    with other genres, 288
    readings
        "A Fighter's Chance," 245–52
        "Rare Earth," 281–86
    strategies for
        argument, 410
        description, 459
        dialogue, 464
        narration, 474
    video, 285
    writing guide, 253–57

Project Gutenberg, 515

pronoun A word that takes the place of a NOUN, such as "she," "anyone," "whoever."

    clarity of, 382
    editing, 383

proofreading, 383–84 The final PROCESS of writing, when a writer checks for correct spelling and punctuation as well as for page order, missing text, and consistent use of FONTS. See also editing; revision; rewriting

proposal, 258–68 A GENRE that argues for a solution to a problem or suggests some action. Key Features: well-defined problem • recommended solution • answers to anticipated questions • call to action • appropriate TONE. See also topic proposal

    abstract for, 197, 199, 200
    for annotated bibliography, 207
    choosing, 68

proposal (cont.)
> key features, 262–63
> with other genres, 288
> reading: "Just How Dishonest Are Most Students?," 258–62
> scientific, 314
> strategies for
>> argument, 410
>> cause-and-effect analysis, 405
>> comparison and contrast, 437
> topic proposal
>> key features, 267–68
>> reading: "Social Media and Data Privacy," 266–67
> writing guide, 263–66

ProQuest Central, 516
Psychology in Your Life (Grison et al.), 29
PsycINFO, 517
PubMed, 517

pull quote, 665 A brief excerpt set off within a text in order to highlight certain information. Pull quotes are often set in a different FONT or color.

punctuation, with dialogue and quotations, 465, 546-47

purpose, 59–60 A writer's goal: to explore ideas, to express oneself, to entertain, to demonstrate learning, to inform, to persuade, and so on. Purpose is one element of the RHETORICAL SITUATION.

Q

qualifying
> claims, 412
> position, 187

thesis, 348–49

qualifying word, 412, A word such as "frequently," "often," "generally," "sometimes," or "rarely" that limits a CLAIM in some way.

question marks, 547

questioning A PROCESS of GENERATING IDEAS AND TEXT about a topic—asking, for example, "What?," "Who?," "When?," "Where?," "How?," and "Why?" or other questions.
> beginning by, 354
> generating ideas by, 337
> writing as inquiry and, 329–32

questionnaire research, 521–23
questions
> begging the question, 428
> in beginnings, 99
> in interviews for profiles, 255
> research questions, 495–96
> responding to, in proposals, 263
> thesis statements and, 347–48
Quindlen, Anna, 353

quotation The use of someone else's words exactly as they were spoken or written. Quoting is most effective when wording makes a point so well that no re-wording will do it justice. Quotations need to be acknowledged with DOCUMENTATION.
> acknowledging sources, 556, 558
> block style vs. in text, 545
> deciding whether to quote, paraphrase, or summarize, 544
> punctuation with, 546–47
> signal phrases and, 551–53
> in summary and response essay, 35
> as textual evidence, 420

quotation marks, 465

R

Rabin, Roni Caryn, 414–15
"Rare Earth" (Jones), 281–86
rationale, in proposals, 268
Raymo, Chet, 424
readers, guiding. *See* cueing devices
The Reader's Guide to Periodical Literature, 517
reading
    critical reading, 20–25
        believing and doubting, 20–21
        how text works, 21–23
        identifying patterns, 23–25
        research sources, 532–33
    fields of study and, 298–308
        advice, 299–304
        career-focused fields, 308
        humanities, 304–5
        rhetorical situation, 298–99
        sciences, 306–7
        social studies, 305–6
    rhetorical reading, 25–28
        analyzing argument, 26–27
        considering larger context, 27–28
        rhetorical situation, 25–26
    strategies, 12–20
    synthesizing ideas and, 535–39
"Reading, Writing, and Riding: A Literacy Narrative" (Herrera Gutierrez), 85–90

reason Support for a CLAIM or POSITION. A reason, in turn, requires its own support in the form of evidence.
    in academic writing, 5–6
    in arguments, 413–14
    in evaluations, 218, 221
    in position papers, 181, 187–89

"The Reason College Costs More Than You Think" (Marcus)
    summary and responses, 35, 37–39
    text, 149–52
recommended solutions. *See* calls for action
reference management systems, 497, 500

references The list of sources at the end of a text prepared in APA STYLE.
    articles and other short works, 629–34
    audio, visual, and other sources, 639–44
    authors and other contributors, 626–29
    books, parts of books, and reports, 634–39
    sources not covered by APA, 644

reference works
    bibliographies, 514
    general and specialized, 513–14
    preliminary research and, 495

reflecting, 391–401 A set of processes that help writers take stock of their writing and learning in order to apply their knowledge to other writing situations.
    as academic habit of mind, 52
    after writing, 392–401
    formal reflection
        insights for, 394–96
        organizing, 398–401
        support for, 396–98
    on literacy portfolio, 390
    strategies for, 456
    in summary and response essays, 38–39
    while writing, 391–92

refuting other positions
    in arguments, 426
    in evaluations, 220
    in position papers, 189

RefWorks, 500

Reitz, Patricia, 472

relative pronoun A PRONOUN such as "that," "which," "who," "whoever," "whom," or "whomever" that introduces a SUBORDINATE CLAUSE: The professor <u>who</u> gave the lecture is my adviser.

"Remembering My Childhood on the Continent of Africa" (Sedaris), 439–40

remix, 280–92 A new text that results from the transformation of a previous text in order to respond to a new RHETORICAL SITUATION.
  choosing, 68
  key features, 287
  reading: "Rare Earth," 281–86
  typical ways of remixing genres, 287–88
  writing guide, 289–92

repetition, in presentations, 698

reporting, 140–63 A writing GENRE that presents information to readers on a subject. Key Features: tightly focused TOPIC • accurate, well-researched information • various writing STRATEGIES • clear DEFINITIONS • appropriate DESIGN. *See also* lab report
  choosing, 67
  key features, 152–53
  lab reports, 322
  with other genres, 288
  readings
    "Edible Magic," 146–49
    "The Reason College Costs More Than You Think," 149–52
    "Sleepless Nights of a University Student," 140–45
  research reports, 316–17, 321–22

rewriting, 379

writing guide
  choosing a topic, 154–55
  considering the rhetorical situation, 155
  design, 160
  drafting, 158–59
  editing and proofreading, 161–62
  generating ideas and text, 156–57
  organizing, 157–58
  responses and revision, 160–61
  taking stock, 162–63
  ways of rewriting, 379

research
  genres
    literature reviews, 212
    position papers, 185
    profiles, 255
    reports, 153, 157
  starting
    choosing a topic, 493–94
    keeping track of sources, 499–500
    librarian consultation and preliminary research, 494–95
    research question, 495–96
    rhetorical situation, 492–93
    rough outline, 497
    schedules for, 491–92
    tentative thesis, 496–97
    working bibliography, 497–99

research reports, 316–17, 321–22

researched essay, 312–13

researchers, conversation among, 303–4

"Researching Hunger and Poverty" (Kelly), 203–4

resources, in proposals, 268

responding to objections. *See* multiple perspectives, incorporating
responding to texts
    guidelines, 36–39
    summary and response essays
        key features, 42–44
        sample essay: "Guns and Cars Are Different," 40–42
        writing guide, 44–45

response, 372–74 A PROCESS of writing in which a reader gives the writer their thoughts about the writer's title, beginning, THESIS, support and DOCUMENTATION, ORGANIZING, STANCE, treatment of AUDIENCE, achievement of PURPOSE, handling of the GENRE, ending, and other matters.

    genres and
        literacy narratives, 100–101
        position papers, 193–94
        proposals, 263
        reports, 160–61
        textual analyses, 129, 138
restating, of thesis, 137
restrictive element. *See* essential element

résumé A GENRE that summarizes someone's academic and employment history, generally written to submit to potential employers. Key Features: organization that suits goals and experience • succinctness • design that highlights key information. *See* the ebook at digital.wwnorton.com/fieldguide6 for a chapter on Résumés and Job Letters.

    reverse chronological order, 475
"Rethinking the Meat-Guzzler" (Bittman), 415
reverse chronological order, 475
reviews, 209–13, 306
    key features, 212–13
    sample review: "Zombie Film Scholarship: A Review of the Literature," 210–12
    taking stock, 213

revision, 375–77 The PROCESS of making substantive changes to a draft so that it contains all the necessary content and presents it in an appropriate organization. During revision, writers generally move from whole-text issues to details with the goals of sharpening their focus and strengthening their position.

rewriting, 378–79 A PROCESS of composing a new draft from another perspective—with a different POINT OF VIEW, AUDIENCE, STANCE, GENRE, or MEDIUM, for example.

rhetorical context, 25

rhetorical situation, 57–77 The CONTEXT in which writing or other communication takes place, including PURPOSE, AUDIENCE, GENRE, STANCE, and MEDIA/DESIGN.

    elements of
        audience, 61–64
        genre, 65–71
        media/design, 75–77, 662–63, 664–65
        purpose, 59–60
        stance, 72–74
        visuals, 674
    fields of study, 309–10
    genres and
        abstracts, 198
        annotated bibliographies, 205
        essay exams, 483–84
        evaluations, 219

rhetorical situation (cont.)

explorations, 276–77
literacy narratives, 95
literary analyses, 229
memoirs, 241–42
portfolios, 385–86
position papers, 184–85
presentations, 698–99
profiles, 254
proposals, 263–64
remixes, 289–90
reports, 155
research, 492–93
textual analyses, 124
processes and
arguments, 422, 429–30
cause-and-effect analysis, 408–9
classification and division, 435–36
comparison and contrast, 443–44
definition, 454–55
description, 463
dialogue, 468
narration, 482
process explanation, 473
reading across fields of study, 298–99
reflecting on, 393
rhetorical reading, 25–26

"Richness in the Eye of the Beholder"
(Parsons), 131–34
Ricker, K., 323
"Risk" (Roberts), 406–7
Roberts, Paul, 406–7
Rockwell, Norman, 449

Rogerian argument, 422–23 A technique for ARGUING that aims to solve conflicts by seeking common ground among people who disagree.

S

Safire, William, 24–25
SAGE Knowledge, 514, 515
"Salvation" (Hughes), 478
sample research papers, 672
APA style, 647–55
MLA style, 607–14
A Sand County Almanac (Leopold), 475
Sandel, Michael J., 18–19
Sanders, Scott Russell, 458, 461–62
scenarios, 418–19
schedules
for drafting, 364
research, 491–92
Schembri, Frankie, 146–49
Schlosser, Eric, 432–33
scholarly research sources, 502–3
Schunk, Brianna, 6–7, 171–77
science writing, 313–15, 320–22
sciences, reading texts in, 306–7
scientific proposal, 314
scope, statements of, 204
Scott, Robert F., 476–77
Scott's Last Expedition: The Journals, 476–77
Scrible, 500
search engines, 509–11

secondary source, 304–5, 501–2 An ANALYSIS or INTERPRETATION of a PRIMARY SOURCE. In writing about the Revolutionary War, a researcher would likely consider the Declaration of Independence a primary source and a textbook's description of how the document was written a secondary source.

The Secret Knowledge of Water (Childs), 419–20, 442
Sedaris, David, 439–40

semicolons, 547
sensory details, 253, 458

sentence fragment A group of words that is capitalized and punctuated as a sentence but is not one, either because it lacks a SUBJECT, a VERB, or both, or because it begins with a word that makes it a SUBORDINATE CLAUSE.

sentences
    complete, 381
    editing, 381–82
sequences, transitions used with, 362
setting, describing, 96, 99
"Sex, Lies, and Conversation: Why Is It So Hard for Men and Women to Talk to Each Other?" (Tannen), 359

sexist language, 383 Language that stereotypes or ignores women or men or needlessly calls attention to gender.

signal phrase A phrase used to attribute quoted, paraphrased, or summarized material to a source, as in "she said" or "according to Kristof."
    APA style and, 618–19
    with dialogue, 465
    identifying authorities with, 416
    integrating sources and, 551–54
    MLA style and, 567
    in summary and response
        essay, 34–35
signal verbs, 553
significance
    in endings, 99
    in explorations, 277
    in literacy narrative, 94, 97
    in memoirs, 241, 242
similarities, transitions used with, 362

simile, 441–42 A figure of speech that uses "like" or "as" to compare two items. *See also* figurative language; metaphor

Singer, Audrey, 350–51
single-subject indexes and databases, 517

singular "they," 383 The use of "they," "them," and "their" to refer to a person whose gender is unknown or not relevant to the context. Traditionally, "they" has referred only to plural items, but the use of the singular "they" is now becoming more accepted.

Skeptics and True Believers: The Exhilarating Connection between Science and Religion (Raymo), 424
skimming, 13, 15, 32
Skype, 693
"Sleepless Nights of a University Student" (Tingling), 140–45
slides, presentation, 698

slippery slope, 429 A FALLACY that asserts, without EVIDENCE, that one event will lead to a series of other events that will end in disaster.

Sloan, John Henry, 439
"Snakes" (McAdory), 457–58
social media, 685
"Social Media and Data Privacy" (Thoms), 266–67
social media searches, 510
Social Sciences Index, 517
social sciences writing, 315–17
social studies, reading texts in, 305–6
solutions
    best, 264
    desirable, 264
    in exploratory essays, 278
    potential, 264
    recommended (*see* calls for action)

"Some Covid Survivors Haunted by Loss of Smell and Taste" (Rabin), 414–15
Sommers, Jennifer, 196–97
sound, using, 680
sources, research
    acknowledging, 555–58
    books
        ebooks, 515
        library catalog, 514–15
    field research
        interviewing experts, 518–20
        observation, 520–21
        questionnaires and surveys, 521–23
    genres
        annotated bibliographies, 206
        literary analyses, 233
    integrating (*see* integrating sources)
    internet research, 509–11
    keeping track of, 499–500
    keyword searches
        advanced searching, 508–9
        databases and, 507–8
        word clouds and, 506–7
    library research overview, 511–12
    multimedia sources, 518
    periodicals (*see* periodical articles)
    reference works
        bibliographies, 514
        general, 513
        specialized, 513–14
    search engines
        Google and *Google Scholar*, 510
        image, video, and audio platforms, 511
    types of
        primary and secondary, 501–2
        scholarly and popular, 502–5
    websites
        digital archives, 511
        government sites, 511
        image, video, and audio platforms, 511
        news sites, 511
        Wikipedia, 509–10
spatial organization, 135
specialized reference works, 513–14
specific details, 457–58
speed of reading, 13–14
stable URLs, 516

stance, 72–74 A writer's or speaker's attitude toward their subject—for example, reasonable, neutral, angry, curious. Stance is conveyed through TONE. *See also* rhetorical situation
    in academic contexts, 6–7
    reading across fields of study, 300

Stanley, Jason, 35
Staples, Brent, 478–79
"Statement of Teaching Philosophy" (Tams), 319–20
stationary vantage points, 460
Statistical Abstract of the United States, 513
statistics
    reflection on, 398
    sources of, 513
    as type of evidence, 415
stereotyped language, 383
Stewart, Jude, 535–37
"Still Needing the F Word" (Quindlen), 353
stipulative definitions, 453
story, 93, 240

storyboard, 291, 338, 339 A visual representation of images and text for a planned multimedia project.

strategy, 403–88 A pattern for ORGANIZING text to ANALYZE CAUSE AND EFFECT, ARGUE, CLASSIFY AND DIVIDE, COMPARE AND CONTRAST, DEFINE, DESCRIBE, EXPLAIN A PROCESS, or NARRATE.

straw man fallacy, 189, 428
structure
    explorations, 275
    presentations, 697
"The Student Loan Trap: When Debt Delays
    Life" (Lehman), 353
study group, 486
style, literary analyses, 233

subject A word or word group, usually including at least one NOUN or PRONOUN plus its MODIFIERS, that tells who or what a sentence or CLAUSE is about. In the sentence "A frustrated group of commuters waited for the late bus," the subject is "A frustrated group of commuters."
    in explorations, 277
    in profiles, 252–55

subjective descriptions, 459–60

subordinate clause A clause that begins with a SUBORDINATING WORD and therefore cannot stand alone as a sentence: She feels good <u>when she exercises</u>. My roommate, <u>who was a physics major</u>, tutors students in science.

subordinating word A word, such as a RELATIVE PRONOUN or a subordinating conjunction, that introduces a SUBORDINATE CLAUSE: The ice sculpture melted <u>because</u> the ballroom was too hot. Common subordinating words include "although," "as," "because," "if," "since," "that," "which," and "why."

Sullivan, Andrew, 424–25
Sullivan, Kathleen M., 453–54

summary, 33–35, 550–51 The use of one's own words and sentence structure to condense someone else's text into a briefer version that gives the main ideas of the original. As with PARAPHRASING and QUOTATION, summarizing requires DOCUMENTATION.
    choosing, 67
    essay questions, 485
    genres
        abstracts, 198, 199
        annotated bibliographies, 207
        literacy narratives, 97
        literature reviews, 212
        position papers, 191–92
        presentation, 697
        reports, 159
        textual analyses, 123, 125
    integrating sources, 544, 550–51
    as reading strategy, 20
    signal phrases, 551–53
    textual evidence, 420
    transitions, 362

summary and response essay, 33–45 A GENRE of writing that demonstrates one's ability to convey a text's main ideas in condensed form and to engage with those ideas by ARGUING a position, ANALYZING the text, or writing a REFLECTION on its content. Key Features: clearly identified author and title • concise summary of the text • an explicit response • support for that response
    key features, 42–44
    sample essay: "Guns and Cars Are
        Different" (MacLeod), 40–42
    writing guide, 44–45

support. *See* evidence
survey research, 521–23
The Swerve (Greenblatt), 300

synthesizing ideas, 535–41 Bringing together ideas and information from multiple sources in order to discover patterns and gain new insights and perspectives.
    in literature reviews, 210
    reading across fields of study, 301
    in reading process, 535–39
    in reports, 153
    to support own ideas, 541
    using notes, 539–40

T

tables, 676, 677
taking notes
    integrating sources, 542–44
    plagiarism and, 559
    synthesizing ideas using, 539–40
talking, to generate ideas, 336
"Talking with Granddad" (Diehl), 269–74
Taking Stock of Your Work, 102, 139, 162, 194, 200, 209, 213, 222, 234, 243, 257, 265, 279, 292
Tams, Kelly, 319–20
Tan, Amy, 356–57
Tannen, Deborah, 359
Tanner, S., 321
teaching philosophy statement, 319–20
technology writing, 320–22
"Teen Film$" (Benton et al.), 202–3
tenses. *See* verb tenses
tentative thesis statements
    evaluations, 220
    reports, 156
    research, 496–97
    textual analyses, 134

text-by-text organization, 135
texting, 685

textual analysis, 104–39 A writing GENRE in which a writer looks at what a text says and how it says it. Key Features: SUMMARY of the text • attention to context • clear INTERPRETATION or judgment • reasonable support for conclusions. *See also* analysis; literary analysis
    choosing, 66–67
    combining genres in, 70
    key features, 123
    with other genres, 484, 485
    readings
        "The Architecture of Inequality: On Bong Joon-ho's *Parasite*," 105–11
        "Our Declaration," 111–16
        "Why It Worked: A Rhetorical Analysis of Obama's Speech on Race," 116–22
    strategies, 431
    writing guide
        choosing a text, 124
        considering rhetorical situation, 124
        design, 137
        drafting, 136–37
        editing and proofreading, 138
        organizing, 134–35
        responses and revision, 138
        taking stock, 139
        tentative thesis, 134
        visual texts, 128–34
        ways of rewriting, 378
        written texts, 124–28

textual evidence, 420
Theatre in Video, 518
thematic organization, 135
themes, 228

thesis, 347–49, 413 A statement that identifies the **TOPIC** and main point of a piece of writing, giving readers an idea of what the text will cover.

    in academic writing, 5

    beginning with, 136, 158, 347–49

    drafting, 413

    genres and

        arguments, 413

        evaluations, 220

        explorations, 277

        literary analyses, 228, 231–32

        position papers, 186–87

        reports, 156–58

        textual analyses, 134

    reading, 14

    research and, 496–97

    as research source, 516

    Rogerian argument, 423

"they," as singular pronoun, 383

Think Like a Chef (Colicchio), 446

"This Is the End of the World: The Black Death" (Tuchman), 480–81

Thoms, Catherine, 266–67

time, signaling

    sequences

        chronological order, 474–75

        flashbacks, 476

        reverse chronological order, 475

        time markers, 476–78

        transitions, 478

    transitions, 362

timelines, 303, 676, 678

timeliness of sources, 206

TinEye, 511, 529

Tingling, Renae, 140–45

titles of essays

    as cueing device, 363

genres and

    literacy narratives, 100

    position papers, 192

    reports, 159

    textual analyses, 137

tone, 72–74 The way a writer's or speaker's **STANCE** toward the readers and subject is reflected in the text.

    editing, 382

    in presentations, 697–98

    rhetorical situation and

        audience, 64

        genre, 70

        stance, 72–74

    types of

        appropriate, 263

        authoritative, 6–7

        speculative, 275–76

        trustworthy, 182

topic, 347 The specific subject written about in a text. A topic should be narrow enough to cover, not too broad or general, and needs to be developed appropriately for its **AUDIENCE** and **PURPOSE**.

    in explorations, 274

    in reports, 152, 154–56

topic proposal, 266–68 A statement of intent to examine a topic; also called a proposal **ABSTRACT**. Some instructors require a topic proposal in order to assess the feasibility of the writing project that a student has in mind. Key Features: concise discussion of the subject • clear statement of the intended focus • rationale for choosing the subject • mention of resources

    key features, 267–68

    reading: "Social Media and Data Privacy," 266–67

topic sentence, 358–60 A sentence, often at the beginning of a paragraph, that states the paragraph's main point. The details in the rest of the paragraph should support the topic sentence.
> as cueing device, 358–60
> editing, 380

transfer of learning The process of applying the skills, concepts, habits of mind, and processes learned in one context to a new context.

transition, 361–62 A word or PHRASE that helps to connect sentences and paragraphs and to guide readers through a text. Transitions can help to show comparisons (also, similarly); contrasts (but, instead); examples (for instance, in fact); sequence (finally, next); time (at first, meanwhile); and more.
> as cueing device, 361–62
> editing and, 381, 382
> in narration, 478
> presentation, 697
> reading, 14

Traub, James, 460–61
"The Trouble with Fries" (Gladwell), 470
trustworthy tone, 182
Tuchman, Barbara, 480–81
Tuomey, K., 323
"Turkey Finds Its Inner Duck (and Chicken)" (Hesser), 441–42
Turkle, Sherry, 479–80

U

unfamiliar topics, reports about, 157
University of Chicago Press documentation style, 561

URLs, keeping track of, 516
USA.gov, 511

V

values, appeals to, 182

vantage point, 460–61 The physical position from which a writer DESCRIBES something.

verb A word that expresses an action (dance, talk) or a state of being (be, seem). A verb is an essential element of a sentence or CLAUSE. Verbs have four forms: base form (smile), past tense (smiled), past participle (smiled), and present participle (smiling).

verb tenses
> consistency in, 102
> in literary analyses, 233
> signal phrases and, 553–54
Vidal, John, 442
video
> acknowledging sources, 557
> explainer, 286
> fact-checking, 529, 532
video platforms, research using, 511
video profiles, 285

visual, 673–83 A photograph, chart, graph, table, video, or similar item used as part of a writer's text.
> acknowledging sources, 557
> analyzing, 128–34
> as evidence, 420–21
> generating ideas and text with, 337–39
> guidelines
>> adding links, 681–82
>> diagrams, maps, flowcharts, timelines, 676

editing, 682–83
graphs, charts, tables, 676
infographics, 679–80
rhetorical situation, 674
using sound, 680
reading, 28–32
reflection on, 398
uses
comparison and contrast, 440–41
presentations, 700–701
process explanation, 471–72

vocabulary, for reading across fields of
study, 299–300
Vodanovich, Stephen J., 196–97
Volvo.com, 426–27
Vowell, Sarah, 356

W

Ward, S., 318
Warnock, J. N., 321
Washington, Jerome, 354
"The Ways of Silencing" (Stanley), 35
"We, the Public, Place the Best Athletes on
Pedestals" (Moller), 416–18
*We the People: An Introduction to American
Politics* (Ginsberg et al.), 451, 452
web conferencing tools, 691, 693
websites
searching with, 509–11
digital archives, 511
government sites, 511
image, video, and audio platforms,
511
news sites, 511
Wikipedia, 509–10
writing for, 685–86
Webster's Third New International Dictionary, 513

Wechsler, Henry, 357–58
Weinberg, Bennett Alan, 435
Weir, Margaret, 451, 452
"What Does Democracy Mean Now?"
(Mejía), 448
"What Is a Homosexual?" (Sullivan),
424–25
"What Wounds Deserve the Purple Heart?"
(Sandel), 18–19
"What You See Is the Real You" (Gaylin), 355

whataboutism, 427 A FALLACY that results
when someone responds to criticism by
accusing the attacker of hypocrisy, but not
answering the criticism itself. Also known
as "You too."

"What's Your Pronoun? Beyond He and She"
(Baron), 360
White, E. B., 452
white space, 672
"Why It Worked: A Rhetorical Analysis
of Obama's Speech on Race" (Clark),
116–22
Wikipedia, 495, 509–10
Williams, Terry Tempest, 476
"Witnessing" (Fontaine), 459–60
"Women in Science: A Social Analysis"
(Keller), 354
word clouds, 506–7
word maps, 302
word origins, definitions and, 448, 450
words, editing, 382–83

working bibliography, 497–99 A record of all
sources consulted in research providing all
the bibliographic information necessary for
DOCUMENTATION including author, title, and
publication information.

working outlines, 340, 345

works-cited list, 574–605, 613–14 A list at the end of a researched text prepared in MLA STYLE that contains full bibliographic information for all the sources cited in the text.

    articles and other short works, 582–89

    audio, visual, and other sources, 599–605

    authors and contributors, 580–82

    books and parts of books, 590–95

    personal communication and social media, 598

    websites, 595–97

The World Almanac Book of Facts, 513

The World of Caffeine (Weinberg and Bealer), 435

"World Trade Center" (*GreatBuildings.com*), 459

Wouldn't Take Nothing for My Journey Now (Angelou), 477–78

WPA outcomes, 8–10

A Writer Teaches Writing (Murray), 377

writer's block, 366

writing, processes of, 327–28

writing context. *See* context

writing online, 684–87

    blogs, 687

    email and texts, 685

    social media, 685

    websites, 685–86

writing portfolios

    assessing your work, 388–89

    organizing, 387–88

    what to include, 386–87

Y

you too (fallacy). *See* whataboutism

YouTube, 511

Z

Zisch, Rebecca, 202–3

"Zombie Film Scholarship: A Review of the Literature" (Carroll), 210–12

Zoom, 693

Zotero, 497, 500

The Norton Writer's Prize

"I have something to say to the world, and I have taken English 12 in order to say it well." —**W. E. B. Du Bois**

The Norton Writer's Prize recognizes outstanding original nonfiction by undergraduates. All entries are considered for possible publication in Norton texts—in fact, many of the essays that appear in this book were nominated for the prize.

The contest is open to students age 17 and above who are enrolled in an accredited 2- or 4-year college or university. Three cash prizes of $1,000 apiece are awarded annually for coursework submitted during the academic year, one in each of the following three categories:

- Writing by a first-year student in a 2- or 4-year college or university
- Writing by a student in a 2-year college or university
- Writing by a student in a 4-year college or university

Submissions must be between 1,000 and 3,000 words in length. Literacy narratives, literary and other textual analyses, reports, profiles, evaluations, arguments, memoirs, proposals, multimodal pieces, and other forms of original nonfiction will be considered if written by a student age 17 or above in fulfillment of an undergraduate course requirement at an eligible institution. Entries submitted in accordance with the Official Contest Rules will be considered for all applicable prizes, but no more than one prize will be awarded to any single entry.

For full contest rules, eligibility, and instructions on how to enter or nominate students, please visit **wwnorton.com/norton-writers-prize**. For questions, please email us at **composition@wwnorton.com**

Current and former students of individuals acting as judges are not eligible to enter or win, and any entry recognized by any of the judges will be automatically disqualified. Employees of W. W. Norton & Company, Inc. ("Sponsor"), including Sponsor's corporate affiliates and subsidiaries, as well as such individuals' children and persons living in any of their households are not eligible to enter; nor are authors published by Sponsor, children of Sponsor's authors, previous contest winners (including runners-up) and persons living in their respective households. Void where prohibited. Must be 17 or older at the time of entry. Other restrictions apply.

A Directory to MLA Style

IN-TEXT DOCUMENTATION

1. Author named in a signal phrase 568
2. Author named in parentheses 568
3. Two or more works by the same author 568
4. Authors with the same last name 569
5. Two or more authors 569
6. Organization or government as author 570
7. Author unknown 570
8. Literary works 570
9. Work in an anthology 571
10. Encyclopedia or dictionary 571
11. Legal documents 571
12. Sacred text 572
13. Multivolume work 572
14. Two or more works cited together 572
15. Source quoted in another source 573
16. Work without page numbers 573
17. An entire work or a one-page article 574

MLA LIST OF WORKS CITED

CORE ELEMENTS

AUTHORS AND CONTRIBUTORS

1. One author 580
2. Two authors 580
3. Three or more authors 580
4. Two or more works by the same author 580
5. Author and editor or translator 581
6. No author or editor 581
7. Organization or government as author 582

ARTICLES AND OTHER SHORT WORKS

Documentation Maps 583, 584, 587

8. Article in a journal 582
9. Article in a magazine 585
10. Article in a news publication 585
11. Article accessed through a database 586
12. Entry in a reference work 586
13. Editorial or op-ed 588
14. Letter to the editor 588
15. Review 589
16. Comment on an online article 589

BOOKS AND PARTS OF BOOKS

Documentation Map 591

17. Basic entries for a book 590
18. Anthology or edited collection 590
19. Work in an anthology 592
20. Multivolume work 592
21. Book in a series 593
22. Graphic narrative or comic book 593
23. Sacred text 593
24. Edition other than the first 594
25. Republished work 594
26. Foreword, introduction, preface, or afterword 594
27. Published letter 594
28. Paper heard at a conference 594
29. Dissertation 595

WEBSITES

Documentation Map 596

30. Entire website 595
31. Work on a website 597
32. Blog entry 597
33. Wiki 597

PERSONAL COMMUNICATION AND SOCIAL MEDIA

34. Personal letter 598
35. Email or text message 598
36. Post to *Twitter*, *Instagram*, or other social media 598

AUDIO, VISUAL, AND OTHER SOURCES

37. Advertisement 599
38. Art 599
39. Cartoon 600
40. Supreme Court case 600
41. Film 600
42. TV show episode 601
43. Online video 602
44. Presentation on *Zoom* or other virtual platform 602
45. Interview 602
46. Map 603
47. Musical score 603
48. Oral presentation 603
49. Podcast 604
50. Radio program 604
51. Sound recording 604
52. Video game 605